D1508294

BEST
CUSTOMERS

BEST CUSTOMERS

DEMOGRAPHICS OF CONSUMER DEMAND

BY CHERYL RUSSELL AND SUSAN MITCHELL

New Strategist Publications, Inc.
Ithaca, New York

New Strategist Publications, Inc.
P.O. Box 242, Ithaca, New York 14851
800-848-0842
www.newstrategist.com

ISBN 1-885070-26-8

Printed in the United States of America

Table of Contents

Introduction

Welcome to the first edition of *Best Customers: Demographics of Consumer Demand.*
Best Customers is a unique examination of how changing demographics are reshaping the consumer marketplace. It reveals who the best and biggest customers are for hundreds of individual products and services, alerting marketers to potential booms and busts in the years ahead.

Based on data from the Bureau of Labor Statistics' 1997 Consumer Expenditure Survey, *Best Customers* examines spending patterns by the demographic characteristics of households. For most consumer products and services, demographics drive demand. *Best Customers* analyzes household spending on 300 products and services by age of householder, household income, household type, and region of residence. It identifies which households spend the most on a product or service (the best customers) and which control the largest share of spending (the biggest customers).

Household demographics are not static, but ever changing. The aging of the population is reshaping consumer demand, bringing boom times to some businesses and bad times to others. *Best Customers* reveals the coming peaks and valleys, allowing marketers to prepare for what lies ahead.

The Demographic Trends

Three major demographic trends are reshaping consumer markets: the middle-aging of the baby-boom generation, the coming-of-age of the Millennial generation, and the growing sophistication of older Americans.

The baby-boom generation, born between 1946 and 1964, spanned ages 33 through 51 in 1997. Boomers number 78 million and account for 29 percent of the population. During the next few years, boomers will almost entirely fill the 35-to-54 age group. Not only are 35-to-54-year-olds in their peak earning years, but they are also raising children, making them doubly important consumers because they control the spending of not just one generation but two. The aging of the highly educated, individualistic, and fun-loving baby-boom generation is behind many of the spending trends examined in *Best Customers.*

Today's children belong to the Millennial generation, born from 1977 through 1994 and spanning the ages of 3 through 20 in 1997. Millennials number 71 million and account for 26 percent of the population. Most are the children of boomers. As this large age group enters its teens and twenties, it is replacing the much smaller

Generation X. Consequently, demand for products and services for young people is growing after years of decline. As Millennials become twentysomethings during the next decade, they will energize many languishing consumer markets.

Perhaps no segment of the population is changing more rapidly than the 55-plus age group. The older population is becoming increasingly sophisticated as better educated and more affluent generations join its ranks. Spending by older Americans is growing, especially on discretionary items such as entertainment and travel. As boomers move into the 55-plus age group, the spending of the older population will become increasingly important to most businesses.

The Spending Data

Best Customers is based on unpublished data collected by the Bureau of Labor Statistics' Consumer Expenditure Survey, an ongoing, nationwide survey of household spending. The Consumer Expenditure Survey is a complete accounting of household expenditures, including everything from big-ticket items such as homes and cars, to small purchases like laundry detergent and film. The survey collects spending records from 25,000 U.S. households each year. It does not include expenditures by government, business, or institutions. The lag time between data collection and publication is about two years.

The Consumer Expenditure Survey uses consumer units rather than households as its sampling unit. In this book, the terms "consumer unit" and "household" are used interchangeably. A "consumer unit" is defined by the Bureau of Labor Statistics as "a single person or group of persons in a sample household related by blood, marriage, adoption or other legal arrangement or who share responsibility for at least two out of three major types of expenses—food, housing, and other expenses." For more information about the Consumer Expenditure Survey and consumer units, see Appendix A.

Three types of household spending figures are shown in this book: average spending, indexed spending, and market share. The Bureau of Labor Statistics (BLS) produces the average spending figures shown in *Best Customers*. The indexes and market shares have been calculated by the authors.

How to Use This Book

Best Customers is divided into 19 chapters, arranged alphabetically, with each chapter focusing on one of the major spending categories as defined by the Bureau of Labor Statistics—such as food at home, transportation, entertainment, and so on. Computer and travel spending are separate chapters in *Best Customers* but are not separate categories in the Consumer Expenditure Survey. The BLS includes computer spending in housing, and it includes the travel categories in food, housing, and transportation. Within each chapter, individual products and services are arranged alphabetically.

Almost every individual product and service included in the Consumer Expenditure Survey is analyzed in *Best Customers*. Three types of items are excluded: "other" categories, such as "other food at home," for which an analysis of spending patterns cannot provide meaningful conclusions; a few products and services with spending patterns considered unreliable by the authors; and spending categories that are not consumer markets—such as federal income taxes, Social Security taxes, and vehicle registration.

Each table in *Best Customers* analyzes household spending on a particular product or service, showing average spending, indexed spending, and market share of spending by age of householder, household income, household type, and region of residence. Each table is accompanied by a page of text identifying the best and biggest customers and predicting trends in spending based on the nation's changing demographics.

• **Average Spending** The average spending figures in *Best Customers* are unpublished data from the Bureau of Labor Statistics' 1997 Consumer Expenditure Survey. The Bureau of Labor Statistics calculates average spending for all households in a segment, not just for those who bought an item. When examining the averages, it is important to remember that by including both purchasers and nonpurchasers in the calculation of the average, the average spending amount is often greatly reduced— especially for infrequently purchased items. For example, the average household spent $232 on day care centers in 1997. Since only a small percentage of households spend money on day care, this figure greatly underestimates the amount spent on day care centers by those who make use of them. To get a more realistic idea of how much buyers spend on an item, Appendix B shows the percentage of households that purchased individual products and services during an average quarter of 1997, and the amount spent by purchasers per quarter. According to Appendix B, only 5.79 percent of households spent on day care centers during an average quarter of 1997. The purchasers spent an average of $693 per quarter, for an estimated annual cost of $2,772—a much more realistic figure than the average of $232 for all households.

For frequently purchased items—such as milk—the average spending figures give a fairly accurate account of actual spending. But for most of the products and services examined in *Best Customers*, the average spending figures are less revealing than the indexes and market shares.

Average spending figures are useful in determining the market potential of a product or service in a local area. By multiplying the average amount married couples spend on children's clothing by the number of married couples in the

Pittsburgh metropolitan area, for example, marketers can estimate the size of the market for children's clothing in Pittsburgh. The Pittsburgh newspaper could show those figures to potential advertisers to prove the demand for children's clothing in its readership area.

• **Indexed Spending (Best Customers)** The indexed spending figures compare the spending of each demographic segment with that of the average household. To compute the indexes, the authors divided the amount spent by each demographic segment by the amount spent by the average household and multiplied the resulting figure by 100. An index of 100 is the average for all households. An index of 125 means average spending by households in a segment is 25 percent above average (100 plus 25). An index of 75 means average spending by households in a segment is 25 percent below average (100 minus 25). Indexed spending figures identify the best customers of a product or service. Householders aged 45 to 54, for example, spend 79 percent more than the average household on outdoor furniture (with an index of 179). This is a higher index than that of any other age group, making householders aged 45 to 54 the best customers of outdoor furniture. Householders aged 25 to 34 spend 32 percent less than average on outdoor furniture (with an index of just 68), meaning they are a weaker or under-served market for this product.

Spending indexes reveal hidden markets—household segments with a high propensity to buy a particular product or service but which are overshadowed by larger household segments that account for a bigger share of the total market. For example, householders aged 55 to 64 spend 26 percent more than the average household on women's shoes (with an index of 126), making them the best customers of this item. In contrast, householders aged 35 to 44 spend only an average amount on women's shoes (with an index of 100). But the spending of the older age group is overshadowed by the spending of the more numerous 35-to-44-year-olds. The younger adults accounted for a 23 percent share of total spending on women's shoes in 1997, versus the 15 percent share accounted for by 55-to-64-year-olds. While market share is important to businesses, those that track market share alone run the risk of ignoring the customers who spend the most on their products.

• **Market Share (Biggest Customers)** To produce market share figures, the authors first calculated the total amount all households spend on each item. This was done by multiplying average household spending on an item by the total number of households (105,576,000). The authors then calculated total household spending by item for each demographic segment. This was done by multiplying the segment's average spending on an item by the number of households in the segment. To calculate the percentage of total spending on an item that is controlled by each demographic segment—i.e., its market share—the authors divided each segment's spending on an item by total household spending on the item.

Market shares reveal the biggest customers—the demographic segments that account for the largest share of spending on a particular product or service. In 1997, for example, married couples without children at home (most of them empty nesters) accounted for 62 percent of total household spending on ship fares. The cruise industry could reach the great majority of its customers if it targeted only this demographic segment. Of course, by single-mindedly targeting the biggest customers, businesses cannot nurture potential growth markets. An additional danger of focusing only on the biggest customers is that businesses can end up ignoring their best customers. This is especially problematic because market shares are unstable, thanks to baby booms and busts over the past half century. Right now the biggest customers of hunting and fishing equipment, for example, are householders aged 35 to 44, accounting for 29 percent of total household spending on this item. As the baby-boom generation exits the 35-to-44 age group during the next few years, however, the market share controlled by these householders will shrink, only to be surpassed by the share controlled by 55-to-64-year-olds—who are, in fact, the best customers of hunting and fishing equipment (with a spending index of 173). Marketers who ignore their best customers in favor of their biggest customers may end up with no customers.

• **Age of Householder** Age is one of the best predictors of spending because lifestage determines most consumer wants and needs. Ongoing changes in the age structure of the population will have a profound effect on consumer spending. This is why *Best Customers* explores spending by age in so much detail, using it as the primary guide to consumer trends in the years ahead. Below is a chart showing projected changes in the number of households between 1997 and 2002:

Percent Change in Households by Age, 1997 to 2002

Total households	**4.9%**
Under age 25	8.3
Aged 25 to 34	−7.1
Aged 35 to 44	−1.0
Aged 45 to 54	15.6
Aged 55 to 64	20.5
Aged 65 to 74	−2.2
Aged 75 or older	9.2

Source: TGE Demographics, Inc., Honeoye Falls, New York

Changes in the size of age groups will dramatically affect spending in many categories. Fewer young adults will mean less spending on products and services for infants. More fiftysomethings will mean higher spending on travel. In addition, the attitudes and behavior of age groups will change as they fill with new cohorts. These demographic trends are behind many of the predictions made by the authors about spending trends in the future.

• **Household Income** It's no surprise that the richest households spend the most. For most of the products and services examined in *Best Customers*, households with the highest incomes appear to be the best and biggest customers. Yet the story behind spending is more complex than income alone. Most spending is driven by lifestage (age) or lifestyle (household type), and secondarily by income. That's why *Best Customers* identifies high-income households as the best and biggest customers only when income has an extraordinary effect on spending or when an item is a purely discretionary expense—such as spending on indoor plants and fresh flowers. While most businesses would do well to target the affluent, they would find it difficult to design a product or craft a message if they ignore the lifestage and lifestyle reasons for the spending.

Note: Average household spending figures by income are slightly different from those by age, household type, or region. Spending by income is calculated by the Bureau of Labor Statistics using only those householders who reveal their incomes to BLS interviewers (called complete income reporters). In contrast, average spending figures by age, household type, and region are based on all households.

• **Household Type** Household type is one of the most important determinants of spending for several reasons. The presence of children, for example, means the household will spend on products and services children want and need. Not only that, but households with children tend to include more people than those without children, and household size is an important determinant of spending. Because married couples head most of the nation's households, they account for the majority of spending in most categories. But single parents are important in some markets, and single-person households have growing clout because they are becoming a larger share of households. The most important household change occurring in the next five to ten years, however, will be the rapid expansion in the number of married couples without children at home as boomers become empty nesters. At the same time, the number of married couples with preschoolers will decline as Generation Xers enter the 25-to-34 age group.

Note: Market shares by household type will not sum to 100 percent because not all household types are shown.

• **Region** For many products and services, regional differences in spending are small. But for some items, regional spending differences are pronounced. There are several reasons for this including differences in regional economies, climates, physical infrastructure, racial and ethnic composition, and access to resources. Differences in regional population growth rates will affect household spending levels in the years ahead, and these are noted in the affected categories.

Appendices

Best Customers includes four appendices and a glossary of terms.

• **Appendix A** describes the Consumer Expenditure Survey in more detail and tells readers how to contact the Bureau of Labor Statistics.

• **Appendix B** shows the percentage of households that purchased each product or service examined in the Consumer Expenditure Survey during an average quarter of 1997. It also shows how much the purchasers spent on an item during an average quarter. In some cases, the quarterly spending figure alone is a good estimate of how much a typical purchaser spends. Take refrigerators, for example, which are a one-time rather than an ongoing expense. In an average quarter of 1997, 1.6 percent of homeowners bought a refrigerator, spending $751 on the item. For ongoing expenses, however, the quarterly spending figure should be multiplied by four to get an estimate of how much people spend annually on the product or service. Fifty-two percent of households bought women's clothes during an average quarter of 1997, for example, spending $207 during the quarter. The annual spending of householders who buy women's clothes can be reasonably estimated at $828 (or $207 times 4). Appendix B not only supplies readers with invaluable insight into the propensity of households to buy individual products and services, but also provides a more realistic idea of how much purchasers spend.

• **Appendix C** ranks all the products and services analyzed in *Best Customers* by the amount the average household spends on them, from highest to lowest. It shows which categories are most important to the household budget. The relative standing of products and services is often surprising. To know that gasoline is the 5th biggest expense of the average household puts the media's focus on gasoline prices into perspective. The fact that federal income taxes, Social Security taxes, and property taxes are the 1st, 3rd, and 6th biggest household expenses explains why so many people feel financially strapped. Some of the tax items included in the list are not analyzed in the book because they are not consumer markets. The authors have included them in the ranking, however, because they are such an important part of spending.

• **Appendix D** shows trends in household spending by major category between 1987 and 1997, after adjusting for inflation. Average household spending barely rose during the decade once inflation is factored in. Spending fell sharply for many discretionary items, such as alcoholic beverages, furniture, and reading material. Spending rose for many nondiscretionary categories such as health care, mortgage interest, and telephone service. While consumer spending has been growing strongly at the national level since the early 1990s, that growth is due to the expanding number of upper-income households rather than any spending spree by the average household. Now that the baby-boom generation is entering its peak-earning years, the number of affluent households is growing. The average household, however, is keeping a tight grip on its wallet.

For More Information

Best Customers examines the demographics of spending on individual products and services and describes how changing demographics will elevate or dampen spending in the future. An alternative way to analyze spending is to look at spending patterns by product within a single demographic segment—such as age or region, for example. New Strategist offers this alternative analysis of consumer spending in a companion volume entitled *Household Spending: Who Spends How Much on What*. The 5th edition is available for $94.95 by calling New Strategist at 1-800-848-0842. Or visit New Strategist's web site at <www.newstrategist.com> to order books and see tables of contents and sample pages from *Household Spending* and other reference books from New Strategist Publications.

Chapter 1.

Alcoholic Beverages

Alcoholic Beverages

The average household spends little on alcoholic beverages—a total of just $309.22 in 1997. Beer accounts for the largest share of the alcoholic beverage dollar, followed by wine and whiskey.

The market for alcoholic beverages has suffered in recent years, with household spending on this item falling 24 percent between 1987 and 1997 after adjusting for inflation. Not only has the young-adult population (the biggest beer drinkers) declined as Generation X filled the twentysomething age group, but the baby-boom generation has been busy raising children. Generally, parents with children under age 18 at home spend far less than the average household on alcoholic beverages.

A turn-around is likely in the market for alcoholic beverages, however. Empty nesters spend far more than parents on wine and whiskey. As the baby-boom nest empties during the next few decades, spending on alcoholic beverages is likely to rise.

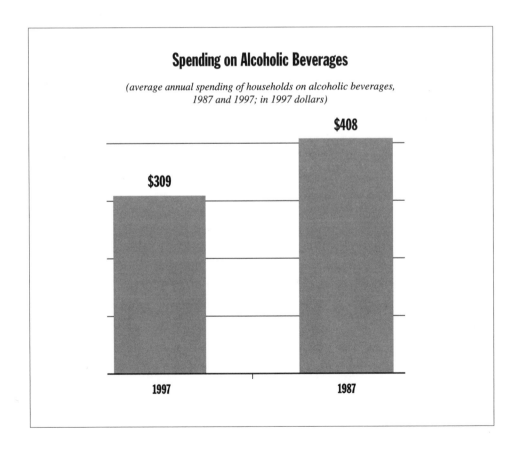

Spending on Alcoholic Beverages

(average annual spending of households on alcoholic beverages, 1987 and 1997; in 1997 dollars)

$408

$309

1997

1987

Alcoholic Beverage Spending

(average annual spending of households on alcoholic beverages, and percent distribution of spending by type, 1997)

Total spending on alcoholic beverages	**$309.22**	**100.0%**
Beer and ale	130.42	42.2
Wine	79.62	25.7
Whiskey	13.4	4.3

Note: Numbers will not add to total because not all categories are shown, including alcoholic beverages purchased on trips which is in the Travel chapter.

Beer and Ale

Best customers: • Householders aged 25 to 34

Customer trends: • Beer spending should receive a boost from the growth of the young-adult age group as the children of the baby-boom generation grow up.

Householders aged 25 to 34 spend 36 percent more than the average householder on beer and ale. Many people in this age group do not yet have family responsibilities that prevent them from getting together with friends for a few beers.

Spending on beer and ale is likely to rise in the years ahead as the large Millennial generation replaces the small Generation X in the 25-to-34 age group. Today the oldest Millennials are just 22, barely of legal drinking age. As they inflate the number of young adults during the next decade, the beer industry will see significant gains.

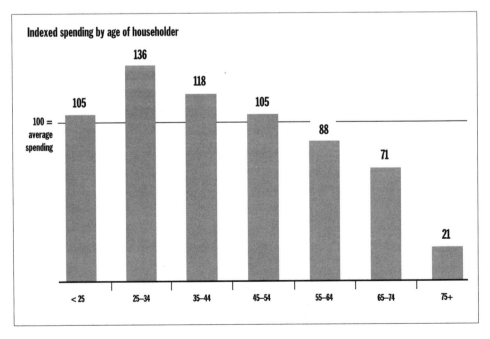

Indexed spending by age of householder

Age	Index
< 25	105
25–34	136
35–44	118
45–54	105
55–64	88
65–74	71
75+	21

100 = average spending

BEER AND ALE

Total households spend $ 13,769,221,920
Average household spends   130.42

	average spending	best customers (index)	biggest customers (market share)
AGE OF HOUSEHOLDER			
Total households	**$130.42**	**100**	**100.0%**
Under age 25	136.82	105	7.5
Aged 25 to 34	177.11	136	25.6
Aged 35 to 44	154.15	118	27.5
Aged 45 to 54	137.20	105	19.3
Aged 55 to 64	115.12	88	10.3
Aged 65 to 74	92.78	71	8.2
Aged 75 or older	26.88	21	1.9
HOUSEHOLD INCOME			
Total households reporting income	**142.03**	**100**	**100.0**
Under $20,000	81.21	57	19.9
$20,000 to $29,999	132.55	93	13.6
$30,000 to $39,999	155.33	109	13.4
$40,000 to $49,999	174.22	123	11.5
$50,000 to $69,999	175.03	123	17.3
$70,000 or more	222.72	157	23.4
HOUSEHOLD TYPE			
Total households	**130.42**	**100**	**100.0**
Married couples	138.29	106	55.4
Married couples, no children	141.27	108	23.1
Married couples, with children	132.73	102	27.4
Oldest child under 6	131.26	101	5.2
Oldest child 6 to 17	129.34	99	14.4
Oldest child 18 or older	140.78	108	7.8
Single parent with child under 18	54.88	42	2.6
Single person	98.71	76	21.7
REGION			
Total households	**130.42**	**100**	**100.0**
Northeast	145.77	112	22.3
Midwest	143.99	110	26.4
South	103.71	80	27.7
West	143.90	110	23.4

Note: For definitions of best and biggest customers, see introduction or glossary.
Source: Calculations by New Strategist based on the 1997 Consumer Expenditure Survey

Whiskey

Best customers:
- Householders aged 35 to 44
- Householders aged 55 to 64
- Married couples without children at home

Customer trends:
- The market should remain stable thanks to younger boomers, who have switched from beer to whiskey.

Married couples without children at home are the best customers of whiskey. They spend 48 percent more than the average household on this item, accounting for nearly one-third of the market. Age is behind this spending. Most of these couples are older and grew up in the era when mixed drinks and hard liquor were more commonly consumed. Householders aged 55 to 64 spend 46 percent more than average on whiskey. There is also a younger group that spends more than average on whiskey: householders aged 35 to 44.

The younger half of the baby-boom generation may give the whiskey market a much-needed boost. Sales of hard liquor slumped years ago, and it appeared that the market would continue to decline as older generations died off. If younger people continue to trade in their beer for whiskey, this should stabilize the market.

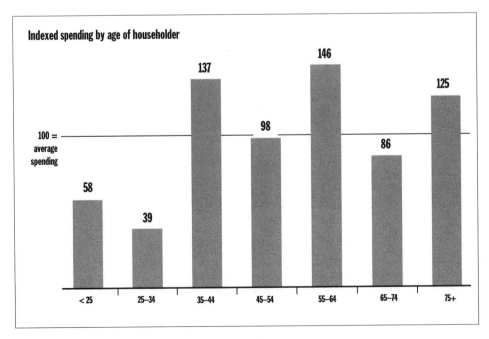

Indexed spending by age of householder

100 = average spending

| < 25 | 25–34 | 35–44 | 45–54 | 55–64 | 65–74 | 75+ |
| 58 | 39 | 137 | 98 | 146 | 86 | 125 |

WHISKEY

Total household spending $1,414,718,400
Average household spends   13.40

	average spending	best customers (index)	biggest customers (market share)
AGE OF HOUSEHOLDER			
Total households	**$13.40**	**100**	**100.0%**
Under age 25	7.72	58	4.1
Aged 25 to 34	5.29	39	7.4
Aged 35 to 44	18.42	137	32.0
Aged 45 to 54	13.19	98	18.0
Aged 55 to 64	19.56	146	17.0
Aged 65 to 74	11.55	86	9.9
Aged 75 or older	16.69	125	11.6
HOUSEHOLD INCOME			
Total households reporting income	**14.43**	**100**	**100.0**
Under $20,000	10.73	74	25.9
$20,000 to $29,999	5.75	40	5.8
$30,000 to $39,999	10.46	72	8.9
$40,000 to $49,999	15.00	104	9.7
$50,000 to $69,999	17.69	123	17.2
$70,000 or more	30.79	213	31.9
HOUSEHOLD TYPE			
Total households	**13.40**	**100**	**100.0**
Married couples	14.68	110	57.3
Married couples, no children	19.86	148	31.6
Married couples, with children	10.77	80	21.6
Oldest child under 6	12.60	94	4.8
Oldest child 6 to 17	9.85	74	10.7
Oldest child 18 or older	11.12	83	6.0
Single parent with child under 18	8.84	66	4.1
Single person	13.52	101	29.0
REGION			
Total households	**13.40**	**100**	**100.0**
Northeast	15.61	116	23.3
Midwest	10.21	76	18.2
South	13.76	103	35.8
West	14.29	107	22.7

Note: Spending on whiskey includes whiskey purchased for home consumption only. For definitions of best and biggest customers, see introduction or glossary.
Source: Calculations by New Strategist based on the 1997 Consumer Expenditure Survey

Wine

Best customers:
- Households with incomes of $70,000 or more
- Married couples without children at home
- Households in the Northeast and West

Customer trends:
- The growing affluence of Americans and the ability of wine merchants to tout potential health benefits should keep this market growing.

The big spenders on wine are those who can afford to drink the very best. Affluent households—those with incomes of $70,000 or more –spend more than two and one-half times as much as the average household on wine. They account for 42 percent of all household spending on wine. Married couples without children at home spend fully 66 percent more than average on wine. Households in the Northeast spend 38 percent more than average while those in the West spend 40 percent more. One factor behind these regional differences is that the Northeast and West are wine-producing regions.

Research showing that moderate wine drinking may be beneficial is already giving the market a boost. Such benefits provide the justification for health-conscious boomers to spend some of their discretionary income on wine. This incentive should keep the wine market growing for some time to come.

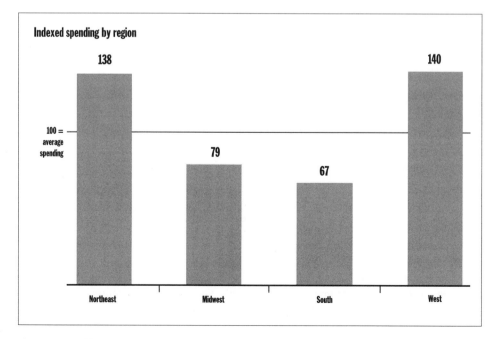

Indexed spending by region

100 = average spending

Northeast 138 Midwest 79 South 67 West 140

WINE

Total household spending	$8,405,961,120		
Average household spends	79.62		

	average spending	best customers (index)	biggest customers (market share)
AGE OF HOUSEHOLDER			
Total households	**$79.62**	**100**	**100.0%**
Under age 25	34.56	43	3.1
Aged 25 to 34	95.33	120	22.6
Aged 35 to 44	84.15	106	24.6
Aged 45 to 54	109.42	137	25.2
Aged 55 to 64	69.07	87	10.1
Aged 65 to 74	83.99	105	12.1
Aged 75 or older	26.19	33	3.1
HOUSEHOLD INCOME			
Total households reporting income	**80.57**	**100**	**100.0**
Under $20,000	28.30	35	12.2
$20,000 to $29,999	49.38	61	9.0
$30,000 to $39,999	63.19	78	9.6
$40,000 to $49,999	69.05	86	8.0
$50,000 to $69,999	107.83	134	18.8
$70,000 or more	223.75	278	41.5
HOUSEHOLD TYPE			
Total households	**79.62**	**100**	**100.0**
Married couples	97.03	122	63.7
Married couples, no children	131.83	166	35.3
Married couples, with children	74.17	93	25.0
Oldest child under 6	58.86	74	3.8
Oldest child 6 to 17	85.97	108	15.7
Oldest child 18 or older	63.22	79	5.7
Single parent with child under 18	37.72	47	3.0
Single person	55.02	69	19.9
REGION			
Total households	**79.62**	**100**	**100.0**
Northeast	110.27	138	27.7
Midwest	62.95	79	18.9
South	53.27	67	23.3
West	111.57	140	29.8

Note: For definitions of best and biggest customers, see introduction or glossary.
Source: Calculations by New Strategist based on the 1997 Consumer Expenditure Survey

Chapter 2.

Apparel

Apparel

Apparel commands a shrinking share of the household budget, behind even entertainment. In 1997, the average household spent $1,729.06 on clothes, shoes, dry cleaning, watches, jewelry, and other apparel products and services.

The apparel industry has been hurt by the shifting spending patterns of Americans. Spending on apparel fell 15 percent between 1987 and 1997, after adjusting for inflation. The average household spent 20 percent less on women's apparel, 22.5 percent less on men's apparel, and 6 to 10 percent less on children's apparel in 1997 than in 1987. Footwear was the only apparel category to see a spending increase during the decade.

In part, the decline in spending on apparel is due to the shift to more casual dress in the workplace. The decline is also the fault of the apparel industry, however. Intent on targeting teens and young adults, the industry has left older women—the best customers of apparel—with little to buy. Women's clothes command the largest share of the apparel dollar—33 percent in 1997.

If the apparel industry better targets its best customers—middle aged women— spending on clothes could rise. But any gains will be limited by the widespread acceptance of casual dress for almost any occasion.

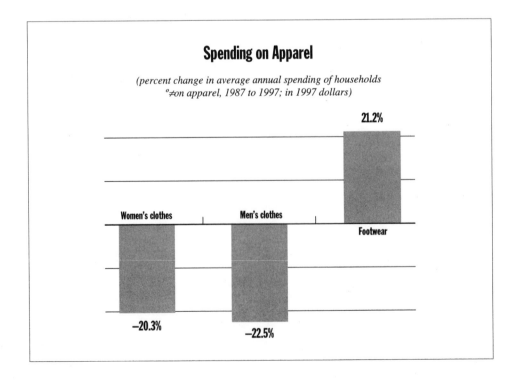

Spending on Apparel

*(percent change in average annual spending of households
°≠on apparel, 1987 to 1997; in 1997 dollars)*

21.2%

Women's clothes

Men's clothes

Footwear

−20.3%

−22.5%

Apparel Spending

(average annual spending of households on apparel, and percent distribution of spending by type, 1997)

Total spending on apparel	**$1,729.06**	**100.0%**
Apparel, women's	574.26	33.2
Apparel, men's	322.98	18.7
Apparel, children's	189.89	11.0
Shoes, women's	157.11	9.1
Jewelry	142.02	8.2
Shoes, men's	100.43	5.8
Apparel, infants'	77.05	4.5
Shoes, children's	56.98	3.3
Laundry and dry cleaning of apparel, professional	31.24	1.8
Watches	29.70	1.7
Laundry and dry cleaning of apparel, coin-operated	20.79	1.2
Sewing material, patterns, and notions for clothing	8.89	0.5
Apparel repair and tailoring	6.10	0.4
Watch and jewelry repair	5.08	0.3
Clothing rental	3.85	0.2
Shoe repair	2.38	0.1

Note: Numbers will not add to total because not all categories are shown.

Apparel Repair and Tailoring

Best customers:
- Householders aged 45 to 74
- Married couples without children
- Households in the Northeast

Customer trends:
- The casualization of dress is likely to curb any growth in this market.

The best customers of apparel repair and tailoring are householders aged 45 to 64, spending 20 to 28 percent more than the average household on this item and accounting for 52 percent of the market. Married couples without children at home, many of them older, spend 62 percent more than average on clothing repair and tailoring. Households in the Northeast spend 47 percent more than average in this category.

The growing casualization of dress at the office and on weekends is likely to curb any growth in this market. Spending on apparel repair and tailoring may even decline, despite the growing number of affluent households.

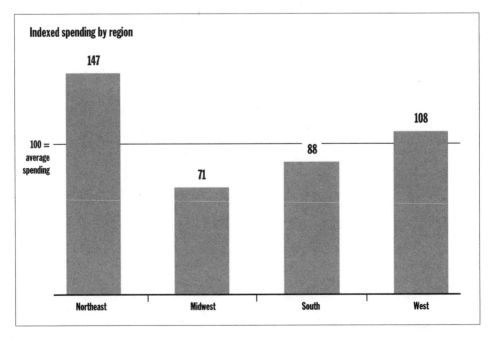

Indexed spending by region

Northeast 147 | Midwest 71 | South 88 | West 108

100 = average spending

APPAREL REPAIR AND TAILORING

Total household spending $644,013,600
Average household spends   6.10

	average spending	best customers (index)	biggest customers (market share)
AGE OF HOUSEHOLDER			
Total households	**$6.10**	**100**	**100.0%**
Under age 25	4.13	68	4.8
Aged 25 to 34	6.20	102	19.2
Aged 35 to 44	4.83	79	18.4
Aged 45 to 54	7.81	128	23.5
Aged 55 to 64	7.30	120	14.0
Aged 65 to 74	7.75	127	14.6
Aged 75 or older	3.65	60	5.6
HOUSEHOLD INCOME			
Total households reporting income	**6.41**	**100**	**100.0**
Under $20,000	2.57	40	14.0
$20,000 to $29,999	6.60	103	15.0
$30,000 to $39,999	5.14	80	9.8
$40,000 to $49,999	5.67	88	8.3
$50,000 to $69,999	7.66	120	16.8
$70,000 or more	15.51	242	36.2
HOUSEHOLD TYPE			
Total households	**6.10**	**100**	**100.0**
Married couples	7.37	121	63.2
Married couples, no children	9.88	162	34.6
Married couples, with children	5.57	91	24.5
Oldest child under 6	5.45	89	4.6
Oldest child 6 to 17	4.84	79	11.5
Oldest child 18 or older	7.11	117	8.4
Single parent with child under 18	2.02	33	2.1
Single person	4.98	82	23.5
REGION			
Total households	**6.10**	**100**	**100.0**
Northeast	8.95	147	29.3
Midwest	4.33	71	17.0
South	5.39	88	30.8
West	6.56	108	22.8

Note: For definitions of best and biggest customers, see introduction or glossary.
Source: Calculations by New Strategist based on the 1997 Consumer Expenditure Survey

Apparel, Children's

Best customers:
- Married couples with school-aged children
- Single parents
- Householders aged 35 to 44

Customer trends
- Likely rise in spending because of growth in the number of fashion-conscious preteens and teens.

The best customers of children's apparel are, naturally, households with children. But spending on children's clothing doesn't become an expensive proposition until children enter school. Married couples with school-aged children spend more than three times as much as the average household on children's apparel, accounting for nearly one-half of the market. Single parents also spend more than average, but less than married couples since their incomes are lower. Spending is high among householders aged 35 to 44 because so many are parents of school-aged children.

Spending on children's clothing is likely to rise during the next few years as the number of preteens and teens, who are highly fashion conscious, increases.

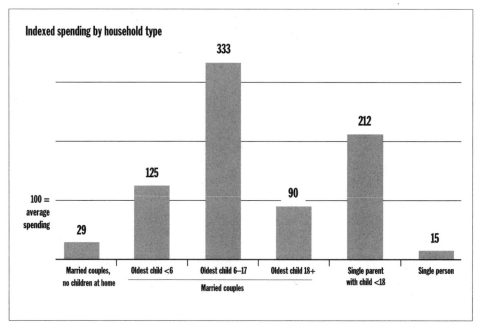

Indexed spending by household type

29	125	333	90	212	15
Married couples, no children at home	Oldest child <6	Oldest child 6–17	Oldest child 18+	Single parent with child <18	Single person
		Married couples			

100 = average spending

APPAREL, CHILDREN'S

Total household spending $20,047,826,640
Average household spends   189.89

	average spending	best customers (index)	biggest customers (market share)
AGE OF HOUSEHOLDER			
Total households	**$189.89**	**100**	**100.0%**
Under age 25	55.04	29	2.1
Aged 25 to 34	218.46	115	21.7
Aged 35 to 44	378.11	199	46.3
Aged 45 to 54	208.20	110	20.1
Aged 55 to 64	89.91	47	5.5
Aged 65 to 74	64.09	34	3.9
Aged 75 or older	20.26	11	1.0
HOUSEHOLD INCOME			
Total households reporting income	**193.12**	**100**	**100.0**
Under $20,000	95.47	49	17.2
$20,000 to $29,999	152.48	79	11.5
$30,000 to $39,999	193.61	100	12.3
$40,000 to $49,999	255.75	132	12.4
$50,000 to $69,999	258.82	134	18.8
$70,000 or more	352.02	182	27.2
HOUSEHOLD TYPE			
Total households	**189.89**	**100**	**100.0**
Married couples	267.92	141	73.8
Married couples, no children	54.86	29	6.2
Married couples, with children	429.53	226	60.8
Oldest child under 6	237.06	125	6.4
Oldest child 6 to 17	632.60	333	48.5
Oldest child 18 or older	171.08	90	6.5
Single parent with child under 18	402.61	212	13.3
Single person	28.04	15	4.2
REGION			
Total households	**189.89**	**100**	**100.0**
Northeast	183.02	96	19.3
Midwest	214.24	113	27.0
South	180.17	95	33.1
West	185.02	97	20.7

Note: For definitions of best and biggest customers, see introduction or glossary.
Source: Calculations by New Strategist based on the 1997 Consumer Expenditure Survey

Apparel, Infants'

Best customers:
- Householders aged 25 to 34
- Married couples with children under age 6

Customer trends
- The market is likely to remain flat or decline during the next few years, but will pick up again when the Millennial generation begins to have children.

Not surprisingly, the best customers of infant apparel are married couples with children under age 6. They spend nearly seven times as much as the average household on infants' clothes. Typically, parents of preschoolers are aged 25 to 34, which explains why this age group spends more than twice as much as the average household on infants' apparel.

The market for infants' apparel will probably remain flat or even shrink during the next few years because the number of children under age 6 is not expected to expand until the Millennial generation—the oldest of whom turn 23 in 2000—begins to have children. Although today's parents and grandparents often indulge children in many ways, they have become savvy consumers when buying clothes that will soon be outgrown.

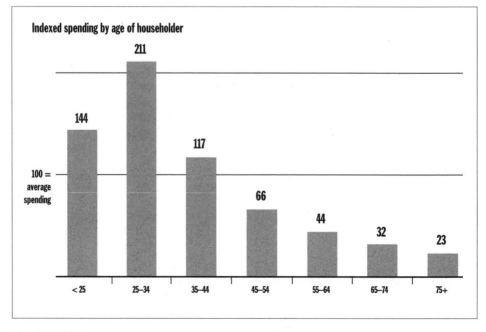

Indexed spending by age of householder

< 25	144
25–34	211
35–44	117
45–54	66
55–64	44
65–74	32
75+	23

100 = average spending

APPAREL, INFANT'S

Total household spending	$8,134,630,800	
Average household spends	77.05	

	average spending	best customers (index)	biggest customers (market share)
AGE OF HOUSEHOLDER			
Total households	**$77.05**	**100**	**100.0%**
Under age 25	110.93	144	10.2
Aged 25 to 34	162.53	211	39.8
Aged 35 to 44	90.00	117	27.2
Aged 45 to 54	50.57	66	12.0
Aged 55 to 64	33.83	44	5.1
Aged 65 to 74	24.54	32	3.7
Aged 75 or older	18.02	23	2.2
HOUSEHOLD INCOME			
Total households reporting income	**83.64**	**100**	**100.0**
Under $20,000	44.33	53	18.5
$20,000 to $29,999	78.38	94	13.7
$30,000 to $39,999	91.62	110	13.4
$40,000 to $49,999	93.45	112	10.4
$50,000 to $69,999	119.92	143	20.1
$70,000 or more	129.02	154	23.1
HOUSEHOLD TYPE			
Total households	**77.05**	**100**	**100.0**
Married couples	111.56	145	75.7
Married couples, no children	40.94	53	11.3
Married couples, with children	161.07	209	56.2
Oldest child under 6	515.56	669	34.4
Oldest child 6 to 17	77.09	100	14.6
Oldest child 18 or older	36.58	47	3.4
Single parent with child under 18	117.49	152	9.6
Single person	11.39	15	4.2
REGION			
Total households	**77.05**	**100**	**100.0**
Northeast	79.89	104	20.7
Midwest	62.86	82	19.5
South	69.06	90	31.3
West	102.69	133	28.3

Note: For definitions of best and biggest customers, see introduction or glossary.
Source: Calculations by New Strategist based on the 1997 Consumer Expenditure Survey

Apparel, Men's

Best customers:
- Householders aged 45 to 54
- Married couples with school-aged or older children

Customer trends
- The preferences of boomers and younger generations for casual clothes will dampen spending on men's apparel for years to come.

Married couples with school-aged or adult children at home are the best customers of men's apparel. Outfitting teen and young-adult sons, as well as dad, explains the higher spending of these households. Married couples with adult children at home spend 68 percent more than average on men's clothes, while those with school-aged children spend 49 percent more than average. Householders aged 45 to 54 are also important customers of men's apparel, spending 41 percent more than average on it. Many men of that age are in management positions that require a more expensive wardrobe.

The growing acceptance of casual dress in the workplace has made it possible for households to reduce their clothing budgets over the years. Boomers and younger generations are fully wedded to comfortable—and generally less expensive—clothing. Consequently, spending on men's apparel is likely to remain flat.

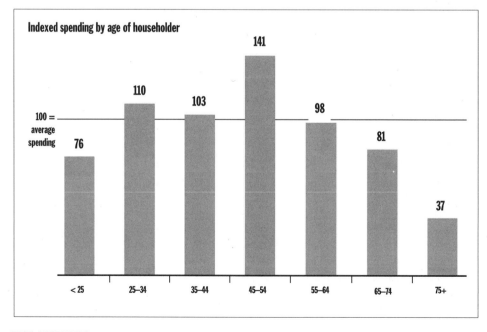

Indexed spending by age of householder

100 = average spending

< 25	25–34	35–44	45–54	55–64	65–74	75+
76	110	103	141	98	81	37

APPAREL, MEN'S

Total household spending $34,098,936,480
Average household spends   322.98

	average spending	best customers (index)	biggest customers (market share)
AGE OF HOUSEHOLDER			
Total households	**$322.98**	**100**	**100.0%**
Under age 25	246.61	76	5.4
Aged 25 to 34	354.62	110	20.7
Aged 35 to 44	332.61	103	24.0
Aged 45 to 54	456.79	141	25.9
Aged 55 to 64	318.05	98	11.5
Aged 65 to 74	261.83	81	9.3
Aged 75 or older	119.57	37	3.4
HOUSEHOLD INCOME			
Total households reporting income	**337.81**	**100**	**100.0**
Under $20,000	143.17	42	14.8
$20,000 to $29,999	214.06	63	9.3
$30,000 to $39,999	342.58	101	12.4
$40,000 to $49,999	358.93	106	9.9
$50,000 to $69,999	505.51	150	21.0
$70,000 or more	724.04	214	32.0
HOUSEHOLD TYPE			
Total households	**322.98**	**100**	**100.0**
Married couples	424.87	132	68.8
Married couples, no children	357.81	111	23.6
Married couples, with children	481.45	149	40.1
Oldest child under 6	405.94	126	6.5
Oldest child 6 to 17	480.72	149	21.7
Oldest child 18 or older	542.65	168	12.1
Single parent with child under 18	92.98	29	1.8
Single person	184.89	57	16.4
REGION			
Total households	**322.98**	**100**	**100.0**
Northeast	347.15	107	21.5
Midwest	352.83	109	26.1
South	270.59	84	29.2
West	351.17	109	23.1

Note: For definitions of best and biggest customers, see introduction or glossary.
Source: Calculations by New Strategist based on the 1997 Consumer Expenditure Survey

Apparel, Women's

Best customers:
- Householders aged 45 to 54
- Married couples with adult children

Customer trends:
- Likely growth in the market as the number of young women increases and the clothing industry learns to make clothes for real women.

Married couples with adult children at home are the best customers of women's apparel. These households spend 58 percent more than average on this category, in part because many have teen and young-adult daughters at home. Householders aged 45 to 54 also spend more than the average household on women's apparel. Many of these households include professional women who buy business wear in addition to casual clothes.

The market for women's clothing has suffered from the failure of designers to make clothes that look good on forty- and fiftysomething women, the best customers of women's apparel. Some clothing companies have begun to address this problem, a remedy that should boost sales. The growing number of young women should also energize the market for women's clothes.

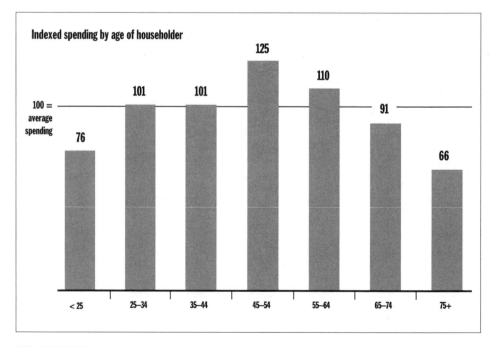

Indexed spending by age of householder

< 25	25–34	35–44	45–54	55–64	65–74	75+
76	101	101	125	110	91	66

100 = average spending

APPAREL, WOMEN'S

Total household spending	$60,628,073,760
Average household spends	574.26

	average spending	best customers (index)	biggest customers (market share)
AGE OF HOUSEHOLDER			
Total households	**$574.26**	**100**	**100.0%**
Under age 25	433.57	76	5.4
Aged 25 to 34	579.56	101	19.0
Aged 35 to 44	578.03	101	23.4
Aged 45 to 54	718.98	125	22.9
Aged 55 to 64	633.07	110	12.9
Aged 65 to 74	521.12	91	10.4
Aged 75 or older	381.05	66	6.2
HOUSEHOLD INCOME			
Total households reporting income	**591.18**	**100**	**100.0**
Under $20,000	295.81	50	17.4
$20,000 to $29,999	485.04	82	12.0
$30,000 to $39,999	559.59	95	11.6
$40,000 to $49,999	527.76	89	8.3
$50,000 to $69,999	902.92	153	21.4
$70,000 or more	1,134.43	192	28.7
HOUSEHOLD TYPE			
Total households	**574.26**	**100**	**100.0**
Married couples	703.72	123	64.1
Married couples, no children	717.80	125	26.7
Married couples, with children	688.06	120	32.2
Oldest child under 6	502.24	87	4.5
Oldest child 6 to 17	654.78	114	16.6
Oldest child 18 or older	908.29	158	11.4
Single parent with child under 18	436.18	76	4.8
Single person	365.92	64	18.3
REGION			
Total households	**574.26**	**100**	**100.0**
Northeast	623.51	109	21.7
Midwest	592.49	103	24.7
South	547.05	95	33.2
West	552.42	96	20.4

Note: For definitions of best and biggest customers, see introduction or glossary.
Source: Calculations by New Strategist based on the 1997 Consumer Expenditure Survey

Clothing Rental

Best customers:
- Householders aged 35 to 54
- Married couples with adult children
- Households in the Northeast and West

Customer trends:
- As the children of boomers enter the age for proms and weddings, this market should grow.

People rent clothing for work (uniforms) and for special occasions (formal wear). The best customers of clothing rental are married couples with adult children at home. Many couples with older children are renting tuxedos for proms and weddings. They spend nearly two and one-half times as much as the average household on clothing rental. Householders aged 45 to 54 spend 42 percent more than average while those aged 35 to 44 spend 38 percent more than average. People in these age groups are likely to have older children at home. Households in the West and Northeast, where formal events are more common than in other regions, also spend more than average.

As the children of boomers enter the teen and young-adult age groups when proms and weddings are common events, the market for clothing rental should get a boost.

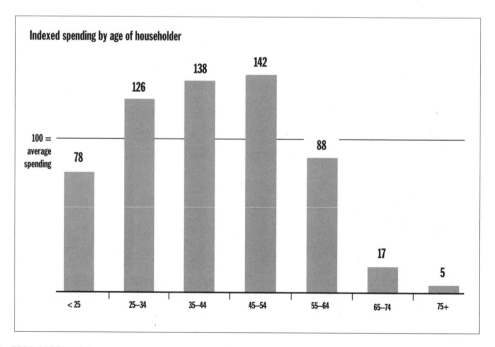

Indexed spending by age of householder

100 = average spending

< 25	25–34	35–44	45–54	55–64	65–74	75+
78	126	138	142	88	17	5

CLOTHING RENTAL

Total household spending $406,467,600
Average household spends   3.85

	average spending	best customers (index)	biggest customers (market share)
AGE OF HOUSEHOLDER			
Total households	**$3.85**	**100**	**100.0%**
Under age 25	3.01	78	5.6
Aged 25 to 34	4.87	126	23.9
Aged 35 to 44	5.31	138	32.1
Aged 45 to 54	5.46	142	26.0
Aged 55 to 64	3.37	88	10.2
Aged 65 to 74	0.67	17	2.0
Aged 75 or older	0.18	5	0.4
HOUSEHOLD INCOME			
Total households reporting income	**4.00**	**100**	**100.0**
Under $20,000	1.48	37	12.9
$20,000 to $29,999	1.71	43	6.2
$30,000 to $39,999	6.25	156	19.1
$40,000 to $49,999	3.20	80	7.5
$50,000 to $69,999	8.02	201	28.1
$70,000 or more	7.00	175	26.2
HOUSEHOLD TYPE			
Total households	**3.85**	**100**	**100.0**
Married couples	5.59	145	75.9
Married couples, no children	3.30	86	18.3
Married couples, with children	6.89	179	48.1
Oldest child under 6	3.58	93	4.8
Oldest child 6 to 17	6.92	180	26.1
Oldest child 18 or older	9.20	239	17.2
Single parent with child under 18	1.42	37	2.3
Single person	1.51	39	11.3
REGION			
Total households	**3.85**	**100**	**100.0**
Northeast	4.65	121	24.1
Midwest	2.80	73	17.4
South	3.62	94	32.8
West	4.69	122	25.9

Note: For definitions of best and biggest customers, see introduction or glossary.
Source: Calculations by New Strategist based on the 1997 Consumer Expenditure Survey

Jewelry

Best customers:
- Households with incomes of $70,000 or more
- Married couples with adult children at home

Customer trends
- Self-indulgent boomers with financial gains from the stock market should keep this market healthy.

The biggest spenders on jewelry are those with the most money to spend: households with incomes of $70,000 or more. This income group spends more than two and one-half times what the average household spends on jewelry, accounting for 41 percent of the market. Spending on jewelry by married couples with adult children at home is also considerably higher than average. Typically, these are dual-earner households in their peak earning years, meaning they have more money to spend. And, of course, middle-aged couples are a prime market for gifts of jewelry to celebrate 25th wedding anniversaries or 50th birthdays.

Older boomers are now in their peak earning years and many have seen their fortunes recently boosted by the stock market. Their desire to indulge themselves—and please their spouses—should benefit the jewelry market for now. But jewelry retailers are likely to face stiff competition from the Internet as tech-savvy buyers search for the best price.

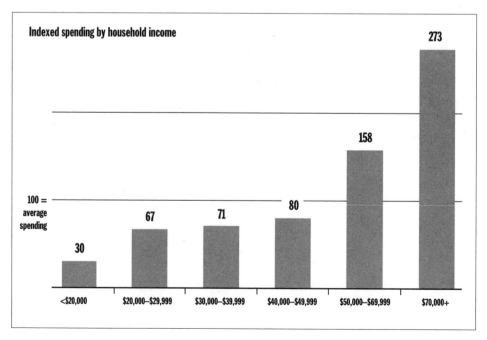

Indexed spending by household income

100 = average spending

<$20,000	$20,000–$29,999	$30,000–$39,999	$40,000–$49,999	$50,000–$69,999	$70,000+
30	67	71	80	158	273

JEWELRY

Total household spending	$14,993,903,520
Average household spends	142.02

	average spending	best customers (index)	biggest customers (market share)
AGE OF HOUSEHOLDER			
Total households	**$142.02**	**100**	**100.0%**
Under age 25	69.49	49	3.5
Aged 25 to 34	177.37	125	23.6
Aged 35 to 44	150.84	106	24.7
Aged 45 to 54	208.88	147	26.9
Aged 55 to 64	119.10	84	9.8
Aged 65 to 74	129.51	91	10.5
Aged 75 or older	27.23	19	1.8
HOUSEHOLD INCOME			
Total households reporting income	**144.54**	**100**	**100.0**
Under $20,000	43.36	30	10.4
$20,000 to $29,999	97.32	67	9.8
$30,000 to $39,999	102.45	71	8.7
$40,000 to $49,999	115.34	80	7.5
$50,000 to $69,999	229.08	158	22.2
$70,000 or more	394.22	273	40.8
HOUSEHOLD TYPE			
Total households	**142.02**	**100**	**100.0**
Married couples	189.64	134	69.8
Married couples, no children	196.61	138	29.5
Married couples, with children	186.42	131	35.3
Oldest child under 6	75.55	53	2.7
Oldest child 6 to 17	178.49	126	18.3
Oldest child 18 or older	294.90	208	14.9
Single parent with child under 18	63.31	45	2.8
Single person	36.94	26	7.5
REGION			
Total households	**142.02**	**100**	**100.0**
Northeast	222.64	157	31.3
Midwest	92.81	65	15.6
South	120.92	85	29.7
West	155.56	110	23.3

Note: For definitions of best and biggest customers, see introduction or glossary.
Source: Calculations by New Strategist based on the 1997 Consumer Expenditure Survey

Laundry and Dry Cleaning of Apparel, Coin-Operated

Best customers:
- Householders under age 35
- Married couples with children under age 6
- Single parents

Customer trends
- Growing number of young adults means more customers for laundromats in the years ahead.

Most young householders have relatively low incomes and rent homes that lack washers and dryers, making them some of the best customers of coin-operated laundries. Householders under age 35 spend 35 to 39 percent more than average on coin-operated apparel cleaning. What truly drives households to spend on laundry, however, is the presence of children in the home. The very best customers of coin-operated laundries are married couples with children under age 6, who spent 72 percent more than average on this item in 1997. Single parents spend 60 percent more than average.

During the next few years, the number of twentysomethings will grow as the Millennial generation enters the age group. Laundromats will see more customers and increased revenues.

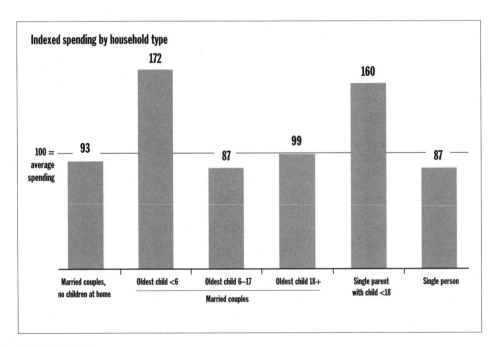

Indexed spending by household type

100 = average spending

Married couples, no children at home	Oldest child <6	Oldest child 6–17	Oldest child 18+	Single parent with child <18	Single person
93	172	87	99	160	87

Married couples

LAUNDRY AND DRY CLEANING OF APPAREL, COIN-OPERATED

Total household spending $2,194,925,040
Average household spends   20.79

	average spending	best customers (index)	biggest customers (market share)
AGE OF HOUSEHOLDER			
Total households	**$20.79**	**100**	**100.0%**
Under age 25	28.15	135	9.6
Aged 25 to 34	28.97	139	26.3
Aged 35 to 44	24.07	116	26.9
Aged 45 to 54	21.25	102	18.7
Aged 55 to 64	20.79	100	11.7
Aged 65 to 74	6.63	32	3.7
Aged 75 or older	6.59	32	3.0
HOUSEHOLD INCOME			
Total households reporting income	**20.94**	**100**	**100.0**
Under $20,000	20.83	99	34.6
$20,000 to $29,999	17.80	85	12.4
$30,000 to $39,999	18.26	87	10.7
$40,000 to $49,999	12.93	62	5.8
$50,000 to $69,999	20.66	99	13.8
$70,000 or more	32.02	153	22.9
HOUSEHOLD TYPE			
Total households	**20.79**	**100**	**100.0**
Married couples	21.58	104	54.3
Married couples, no children	19.34	93	19.9
Married couples, with children	22.53	108	29.1
Oldest child under 6	35.70	172	8.8
Oldest child 6 to 17	18.06	87	12.6
Oldest child 18 or older	20.52	99	7.1
Single parent with child under 18	33.36	160	10.1
Single person	17.99	87	24.9
REGION			
Total households	**20.79**	**100**	**100.0**
Northeast	21.92	105	21.1
Midwest	21.91	105	25.2
South	20.58	99	34.5
West	18.88	91	19.3

Note: For definitions of best and biggest customers, see introduction or glossary.
Source: Calculations by New Strategist based on the 1997 Consumer Expenditure Survey

Laundry and Dry Cleaning of Apparel, Professional

Best customers:	• **Householders aged 45 to 54** • **Households with incomes of $70,000 or more** • **Married couples with children under age 6** • **Married couples with adult children**
Customer trends:	• **Declining market because of the trend toward more casual clothing both at work and at home.**

Because affluent households are more likely to buy clothes that require professional dry cleaning, households with incomes of $70,000 or more are the best customers of professional laundry and dry cleaning. They spend well over two and one-half times as much as the average household and account for 41 percent of the market. Householders aged 45 to 54 make up a large share of affluent households, so it is no surprise that they also spend more than average. Married couples with preschoolers and those with adult children at home also spend more than average on professional laundry and dry cleaning.

The preference of younger generations for casual clothing means slowing growth or even decline in the demand for professional laundry and dry cleaning. As boomers retire beginning in about ten years, the market for professional laundry and dry cleaning could experience a downturn.

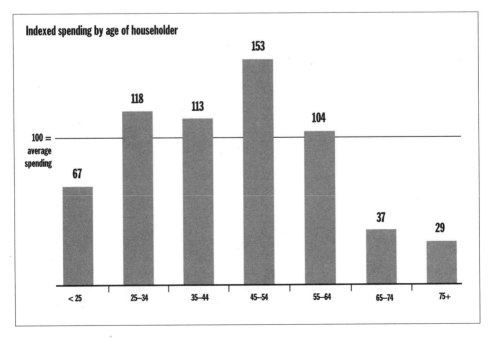

Indexed spending by age of householder

Age	< 25	25–34	35–44	45–54	55–64	65–74	75+
Index	67	118	113	153	104	37	29

100 = average spending

LAUNDRY AND DRY CLEANING OF APPAREL, PROFESSIONAL

Total household spending	$3,298,194,240	
Average household spends	31.24	

	average spending	best customers (index)	biggest customers (market share)
AGE OF HOUSEHOLDER			
Total households	**$31.24**	**100**	**100.0%**
Under age 25	20.96	67	4.8
Aged 25 to 34	36.97	118	22.3
Aged 35 to 44	35.18	113	26.2
Aged 45 to 54	47.72	153	28.0
Aged 55 to 64	32.50	104	12.1
Aged 65 to 74	11.56	37	4.2
Aged 75 or older	9.14	29	2.7
HOUSEHOLD INCOME			
Total households reporting income	**30.57**	**100**	**100.0**
Under $20,000	13.29	43	15.1
$20,000 to $29,999	19.58	64	9.4
$30,000 to $39,999	24.37	80	9.7
$40,000 to $49,999	16.26	53	5.0
$50,000 to $69,999	41.72	136	19.2
$70,000 or more	84.45	276	41.3
HOUSEHOLD TYPE			
Total households	**31.24**	**100**	**100.0**
Married couples	39.52	127	66.1
Married couples, no children	34.08	109	23.3
Married couples, with children	43.50	139	37.4
Oldest child under 6	49.91	160	8.2
Oldest child 6 to 17	38.89	124	18.1
Oldest child 18 or older	47.41	152	10.9
Single parent with child under 18	21.01	67	4.2
Single person	22.46	72	20.7
REGION			
Total households	**31.24**	**100**	**100.0**
Northeast	35.89	115	22.9
Midwest	31.09	100	23.8
South	33.33	107	37.2
West	23.84	76	16.2

Note: For definitions of best and biggest customers, see introduction or glossary.
Source: Calculations by New Strategist based on the 1997 Consumer Expenditure Survey

Sewing Material, Patterns, and Notions for Clothing

Best customers:
- Householders aged 55 to 74
- Married couples without children at home
- Married couples with adult children
- Households in the South and West

Customer trends:
- The sewing market is likely to decline since younger generations have neither the time nor the need to make their own clothes.

Married couples with adult children at home are the best customers of sewing supplies, spending more than twice as much as the average household on this item. Married couples without children at home spend 71 percent more than average on sewing supplies. An important factor behind the higher spending of these households is age—couples without children at home tend to be older, and householders aged 55 to 74 are higher-than-average spenders on sewing supplies. Households in the South and West also spend considerably more than average on sewing materials.

Older women are far more likely than younger ones to make clothes for themselves and other family members. Spending on sewing supplies for making clothes will decline because younger people who never learned how to sew are unlikely to take it up.

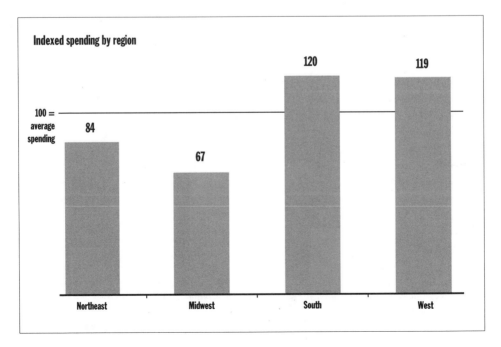

Indexed spending by region

100 = average spending

Northeast	Midwest	South	West
84	67	120	119

SEWING MATERIAL, PATTERNS, AND NOTIONS FOR CLOTHING

Total household spending $938,570,640
Average household spends   8.89

	average spending	best customers (index)	biggest customers (market share)
AGE OF HOUSEHOLDER			
Total households	**$8.89**	**100**	**100.0%**
Under age 25	0.58	7	0.5
Aged 25 to 34	5.85	66	12.4
Aged 35 to 44	10.22	115	26.7
Aged 45 to 54	11.30	127	23.3
Aged 55 to 64	13.90	156	18.2
Aged 65 to 74	12.42	140	16.0
Aged 75 or older	3.29	37	3.4
HOUSEHOLD INCOME			
Total households reporting income	**10.04**	**100**	**100.0**
Under $20,000	3.96	39	13.7
$20,000 to $29,999	9.75	97	14.2
$30,000 to $39,999	13.67	136	16.6
$40,000 to $49,999	8.33	83	7.8
$50,000 to $69,999	17.61	175	24.6
$70,000 or more	15.06	150	22.4
HOUSEHOLD TYPE			
Total households	**8.89**	**100**	**100.0**
Married couples	13.85	156	81.5
Married couples, no children	15.23	171	36.6
Married couples, with children	13.21	149	39.9
Oldest child under 6	4.76	54	2.8
Oldest child 6 to 17	13.28	149	21.7
Oldest child 18 or older	20.15	227	16.3
Single parent with child under 18	3.24	36	2.3
Single person	2.67	30	8.6
REGION			
Total households	**8.89**	**100**	**100.0**
Northeast	7.50	84	16.9
Midwest	5.98	67	16.1
South	10.64	120	41.8
West	10.57	119	25.3

Note: For definitions of best and biggest customers, see introduction or glossary.
Source: Calculations by New Strategist based on the 1997 Consumer Expenditure Survey

Shoe Repair

Best customers:
- Householders aged 45 to 54
- Married couples without children at home
- Married couples with adult children

Customer trends:
- If the economy continues to boom, the market for shoe repair may rise as people indulge in more expensive shoes.

Americans live in a throwaway culture. Rather than repair things, we throw them out and replace them. This is as true for shoes as it is for other items, but there are exceptions. People who can afford high-quality shoes are likely to repair rather than replace them. Householders aged 45 to 54, who are in their peak earnings years, spend more than average on shoe repair, as do married couples without children at home and those who live with adult children.

The market for shoe repair may get a boost if the economy continues to pump up incomes. The growing number of affluent households means more high-quality shoes that merit repair rather than replacement.

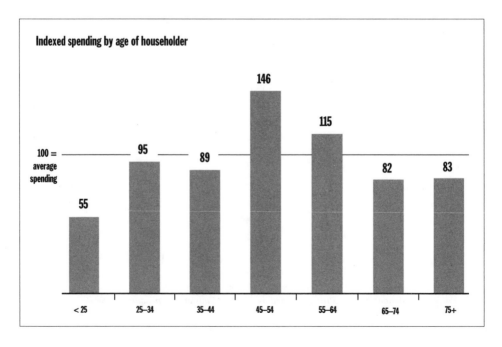

Indexed spending by age of householder

< 25	25–34	35–44	45–54	55–64	65–74	75+
55	95	89	146	115	82	83

100 = average spending

SHOE REPAIR

Total household spending	$251,270,880		
Average household spends	2.38		

	average spending	best customers (index)	biggest customers (market share)
AGE OF HOUSEHOLDER			
Total households	**$2.38**	**100**	**100.0%**
Under age 25	1.31	55	3.9
Aged 25 to 34	2.27	95	18.0
Aged 35 to 44	2.13	89	20.8
Aged 45 to 54	3.47	146	26.7
Aged 55 to 64	2.74	115	13.4
Aged 65 to 74	1.95	82	9.4
Aged 75 or older	1.98	83	7.7
HOUSEHOLD INCOME			
Total households reporting income	**2.47**	**100**	**100.0**
Under $20,000	1.41	57	19.9
$20,000 to $29,999	1.68	68	9.9
$30,000 to $39,999	1.26	51	6.2
$40,000 to $49,999	1.72	70	6.5
$50,000 to $69,999	3.60	146	20.5
$70,000 or more	6.10	247	36.9
HOUSEHOLD TYPE			
Total households	**2.38**	**100**	**100.0**
Married couples	3.37	142	74.0
Married couples, no children	3.68	155	33.0
Married couples, with children	3.27	137	36.9
Oldest child under 6	2.29	96	4.9
Oldest child 6 to 17	3.23	136	19.7
Oldest child 18 or older	4.04	170	12.2
Single parent with child under 18	0.57	24	1.5
Single person	1.58	66	19.1
REGION			
Total households	**2.38**	**100**	**100.0**
Northeast	1.74	73	14.6
Midwest	2.03	85	20.4
South	2.46	103	36.1
West	3.26	137	29.1

Note: For definitions of best and biggest customers, see introduction or glossary.
Source: Calculations by New Strategist based on the 1997 Consumer Expenditure Survey

Shoes, Children's

Best customers:	• Married couples with school-aged children
	• Single parents
	• Householders aged 35 to 44
Customer trends:	• Stable for the near future since the number of school-aged children is at a peak.

Married couples with school-aged children are the best customers of children's shoes. They spend more than three times as much as the average household on this category. In contrast, parents of preschoolers are average spenders on children's shoes. When children enter school, they need a greater variety of shoes, and they develop definite opinions about which shoes are cool—usually not the inexpensive ones. Single parents spend more than twice the average on children's shoes, but their spending is lower than married couples' because their incomes are lower. Householders aged 35 to 44 spend twice as much as average on children's shoes. Most people in this age group have school-aged children.

Children have trained their parents to spend just as much, if not more, on their shoes as on shoes for mom and dad. Parents aren't about to become cost cutters in this category, suggesting stability in the market. Another factor that will maintain the status quo is the peaking number of school-aged children.

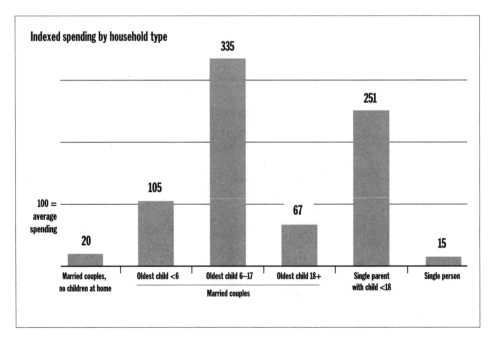

Indexed spending by household type

335 — Oldest child 6–17 (Married couples)
251 — Single parent with child <18
105 — Oldest child <6 (Married couples)
100 = average spending
67 — Oldest child 18+ (Married couples)
20 — Married couples, no children at home
15 — Single person

SHOES, CHILDREN'S

Total household spending	$6,015,720,480
Average household spends	56.98

	average spending	best customers (index)	biggest customers (market share)
AGE OF HOUSEHOLDER			
Total households	**$56.98**	**100**	**100.0%**
Under age 25	23.28	41	2.9
Aged 25 to 34	80.59	141	26.7
Aged 35 to 44	111.85	196	45.7
Aged 45 to 54	51.11	90	16.4
Aged 55 to 64	30.80	54	6.3
Aged 65 to 74	11.46	20	2.3
Aged 75 or older	5.29	9	0.9
HOUSEHOLD INCOME			
Total households reporting income	**62.24**	**100**	**100.0**
Under $20,000	45.14	73	25.3
$20,000 to $29,999	55.62	89	13.1
$30,000 to $39,999	70.91	114	13.9
$40,000 to $49,999	66.55	107	10.0
$50,000 to $69,999	72.17	116	16.3
$70,000 or more	86.78	139	20.8
HOUSEHOLD TYPE			
Total households	**56.98**	**100**	**100.0**
Married couples	73.73	129	67.7
Married couples, no children	11.19	20	4.2
Married couples, with children	122.75	215	57.9
Oldest child under 6	59.74	105	5.4
Oldest child 6 to 17	191.07	335	48.8
Oldest child 18 or older	37.99	67	4.8
Single parent with child under 18	143.15	251	15.8
Single person	8.42	15	4.2
REGION			
Total households	**56.98**	**100**	**100.0**
Northeast	47.64	84	16.7
Midwest	51.72	91	21.7
South	62.62	110	38.3
West	62.30	109	23.2

Note: For definitions of best and biggest customers, see introduction or glossary.
Source: Calculations by New Strategist based on the 1997 Consumer Expenditure Survey

Shoes, Men's

Best customers:
- Married couples with school-aged children
- Married couples with adult children

Customer trends:
- The market for men's shoes should begin to grow as the number of young men grows.

Married couples with older children are the biggest spenders on men's shoes. They spend twice as much as the average household. Spending is higher in these households because many are buying for adult sons as well as for dad. Married couples with school-aged children spend 54 percent more than average on men's shoes.

The demand for men's shoes is driven largely by population trends. Because the number of young men is beginning to grow as the children of boomers come of age, the market for men's shoes should get a boost.

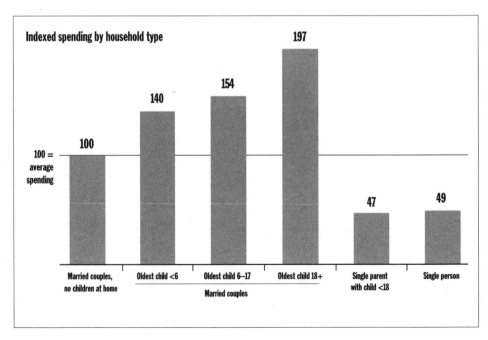

Indexed spending by household type

100	140	154	197	47	49

100 = average spending

Married couples, no children at home | Oldest child <6 | Oldest child 6–17 | Oldest child 18+ | Single parent with child <18 | Single person

Married couples

SHOES, MEN'S

Total household spending	$10,602,997,680
Average household spends	100.43

	average spending	best customers (index)	biggest customers (market share)
AGE OF HOUSEHOLDER			
Total households	**$100.43**	**100**	**100.0%**
Under age 25	110.94	110	7.8
Aged 25 to 34	99.85	99	18.8
Aged 35 to 44	121.33	121	28.1
Aged 45 to 54	117.18	117	21.4
Aged 55 to 64	108.78	108	12.6
Aged 65 to 74	83.29	83	9.5
Aged 75 or older	19.39	19	1.8
HOUSEHOLD INCOME			
Total households reporting income	**102.71**	**100**	**100.0**
Under $20,000	71.09	69	24.1
$20,000 to $29,999	98.94	96	14.1
$30,000 to $39,999	90.51	88	10.8
$40,000 to $49,999	74.51	73	6.8
$50,000 to $69,999	156.32	152	21.4
$70,000 or more	159.97	156	23.3
HOUSEHOLD TYPE			
Total households	**100.43**	**100**	**100.0**
Married couples	133.19	133	69.3
Married couples, no children	100.51	100	21.4
Married couples, with children	163.04	162	43.6
Oldest child under 6	141.07	140	7.2
Oldest child 6 to 17	154.71	154	22.4
Oldest child 18 or older	198.13	197	14.2
Single parent with child under 18	47.62	47	3.0
Single person	48.87	49	14.0
REGION			
Total households	**100.43**	**100**	**100.0**
Northeast	105.91	105	21.1
Midwest	96.98	97	23.1
South	104.46	104	36.3
West	92.81	92	19.6

Note: For definitions of best and biggest customers, see introduction or glossary.
Source: Calculations by New Strategist based on the 1997 Consumer Expenditure Survey

Shoes, Women's

Women own a greater number and variety of shoes than men or children do because each of their roles—mother, wife, career woman, health club member—requires a different pair of shoes. The best customers of women's shoes are those who don't have to devote their shoe-buying dollars to children's feet. Married couples with adult children at home spend 34 percent more than average on women's shoes. Those without children at home spend 29 percent more than average.

The biggest spenders on women's shoes, householders aged 55 to 64, will soon fill with aging boomers. This growth should fuel the market as empty-nest boomers indulge in shoes for themselves.

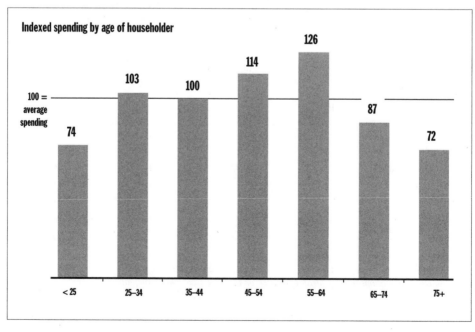

Indexed spending by age of householder

100 = average spending

< 25	25–34	35–44	45–54	55–64	65–74	75+
74	103	100	114	126	87	72

SHOES, WOMEN'S

Total household spending $16,587,045,360
Average household spends   157.11

	average spending	best customers (index)	biggest customers (market share)
AGE OF HOUSEHOLDER			
Total households	**$157.11**	**100**	**100.0%**
Under age 25	116.01	74	5.2
Aged 25 to 34	161.49	103	19.4
Aged 35 to 44	156.94	100	23.2
Aged 45 to 54	178.65	114	20.8
Aged 55 to 64	197.83	126	14.7
Aged 65 to 74	137.24	87	10.0
Aged 75 or older	112.93	72	6.7
HOUSEHOLD INCOME			
Total households reporting income	**160.65**	**100**	**100.0**
Under $20,000	100.68	63	21.8
$20,000 to $29,999	106.00	66	9.6
$30,000 to $39,999	177.80	111	13.5
$40,000 to $49,999	201.91	126	11.8
$50,000 to $69,999	221.67	138	19.4
$70,000 or more	247.46	154	23.0
HOUSEHOLD TYPE			
Total households	**157.11**	**100**	**100.0**
Married couples	186.61	119	62.1
Married couples, no children	202.16	129	27.5
Married couples, with children	176.99	113	30.3
Oldest child under 6	128.33	82	4.2
Oldest child 6 to 17	180.86	115	16.7
Oldest child 18 or older	209.82	134	9.6
Single parent with child under 18	129.31	82	5.2
Single person	105.00	67	19.2
REGION			
Total households	**157.11**	**100**	**100.0**
Northeast	185.22	118	23.6
Midwest	149.29	95	22.7
South	155.48	99	34.5
West	142.57	91	19.3

Note: For definitions of best and biggest customers, see introduction or glossary.
Source: Calculations by New Strategist based on the 1997 Consumer Expenditure Survey

Watch and Jewelry Repair

Best customers:
- Householders aged 55 to 74
- Married couples without children at home
- Households in the West

Customer trends:
- Possible increase as boomers inherit family heirlooms.

Older Americans are more likely than younger people to own valuable watches and jewelry, some of which are heirlooms with strong sentimental value. They are also more likely to have incomes that allow them to buy expensive watches and jewelry rather than cheaper disposable items. Consequently, the best customers for watch and jewelry repair are householders aged 55 to 74. This age group spends 30 to 34 percent more than the average household on watch and jewelry repair. Households in the West also spend more than average on this category.

As boomers inherit the family jewels during the next few years, demand for watch and jewelry repair should grow.

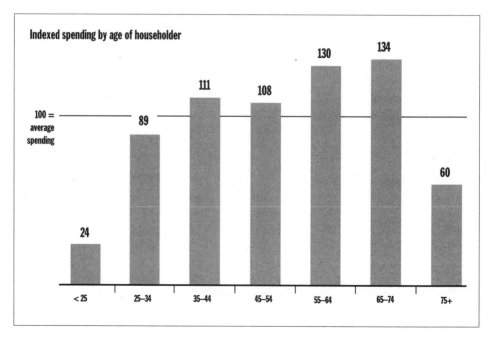

Indexed spending by age of householder

100 = average spending

< 25	25–34	35–44	45–54	55–64	65–74	75+
24	89	111	108	130	134	60

WATCH AND JEWELRY REPAIR

Total household spending $536,326,080
Average household spends   5.08

	average spending	best customers (index)	biggest customers (market share)
AGE OF HOUSEHOLDER			
Total households	**$5.08**	**100**	**100.0%**
Under age 25	1.23	24	1.7
Aged 25 to 34	4.53	89	16.8
Aged 35 to 44	5.63	111	25.8
Aged 45 to 54	5.47	108	19.7
Aged 55 to 64	6.58	130	15.1
Aged 65 to 74	6.79	134	15.3
Aged 75 or older	3.04	60	5.6
HOUSEHOLD INCOME			
Total households reporting income	**5.54**	**100**	**100.0**
Under $20,000	3.23	58	20.3
$20,000 to $29,999	3.64	66	9.6
$30,000 to $39,999	3.98	72	8.8
$40,000 to $49,999	4.54	82	7.7
$50,000 to $69,999	9.88	178	25.0
$70,000 or more	10.64	192	28.7
HOUSEHOLD TYPE			
Total households	**5.08**	**100**	**100.0**
Married couples	6.34	125	65.3
Married couples, no children	7.07	139	29.7
Married couples, with children	5.59	110	29.6
Oldest child under 6	5.45	107	5.5
Oldest child 6 to 17	6.42	126	18.4
Oldest child 18 or older	4.03	79	5.7
Single parent with child under 18	4.82	95	6.0
Single person	3.52	69	19.9
REGION			
Total households	**5.08**	**100**	**100.0**
Northeast	5.19	102	20.4
Midwest	5.01	99	23.6
South	3.92	77	26.9
West	6.98	137	29.2

Note: For definitions of best and biggest customers, see introduction or glossary.
Source: Calculations by New Strategist based on the 1997 Consumer Expenditure Survey

Watches

Best customers:
- Householders aged 35 to 44
- Households with incomes of $30,000 to $39,999
- Married couples with children under age 6

Customer trends:
- Market may level off since the number of 35-to-44-year-olds will decline as Generation X fills the age group.

Households with incomes of $30,000 to $39,999 are the best customers of watches. These households spend more than twice as much as the average household on timepieces. Young, time-pressed parents are also among the best customers of watches. Householders aged 35 to 44 spend 84 percent more than average on watches and account for 43 percent of the market. Married couples with preschoolers spend 72 percent more than average.

The number of people aged 35 to 44 will soon begin to decline as the small Generation X replaces the youngest boomers in the age group. This could erode the market unless retailers are successful in targeting older customers who can afford higher-quality, more expensive watches.

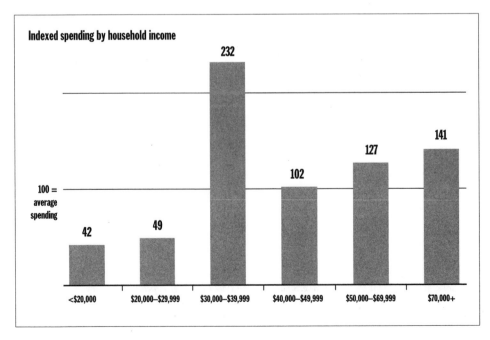

Indexed spending by household income

<$20,000	$20,000–$29,999	$30,000–$39,999	$40,000–$49,999	$50,000–$69,999	$70,000+
42	49	232	102	127	141

100 = average spending

WATCHES

Total household spending	$3,135,607,200	
Average household spends	29.70	

	average spending	best customers (index)	biggest customers (market share)
AGE OF HOUSEHOLDER			
Total households	**$29.70**	**100**	**100.0%**
Under age 25	21.69	73	5.2
Aged 25 to 34	32.63	110	20.7
Aged 35 to 44	54.58	184	42.8
Aged 45 to 54	13.54	46	8.4
Aged 55 to 64	36.67	123	14.4
Aged 65 to 74	20.83	70	8.0
Aged 75 or older	2.98	10	0.9
HOUSEHOLD INCOME			
Total households reporting income	**30.26**	**100**	**100.0**
Under $20,000	12.79	42	14.7
$20,000 to $29,999	14.75	49	7.1
$30,000 to $39,999	70.20	232	28.4
$40,000 to $49,999	30.98	102	9.6
$50,000 to $69,999	38.33	127	17.8
$70,000 or more	42.58	141	21.0
HOUSEHOLD TYPE			
Total households	**29.70**	**100**	**100.0**
Married couples	35.07	118	61.7
Married couples, no children	26.32	89	18.9
Married couples, with children	39.54	133	35.8
Oldest child under 6	51.23	172	8.9
Oldest child 6 to 17	37.09	125	18.2
Oldest child 18 or older	34.71	117	8.4
Single parent with child under 18	20.16	68	4.3
Single person	21.63	73	20.9
REGION			
Total households	**29.70**	**100**	**100.0**
Northeast	34.52	116	23.2
Midwest	19.80	67	15.9
South	29.92	101	35.1
West	35.74	120	25.6

Note: For definitions of best and biggest customers, see introduction or glossary.
Source: Calculations by New Strategist based on the 1997 Consumer Expenditure Survey

Chapter 3.

Computers

Computers

A few short years ago, the average household spent nothing on computers. Today, computers have become an important expenditure category. Among the hundreds of individual products and services examined in this book (see Appendix C), computer hardware for nonbusiness use ranks 44th, ahead of jewelry, day care, and physician's services.

The average household spent $210.50 in 1997 on nonbusiness computer hardware and software, as well as online and repair services. This amount seems small because it includes both purchasers and nonpurchases. Among the 3.6 percent of households purchasing a computer during an average quarter of 1997, spending amounted to $1,132.73 (see Appendix B).

The biggest spenders on computers for nonbusiness use are families with school-aged or older children at home. Baby-boom parents, encouraging their children to become computer literate, are the driving force behind spending on computers. Spending in this category has nowhere to go but up as computers become universally owned and online access becomes as necessary to daily life as telephones or televisions.

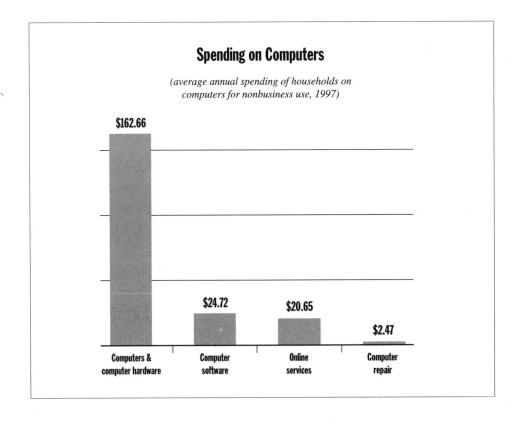

Spending on Computers

(average annual spending of households on computers for nonbusiness use, 1997)

$162.66 — Computers & computer hardware
$24.72 — Computer software
$20.65 — Online services
$2.47 — Computer repair

Computer Spending

(average annual spending of households on computer hardware, software, and services for nonbusiness use, and percent distribution of spending by type, 1997)

Total spending on computer equipment and services for nonbusiness use	**$210.50**	**100.0%**
Computers and computer hardware for nonbusiness use	162.66	77.3
Computer software and accessories for nonbusiness use	24.72	11.7
Computer information services	20.65	9.8
Computer systems for nonbusiness use, repair	2.47	1.2

Computer Information Services

Best customers:
- Householders aged 25 to 54
- Married couples with school-aged or adult children at home

Customer trends:
- Continued strong growth as more Americans discover the benefits of the Internet.

Householders aged 25 to 54 are the best customers of computer information services, spending 21 to 57 percent more than the average household on this item. Many subscribe to services beyond basic Internet access, such as financial services and news providers. Married couples with children at home spend 60 percent more than average on computer information services as they seek the convenience of online information and shopping and encourage their children to become computer literate.

The market for computer information services should remain strong as more households with computers subscribe. The growing number of school-aged children will also contribute to the expansion of this market.

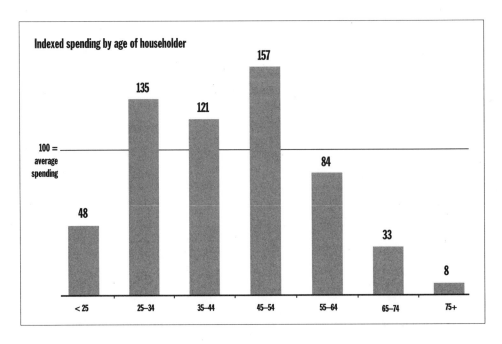

Indexed spending by age of householder

100 = average spending

< 25	25–34	35–44	45–54	55–64	65–74	75+
48	135	121	157	84	33	8

COMPUTER INFORMATION SERVICES

Total household spending	$2,180,144,400	
Average household spends	20.65	

	average spending	best customers (index)	biggest customers (market share)
AGE OF HOUSEHOLDER			
Total households	**$20.65**	**100**	**100.0%**
Under age 25	9.82	48	3.4
Aged 25 to 34	27.81	135	25.4
Aged 35 to 44	25.01	121	28.2
Aged 45 to 54	32.35	157	28.7
Aged 55 to 64	17.31	84	9.8
Aged 65 to 74	6.87	33	3.8
Aged 75 or older	1.71	8	0.8
HOUSEHOLD INCOME			
Total households reporting income	**21.35**	**100**	**100.0**
Under $20,000	5.22	24	8.5
$20,000 to $29,999	10.14	47	6.9
$30,000 to $39,999	16.04	75	9.2
$40,000 to $49,999	23.02	108	10.1
$50,000 to $69,999	34.15	160	22.5
$70,000 or more	61.19	287	42.8
HOUSEHOLD TYPE			
Total households	**20.65**	**100**	**100.0**
Married couples	27.34	132	69.2
Married couples, no children	21.46	104	22.2
Married couples, with children	33.01	160	43.0
Oldest child under 6	32.57	158	8.1
Oldest child 6 to 17	34.20	166	24.1
Oldest child 18 or older	30.92	150	10.8
Single parent with child under 18	10.87	53	3.3
Single person	13.44	65	18.7
REGION			
Total households	**20.65**	**100**	**100.0**
Northeast	25.11	122	24.3
Midwest	15.95	77	18.5
South	17.66	86	29.8
West	26.68	129	27.4

Note: For definitions of best and biggest customers, see introduction or glossary.
Source: Calculations by New Strategist based on the 1997 Consumer Expenditure Survey

Computer Software and Accessories for Nonbusiness Use

Best customers:
- Householders aged 35 to 54
- Married couples with school-aged or adult children at home
- Households in the West

Customer trends:
- The large school-aged population should keep software sales healthy.

Married couples with school-aged or older children at home are the best customers of computer software, spending more than twice as much as the average household on this item. Householders aged 35 to 54 also spend more than average because many such households include school-aged and older children. Households in the West spend 48 percent more than average on computer software.

Software sales should remain brisk since the majority of households now own computers. The presence of a large school-aged population also contributes to a healthy market since many parents are eager to buy educational and recreational software for their children.

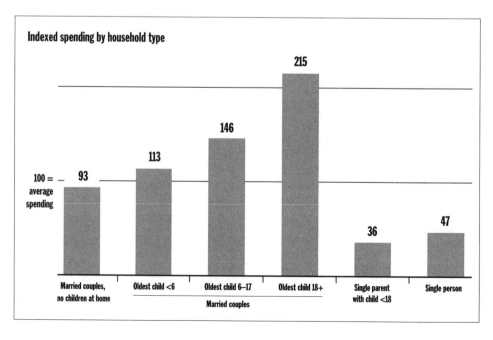

Indexed spending by household type

- Married couples, no children at home: 93
- Oldest child <6: 113
- Oldest child 6–17: 146
- Oldest child 18+: 215
- Single parent with child <18: 36
- Single person: 47

100 = average spending

Married couples

COMPUTER SOFTWARE AND ACCESSORIES FOR NONBUSINESS USE

Total household spending $2,609,838,720
Average household spends   24.72

	average spending	best customers (index)	biggest customers (market share)
AGE OF HOUSEHOLDER			
Total households	**$24.72**	**100**	**100.0%**
Under age 25	11.49	46	3.3
Aged 25 to 34	26.87	109	20.5
Aged 35 to 44	33.88	137	31.9
Aged 45 to 54	38.36	155	28.4
Aged 55 to 64	21.00	85	9.9
Aged 65 to 74	10.54	43	4.9
Aged 75 or older	2.88	12	1.1
HOUSEHOLD INCOME			
Total households reporting income	**26.83**	**100**	**100.0**
Under $20,000	7.97	30	10.3
$20,000 to $29,999	10.91	41	5.9
$30,000 to $39,999	17.65	66	8.0
$40,000 to $49,999	33.13	123	11.5
$50,000 to $69,999	48.73	182	25.5
$70,000 or more	69.32	258	38.6
HOUSEHOLD TYPE			
Total households	**24.72**	**100**	**100.0**
Married couples	32.09	130	67.9
Married couples, no children	23.01	93	19.9
Married couples, with children	39.09	158	42.5
Oldest child under 6	28.00	113	5.8
Oldest child 6 to 17	36.02	146	21.2
Oldest child 18 or older	53.23	215	15.5
Single parent with child under 18	8.94	36	2.3
Single person	11.62	47	13.5
REGION			
Total households	**24.72**	**100**	**100.0**
Northeast	23.21	94	18.8
Midwest	21.78	88	21.1
South	20.33	82	28.7
West	36.67	148	31.5

Note: For definitions of best and biggest customers, see introduction or glossary.
Source: Calculations by New Strategist based on the 1997 Consumer Expenditure Survey

Computer Systems for Nonbusiness Use, Repair

Best customers:
- Householders aged 65 to 74
- Married couples without children
- Households in the South

Customer trends:
- Little or no growth as long as computers become obsolete so quickly.

The best customers of nonbusiness computer system repair are householders aged 65 to 74, spending 67 percent more than average. Unlike younger householders, older people have been slow to adopt new technologies. As they discover computers, they need assistance in setting up equipment and installing hardware, services that are classified as "repair." Married couples without children at home (who tend to be older householders) spend 32 percent more than average on computer repairs, while householders in the South spend 25 percent more.

The market for computer repair isn't likely to grow much, if at all, because computers are getting easier to work with and Americans are becoming more comfortable with them. Perhaps the most limiting factor in this market, however, is the quick obsolescence of today's machines. So long as new computers replace older models every few years, the market for nonbusiness computer repair will remain flat.

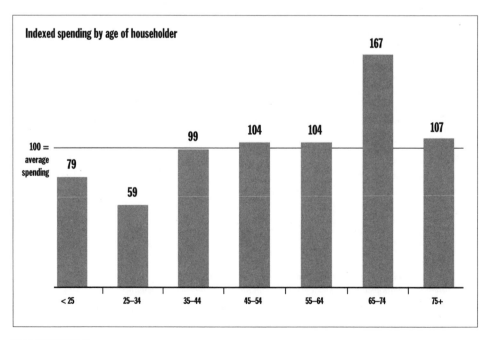

Indexed spending by age of householder

< 25	25–34	35–44	45–54	55–64	65–74	75+
79	59	99	104	104	167	107

100 = average spending

COMPUTER SYSTEMS FOR NONBUSINESS USE, REPAIR

Total household spending $260,772,720
Average household spends   2.47

	average spending	best customers (index)	biggest customers (market share)
Age of householder			
Total households	**$2.47**	**100**	**100.0%**
Under age 25	1.96	79	5.6
Aged 25 to 34	1.46	59	11.2
Aged 35 to 44	2.45	99	23.1
Aged 45 to 54	2.58	104	19.1
Aged 55 to 64	2.57	104	12.1
Aged 65 to 74	4.13	167	19.2
Aged 75 or older	2.64	107	9.9
HOUSEHOLD INCOME			
Total households reporting income	**2.70**	**100**	**100.0**
Under $20,000	1.04	39	13.5
$20,000 to $29,999	3.82	141	20.7
$30,000 to $39,999	1.84	68	8.3
$40,000 to $49,999	2.05	76	7.1
$50,000 to $69,999	5.50	204	28.6
$70,000 or more	3.93	146	21.8
HOUSEHOLD TYPE			
Total households	**2.47**	**100**	**100.0**
Married couples	2.77	112	58.6
Married couples, no children	3.27	132	28.3
Married couples, with children	2.63	106	28.6
Oldest child under 6	2.90	117	6.0
Oldest child 6 to 17	2.78	113	16.4
Oldest child 18 or older	2.15	87	6.3
Single parent with child under 18	2.60	105	6.6
Single person	2.10	85	24.4
REGION			
Total households	**2.47**	**100**	**100.0**
Northeast	2.20	89	17.8
Midwest	1.94	79	18.8
South	3.09	125	43.6
West	2.33	94	20.0

Note: For definitions of best and biggest customers, see introduction or glossary.
Source: Calculations by New Strategist based on the 1997 Consumer Expenditure Survey

Computers and Computer Hardware for Nonbusiness Use

Best customers:
- Householders aged 45 to 54
- Married couples with school-aged or adult children at home

Customer trends:
- Continued strong growth as more households buy computers and others upgrade their equipment.

Households with school-aged or older children spend 61 percent more than the average household on computers and computer hardware as they rush to include their children in the computer revolution. These households buy a lot more than the standard desktop computer. They also buy color printers, scanners, and other bells and whistles that add fun and functionality to computing. Householders aged 45 to 54 have the highest incomes, on average, and their 64 percent above-average spending on computer hardware reflects this fact.

Spending on computers and computer hardware for nonbusiness use should continue to grow strongly as more households buy computers and others upgrade their equipment.

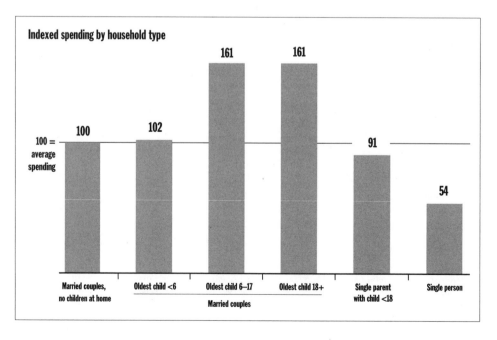

Indexed spending by household type

Married couples, no children at home	Oldest child <6	Oldest child 6–17	Oldest child 18+	Single parent with child <18	Single person
100	102	161	161	91	54

100 = average spending

Married couples

COMPUTERS AND COMPUTER HARDWARE FOR NONBUSINESS USE

Total household spending $17,172,992,160
Average household spends   162.66

	average spending	best customers (index)	biggest customers (market share)
Age of householder			
Total households	**$162.66**	**100**	**100.0%**
Under age 25	103.55	64	4.5
Aged 25 to 34	149.92	92	17.4
Aged 35 to 44	191.32	118	27.4
Aged 45 to 54	266.71	164	30.0
Aged 55 to 64	176.61	109	12.7
Aged 65 to 74	94.28	58	6.6
Aged 75 or older	23.90	15	1.4
HOUSEHOLD INCOME			
Total households reporting income	**169.01**	**100**	**100.0**
Under $20,000	47.57	28	9.8
$20,000 to $29,999	90.23	53	7.8
$30,000 to $39,999	136.13	81	9.8
$40,000 to $49,999	195.30	116	10.8
$50,000 to $69,999	284.28	168	23.6
$70,000 or more	431.19	255	38.1
HOUSEHOLD TYPE			
Total households	**162.66**	**100**	**100.0**
Married couples	208.48	128	67.0
Married couples, no children	162.63	100	21.3
Married couples, with children	243.32	150	40.2
Oldest child under 6	165.56	102	5.2
Oldest child 6 to 17	261.49	161	23.4
Oldest child 18 or older	262.16	161	11.6
Single parent with child under 18	148.25	91	5.7
Single person	87.47	54	15.4
REGION			
Total households	**162.66**	**100**	**100.0**
Northeast	186.56	115	22.9
Midwest	143.86	88	21.1
South	131.38	81	28.2
West	212.69	131	27.8

Note: For definitions of best and biggest customers, see introduction or glossary.
Source: Calculations by New Strategist based on the 1997 Consumer Expenditure Survey

Chapter 4.

Education

Education

Spending by the average household on education reveals little, since few households have educational expenses in a given year, driving down the averages. In 1997, the average household spent $570.70 on education, including $326.09 for college tuition. With public colleges costing thousands of dollars a year, and private colleges costing tens of thousands, this figure is artificially low. A more realistic spending figure for college tuition can be found in Appendix B, which shows the spending of purchasers only. During an average quarter of 1997, just 5 percent of households paid for college tuition. These purchasers spent $1,471.53 per quarter—or, if multiplied by four to approximate an annual cost, $5,886 for tuition.

More important than the average spending figures, however, are the patterns of spending by demographic characteristic. Householders under age 25 and those aged 45 to 54 are the biggest spenders on college tuition. The younger householders are paying for their own college education, while the older ones are paying for their children's education. With boomers now entering the 45-to-54 age group, and with an expanding teen and young-adult population, spending on education will rise steadily for years to come.

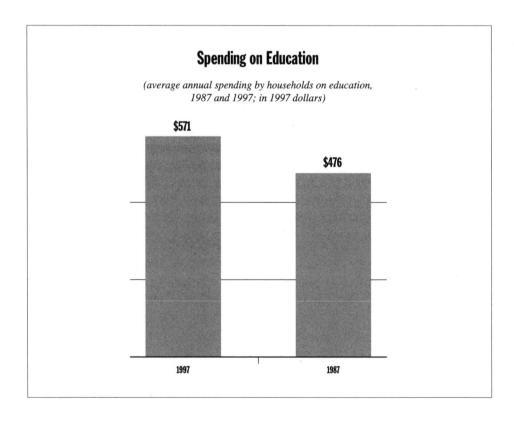

Spending on Education

(average annual spending by households on education, 1987 and 1997; in 1997 dollars)

$571

$476

1997

1987

Education Spending

(average annual spending of households on education, and percent distribution of spending by type, 1997)

Total spending on education	**$570.70**	**100.0%**
Tuition, college	326.09	57.1
Tuition, elementary and high school	90.14	15.8
Books and supplies, college	47.48	8.3
Books and supplies, elementary and high school	12.22	2.1
Books and supplies, day care and nursery school	3.13	0.5

Note: Numbers will not add to total because not all categories are shown.

Books and Supplies, College

Best customers:	• **Householders under age 25**
	• **Married couples with adult children**
	• **People living alone**
Customer trends:	• **Growth is likely since the college-aged population is increasing and the percentage of people attending college is rising. The market faces competition from electronic information sources, however.**

Householders under age 25 are the best customers of college books and supplies, spending more than four times as much as the average household. They are young adults attending college. Married couples with adult children at home spend more than twice as much as the average household on this item because many have children attending college. Householders aged 45 to 54 spend 51 percent more than average on college books and supplies because they are parents of college students.

The size of the young-adult population will increase for the next few years and a growing proportion of young adults will attend college. The market for college books and supplies is likely to expand because of these trends. The outlook is not entirely positive, however, because traditional textbook publishers face competition from companies delivering text and reference information via electronic media.

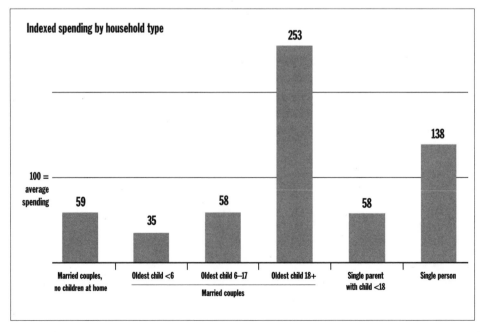

Indexed spending by household type

100 = average spending

Married couples, no children at home	Oldest child <6	Oldest child 6–17	Oldest child 18+	Single parent with child <18	Single person
59	35	58	253	58	138

Married couples

BOOKS AND SUPPLIES, COLLEGE

Total household spending	**$5,053,923,120**
Average household spends	**47.87**

	average spending	best customers (index)	biggest customers (market share)
AGE OF HOUSEHOLDER			
Total households	**$47.87**	**100**	**100.0%**
Under age 25	226.59	473	33.6
Aged 25 to 34	40.32	84	15.9
Aged 35 to 44	27.27	57	13.3
Aged 45 to 54	72.19	151	27.6
Aged 55 to 64	24.65	51	6.0
Aged 65 to 74	12.46	26	3.0
Aged 75 or older	3.07	6	0.6
HOUSEHOLD INCOME			
Total households reporting income	**47.48**	**100**	**100.0**
Under $20,000	57.21	120	42.0
$20,000 to $29,999	29.81	63	9.2
$30,000 to $39,999	31.52	66	8.1
$40,000 to $49,999	33.70	71	6.6
$50,000 to $69,999	43.89	92	13.0
$70,000 or more	67.10	141	21.1
HOUSEHOLD TYPE			
Total households	**47.87**	**100**	**100.0**
Married couples	41.21	86	45.4
Married couples, no children	28.19	59	12.6
Married couples, with children	50.80	106	28.5
Oldest child under 6	16.81	35	1.8
Oldest child 6 to 17	27.99	58	8.5
Oldest child 18 or older	121.26	253	18.2
Single parent with child under 18	27.63	58	3.6
Single person	66.18	138	39.7
REGION			
Total households	**47.87**	**100**	**100.0**
Northeast	65.82	137	27.5
Midwest	38.75	81	19.3
South	37.91	79	27.6
West	57.60	120	25.6

Note: For definitions of best and biggest customers, see introduction or glossary.
Source: Calculations by New Strategist based on the 1997 Consumer Expenditure Survey

Books and Supplies, Day Care and Nursery School

Best customers:
- **Householders aged 35 to 44**
- **Households with incomes of $70,000 or more**
- **Married couples with school-aged or adult children at home**

Customer trends:
- **Continued increase in the share of working mothers may offset the decline in the number of young children, resulting in a stable market.**

The best customers of day care and nursery school books and supplies are households with incomes of $70,000 or more. These households spend two and one-half times as much as the average household on this item. Married couples with school-aged children spend almost three times as much as the average household. Among married couples with children aged 18 or older at home, spending on day care and nursery school books and supplies is twice the average. Many of these householders are grandparents of children enrolled in day care programs. Householders aged 35 to 44 spend much more than average on this item because most are parents of preschool or school-aged children.

The number of young children is now falling slightly. Ordinarily, this would result in a decline in the market for day care and nursery school books and supplies. But the percentage of mothers who work is rising, offsetting the decline.

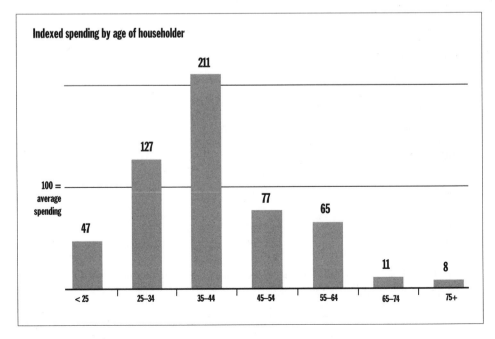

Indexed spending by age of householder

< 25	25–34	35–44	45–54	55–64	65–74	75+
47	127	211	77	65	11	8

100 = average spending

BOOKS AND SUPPLIES, DAY CARE AND NURSERY SCHOOL

Total household spending	$330,452,880		
Average household spends	3.13		

	average spending	best customers (index)	biggest customers (market share)
AGE OF HOUSEHOLDER			
Total households	**$3.13**	**100**	**100.0%**
Under age 25	1.47	47	3.3
Aged 25 to 34	3.97	127	23.9
Aged 35 to 44	6.59	211	49.0
Aged 45 to 54	2.42	77	14.2
Aged 55 to 64	2.05	65	7.6
Aged 65 to 74	0.35	11	1.3
Aged 75 or older	0.26	8	0.8
HOUSEHOLD INCOME			
Total households reporting income	**2.95**	**100**	**100.0**
Under $20,000	0.98	33	11.6
$20,000 to $29,999	1.77	60	8.8
$30,000 to $39,999	2.86	97	11.9
$40,000 to $49,999	4.05	137	12.8
$50,000 to $69,999	3.65	124	17.4
$70,000 or more	7.45	253	37.8
HOUSEHOLD TYPE			
Total households	**3.13**	**100**	**100.0**
Married couples	4.83	154	80.7
Married couples, no children	0.96	31	6.5
Married couples, with children	7.49	239	64.3
Oldest child under 6	4.42	141	7.3
Oldest child 6 to 17	8.91	285	41.4
Oldest child 18 or older	6.79	217	15.6
Single parent with child under 18	0.65	21	1.3
Single person	1.40	45	12.8
REGION			
Total households	**3.13**	**100**	**100.0**
Northeast	1.57	50	10.0
Midwest	2.90	93	22.1
South	3.49	112	38.9
West	4.28	137	29.0

Note: For definitions of best and biggest customers, see introduction or glossary.
Source: Calculations by New Strategist based on the 1997 Consumer Expenditure Survey

Books and Supplies, Elementary and High School

Best customers:	• Householders aged 35 to 44
	• Married couples with school-aged children
Customer trends:	• Stable for now, but the market faces competition from the Internet and CD-ROM—based texts and reference materials.

The best customers of elementary and high school books and supplies are parents of school-aged children. Married couples whose oldest child is aged 6 to 17 spend four times as much as the average household on this item, accounting for 60 percent of the market for elementary and high school books and supplies. Householders aged 35 to 44, who make up a large proportion of the parents of school-aged children, spend more than twice as much as the average household on this item.

The market for elementary and high school books and supplies should remain stable in the near future. Eventually, however, reference materials on the Internet and on CD-ROM will cut into the market.

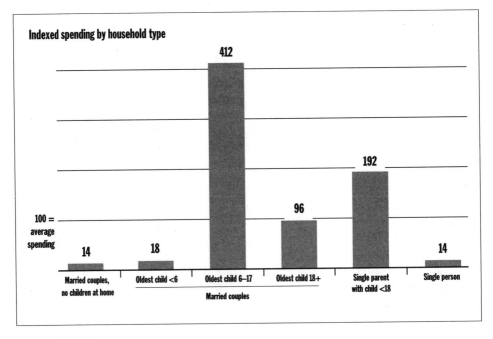

Indexed spending by household type

BOOKS AND SUPPLIES, ELEMENTARY AND HIGH SCHOOL

Total household spending $1,290,138,720
Average household spends   12.22

	average spending	best customers (index)	biggest customers (market share)
AGE OF HOUSEHOLDER			
Total households	**$12.22**	**100**	**100.0%**
Under age 25	2.64	22	1.5
Aged 25 to 34	11.97	98	18.5
Aged 35 to 44	27.15	222	51.7
Aged 45 to 54	15.48	127	23.2
Aged 55 to 64	3.94	32	3.8
Aged 65 to 74	1.06	9	1.0
Aged 75 or older	0.46	4	0.4
HOUSEHOLD INCOME			
Total households reporting income	**12.88**	**100**	**100.0**
Under $20,000	5.05	39	13.7
$20,000 to $29,999	8.33	65	9.4
$30,000 to $39,999	14.24	111	13.5
$40,000 to $49,999	15.30	119	11.1
$50,000 to $69,999	25.32	197	27.6
$70,000 or more	21.23	165	24.6
HOUSEHOLD TYPE			
Total households	**12.22**	**100**	**100.0**
Married couples	17.98	147	76.9
Married couples, no children	1.68	14	2.9
Married couples, with children	30.84	252	67.8
Oldest child under 6	2.22	18	0.9
Oldest child 6 to 17	50.38	412	60.0
Oldest child 18 or older	11.77	96	6.9
Single parent with child under 18	23.49	192	12.1
Single person	1.66	14	3.9
REGION			
Total households	**12.22**	**100**	**100.0**
Northeast	7.30	60	11.9
Midwest	15.13	124	29.6
South	12.36	101	35.3
West	13.35	109	23.2

Note: For definitions of best and biggest customers, see introduction or glossary.
Source: Calculations by New Strategist based on the 1997 Consumer Expenditure Survey

Tuition, College

Best customers:
- Married couples with adult children
- Householders under age 25
- Householders aged 45 to 54

Customer trends:
- Market will increase as the college-aged population grows and more young people attend college.

Married couples with adult children at home spend the most on college tuition. These households spend more than three times as much as the average household as they put their children through college. Householders aged 45 to 54 spend twice as much as average because many in this age group are parents of college-aged children. Spending on college tuition by householders under age 25 is two and one-half times the average. These young adults are putting themselves through college.

Spending on college tuition will continue to increase as the college-aged population grows and a larger percentage of high school graduates attend college.

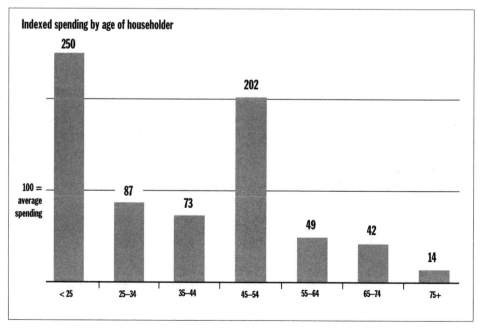

Indexed spending by age of householder

250   87   73   202   49   42   14

100 = average spending

< 25   25–34   35–44   45–54   55–64   65–74   75+

TUITION, COLLEGE

Total household spending $34,427,277,840
Average household spends 326.09

	average spending	best customers (index)	biggest customers (market share)
AGE OF HOUSEHOLDER			
Total households	**$326.09**	**100**	**100.0%**
Under age 25	815.97	250	17.8
Aged 25 to 34	284.67	87	16.5
Aged 35 to 44	239.60	73	17.1
Aged 45 to 54	657.12	202	36.9
Aged 55 to 64	158.32	49	5.7
Aged 65 to 74	136.53	42	4.8
Aged 75 or older	44.48	14	1.3
HOUSEHOLD INCOME			
Total households reporting income	**303.14**	**100**	**100.0**
Under $20,000	252.69	83	29.0
$20,000 to $29,999	161.19	53	7.8
$30,000 to $39,999	191.04	63	7.7
$40,000 to $49,999	237.13	78	7.3
$50,000 to $69,999	347.45	115	16.1
$70,000 or more	650.78	215	32.1
HOUSEHOLD TYPE			
Total households	**326.09**	**100**	**100.0**
Married couples	370.66	114	59.4
Married couples, no children	285.23	87	18.7
Married couples, with children	456.00	140	37.6
Oldest child under 6	192.06	59	3.0
Oldest child 6 to 17	255.09	78	11.4
Oldest child 18 or older	1,051.35	322	23.2
Single parent with child under 18	135.47	42	2.6
Single person	323.52	99	28.5
REGION			
Total households	**326.09**	**100**	**100.0**
Northeast	463.28	142	28.4
Midwest	309.20	95	22.7
South	226.95	70	24.3
West	378.87	116	24.7

Note: For definitions of best and biggest customers, see introduction or glossary.
Source: Calculations by New Strategist based on the 1997 Consumer Expenditure Survey

Tuition, Elementary and High School

Best customers:
- Married couples with school-aged children
- Single parents
- Households in the Northeast

Customer trends:
- Unless public schools can improve their reputations, spending on elementary and high school tuition is likely to increase.

It's no surprise that parents of school-aged children are the best customers of elementary and high school tuition. Married couples whose oldest child is aged 6 to 17 spend almost four times as much as the average household on private school tuition, accounting for 54 percent of the market. Single parents with children under age 18 spend three times the average. Households in the Northeast spend 68 percent more than average on this item.

Dissatisfaction with the public school system is at an all-time high. Unless public schools are able to improve their reputations, more Americans are likely to send their children to private school for at least a few years, boosting spending in this category.

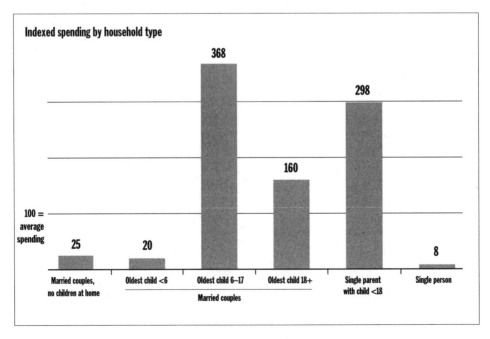

Indexed spending by household type

Married couples, no children at home	Oldest child <6	Oldest child 6–17	Oldest child 18+	Single parent with child <18	Single person
25	20	368	160	298	8

Married couples

100 = average spending

TUITION, ELEMENTARY AND HIGH SCHOOL

Total household spending $2,033,393,760
Average household spends   90.14

	average spending	best customers (index)	biggest customers (market share)
AGE OF HOUSEHOLDER			
Total households	**$90.14**	**100**	**100.0%**
Under age 25	1.87	2	0.1
Aged 25 to 34	44.31	49	9.3
Aged 35 to 44	175.15	194	45.2
Aged 45 to 54	177.85	197	36.1
Aged 55 to 64	28.26	31	3.7
Aged 65 to 74	43.80	49	5.6
Aged 75 or older	–	–	–
HOUSEHOLD INCOME			
Total households reporting income	**87.97**	**100**	**100.0**
Under $20,000	7.92	9	3.1
$20,000 to $29,999	86.53	98	14.4
$30,000 to $39,999	45.88	52	6.4
$40,000 to $49,999	89.98	102	9.6
$50,000 to $69,999	179.42	204	28.6
$70,000 or more	223.22	254	37.9
HOUSEHOLD TYPE			
Total households	**90.14**	**100**	**100.0**
Married couples	130.93	145	76.0
Married couples, no children	22.60	25	5.4
Married couples, with children	221.24	245	66.0
Oldest child under 6	17.77	20	1.0
Oldest child 6 to 17	331.30	368	53.5
Oldest child 18 or older	144.12	160	11.5
Single parent with child under 18	268.57	298	18.7
Single person	7.07	8	2.3
REGION			
Total households	**90.14**	**100**	**100.0**
Northeast	151.28	168	33.5
Midwest	62.89	70	16.7
South	81.41	90	31.5
West	77.63	86	18.3

Note: (–) means sample is too small to make a reliable estimate. For definitions of best and biggest customers, see introduction or glossary.
Source: Calculations by New Strategist based on the 1997 Consumer Expenditure Survey

Chapter 5.

Entertainment

Entertainment

Americans spend more on entertainment than they do on clothes, a total of $1,813.28 in 1997. During the past decade, the average household boosted its spending on entertainment by a substantial 8 percent, after adjusting for inflation—despite cuts in spending on most other discretionary items. Spending rose 14 percent for miscellaneous entertainment supplies and equipment, a category that includes athletic gear, tents, backpacks, skis, snorkels, bicycles, fishing tackle and all the other paraphernalia that fills our closets and garages.

The biggest spenders on entertainment are householders with children, money, or time. Younger adults spend big on the entertainment items favored by children, such as recreational lessons. Those aged 45 to 54 spend the most on expensive items such as motor boats. Older householders spend the most on entertainment items that require more free time to enjoy, such as club memberships, motorized campers, and hunting and fishing equipment.

Spending on entertainment will rise along with the economic fortunes of Americans. Growth in spending will receive an added boost from an increasingly active older population with the time, money, and desire to have fun.

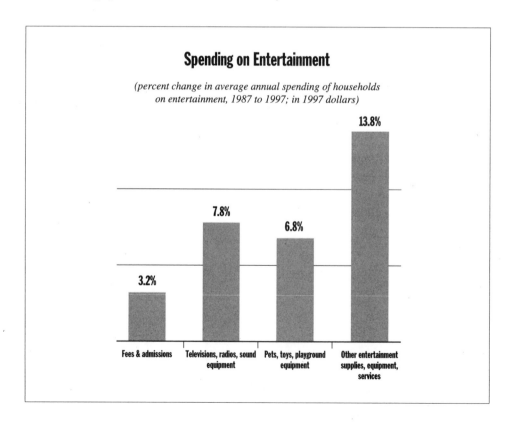

Spending on Entertainment

(percent change in average annual spending of households on entertainment, 1987 to 1997; in 1997 dollars)

- Fees & admissions: 3.2%
- Televisions, radios, sound equipment: 7.8%
- Pets, toys, playground equipment: 6.8%
- Other entertainment supplies, equipment, services: 13.8%

Entertainment Spending

(average annual spending of households on entertainment, and percent distribution of spending on entertainment by type, 1997)

Total spending on entertainment	**$1,813.28**	**100.0%**
Cable TV or community antenna	262.34	14.5
Movie, theater, opera, ballet tickets	128.64	7.1
Toys, games, hobbies, and tricycles	127.68	7.0
Motor boats	109.17	6.0
Fees for participant sports	102.92	5.7
Pet food	87.23	4.8
Social, recreation, and civic club memberships	75.12	4.1
Fees for recreational lessons	67.17	3.7
Television sets	65.80	3.6
Athletic gear, game tables, exercise equipment	60.02	3.3
Pet purchase, supplies, medicine, services	57.32	3.2
Veterinary services	53.49	2.9
Admission to sporting events	47.49	2.6
Sound equipment and accessories	42.29	2.3
Videotape, disc, film rental	40.30	2.2
CDs, audio tapes, records	39.41	2.2
Film processing	29.36	1.6
VCRs and video disc players	26.58	1.5
Motorized campers	26.17	1.4
Musical instruments and accessories	23.96	1.3
Photographer's fees	23.45	1.3
Video cassettes, tapes, and discs	22.15	1.2
Film	21.36	1.2
Video game hardware and software	19.74	1.1
Hunting and fishing equipment	16.11	0.9
Bicycles	15.27	0.8
Photographic equipment	14.19	0.8
Radios	11.76	0.6
CD, tape, record, video mail order clubs	10.59	0.6
Docking and landing fees	9.52	0.5
Camping equipment	9.34	0.5
TV, radio, sound equipment repair	6.65	0.4
Winter sports equipment	5.50	0.3
Water sports equipment	4.52	0.2
Satellite dishes	3.41	0.2
Recreational vehicle rental	3.35	0.2
Musical instruments, rental and repair	1.64	0.1

Note: Numbers will not add to total because not all categories are shown, including recreation expenses on out-of-town trips which is in the Travel chapter.

Admission to Sporting Events

(includes spending on admissions to sporting events while on out-of-town trips,
also shown separately in the Travel section)

Best customers:
- Households with children aged 6 or older
- Householders aged 35 to 54
- Households with incomes of $70,000 or more
- Households in the West

Customer trends:
- Possible slowdown as technology allows more events to be seen from the comfort of home.

Householders with children aged 6 or older spend more on admissions to sporting events than any other household type. Those with children aged 18 or older spend 60 percent more than average. Householders aged 35 to 54 also spend significantly more than the average household on admissions to sporting events—accounting for 56 percent of the market—because many have school-aged or older children at home. High-income households and households in the West are also big spenders on admissions to sporting events.

The future health of this market is questionable. Spending on admissions to sporting events is likely to grow slowly or not at all in the years ahead because of the expanding availability of televised sports.

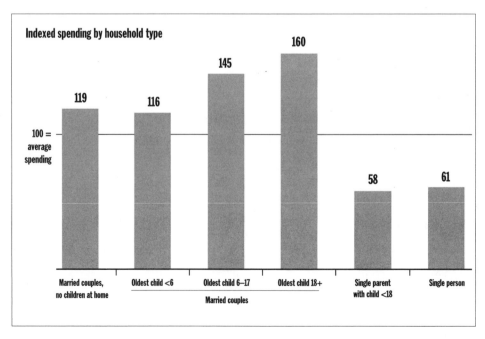

Indexed spending by household type

Married couples, no children at home	Oldest child <6	Oldest child 6–17	Oldest child 18+	Single parent with child <18	Single person
119	116	145	160	58	61

100 = average spending

Married couples

Admission to Sporting Events

Total households spend	$5,013,804,000	
Average household spends	47.49	

	average spending	best customers (index)	biggest customers (market share)
AGE OF HOUSEHOLDER			
Total households	**$47.49**	**100**	**100.0%**
Under age 25	39.12	82	5.9
Aged 25 to 34	43.16	91	17.1
Aged 35 to 44	62.77	132	30.7
Aged 45 to 54	65.68	138	25.3
Aged 55 to 64	38.85	82	9.5
Aged 65 to 74	39.21	83	9.5
Aged 75 or older	9.63	20	1.9
HOUSEHOLD INCOME			
Total households reporting income	**50.62**	**100**	**100.0**
Under $20,000	17.09	34	11.8
$20,000 to $29,999	25.98	51	7.5
$30,000 to $39,999	40.62	80	9.8
$40,000 to $49,999	48.52	96	9.0
$50,000 to $69,999	69.54	137	19.3
$70,000 or more	144.57	286	42.7
HOUSEHOLD TYPE			
Total households	**47.49**	**100**	**100.0**
Married couples	62.20	131	68.5
Married couples, no children	56.52	119	25.4
Married couples, with children	68.24	144	38.6
Oldest child under 6	55.27	116	6.0
Oldest child 6 to 17	68.95	145	21.1
Oldest child 18 or older	76.08	160	11.5
Single parent with child under 18	27.77	58	3.7
Single person	28.84	61	17.4
REGION			
Total households	**47.49**	**100**	**100.0**
Northeast	42.26	89	17.8
Midwest	48.79	103	24.5
South	40.16	85	29.5
West	62.96	133	28.2

Note: For definitions of best and biggest customers, see introduction or glossary.
Source: Calculations by New Strategist based on the 1997 Consumer Expenditure Survey

Athletic Gear, Game Tables, Exercise Equipment

Best customers:
- Married couples with school-aged children
- Households with incomes of $70,000 or more
- Households in the Midwest

Customer trends:
- The growing health consciousness of the baby-boom generation should spur growth in this market during the next few years.

Children drive much of the spending in this category. Married couples with school-aged children spend two and one-half times as much as the average household on athletic gear, game tables, and exercise equipment. Households with incomes of $70,000 or more also spend two and one-half times as much as the average household on these items. Not only are affluent households better able to afford sports equipment, they are also more likely to have houses large enough to accommodate them. Households in the Midwest, where winters are too harsh for regular outdoor exercise, spend 51 percent more than average.

Americans' health consciousness should grow as the baby-boom generation ages, stimulating the market for athletic gear, game tables, and exercise equipment.

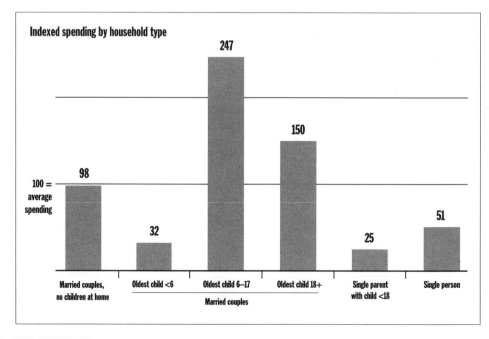

Indexed spending by household type

247 — Oldest child 6–17 (Married couples)
150 — Oldest child 18+ (Married couples)
98 — Married couples, no children at home
32 — Oldest child <6 (Married couples)
25 — Single parent with child <18
51 — Single person

100 = average spending

ATHLETIC GEAR, GAME TABLES, EXERCISE EQUIPMENT

Total household spending $6,336,671,520
Average household spends   60.02

	average spending	best customers (index)	biggest customers (market share)
AGE OF HOUSEHOLDER			
Total households	**$60.02**	**100**	**100.0%**
Under age 25	50.92	85	6.0
Aged 25 to 34	41.18	69	12.9
Aged 35 to 44	89.60	149	34.7
Aged 45 to 54	101.94	170	31.1
Aged 55 to 64	48.84	81	9.5
Aged 65 to 74	16.32	27	3.1
Aged 75 or older	19.25	32	3.0
HOUSEHOLD INCOME			
Total households reporting income	**61.04**	**100**	**100.0**
Under $20,000	29.56	48	16.9
$20,000 to $29,999	24.64	40	5.9
$30,000 to $39,999	49.03	80	9.8
$40,000 to $49,999	33.00	54	5.1
$50,000 to $69,999	102.16	167	23.5
$70,000 or more	156.03	256	38.2
HOUSEHOLD TYPE			
Total households	**60.02**	**100**	**100.0**
Married couples	81.91	136	71.4
Married couples, no children	58.64	98	20.9
Married couples, with children	105.21	175	47.1
Oldest child under 6	19.00	32	1.6
Oldest child 6 to 17	148.50	247	36.0
Oldest child 18 or older	90.11	150	10.8
Single parent with child under 18	15.13	25	1.6
Single person	30.32	51	14.5
REGION			
Total households	**60.02**	**100**	**100.0**
Northeast	68.57	114	22.8
Midwest	90.90	151	36.2
South	40.48	67	23.5
West	49.48	82	17.5

Note: For definitions of best and biggest customers, see introduction or glossary.
Source: Calculations by New Strategist based on the 1997 Consumer Expenditure Survey

Bicycles

Best customers:
- Married couples with school-aged children
- Householders aged 25 to 44
- Households in the West

Customer trends:
- Many localities, especially those in areas with moderate climates, are constructing walking and bicycling trails. This should benefit the market for bicycles.

Bicycling has long been a favorite activity of children. This is why married couples with school-aged children spend two and one-half times as much as the average household on bicycles. Householders aged 25 to 44 spend 60 to 67 percent more than average on bicycles for the same reason: they are buying bikes for their children. The mild weather enjoyed nearly year-round by much of the West undoubtedly contributes to the fact that households in the region spend 65 percent more than average on bicycles.

Increasingly crowded highways could drive bicycles off the road and dampen sales. But many communities are building paved walking and cycling trails that enable children and adults to bicycle in safety. This should help counteract the effects of highway congestion.

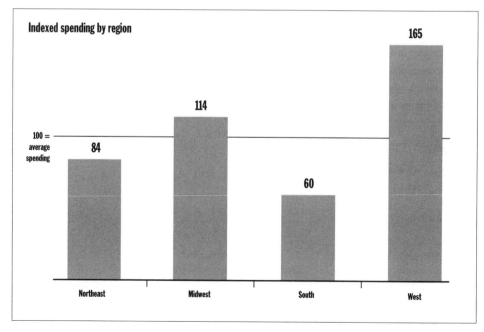

Indexed spending by region

100 = average spending

Northeast 84
Midwest 114
South 60
West 165

BICYCLES

Total household spending	$1,612,145,520	
Average household spends	15.27	

	average spending	best customers (index)	biggest customers (market share)
Age of householder			
Total households	**$15.27**	**100**	**100.0%**
Under age 25	9.03	59	4.2
Aged 25 to 34	25.55	167	31.6
Aged 35 to 44	24.44	160	37.2
Aged 45 to 54	16.11	106	19.3
Aged 55 to 64	7.86	51	6.0
Aged 65 to 74	1.49	10	1.1
Aged 75 or older	0.90	6	0.5
HOUSEHOLD INCOME			
Total households reporting income	**16.25**	**100**	**100.0**
Under $20,000	5.11	31	10.9
$20,000 to $29,999	14.58	90	13.1
$30,000 to $39,999	22.24	137	16.7
$40,000 to $49,999	13.21	81	7.6
$50,000 to $69,999	24.43	150	21.1
$70,000 or more	33.18	204	30.5
HOUSEHOLD TYPE			
Total households	**15.27**	**100**	**100.0**
Married couples	19.05	125	65.2
Married couples, no children	9.42	62	13.2
Married couples, with children	28.73	188	50.6
Oldest child under 6	17.73	116	6.0
Oldest child 6 to 17	41.14	269	39.2
Oldest child 18 or older	11.47	75	5.4
Single parent with child under 18	9.80	64	4.0
Single person	7.82	51	14.7
REGION			
Total households	**15.27**	**100**	**100.0**
Northeast	12.77	84	16.7
Midwest	17.45	114	27.3
South	9.17	60	21.0
West	25.20	165	35.1

Note: For definitions of best and biggest customers, see introduction or glossary.
Source: Calculations by New Strategist based on the 1997 Consumer Expenditure Survey

Cable TV or Community Antenna

Best customers:
- Married couples with adult children

Customer trends:
- Spending may decline as competition grows. New offerings, such as Internet access, will be needed to stimulate growth in this mature market.

The best customers of cable TV or community antenna are married couples with adult children at home. Most of these households have multiple television sets to accommodate the different viewing habits of family members.

Cable TV or community antenna has almost reached saturation level in American households. New offerings, such as Internet access, will be needed to keep the market growing. In some areas of the country, the market for cable TV is becoming more competitive and this could reduce spending. But spending is likely to rise in areas with little competition as deregulated cable providers boost prices.

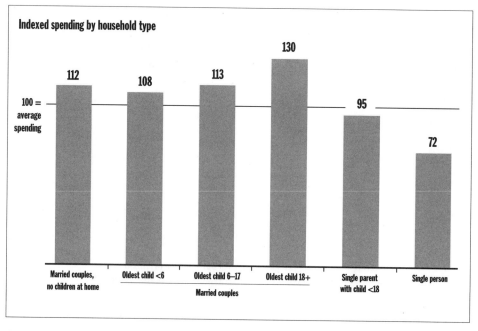

Indexed spending by household type

Married couples, no children at home	Oldest child <6	Oldest child 6–17	Oldest child 18+	Single parent with child <18	Single person
112	108	113	130	95	72

100 = average spending

Married couples

CABLE TV OR COMMUNITY ANTENNA

Total household spending	$27,696,807,840		
Average household spends	262.34		

	average spending	best customers (index)	biggest customers (market share)
AGE OF HOUSEHOLDER			
Total households	**$262.34**	**100**	**100.0%**
Under age 25	134.87	51	3.7
Aged 25 to 34	249.97	95	18.0
Aged 35 to 44	279.52	107	24.8
Aged 45 to 54	307.55	117	21.5
Aged 55 to 64	293.31	112	13.0
Aged 65 to 74	266.65	102	11.7
Aged 75 or older	208.69	80	7.4
HOUSEHOLD INCOME			
Total households reporting income	**265.14**	**100**	**100.0**
Under $20,000	187.40	71	24.6
$20,000 to $29,999	247.59	93	13.6
$30,000 to $39,999	264.24	100	12.2
$40,000 to $49,999	314.13	118	11.1
$50,000 to $69,999	326.88	123	17.3
$70,000 or more	375.53	142	21.2
HOUSEHOLD TYPE			
Total households	**262.34**	**100**	**100.0**
Married couples	303.07	116	60.4
Married couples, no children	294.72	112	24.0
Married couples, with children	305.33	116	31.3
Oldest child under 6	284.45	108	5.6
Oldest child 6 to 17	295.66	113	16.4
Oldest child 18 or older	339.81	130	9.3
Single parent with child under 18	249.03	95	6.0
Single person	188.04	72	20.6
REGION			
Total households	**262.34**	**100**	**100.0**
Northeast	296.03	113	22.5
Midwest	249.61	95	22.7
South	267.71	102	35.6
West	236.17	90	19.1

Note: For definitions of best and biggest customers, see introduction or glossary.
Source: Calculations by New Strategist based on the 1997 Consumer Expenditure Survey

Camping Equipment

Best customers: • Married couples with school-aged or older children

Customer trends: • Sales of camping equipment should benefit from the growing number of families with school-aged or older children.

Camping is a family activity, which is why married couples with school-aged children are the best customers of camping equipment. They spend three times as much as the average household on this item, accounting for 44 percent of the market. Married couples with adult children at home are also big spenders on camping equipment.

Americans like to enjoy nature without giving up the comforts of home. Camping equipment sales have benefited from new materials and technologies that enable families to rough it in comfort. The most important factor driving spending on camping equipment, however, is the growing number of families with children old enough to enjoy the activity.

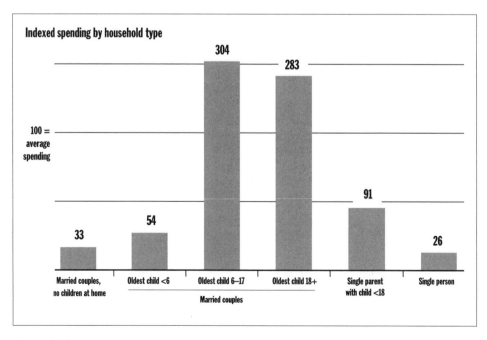

Indexed spending by household type

- 100 = average spending

33	54	304	283	91	26
Married couples, no children at home	Oldest child <6	Oldest child 6–17	Oldest child 18+	Single parent with child <18	Single person
		Married couples			

CAMPING EQUIPMENT

Total household spending $986,079,840
Average household spends   9.34

	average spending	best customers (index)	biggest customers (market share)
AGE OF HOUSEHOLDER			
Total households	**$9.34**	**100**	**100.0%**
Under age 25	10.36	111	7.9
Aged 25 to 34	8.23	88	16.6
Aged 35 to 44	13.86	148	34.5
Aged 45 to 54	15.08	161	29.6
Aged 55 to 64	2.69	29	3.4
Aged 65 to 74	7.06	76	8.7
Aged 75 or older	–	–	–
HOUSEHOLD INCOME			
Total households reporting income	**8.56**	**100**	**100.0**
Under $20,000	5.13	60	20.9
$20,000 to $29,999	5.79	68	9.9
$30,000 to $39,999	6.03	70	8.6
$40,000 to $49,999	4.46	52	4.9
$50,000 to $69,999	7.39	86	12.1
$70,000 or more	24.07	281	42.0
HOUSEHOLD TYPE			
Total households	**9.34**	**100**	**100.0**
Married couples	13.08	140	73.2
Married couples, no children	3.04	33	6.9
Married couples, with children	22.82	244	65.7
Oldest child under 6	5.06	54	2.8
Oldest child 6 to 17	28.38	304	44.2
Oldest child 18 or older	26.47	283	20.4
Single parent with child under 18	8.52	91	5.7
Single person	2.45	26	7.5
REGION			
Total households	**9.34**	**100**	**100.0**
Northeast	10.02	107	21.4
Midwest	13.07	140	33.4
South	6.35	68	23.7
West	9.40	101	21.4

Note: (–) means sample is too small to make a reliable estimate. For definitions of best and biggest customers, see introduction or glossary.
Source: Calculations by New Strategist based on the 1997 Consumer Expenditure Survey

CD, Tape, Record, Video Mail Order Clubs

Best customers:
- Married couples with school-aged or older children
- Householders aged 45 to 54

Customer trends:
- Spending will decline as competition from online sellers heats up.

Time-pressed families are the best customers of mail order clubs selling CDs, tapes, records, and videos. Married couples with school-aged or older children spend about 40 percent more than the average household on mail order clubs. Many of these purchases are for teens and young-adult children. Householders aged 45 to 54, who often have more money than time, spend 33 percent more than average on this item.

Mail order clubs appeal to consumers by offering a large selection, good prices, and convenience. But as online sellers of music and videos proliferate, traditional mail order clubs will lose much of their appeal.

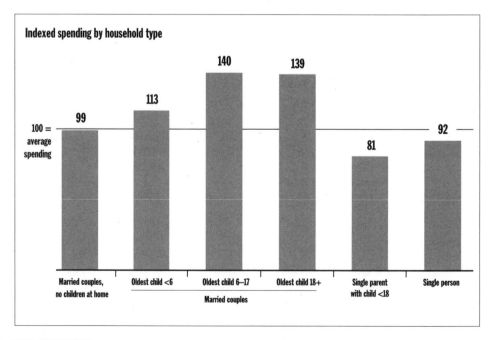

Indexed spending by household type

99	113	140	139	81	92
Married couples, no children at home	Oldest child <6	Oldest child 6–17	Oldest child 18+	Single parent with child <18	Single person

100 = average spending

Married couples

CD, TAPE, RECORD, VIDEO MAIL ORDER CLUBS

Total household spending	$1,118,049,840
Average household spends	10.59

	average spending	best customers (index)	biggest customers (market share)
AGE OF HOUSEHOLDER			
Total households	**$10.59**	**100**	**100.0%**
Under age 25	12.71	120	8.5
Aged 25 to 34	13.60	128	24.2
Aged 35 to 44	11.19	106	24.6
Aged 45 to 54	14.07	133	24.3
Aged 55 to 64	8.67	82	9.6
Aged 65 to 74	5.07	48	5.5
Aged 75 or older	3.68	35	3.2
HOUSEHOLD INCOME			
Total households reporting income	**11.02**	**100**	**100.0**
Under $20,000	6.97	63	22.0
$20,000 to $29,999	6.52	59	8.6
$30,000 to $39,999	12.57	114	13.9
$40,000 to $49,999	11.36	103	9.6
$50,000 to $69,999	14.05	127	17.9
$70,000 or more	20.50	186	27.8
HOUSEHOLD TYPE			
Total households	**10.59**	**100**	**100.0**
Married couples	12.08	114	59.6
Married couples, no children	10.47	99	21.1
Married couples, with children	14.24	134	36.1
Oldest child under 6	11.95	113	5.8
Oldest child 6 to 17	14.79	140	20.3
Oldest child 18 or older	14.76	139	10.0
Single parent with child under 18	8.54	81	5.1
Single person	9.76	92	26.5
REGION			
Total households	**10.59**	**100**	**100.0**
Northeast	8.50	80	16.0
Midwest	12.83	121	28.9
South	9.14	86	30.1
West	12.41	117	24.9

Note: For definitions of best and biggest cus   see introduction or glossary.
Source: Calculations by New Strategist base   097 Consumer Expenditure Survey

CDs, Audio Tapes, Records

Best customers:	• Householders under age 25
	• Married couples with school-aged or older children
	• Households in the West
Customer trends:	• The market should get a boost from the expanding teen and young-adult population, but new technologies could pose a threat in the future.

The youngest householders are the best customers of CDs, audio tapes, and records. They spend 51 percent more than average on these items. Married couples with school-aged children spend 48 percent more than average, while those with adult children at home spend 34 percent more. Households in the West spend 36 percent more than the average household on this category.

The number of teens and young adults will grow in the next decade. This growth, in combination with continued strong music buying by boomers and Generation Xers, should benefit sales of CDs and audio tapes. (Record sales have become negligible.) But new technologies allowing people to download music from the Internet could threaten the market in the future.

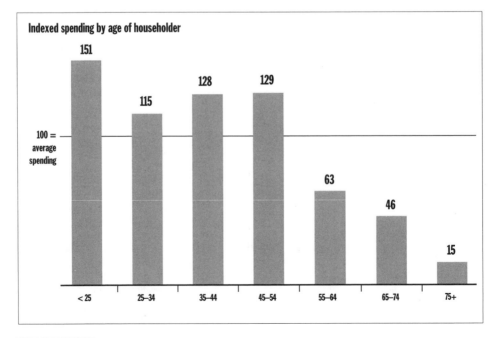

Indexed spending by age of householder

CDs, AUDIO TAPES, RECORDS

Total household spending $4,160,750,160
Average household spends   39.41

	average spending	best customers (index)	biggest customers (market share)
AGE OF HOUSEHOLDER			
Total households	**$39.41**	**100**	**100.0%**
Under age 25	59.62	151	10.7
Aged 25 to 34	45.21	115	21.6
Aged 35 to 44	50.54	128	29.8
Aged 45 to 54	50.96	129	23.7
Aged 55 to 64	25.00	63	7.4
Aged 65 to 74	18.01	46	5.2
Aged 75 or older	6.09	15	1.4
HOUSEHOLD INCOME			
Total households reporting income	**41.96**	**100**	**100.0**
Under $20,000	21.47	51	17.8
$20,000 to $29,999	28.37	68	9.9
$30,000 to $39,999	39.93	95	11.6
$40,000 to $49,999	43.29	103	9.6
$50,000 to $69,999	56.88	136	19.0
$70,000 or more	89.80	214	32.0
HOUSEHOLD TYPE			
Total households	**39.41**	**100**	**100.0**
Married couples	43.58	111	57.8
Married couples, no children	29.63	75	16.0
Married couples, with children	53.48	136	36.5
Oldest child under 6	41.17	104	5.4
Oldest child 6 to 17	58.16	148	21.5
Oldest child 18 or older	52.80	134	9.6
Single parent with child under 18	30.03	76	4.8
Single person	34.75	88	25.3
REGION			
Total households	**39.41**	**100**	**100.0**
Northeast	38.56	98	19.5
Midwest	37.63	95	22.8
South	32.52	83	28.8
West	53.53	136	28.9

Note: For definitions of best and biggest customers, see introduction or glossary.
Source: Calculations by New Strategist based on the 1997 Consumer Expenditure Survey

Docking and Landing Fees

Best customers:	• Householders aged 45 to 54
	• Households with incomes of $70,000 or more
	• Married couples without children
	• Households in the Northeast
Customer trends:	• If the economy remains strong, the market for docking and landing fees will reap some of the benefits.

The most affluent households are the best customers of docking and landing fees, spending three and one-half times as much as the average household on this item. These households account for more than half the market. Households in the Northeast spend 53 percent more than average. This is due to the combination of the region's relatively high incomes and the need to dock boats during the winter.

Docking and landing fees are a discretionary expense. As long as the economy remains strong, the market should benefit as the well-to-do seek new ways to spend their money.

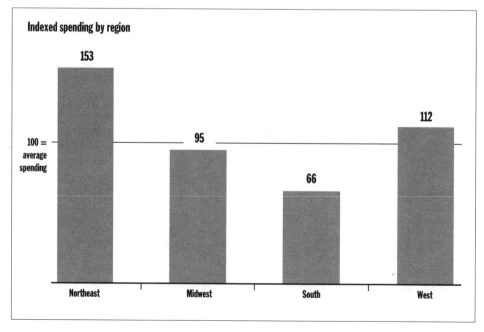

Indexed spending by region

100 = average spending

Northeast 153 · Midwest 95 · South 66 · West 112

DOCKING AND LANDING FEES

Total household spending $1,005,083,520
Average household spends   9.52

	average spending	best customers (index)	biggest customers (market share)
AGE OF HOUSEHOLDER			
Total households	**$9.52**	**100**	**100.0%**
Under age 25	0.10	1	0.1
Aged 25 to 34	6.57	69	13.0
Aged 35 to 44	5.04	53	12.3
Aged 45 to 54	24.86	261	47.8
Aged 55 to 64	9.08	95	11.1
Aged 65 to 74	11.24	118	13.5
Aged 75 or older	2.06	22	2.0
HOUSEHOLD INCOME			
Total households reporting income	**8.96**	**100**	**100.0**
Under $20,000	3.12	35	12.1
$20,000 to $29,999	4.18	47	6.8
$30,000 to $39,999	10.60	118	14.5
$40,000 to $49,999	4.55	51	4.7
$50,000 to $69,999	4.92	55	7.7
$70,000 or more	32.45	362	54.1
HOUSEHOLD TYPE			
Total households	**9.52**	**100**	**100.0**
Married couples	14.15	149	77.7
Married couples, no children	24.55	258	55.0
Married couples, with children	6.55	69	18.5
Oldest child under 6	2.04	21	1.1
Oldest child 6 to 17	6.28	66	9.6
Oldest child 18 or older	10.30	108	7.8
Single parent with child under 18	1.18	12	0.8
Single person	4.32	45	13.0
REGION			
Total households	**9.52**	**100**	**100.0**
Northeast	14.58	153	30.6
Midwest	9.01	95	22.6
South	6.28	66	23.0
West	10.64	112	23.7

Note: For definitions of best and biggest customers, see introduction or glossary.
Source: Calculations by New Strategist based on the 1997 Consumer Expenditure Survey

Fees for Participant Sports

(includes spending on fees for participant sports while on out-of-town trips, also shown separately in the Travel section)

Best customers:	• Householders aged 45 to 54
	• Households with incomes of $70,000 or more
	• Married couples with school-aged children
Customer trends:	• Stable market thanks to the large number of active and affluent boomers.

Fees for participant sports include a broad range of activities from greens fees for golfers to fees for children's sports leagues. Those who spend the most on fees for participant sports are households with incomes of $70,000 or more. Spending by the most affluent households is more than two and one-half times as much as that of the average household, accounting for 42 percent of the market. Married couples with school-aged children spend 53 percent more than average on the category, while householder aged 45 to 54 spend 44 percent more.

Millions of active boomers in their peak-earning years will keep the market for participant sports fees growing in the future.

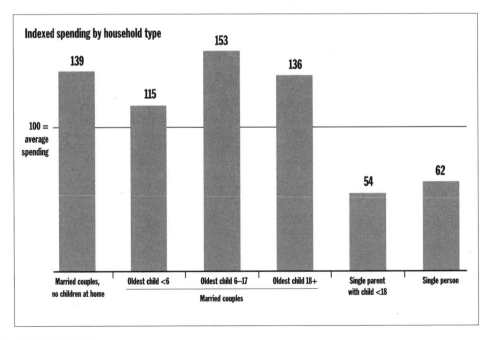

Indexed spending by household type

100 = average spending

Married couples, no children at home	Oldest child <6	Oldest child 6–17	Oldest child 18+	Single parent with child <18	Single person
139	115	153	136	54	62

Married couples

FEES FOR PARTICIPANT SPORTS

Total household spending $10,865,881,920
Average household spends   102.92

	average spending	best customers (index)	biggest customers (market share)
AGE OF HOUSEHOLDER			
Total households	**$102.92**	**100**	**100.0%**
Under age 25	53.35	52	3.7
Aged 25 to 34	99.14	96	18.2
Aged 35 to 44	115.43	112	26.1
Aged 45 to 54	148.27	144	26.4
Aged 55 to 64	101.48	99	11.5
Aged 65 to 74	84.41	82	9.4
Aged 75 or older	52.55	51	4.8
HOUSEHOLD INCOME			
Total households reporting income	**107.14**	**100**	**100.0**
Under $20,000	34.41	32	11.2
$20,000 to $29,999	59.96	56	8.2
$30,000 to $39,999	73.07	68	8.3
$40,000 to $49,999	106.78	100	9.3
$50,000 to $69,999	163.89	153	21.5
$70,000 or more	297.50	278	41.5
HOUSEHOLD TYPE			
Total households	**102.92**	**100**	**100.0**
Married couples	140.39	136	71.3
Married couples, no children	143.17	139	29.7
Married couples, with children	145.29	141	38.0
Oldest child under 6	118.80	115	5.9
Oldest child 6 to 17	157.39	153	22.2
Oldest child 18 or older	139.75	136	9.8
Single parent with child under 18	55.96	54	3.4
Single person	64.24	62	17.9
REGION			
Total households	**102.92**	**100**	**100.0**
Northeast	114.03	111	22.1
Midwest	108.32	105	25.1
South	73.72	72	25.0
West	134.38	131	27.7

Note: For definitions of best and biggest customers, see introduction or glossary.
Source: Calculations by New Strategist based on the 1997 Consumer Expenditure Survey

Fees for Recreational Lessons

(includes spending on fees for recreational lessons while on out-of-town trips,
also shown separately in the Travel section)

Best customers:
- Householders aged 35 to 54
- Married couples with school-aged children
- Households with incomes of $70,000 or more

Customer trends:
- Today's parents will keep the market for recreational lessons strong as they chauffeur their children from one activity to another.

Married couples with school-aged children spend three-and-one-times as much as the average household on fees for recreational lessons as they make sure their children learn how to ski, swim, and play tennis. Householders aged 35 to 44, most of whom are parents of school-aged children, spend 94 percent more than average on this item, while those aged 45 to 54 spend 71 percent more. The most affluent households account for over one-half of all spending in this category.

Today's parents organize their children's lives as tightly as their own. A significant part of children's weekly schedule is devoted to lessons. There are no signs of this trend letting up, ensuring the health of this market for some time to come.

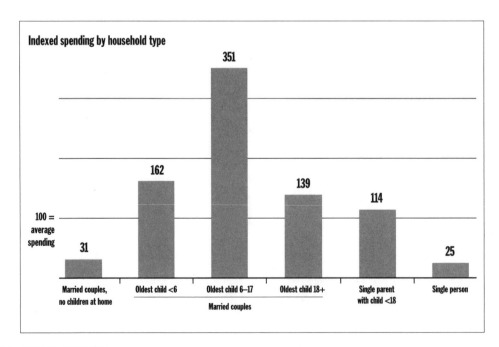

Indexed spending by household type

Household type	Index
Married couples, no children at home	31
Married couples — Oldest child <6	162
Married couples — Oldest child 6–17	351
Married couples — Oldest child 18+	139
Single parent with child <18	114
Single person	25

100 = average spending

FEES FOR RECREATIONAL LESSONS

Total household spending	$7,091,539,920
Average household spends	67.17

	average spending	best customers (index)	biggest customers (market share)
AGE OF HOUSEHOLDER			
Total households	**$67.17**	**100**	**100.0%**
Under age 25	9.38	14	1.0
Aged 25 to 34	47.37	71	13.3
Aged 35 to 44	130.42	194	45.2
Aged 45 to 54	114.59	171	31.3
Aged 55 to 64	31.49	47	5.5
Aged 65 to 74	17.52	26	3.0
Aged 75 or older	5.86	9	0.8
HOUSEHOLD INCOME			
Total households reporting income	**67.09**	**100**	**100.0**
Under $20,000	13.87	21	7.2
$20,000 to $29,999	27.01	40	5.9
$30,000 to $39,999	29.94	45	5.5
$40,000 to $49,999	56.39	84	7.9
$50,000 to $69,999	93.06	139	19.5
$70,000 or more	242.93	362	54.1
HOUSEHOLD TYPE			
Total households	**67.17**	**100**	**100.0**
Married couples	104.94	156	81.7
Married couples, no children	20.65	31	6.6
Married couples, with children	173.19	258	69.3
Oldest child under 6	108.56	162	8.3
Oldest child 6 to 17	235.63	351	51.0
Oldest child 18 or older	93.11	139	10.0
Single parent with child under 18	76.40	114	7.1
Single person	16.46	25	7.0
REGION			
Total households	**67.17**	**100**	**100.0**
Northeast	92.89	138	27.6
Midwest	63.65	95	22.6
South	46.01	68	23.9
West	81.66	122	25.8

Note: For definitions of best and biggest customers, see introduction or glossary.
Source: Calculations by New Strategist based on the 1997 Consumer Expenditure Survey

Film

Best customers: • Married couples with children

Customer trends: • Stable market for now, but new technologies, such as digital cameras, are a threat to the market.

Married couples with preschoolers spend twice as much as the average household on film. Those with school-aged or older children spend 47 percent more than average as they photograph the milestones of their children's lives. Overall, married couples with children of any age at home control 43 percent of spending on film.

The market for film is stable now, but it is threatened by new technologies. As the quality of digital cameras and color printers improves and their prices fall, spending on film will decline.

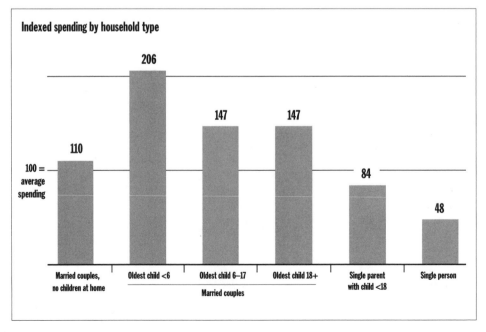

Indexed spending by household type

Married couples, no children at home	Oldest child <6	Oldest child 6–17	Oldest child 18+	Single parent with child <18	Single person
110	206	147	147	84	48

Married couples

100 = average spending

FILM

Total household spending	$2,255,103,360		
Average household spends	21.36		

	average spending	best customers (index)	biggest customers (market share)
AGE OF HOUSEHOLDER			
Total households	**$21.36**	**100**	**100.0%**
Under age 25	11.97	56	4.0
Aged 25 to 34	22.41	105	19.8
Aged 35 to 44	28.47	133	31.0
Aged 45 to 54	27.09	127	23.2
Aged 55 to 64	20.16	94	11.0
Aged 65 to 74	15.69	73	8.4
Aged 75 or older	5.89	28	2.6
HOUSEHOLD INCOME			
Total households reporting income	**21.93**	**100**	**100.0**
Under $20,000	8.75	40	13.9
$20,000 to $29,999	15.51	71	10.3
$30,000 to $39,999	19.73	90	11.0
$40,000 to $49,999	24.11	110	10.3
$50,000 to $69,999	34.60	158	22.1
$70,000 or more	47.44	216	32.3
HOUSEHOLD TYPE			
Total households	**21.36**	**100**	**100.0**
Married couples	29.11	136	71.3
Married couples, no children	23.57	110	23.5
Married couples, with children	33.86	159	42.6
Oldest child under 6	43.99	206	10.6
Oldest child 6 to 17	31.50	147	21.5
Oldest child 18 or older	31.40	147	10.6
Single parent with child under 18	18.02	84	5.3
Single person	10.33	48	13.9
REGION			
Total households	**21.36**	**100**	**100.0**
Northeast	23.24	109	21.7
Midwest	21.32	100	23.9
South	17.08	80	27.9
West	26.68	125	26.5

Note: For definitions of best and biggest customers, see introduction or glossary.
Source: Calculations by New Strategist based on the 1997 Consumer Expenditure Survey

Film Processing

Best customers: • Married couples with children

Customer trends: • Digital cameras and photos threaten the market for film processing.

The best customers of film processing are parents. Spending on film processing by married couples with children under age 6 is more than double that of the average household. The desire to snap shots of their adorable offspring wanes somewhat as children get older. Married couples with school-aged or older children spend 44 percent more than average on film processing.

As is true for film, the market for film processing is threatened by digital cameras and photos. Expect to see spending decline.

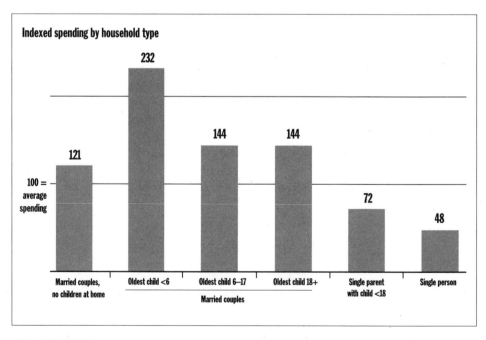

Indexed spending by household type

121	232	144	144	72	48
Married couples, no children at home	Oldest child <6	Oldest child 6–17	Oldest child 18+	Single parent with child <18	Single person
		Married couples			

100 = average spending

FILM PROCESSING

Total household spending	$3,099,711,360
Average household spends	29.36

	average spending	best customers (index)	biggest customers (market share)
AGE OF HOUSEHOLDER			
Total households	**$29.36**	**100**	**100.0%**
Under age 25	17.48	60	4.2
Aged 25 to 34	31.59	108	20.3
Aged 35 to 44	37.19	127	29.5
Aged 45 to 54	38.47	131	24.0
Aged 55 to 64	29.96	102	11.9
Aged 65 to 74	19.94	68	7.8
Aged 75 or older	7.31	25	2.3
HOUSEHOLD INCOME			
Total households reporting income	**30.86**	**100**	**100.0**
Under $20,000	11.16	36	12.6
$20,000 to $29,999	19.81	64	9.4
$30,000 to $39,999	25.92	84	10.3
$40,000 to $49,999	33.59	109	10.2
$50,000 to $69,999	47.98	155	21.8
$70,000 or more	73.80	239	35.7
HOUSEHOLD TYPE			
Total households	**29.36**	**100**	**100.0**
Married couples	41.19	140	73.4
Married couples, no children	35.56	121	25.8
Married couples, with children	47.15	161	43.2
Oldest child under 6	68.06	232	11.9
Oldest child 6 to 17	42.23	144	20.9
Oldest child 18 or older	42.15	144	10.3
Single parent with child under 18	21.15	72	4.5
Single person	14.22	48	13.9
REGION			
Total households	**29.36**	**100**	**100.0**
Northeast	32.25	110	21.9
Midwest	29.35	100	23.9
South	23.28	79	27.7
West	36.66	125	26.5

Note: For definitions of best and biggest customers, see introduction or glossary.
Source: Calculations by New Strategist based on the 1997 Consumer Expenditure Survey

Hunting and Fishing Equipment

Best customers:
- Householders aged 55 to 64
- Married couples with adult children
- Households in the Midwest

Customer trends:
- No change in the near future since growing numbers of older people will be offset by fewer early retirees.

The best customers of hunting and fishing equipment are older Americans with grown children. Married couples with adult children at home spend three times as much as the average household on hunting and fishing equipment. Householders aged 55 to 64 spend 73 percent more than average. Households in the Midwest spend 42 percent more on this item.

The number of 55-to-64-year-olds will begin to rise in the next few years as the baby-boom generation enters the age group. This trend suggests potential growth in spending on hunting and fishing equipment. But if the predicted decline in early retirement materializes, few boomers will have the time to do much hunting or fishing.

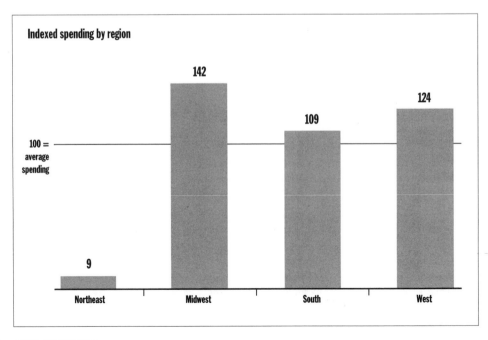

Indexed spending by region

- Northeast: 9
- Midwest: 142
- South: 109
- West: 124

100 = average spending

HUNTING AND FISHING EQUIPMENT

Total household spending $1,700,829,360
Average household spends   16.11

	average spending	best customers (index)	biggest customers (market share)
AGE OF HOUSEHOLDER			
Total households	**$16.11**	**100**	**100.0%**
Under age 25	4.86	30	2.1
Aged 25 to 34	16.21	101	19.0
Aged 35 to 44	20.00	124	28.9
Aged 45 to 54	20.56	128	23.4
Aged 55 to 64	27.91	173	20.2
Aged 65 to 74	8.84	55	6.3
Aged 75 or older	0.70	4	0.4
HOUSEHOLD INCOME			
Total households reporting income	**18.35**	**100**	**100.0**
Under $20,000	5.98	33	11.4
$20,000 to $29,999	10.51	57	8.4
$30,000 to $39,999	25.60	140	17.1
$40,000 to $49,999	11.87	65	6.0
$50,000 to $69,999	28.88	157	22.1
$70,000 or more	42.49	232	34.6
HOUSEHOLD TYPE			
Total households	**16.11**	**100**	**100.0**
Married couples	22.96	143	74.5
Married couples, no children	19.54	121	25.9
Married couples, with children	28.36	176	47.3
Oldest child under 6	27.13	168	8.7
Oldest child 6 to 17	17.70	110	16.0
Oldest child 18 or older	50.82	315	22.7
Single parent with child under 18	5.18	32	2.0
Single person	7.39	46	13.2
REGION			
Total households	**16.11**	**100**	**100.0**
Northeast	1.38	9	1.7
Midwest	22.86	142	33.9
South	17.51	109	37.9
West	19.95	124	26.3

Note: For definitions of best and biggest customers, see introduction or glossary.
Source: Calculations by New Strategist based on the 1997 Consumer Expenditure Survey

Motor Boats

Best customers:
- Households with incomes of $70,000 or more
- Householders aged 45 to 54
- Married couples with adult children
- Households in the West

Customer trends:
- Strong spending as affluent older boomers look for ways to have fun with their money.

Households with incomes of $70,000 or more are by far the best customers of motor boats. These households spend more than four times as much as the average household on motor boats, accounting for 64 percent of the market. Households with adult children at home spend three times the average. Householders aged 45 to 54 spend twice as much as the average household on motor boats, while households in the West spend 89 percent more than average.

Nothing boosts boat sales like the nouveau riche. Older boomers are in their peak earning years (ages 45 to 54) and many have seen their wealth grow thanks to the surging stock market. This generation's financial gains should lift boat sales.

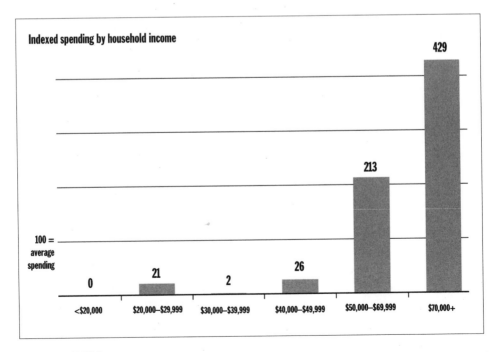

Indexed spending by household income

| | 429 |
| 213 |
| 100 = average spending |
| 0 | 21 | 2 | 26 |

| <$20,000 | $20,000–$29,999 | $30,000–$39,999 | $40,000–$49,999 | $50,000–$69,999 | $70,000+ |

MOTOR BOATS

Total household spending	$11,525,731,920		
Average household spends	109.17		

	average spending	best customers (index)	biggest customers (market share)
AGE OF HOUSEHOLDER			
Total households	**$109.17**	**100**	**100.0%**
Under age 25	–	–	–
Aged 25 to 34	175.59	161	30.3
Aged 35 to 44	102.07	93	21.7
Aged 45 to 54	218.43	200	36.7
Aged 55 to 64	94.51	87	10.1
Aged 65 to 74	9.67	9	1.0
Aged 75 or older	1.58	1	0.1
HOUSEHOLD INCOME			
Total households reporting income	**99.84**	**100**	**100.0**
Under $20,000	0.32	0	0.1
$20,000 to $29,999	21.32	21	3.1
$30,000 to $39,999	2.28	2	0.3
$40,000 to $49,999	26.34	26	2.5
$50,000 to $69,999	213.10	213	30.0
$70,000 or more	427.85	429	64.1
HOUSEHOLD TYPE			
Total households	**109.17**	**100**	**100.0**
Married couples	178.30	163	85.4
Married couples, no children	226.52	207	44.3
Married couples, with children	166.98	153	41.1
Oldest child under 6	96.59	88	4.6
Oldest child 6 to 17	106.34	97	14.2
Oldest child 18 or older	340.06	311	22.4
Single parent with child under 18	21.00	19	1.2
Single person	29.89	27	7.9
REGION			
Total households	**109.17**	**100**	**100.0**
Northeast	78.20	72	14.3
Midwest	120.17	110	26.3
South	59.92	55	19.1
West	206.82	189	40.2

Note: (–) means sample is too small to make a reliable estimate. For definitions of best and biggest customers, see introduction or glossary.
Source: Calculations by New Strategist based on the 1997 Consumer Expenditure Survey

Motorized Campers

Best customers:
- Householders aged 55 to 64
- Households with incomes of $70,000 or more
- Married couples without children at home

Customer trends:
- Growing numbers of empty nesters will drive up sales in this market.

The best customers of motorized campers are people with time and money on their hands. Householders aged 55 to 64 spend three and one-half times as much as the average household on motorized campers. Households with incomes of $70,000 or more spend four and one-half times as much as the average household on this item. Spending on motorized campers by married couples without children at home is three times the average.

As boomers become empty nesters they will have more time to travel. This lifestyle change will translate into increased sales of motorized campers.

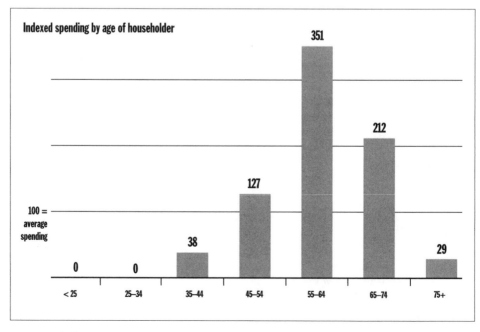

Indexed spending by age of householder

<25	25–34	35–44	45–54	55–64	65–74	75+
0	0	38	127	351	212	29

100 = average spending

MOTORIZED CAMPERS

Total household spending	$2,762,923,920
Average household spends	26.17

	average spending	best customers (index)	biggest customers (market share)
AGE OF HOUSEHOLDER			
Total households	**$26.17**	**100**	**100.0%**
Under age 25	–	–	–
Aged 25 to 34	–	–	–
Aged 35 to 44	9.84	38	8.7
Aged 45 to 54	33.31	127	23.3
Aged 55 to 64	91.88	351	41.0
Aged 65 to 74	55.35	212	24.3
Aged 75 or older	7.59	29	2.7
HOUSEHOLD INCOME			
Total households reporting income	**21.87**	**100**	**100.0**
Under $20,000	–	–	–
$20,000 to $29,999	29.75	136	19.9
$30,000 to $39,999	–	–	–
$40,000 to $49,999	–	–	–
$50,000 to $69,999	20.25	93	13.0
$70,000 or more	98.20	449	67.1
HOUSEHOLD TYPE			
Total households	**26.17**	**100**	**100.0**
Married couples	48.69	186	97.3
Married couples, no children	79.97	306	65.2
Married couples, with children	18.90	72	19.4
Oldest child under 6	–	–	–
Oldest child 6 to 17	31.60	121	17.6
Oldest child 18 or older	6.71	26	1.8
Single parent with child under 18	–	–	–
Single person	–	–	–
REGION			
Total households	**26.17**	**100**	**100.0**
Northeast	–	–	–
Midwest	43.38	166	39.6
South	32.38	124	43.2
West	21.19	81	17.2

Note: (–) means sample is too small to make a reliable estimate. For definitions of best and biggest customers, see introduction or glossary.
Source: Calculations by New Strategist based on the 1997 Consumer Expenditure Survey

Movie, Theater, Opera, Ballet Tickets

(includes spending on movie, theater, opera, and ballet tickets while on out-of-town trips, also shown separately in the Travel section)

Best customers:	• Married couples with school-aged or adult children
	• Householders aged 45 to 54
Customer trends:	• Movie theaters will benefit from the growing teen population, while live arts performances should grow in popularity as empty-nest boomers enjoy more free time.

The best customers for movie, theater, opera, and ballet tickets are households with children. Married couples with school-aged children spend 38 percent more than average on this item, while those with adult children at home spend 43 percent more. Householders aged 45 to 54 spend 32 percent more than average on tickets.

Movie theaters will reap the rewards of a growing teen population during the next few years. The future also looks bright for live arts events. Innovative offerings by opera, theater, and ballet companies are likely to bring more people in the door, especially as nests empty and boomers gain more free time.

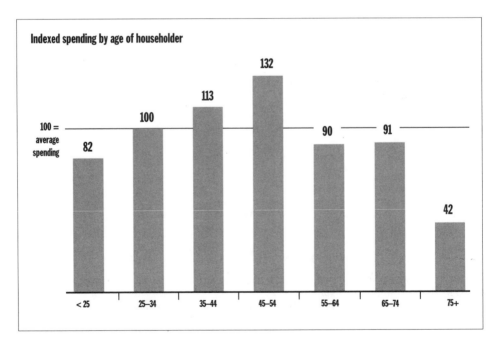

Indexed spending by age of householder

100 = average spending

< 25	25–34	35–44	45–54	55–64	65–74	75+
82	100	113	132	90	91	42

MOVIE, THEATER, OPERA, BALLET TICKETS

Total household spending $13,581,296,640
Average household spends 128.64

	average spending	best customers (index)	biggest customers (market share)
AGE OF HOUSEHOLDER			
Total households	**$128.64**	**100**	**100.0%**
Under age 25	105.62	82	5.8
Aged 25 to 34	128.52	100	18.8
Aged 35 to 44	145.97	113	26.4
Aged 45 to 54	169.60	132	24.2
Aged 55 to 64	115.28	90	10.5
Aged 65 to 74	116.96	91	10.4
Aged 75 or older	53.76	42	3.9
HOUSEHOLD INCOME			
Total households reporting income	**134.36**	**100**	**100.0**
Under $20,000	58.74	44	15.2
$20,000 to $29,999	89.57	67	9.7
$30,000 to $39,999	111.35	83	10.1
$40,000 to $49,999	144.35	107	10.0
$50,000 to $69,999	173.99	129	18.2
$70,000 or more	329.66	245	36.7
HOUSEHOLD TYPE			
Total households	**128.64**	**100**	**100.0**
Married couples	155.63	121	63.3
Married couples, no children	141.85	110	23.5
Married couples, with children	168.68	131	35.3
Oldest child under 6	121.38	94	4.9
Oldest child 6 to 17	177.90	138	20.1
Oldest child 18 or older	183.88	143	10.3
Single parent with child under 18	90.31	70	4.4
Single person	94.42	73	21.1
REGION			
Total households	**128.64**	**100**	**100.0**
Northeast	147.48	115	22.9
Midwest	127.93	99	23.8
South	101.42	79	27.5
West	156.47	122	25.8

Note: For definitions of best and biggest customers, see introduction or glossary.
Source: Calculations by New Strategist based on the 1997 Consumer Expenditure Survey

Musical Instruments and Accessories

| Best customers: | • Married couples with school-aged children |
| | • Households with incomes of $70,000 or more |

| Customer trends: | • Growth likely as the school-aged population expands. |

Married couples with school-aged children spend two and one-half times as much as the average household on musical instruments and accessories. Households with high incomes also spend at this level. Affluent Americans are in the best position to provide their children with music lessons and to buy instruments for them, accounting for 41 percent of the market.

The market for musical instruments and accessories should grow during the next few years. The number of school-aged children will rise, and since many of their parents are in their peak-earning years they will be able to afford instruments for their children.

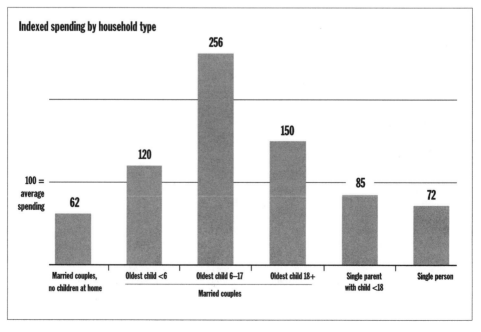

Indexed spending by household type

Married couples, no children at home	Oldest child <6	Oldest child 6–17	Oldest child 18+	Single parent with child <18	Single person
62	120	256	150	85	72

Married couples

100 = average spending

MUSICAL INSTRUMENTS AND ACCESSORIES

Total household spending	$2,529,600,960		
Average household spends	23.96		

	average spending	best customers (index)	biggest customers (market share)
AGE OF HOUSEHOLDER			
Total households	**$23.96**	**100**	**100.0%**
Under age 25	18.10	76	5.4
Aged 25 to 34	19.82	83	15.6
Aged 35 to 44	39.46	165	38.3
Aged 45 to 54	29.34	122	22.4
Aged 55 to 64	11.80	49	5.7
Aged 65 to 74	18.15	76	8.7
Aged 75 or older	9.93	41	3.9
HOUSEHOLD INCOME			
Total households reporting income	**24.88**	**100**	**100.0**
Under $20,000	10.13	41	14.2
$20,000 to $29,999	36.18	145	21.2
$30,000 to $39,999	15.62	63	7.7
$40,000 to $49,999	16.81	68	6.3
$50,000 to $69,999	17.88	72	10.1
$70,000 or more	67.43	271	40.5
HOUSEHOLD TYPE			
Total households	**23.96**	**100**	**100.0**
Married couples	31.82	133	69.4
Married couples, no children	14.86	62	13.2
Married couples, with children	48.34	202	54.2
Oldest child under 6	28.69	120	6.2
Oldest child 6 to 17	61.37	256	37.3
Oldest child 18 or older	36.03	150	10.8
Single parent with child under 18	20.35	85	5.3
Single person	17.19	72	20.6
REGION			
Total households	**23.96**	**100**	**100.0**
Northeast	13.86	58	11.6
Midwest	26.54	111	26.5
South	24.41	102	35.5
West	29.84	125	26.5

Note: For definitions of best and biggest customers, see introduction or glossary.
Source: Calculations by New Strategist based on the 1997 Consumer Expenditure Survey

Musical Instruments, Rental and Repair

Best customers:
- Householders aged 35 to 44
- Married couples with school-aged children

Customer trends:
- Spending should remain stable, along with the number of school-aged children.

Many parents rent rather than buy musical instruments for their children. Consequently, the best customers for rental and repair of musical instruments are married couples with school-aged children. They spend four and one-half times as much as the average household on this item. Householders aged 35 to 44 spend almost two and one-half times as much as average because most of these households include school-aged children.

Some school districts have reduced or eliminated music programs to save money or to make more time for other subjects. If this trend spreads, the market for musical instrument rental and repair will decline. For now, however, burgeoning numbers of school-aged children should stabilize spending in this category.

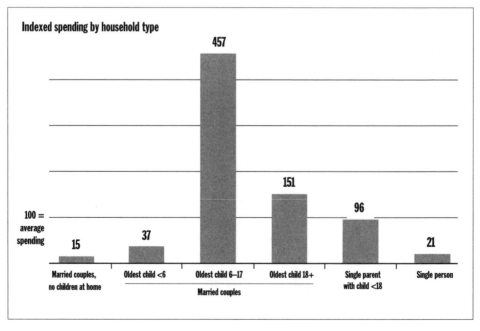

Indexed spending by household type

Married couples, no children at home	Oldest child <6	Oldest child 6–17	Oldest child 18+	Single parent with child <18	Single person
15	37	457	151	96	21

Married couples

100 = average spending

MUSICAL INSTRUMENTS, RENTAL AND REPAIR

Total household spending $173,144,640
Average household spends   1.64

	average spending	best customers (index)	biggest customers (market share)
AGE OF HOUSEHOLDER			
Total households	**$1.64**	**100**	**100.0%**
Under age 25	0.14	9	0.6
Aged 25 to 34	0.92	56	10.6
Aged 35 to 44	3.94	240	55.9
Aged 45 to 54	2.09	127	23.3
Aged 55 to 64	0.51	31	3.6
Aged 65 to 74	0.64	39	4.5
Aged 75 or older	0.29	18	1.6
HOUSEHOLD INCOME			
Total households reporting income	**1.78**	**100**	**100.0**
Under $20,000	0.45	25	8.9
$20,000 to $29,999	0.96	54	7.9
$30,000 to $39,999	1.15	65	7.9
$40,000 to $49,999	2.59	146	13.6
$50,000 to $69,999	3.90	219	30.8
$70,000 or more	3.71	208	31.2
HOUSEHOLD TYPE			
Total households	**1.64**	**100**	**100.0**
Married couples	2.69	164	85.8
Married couples, no children	0.25	15	3.3
Married couples, with children	4.83	295	79.2
Oldest child under 6	0.60	37	1.9
Oldest child 6 to 17	7.49	457	66.4
Oldest child 18 or older	2.48	151	10.9
Single parent with child under 18	1.58	96	6.0
Single person	0.34	21	6.0
REGION			
Total households	**1.64**	**100**	**100.0**
Northeast	1.96	120	23.9
Midwest	1.84	112	26.8
South	0.88	54	18.7
West	2.39	146	31.0

Note: For definitions of best and biggest customers, see introduction or glossary.
Source: Calculations by New Strategist based on the 1997 Consumer Expenditure Survey

Pet Food

Best customers:
- Householders aged 55 to 64
- Married couples without children
- Married couples with adult children

Customer trends:
- Growth is likely as the number of empty-nest households rises.

As America ages, it is becoming a nation of pet owners. The best customers of pet food are older Americans who no longer have young children at home. Householders aged 55 to 64 spend 50 percent more than the average household on pet food. Married couples without children at home spend 30 percent more, while those with adult children in the household spend 32 percent more than average on pet food.

The market for pet food should grow in the coming years as expanding numbers of empty nesters fill the void left by grown children with dogs and cats.

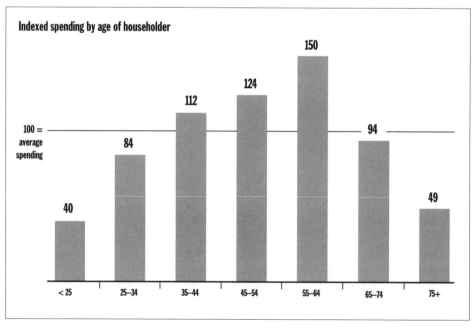

Indexed spending by age of householder

Age	Index
< 25	40
25–34	84
35–44	112
45–54	124
55–64	150
65–74	94
75+	49

100 = average spending

PET FOOD

Total household spending	$9,209,394,480		
Average household spends	87.23		

	average spending	best customers (index)	biggest customers (market share)
AGE OF HOUSEHOLDER			
Total households	**$87.23**	**100**	**100.0%**
Under age 25	34.91	40	2.8
Aged 25 to 34	73.32	84	15.9
Aged 35 to 44	97.85	112	26.1
Aged 45 to 54	108.16	124	22.7
Aged 55 to 64	130.65	150	17.5
Aged 65 to 74	81.84	94	10.8
Aged 75 or older	42.68	49	4.6
HOUSEHOLD INCOME			
Total households reporting income	**94.36**	**100**	**100.0**
Under $20,000	59.01	63	21.8
$20,000 to $29,999	82.82	88	12.8
$30,000 to $39,999	85.54	91	11.1
$40,000 to $49,999	99.63	106	9.9
$50,000 to $69,999	138.96	147	20.7
$70,000 or more	147.96	157	23.4
HOUSEHOLD TYPE			
Total households	**87.23**	**100**	**100.0**
Married couples	111.63	128	66.9
Married couples, no children	113.78	130	27.8
Married couples, with children	101.80	117	31.4
Oldest child under 6	76.78	88	4.5
Oldest child 6 to 17	105.66	121	17.6
Oldest child 18 or older	114.94	132	9.5
Single parent with child under 18	55.75	64	4.0
Single person	51.36	59	16.9
REGION			
Total households	**87.23**	**100**	**100.0**
Northeast	86.47	99	19.8
Midwest	76.65	88	21.0
South	87.29	100	34.9
West	99.35	114	24.2

Note: For definitions of best and biggest customers, see introduction or glossary.
Source: Calculations by New Strategist based on the 1997 Consumer Expenditure Survey

Pet Purchase, Supplies, Medicine, Services

Best customers:	• **Married couples with adult children**
	• **Householders aged 35 to 54**
Customer trends:	• **The market for pets and supplies will increase as the population ages and more people turn to pets for companionship.**

Many people are content to pick up a pooch at the pound. But if they can afford it, some prefer to spend big on a pedigreed cat or dog, then lavish the pet with fancy toys, beds, and other products. The best customers of pets and pet supplies are married couples with adult children at home. They spend 64 percent more than the average household on this item. Householders aged 35 to 54 spend 35 to 45 percent more.

The aging of the American population is good news for purveyors of pets and pet supplies since older people often turn to pets for companionship.

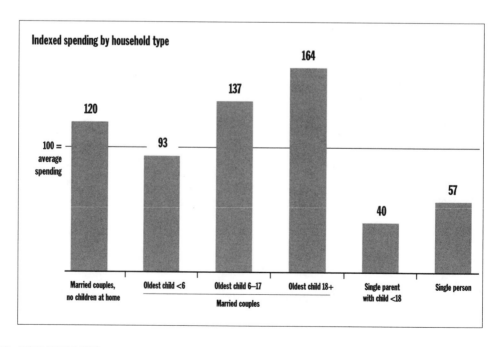

Indexed spending by household type

PET PURCHASE, SUPPLIES, MEDICINE, SERVICES

Total household spending	$6,051,616,320
Average household spends	57.32

	average spending	best customers (index)	biggest customers (market share)
AGE OF HOUSEHOLDER			
Total households	**$57.32**	**100**	**100.0%**
Under age 25	35.36	62	4.4
Aged 25 to 34	50.99	89	16.8
Aged 35 to 44	77.15	135	31.3
Aged 45 to 54	83.09	145	26.6
Aged 55 to 64	60.61	106	12.3
Aged 65 to 74	32.74	57	6.6
Aged 75 or older	14.39	25	2.3
HOUSEHOLD INCOME			
Total households reporting income	**57.97**	**100**	**100.0**
Under $20,000	19.83	34	11.9
$20,000 to $29,999	44.64	77	11.2
$30,000 to $39,999	45.39	78	9.6
$40,000 to $49,999	68.56	118	11.1
$50,000 to $69,999	69.81	120	16.9
$70,000 or more	149.02	257	38.4
HOUSEHOLD TYPE			
Total households	**57.32**	**100**	**100.0**
Married couples	76.68	134	70.0
Married couples, no children	68.77	120	25.6
Married couples, with children	77.65	135	36.4
Oldest child under 6	53.57	93	4.8
Oldest child 6 to 17	78.75	137	20.0
Oldest child 18 or older	94.23	164	11.8
Single parent with child under 18	23.07	40	2.5
Single person	32.45	57	16.3
REGION			
Total households	**57.32**	**100**	**100.0**
Northeast	48.34	84	16.8
Midwest	56.01	98	23.3
South	53.00	92	32.3
West	73.88	129	27.4

Note: For definitions of best and biggest customers, see introduction or glossary.
Source: Calculations by New Strategist based on the 1997 Consumer Expenditure Survey

Photographer's Fees

Best customers:	• Householders aged 25 to 34
	• Married couples with adult children
Customer trends:	• The market will grow as the number of people at the prime age for graduations and weddings increases.

Today even relatively inexpensive cameras can produce high-quality pictures, but Americans still hire a professional to immortalize some moments. Graduations and weddings are the professional photographer's bread and butter. In married-couple households where the oldest child is aged 18 or older, spending on photographer's fees is three times that of the average household. Householders aged 25 to 34—the age at which weddings are common—spend almost twice as much as the average household on this item.

So far, technology hasn't been able to trump talent. For preserving really important moments Americans will continue to hire photographers. This market will get a boost as the Millennial generation—the children of baby boomers—enters the ages when graduations and weddings are most common.

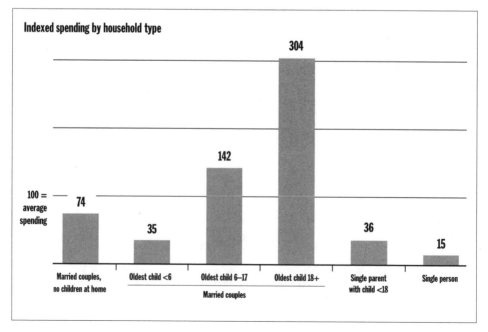

Indexed spending by household type

PHOTOGRAPHER'S FEES

Total household spending $2,475,757,200
Average household spends   23.45

	average spending	best customers (index)	biggest customers (market share)
AGE OF HOUSEHOLDER			
Total households	**$23.45**	**100**	**100.0%**
Under age 25	2.91	12	0.9
Aged 25 to 34	46.04	196	37.0
Aged 35 to 44	30.51	130	30.3
Aged 45 to 54	26.58	113	20.8
Aged 55 to 64	0.61	3	0.3
Aged 65 to 74	1.58	7	0.8
Aged 75 or older	28.70	122	11.4
HOUSEHOLD INCOME			
Total households reporting income	**25.37**	**100**	**100.0**
Under $20,000	22.87	90	31.4
$20,000 to $29,999	8.17	32	4.7
$30,000 to $39,999	14.06	55	6.8
$40,000 to $49,999	20.79	82	7.7
$50,000 to $69,999	34.59	136	19.1
$70,000 or more	53.00	209	31.2
HOUSEHOLD TYPE			
Total households	**23.45**	**100**	**100.0**
Married couples	28.68	122	64.0
Married couples, no children	17.28	74	15.7
Married couples, with children	37.74	161	43.3
Oldest child under 6	8.21	35	1.8
Oldest child 6 to 17	33.34	142	20.7
Oldest child 18 or older	71.23	304	21.8
Single parent with child under 18	8.40	36	2.2
Single person	3.62	15	4.4
REGION			
Total households	**23.45**	**100**	**100.0**
Northeast	31.96	136	27.2
Midwest	32.64	139	33.3
South	15.30	65	22.8
West	18.56	79	16.8

Note: For definitions of best and biggest customers, see introduction or glossary.
Source: Calculations by New Strategist based on the 1997 Consumer Expenditure Survey

Photographic Equipment

Best customers:
- Married couples with children under age 6
- Married couples with adult children

Customer trends:
- The number of preschoolers is poised to decline, which may reduce spending unless manufacturers can tantalize buyers with new offerings.

The best customers of photographic equipment are parents. Married couples with children under age 6 spend two and one-half times as much as the average household on photographic equipment. Married couples with adult children at home spend twice as much as the average household. Many of these householders are motivated to buy photographic equipment so they can capture their children's graduations and weddings.

The number of preschoolers will decline slightly in the next few years. This could precipitate a decline in spending on photographic equipment. But new offerings, such as digital cameras, may prompt other segments of the population to buy.

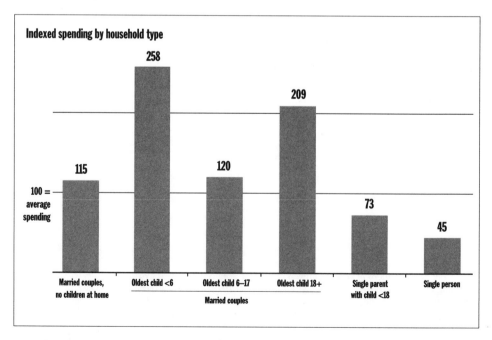

Indexed spending by household type

- Married couples, no children at home: 115
- Oldest child <6: 258
- Oldest child 6–17: 120
- Oldest child 18+: 209
- Single parent with child <18: 73
- Single person: 45

100 = average spending

Married couples

PHOTOGRAPHIC EQUIPMENT

Total household spending	$1,498,123,440	
Average household spends	14.19	

	average spending	best customers (index)	biggest customers (market share)
AGE OF HOUSEHOLDER			
Total households	**$14.19**	**100**	**100.0%**
Under age 25	9.03	64	4.5
Aged 25 to 34	14.27	101	19.0
Aged 35 to 44	21.52	152	35.3
Aged 45 to 54	16.65	117	21.5
Aged 55 to 64	15.58	110	12.8
Aged 65 to 74	7.62	54	6.2
Aged 75 or older	1.17	8	0.8
HOUSEHOLD INCOME			
Total households reporting income	**14.83**	**100**	**100.0**
Under $20,000	4.72	32	11.1
$20,000 to $29,999	8.40	57	8.3
$30,000 to $39,999	13.48	91	11.1
$40,000 to $49,999	14.10	95	8.9
$50,000 to $69,999	27.93	188	26.4
$70,000 or more	33.92	229	34.2
HOUSEHOLD TYPE			
Total households	**14.19**	**100**	**100.0**
Married couples	20.17	142	74.3
Married couples, no children	16.27	115	24.5
Married couples, with children	24.14	170	45.7
Oldest child under 6	36.57	258	13.3
Oldest child 6 to 17	17.03	120	17.5
Oldest child 18 or older	29.64	209	15.0
Single parent with child under 18	10.30	73	4.6
Single person	6.34	45	12.8
REGION			
Total households	**14.19**	**100**	**100.0**
Northeast	13.32	94	18.8
Midwest	16.53	116	27.8
South	11.75	83	28.9
West	16.39	116	24.5

Note: For definitions of best and biggest customers, see introduction or glossary.
Source: Calculations by New Strategist based on the 1997 Consumer Expenditure Survey

Radios

Radios are the most affordable type of electronic home entertainment. Most are inexpensive, and listeners don't have to pay to receive programming. This is why single parents are the best customers of radios. They spend four times as much as the average household on this item. Householders aged 65 to 74, who grew up in radio's golden years, spend twice as much as the average household on radios.

Radio is a relatively old-fashioned medium, but spending on radio receivers shows no signs of letting up. Cable companies have tried to lure customers away by providing music channels, but so far they have made little headway. The market for radios should remain stable.

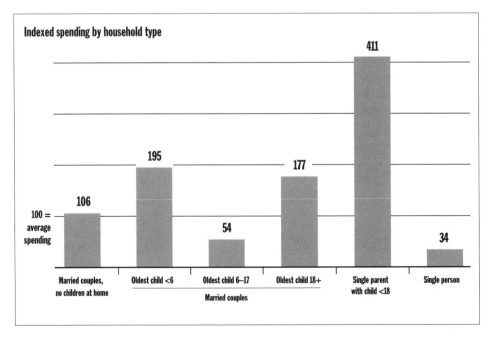

Indexed spending by household type

100 = average spending

Married couples, no children at home	Oldest child <6	Oldest child 6–17	Oldest child 18+	Single parent with child <18	Single person
106	195	54	177	411	34

Married couples

RADIOS

Total household spending	$1,241,573,760	
Average household spends	11.76	

	average spending	best customers (index)	biggest customers (market share)
AGE OF HOUSEHOLDER			
Total households	**$11.76**	**100**	**100.0%**
Under age 25	0.61	5	0.4
Aged 25 to 34	19.99	170	32.1
Aged 35 to 44	5.40	46	10.7
Aged 45 to 54	12.54	107	19.5
Aged 55 to 64	11.47	98	11.4
Aged 65 to 74	27.70	236	27.0
Aged 75 or older	–	–	–
HOUSEHOLD INCOME			
Total households reporting income	**13.28**	**100**	**100.0**
Under $20,000	15.86	119	41.6
$20,000 to $29,999	2.30	17	2.5
$30,000 to $39,999	30.96	233	28.5
$40,000 to $49,999	6.31	48	4.4
$50,000 to $69,999	12.21	92	12.9
$70,000 or more	8.94	67	10.1
HOUSEHOLD TYPE			
Total households	**11.76**	**100**	**100.0**
Married couples	13.72	117	61.0
Married couples, no children	12.48	106	22.6
Married couples, with children	13.71	117	31.3
Oldest child under 6	22.98	195	10.1
Oldest child 6 to 17	6.32	54	7.8
Oldest child 18 or older	20.82	177	12.7
Single parent with child under 18	48.35	411	25.8
Single person	4.02	34	9.8
REGION			
Total households	**11.76**	**100**	**100.0**
Northeast	11.90	101	20.2
Midwest	11.88	101	24.1
South	15.03	128	44.6
West	6.33	54	11.4

Note: (–) means sample is too small to make a reliable estimate. For definitions of best and biggest customers, see introduction or glossary.
Source: Calculations by New Strategist based on the 1997 Consumer Expenditure Survey

Recreational Vehicle Rental

Best customers:
- Married couples without children
- Households with incomes of $70,000 or more
- Households in the Northeast

Customer trends:
- Stable market for now, but growth is possible as the number of child-free households increases.

Married couples without children at home, who are free to travel for extended periods of time, spend more than three times the average amount on the rental of recreational vehicles. This household type—which includes young couples who have not yet had children as well as older couples whose children are grown—accounts for 72 percent of the market. Householders aged 25 to 34 and those aged 55 to 64 (the age groups with many childless couples) are also above-average spenders on this item. Households in the Northeast spend more than twice as much as the average household on the rental of recreational vehicles.

Rentals of recreational vehicles should remain stable for now. In the future, this market may get a boost as the number of households without children—at both ends of the age spectrum—increases.

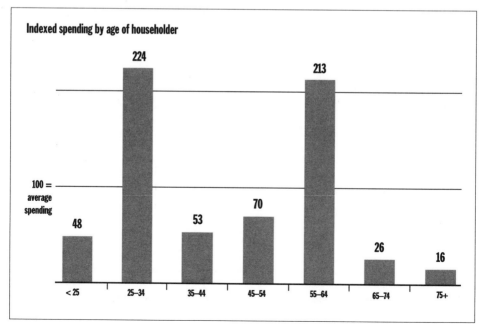

Indexed spending by age of householder

Age	Index
< 25	48
25–34	224
35–44	53
45–54	70
55–64	213
65–74	26
75+	16

100 = average spending

RECREATIONAL VEHICLE RENTAL

Total household spending	$353,679,600		
Average household spends	3.35		

	average spending	best customers (index)	biggest customers (market share)
AGE OF HOUSEHOLDER			
Total households	**$3.35**	**100**	**100.0%**
Under age 25	1.61	48	3.4
Aged 25 to 34	7.49	224	42.2
Aged 35 to 44	1.79	53	12.4
Aged 45 to 54	2.34	70	12.8
Aged 55 to 64	7.12	213	24.8
Aged 65 to 74	0.86	26	2.9
Aged 75 or older	0.55	16	1.5
HOUSEHOLD INCOME			
Total households reporting income	**3.86**	**100**	**100.0**
Under $20,000	0.42	11	3.8
$20,000 to $29,999	1.20	31	4.5
$30,000 to $39,999	7.32	190	23.2
$40,000 to $49,999	2.95	76	7.1
$50,000 to $69,999	1.75	45	6.4
$70,000 or more	14.21	368	55.0
HOUSEHOLD TYPE			
Total households	**3.35**	**100**	**100.0**
Married couples	5.64	168	88.0
Married couples, no children	11.35	339	72.3
Married couples, with children	1.95	58	15.6
Oldest child under 6	1.01	30	1.6
Oldest child 6 to 17	2.70	81	11.7
Oldest child 18 or older	1.10	33	2.4
Single parent with child under 18	0.65	19	1.2
Single person	1.01	30	8.7
REGION			
Total households	**3.35**	**100**	**100.0**
Northeast	7.84	234	46.8
Midwest	2.79	83	19.9
South	2.22	66	23.1
West	1.63	49	10.3

Note: For definitions of best and biggest customers, see introduction or glossary.
Source: Calculations by New Strategist based on the 1997 Consumer Expenditure Survey

Satellite Dishes

Best customers:
- Householders aged 35 to 64
- Married couples with adult children
- Married couples without children
- Households in the West

Customer trends:
- Uncertain future as regulations regarding the broadcast of local stations are negotiated.

Householders aged 35 to 64 are the best customers of satellite dishes, spending 36 to 52 percent more than the average household on this item. Married couples without children at home spend 69 percent more than average, while those with adult children at home spend 95 percent more. Households in the West spend 40 percent more than average on satellite dishes.

Spending on satellite dishes is not likely to grow because cable is so widespread.

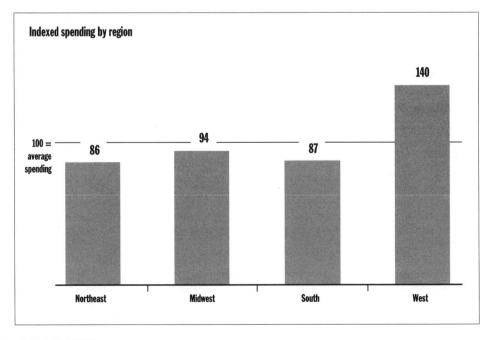

Indexed spending by region

100 = average spending

Northeast	Midwest	South	West
86	94	87	140

SATELLITE DISHES

Total household spending	$360,014,160		
Average household spends	3.41		

	average spending	best customers (index)	biggest customers (market share)
AGE OF HOUSEHOLDER			
Total households	**$3.41**	**100**	**100.0%**
Under age 25	–	–	–
Aged 25 to 34	2.72	80	15.0
Aged 35 to 44	4.83	142	33.0
Aged 45 to 54	4.63	136	24.9
Aged 55 to 64	5.17	152	17.7
Aged 65 to 74	1.57	46	5.3
Aged 75 or older	1.52	45	4.1
HOUSEHOLD INCOME			
Total households reporting income	**2.98**	**100**	**100.0**
Under $20,000	0.70	23	8.2
$20,000 to $29,999	0.99	33	4.9
$30,000 to $39,999	2.06	69	8.5
$40,000 to $49,999	6.43	216	20.2
$50,000 to $69,999	7.83	263	36.9
$70,000 or more	4.26	143	21.4
HOUSEHOLD TYPE			
Total households	**3.41**	**100**	**100.0**
Married couples	4.59	135	70.4
Married couples, no children	5.76	169	36.0
Married couples, with children	3.48	102	27.4
Oldest child under 6	1.73	51	2.6
Oldest child 6 to 17	2.54	74	10.8
Oldest child 18 or older	6.64	195	14.0
Single parent with child under 18	0.81	24	1.5
Single person	1.38	40	11.6
REGION			
Total households	**3.41**	**100**	**100.0**
Northeast	2.94	86	17.2
Midwest	3.21	94	22.5
South	2.98	87	30.5
West	4.79	140	29.8

Note: (–) means sample is too small to make a reliable estimate. For definitions of best and biggest customers, see introduction or glossary.
Source: Calculations by New Strategist based on the 1997 Consumer Expenditure Survey

Social, Recreation, and Civic Club Memberships

Best customers:
- Households with incomes of $70,000 or more
- Married couples with adult children
- Households in the West

Customer trends:
- If clubs can reinvent themselves to appeal to aging boomers, spending in this category could rise as boomers gain more free time.

Households with incomes of $70,000 or more spend three times as much as the average household on social, recreation, and civic club memberships. This category includes a broad range of organizations from health clubs to country clubs and fraternal organizations. Married couples with adult children at home spend 50 percent more than average on club memberships. Households in the West spend 40 percent more than average.

While membership in social and fraternal organizations has waned over the past few decades, health clubs have enjoyed rapid growth. To remain viable in the future, clubs of all kinds will have to reinvent themselves to appeal to aging boomers.

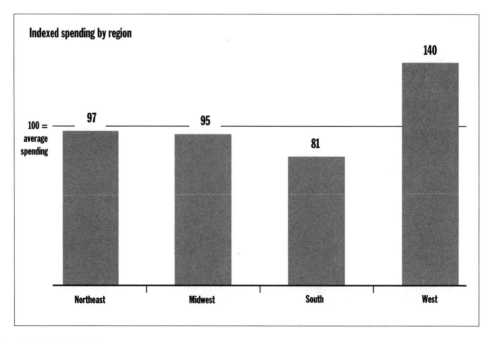

Indexed spending by region

100 = average spending

Northeast	Midwest	South	West
97	95	81	140

SOCIAL, RECREATION, AND CIVIC CLUB MEMBERSHIPS

Total household spending $7,930,869,120
Average household spends   75.12

	average spending	best customers (index)	biggest customers (market share)
AGE OF HOUSEHOLDER			
Total households	**$75.12**	**100**	**100.0%**
Under age 25	31.69	42	3.0
Aged 25 to 34	59.71	79	15.0
Aged 35 to 44	69.41	92	21.5
Aged 45 to 54	104.50	139	25.5
Aged 55 to 64	97.69	130	15.2
Aged 65 to 74	98.87	132	15.1
Aged 75 or older	38.39	51	4.8
HOUSEHOLD INCOME			
Total households reporting income	**78.75**	**100**	**100.0**
Under $20,000	25.78	33	11.4
$20,000 to $29,999	45.76	58	8.5
$30,000 to $39,999	49.24	63	7.6
$40,000 to $49,999	83.42	106	9.9
$50,000 to $69,999	105.60	134	18.8
$70,000 or more	230.40	293	43.7
HOUSEHOLD TYPE			
Total households	**75.12**	**100**	**100.0**
Married couples	96.21	128	67.0
Married couples, no children	107.78	143	30.6
Married couples, with children	95.04	127	34.0
Oldest child under 6	75.40	100	5.2
Oldest child 6 to 17	93.16	124	18.0
Oldest child 18 or older	112.89	150	10.8
Single parent with child under 18	38.58	51	3.2
Single person	52.88	70	20.2
REGION			
Total households	**75.12**	**100**	**100.0**
Northeast	72.90	97	19.4
Midwest	71.50	95	22.7
South	60.52	81	28.1
West	105.25	140	29.8

Note: For definitions of best and biggest customers, see introduction or glossary.
Source: Calculations by New Strategist based on the 1997 Consumer Expenditure Survey

Sound Equipment and Accessories

Best customers:
- Married couples with school-aged or older children
- Households in the West

Customer trends:
- The growing teen and young-adult population should boost spending on sound equipment and accessories.

The bedrooms of the nation's children are well-stocked with electronics. This is the reason why spending on sound equipment and accessories by parents is higher than average. Married couples with school-aged children spend 46 percent more than the average household on sound equipment and accessories. Those with adult children at home spend 53 percent more than average. Households in the West, where the entertainment industry reigns, spend 33 percent more than average on sound equipment and accessories.

The growing teen population, combined with teens' love of music, will boost spending on sound equipment and accessories for the next few years.

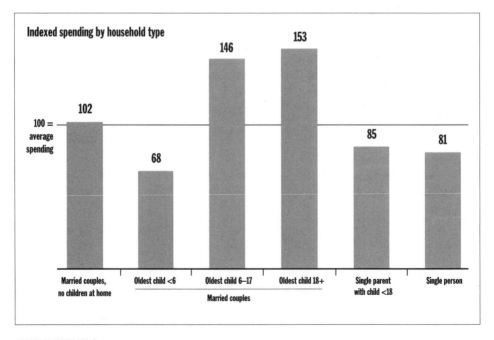

Indexed spending by household type

Married couples, no children at home	Oldest child <6	Oldest child 6–17	Oldest child 18+	Single parent with child <18	Single person
102	68	146	153	85	81

100 = average spending

Married couples

SOUND EQUIPMENT AND ACCESSORIES

Total household spending	$4,464,809,040	
Average household spends	42.29	

	average spending	best customers (index)	biggest customers (market share)
AGE OF HOUSEHOLDER			
Total households	**$42.29**	**100**	**100.0%**
Under age 25	43.38	103	7.3
Aged 25 to 34	50.43	119	22.5
Aged 35 to 44	54.12	128	29.8
Aged 45 to 54	48.63	115	21.1
Aged 55 to 64	33.90	80	9.4
Aged 65 to 74	29.38	69	8.0
Aged 75 or older	10.49	25	2.3
HOUSEHOLD INCOME			
Total households reporting income	**45.81**	**100**	**100.0**
Under $20,000	18.74	41	14.3
$20,000 to $29,999	43.28	94	13.8
$30,000 to $39,999	32.74	71	8.7
$40,000 to $49,999	34.50	75	7.0
$50,000 to $69,999	42.54	93	13.0
$70,000 or more	86.53	189	28.2
HOUSEHOLD TYPE			
Total households	**42.29**	**100**	**100.0**
Married couples	49.58	117	61.3
Married couples, no children	43.34	102	21.9
Married couples, with children	56.23	133	35.7
Oldest child under 6	28.79	68	3.5
Oldest child 6 to 17	61.90	146	21.3
Oldest child 18 or older	64.70	153	11.0
Single parent with child under 18	36.09	85	5.4
Single person	34.09	81	23.2
REGION			
Total households	**42.29**	**100**	**100.0**
Northeast	29.93	71	14.1
Midwest	36.23	86	20.5
South	45.05	107	37.2
West	56.15	133	28.2

Note: For definitions of best and biggest customers, see introduction or glossary.
Source: Calculations by New Strategist based on the 1997 Consumer Expenditure Survey

Television Sets

Best customers: • Married couples with adult children

Customer trends: • Little growth in the immediate future as shoppers wait for the dust to settle around changing television technology.

Most U.S. households have not one, but two television sets. New technologies, such as big screens, have kept the television market from stagnating despite this saturation. Married couples with adult children at home are the best customers of television sets, spending 77 percent more than the average household. Many are buying sets for college-bound children or getting an additional set to avoid arguments about who controls the remote.

Sales of television sets are likely to decline during the next few years as consumers wait for new television technologies to take hold. After the dust settles and prices drop, sales of new television sets will take off.

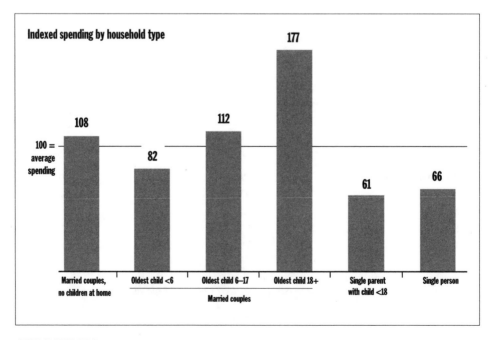

Indexed spending by household type

108	82	112	177	61	66
Married couples, no children at home	Oldest child <6	Oldest child 6–17	Oldest child 18+	Single parent with child <18	Single person

100 = average spending

Married couples

TELEVISION SETS

Total household spending $6,946,900,800
Average household spends   65.80

	average spending	best customers (index)	biggest customers (market share)
AGE OF HOUSEHOLDER			
Total households	**$65.80**	**100**	**100.0%**
Under age 25	52.84	80	5.7
Aged 25 to 34	62.71	95	18.0
Aged 35 to 44	73.82	112	26.1
Aged 45 to 54	78.77	120	21.9
Aged 55 to 64	76.17	116	13.5
Aged 65 to 74	49.06	75	8.6
Aged 75 or older	44.04	67	6.2
HOUSEHOLD INCOME			
Total households reporting income	**66.10**	**100**	**100.0**
Under $20,000	42.81	65	22.6
$20,000 to $29,999	41.28	62	9.1
$30,000 to $39,999	52.93	80	9.8
$40,000 to $49,999	74.79	113	10.6
$50,000 to $69,999	112.39	170	23.9
$70,000 or more	106.43	161	24.1
HOUSEHOLD TYPE			
Total households	**65.80**	**100**	**100.0**
Married couples	80.66	123	64.1
Married couples, no children	71.33	108	23.1
Married couples, with children	81.43	124	33.3
Oldest child under 6	54.16	82	4.2
Oldest child 6 to 17	73.82	112	16.3
Oldest child 18 or older	116.36	177	12.7
Single parent with child under 18	39.94	61	3.8
Single person	43.40	66	18.9
REGION			
Total households	**65.80**	**100**	**100.0**
Northeast	72.31	110	22.0
Midwest	61.04	93	22.2
South	67.06	102	35.6
West	62.96	96	20.3

Note: For definitions of best and biggest customers, see introduction or glossary.
Source: Calculations by New Strategist based on the 1997 Consumer Expenditure Survey

Toys, Games, Hobbies, and Tricycles

Best customers: • Married couples with children under age 18

Customer trends: • Slowdown likely as the number of preschoolers declines slightly in the near future.

The best customers of toys, games, hobbies, and tricycles are parents. Married couples with children under age 6 spend more than twice as much as the average household on this category. Those with school-aged children spend 65 percent more than average.

The number of preschoolers will decline slightly in the next few years. This could slow sales of toys, games, hobbies, and tricycles unless sales to older children rise to take up the slack.

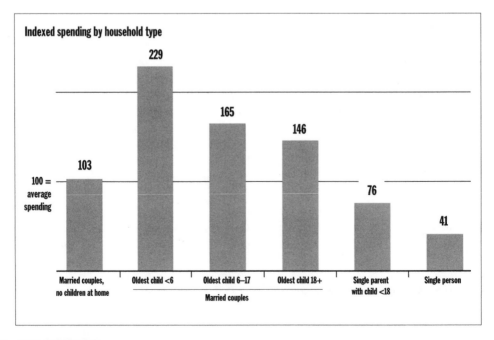

Indexed spending by household type

103	229	165	146	76	41
Married couples, no children at home	Oldest child <6	Oldest child 6–17	Oldest child 18+	Single parent with child <18	Single person
		Married couples			

100 = average spending

TOYS, GAMES, HOBBIES, AND TRICYCLES

Total household spending $13,479,943,680
Average household spends   127.68

	average spending	best customers (index)	biggest customers (market share)
AGE OF HOUSEHOLDER			
Total households	**$127.68**	**100**	**100.0%**
Under age 25	90.10	71	5.0
Aged 25 to 34	172.45	135	25.5
Aged 35 to 44	167.61	131	30.5
Aged 45 to 54	115.52	90	16.6
Aged 55 to 64	124.56	98	11.4
Aged 65 to 74	82.29	64	7.4
Aged 75 or older	55.67	44	4.1
HOUSEHOLD INCOME			
Total households reporting income	**130.24**	**100**	**100.0**
Under $20,000	54.17	42	14.5
$20,000 to $29,999	87.09	67	9.8
$30,000 to $39,999	137.38	105	12.9
$40,000 to $49,999	128.55	99	9.2
$50,000 to $69,999	237.56	182	25.6
$70,000 or more	240.17	184	27.6
HOUSEHOLD TYPE			
Total households	**127.68**	**100**	**100.0**
Married couples	179.74	141	73.6
Married couples, no children	131.70	103	22.0
Married couples, with children	222.26	174	46.8
Oldest child under 6	292.99	229	11.8
Oldest child 6 to 17	210.56	165	24.0
Oldest child 18 or older	186.75	146	10.5
Single parent with child under 18	96.47	76	4.7
Single person	51.82	41	11.7
REGION			
Total households	**127.68**	**100**	**100.0**
Northeast	130.75	102	20.5
Midwest	140.59	110	26.3
South	108.93	85	29.8
West	140.49	110	23.4

Note: For definitions of best and biggest customers, see introduction or glossary.
Source: Calculations by New Strategist based on the 1997 Consumer Expenditure Survey

TV, Radio, Sound Equipment Repair

Best customers:	• **Married couples with adult children.**
Customer trends:	• **The market may get a temporary boost as people try to keep their old TV sets running until prices on high-tech digital sets come down.**

Married couples with adult children at home are the best customers of television, radio, and sound equipment repair. These households spend 70 percent more than average on this category.

The market for TV, radio, and sound equipment repair may get a short-term boost as Americans opt to repair rather than replace television sets while they wait for prices of new high-tech sets to decline. Apart from high-end equipment, however, prices for electronics have fallen to the point at which Americans are more likely to buy new television, radio, and sound equipment rather than pay for repairs.

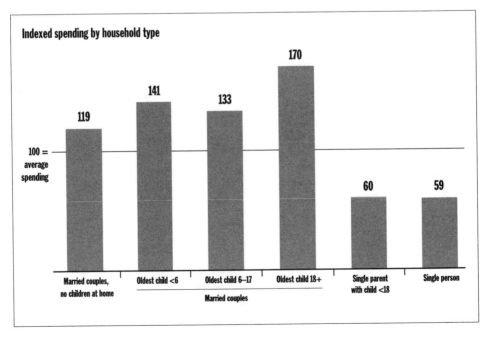

Indexed spending by household type

TV, RADIO, SOUND EQUIPMENT REPAIR

Total household spending	$702,080,400
Average household spends	6.65

	average spending	best customers (index)	biggest customers (market share)
AGE OF HOUSEHOLDER			
Total households	**$6.65**	**100**	**100.0%**
Under age 25	2.78	42	3.0
Aged 25 to 34	6.80	102	19.3
Aged 35 to 44	6.81	102	23.8
Aged 45 to 54	7.58	114	20.9
Aged 55 to 64	6.77	102	11.9
Aged 65 to 74	7.81	117	13.5
Aged 75 or older	5.54	83	7.8
HOUSEHOLD INCOME			
Total households reporting income	**7.31**	**100**	**100.0**
Under $20,000	3.79	52	18.1
$20,000 to $29,999	6.28	86	12.5
$30,000 to $39,999	5.02	69	8.4
$40,000 to $49,999	10.76	147	13.8
$50,000 to $69,999	9.79	134	18.8
$70,000 or more	13.89	190	28.4
HOUSEHOLD TYPE			
Total households	**6.65**	**100**	**100.0**
Married couples	8.65	130	68.0
Married couples, no children	7.89	119	25.3
Married couples, with children	9.61	145	38.8
Oldest child under 6	9.35	141	7.2
Oldest child 6 to 17	8.86	133	19.4
Oldest child 18 or older	11.31	170	12.2
Single parent with child under 18	3.96	60	3.7
Single person	3.95	59	17.1
REGION			
Total households	**6.65**	**100**	**100.0**
Northeast	6.63	100	19.9
Midwest	6.73	101	24.2
South	6.03	91	31.6
West	7.61	114	24.3

Note: For definitions of best and biggest customers, see introduction or glossary.
Source: Calculations by New Strategist based on the 1997 Consumer Expenditure Survey

VCRs and Video Disk Players

Best customers:
- Married couples with children under age 6
- Married couples with adult children

Customer trends:
- This mature market is secure for the moment, but faces eventual threats from new technologies.

The best customers of VCRs and video disk players are parents buying for children. Married couples with adult children at home spend 71 percent more than average on VCRs and video disk players. Many are buying video equipment for college-bound kids. Married couples with preschoolers spend 55 percent more than average as they satisfy the demand to view Barney or the Teletubbies over and over again.

The market for VCRs is mature, and digital video disk players have yet to catch on beyond early adopters. The market is stable for now, but it will face threats from new offerings such as video on demand from cable companies.

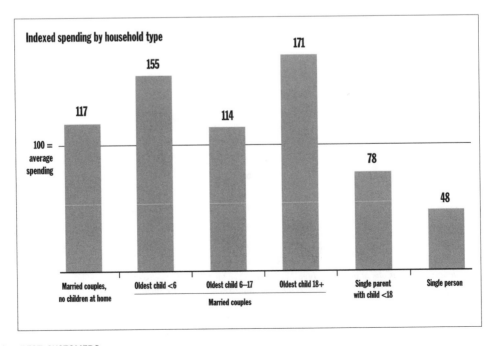

Indexed spending by household type

100 = average spending

Married couples, no children at home	Oldest child <6	Oldest child 6–17	Oldest child 18+	Single parent with child <18	Single person
117	155	114	171	78	48

Married couples

VCRs AND VIDEO DISC PLAYERS

Total household spending	$2,806,210,080		
Average household spends	26.58		

	average spending	best customers (index)	biggest customers (market share)
AGE OF HOUSEHOLDER			
Total households	**$26.58**	**100**	**100.0%**
Under age 25	26.89	101	7.2
Aged 25 to 34	34.12	128	24.2
Aged 35 to 44	26.76	101	23.4
Aged 45 to 54	32.01	120	22.1
Aged 55 to 64	29.55	111	13.0
Aged 65 to 74	13.95	52	6.0
Aged 75 or older	11.78	44	4.1
HOUSEHOLD INCOME			
Total households reporting income	**28.25**	**100**	**100.0**
Under $20,000	12.28	43	15.1
$20,000 to $29,999	24.05	85	12.4
$30,000 to $39,999	28.41	101	12.3
$40,000 to $49,999	37.30	132	12.3
$50,000 to $69,999	37.43	132	18.6
$70,000 or more	55.16	195	29.2
HOUSEHOLD TYPE			
Total households	**26.58**	**100**	**100.0**
Married couples	35.86	135	70.5
Married couples, no children	31.17	117	25.0
Married couples, with children	36.44	137	36.9
Oldest child under 6	41.11	155	8.0
Oldest child 6 to 17	30.37	114	16.6
Oldest child 18 or older	45.40	171	12.3
Single parent with child under 18	20.71	78	4.9
Single person	12.70	48	13.7
REGION			
Total households	**26.58**	**100**	**100.0**
Northeast	24.79	93	18.6
Midwest	26.24	99	23.6
South	23.13	87	30.4
West	34.32	129	27.4

Note: For definitions of best and biggest customers, see introduction or glossary.
Source: Calculations by New Strategist based on the 1997 Consumer Expenditure Survey

Veterinary Services

Best customers:
- Householders aged 45 to 54
- Married couples with school-aged or adult children
- Married couples without children

Customer trends:
- As the nation grows older, the number of pet owners is likely to increase, boosting demand for veterinary services.

Householders aged 45 to 54 spend 62 percent more than the average household on veterinary services. Married couples with school-aged children spend 32 percent more, and those with preschoolers spend 3 percent less'. Married couples without children at home, many of them older, spend 42 percent more than average on this item.

Americans love their pets. As the nation grows older, the number of pet owners is likely to increase. This should boost the demand for veterinary services.

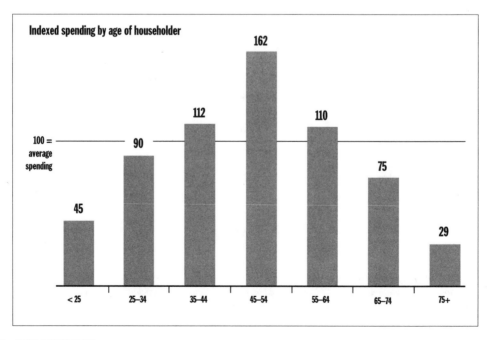

Indexed spending by age of householder

100 = average spending

| <25 | 25–34 | 35–44 | 45–54 | 55–64 | 65–74 | 75+ |
| 45 | 90 | 112 | 162 | 110 | 75 | 29 |

VETERINARY SERVICES

Total household spending	$5,647,260,240
Average household spends	53.49

	average spending	best customers (index)	biggest customers (market share)
AGE OF HOUSEHOLDER			
Total households	**$53.49**	**100**	**100.0%**
Under age 25	23.98	45	3.2
Aged 25 to 34	48.02	90	16.9
Aged 35 to 44	60.01	112	26.1
Aged 45 to 54	86.48	162	29.6
Aged 55 to 64	58.78	110	12.8
Aged 65 to 74	40.12	75	8.6
Aged 75 or older	15.70	29	2.7
HOUSEHOLD INCOME			
Total households reporting income	**55.38**	**100**	**100.0**
Under $20,000	23.97	43	15.1
$20,000 to $29,999	39.84	72	10.5
$30,000 to $39,999	40.58	73	9.0
$40,000 to $49,999	62.05	112	10.5
$50,000 to $69,999	92.90	168	23.5
$70,000 or more	116.48	210	31.4
HOUSEHOLD TYPE			
Total households	**53.49**	**100**	**100.0**
Married couples	70.05	131	68.5
Married couples, no children	75.72	142	30.2
Married couples, with children	68.86	129	34.6
Oldest child under 6	52.08	97	5.0
Oldest child 6 to 17	70.62	132	19.2
Oldest child 18 or older	77.30	145	10.4
Single parent with child under 18	25.35	47	3.0
Single person	29.52	55	15.9
REGION			
Total households	**53.49**	**100**	**100.0**
Northeast	54.36	102	20.3
Midwest	50.17	94	22.4
South	49.46	92	32.3
West	63.01	118	25.0

Note: For definitions of best and biggest customers, see introduction or glossary.
Source: Calculations by New Strategist based on the 1997 Consumer Expenditure Survey

Video Cassettes, Tapes, and Discs

Best customers:	• Married couples with children under age 6
	• Married couples with school-aged children
Customer trends:	• Stable market for now, but it faces eventual threat from new technologies.

Although many adults buy video cassettes, tapes, and discs for themselves, there can be no doubt that children are the driving force behind sales of these items. Young children especially like to watch the same video over and over again, and it quickly becomes cost-effective to buy rather than rent. Married couples with preschoolers spend 64 percent more than average on video cassettes, tapes, and discs. Those with school-aged children spend 46 percent more than average.

The market for video cassettes, tapes, and discs should remain stable for now. Eventually, however, new technologies that enable consumers to download videos from the Internet will challenge current formats.

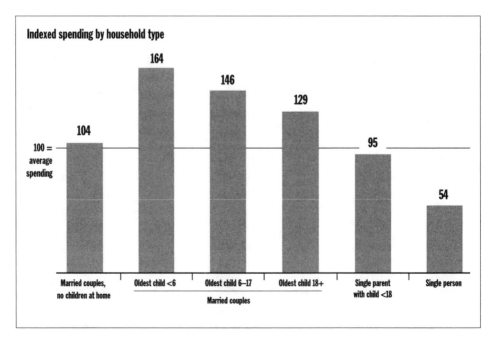

Indexed spending by household type

- Married couples, no children at home: 104
- Oldest child <6: 164
- Oldest child 6–17: 146
- Oldest child 18+: 129
- Single parent with child <18: 95
- Single person: 54

100 = average spending

Married couples

VIDEO CASSETTES, TAPES, AND DISCS

Total household spending	$2,338,508,400
Average household spends	22.15

	average spending	best customers (index)	biggest customers (market share)
AGE OF HOUSEHOLDER			
Total households	**$22.15**	**100**	**100.0%**
Under age 25	14.79	67	4.7
Aged 25 to 34	28.30	128	24.1
Aged 35 to 44	25.71	116	27.0
Aged 45 to 54	24.80	112	20.5
Aged 55 to 64	24.13	109	12.7
Aged 65 to 74	16.68	75	8.6
Aged 75 or older	5.41	24	2.3
HOUSEHOLD INCOME			
Total households reporting income	**23.81**	**100**	**100.0**
Under $20,000	11.99	50	17.5
$20,000 to $29,999	20.45	86	12.5
$30,000 to $39,999	25.87	109	13.3
$40,000 to $49,999	30.38	128	11.9
$50,000 to $69,999	32.57	137	19.2
$70,000 or more	40.60	171	25.5
HOUSEHOLD TYPE			
Total households	**22.15**	**100**	**100.0**
Married couples	28.35	128	66.9
Married couples, no children	22.94	104	22.1
Married couples, with children	32.06	145	38.9
Oldest child under 6	36.42	164	8.5
Oldest child 6 to 17	32.25	146	21.2
Oldest child 18 or older	28.54	129	9.3
Single parent with child under 18	21.07	95	6.0
Single person	11.91	54	15.4
REGION			
Total households	**22.15**	**100**	**100.0**
Northeast	16.97	77	15.3
Midwest	25.83	117	27.9
South	19.62	89	30.9
West	27.01	122	25.9

Note: For definitions of best and biggest customers, see introduction or glossary.
Source: Calculations by New Strategist based on the 1997 Consumer Expenditure Survey

Video Game Hardware and Software

Best customers:	• Householders aged 35 to 44
	• Married couples with school-aged children
Customer trends:	• The market will continue to grow as the number of teens increases and the quality of games improves.

Although violent video games have come under fire for several years now, the popularity of this technology shows no sign of waning. Parents still spend a considerable amount of money on video game hardware and software. Married couples with school-aged children spend two and one-half times as much as the average household on video game hardware and software. Householders aged 35 to 44 spend 56 percent more than average, primarily because most have school-aged children.

The quality of video games has been steadily improving, keeping sales strong. The number of teenagers is rising, and this bodes well for the market. Eventual threats include new technologies that allow home computers to function as game machines and a backlash against the industry's frequently violent offerings.

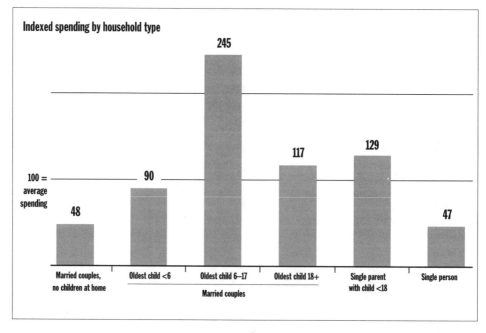

Indexed spending by household type

VIDEO GAME HARDWARE AND SOFTWARE

Total household spending $2,084,070,240
Average household spends   19.74

	average spending	best customers (index)	biggest customers (market share)
AGE OF HOUSEHOLDER			
Total households	$19.74	100	100.0%
Under age 25	24.46	124	8.8
Aged 25 to 34	26.25	133	25.1
Aged 35 to 44	30.76	156	36.2
Aged 45 to 54	21.12	107	19.6
Aged 55 to 64	11.15	56	6.6
Aged 65 to 74	5.10	26	3.0
Aged 75 or older	1.56	8	0.7
HOUSEHOLD INCOME			
Total households reporting income	20.40	100	100.0
Under $20,000	9.53	47	16.3
$20,000 to $29,999	16.14	79	11.6
$30,000 to $39,999	17.47	86	10.5
$40,000 to $49,999	34.56	169	15.8
$50,000 to $69,999	28.28	139	19.5
$70,000 or more	35.99	176	26.4
HOUSEHOLD TYPE			
Total households	19.74	100	100.0
Married couples	24.67	125	65.3
Married couples, no children	9.41	48	10.2
Married couples, with children	35.72	181	48.6
Oldest child under 6	17.75	90	4.6
Oldest child 6 to 17	48.28	245	35.6
Oldest child 18 or older	23.14	117	8.4
Single parent with child under 18	25.42	129	8.1
Single person	9.26	47	13.5
REGION			
Total households	19.74	100	100.0
Northeast	21.31	108	21.6
Midwest	20.33	103	24.6
South	18.20	92	32.2
West	20.15	102	21.7

Note: For definitions of best and biggest customers, see introduction or glossary.
Source: Calculations by New Strategist based on the 1997 Consumer Expenditure Survey

Videotape, Disc, Film Rental

Best customers:
- Householders aged 25 to 44
- Married couples with school-aged children

Customer trends:
- New technologies pose a serious threat to this market.

The best customers for videotape, disc, and film rentals are children. Married couples with school-aged children spend 76 percent more than the average household on video rentals as they seek a few minutes of peace and quiet. Householders aged 35 to 44, many of whom are parents of school-aged children, spend 44 percent more than average. Householders aged 25 to 34 spend 39 percent more than average.

Although the market for video rentals is safe for the moment, new technology eventually will undermine this market. If families can get their favorite movies delivered straight to their television, running to the store for a video will become a thing of the past.

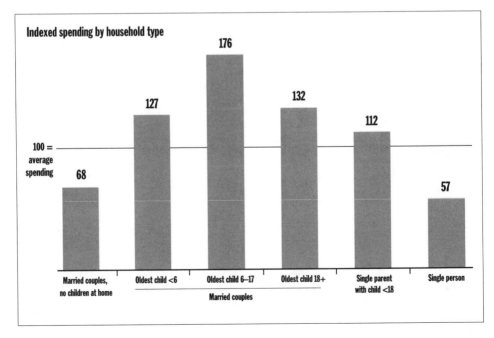

Indexed spending by household type

Married couples, no children at home	68	
Oldest child <6	127	
Oldest child 6–17	176	
Oldest child 18+	132	
Single parent with child <18	112	
Single person	57	

100 = average spending

Married couples

VIDEOTAPE, DISC, FILM RENTAL

Total household spending $4,254,712,800
Average household spends   40.30

	average spending	best customers (index)	biggest customers (market share)
AGE OF HOUSEHOLDER			
Total households	**$40.30**	**100**	**100.0%**
Under age 25	43.73	109	7.7
Aged 25 to 34	56.16	139	26.3
Aged 35 to 44	57.87	144	33.4
Aged 45 to 54	48.37	120	22.0
Aged 55 to 64	22.63	56	6.6
Aged 65 to 74	10.45	26	3.0
Aged 75 or older	4.67	12	1.1
HOUSEHOLD INCOME			
Total households reporting income	**42.63**	**100**	**100.0**
Under $20,000	21.66	51	17.7
$20,000 to $29,999	34.47	81	11.8
$30,000 to $39,999	46.01	108	13.2
$40,000 to $49,999	52.93	124	11.6
$50,000 to $69,999	61.77	145	20.3
$70,000 or more	72.26	170	25.3
HOUSEHOLD TYPE			
Total households	**40.30**	**100**	**100.0**
Married couples	47.95	119	62.2
Married couples, no children	27.46	68	14.5
Married couples, with children	62.40	155	41.6
Oldest child under 6	51.30	127	6.5
Oldest child 6 to 17	70.90	176	25.6
Oldest child 18 or older	53.13	132	9.5
Single parent with child under 18	45.14	112	7.0
Single person	22.95	57	16.4
REGION			
Total households	**40.30**	**100**	**100.0**
Northeast	34.74	86	17.2
Midwest	39.85	99	23.6
South	37.57	93	32.5
West	50.52	125	26.6

Note: For definitions of best and biggest customers, see introduction or glossary.
Source: Calculations by New Strategist based on the 1997 Consumer Expenditure Survey

Water Sports Equipment

Best customers:	• Householders aged 35 to 54
	• Households with incomes of $70,000 or more
	• Married couples with school-aged children
	• Households in the West
Customer trends:	• Sales of water sports equipment should get a boost from the rising number of teens and young adults.

Households with incomes of $70,000 or more spend far more than the average household on water sports equipment. Spending by these households is more than four times the average, accounting for 65 percent of the market. Households with school-aged children spend more than double the average on this category. Householders aged 35 to 44 spend 74 percent more, while those aged 45 to 54 spend 81 percent more. Households in the West spend 36 percent more than average on water sports equipment.

Americans of all ages love to play in the water, but young people (who still look good in bathing suits) drive the market. As the number of teens and young adults increases in the coming years, sales of water sports equipment should rise.

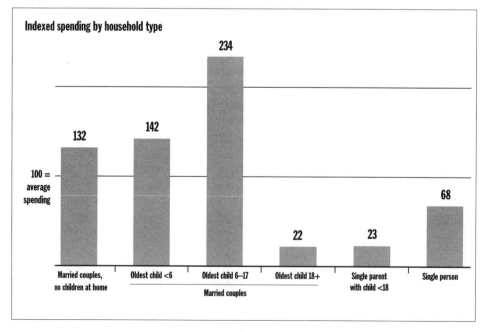

Indexed spending by household type

100 = average spending

Married couples, no children at home — 132
Oldest child <6 — 142
Oldest child 6–17 — 234
Oldest child 18+ — 22
(Married couples)
Single parent with child <18 — 23
Single person — 68

WATER SPORTS EQUIPMENT

Total household spending $477,203,520
Average household spends   4.52

	average spending	best customers (index)	biggest customers (market share)
AGE OF HOUSEHOLDER			
Total households	**$4.52**	**100**	**100.0%**
Under age 25	0.67	15	1.1
Aged 25 to 34	4.55	101	19.0
Aged 35 to 44	7.87	174	40.5
Aged 45 to 54	8.19	181	33.2
Aged 55 to 64	1.57	35	4.1
Aged 65 to 74	0.69	15	1.8
Aged 75 or older	0.26	6	0.5
HOUSEHOLD INCOME			
Total households reporting income	**5.42**	**100**	**100.0**
Under $20,000	0.54	10	3.4
$20,000 to $29,999	2.86	53	7.7
$30,000 to $39,999	3.00	55	6.8
$40,000 to $49,999	2.38	44	4.1
$50,000 to $69,999	4.88	90	12.6
$70,000 or more	23.70	437	65.4
HOUSEHOLD TYPE			
Total households	**4.52**	**100**	**100.0**
Married couples	6.36	141	73.6
Married couples, no children	5.97	132	28.2
Married couples, with children	7.23	160	43.0
Oldest child under 6	6.40	142	7.3
Oldest child 6 to 17	10.59	234	34.1
Oldest child 18 or older	1.00	22	1.6
Single parent with child under 18	1.03	23	1.4
Single person	3.08	68	19.6
REGION			
Total households	**4.52**	**100**	**100.0**
Northeast	4.88	108	21.6
Midwest	4.12	91	21.8
South	3.62	80	27.9
West	6.13	136	28.8

Note: For definitions of best and biggest customers, see introduction or glossary.
Source: Calculations by New Strategist based on the 1997 Consumer Expenditure Survey

Winter Sports Equipment

Best customers:

- Householders under age 25
- Married couples with school-aged or older children
- Households with incomes of $70,000 or more
- Households in the West

Customer trends:

- A booming economy and the growing number of young people is good news for sales of winter sports equipment.

The best customers of winter sports equipment are households with incomes of $70,000 or more, spending three times as much as the average household. Married couples with school-aged children spend twice as much, while those with adult children at home spend nearly three times the average. Spending by householders under age 25 is twice the average. Households in the West, where skiing and winter resorts are plentiful, spend 81 percent more than average. In the Northeast, which also has a thriving winter sports industry, households spend 56 percent more than average on this item.

The booming economy should benefit sales of winter sports equipment. The growing population of teens and young adults also should keep sales brisk.

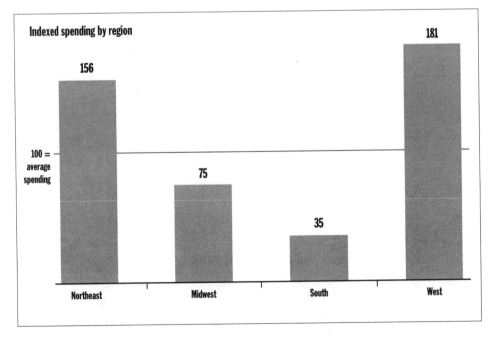

Indexed spending by region

100 = average spending

| Northeast | Midwest | South | West |
| 156 | 75 | 35 | 181 |

WINTER SPORTS EQUIPMENT

Total household spending	$580,668,000		
Average household spends	5.50		

	average spending	best customers (index)	biggest customers (market share)
AGE OF HOUSEHOLDER			
Total households	**$5.50**	**100**	**100.0%**
Under age 25	11.59	211	15.0
Aged 25 to 34	3.70	67	12.7
Aged 35 to 44	10.25	186	43.4
Aged 45 to 54	6.80	124	22.7
Aged 55 to 64	2.28	41	4.8
Aged 65 to 74	0.60	11	1.3
Aged 75 or older	0.13	2	0.2
HOUSEHOLD INCOME			
Total households reporting income	**5.48**	**100**	**100.0**
Under $20,000	2.11	38	13.4
$20,000 to $29,999	1.76	32	4.7
$30,000 to $39,999	1.39	25	3.1
$40,000 to $49,999	8.16	149	13.9
$50,000 to $69,999	7.96	145	20.4
$70,000 or more	16.31	298	44.5
HOUSEHOLD TYPE			
Total households	**5.50**	**100**	**100.0**
Married couples	6.68	121	63.5
Married couples, no children	1.74	32	6.8
Married couples, with children	11.29	205	55.2
Oldest child under 6	5.38	98	5.0
Oldest child 6 to 17	11.15	203	29.5
Oldest child 18 or older	15.78	287	20.6
Single parent with child under 18	4.00	73	4.6
Single person	5.17	94	27.0
REGION			
Total households	**5.50**	**100**	**100.0**
Northeast	8.59	156	31.2
Midwest	4.11	75	17.9
South	1.95	35	12.4
West	9.98	181	38.5

Note: For definitions of best and biggest customers, see introduction or glossary.
Source: Calculations by New Strategist based on the 1997 Consumer Expenditure Survey

Chapter 6.

Financial Products & Services

Financial Products and Services

The average American household spends almost as much on financial and miscellaneous products and services, including taxes, as it does on shelter—fully $8,312.76 in 1997. This chapter examines only those financial products and services for which there are customers, such as life insurance and legal fees. It does not examine spending on Social Security taxes or other government retirement programs, nor does it examine federal, state, or local tax payments since none is under the control of individual consumers. These mandatory financial expenses account for two-thirds of spending in this category.

Discretionary spending on financial products and services is directly linked to income. Those with the highest incomes spend the most on life insurance, accounting fees, contributions to charities, and most of the other categories shown here. During the recession of the early 1990s, many households trimmed their spending on financial items, including cash contributions and life insurance. But they spent more on pensions and Social Security. With the baby-boom generation entering its peak earning years, spending on financial products and services is likely to grow substantially.

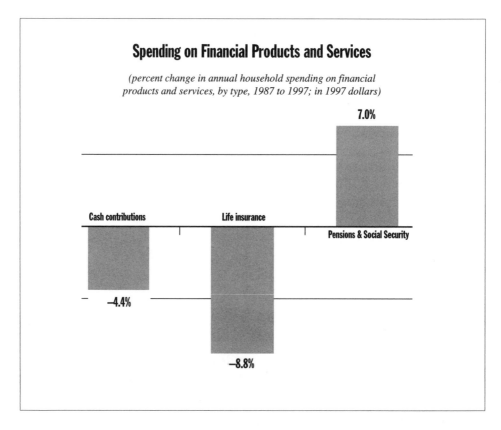

Spending on Financial Products and Services

(percent change in annual household spending on financial products and services, by type, 1987 to 1997; in 1997 dollars)

7.0%

Cash contributions

Life insurance

Pensions & Social Security

−4.4%

−8.8%

Financial Spending

(average annual spending of households on financial and miscellaneous products and services, and percent distribution of spending by type, 1997)

Total spending on financial products and services	**$8,312.76**	**100.0%**
Contributions to religious organizations	390.25	4.7
Insurance, life and other personal except health	378.63	4.6
Retirement accounts, nonpayroll deposits	376.65	4.5
Pensions, deductions for private	339.22	4.1
Contributions of cash to nonhousehold members including students, alimony, child support	253.98	3.1
Finance charges, except mortgage and vehicle	249.40	3.0
Gifts of cash, stocks, bonds to nonhousehold members	225.03	2.7
Legal fees	135.79	1.6
Occupational expenses, union and professional dues	102.65	1.2
Contributions to charities	101.95	1.2
Funeral expenses	63.05	0.8
Accounting fees	48.99	0.6
Bank service charges	24.51	0.3
Cemetery lots, vaults, and maintenance fees	19.65	0.2
Contributions to educational organizations	16.88	0.2
Safe deposit box rental	6.69	0.1
Contributions to political organizations	6.20	0.1
Credit card memberships	3.98	0.0

Note: Numbers will not add to total because not all categories are shown, including Social Security and federal, state, and local taxes.

Accounting Fees

Best customers:
- Households with incomes of $70,000 or more
- Households in the West
- Married couples without children at home
- Householders aged 45 to 64

Customer trends:
- Potentially rapid growth in the next few years, but competition from software packages will intensify as the computer-literate baby-boom generation ages

Households with incomes of $70,000 or more spend nearly three times as much as the average household on accounting fees. Not only do affluent householders have more money to manage than others, but their finances are usually more complex and often require an expert's advice. Other good customers of accountants are householders aged 45 to 64. They are the ones most likely to be in their peak earning years.

Accounting firms have an opportunity to expand rapidly in the years ahead because of the aging of the baby-boom generation into the 45-to-64 age group. But growth may be curbed by the high level of computer literacy among boomers. Unlike today's older Americans, boomers are technologically savvy and most have computers at home. Tax preparation and financial-planning software could siphon off millions of potential customers.

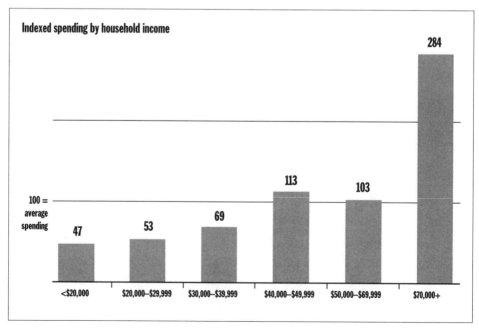

Indexed spending by household income

47	53	69	113	103	284
<$20,000	$20,000–$29,999	$30,000–$39,999	$40,000–$49,999	$50,000–$69,999	$70,000+

100 = average spending

Accounting fees

Total household spending	$5,172,168,240
Average household spends	48.99

	average spending	best customers (index)	biggest customers (market share)
AGE OF HOUSEHOLDER			
Total households	**$48.99**	**100**	**100.0%**
Under age 25	7.06	14	1.0
Aged 25 to 34	30.03	61	11.6
Aged 35 to 44	52.61	107	25.0
Aged 45 to 54	65.26	133	24.4
Aged 55 to 64	63.25	129	15.1
Aged 65 to 74	58.49	119	13.7
Aged 75 or older	48.79	100	9.3
HOUSEHOLD INCOME			
Total households reporting income	**50.62**	**100**	**100.0**
Under $20,000	23.78	47	16.4
$20,000 to $29,999	26.84	53	7.7
$30,000 to $39,999	34.71	69	8.4
$40,000 to $49,999	57.45	113	10.6
$50,000 to $69,999	52.21	103	14.5
$70,000 or more	143.65	284	42.4
HOUSEHOLD TYPE			
Total households	**48.99**	**100**	**100.0**
Married couples	60.83	124	64.9
Married couples, no children	72.72	148	31.7
Married couples, with children	56.69	116	31.1
Oldest child under 6	59.98	122	6.3
Oldest child 6 to 17	49.90	102	14.8
Oldest child 18 or older	68.08	139	10.0
Single parent with child under 18	28.74	59	3.7
Single person	39.35	80	23.1
REGION			
Total households	**48.99**	**100**	**100.0**
Northeast	54.13	110	22.1
Midwest	42.30	86	20.6
South	33.66	69	24.0
West	76.86	157	33.3

Note: For definitions of best and biggest customers, see introduction or glossary.
Source: Calculations by New Strategist based on the 1997 Consumer Expenditure Survey

Bank Service Charges

Best customers:	• Householders aged 35 to 54
	• Married couples with school-aged or older children
Customer trends:	• Fed up with service charges, consumers are unlikely to accept further increases without a backlash.

Married couples with school-aged children spend 49 percent more than the average household on bank service charges, while householders aged 35 to 54 spend about one-third more than average. Many banks waive service charges for older Americans, so younger adults must pay more to make up the difference.

Banks have been raising existing charges and tacking on new ones for a variety of services. So far consumers have accepted the increased costs, but there are signs of rebellion (read, "demands for regulation"). It is unlikely that bank service charges can increase much more in the near future.

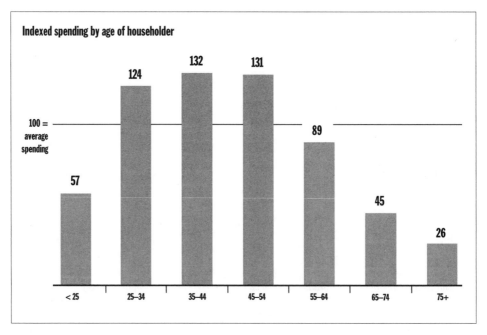

Indexed spending by age of householder

100 = average spending

< 25	25–34	35–44	45–54	55–64	65–74	75+
57	124	132	131	89	45	26

BANK SERVICE CHARGES

Total household spending $2,587,667,760
Average household spends   24.51

	average spending	best customers (index)	biggest customers (market share)
AGE OF HOUSEHOLDER			
Total households	**$24.51**	**100**	**100.0%**
Under age 25	13.86	57	4.0
Aged 25 to 34	30.42	124	23.4
Aged 35 to 44	32.40	132	30.8
Aged 45 to 54	32.00	131	23.9
Aged 55 to 64	21.80	89	10.4
Aged 65 to 74	10.99	45	5.1
Aged 75 or older	6.26	26	2.4
HOUSEHOLD INCOME			
Total households reporting income	**25.65**	**100**	**100.0**
Under $20,000	14.64	57	19.9
$20,000 to $29,999	26.12	102	14.9
$30,000 to $39,999	29.11	113	13.9
$40,000 to $49,999	29.40	115	10.7
$50,000 to $69,999	36.12	141	19.8
$70,000 or more	35.81	140	20.9
HOUSEHOLD TYPE			
Total households	**24.51**	**100**	**100.0**
Married couples	28.10	115	59.9
Married couples, no children	20.34	83	17.7
Married couples, with children	33.88	138	37.2
Oldest child under 6	28.98	118	6.1
Oldest child 6 to 17	36.41	149	21.6
Oldest child 18 or older	32.25	132	9.5
Single parent with child under 18	20.73	85	5.3
Single person	16.99	69	19.9
REGION			
Total households	**24.51**	**100**	**100.0**
Northeast	19.19	78	15.6
Midwest	20.47	84	20.0
South	26.51	108	37.7
West	30.77	126	26.7

Note: For definitions of best and biggest customers, see introduction or glossary.
Source: Calculations by New Strategist based on the 1997 Consumer Expenditure Survey

Cemetery Lots, Vaults, and Maintenance Fees

Best customers:
- Householders aged 65 or older
- Married couples with adult children at home
- Households in the South

Customer trends:
- Robust spending in the short term, but in the long run, boomer preference for cremation may curtail spending.

Householders aged 65 or older spend nearly three times as much as the average household on cemetery lots, vaults, and maintenance fees, accounting for 58 percent of spending in this category. Many are paying to bury spouses or other family members, while some are buying lots for themselves. Married couples with adult children at home (many of whom are older householders) spend more than twice the average. Households in the South spend 39 percent more than average.

Spending should be robust due to the rapid growth in the number of very old Americans. Future sales could be curtailed by the preference of many baby boomers for cremation rather than interment.

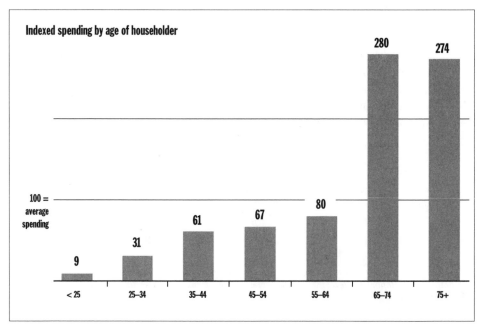

Indexed spending by age of householder

< 25	25–34	35–44	45–54	55–64	65–74	75+
9	31	61	67	80	280	274

100 = average spending

CEMETERY LOTS, VAULTS, AND MAINTENANCE FEES

Total household spending	$2,074,568,400
Average household spends	19.65

	average spending	best customers (index)	biggest customers (market share)
AGE OF HOUSEHOLDER			
Total households	**$19.65**	**100**	**100.0%**
Under age 25	1.82	9	0.7
Aged 25 to 34	6.09	31	5.8
Aged 35 to 44	12.01	61	14.2
Aged 45 to 54	13.18	67	12.3
Aged 55 to 64	15.79	80	9.4
Aged 65 to 74	55.08	280	32.1
Aged 75 or older	53.81	274	25.5
HOUSEHOLD INCOME			
Total households reporting income	**20.06**	**100**	**100.0**
Under $20,000	15.15	76	26.3
$20,000 to $29,999	18.15	90	13.2
$30,000 to $39,999	28.53	142	17.4
$40,000 to $49,999	25.28	126	11.8
$50,000 to $69,999	35.30	176	24.7
$70,000 or more	8.85	44	6.6
HOUSEHOLD TYPE			
Total households	**19.65**	**100**	**100.0**
Married couples	24.86	127	66.2
Married couples, no children	25.41	129	27.6
Married couples, with children	23.07	117	31.6
Oldest child under 6	4.70	24	1.2
Oldest child 6 to 17	17.80	91	13.2
Oldest child 18 or older	46.88	239	17.2
Single parent with child under 18	0.75	4	0.2
Single person	18.51	94	27.1
REGION			
Total households	**19.65**	**100**	**100.0**
Northeast	11.48	58	11.7
Midwest	16.59	84	20.2
South	27.35	139	48.6
West	18.15	92	19.6

Note: For definitions of best and biggest customers, see introduction or glossary.
Source: Calculations by New Strategist based on the 1997 Consumer Expenditure Survey

Contributions of Cash to Non-Household Members

(includes financial support for college students, alimony, and child support)

Best customers:
- Householders aged 45 to 54
- Households with incomes of $70,000 or more

Customer trends:
- With divorce rates still high and more children going to college, spending on this category isn't likely to decline any time soon.

Households with incomes of $70,000 or more spend two and one-half times as much as the average household on contributions of cash to non-household members. This category includes money for children attending college, alimony, and child support. Householders aged 45 to 54 spend twice as much as the average household on this item. Many are parents of college students, but others are paying child support.

Alimony payments are much less common than they once were since both spouses work in most families. Divorce is still common, however, and a growing proportion of children attend college. Spending in this category is likely to remain stable.

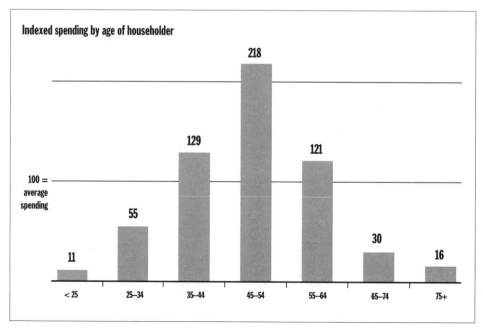

Indexed spending by age of householder

	11	55	129	218	121	30	16
	< 25	25–34	35–44	45–54	55–64	65–74	75+

100 = average spending

CONTRIBUTIONS OF CASH TO NON-HOUSEHOLD MEMBERS INCLUDING STUDENTS, ALIMONY, CHILD SUPPORT

Total household spending $26,814,192,480
Average household spends 253.98

	average spending	best customers (index)	biggest customers (market share)
AGE OF HOUSEHOLDER			
Total households	**$253.98**	**100**	**100.0%**
Under age 25	26.94	11	0.8
Aged 25 to 34	140.18	55	10.4
Aged 35 to 44	326.86	129	29.9
Aged 45 to 54	553.08	218	39.9
Aged 55 to 64	306.14	121	14.1
Aged 65 to 74	76.11	30	3.4
Aged 75 or older	40.85	16	1.5
HOUSEHOLD INCOME			
Total households reporting income	**265.70**	**100**	**100.0**
Under $20,000	63.01	24	8.3
$20,000 to $29,999	207.01	78	11.4
$30,000 to $39,999	249.45	94	11.5
$40,000 to $49,999	373.23	140	13.1
$50,000 to $69,999	356.75	134	18.8
$70,000 or more	655.82	247	36.9
HOUSEHOLD TYPE			
Total households	**253.98**	**100**	**100.0**
Married couples	244.65	96	50.4
Married couples, no children	256.70	101	21.6
Married couples, with children	252.09	99	26.7
Oldest child under 6	124.71	49	2.5
Oldest child 6 to 17	288.48	114	16.5
Oldest child 18 or older	269.58	106	7.6
Single parent with child under 18	193.82	76	4.8
Single person	264.16	104	29.9
REGION			
Total households	**253.98**	**100**	**100.0**
Northeast	234.10	92	18.4
Midwest	286.88	113	27.0
South	256.73	101	35.3
West	231.14	91	19.3

Note: For definitions of best and biggest customers, see introduction or glossary.
Source: Calculations by New Strategist based on the 1997 Consumer Expenditure Survey

Contributions to Charities

Best customers:	• Householders aged 75 or older
	• Households with incomes of $70,000 or more
	• Married couples without children at home
Customer trends:	• Stock market gains are creating a larger pool of potential donors, but charities need to do more to convince younger people to give.

Affluent households spend three times as much as the average household on charitable contributions, accounting for nearly half of all giving. While households with lower incomes often give a larger share of their income, they do not have the resources to match the amounts given by wealthy households. Householders aged 75 or older give 87 percent more to charity than the average household. Many are giving their assets away before death to avoid estate taxes. Married couples without children at home (many of whom are older) contribute twice as much as average.

With so much wealth being generated by the stock market, charitable contributions should increase. But middle-aged and younger adults are wary of organizations asking for handouts. Charities need to do more to convince skeptical younger generations to part with their money.

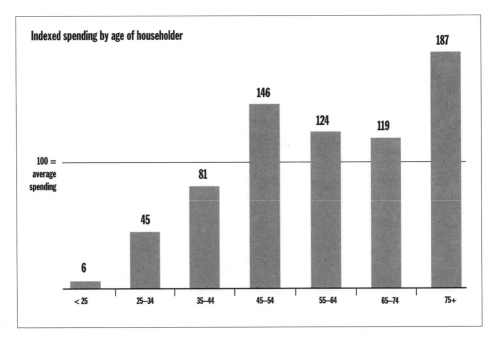

Indexed spending by age of householder

< 25	25–34	35–44	45–54	55–64	65–74	75+
6	45	81	146	124	119	187

100 = average spending

CONTRIBUTIONS TO CHARITIES

Total household spending $10,763,473,200
Average household spends   101.95

	average spending	best customers (index)	biggest customers (market share)
AGE OF HOUSEHOLDER			
Total households	**$101.95**	**100**	**100.0%**
Under age 25	5.96	6	0.4
Aged 25 to 34	45.97	45	8.5
Aged 35 to 44	82.80	81	18.9
Aged 45 to 54	148.43	146	26.7
Aged 55 to 64	126.73	124	14.5
Aged 65 to 74	121.11	119	13.6
Aged 75 or older	190.42	187	17.4
HOUSEHOLD INCOME			
Total households reporting income	**112.21**	**100**	**100.0**
Under $20,000	57.93	52	18.0
$20,000 to $29,999	37.33	33	4.9
$30,000 to $39,999	64.37	57	7.0
$40,000 to $49,999	106.80	95	8.9
$50,000 to $69,999	98.60	88	12.3
$70,000 or more	367.17	327	48.9
HOUSEHOLD TYPE			
Total households	**101.95**	**100**	**100.0**
Married couples	149.77	147	76.8
Married couples, no children	201.32	197	42.1
Married couples, with children	124.27	122	32.8
Oldest child under 6	131.21	129	6.6
Oldest child 6 to 17	132.33	130	18.9
Oldest child 18 or older	102.99	101	7.3
Single parent with child under 18	25.60	25	1.6
Single person	49.15	48	13.8
REGION			
Total households	**101.95**	**100**	**100.0**
Northeast	91.37	90	17.9
Midwest	129.56	127	30.4
South	87.66	86	30.0
West	104.32	102	21.7

Note: For definitions of best and biggest customers, see introduction or glossary.
Source: Calculations by New Strategist based on the 1997 Consumer Expenditure Survey

Contributions to Educational Organizations

Best customers:
- Householders aged 45 to 54
- Households with incomes of $70,000 or more
- Married couples with children under age 6
- Households in the West

Customer trends:
- Concern about the quality of education should boost contributions to educational organizations in the years ahead.

Households with incomes of $70,000 or more spend three times as much as the average household on contributions to educational organizations. Married couples with preschoolers contribute more than twice the average. Many are helping support nonprofit day care and nursery schools attended by their children. Householders aged 45 to 54, many of whom have children in college, contribute 80 percent more to educational organizations than the average household. Households in the West contribute 40 percent more than average.

Americans are deeply concerned about education. If they believe their donations will help improve the quality of education, they may increase their giving. Also, because a growing share of Americans are college graduates, the potential donor pool is expanding. This should boost contributions.

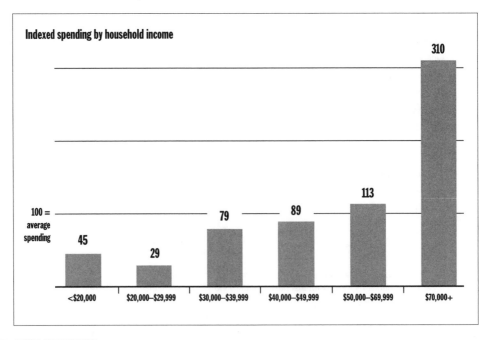

Indexed spending by household income

100 = average spending

<$20,000	$20,000–$29,999	$30,000–$39,999	$40,000–$49,999	$50,000–$69,999	$70,000+
45	29	79	89	113	310

CONTRIBUTIONS TO EDUCATIONAL ORGANIZATIONS

Total household spending $ 1,782,122,880
Average household spends   16.88

	average spending	best customers (index)	biggest customers (market share)
AGE OF HOUSEHOLDER			
Total households	**$16.88**	**100**	**100.0%**
Under age 25	0.39	2	0.2
Aged 25 to 34	13.39	79	15.0
Aged 35 to 44	14.67	87	20.2
Aged 45 to 54	30.35	180	32.9
Aged 55 to 64	11.00	65	7.6
Aged 65 to 74	16.18	96	11.0
Aged 75 or older	23.81	141	13.1
HOUSEHOLD INCOME			
Total households reporting income	**18.37**	**100**	**100.0**
Under $20,000	8.23	45	15.6
$20,000 to $29,999	5.25	29	4.2
$30,000 to $39,999	14.52	79	9.7
$40,000 to $49,999	16.39	89	8.3
$50,000 to $69,999	20.82	113	15.9
$70,000 or more	56.93	310	46.3
HOUSEHOLD TYPE			
Total households	**16.88**	**100**	**100.0**
Married couples	24.51	145	75.9
Married couples, no children	21.02	125	26.6
Married couples, with children	26.30	156	41.9
Oldest child under 6	40.95	243	12.5
Oldest child 6 to 17	28.06	166	24.2
Oldest child 18 or older	12.25	73	5.2
Single parent with child under 18	6.69	40	2.5
Single person	10.95	65	18.6
REGION			
Total households	**16.88**	**100**	**100.0**
Northeast	20.19	120	23.9
Midwest	17.97	106	25.4
South	10.11	60	20.9
West	23.69	140	29.8

Note: For definitions of best and biggest customers, see introduction or glossary.
Source: Calculations by New Strategist based on the 1997 Consumer Expenditure Survey

Contributions to Political Organizations

Best customers:	• **Householders aged 45 to 64**
	• **Households with incomes of $70,000 or more**
	• **Married couples without children**
Customer trends:	• **Contributions to political organizations may decline as cynical baby boomers enter the ages of greatest giving.**

Households with incomes of $70,000 or more contribute four times as much as the average household to political organizations, accounting for 59 percent of all political contributions. Householders aged 45 to 64 spend over 60 percent more than average. These households not only have more money than younger people, they are also more politically active. Households in the Northeast and the Midwest also contribute more than average to political organizations.

Younger generations have been disillusioned by politics. As baby boomers age into the prime years of political donation, contributions may decline.

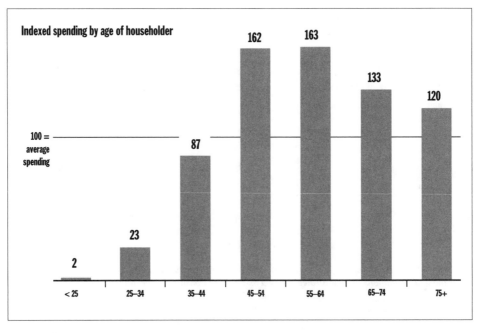

Indexed spending by age of householder

< 25	25–34	35–44	45–54	55–64	65–74	75+
2	23	87	162	163	133	120

100 = average spending

CONTRIBUTIONS TO POLITICAL ORGANIZATIONS

Total household spending $654,571,200
Average household spends   6.20

	average spending	best customers (index)	biggest customers (market share)
AGE OF HOUSEHOLDER			
Total households	**$6.20**	**100**	**100.0%**
Under age 25	0.15	2	0.2
Aged 25 to 34	1.44	23	4.4
Aged 35 to 44	5.39	87	20.2
Aged 45 to 54	10.04	162	29.7
Aged 55 to 64	10.12	163	19.0
Aged 65 to 74	8.27	133	15.3
Aged 75 or older	7.47	120	11.2
HOUSEHOLD INCOME			
Total households reporting income	**7.27**	**100**	**100.0**
Under $20,000	2.59	36	12.4
$20,000 to $29,999	2.40	33	4.8
$30,000 to $39,999	2.32	32	3.9
$40,000 to $49,999	5.91	81	7.6
$50,000 to $69,999	6.32	87	12.2
$70,000 or more	28.73	395	59.1
HOUSEHOLD TYPE			
Total households	**6.20**	**100**	**100.0**
Married couples	8.76	141	73.9
Married couples, no children	12.03	194	41.4
Married couples, with children	7.34	118	31.8
Oldest child under 6	3.30	53	2.7
Oldest child 6 to 17	8.06	130	18.9
Oldest child 18 or older	8.77	141	10.2
Single parent with child under 18	0.60	10	0.6
Single person	4.22	68	19.6
REGION			
Total households	**6.20**	**100**	**100.0**
Northeast	8.32	134	26.8
Midwest	8.66	140	33.4
South	4.45	72	25.0
West	4.30	69	14.7

Note: For definitions of best and biggest customers, see introduction or glossary.
Source: Calculations by New Strategist based on the 1997 Consumer Expenditure Survey

Contributions to Religious Organizations

Best customers:	• Married couples without children
	• Married couples with school-aged or adult children
	• Householders aged 45 to 64
	• Households in the South
Customer trends:	• Less formal attachment to religious organizations among younger generations may reduce contributions.

Married couples with adult children at home contribute 66 percent more than the average household to religious organizations. Those with school-aged children contribute 48 percent more than average. While younger generations of Americans are less likely than their elders to attend religious services, their children often get them in the door—which is the key to getting contributions. Households in the South contribute 20 percent more than average to religious organizations. Southerners are more likely than people in other regions to consider themselves very religious and to attend services, which is why the region is sometimes referred to as the "Bible belt."

Although many younger people go to church for the sake of their children, they are still less likely than their elders to be involved in formal religion. Unless this trend is reversed, religious organizations could see contributions decline.

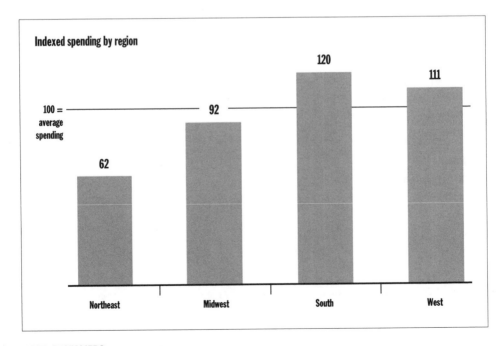

Indexed spending by region

100 = average spending

Northeast 62 · Midwest 92 · South 120 · West 111

CONTRIBUTIONS TO RELIGIOUS ORGANIZATIONS

Total household spending $41,201,034,000
Average household spends   390.25

	average spending	best customers (index)	biggest customers (market share)
AGE OF HOUSEHOLDER			
Total households	**$390.25**	**100**	**100.0%**
Under age 25	108.95	28	2.0
Aged 25 to 34	238.54	61	11.5
Aged 35 to 44	396.82	102	23.7
Aged 45 to 54	533.86	137	25.1
Aged 55 to 64	510.10	131	15.2
Aged 65 to 74	447.26	115	13.1
Aged 75 or older	392.93	101	9.4
HOUSEHOLD INCOME			
Total households reporting income	**426.74**	**100**	**100.0**
Under $20,000	171.44	40	14.0
$20,000 to $29,999	373.58	88	12.8
$30,000 to $39,999	358.01	84	10.3
$40,000 to $49,999	456.67	107	10.0
$50,000 to $69,999	585.44	137	19.3
$70,000 or more	962.02	225	33.7
HOUSEHOLD TYPE			
Total households	**390.25**	**100**	**100.0**
Married couples	582.44	149	78.0
Married couples, no children	567.42	145	31.0
Married couples, with children	580.89	149	40.0
Oldest child under 6	492.12	126	6.5
Oldest child 6 to 17	578.97	148	21.6
Oldest child 18 or older	648.28	166	11.9
Single parent with child under 18	165.55	42	2.7
Single person	180.25	46	13.3
REGION			
Total households	**390.25**	**100**	**100.0**
Northeast	243.85	62	12.5
Midwest	357.17	92	21.9
South	469.44	120	42.0
West	435.10	111	23.7

Note: For definitions of best and biggest customers, see introduction or glossary.
Source: Calculations by New Strategist based on the 1997 Consumer Expenditure Survey

Credit Card Memberships

Best customers:
- Householders aged 55 to 64
- Households with incomes of $70,000 or more
- Married couples without children at home
- Households in the Northeast

Customer trends:
- A decline in spending is likely as consumers shop around for the best deals.

A growing number of credit cards do not charge membership fees, especially if cardholders carry a balance. But some credit cards—particularly those offering other benefits such as discounts on products—still charge fees. Affluent households spend nearly two and one-half times as much as the average household on credit card membership fees. Householders aged 55 to 64 spend 72 percent more than average. Married couples without children at home, many of whom are older householders, spend 48 percent more. Householders in the Northeast spend 43 percent more than average on credit card memberships.

Many credit card issuers have dropped or reduced membership charges in favor of higher fees for late payments, cash advances, and other services. A continued decline in spending on credit card memberships is likely as savvy consumers shop around for the best deals.

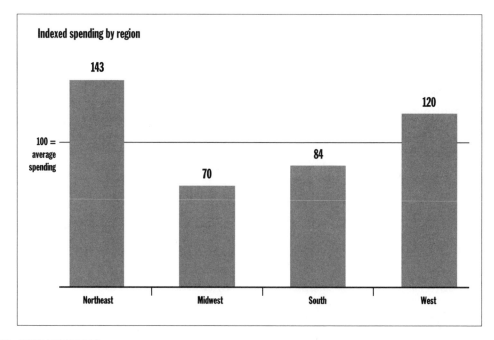

Indexed spending by region

Northeast	Midwest	South	West
143	70	84	120

100 = average spending

CREDIT CARD MEMBERSHIPS

	average spending	best customers (index)	biggest customers (market share)
Total household spending	$420,192,480		
Average household spends	3.98		

AGE OF HOUSEHOLDER

	average spending	best customers (index)	biggest customers (market share)
Total households	**$3.98**	**100**	**100.0%**
Under age 25	1.92	48	3.4
Aged 25 to 34	3.71	93	17.6
Aged 35 to 44	4.20	106	24.5
Aged 45 to 54	4.43	111	20.4
Aged 55 to 64	6.86	172	20.1
Aged 65 to 74	3.32	83	9.6
Aged 75 or older	1.87	47	4.4

HOUSEHOLD INCOME

Total households reporting income	**4.32**	**100**	**100.0**
Under $20,000	1.47	34	11.9
$20,000 to $29,999	4.43	103	15.0
$30,000 to $39,999	3.64	84	10.3
$40,000 to $49,999	4.63	107	10.0
$50,000 to $69,999	5.67	131	18.4
$70,000 or more	9.97	231	34.5

HOUSEHOLD TYPE

Total households	**3.98**	**100**	**100.0**
Married couples	4.94	124	64.9
Married couples, no children	5.88	148	31.5
Married couples, with children	4.27	107	28.8
Oldest child under 6	4.83	121	6.2
Oldest child 6 to 17	4.53	114	16.6
Oldest child 18 or older	3.36	84	6.1
Single parent with child under 18	1.76	44	2.8
Single person	2.66	67	19.2

REGION

Total households	**3.98**	**100**	**100.0**
Northeast	5.68	143	28.5
Midwest	2.79	70	16.8
South	3.34	84	29.3
West	4.77	120	25.5

Note: For definitions of best and biggest customers, see introduction or glossary.
Source: Calculations by New Strategist based on the 1997 Consumer Expenditure Survey

Finance Charges, Except Mortgage and Vehicle

Best customers:
- Married couples with children
- Householders aged 25 to 54
- Households in the West

Customer trends:
- Lower interest rates will reduce spending on finance charges.

The cost of childrearing is evident in spending on finance charges. Parents of young children spend the most on finance charges as they struggle to pay for growing families on relatively low incomes. Married couples with children under age 6 spend 62 percent more than the average household on finance charges. Parents of older children also spend more than average on this item. Householders aged 25 to 54 spend more on finance charges than the average household because most are raising children. Households in the West spend 24 percent more than average on finance charges.

Lower interest rates are reducing finance charges, and there is some evidence of Americans paying down their debts. In the years ahead, spending on finance charges is likely to decline.

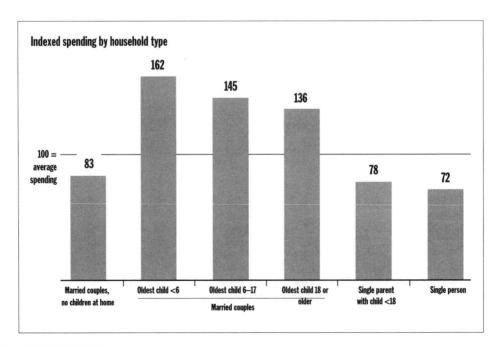

Indexed spending by household type

Married couples, no children at home	Oldest child <6	Oldest child 6–17	Oldest child 18 or older	Single parent with child <18	Single person
83	162	145	136	78	72

100 = average spending

Married couples

FINANCE CHARGES, EXCEPT MORTGAGE AND VEHICLE

Total household spending $26,330,654,400
Average household spends   249.40

	average spending	best customers (index)	biggest customers (market share)
AGE OF HOUSEHOLDER			
Total households	**$249.40**	**100**	**100.0%**
Under age 25	148.59	60	4.2
Aged 25 to 34	299.73	120	22.7
Aged 35 to 44	323.98	130	30.2
Aged 45 to 54	316.08	127	23.2
Aged 55 to 64	251.49	101	11.8
Aged 65 to 74	126.40	51	5.8
Aged 75 or older	55.65	22	2.1
HOUSEHOLD INCOME			
Total households reporting income	**272.33**	**100**	**100.0**
Under $20,000	140.37	52	18.0
$20,000 to $29,999	230.68	85	12.4
$30,000 to $39,999	288.43	106	13.0
$40,000 to $49,999	370.64	136	12.7
$50,000 to $69,999	413.98	152	21.3
$70,000 or more	412.82	152	22.7
HOUSEHOLD TYPE			
Total households	**249.40**	**100**	**100.0**
Married couples	303.07	122	63.5
Married couples, no children	207.55	83	17.8
Married couples, with children	363.90	146	39.2
Oldest child under 6	403.68	162	8.3
Oldest child 6 to 17	362.43	145	21.1
Oldest child 18 or older	338.43	136	9.8
Single parent with child under 18	193.33	78	4.9
Single person	178.74	72	20.6
REGION			
Total households	**249.40**	**100**	**100.0**
Northeast	207.06	83	16.6
Midwest	222.35	89	21.3
South	255.14	102	35.7
West	310.22	124	26.4

Note: For definitions of best and biggest customers, see introduction or glossary.
Source: Calculations by New Strategist based on the 1997 Consumer Expenditure Survey

Funeral Expenses

Best customers:
- Householders aged 55 to 74
- Households with incomes below $20,000
- People living alone
- Households in the South

Customer trends:
- Strong spending in the short term, but the funeral industry will face challenges as boomers and younger generations choose nontraditional send-offs.

Householders aged 55 to 64 spend nearly three times as much as the average household on funerals, while those aged 65 to 74 spend more than twice the average. These age groups are paying for the funerals of spouses and parents, and some are prepaying their own. People living alone spend 82 percent more than average on funeral expenses, while low-income households spend 56 percent more. In both cases, the higher spending is due to the fact that many older Americans live alone and many have low incomes. Households in the South spend 43 percent more than average on funerals and account for 50 percent of the market. Southerners prefer traditional funerals with all the trimmings.

The large and growing number of very old Americans means spending on funerals will increase during the next decade. But this may be the golden age for the funeral industry. It's likely that many baby boomers and younger people will eschew traditional funerals in favor of ceremonies of their own devising.

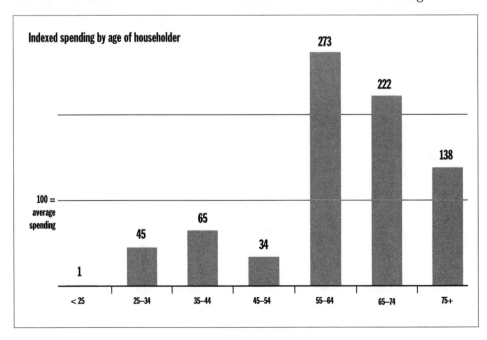

Indexed spending by age of householder

| | | | | | 273 | 222 | 138 |

100 = average spending

| 1 | 45 | 65 | 34 | | | | |

| < 25 | 25–34 | 35–44 | 45–54 | 55–64 | 65–74 | 75+ |

FUNERAL EXPENSES

Total household spending $6,656,566,800
Average household spends   63.05

	average spending	best customers (index)	biggest customers (market share)
AGE OF HOUSEHOLDER			
Total households	**$63.05**	**100**	**100.0%**
Under age 25	0.86	1	0.1
Aged 25 to 34	28.15	45	8.4
Aged 35 to 44	40.98	65	15.1
Aged 45 to 54	21.16	34	6.1
Aged 55 to 64	172.26	273	31.9
Aged 65 to 74	139.94	222	25.5
Aged 75 or older	87.21	138	12.9
HOUSEHOLD INCOME			
Total households reporting income	**69.79**	**100**	**100.0**
Under $20,000	109.18	156	54.5
$20,000 to $29,999	49.37	71	10.3
$30,000 to $39,999	68.55	98	12.0
$40,000 to $49,999	44.23	63	5.9
$50,000 to $69,999	60.26	86	12.1
$70,000 or more	23.91	34	5.1
HOUSEHOLD TYPE			
Total households	**63.05**	**100**	**100.0**
Married couples	34.42	55	28.5
Married couples, no children	36.98	59	12.5
Married couples, with children	30.49	48	13.0
Oldest child under 6	16.53	26	1.3
Oldest child 6 to 17	15.95	25	3.7
Oldest child 18 or older	69.88	111	8.0
Single parent with child under 18	15.55	25	1.5
Single person	114.73	182	52.3
REGION			
Total households	**63.05**	**100**	**100.0**
Northeast	44.40	70	14.1
Midwest	66.56	106	25.2
South	90.03	143	49.8
West	32.32	51	10.9

Note: For definitions of best and biggest customers, see introduction or glossary.
Source: Calculations by New Strategist based on the 1997 Consumer Expenditure Survey

Gifts of Cash, Stocks, Bonds to Non-Household Members

Best customers:
- Householders aged 65 or older
- Married couples without children
- Households in the West

Customer trends:
- Increased gift giving is likely as older generations seek to reduce inheritance taxes by giving some of their assets to their children.

Many older people prefer to dispose of their assets while they are still alive in order to reduce the tax bite for their heirs. Householders aged 75 or older are three and one-half times as likely as the average household to give cash, stocks, and bonds to people who are not household members—usually children or grandchildren. Those aged 65 to 74 give away more than two and one-half times the average. Married couples without children in the household (many of whom are older people) give 42 percent more than average, while households in the West give 51 percent more.

The World War II generation is the wealthiest group of older Americans in history. They are transferring some of this wealth to younger generations, a trend that will accelerate in the coming years.

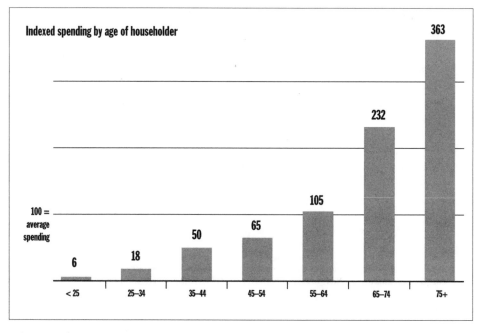

Indexed spending by age of householder

< 25	25–34	35–44	45–54	55–64	65–74	75+
6	18	50	65	105	232	363

100 = average spending

GIFTS OF CASH, STOCKS, BONDS TO NON-HOUSEHOLD MEMBERS

Total household spending $23,757,767,280
Average household spends   225.03

	average spending	best customers (index)	biggest customers (market share)
AGE OF HOUSEHOLDER			
Total households	**$225.03**	**100**	**100.0%**
Under age 25	14.21	6	0.4
Aged 25 to 34	40.94	18	3.4
Aged 35 to 44	112.03	50	11.6
Aged 45 to 54	146.39	65	11.9
Aged 55 to 64	236.53	105	12.3
Aged 65 to 74	521.93	232	26.6
Aged 75 or older	816.02	363	33.8
HOUSEHOLD INCOME			
Total households reporting income	**246.98**	**100**	**100.0**
Under $20,000	165.07	67	23.3
$20,000 to $29,999	367.33	149	21.7
$30,000 to $39,999	148.50	60	7.4
$40,000 to $49,999	213.50	86	8.1
$50,000 to $69,999	113.21	46	6.4
$70,000 or more	547.35	222	33.1
HOUSEHOLD TYPE			
Total households	**225.03**	**100**	**100.0**
Married couples	197.06	88	45.8
Married couples, no children	320.03	142	30.4
Married couples, with children	113.63	50	13.6
Oldest child under 6	261.14	116	6.0
Oldest child 6 to 17	63.91	28	4.1
Oldest child 18 or older	108.68	48	3.5
Single parent with child under 18	21.84	10	0.6
Single person	297.36	132	38.0
REGION			
Total households	**225.03**	**100**	**100.0**
Northeast	161.86	72	14.4
Midwest	182.53	81	19.4
South	220.63	98	34.2
West	339.47	151	32.0

Note: For definitions of best and biggest customers, see introduction or glossary.
Source: Calculations by New Strategist based on the 1997 Consumer Expenditure Survey

Insurance, Life and Other Personal Except Health

Best customers:
- Householders aged 45 to 54
- Households with incomes of $70,000 or more
- Married couples with school-aged or older children

Customer trends:
- A spending decline is likely as people invest in higher-return alternatives.

The need for life and other forms of personal insurance, such as disability insurance, is greater for those with children and assets to protect. Households with incomes of $70,000 or more spend nearly two and one-half times as much as the average household on life and other personal insurance, not including health insurance. Married couples with school-aged or older children spend over 50 percent more than the average household on this item. Householders aged 45 to 54, most of whom have children, spend 60 percent more than average.

Spending on life and other personal insurance has suffered from the relatively low returns these financial products offer, and this trend is likely to continue. Boomers and younger generations are more likely to turn to stocks and mutual funds as a form of insurance, reasoning that they can better protect their families by building as much wealth as possible.

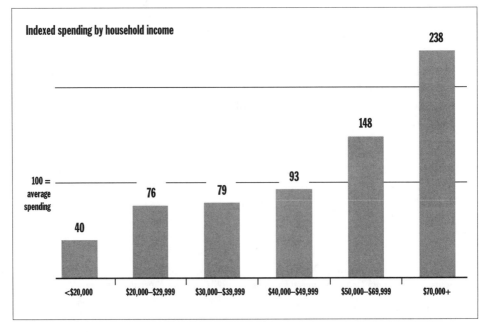

Indexed spending by household income

100 = average spending

<$20,000	$20,000–$29,999	$30,000–$39,999	$40,000–$49,999	$50,000–$69,999	$70,000+
40	76	79	93	148	238

INSURANCE, LIFE AND OTHER PERSONAL EXCEPT HEALTH

Total household spending	$39,974,240,880	
Average household spends	378.63	

	average spending	best customers (index)	biggest customers (market share)
AGE OF HOUSEHOLDER			
Total households	**$378.63**	**100**	**100.0%**
Under age 25	47.37	13	0.9
Aged 25 to 34	239.19	63	11.9
Aged 35 to 44	383.21	101	23.5
Aged 45 to 54	604.14	160	29.2
Aged 55 to 64	522.55	138	16.1
Aged 65 to 74	406.19	107	12.3
Aged 75 or older	244.48	65	6.0
HOUSEHOLD INCOME			
Total households reporting income	**386.53**	**100**	**100.0**
Under $20,000	155.97	40	14.1
$20,000 to $29,999	295.49	76	11.2
$30,000 to $39,999	306.45	79	9.7
$40,000 to $49,999	359.74	93	8.7
$50,000 to $69,999	571.47	148	20.8
$70,000 or more	921.31	238	35.6
HOUSEHOLD TYPE			
Total households	**378.63**	**100**	**100.0**
Married couples	544.35	144	75.2
Married couples, no children	519.23	137	29.3
Married couples, with children	568.09	150	40.3
Oldest child under 6	458.38	121	6.2
Oldest child 6 to 17	591.68	156	22.7
Oldest child 18 or older	598.82	158	11.4
Single parent with child under 18	176.11	47	2.9
Single person	169.76	45	12.9
REGION			
Total households	**378.63**	**100**	**100.0**
Northeast	385.70	102	20.3
Midwest	360.79	95	22.8
South	421.48	111	38.8
West	321.69	85	18.0

Note: For definitions of best and biggest customers, see introduction or glossary.
Source: Calculations by New Strategist based on the 1997 Consumer Expenditure Survey

Legal Fees

Best customers:
- Householders aged 35 to 54
- Single parents
- Households in the Northeast

Customer trends:
- As mediation becomes more common for resolving divorce and custody disputes, spending on legal fees could fall.

Single parents spend 57 percent more than the average household on legal fees. Divorce and custodial disputes are behind this higher spending. Householders aged 35 to 44 spend 39 percent more than average on legal fees, and those aged 45 to 54 spend 30 percent more. Spending is higher in these age groups because they are more prone to divorce and have complicated property and custody issues to resolve. Households in the Northeast spend 28 percent more than average on legal fees.

Increasingly, mediation is being used as an alternative to the courts to resolve divorce and custody disputes. This is likely to reduce spending on legal fees.

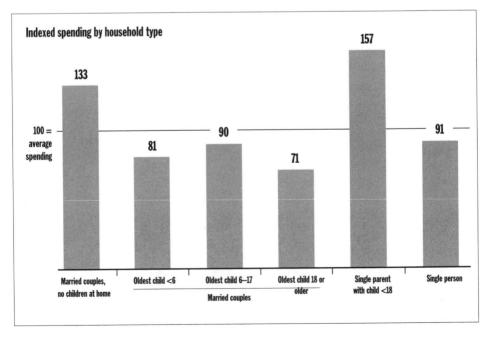

Indexed spending by household type

Married couples, no children at home	Oldest child <6	Oldest child 6–17	Oldest child 18 or older	Single parent with child <18	Single person
133	81	90	71	157	91

100 = average spending

Married couples

LEGAL FEES

Total household spending	$14,336,165,040		
Average household spends	135.79		

	average spending	best customers (index)	biggest customers (market share)
AGE OF HOUSEHOLDER			
Total households	**$135.79**	**100**	**100.0%**
Under age 25	19.29	14	1.0
Aged 25 to 34	97.78	72	13.6
Aged 35 to 44	188.48	139	32.3
Aged 45 to 54	176.31	130	23.8
Aged 55 to 64	191.07	141	16.4
Aged 65 to 74	128.12	94	10.8
Aged 75 or older	30.45	22	2.1
HOUSEHOLD INCOME			
Total households reporting income	**124.33**	**100**	**100.0**
Under $20,000	81.51	66	22.8
$20,000 to $29,999	123.94	100	14.6
$30,000 to $39,999	112.93	91	11.1
$40,000 to $49,999	226.99	183	17.1
$50,000 to $69,999	115.47	93	13.0
$70,000 or more	177.89	143	21.4
HOUSEHOLD TYPE			
Total households	**135.79**	**100**	**100.0**
Married couples	137.18	101	52.8
Married couples, no children	180.91	133	28.4
Married couples, with children	112.72	83	22.3
Oldest child under 6	109.72	81	4.2
Oldest child 6 to 17	121.92	90	13.1
Oldest child 18 or older	96.26	71	5.1
Single parent with child under 18	212.71	157	9.8
Single person	123.00	91	26.0
REGION			
Total households	**135.79**	**100**	**100.0**
Northeast	174.15	128	25.6
Midwest	152.73	112	26.9
South	113.26	83	29.1
West	117.65	87	18.4

Note: For definitions of best and biggest customers, see introduction or glossary.
Source: Calculations by New Strategist based on the 1997 Consumer Expenditure Survey

Occupational Expenses, Union and Professional Dues

Best customers:
- Householders aged 45 to 54
- Households with incomes of $70,000 or more
- Married couples with adult children

Customer trends:
- Spending should remain stable as an increase in those paying professional fees offsets a decline in union membership.

Households with incomes of $70,000 or more spend two and one-half times as much as the average household on union and professional fees. Membership in a profession or union is one reason why these households have such high incomes. Married couples with adult children at home spend much more than average on this item because they often include three workers. Householders aged 45 to 54, who are at the peak of their careers, spend 96 percent more than the average household on union dues and professional dues.

Union membership is down, but college graduation rates are up, which means more people are joining the professions. Professional fees should offset some of the decline in union dues, keeping spending in this category stable.

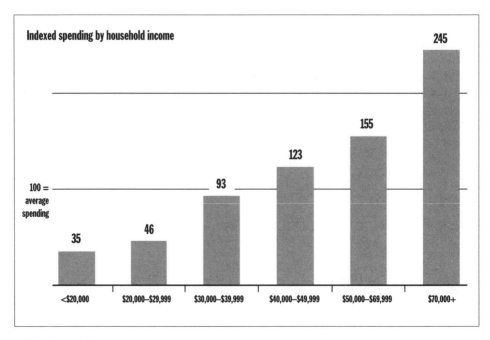

Indexed spending by household income

100 = average spending

<$20,000	$20,000–$29,999	$30,000–$39,999	$40,000–$49,999	$50,000–$69,999	$70,000+
35	46	93	123	155	245

OCCUPATIONAL EXPENSES, UNION AND PROFESSIONAL DUES

Total household spending $10,837,376,400
Average household spends   102.65

	average spending	best customers (index)	biggest customers (market share)
AGE OF HOUSEHOLDER			
Total households	**$102.65**	**100**	**100.0%**
Under age 25	38.61	38	2.7
Aged 25 to 34	101.85	99	18.7
Aged 35 to 44	131.14	128	29.7
Aged 45 to 54	201.02	196	35.9
Aged 55 to 64	88.10	86	10.0
Aged 65 to 74	21.54	21	2.4
Aged 75 or older	6.50	6	0.6
HOUSEHOLD INCOME			
Total households reporting income	**115.16**	**100**	**100.0**
Under $20,000	40.28	35	12.2
$20,000 to $29,999	52.80	46	6.7
$30,000 to $39,999	106.54	93	11.3
$40,000 to $49,999	141.08	123	11.5
$50,000 to $69,999	177.96	155	21.7
$70,000 or more	282.42	245	36.7
HOUSEHOLD TYPE			
Total households	**102.65**	**100**	**100.0**
Married couples	123.83	121	63.1
Married couples, no children	89.02	87	18.5
Married couples, with children	159.18	155	41.7
Oldest child under 6	121.78	119	6.1
Oldest child 6 to 17	127.77	124	18.1
Oldest child 18 or older	249.50	243	17.5
Single parent with child under 18	172.54	168	10.5
Single person	63.91	62	17.9
REGION			
Total households	**102.65**	**100**	**100.0**
Northeast	99.87	97	19.4
Midwest	122.32	119	28.5
South	74.84	73	25.4
West	128.80	125	26.7

Note: For definitions of best and biggest customers, see introduction or glossary.
Source: Calculations by New Strategist based on the 1997 Consumer Expenditure Survey

Pensions, Deductions for Private

Best customers:
- Householders aged 35 to 54
- Households with incomes of $70,000 or more
- Married couples with preschoolers

Customer trends:
- Strong growth as fears of inadequate retirement income spurs Americans to put more money into pensions.

With many company pensions now requiring contributions from employees, it is no surprise that the households contributing the most are those with the highest incomes. Households with incomes of $70,000 or more spend more than three times the average on deductions for private pensions (such as 401(k) plans). Householders aged 45 to 54 spend 65 percent more than average, while those aged 35 to 44 spend 46 percent more. Married couples with children under age 6, who have yet to face the mounting expenses of school-aged children, are getting a head start on their retirement. They spend twice the average on contributions to private pensions.

Many middle-aged and young adults do not believe Social Security will provide them with any retirement benefits. Spending on contributions to private pensions will rise as these workers save for the future.

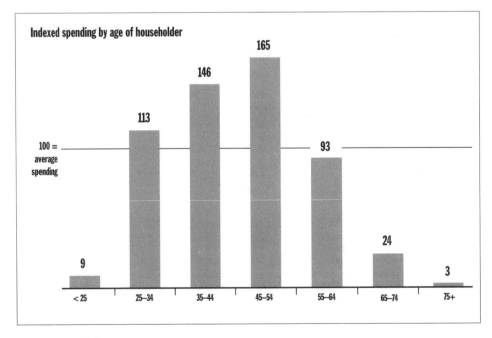

Indexed spending by age of householder

100 = average spending

<25	25–34	35–44	45–54	55–64	65–74	75+
9	113	146	165	93	24	3

PENSIONS, DEDUCTIONS FOR PRIVATE

| Total household spending | $35,813,490,720 |
| Average household spends | 339.22 |

	average spending	best customers (index)	biggest customers (market share)
AGE OF HOUSEHOLDER			
Total households	**$339.22**	**100**	**100.0%**
Under age 25	29.17	9	0.6
Aged 25 to 34	382.84	113	21.3
Aged 35 to 44	496.46	146	34.0
Aged 45 to 54	558.87	165	30.2
Aged 55 to 64	316.65	93	10.9
Aged 65 to 74	80.48	24	2.7
Aged 75 or older	9.24	3	0.3
HOUSEHOLD INCOME			
Total households reporting income	**416.13**	**100**	**100.0**
Under $20,000	12.18	3	1.0
$20,000 to $29,999	100.56	24	3.5
$30,000 to $39,999	239.57	58	7.0
$40,000 to $49,999	393.66	95	8.8
$50,000 to $69,999	720.22	173	24.3
$70,000 or more	1,538.59	370	55.3
HOUSEHOLD TYPE			
Total households	**339.22**	**100**	**100.0**
Married couples	483.70	143	74.6
Married couples, no children	429.96	127	27.0
Married couples, with children	547.65	161	43.4
Oldest child under 6	727.55	214	11.0
Oldest child 6 to 17	507.94	150	21.8
Oldest child 18 or older	499.30	147	10.6
Single parent with child under 18	163.31	48	3.0
Single person	178.99	53	15.2
REGION			
Total households	**339.22**	**100**	**100.0**
Northeast	243.16	72	14.3
Midwest	332.59	98	23.4
South	308.16	91	31.7
West	488.01	144	30.6

Note: For definitions of best and biggest customers, see introduction or glossary.
Source: Calculations by New Strategist based on the 1997 Consumer Expenditure Survey

Retirement Accounts, Nonpayroll Deposit

Best customers:
- Householders aged 45 to 64
- Households with incomes of $70,000 or more
- Married couples with school-aged children
- Households in the Northeast

Customer trends:
- Spending on retirement accounts will increase as boomers build their nest eggs.

The most affluent households spend the most on retirement accounts such as IRAs. These households spend well over three and one-half times as much as the average household on retirement contributions, accounting for 55 percent of all spending in this category. Householders nearing retirement age (55 to 64) spend 64 percent more, but those ten years younger spend just as much. Married couples with school-aged children usually have two earners in the household, which explains why they spend 52 percent more than average on retirement accounts. Households in the Northeast spend 40 percent more than average.

Boomers have been faulted for not putting enough away for retirement, but in reality they are just reaching the age at which most people begin saving in earnest. Spending on retirement accounts will increase substantially as boomers build their nest eggs.

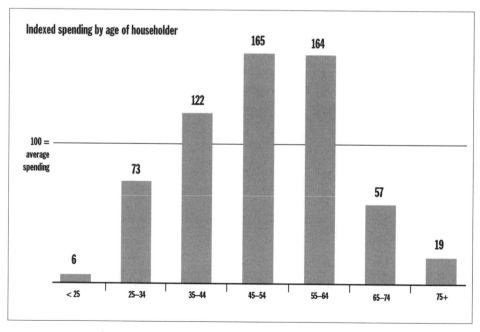

Indexed spending by age of householder

< 25	25–34	35–44	45–54	55–64	65–74	75+
6	73	122	165	164	57	19

100 = average spending

RETIREMENT ACCOUNTS, NONPAYROLL DEPOSITS

Total household spending	$39,765,200,400
Average household spends	376.65

	average spending	best customers (index)	biggest customers (market share)
AGE OF HOUSEHOLDER			
Total households	**$376.65**	**100**	**100.0%**
Under age 25	20.80	6	0.4
Aged 25 to 34	274.66	73	13.8
Aged 35 to 44	457.99	122	28.3
Aged 45 to 54	619.96	165	30.2
Aged 55 to 64	617.06	164	19.1
Aged 65 to 74	214.26	57	6.5
Aged 75 or older	71.60	19	1.8
HOUSEHOLD INCOME			
Total households reporting income	**416.13**	**100**	**100.0**
Under $20,000	12.18	3	1.0
$20,000 to $29,999	100.56	24	3.5
$30,000 to $39,999	239.57	58	7.0
$40,000 to $49,999	393.66	95	8.8
$50,000 to $69,999	720.22	173	24.3
$70,000 or more	1,538.59	370	55.3
HOUSEHOLD TYPE			
Total households	**376.65**	**100**	**100.0**
Married couples	542.22	144	75.3
Married couples, no children	554.24	147	31.4
Married couples, with children	540.63	144	38.6
Oldest child under 6	500.50	133	6.8
Oldest child 6 to 17	571.77	152	22.1
Oldest child 18 or older	506.34	134	9.7
Single parent with child under 18	127.91	34	2.1
Single person	216.12	57	16.5
REGION			
Total households	**376.65**	**100**	**100.0**
Northeast	527.30	140	28.0
Midwest	362.25	96	23.0
South	264.38	70	24.5
West	435.58	116	24.6

Note: For definitions of best and biggest customers, see introduction or glossary.
Source: Calculations by New Strategist based on the 1997 Consumer Expenditure Survey

Safe Deposit Box Rental

Best customers:	• Householders aged 65 or older
	• Married couples without children
	• Married couples with adult children
Customer trends:	• Spending will decline as paper documents give way to electronic records and fewer people feel the need to rent safe deposit boxes.

Older Americans are the best customers of safe deposit box rentals because they grew up in an era when only a single paper copy of many important documents existed. Householders aged 65 or older spend 77 to 78 percent more than the average household on safe deposit boxes, accounting for 37 percent of the market.

Many people still use safe deposit boxes to protect jewelry and ensure the safety of important papers in case of theft or disaster at home. But electronic record-keeping is reducing the need for safe deposit boxes, which should reduce spending on this item in the future.

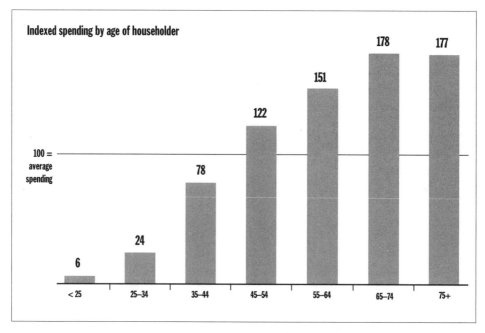

Indexed spending by age of householder

100 = average spending

< 25	25–34	35–44	45–54	55–64	65–74	75+
6	24	78	122	151	178	177

SAFE DEPOSIT BOX RENTAL

	average spending	best customers (index)	biggest customers (market share)
Total household spending	$706,303,440		
Average household spends	6.69		

AGE OF HOUSEHOLDER

	average spending	best customers (index)	biggest customers (market share)
Total households	**$6.69**	**100**	**100.0%**
Under age 25	0.42	6	0.4
Aged 25 to 34	1.63	24	4.6
Aged 35 to 44	5.24	78	18.2
Aged 45 to 54	8.13	122	22.3
Aged 55 to 64	10.13	151	17.7
Aged 65 to 74	11.88	178	20.4
Aged 75 or older	11.85	177	16.5

HOUSEHOLD INCOME

Total households reporting income	**6.65**	**100**	**100.0**
Under $20,000	4.59	69	24.0
$20,000 to $29,999	4.51	68	9.9
$30,000 to $39,999	5.26	79	9.7
$40,000 to $49,999	6.48	97	9.1
$50,000 to $69,999	7.68	115	16.2
$70,000 or more	13.82	208	31.1

HOUSEHOLD TYPE

Total households	**6.69**	**100**	**100.0**
Married couples	8.46	126	66.1
Married couples, no children	11.06	165	35.3
Married couples, with children	6.90	103	27.7
Oldest child under 6	2.81	42	2.2
Oldest child 6 to 17	6.85	102	14.9
Oldest child 18 or older	9.94	149	10.7
Single parent with child under 18	2.04	30	1.9
Single person	5.89	88	25.3

REGION

Total households	**6.69**	**100**	**100.0**
Northeast	6.47	97	19.3
Midwest	6.95	104	24.8
South	7.02	105	36.6
West	6.08	91	19.3

Note: For definitions of best and biggest customers, see introduction or glossary.
Source: Calculations by New Strategist based on the 1997 Consumer Expenditure Survey

Chapter 7.

Food at Home

Food at Home

The average household spends a lot of money on food, but less than it did a decade ago. Between 1987 and 1997, spending on food-at-home fell 3 percent, to $2,880, after adjusting for inflation. Behind the decline is a shift in eating habits, with the average household spending less on meats and more on poultry, less on eggs and dairy products and more on cereals. Nevertheless, the average household still spends more on beef than any other food—over $200 in 1997. Fresh fruit ranks second, followed by poultry, fresh vegetables, and carbonated drinks.

The best customers of most foods are the largest households—married couples with children at home. Convenience has become the key to selling to these busy families as supermarkets compete with restaurants for carry-out and even sit-down meals. But grocery store managers cannot market solely to the largest households and ignore everyone else. Older Americans have distinct tastes, such as their preference for coffee over carbonated drinks. The baby-boom generation is certain to demand healthier foods as it ages. These demographic trends will keep the food -at-home market in flux for years to come.

Food-at-Home Spending

(average annual spending of households on food at home, and percent distribution of spending by type, 1997)

Total spending on food-at-home	**$2,880.00**	**100.0%**
Beef	223.55	7.8
Fruit, fresh	150.47	5.2
Poultry	145.01	5.0
Vegetables, fresh	142.75	5.0
Carbonated drinks	133.45	4.6
Milk, fresh	118.78	4.1
Cheese	94.33	3.3
Cereal, ready-to-eat and cooked	91.15	3.2
Fish and seafood	88.54	3.1
Bread	83.43	2.9
Candy and chewing gum	69.26	2.4
Potato chips and other snacks	66.83	2.3
Lunch meats (cold cuts)	65.55	2.3
Ice cream and related products	52.91	1.8
Coffee	48.80	1.7
Fruit juice, canned and bottled	47.43	1.6
Cookies	45.01	1.6

Biscuits and rolls	$40.96	1.4%
Sauces and gravies	39.86	1.4
Pork chops	39.23	1.4
Ham	37.28	1.3
Vegetables, canned	35.85	1.2
Cakes and cupcakes	34.51	1.2
Soup, canned and packaged	32.87	1.1
Eggs	32.59	1.1
Pork, except bacon, frankfurters, ham, pork chops, sausage	31.07	1.1
Pasta, cornmeal, and other cereal products	28.03	1.0
Baby food	27.86	1.0
Vegetables, frozen	26.57	0.9
Bacon	25.42	0.9
Salad dressings	24.68	0.9
Fats and oils	24.50	0.9
Sausage	24.12	0.8
Bakery products, frozen and refrigerated	23.35	0.8
Crackers	23.26	0.8
Sweet rolls, coffee cakes, and doughnuts	23.13	0.8
Frankfurters	22.83	0.8
Jams, preserves, and other sweets	22.63	0.8
Frozen meals	20.73	0.7
Fruit juice, fresh	19.82	0.7
Fruit-flavored drinks, noncarbonated	19.22	0.7
Salt, spices, and other seasonings	19.07	0.7
Sugar	18.93	0.7
Rice	18.37	0.6
Nuts	17.70	0.6
Baking needs and miscellaneous products	16.65	0.6
Salads, prepared	15.05	0.5
Flour, prepared mixes	15.04	0.5
Tea	14.76	0.5
Butter	14.63	0.5
Fruit, canned	13.97	0.5
Pies, tarts, and turnovers	13.50	0.5
Fruit juice, frozen	13.01	0.5
Margarine	11.74	0.4
Peanut butter	11.63	0.4
Olives, pickles, and relishes	10.54	0.4
Desserts, prepared	9.95	0.3
Flour	8.79	0.3
Nondairy cream and imitation milk	8.50	0.3
Vegetable juices	7.50	0.3
Artificial sweeteners	3.48	0.1

Note: Numbers will not add to total because not all categories are shown, including food on out-of-town trips, which is in the Travel chapter.

Artificial Sweeteners

Best customers:
- Householders aged 55 or older
- Married couples with adult children
- Married couples without children
- Households in the South

Customer trends:
- A spending decline is likely as young soda drinkers replace older coffee and tea drinkers.

Older people are more likely to count calories than young adults. Consequently, householders aged 65 to 74 are the best customers of artificial sweeteners, spending 46 percent more than the average household on them. Married couples with adult children at home spend more than twice as much as the average household, while households in the South spend 58 percent more than average.

Younger generations are more likely than their elders to prefer presweetened drinks, such as carbonated beverages, to coffee or tea. As older generations are replaced by younger ones, spending on artificial sweeteners is likely to decline.

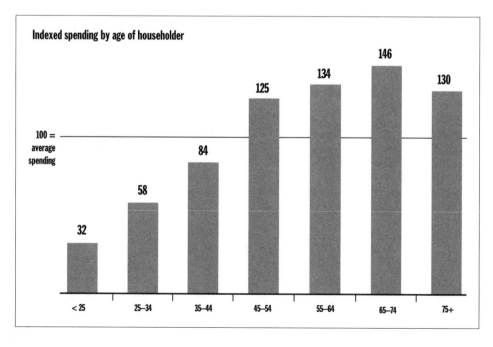

Indexed spending by age of householder

100 = average spending

< 25	25–34	35–44	45–54	55–64	65–74	75+
32	58	84	125	134	146	130

ARTIFICIAL SWEETENERS

Total household spending $367,404,480
Average household spends 3.48

	average spending	best customers (index)	biggest customers (market share)
AGE OF HOUSEHOLDER			
Total households	**$3.48**	**100**	**100.0%**
Under age 25	1.13	32	2.3
Aged 25 to 34	2.02	58	11.0
Aged 35 to 44	2.94	84	19.7
Aged 45 to 54	4.36	125	23.0
Aged 55 to 64	4.65	134	15.6
Aged 65 to 74	5.07	146	16.7
Aged 75 or older	4.51	130	12.1
HOUSEHOLD INCOME			
Total households reporting income	**3.45**	**100**	**100.0**
Under $20,000	3.28	95	33.1
$20,000 to $29,999	4.12	119	17.4
$30,000 to $39,999	2.07	60	7.3
$40,000 to $49,999	2.67	77	7.2
$50,000 to $69,999	3.52	102	14.3
$70,000 or more	4.75	138	20.6
HOUSEHOLD TYPE			
Total households	**3.48**	**100**	**100.0**
Married couples	4.64	133	69.7
Married couples, no children	5.09	146	31.2
Married couples, with children	3.96	114	30.6
Oldest child under 6	0.84	24	1.2
Oldest child 6 to 17	3.29	95	13.8
Oldest child 18 or older	7.91	227	16.3
Single parent with child under 18	2.24	64	4.0
Single person	1.62	47	13.4
REGION			
Total households	**3.48**	**100**	**100.0**
Northeast	3.96	114	22.7
Midwest	1.74	50	11.9
South	5.50	158	55.1
West	1.73	50	10.6

Note: For definitions of best and biggest customers, see introduction or glossary.
Source: Calculations by New Strategist based on the 1997 Consumer Expenditure Survey

Baby Food

Best customers:
- Householders aged 25 to 34
- Married couples with children under age 6

Customer trends:
- Spending is likely to decline as the smaller Generation X fills the young-parent age group.

Not surprisingly, the best customers of baby food are married couples with children under age 6. These households spend nearly nine times as much as the average household on baby food and account for 45 percent of the market. Households headed by people aged 25 to 34 (the age group most likely to have infants) spend two and one-half times the average and account for 49 percent of the market.

As the relatively small Generation X fills the 25-to-34 age group, when people typically become parents, spending on baby food could decline. But the larger Millennial generation will enter the age group in a few years, boosting spending once again.

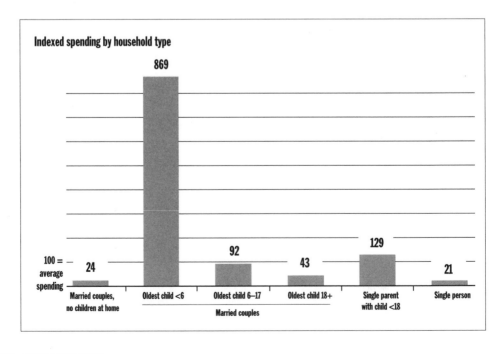

Indexed spending by household type

Married couples, no children at home	Oldest child <6	Oldest child 6–17	Oldest child 18+	Single parent with child <18	Single person
24	869	92	43	129	21

100 = average spending

Married couples

BABY FOOD

Total household spending	$2,941,347,360		
Average household spends	27.86		

	average spending	best customers (index)	biggest customers (market share)
AGE OF HOUSEHOLDER			
Total households	**$27.86**	**100**	**100.0%**
Under age 25	30.51	110	7.8
Aged 25 to 34	71.82	258	48.6
Aged 35 to 44	33.21	119	27.7
Aged 45 to 54	11.85	43	7.8
Aged 55 to 64	10.30	37	4.3
Aged 65 to 74	8.03	29	3.3
Aged 75 or older	3.08	11	1.0
HOUSEHOLD INCOME			
Total households reporting income	**28.65**	**100**	**100.0**
Under $20,000	15.47	54	18.8
$20,000 to $29,999	25.89	90	13.2
$30,000 to $39,999	44.42	155	19.0
$40,000 to $49,999	20.24	71	6.6
$50,000 to $69,999	39.20	137	19.2
$70,000 or more	42.82	149	22.3
HOUSEHOLD TYPE			
Total households	**27.86**	**100**	**100.0**
Married couples	40.55	146	76.1
Married couples, no children	6.55	24	5.0
Married couples, with children	69.04	248	66.6
Oldest child under 6	242.24	869	44.7
Oldest child 6 to 17	25.55	92	13.3
Oldest child 18 or older	11.95	43	3.1
Single parent with child under 18	35.92	129	8.1
Single person	5.77	21	5.9
REGION			
Total households	**27.86**	**100**	**100.0**
Northeast	25.65	92	18.4
Midwest	22.44	81	19.2
South	27.78	100	34.8
West	35.93	129	27.4

Note: For definitions of best and biggest customers, see introduction or glossary.
Source: Calculations by New Strategist based on the 1997 Consumer Expenditure Survey

Bacon

Best customers:
- Householders aged 55 to 64
- Married couples with adult children
- Households in the South

Customer trends:
- Spending could decline because younger generations are less likely to buy bacon or know how to cook it.

Householders aged 55 to 64 spend 27 percent more than the average household on bacon. Married couples with adult children at home spend 54 percent more than average on this item. Households in the South, where consumption of beef and pork is well above average, spend 14 percent more than the average household on bacon.

Spending on bacon may fall as younger generations, who have little time to cook bacon (and may not even know how), replace older bacon eaters.

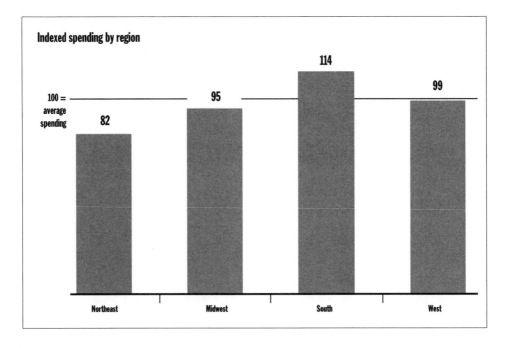

Indexed spending by region

100 = average spending

Northeast	Midwest	South	West
82	95	114	99

BACON

Total household spending	$2,683,741,920
Average household spends	25.42

	average spending	best customers (index)	biggest customers (market share)
AGE OF HOUSEHOLDER			
Total households	**$25.42**	**100**	**100.0%**
Under age 25	17.04	67	4.8
Aged 25 to 34	21.19	83	15.7
Aged 35 to 44	27.36	108	25.0
Aged 45 to 54	29.49	116	21.3
Aged 55 to 64	32.31	127	14.8
Aged 65 to 74	23.50	92	10.6
Aged 75 or older	21.70	85	7.9
HOUSEHOLD INCOME			
Total households reporting income	**26.23**	**100**	**100.0**
Under $20,000	24.25	92	32.2
$20,000 to $29,999	27.26	104	15.2
$30,000 to $39,999	27.59	105	12.9
$40,000 to $49,999	20.91	80	7.5
$50,000 to $69,999	24.87	95	13.3
$70,000 or more	32.74	125	18.7
HOUSEHOLD TYPE			
Total households	**25.42**	**100**	**100.0**
Married couples	32.67	129	67.2
Married couples, no children	25.80	101	21.7
Married couples, with children	34.89	137	36.9
Oldest child under 6	36.23	143	7.3
Oldest child 6 to 17	32.24	127	18.5
Oldest child 18 or older	39.11	154	11.1
Single parent with child under 18	23.15	91	5.7
Single person	9.84	39	11.1
REGION			
Total households	**25.42**	**100**	**100.0**
Northeast	20.87	82	16.4
Midwest	24.22	95	22.8
South	29.00	114	39.8
West	25.23	99	21.1

Note: For definitions of best and biggest customers, see introduction or glossary.
Source: Calculations by New Strategist based on the 1997 Consumer Expenditure Survey

Bakery Products, Frozen and Refrigerated

Best customers:	• Married couples with school-aged children
Customer trends:	• Spending should increase along with the number of dual-income couples with school-aged children.

Today's busy parents don't have much time to bake from scratch, so they often buy frozen or refrigerated bakery products—such as refrigerated cookies that require no more than slicing and heating. Not surprisingly, married couples with school-aged children are the best customers of frozen and refrigerated bakery products, spending 81 percent more than the average household on this item.

Spending on frozen and refrigerated bakery products is likely to rise along with the number of busy dual-income couples with school-aged children.

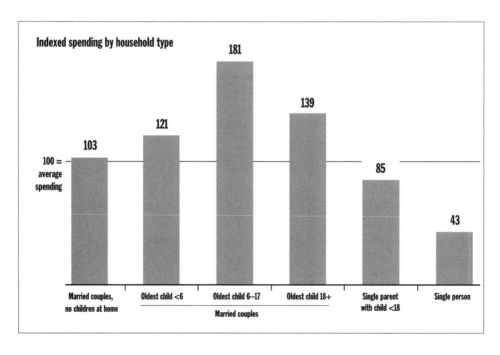

Indexed spending by household type

Married couples, no children at home	Oldest child <6	Oldest child 6–17	Oldest child 18+	Single parent with child <18	Single person
103	121	181	139	85	43

Married couples

100 = average spending

BAKERY PRODUCTS, FROZEN AND REFRIGERATED

Total household spending $2,465,199,600
Average household spends   23.35

	average spending	best customers (index)	biggest customers (market share)
AGE OF HOUSEHOLDER			
Total households	**$23.35**	**100**	**100.0%**
Under age 25	11.49	49	3.5
Aged 25 to 34	21.98	94	17.8
Aged 35 to 44	29.40	126	29.3
Aged 45 to 54	27.39	117	21.5
Aged 55 to 64	21.34	91	10.7
Aged 65 to 74	22.86	98	11.2
Aged 75 or older	16.72	72	6.7
HOUSEHOLD INCOME			
Total households reporting income	**23.43**	**100**	**100.0**
Under $20,000	15.75	67	23.4
$20,000 to $29,999	17.77	76	11.1
$30,000 to $39,999	24.53	105	12.8
$40,000 to $49,999	29.24	125	11.7
$50,000 to $69,999	33.56	143	20.1
$70,000 or more	32.15	137	20.5
HOUSEHOLD TYPE			
Total households	**23.35**	**100**	**100.0**
Married couples	31.24	134	70.0
Married couples, no children	23.96	103	21.9
Married couples, with children	36.74	157	42.3
Oldest child under 6	28.14	121	6.2
Oldest child 6 to 17	42.38	181	26.4
Oldest child 18 or older	32.57	139	10.0
Single parent with child under 18	19.85	85	5.3
Single person	10.11	43	12.4
REGION			
Total households	**23.35**	**100**	**100.0**
Northeast	22.16	95	19.0
Midwest	22.96	98	23.5
South	25.95	111	38.8
West	20.73	89	18.9

Note: For definitions of best and biggest customers, see introduction or glossary.
Source: Calculations by New Strategist based on the 1997 Consumer Expenditure Survey

Baking Needs and Miscellaneous Products

Best customers:	• **Householders aged 55 to 64**
	• **Married couples without children at home**
	• **Married couples with school-aged children**
	• **Households in the West**
Customer trends:	• **A spending decline is likely as the cooking-averse baby-boom generation ages.**

Although cooking from scratch is a lot less common than it once was, many people still enjoy whipping up a home-cooked meal or dessert. The best customers of baking products are older householders. Those aged 55 to 64 spend 31 percent more than the average household on this item. Married couples without children at home, most of whom are older, spend 36 percent more than average on baking needs.

Spending on baking needs is likely to decline as the number of busy dual-income couples rises and as the cooking-averse baby-boom generation ages.

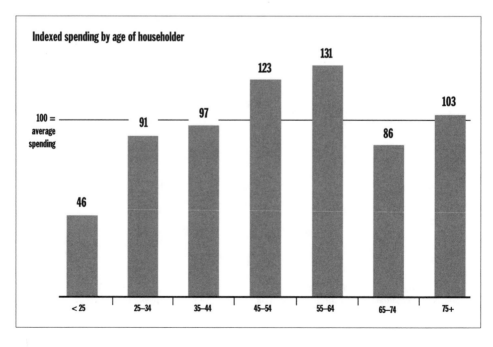

Indexed spending by age of householder

100 = average spending

< 25	25–34	35–44	45–54	55–64	65–74	75+
46	91	97	123	131	86	103

BAKING NEEDS AND MISCELLANEOUS PRODUCTS

Total household spending $1,757,840,400
Average household spends   16.65

	average spending	best customers (index)	biggest customers (market share)
AGE OF HOUSEHOLDER			
Total households	**$16.65**	**100**	**100.0%**
Under age 25	7.59	46	3.2
Aged 25 to 34	15.10	91	17.1
Aged 35 to 44	16.20	97	22.6
Aged 45 to 54	20.55	123	22.6
Aged 55 to 64	21.78	131	15.3
Aged 65 to 74	14.26	86	9.8
Aged 75 or older	17.07	103	9.5
HOUSEHOLD INCOME			
Total households reporting income	**17.07**	**100**	**100.0**
Under $20,000	11.10	65	22.7
$20,000 to $29,999	18.59	109	15.9
$30,000 to $39,999	14.50	85	10.4
$40,000 to $49,999	19.20	112	10.5
$50,000 to $69,999	24.28	142	20.0
$70,000 or more	22.92	134	20.1
HOUSEHOLD TYPE			
Total households	**16.65**	**100**	**100.0**
Married couples	21.89	131	68.7
Married couples, no children	22.60	136	29.0
Married couples, with children	20.67	124	33.4
Oldest child under 6	18.43	111	5.7
Oldest child 6 to 17	21.87	131	19.1
Oldest child 18 or older	20.12	121	8.7
Single parent with child under 18	13.52	81	5.1
Single person	8.73	52	15.1
REGION			
Total households	**16.65**	**100**	**100.0**
Northeast	16.15	97	19.4
Midwest	16.34	98	23.5
South	15.00	90	31.4
West	20.03	120	25.6

Note: For definitions of best and biggest customers, see introduction or glossary.
Source: Calculations by New Strategist based on the 1997 Consumer Expenditure Survey

Beef

Best customers:	• Married couples with school-aged or older children
Customer trends:	• Spending should remain stable as the beef industry fights to retain market share.

The largest households spend the most on beef. Married couples with school-aged or older children are the best customers of beef because they have the most people to feed. Married couples with school-aged or older children spend 52 to 55 percent more than the average household on this item. Householders aged 35 to 54 spend 18 to 27 percent more because they have the largest households.

Health concerns have led to a decline in beef consumption over the past few years, and Americans substitute poultry and fish for hamburgers and steaks. The beef industry has been fighting back, and it's likely that spending on beef will stabilize—unless new health concerns arise.

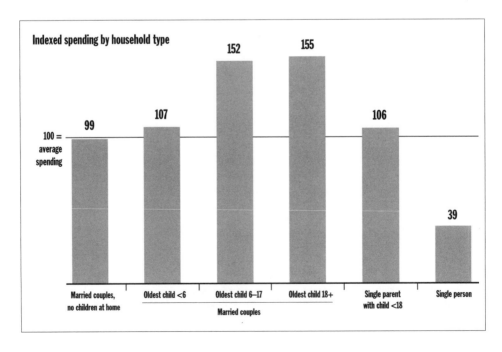

Indexed spending by household type

100 = average spending

- Married couples, no children at home: 99
- Oldest child <6: 107
- Oldest child 6–17: 152
- Oldest child 18+: 155
- Single parent with child <18: 106
- Single person: 39

Married couples

BEEF

Total household spending	$23,601,514,800
Average household spends	223.55

	average spending	best customers (index)	biggest customers (market share)
AGE OF HOUSEHOLDER			
Total households	**$223.55**	**100**	**100.0%**
Under age 25	124.93	56	4.0
Aged 25 to 34	219.46	98	18.5
Aged 35 to 44	264.29	118	27.5
Aged 45 to 54	284.29	127	23.3
Aged 55 to 64	231.02	103	12.1
Aged 65 to 74	190.43	85	9.8
Aged 75 or older	128.49	57	5.3
HOUSEHOLD INCOME			
Total households reporting income	**226.37**	**100**	**100.0**
Under $20,000	164.91	73	25.4
$20,000 to $29,999	218.85	97	14.1
$30,000 to $39,999	237.96	105	12.9
$40,000 to $49,999	238.09	105	9.8
$50,000 to $69,999	291.28	129	18.1
$70,000 or more	292.01	129	19.3
HOUSEHOLD TYPE			
Total households	**223.55**	**100**	**100.0**
Married couples	285.95	128	66.9
Married couples, no children	221.98	99	21.2
Married couples, with children	320.00	143	38.5
Oldest child under 6	239.93	107	5.5
Oldest child 6 to 17	340.11	152	22.1
Oldest child 18 or older	346.40	155	11.1
Single parent with child under 18	237.38	106	6.7
Single person	87.80	39	11.3
REGION			
Total households	**223.55**	**100**	**100.0**
Northeast	214.34	96	19.2
Midwest	206.77	92	22.1
South	234.59	105	36.6
West	232.79	104	22.1

Note: For definitions of best and biggest customers, see introduction or glossary.
Source: Calculations by New Strategist based on the 1997 Consumer Expenditure Survey

Biscuits and Rolls

Best customers:
- Married couples with school-aged or older children
- Households in the Northeast

Customer trends:
- Spending could rise as prepared foods become more popular.

The larger the household, the more it spends on biscuits and rolls. Married couples with adult children at home spend 64 percent more than the average household on biscuits and rolls. Those with school-aged children spend 56 percent more than average on this item. Households in the Northeast spend 26 percent more than average on biscuits and rolls, perhaps because Northeastern householders are less likely to make these items from scratch than householders in other regions.

Spending on biscuits and rolls could rise as busy householders opt for the convenience of buying prepared foods rather than cooking from scratch.

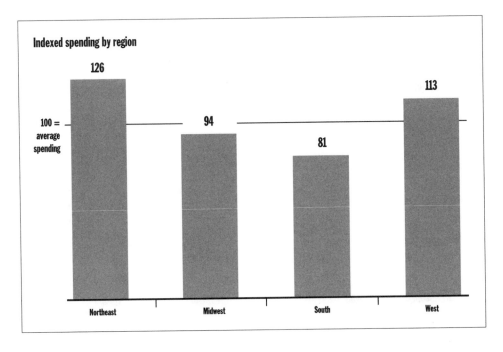

Indexed spending by region

100 = average spending

Northeast 126 Midwest 94 South 81 West 113

BISCUITS AND ROLLS

Total household spending $4,324,392,960
Average household spends   40.96

	average spending	best customers (index)	biggest customers (market share)
AGE OF HOUSEHOLDER			
Total households	**$40.96**	**100**	**100.0%**
Under age 25	20.75	51	3.6
Aged 25 to 34	34.73	85	16.0
Aged 35 to 44	48.86	119	27.7
Aged 45 to 54	55.68	136	24.9
Aged 55 to 64	41.92	102	11.9
Aged 65 to 74	34.75	85	9.7
Aged 75 or older	28.93	71	6.6
HOUSEHOLD INCOME			
Total households reporting income	**42.66**	**100**	**100.0**
Under $20,000	22.75	53	18.6
$20,000 to $29,999	33.50	79	11.5
$30,000 to $39,999	39.85	93	11.4
$40,000 to $49,999	51.44	121	11.3
$50,000 to $69,999	53.99	127	17.8
$70,000 or more	81.60	191	28.6
HOUSEHOLD TYPE			
Total households	**40.96**	**100**	**100.0**
Married couples	55.40	135	70.7
Married couples, no children	44.57	109	23.2
Married couples, with children	62.23	152	40.8
Oldest child under 6	52.36	128	6.6
Oldest child 6 to 17	63.80	156	22.7
Oldest child 18 or older	67.32	164	11.8
Single parent with child under 18	27.15	66	4.2
Single person	17.00	42	11.9
REGION			
Total households	**40.96**	**100**	**100.0**
Northeast	51.61	126	25.2
Midwest	38.54	94	22.5
South	33.11	81	28.2
West	46.32	113	24.0

Note: For definitions of best and biggest customers, see introduction or glossary.
Source: Calculations by New Strategist based on the 1997 Consumer Expenditure Survey

Bread

Best customers: • Married couples with school-aged or older children

Customer trends: • Spending may rise along with the number of households with teens and young
                                           adults.

The largest households spend the most on bread. The best customers of bread are married couples with at least one adult child at home. They spend 59 percent more than the average household on bread. Married couples with school-aged children at home spend 30 percent more than average on bread.

Spending on bread may increase as the children of boomers grow up and an expanding number of households include teens and young adults.

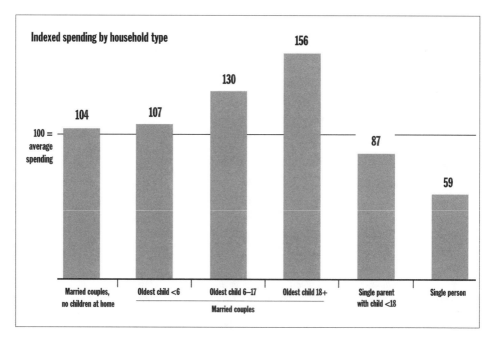

Indexed spending by household type

104	107	130	156	87	59

100 = average spending

Married couples, no children at home | Oldest child <6 | Oldest child 6–17 | Oldest child 18+ | Single parent with child <18 | Single person

Married couples

BREAD

Total household spending	$8,808,205,680		
Average household spends	83.43		

	average spending	best customers (index)	biggest customers (market share)
AGE OF HOUSEHOLDER			
Total households	**$83.43**	**100**	**100.0%**
Under age 25	46.93	56	4.0
Aged 25 to 34	76.65	92	17.3
Aged 35 to 44	89.66	107	25.0
Aged 45 to 54	100.88	121	22.2
Aged 55 to 64	93.33	112	13.0
Aged 65 to 74	85.75	103	11.8
Aged 75 or older	63.11	76	7.0
HOUSEHOLD INCOME			
Total households reporting income	**86.16**	**100**	**100.0**
Under $20,000	64.09	74	25.9
$20,000 to $29,999	88.56	103	15.0
$30,000 to $39,999	92.03	107	13.1
$40,000 to $49,999	90.87	105	9.9
$50,000 to $69,999	89.83	104	14.6
$70,000 or more	120.36	140	20.9
HOUSEHOLD TYPE			
Total households	**83.43**	**100**	**100.0**
Married couples	102.73	123	64.4
Married couples, no children	86.79	104	22.2
Married couples, with children	110.05	132	35.5
Oldest child under 6	89.65	107	5.5
Oldest child 6 to 17	108.57	130	18.9
Oldest child 18 or older	130.05	156	11.2
Single parent with child under 18	72.51	87	5.5
Single person	48.99	59	16.9
REGION			
Total households	**83.43**	**100**	**100.0**
Northeast	95.87	115	23.0
Midwest	87.85	105	25.2
South	73.39	88	30.7
West	83.16	100	21.2

Note: For definitions of best and biggest customers, see introduction or glossary.
Source: Calculations by New Strategist based on the 1997 Consumer Expenditure Survey

Butter

Best customers:
- Married couples with adult children
- Households in the Northeast

Customer trends:
- A spending decline is likely as people try to cut their fat intake.

The best customers of butter are married couples with adult children at home. They spend 81 percent more than the average household on butter, largely because there are more people in the household. Northeastern households spend 39 percent more than average on this item thanks to the region's large dairy industry.

Many health-conscious Americans are shying away from butter because of its high fat content. Consequently, spending on butter is likely to decline.

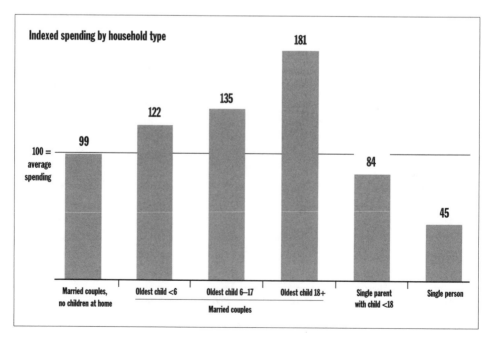

Indexed spending by household type

99	122	135	181	84	45

100 = average spending

| Married couples, no children at home | Oldest child <6 | Oldest child 6–17 | Oldest child 18+ | Single parent with child <18 | Single person |

Married couples

BUTTER

Total household spending	$1,544,576,880		
Average household spends	14.63		

	average spending	best customers (index)	biggest customers (market share)
AGE OF HOUSEHOLDER			
Total households	**$14.63**	**100**	**100.0%**
Under age 25	6.73	46	3.3
Aged 25 to 34	14.15	97	18.2
Aged 35 to 44	15.76	108	25.1
Aged 45 to 54	18.17	124	22.8
Aged 55 to 64	16.98	116	13.5
Aged 65 to 74	13.95	95	10.9
Aged 75 or older	10.46	71	6.7
HOUSEHOLD INCOME			
Total households reporting income	**15.08**	**100**	**100.0**
Under $20,000	10.55	70	24.4
$20,000 to $29,999	14.33	95	13.9
$30,000 to $39,999	13.90	92	11.3
$40,000 to $49,999	16.52	110	10.2
$50,000 to $69,999	19.73	131	18.4
$70,000 or more	21.49	143	21.3
HOUSEHOLD TYPE			
Total households	**14.63**	**100**	**100.0**
Married couples	18.76	128	67.1
Married couples, no children	14.49	99	21.1
Married couples, with children	21.11	144	38.8
Oldest child under 6	17.87	122	6.3
Oldest child 6 to 17	19.80	135	19.7
Oldest child 18 or older	26.42	181	13.0
Single parent with child under 18	12.35	84	5.3
Single person	6.60	45	13.0
REGION			
Total households	**14.63**	**100**	**100.0**
Northeast	20.39	139	27.8
Midwest	13.25	91	21.6
South	11.68	80	27.9
West	15.57	106	22.6

Note: For definitions of best and biggest customers, see introduction or glossary.
Source: Calculations by New Strategist based on the 1997 Consumer Expenditure Survey

Cakes and Cupcakes

Best customers:
- Householders aged 35 to 44
- Married couples with school-aged or older children

Customer trends:
- More school-aged children means more spending on cakes and cupcakes.

Children are the driving force behind spending on cakes and cupcakes. Married couples with school-aged children spend 57 percent more than the average household on this item. Married couples with adult children at home spend 59 percent more than average. Householders aged 35 to 44 spend 38 percent more than average on cakes and cupcakes because most have children at home.

Spending on cakes and cupcakes is likely to increase in the next few years as the number of households with school-aged and older children expands.

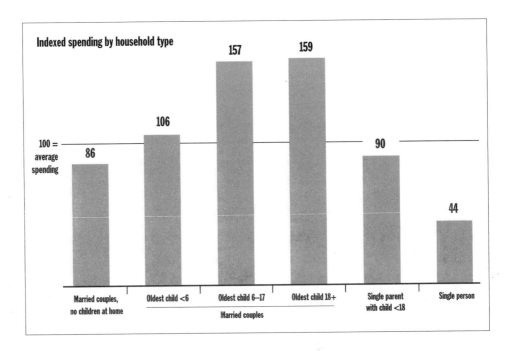

Indexed spending by household type

86	106	157	159	90	44

100 = average spending

Married couples, no children at home | Oldest child <6 | Oldest child 6–17 | Oldest child 18+ | Single parent with child <18 | Single person

Married couples

CAKES AND CUPCAKES

Total household spending	$3,643,427,760
Average household spends	34.51

	average spending	best customers (index)	biggest customers (market share)
AGE OF HOUSEHOLDER			
Total households	**$34.51**	**100**	**100.0%**
Under age 25	18.37	53	3.8
Aged 25 to 34	33.47	97	18.3
Aged 35 to 44	47.73	138	32.2
Aged 45 to 54	44.61	129	23.7
Aged 55 to 64	30.13	87	10.2
Aged 65 to 74	24.94	72	8.3
Aged 75 or older	15.75	46	4.2
HOUSEHOLD INCOME			
Total households reporting income	**34.41**	**100**	**100.0**
Under $20,000	23.31	68	23.6
$20,000 to $29,999	31.86	93	13.5
$30,000 to $39,999	30.80	90	10.9
$40,000 to $49,999	46.27	134	12.6
$50,000 to $69,999	45.28	132	18.5
$70,000 or more	47.05	137	20.4
HOUSEHOLD TYPE			
Total households	**34.51**	**100**	**100.0**
Married couples	44.76	130	67.8
Married couples, no children	29.51	86	18.2
Married couples, with children	50.63	147	39.4
Oldest child under 6	36.55	106	5.4
Oldest child 6 to 17	54.29	157	22.9
Oldest child 18 or older	55.00	159	11.5
Single parent with child under 18	31.15	90	5.7
Single person	15.32	44	12.8
REGION			
Total households	**34.51**	**100**	**100.0**
Northeast	39.45	114	22.8
Midwest	30.02	87	20.8
South	34.37	100	34.7
West	35.13	102	21.6

Note: For definitions of best and biggest customers, see introduction or glossary.
Source: Calculations by New Strategist based on the 1997 Consumer Expenditure Survey

Candy and Chewing Gum

Best customers:
- Married couples with school-aged or older children

Customer trends:
- Spending on candy and chewing gum is likely to increase as the teen and young-adult population expands.

Households with children are the best customers of candy and chewing gum. Married couples with school-aged children spend 65 percent more than the average household on this item. Those with adult children at home spend 41 percent more than average. Spending on candy and chewing gum is above average for householders aged 35 to 54, who are likely to have school-aged or older children at home. It is also above average for householders aged 55 to 64—many of them buying sweets for grandchildren.

Spending on candy and chewing gum should rise as the number of households with teens and young adults expands.

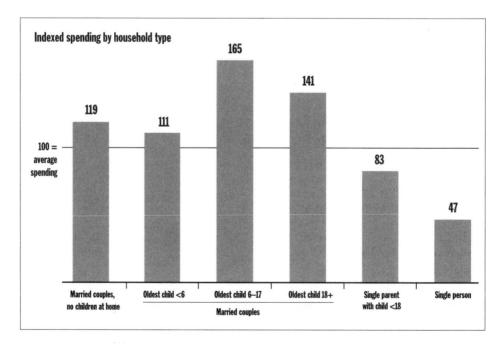

Indexed spending by household type

119	111	165	141	83	47
Married couples, no children at home	Oldest child <6	Oldest child 6–17	Oldest child 18+	Single parent with child <18	Single person

100 = average spending

Married couples

CANDY AND CHEWING GUM

Total household spending	$7,312,193,760		
Average household spends	69.26		

	average spending	best customers (index)	biggest customers (market share)
AGE OF HOUSEHOLDER			
Total households	**$69.26**	**100**	**100.0%**
Under age 25	31.32	45	3.2
Aged 25 to 34	63.50	92	17.3
Aged 35 to 44	80.12	116	26.9
Aged 45 to 54	87.68	127	23.2
Aged 55 to 64	79.66	115	13.4
Aged 65 to 74	62.83	91	10.4
Aged 75 or older	44.90	65	6.0
HOUSEHOLD INCOME			
Total households reporting income	**71.95**	**100**	**100.0**
Under $20,000	43.50	60	21.1
$20,000 to $29,999	57.92	81	11.8
$30,000 to $39,999	78.54	109	13.3
$40,000 to $49,999	81.44	113	10.6
$50,000 to $69,999	98.67	137	19.2
$70,000 or more	112.03	156	23.3
HOUSEHOLD TYPE			
Total households	**69.26**	**100**	**100.0**
Married couples	93.28	135	70.4
Married couples, no children	82.75	119	25.5
Married couples, with children	101.74	147	39.5
Oldest child under 6	76.67	111	5.7
Oldest child 6 to 17	114.20	165	24.0
Oldest child 18 or older	97.61	141	10.1
Single parent with child under 18	57.73	83	5.2
Single person	32.44	47	13.5
REGION			
Total households	**69.26**	**100**	**100.0**
Northeast	64.06	92	18.5
Midwest	73.60	106	25.4
South	65.36	94	32.9
West	75.46	109	23.1

Note: For definitions of best and biggest customers, see introduction or glossary.
Source: Calculations by New Strategist based on the 1997 Consumer Expenditure Survey

Carbonated Drinks

Best customers: • Married couples with school-aged or older children

Customer trends: • Spending on carbonated drinks is likely to rise as the population of teens and young adults expands.

Americans spend a lot of money on carbonated beverages. The only grocery items on which the average household spends more are beef, fruit, vegetables, and poultry. Married couples with children spend even more than the average household on carbonated drinks, in part because they have larger households. Married couples with school-aged children spend 50 percent more, while those with adult children at home spend 59 percent more.

Although carbonated drinks face growing competition from sports drinks, iced teas, and fruit drinks, spending on them is likely to rise as the population of teens and young adults expands.

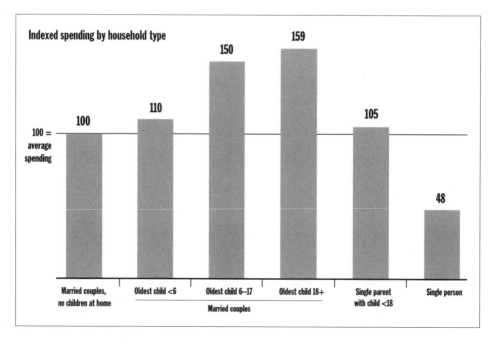

Indexed spending by household type

Married couples, no children at home	Oldest child <6	Oldest child 6–17	Oldest child 18+	Single parent with child <18	Single person
100	110	150	159	105	48

100 = average spending

Married couples

CARBONATED DRINKS

Total household spending	$14,089,117,200
Average household spends	133.45

	average spending	best customers (index)	biggest customers (market share)
AGE OF HOUSEHOLDER			
Total households	**$133.45**	**100**	**100.0%**
Under age 25	103.37	77	5.5
Aged 25 to 34	127.28	95	18.0
Aged 35 to 44	167.43	125	29.2
Aged 45 to 54	165.52	124	22.7
Aged 55 to 64	143.38	107	12.5
Aged 65 to 74	99.53	75	8.6
Aged 75 or older	54.40	41	3.8
HOUSEHOLD INCOME			
Total households reporting income	**139.44**	**100**	**100.0**
Under $20,000	95.08	68	23.7
$20,000 to $29,999	130.55	94	13.7
$30,000 to $39,999	157.72	113	13.8
$40,000 to $49,999	162.55	117	10.9
$50,000 to $69,999	177.36	127	17.9
$70,000 or more	180.72	130	19.4
HOUSEHOLD TYPE			
Total households	**133.45**	**100**	**100.0**
Married couples	168.84	127	66.2
Married couples, no children	133.48	100	21.3
Married couples, with children	191.71	144	38.6
Oldest child under 6	147.14	110	5.7
Oldest child 6 to 17	199.87	150	21.8
Oldest child 18 or older	212.49	159	11.4
Single parent with child under 18	140.19	105	6.6
Single person	63.76	48	13.7
REGION			
Total households	**133.45**	**100**	**100.0**
Northeast	112.28	84	16.8
Midwest	140.15	105	25.1
South	143.64	108	37.6
West	129.32	97	20.6

Note: For definitions of best and biggest customers, see introduction or glossary.
Source: Calculations by New Strategist based on the 1997 Consumer Expenditure Survey

Cereal, Ready-to-Eat and Cooked

Best customers:
- Householders aged 35 to 44
- Married couples with children

Customer trends:
- The desire for convenience ensures a steady rise in spending on ready-to-eat cereal.

Married couples with children are the best customers of ready-to-eat and cooked cereals. Those with school-aged children spend 67 percent more than average on this item, while those with adult children at home spend 57 percent more. Married couples with preschoolers spend 28 percent more than average. Householders aged 35 to 44, most of whom are parents, spend 25 percent more than average on cereal.

Ready-to-eat cereal is convenient for busy families, and many are supplemented with vitamins and minerals—reassuring parents that their children are eating properly. Spending on cereal will continue to rise as the number of families with teens and young adults expands.

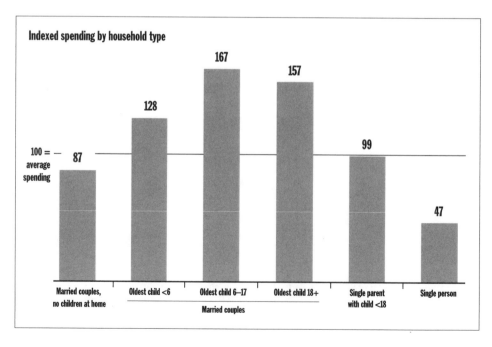

Indexed spending by household type

87	128	167	157	99	47

100 = average spending

Married couples, no children at home | Oldest child <6 | Oldest child 6–17 | Oldest child 18+ | Single parent with child <18 | Single person

Married couples

CEREAL, READY-TO-EAT AND COOKED

Total household spending	$9,623,252,400	
Average household spends	91.15	

	average spending	best customers (index)	biggest customers (market share)
AGE OF HOUSEHOLDER			
Total households	**$91.15**	**100**	**100.0%**
Under age 25	54.42	60	4.2
Aged 25 to 34	95.75	105	19.8
Aged 35 to 44	114.00	125	29.1
Aged 45 to 54	105.77	116	21.3
Aged 55 to 64	83.87	92	10.7
Aged 65 to 74	74.67	82	9.4
Aged 75 or older	58.44	64	6.0
HOUSEHOLD INCOME			
Total households reporting income	**92.76**	**100**	**100.0**
Under $20,000	64.15	69	24.1
$20,000 to $29,999	75.16	81	11.8
$30,000 to $39,999	106.62	115	14.1
$40,000 to $49,999	98.45	106	9.9
$50,000 to $69,999	112.58	121	17.0
$70,000 or more	139.26	150	22.4
HOUSEHOLD TYPE			
Total households	**91.15**	**100**	**100.0**
Married couples	117.17	129	67.2
Married couples, no children	79.17	87	18.5
Married couples, with children	142.33	156	42.0
Oldest child under 6	116.27	128	6.6
Oldest child 6 to 17	152.55	167	24.3
Oldest child 18 or older	143.52	157	11.3
Single parent with child under 18	90.51	99	6.2
Single person	42.40	47	13.4
REGION			
Total households	**91.15**	**100**	**100.0**
Northeast	99.54	109	21.8
Midwest	92.30	101	24.2
South	82.64	91	31.6
West	95.71	105	22.3

Note: For definitions of best and biggest customers, see introduction or glossary.
Source: Calculations by New Strategist based on the 1997 Consumer Expenditure Survey

Cheese

Best customers: • Married couples with school-aged or older children

Customer trends: • Spending should rise as the teen and young-adult population expands, but is
                                     likely to stabilize or even decline once boomers reach their empty-nest years.

The best customers of cheese are families with children. Married couples with school-aged children spend 57 percent more than the average household on this item, while those with adult children at home spend 53 percent more. Cheese spending drops off in the older age groups as concerns about fat intake limit consumption.

Spending on cheese is likely to increase as the number of households with teens and young adults expands. Once the health-conscious baby-boom generation ages into its fifties and sixties, spending on cheese may decline as health concerns arise.

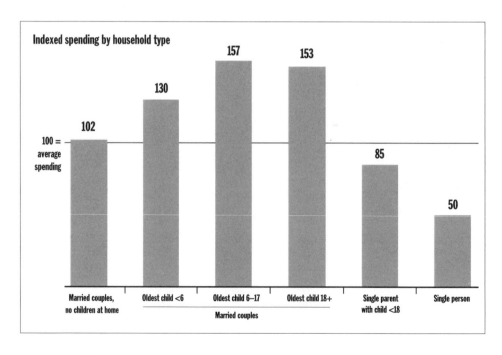

Indexed spending by household type

102	130	157	153	85	50
Married couples, no children at home	Oldest child <6	Oldest child 6–17	Oldest child 18+	Single parent with child <18	Single person
		Married couples			

100 = average spending

CHEESE

Total household spending	$9,958,984,080
Average household spends	94.33

	average spending	best customers (index)	biggest customers (market share)
AGE OF HOUSEHOLDER			
Total households	**$94.33**	**100**	**100.0%**
Under age 25	48.68	52	3.7
Aged 25 to 34	90.62	96	18.1
Aged 35 to 44	118.35	125	29.2
Aged 45 to 54	112.21	119	21.8
Aged 55 to 64	100.60	107	12.4
Aged 65 to 74	78.69	83	9.6
Aged 75 or older	57.93	61	5.7
HOUSEHOLD INCOME			
Total households reporting income	**99.99**	**100**	**100.0**
Under $20,000	64.31	64	22.4
$20,000 to $29,999	83.18	83	12.2
$30,000 to $39,999	101.76	102	12.4
$40,000 to $49,999	122.52	123	11.5
$50,000 to $69,999	120.72	121	16.9
$70,000 or more	159.63	160	23.9
HOUSEHOLD TYPE			
Total households	**94.33**	**100**	**100.0**
Married couples	121.36	129	67.3
Married couples, no children	95.91	102	21.7
Married couples, with children	141.59	150	40.4
Oldest child under 6	122.29	130	6.7
Oldest child 6 to 17	148.46	157	22.9
Oldest child 18 or older	143.91	153	11.0
Single parent with child under 18	80.15	85	5.3
Single person	47.36	50	14.4
REGION			
Total households	**94.33**	**100**	**100.0**
Northeast	94.58	100	20.0
Midwest	96.65	102	24.5
South	89.01	94	32.9
West	100.01	106	22.5

Note: For definitions of best and biggest customers, see introduction or glossary.
Source: Calculations by New Strategist based on the 1997 Consumer Expenditure Survey

Coffee

Best customers: • Householders aged 55 to 74
                         • Married couples with adult children

Customer trends: • Spending is likely to decline unless younger generations become coffee
                           drinkers.

The best customers of coffee are householders aged 55 to 74. Those aged 55 to 64 spend 39 percent more than the average household on coffee, while householders aged 65 to 74 spend 49 percent more. Married couples with adult children spend 47 percent more than average on this item, while those without children at home—most of them older—spend 42 percent more.

Although coffee bars have become almost as popular as pizza joints, the biggest coffee drinkers by far are older Americans. Unless younger generations become bigger coffee drinkers at home, spending on this item will decline.

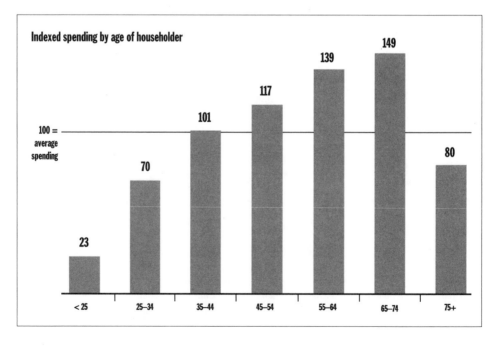

Indexed spending by age of householder

	< 25	25–34	35–44	45–54	55–64	65–74	75+
	23	70	101	117	139	149	80

100 = average spending

COFFEE

Total household spending	$5,152,108,800		
Average household spends	48.80		

	average spending	best customers (index)	biggest customers (market share)
AGE OF HOUSEHOLDER			
Total households	**$48.80**	**100**	**100.0%**
Under age 25	11.35	23	1.7
Aged 25 to 34	34.03	70	13.2
Aged 35 to 44	49.25	101	23.5
Aged 45 to 54	57.12	117	21.4
Aged 55 to 64	67.99	139	16.3
Aged 65 to 74	72.50	149	17.0
Aged 75 or older	39.04	80	7.4
HOUSEHOLD INCOME			
Total households reporting income	**49.87**	**100**	**100.0**
Under $20,000	39.74	80	27.8
$20,000 to $29,999	41.90	84	12.3
$30,000 to $39,999	51.80	104	12.7
$40,000 to $49,999	51.86	104	9.7
$50,000 to $69,999	52.95	106	14.9
$70,000 or more	74.16	149	22.2
HOUSEHOLD TYPE			
Total households	**48.80**	**100**	**100.0**
Married couples	63.10	129	67.6
Married couples, no children	69.08	142	30.2
Married couples, with children	56.48	116	31.1
Oldest child under 6	44.42	91	4.7
Oldest child 6 to 17	53.83	110	16.0
Oldest child 18 or older	71.88	147	10.6
Single parent with child under 18	32.17	66	4.1
Single person	25.81	53	15.2
REGION			
Total households	**48.80**	**100**	**100.0**
Northeast	51.73	106	21.2
Midwest	52.32	107	25.6
South	43.59	89	31.2
West	50.56	104	22.0

Note: For definitions of best and biggest customers, see introduction or glossary.
Source: Calculations by New Strategist based on the 1997 Consumer Expenditure Survey

Cookies

Best customers:
- Married couples with school-aged or older children

Customer trends:
- Spending will rise as the number of households with teens and young adults expands.

Children love cookies, so it's no surprise that the best customers of cookies are families with children. Married couples with school-aged children spend 61 percent more than the average household on cookies. Those with adult children at home spend 60 percent more than average on this item.

The number of school-aged children is growing, and this should boost spending on cookies. In addition, cookie makers are finding new ways to sell their wares—such as individually wrapped, oversized cookies—which should add to spending on this item.

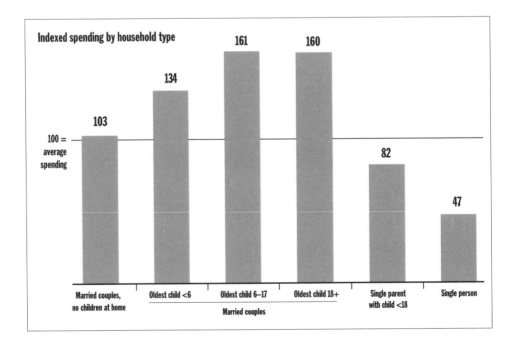

Indexed spending by household type

Married couples, no children at home	103	
Oldest child <6	134	Married couples
Oldest child 6–17	161	
Oldest child 18+	160	
Single parent with child <18	82	
Single person	47	

100 = average spending

COOKIES

Total household spending	$4,751,975,760
Average household spends	45.01

	average spending	best customers (index)	biggest customers (market share)
AGE OF HOUSEHOLDER			
Total households	**$45.01**	**100**	**100.0%**
Under age 25	28.28	63	4.5
Aged 25 to 34	36.95	82	15.5
Aged 35 to 44	55.15	123	28.5
Aged 45 to 54	54.04	120	22.0
Aged 55 to 64	47.60	106	12.3
Aged 65 to 74	44.43	99	11.3
Aged 75 or older	30.29	67	6.3
HOUSEHOLD INCOME			
Total households reporting income	**45.86**	**100**	**100.0**
Under $20,000	32.87	72	25.0
$20,000 to $29,999	39.44	86	12.6
$30,000 to $39,999	48.60	106	13.0
$40,000 to $49,999	49.72	108	10.1
$50,000 to $69,999	50.66	110	15.5
$70,000 or more	71.24	155	23.2
HOUSEHOLD TYPE			
Total households	**45.01**	**100**	**100.0**
Married couples	59.61	132	69.3
Married couples, no children	46.47	103	22.0
Married couples, with children	69.84	155	41.7
Oldest child under 6	60.43	134	6.9
Oldest child 6 to 17	72.60	161	23.5
Oldest child 18 or older	72.13	160	11.5
Single parent with child under 18	37.06	82	5.2
Single person	20.97	47	13.4
REGION			
Total households	**45.01**	**100**	**100.0**
Northeast	50.68	113	22.5
Midwest	42.91	95	22.8
South	41.72	93	32.3
West	47.33	105	22.3

Note: For definitions of best and biggest customers, see introduction or glossary.
Source: Calculations by New Strategist based on the 1997 Consumer Expenditure Survey

Crackers

Best customers:	• Married couples with school-aged or older children
	• Householders aged 35 to 64
Customer trends:	• Spending should rise as an aging population looks for healthy snacks.

The best customers of crackers are married couples with school-aged or older children. These householders spend 50 to 56 percent more than the average household on crackers as they search for a healthier alternative to candy and cookies. The same motivation is behind the higher spending on crackers by householders aged 45 to 64, who spend 20 percent more than average on this item.

Spending on crackers is likely to rise in the years ahead as aging boomers look for healthy snacks and as cracker manufacturers produce a greater variety of products to satisfy this demand.

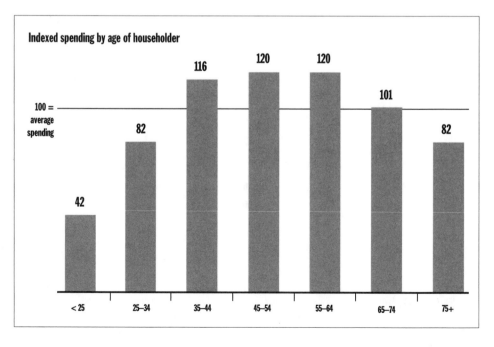

Indexed spending by age of householder

<25	25–34	35–44	45–54	55–64	65–74	75+
42	82	116	120	120	101	82

100 = average spending

CRACKERS

Total household spending	$2,455,697,760
Average household spends	23.26

	average spending	best customers (index)	biggest customers (market share)
AGE OF HOUSEHOLDER			
Total households	**$23.26**	**100**	**100.0%**
Under age 25	9.75	42	3.0
Aged 25 to 34	19.09	82	15.5
Aged 35 to 44	26.89	116	26.9
Aged 45 to 54	27.89	120	22.0
Aged 55 to 64	27.80	120	13.9
Aged 65 to 74	23.45	101	11.6
Aged 75 or older	19.02	82	7.6
HOUSEHOLD INCOME			
Total households reporting income	**24.19**	**100**	**100.0**
Under $20,000	15.76	65	22.7
$20,000 to $29,999	21.19	88	12.8
$30,000 to $39,999	26.33	109	13.3
$40,000 to $49,999	23.29	96	9.0
$50,000 to $69,999	30.90	128	17.9
$70,000 or more	38.29	158	23.7
HOUSEHOLD TYPE			
Total households	**23.26**	**100**	**100.0**
Married couples	30.94	133	69.6
Married couples, no children	27.59	119	25.3
Married couples, with children	33.60	144	38.8
Oldest child under 6	27.43	118	6.1
Oldest child 6 to 17	34.78	150	21.8
Oldest child 18 or older	36.35	156	11.2
Single parent with child under 18	18.70	80	5.0
Single person	11.55	50	14.3
REGION			
Total households	**23.26**	**100**	**100.0**
Northeast	20.73	89	17.8
Midwest	24.52	105	25.2
South	22.53	97	33.8
West	25.36	109	23.2

Note: For definitions of best and biggest customers, see introduction or glossary.
Source: Calculations by New Strategist based on the 1997 Consumer Expenditure Survey

Desserts, Prepared

Best customers:	• Married couples with children
	• Householders aged 35 to 64
Customer trends:	• Spending will increase thanks to the growing number of busy two-earner couples with teens and young adults at home.

The larger the household, the more it spends on prepared desserts—especially if the household includes children. Married couples with adult children at home spend 75 percent more than the average household on prepared desserts. Couples with school-aged children spend 59 percent more, while those with preschoolers spend 50 percent more. Householders spanning the ages from 35 to 64 all spend more than average on prepared desserts.

Spending on prepared desserts will rise in the years ahead as the number of busy two-earner couples with teens and young adults expands.

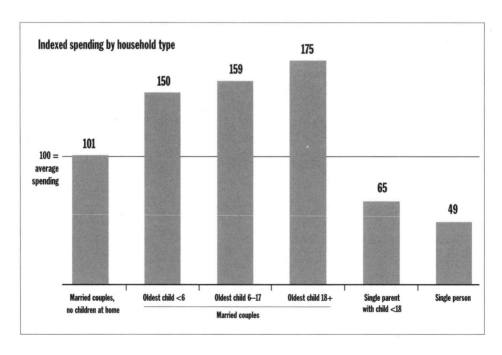

Indexed spending by household type

Married couples, no children at home	Oldest child <6	Oldest child 6–17	Oldest child 18+	Single parent with child <18	Single person
101	150	159	175	65	49

100 = average spending

Married couples

DESSERTS, PREPARED

Total household spending	$1,050,481,200
Average household spends	9.95

	average spending	best customers (index)	biggest customers (market share)
AGE OF HOUSEHOLDER			
Total households	**$9.95**	**100**	**100.0%**
Under age 25	3.82	38	2.7
Aged 25 to 34	8.19	82	15.5
Aged 35 to 44	11.57	116	27.1
Aged 45 to 54	12.58	126	23.2
Aged 55 to 64	11.46	115	13.4
Aged 65 to 74	8.68	87	10.0
Aged 75 or older	9.12	92	8.5
HOUSEHOLD INCOME			
Total households reporting income	**10.54**	**100**	**100.0**
Under $20,000	7.44	71	24.6
$20,000 to $29,999	8.67	82	12.0
$30,000 to $39,999	10.93	104	12.7
$40,000 to $49,999	11.57	110	10.3
$50,000 to $69,999	12.00	114	16.0
$70,000 or more	16.78	159	23.8
HOUSEHOLD TYPE			
Total households	**9.95**	**100**	**100.0**
Married couples	13.51	136	71.0
Married couples, no children	10.01	101	21.5
Married couples, with children	16.03	161	43.3
Oldest child under 6	14.92	150	7.7
Oldest child 6 to 17	15.79	159	23.1
Oldest child 18 or older	17.43	175	12.6
Single parent with child under 18	6.46	65	4.1
Single person	4.91	49	14.2
REGION			
Total households	**9.95**	**100**	**100.0**
Northeast	10.05	101	20.2
Midwest	10.75	108	25.8
South	8.69	87	30.5
West	10.95	110	23.4

Note: For definitions of best and biggest customers, see introduction or glossary.
Source: Calculations by New Strategist based on the 1997 Consumer Expenditure Survey

Eggs

Best customers:	• Married couples with adult children at home
	• Households in the West
	• Householders aged 45 to 64
Customer trends:	• Spending may increase slightly as the reputation of the egg improves.

Americans are eating many fewer eggs than they once did because of health concerns. The best customers of eggs are families with teenaged or adult children, in part because of their larger household size. Married couples with adult children at home spend 46 percent more than the average household on eggs, while those with school-aged children spend 24 percent more. Older householders spend more on eggs than younger ones, and spending is highest in the 45-to-64 age groups. Households in the West spend 25 percent more, thanks to the higher spending of Hispanics on eggs.

The egg's image has improved somewhat due to efforts by the egg industry to tout the nutritional value of its product. Because of this marketing, spending on eggs is likely to remain stable or increase slightly.

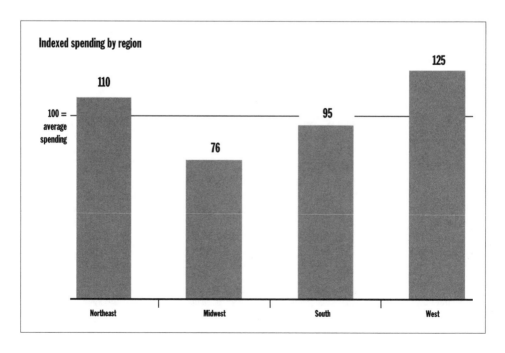

Indexed spending by region

Northeast	Midwest	South	West
110	76	95	125

100 = average spending

EGGS

Total household spending	$3,440,721,840
Average household spends	32.59

	average spending	best customers (index)	biggest customers (market share)
AGE OF HOUSEHOLDER			
Total households	**$32.59**	**100**	**100.0%**
Under age 25	20.42	63	4.5
Aged 25 to 34	28.48	87	16.5
Aged 35 to 44	35.17	108	25.1
Aged 45 to 54	38.29	117	21.5
Aged 55 to 64	37.34	115	13.4
Aged 65 to 74	33.11	102	11.7
Aged 75 or older	26.93	83	7.7
HOUSEHOLD INCOME			
Total households reporting income	**33.59**	**100**	**100.0**
Under $20,000	28.53	85	29.6
$20,000 to $29,999	35.62	106	15.5
$30,000 to $39,999	37.06	110	13.5
$40,000 to $49,999	33.09	99	9.2
$50,000 to $69,999	35.64	106	14.9
$70,000 or more	37.95	113	16.9
HOUSEHOLD TYPE			
Total households	**32.59**	**100**	**100.0**
Married couples	39.95	123	64.1
Married couples, no children	33.97	104	22.2
Married couples, with children	41.30	127	34.1
Oldest child under 6	35.61	109	5.6
Oldest child 6 to 17	40.49	124	18.1
Oldest child 18 or older	47.70	146	10.5
Single parent with child under 18	36.30	111	7.0
Single person	15.14	46	13.3
REGION			
Total households	**32.59**	**100**	**100.0**
Northeast	35.83	110	22.0
Midwest	24.78	76	18.2
South	31.05	95	33.2
West	40.61	125	26.5

Note: For definitions of best and biggest customers, see introduction or glossary.
Source: Calculations by New Strategist based on the 1997 Consumer Expenditure Survey

Fats and Oils

Best customers:
- Married couples with adult children
- Householders aged 45 to 64

Customer trends:
- Spending may decline because fewer households have time to cook and bake.

The best customers of fats and oils are older householders. Those aged 45 to 64 spend 13 to 19 percent more than the average household on this item. People in their fifties and sixties are more likely than younger adults to cook and bake at home, for which they need fats and oils. Married couples with adult children at home spend 49 percent more than average on this item, in part because their households are larger than average.

Spending on fats and oils may decline somewhat as busy two-earner couples with little time to cook replace older generations, who are more likely to cook from scratch.

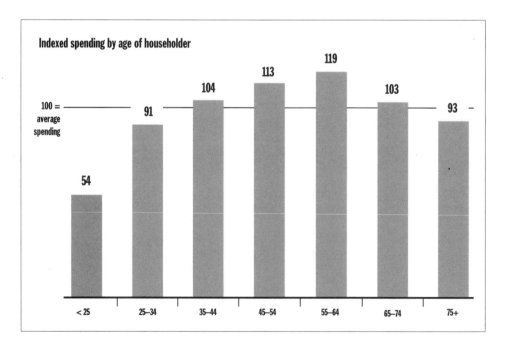

Indexed spending by age of householder

Age	Index
< 25	54
25–34	91
35–44	104
45–54	113
55–64	119
65–74	103
75+	93

100 = average spending

FATS AND OILS

Total household spending	$2,586,612,000
Average household spends	24.50

	average spending	best customers (index)	biggest customers (market share)
AGE OF HOUSEHOLDER			
Total households	**$24.50**	**100**	**100.0%**
Under age 25	13.35	54	3.9
Aged 25 to 34	22.29	91	17.2
Aged 35 to 44	25.59	104	24.3
Aged 45 to 54	27.63	113	20.7
Aged 55 to 64	29.24	119	13.9
Aged 65 to 74	25.12	103	11.8
Aged 75 or older	22.71	93	8.6
HOUSEHOLD INCOME			
Total households reporting income	**25.05**	**100**	**100.0**
Under $20,000	24.08	96	33.5
$20,000 to $29,999	24.81	99	14.5
$30,000 to $39,999	25.59	102	12.5
$40,000 to $49,999	21.58	86	8.1
$50,000 to $69,999	25.39	101	14.2
$70,000 or more	28.15	112	16.8
HOUSEHOLD TYPE			
Total households	**24.50**	**100**	**100.0**
Married couples	30.39	124	64.9
Married couples, no children	26.68	109	23.2
Married couples, with children	30.70	125	33.7
Oldest child under 6	27.15	111	5.7
Oldest child 6 to 17	29.25	119	17.4
Oldest child 18 or older	36.56	149	10.7
Single parent with child under 18	25.02	102	6.4
Single person	10.55	43	12.4
REGION			
Total households	**24.50**	**100**	**100.0**
Northeast	28.31	116	23.1
Midwest	18.05	74	17.6
South	25.96	106	37.0
West	25.76	105	22.3

Note: For definitions of best and biggest customers, see introduction or glossary.
Source: Calculations by New Strategist based on the 1997 Consumer Expenditure Survey

Fish and Seafood

Best customers:
- Married couples with school-aged or older children
- Householders aged 45 to 64
- Households in the Northeast and West

Customer trends:
- Spending will increase as an aging population tries to eat a healthier diet.

Fish is a healthy alternative to beef and has become a more important part of the American diet in recent years. Householders aged 45 to 64 spend 29 to 32 percent more than average on this item as they try to lower their fat intake. Married couples with school-aged or older children at home spend 36 to 55 percent more than the average household on fish and seafood, largely because they have more mouths to feed. Households in the Northeast and the West spend more on this item because of the greater availability of fish and seafood in those regions.

Spending will rise in the years ahead as aging boomers substitute fish for red meat in their diets.

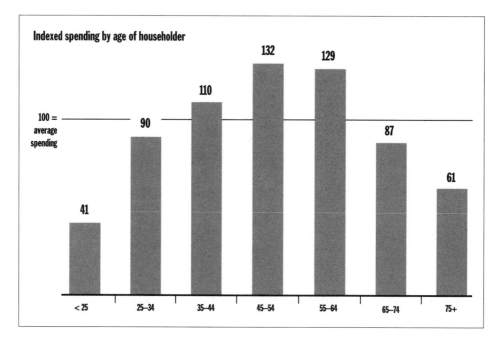

Indexed spending by age of householder

100 = average spending

< 25	25–34	35–44	45–54	55–64	65–74	75+
41	90	110	132	129	87	61

FISH AND SEAFOOD

Total household spending	$9,347,699,040
Average household spends	88.54

	average spending	best customers (index)	biggest customers (market share)
AGE OF HOUSEHOLDER			
Total households	**$88.54**	**100**	**100.0%**
Under age 25	36.56	41	2.9
Aged 25 to 34	80.04	90	17.1
Aged 35 to 44	97.44	110	25.6
Aged 45 to 54	116.59	132	24.1
Aged 55 to 64	114.06	129	15.0
Aged 65 to 74	77.32	87	10.0
Aged 75 or older	53.74	61	5.6
HOUSEHOLD INCOME			
Total households reporting income	**90.67**	**100**	**100.0**
Under $20,000	66.77	74	25.6
$20,000 to $29,999	87.73	97	14.1
$30,000 to $39,999	88.40	97	11.9
$40,000 to $49,999	75.81	84	7.8
$50,000 to $69,999	99.32	110	15.4
$70,000 or more	149.52	165	24.7
HOUSEHOLD TYPE			
Total households	**88.54**	**100**	**100.0**
Married couples	114.37	129	67.5
Married couples, no children	100.01	113	24.1
Married couples, with children	119.48	135	36.3
Oldest child under 6	95.12	107	5.5
Oldest child 6 to 17	120.63	136	19.8
Oldest child 18 or older	137.49	155	11.2
Single parent with child under 18	83.93	95	5.9
Single person	37.48	42	12.2
REGION			
Total households	**88.54**	**100**	**100.0**
Northeast	108.26	122	24.4
Midwest	57.98	65	15.6
South	84.85	96	33.4
West	.109.77	124	26.3

Note: For definitions of best and biggest customers, see introduction or glossary.
Source: Calculations by New Strategist based on the 1997 Consumer Expenditure Survey

Flour

Best customers:
- Householders aged 35 to 64
- Married couples with adult children

Customer trends:
- Spending will decline as younger generations with little time to cook replace older people in the population.

Among age groups, the best customers of flour are householders aged 35 to 64, spending 7 to 23 percent more than the average household on this item. Behind their higher spending is their larger household size. Married couples with adult children at home spend 48 percent more than average, while those with younger children spend 20 to 24 percent more—largely because these households have more mouths to feed.

Spending on flour is likely to decline as younger generations with little time to bake from scratch replace older people in the population.

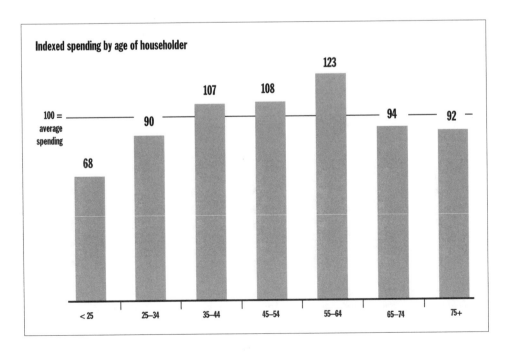

Indexed spending by age of householder

100 = average spending

< 25	25–34	35–44	45–54	55–64	65–74	75+
68	90	107	108	123	94	92

FLOUR

Total household spending	$928,013,040		
Average household spends	8.79		

	average spending	best customers (index)	biggest customers (market share)
AGE OF HOUSEHOLDER			
Total households	**$8.79**	**100**	**100.0%**
Under age 25	6.00	68	4.8
Aged 25 to 34	7.91	90	17.0
Aged 35 to 44	9.43	107	25.0
Aged 45 to 54	9.47	108	19.7
Aged 55 to 64	10.82	123	14.4
Aged 65 to 74	8.22	94	10.7
Aged 75 or older	8.12	92	8.6
HOUSEHOLD INCOME			
Total households reporting income	**8.94**	**100**	**100.0**
Under $20,000	9.18	103	35.8
$20,000 to $29,999	7.54	84	12.3
$30,000 to $39,999	9.41	105	12.9
$40,000 to $49,999	8.10	91	8.5
$50,000 to $69,999	9.67	108	15.2
$70,000 or more	8.82	99	14.7
HOUSEHOLD TYPE			
Total households	**8.79**	**100**	**100.0**
Married couples	10.82	123	64.4
Married couples, no children	8.20	93	19.9
Married couples, with children	11.36	129	34.7
Oldest child under 6	10.52	120	6.2
Oldest child 6 to 17	10.88	124	18.0
Oldest child 18 or older	13.00	148	10.6
Single parent with child under 18	9.18	104	6.6
Single person	3.58	41	11.7
REGION			
Total households	**8.79**	**100**	**100.0**
Northeast	8.94	102	20.3
Midwest	6.89	78	18.7
South	9.49	108	37.7
West	9.63	110	23.3

Note: For definitions of best and biggest customers, see introduction or glossary.
Source: Calculations by New Strategist based on the 1997 Consumer Expenditure Survey

Flour, Prepared Mixes

Best customers:
- Householders aged 35 to 54
- Married couples with children
- Households in the Midwest

Customer trends:
- Spending will rise as busy families look for convenient and time-saving products.

The best customers of prepared flour mixes are families with children. Prepared mixes—such as cake mixes—offer convenience and time savings, commodities of great importance to busy families. Householders aged 35 to 54 spend 22 to 27 percent more than average on prepared flour mixes. Married couples with children spend from 35 to 65 percent more than average. Households in the Midwest spend 21 percent more than average on this item.

Spending on prepared flour mixes will rise in the years ahead along with the number of busy two-earner couples. Competition from prepared desserts may limit spending in the category, however.

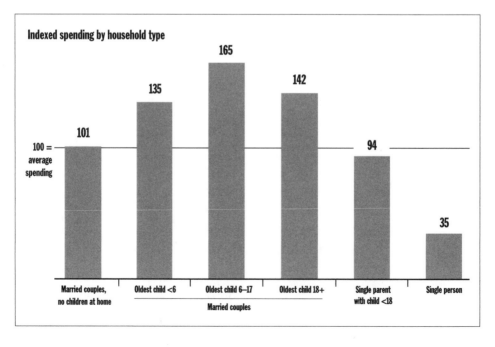

Indexed spending by household type

Married couples, no children at home	Oldest child <6	Oldest child 6–17	Oldest child 18+	Single parent with child <18	Single person
101	135	165	142	94	35

Married couples

100 = average spending

FLOUR, PREPARED MIXES

Total household spending	$1,587,863,040	
Average household spends	15.04	

	average spending	best customers (index)	biggest customers (market share)
AGE OF HOUSEHOLDER			
Total households	**$15.04**	**100**	**100.0%**
Under age 25	7.72	51	3.6
Aged 25 to 34	13.72	91	17.2
Aged 35 to 44	19.05	127	29.5
Aged 45 to 54	18.37	122	22.4
Aged 55 to 64	14.01	93	10.9
Aged 65 to 74	13.60	90	10.4
Aged 75 or older	10.73	71	6.6
HOUSEHOLD INCOME			
Total households reporting income	**16.51**	**100**	**100.0**
Under $20,000	11.77	71	24.8
$20,000 to $29,999	15.46	94	13.7
$30,000 to $39,999	15.24	92	11.3
$40,000 to $49,999	15.35	93	8.7
$50,000 to $69,999	19.56	118	16.6
$70,000 or more	26.75	162	24.2
HOUSEHOLD TYPE			
Total households	**15.04**	**100**	**100.0**
Married couples	20.61	137	71.7
Married couples, no children	15.19	101	21.6
Married couples, with children	22.94	153	41.0
Oldest child under 6	20.33	135	7.0
Oldest child 6 to 17	24.83	165	24.0
Oldest child 18 or older	21.33	142	10.2
Single parent with child under 18	14.08	94	5.9
Single person	5.22	35	10.0
REGION			
Total households	**15.04**	**100**	**100.0**
Northeast	13.05	87	17.3
Midwest	18.16	121	28.9
South	14.04	93	32.6
West	15.05	100	21.3

Note: For definitions of best and biggest customers, see introduction or glossary.
Source: Calculations by New Strategist based on the 1997 Consumer Expenditure Survey

Frankfurters

Hot dogs are a kid's food, which explains why married couples with school-aged children spend 50 percent more than the average household on hot dogs. Those with adult children at home spend 58 percent more than average on this item. Householders aged 35 to 44 spend 31 percent more than average on hot dogs because they are likely to have children at home.

The growing teen and young-adult population should stabilize spending on hot dogs despite health concerns about this product.

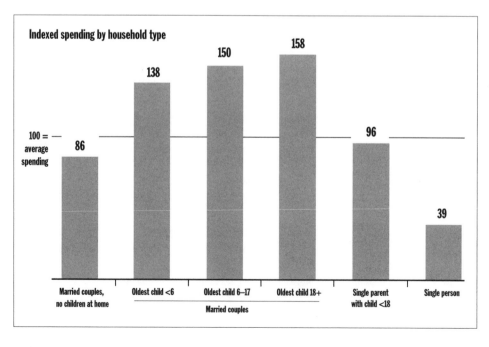

Indexed spending by household type

Married couples, no children at home	Oldest child <6	Oldest child 6–17	Oldest child 18+	Single parent with child <18	Single person
86	138	150	158	96	39

100 = average spending

Married couples

FRANKFURTERS

Total household spending $2,410,300,080
Average household spends   22.83

	average spending	best customers (index)	biggest customers (market share)
AGE OF HOUSEHOLDER			
Total households	**$22.83**	**100**	**100.0%**
Under age 25	13.24	58	4.1
Aged 25 to 34	21.71	95	17.9
Aged 35 to 44	29.95	131	30.5
Aged 45 to 54	26.96	118	21.6
Aged 55 to 64	23.47	103	12.0
Aged 65 to 74	19.12	84	9.6
Aged 75 or older	11.44	50	4.7
HOUSEHOLD INCOME			
Total households reporting income	**23.52**	**100**	**100.0**
Under $20,000	18.42	78	27.3
$20,000 to $29,999	19.74	84	12.3
$30,000 to $39,999	25.70	109	13.4
$40,000 to $49,999	28.41	121	11.3
$50,000 to $69,999	26.97	115	16.1
$70,000 or more	29.98	127	19.1
HOUSEHOLD TYPE			
Total households	**22.83**	**100**	**100.0**
Married couples	29.25	128	67.0
Married couples, no children	19.64	86	18.4
Married couples, with children	34.09	149	40.1
Oldest child under 6	31.50	138	7.1
Oldest child 6 to 17	34.20	150	21.8
Oldest child 18 or older	36.04	158	11.4
Single parent with child under 18	22.03	96	6.1
Single person	8.89	39	11.2
REGION			
Total households	**22.83**	**100**	**100.0**
Northeast	27.11	119	23.7
Midwest	22.47	98	23.5
South	22.41	98	34.2
West	19.95	87	18.6

Note: For definitions of best and biggest customers, see introduction or glossary.
Source: Calculations by New Strategist based on the 1997 Consumer Expenditure Survey

Frozen Meals

Best customers:
- Householders aged 35 to 64
- Married couples with adult children
- Households in the West

Customer trends:
- Spending is likely to decline because more grocery stores are offering fresh prepared meals as an alternative.

There are two markets for frozen meals—busy middle-aged consumers and older people who do not want to bother with cooking. The best customers of frozen meals are householders aged 35 to 64, spending 16 to 30 percent more than the average householder on this item. The oldest householders spend 17 percent more than average on frozen meals. Married couples with adult children at home spend 34 percent more than average, while households in the West spend 27 percent more.

Spending on frozen meals is likely to decline because of the growing number of alternatives—such as fresh prepared meals offered by many supermarkets.

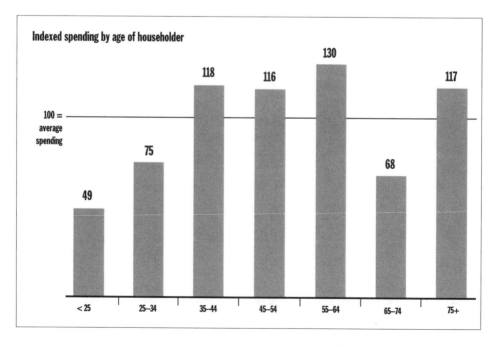

Indexed spending by age of householder

100 = average spending

< 25	25–34	35–44	45–54	55–64	65–74	75+
49	75	118	116	130	68	117

FROZEN MEALS

Total household spending	$2,188,590,480		
Average household spends	20.73		

	average spending	best customers (index)	biggest customers (market share)
AGE OF HOUSEHOLDER			
Total households	**$20.73**	**100**	**100.0%**
Under age 25	10.24	49	3.5
Aged 25 to 34	15.61	75	14.2
Aged 35 to 44	24.49	118	27.5
Aged 45 to 54	24.07	116	21.3
Aged 55 to 64	26.91	130	15.1
Aged 65 to 74	14.04	68	7.8
Aged 75 or older	24.17	117	10.9
HOUSEHOLD INCOME			
Total households reporting income	**21.74**	**100**	**100.0**
Under $20,000	15.77	73	25.3
$20,000 to $29,999	20.14	93	13.5
$30,000 to $39,999	24.31	112	13.7
$40,000 to $49,999	27.12	125	11.7
$50,000 to $69,999	23.62	109	15.3
$70,000 or more	28.52	131	19.6
HOUSEHOLD TYPE			
Total households	**20.73**	**100**	**100.0**
Married couples	22.29	108	56.2
Married couples, no children	19.38	93	20.0
Married couples, with children	24.29	117	31.5
Oldest child under 6	20.93	101	5.2
Oldest child 6 to 17	23.96	116	16.8
Oldest child 18 or older	27.75	134	9.6
Single parent with child under 18	18.11	87	5.5
Single person	18.64	90	25.8
REGION			
Total households	**20.73**	**100**	**100.0**
Northeast	16.49	80	15.9
Midwest	22.22	107	25.6
South	18.55	89	31.2
West	26.43	127	27.1

Note: For definitions of best and biggest customers, see introduction or glossary.
Source: Calculations by New Strategist based on the 1997 Consumer Expenditure Survey

Fruit-Flavored Drinks, Noncarbonated

Best customers:	• Householders aged 35 to 44
	• Married couples with children under 18
Customer trends:	• Spending might rise if manufacturers boosted the nutritional content of these drinks.

Children are the primary consumers of noncarbonated fruit-flavored drinks. Married couples with school-aged children spend more than twice as much as the average household on this item. Couples with preschoolers spend 50 percent more than average. Householders aged 25 to 44 spend 26 to 39 percent more than average, largely because their households include children.

Many parents serve fruit-flavored drinks to their children as an alternative to carbonated beverages. Spending on this item might increase if manufacturers boosted their nutritional content.

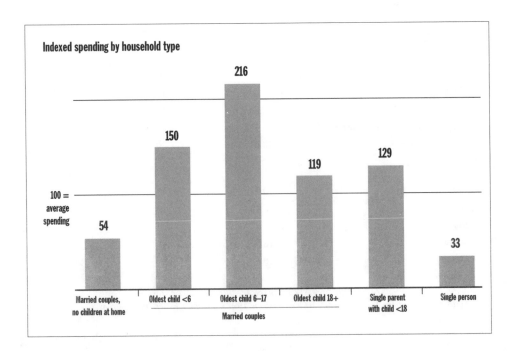

Indexed spending by household type

- Married couples, no children at home: 54
- Oldest child <6: 150
- Oldest child 6–17: 216
- Oldest child 18+: 119
- Single parent with child <18: 129
- Single person: 33

100 = average spending

Married couples

FRUIT-FLAVORED DRINKS, NONCARBONATED

Total household spending	$2,029,170,720
Average household spends	19.22

	average spending	best customers (index)	biggest customers (market share)
AGE OF HOUSEHOLDER			
Total households	**$19.22**	**100**	**100.0%**
Under age 25	22.37	116	8.3
Aged 25 to 34	24.17	126	23.7
Aged 35 to 44	26.73	139	32.4
Aged 45 to 54	19.78	103	18.9
Aged 55 to 64	15.46	80	9.4
Aged 65 to 74	8.62	45	5.1
Aged 75 or older	5.06	26	2.5
HOUSEHOLD INCOME			
Total households reporting income	**19.81**	**100**	**100.0**
Under $20,000	14.14	71	24.9
$20,000 to $29,999	20.39	103	15.0
$30,000 to $39,999	15.31	77	9.4
$40,000 to $49,999	23.35	118	11.0
$50,000 to $69,999	26.01	131	18.4
$70,000 or more	27.60	139	20.8
HOUSEHOLD TYPE			
Total households	**19.22**	**100**	**100.0**
Married couples	24.36	127	66.3
Married couples, no children	10.30	54	11.4
Married couples, with children	33.88	176	47.4
Oldest child under 6	28.74	150	7.7
Oldest child 6 to 17	41.52	216	31.4
Oldest child 18 or older	22.79	119	8.5
Single parent with child under 18	24.84	129	8.1
Single person	6.26	33	9.4
REGION			
Total households	**19.22**	**100**	**100.0**
Northeast	17.37	90	18.1
Midwest	14.81	77	18.4
South	21.52	112	39.1
West	22.08	115	24.4

Note: For definitions of best and biggest customers, see introduction or glossary.
Source: Calculations by New Strategist based on the 1997 Consumer Expenditure Survey

Fruit Juice, Canned and Bottled

Best customers: • Married couples with children under 18

Customer trends: • Stable spending while the children of boomers are still at home.

The best customers of canned and bottled fruit juice are parents with children. Married couples with school-aged children spend 47 percent more than the average household on this item, while those with children under age 6 spend 43 percent more than average. Householders aged 35 to 54 spend 15 percent more than average because they are likely to have children at home.

Spending on canned and bottled juice is likely to remain stable while the baby-boom generation is raising children. Spending may decline after the children of boomers leave home.

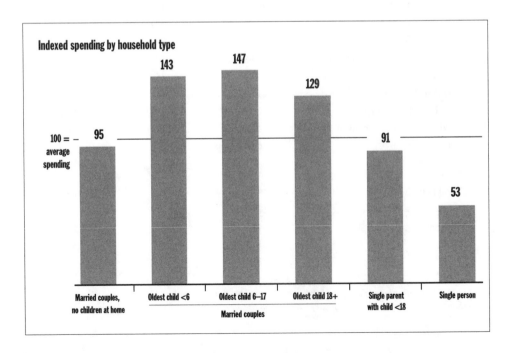

Indexed spending by household type

	143	147			
95			129	91	
100 = average spending					53

Married couples, no children at home	Oldest child <6	Oldest child 6–17	Oldest child 18+	Single parent with child <18	Single person
	Married couples				

FRUIT JUICE, CANNED AND BOTTLED

Total household spending	$5,007,469,680		
Average household spends	47.43		

	average spending	best customers (index)	biggest customers (market share)
AGE OF HOUSEHOLDER			
Total households	**$47.43**	**100**	**100.0%**
Under age 25	30.53	64	4.6
Aged 25 to 34	47.94	101	19.1
Aged 35 to 44	54.50	115	26.7
Aged 45 to 54	54.63	115	21.1
Aged 55 to 64	45.83	97	11.3
Aged 65 to 74	44.55	94	10.8
Aged 75 or older	35.10	74	6.9
HOUSEHOLD INCOME			
Total households reporting income	**48.26**	**100**	**100.0**
Under $20,000	38.52	80	27.8
$20,000 to $29,999	35.96	75	10.9
$30,000 to $39,999	42.90	89	10.9
$40,000 to $49,999	52.32	108	10.1
$50,000 to $69,999	54.85	114	16.0
$70,000 or more	77.18	160	23.9
HOUSEHOLD TYPE			
Total households	**47.43**	**100**	**100.0**
Married couples	59.06	125	65.1
Married couples, no children	44.94	95	20.2
Married couples, with children	67.00	141	38.0
Oldest child under 6	67.73	143	7.3
Oldest child 6 to 17	69.62	147	21.4
Oldest child 18 or older	61.13	129	9.3
Single parent with child under 18	43.14	91	5.7
Single person	25.28	53	15.3
REGION			
Total households	**47.43**	**100**	**100.0**
Northeast	55.24	116	23.3
Midwest	37.26	79	18.8
South	47.37	100	34.8
West	51.49	109	23.1

Note: For definitions of best and biggest customers, see introduction or glossary.
Source: Calculations by New Strategist based on the 1997 Consumer Expenditure Survey

Fruit Juice, Fresh

Best customers:
- Married couples with school-aged or older children
- Householders aged 35 to 54
- Households in the Northeast

Customer trends:
- Spending should rise as the population ages.

As the population ages, juice spending may shift away from canned and bottled toward fresh juice. The best customers of fresh juice are older than the best customers of bottled or canned juice. Householders spanning the ages from 35 to 74 spend more than the average householder on this item. Married couples with school-aged or older children spend 40 to 41 percent more than average on fresh fruit juice, largely because those households are larger. Households in the Northeast spend 33 percent more on fresh juice.

Spending on fresh fruit juice may rise as the population ages. Older householders will buy less of the canned and bottled juices preferred by children and more of the fresh juice preferred by adults.

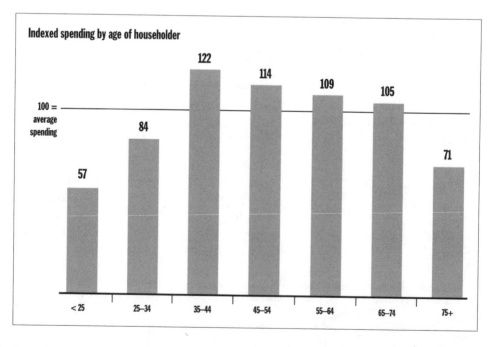

Indexed spending by age of householder

< 25	25–34	35–44	45–54	55–64	65–74	75+
57	84	122	114	109	105	71

100 = average spending

FRUIT JUICE, FRESH

Total household spending $2,092,516,320
Average household spends   19.82

	average spending	best customers (index)	biggest customers (market share)
AGE OF HOUSEHOLDER			
Total households	**$19.82**	**100**	**100.0%**
Under age 25	11.21	57	4.0
Aged 25 to 34	16.59	84	15.8
Aged 35 to 44	24.20	122	28.4
Aged 45 to 54	22.61	114	20.9
Aged 55 to 64	21.60	109	12.7
Aged 65 to 74	20.76	105	12.0
Aged 75 or older	14.02	71	6.6
HOUSEHOLD INCOME			
Total households reporting income	**20.43**	**100**	**100.0**
Under $20,000	14.70	72	25.1
$20,000 to $29,999	15.77	77	11.3
$30,000 to $39,999	23.79	116	14.2
$40,000 to $49,999	19.06	93	8.7
$50,000 to $69,999	22.88	112	15.7
$70,000 or more	33.16	162	24.3
HOUSEHOLD TYPE			
Total households	**19.82**	**100**	**100.0**
Married couples	23.90	121	63.1
Married couples, no children	19.10	96	20.6
Married couples, with children	27.12	137	36.8
Oldest child under 6	24.57	124	6.4
Oldest child 6 to 17	27.75	140	20.4
Oldest child 18 or older	27.97	141	10.1
Single parent with child under 18	20.15	102	6.4
Single person	12.92	65	18.7
REGION			
Total households	**19.82**	**100**	**100.0**
Northeast	26.45	133	26.7
Midwest	17.23	87	20.8
South	15.83	80	27.9
West	22.94	116	24.6

Note: For definitions of best and biggest customers, see introduction or glossary.
Source: Calculations by New Strategist based on the 1997 Consumer Expenditure Survey

Fruit Juice, Frozen

Best customers:
- Married couples with children under 18
- Households in the West

Customer trends:
- Spending is likely to remain stable because frozen juice is popular among children as well as adults.

The best customers of frozen fruit juice are parents with young children. Married couples with preschoolers spend 82 percent more than the average household on frozen fruit juice, while those with school-aged children spend 60 percent more. Frozen fruit juice is not just for kids, however. Householders spanning the ages from 25 to 64 spend more than average on this item. Households in the West spend 32 percent more than average on frozen fruit juice, in part because of the above-average spending by the region's large Hispanic population.

Spending on frozen fruit juice is likely to remain stable because of the popularity of this item among all age groups.

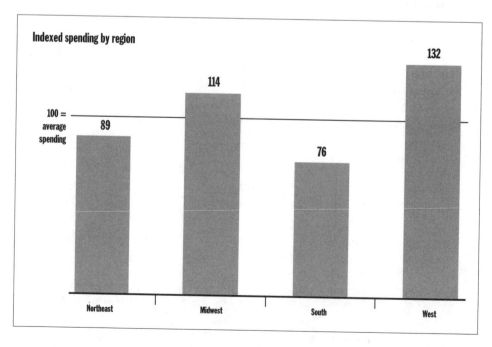

Indexed spending by region

100 = average spending

Northeast 89
Midwest 114
South 76
West 132

FRUIT JUICE, FROZEN

Total household spending	$1,373,543,760
Average household spends	13.01

	average spending	best customers (index)	biggest customers (market share)
AGE OF HOUSEHOLDER			
Total households	**$13.01**	**100**	**100.0%**
Under age 25	5.30	41	2.9
Aged 25 to 34	13.53	104	19.6
Aged 35 to 44	15.88	122	28.4
Aged 45 to 54	13.76	106	19.4
Aged 55 to 64	14.90	115	13.4
Aged 65 to 74	12.28	94	10.8
Aged 75 or older	8.38	64	6.0
HOUSEHOLD INCOME			
Total households reporting income	**13.45**	**100**	**100.0**
Under $20,000	8.79	65	22.8
$20,000 to $29,999	11.77	88	12.8
$30,000 to $39,999	11.82	88	10.7
$40,000 to $49,999	15.95	119	11.1
$50,000 to $69,999	19.05	142	19.9
$70,000 or more	19.94	148	22.2
HOUSEHOLD TYPE			
Total households	**13.01**	**100**	**100.0**
Married couples	17.26	133	69.4
Married couples, no children	13.17	101	21.6
Married couples, with children	20.07	154	41.5
Oldest child under 6	23.68	182	9.4
Oldest child 6 to 17	20.85	160	23.3
Oldest child 18 or older	15.53	119	8.6
Single parent with child under 18	12.37	95	6.0
Single person	5.93	46	13.1
REGION			
Total households	**13.01**	**100**	**100.0**
Northeast	11.53	89	17.7
Midwest	14.84	114	27.3
South	9.91	76	26.6
West	17.23	132	28.1

Note: For definitions of best and biggest customers, see introduction or glossary.
Source: Calculations by New Strategist based on the 1997 Consumer Expenditure Survey

Fruit, Canned

Best customers:
- Married couples with school-aged or older children
- Householders aged 45 or older

Customer trends:
- Spending is likely to decline as younger generations buy fresh rather than canned fruit.

The best customers of canned fruit are older householders. Spending on this item is well above average among householders aged 45 or older, who account for 59 percent of the market. Married couples with school-aged or adult children at home spend 34 to 51 percent more than average on this item, while those without children at home (most of them older) spend 29 percent more than average.

Canned fruit is losing popularity as fresh fruit becomes more widely available year-round and as supermarkets prepare fresh fruit for customers. Spending on canned fruit is likely to decline as younger generations who prefer fresh fruit replace older canned-fruit buyers.

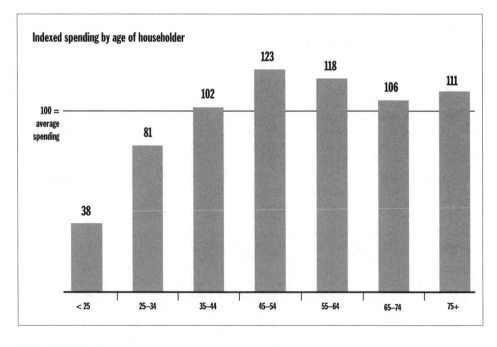

Indexed spending by age of householder

100 = average spending

< 25	25–34	35–44	45–54	55–64	65–74	75+
38	81	102	123	118	106	111

FRUIT, CANNED

Total household spending	$1,474,896,720	
Average household spends	13.97	

	average spending	best customers (index)	biggest customers (market share)
AGE OF HOUSEHOLDER			
Total households	**$13.97**	**100**	**100.0%**
Under age 25	5.27	38	2.7
Aged 25 to 34	11.29	81	15.2
Aged 35 to 44	14.24	102	23.7
Aged 45 to 54	17.14	123	22.5
Aged 55 to 64	16.47	118	13.8
Aged 65 to 74	14.86	106	12.2
Aged 75 or older	15.45	111	10.3
HOUSEHOLD INCOME			
Total households reporting income	**14.20**	**100**	**100.0**
Under $20,000	9.82	69	24.1
$20,000 to $29,999	12.62	89	13.0
$30,000 to $39,999	15.85	112	13.6
$40,000 to $49,999	16.19	114	10.7
$50,000 to $69,999	15.56	110	15.4
$70,000 or more	21.33	150	22.5
HOUSEHOLD TYPE			
Total households	**13.97**	**100**	**100.0**
Married couples	18.75	134	70.2
Married couples, no children	18.07	129	27.6
Married couples, with children	18.97	136	36.5
Oldest child under 6	17.00	122	6.3
Oldest child 6 to 17	18.73	134	19.5
Oldest child 18 or older	21.10	151	10.9
Single parent with child under 18	9.65	69	4.3
Single person	7.19	51	14.8
REGION			
Total households	**13.97**	**100**	**100.0**
Northeast	13.46	96	19.2
Midwest	14.83	106	25.4
South	12.29	88	30.7
West	16.13	115	24.5

Note: For definitions of best and biggest customers, see introduction or glossary.
Source: Calculations by New Strategist based on the 1997 Consumer Expenditure Survey

Fruit, Fresh

Best customers:
- Married couples with adult children
- Householders aged 45 to 64

Customer trends:
- Spending will grow as younger generations, who prefer fresh fruit, replace older buyers of canned fruit.

Americans are eating more fruit than they once did, largely because it is now widely available year-round. The best customers of fresh fruit are married couples with adult children at home, who spend 44 percent more than average, in part because these households are larger. Couples with school-aged children spend 28 percent more than average. Householders aged 45 to 64 spend 12 to 15 percent more than average on fresh fruit.

Spending on fresh fruit will rise as younger generations, who prefer fresh to canned fruit, replace older people in the population. In addition, the sliced pineapples, melons, and other fruits offered by a growing number of supermarkets will boost spending on fruit by making it easier to eat.

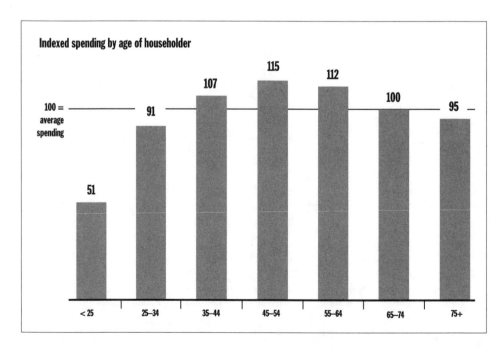

Indexed spending by age of householder

100 = average spending

< 25	25–34	35–44	45–54	55–64	65–74	75+
51	91	107	115	112	100	95

FRUIT, FRESH

Total household spending $15,886,020,720
Average household spends   150.47

	average spending	best customers (index)	biggest customers (market share)
AGE OF HOUSEHOLDER			
Total households	**$150.47**	**100**	**100.0%**
Under age 25	76.78	51	3.6
Aged 25 to 34	137.19	91	17.2
Aged 35 to 44	161.39	107	25.0
Aged 45 to 54	173.73	115	21.2
Aged 55 to 64	168.56	112	13.1
Aged 65 to 74	151.15	100	11.5
Aged 75 or older	142.95	95	8.8
HOUSEHOLD INCOME			
Total households reporting income	**154.00**	**100**	**100.0**
Under $20,000	107.14	70	24.2
$20,000 to $29,999	147.45	96	14.0
$30,000 to $39,999	153.64	100	12.2
$40,000 to $49,999	152.87	99	9.3
$50,000 to $69,999	196.58	128	17.9
$70,000 or more	226.20	147	22.0
HOUSEHOLD TYPE			
Total households	**150.47**	**100**	**100.0**
Married couples	189.28	126	65.8
Married couples, no children	178.78	119	25.4
Married couples, with children	194.23	129	34.7
Oldest child under 6	169.48	113	5.8
Oldest child 6 to 17	193.34	128	18.7
Oldest child 18 or older	216.68	144	10.4
Single parent with child under 18	131.25	87	5.5
Single person	83.24	55	15.9
REGION			
Total households	**150.47**	**100**	**100.0**
Northeast	168.91	112	22.4
Midwest	146.13	97	23.2
South	130.66	87	30.3
West	169.73	113	24.0

Note: For definitions of best and biggest customers, see introduction or glossary.
Source: Calculations by New Strategist based on the 1997 Consumer Expenditure Survey

Ham

Best customers:
- Married couples with school-aged or older children
- Householders aged 45 to 64

Customer trends:
- Stable spending because boomers are less likely than older Americans to cook meals at home.

The best customers of ham are householders aged 45 to 64. They spend 32 percent more than average on this item. Married couples with adult children at home spend 66 percent more than the average household on ham, while those with school-aged children spend 41 percent more than average. Behind the higher spending of couples with children is their larger household size.

The baby-boom generation is now filling the age groups that spend the most on ham. Nevertheless, spending on ham will not change much because boomers are less likely than older Americans to cook meals at home.

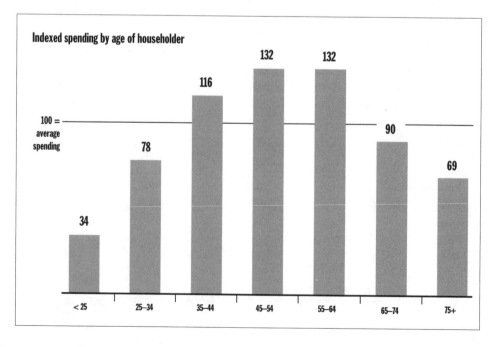

Indexed spending by age of householder

34	78	116	132	132	90	69
< 25	25–34	35–44	45–54	55–64	65–74	75+

100 = average spending

HAM

Total household spending	$3,935,873,280
Average household spends	37.28

	average spending	best customers (index)	biggest customers (market share)
AGE OF HOUSEHOLDER			
Total households	**$37.28**	**100**	**100.0%**
Under age 25	12.84	34	2.4
Aged 25 to 34	29.01	78	14.7
Aged 35 to 44	43.33	116	27.0
Aged 45 to 54	49.18	132	24.2
Aged 55 to 64	49.20	132	15.4
Aged 65 to 74	33.39	90	10.3
Aged 75 or older	25.78	69	6.4
HOUSEHOLD INCOME			
Total households reporting income	**38.45**	**100**	**100.0**
Under $20,000	29.27	76	26.5
$20,000 to $29,999	34.93	91	13.3
$30,000 to $39,999	36.89	96	11.7
$40,000 to $49,999	42.85	111	10.4
$50,000 to $69,999	45.33	118	16.5
$70,000 or more	53.82	140	20.9
HOUSEHOLD TYPE			
Total households	**37.28**	**100**	**100.0**
Married couples	49.85	134	69.9
Married couples, no children <18	44.20	119	25.3
Married couples, with children <18	52.43	141	37.8
Oldest child under 6	41.38	111	5.7
Oldest child 6 to 17	52.38	141	20.4
Oldest child 18+	61.74	166	11.9
Single parent with child <18	35.03	94	5.9
Single person	12.70	34	9.8
REGION			
Total households	**37.28**	**100**	**100.0**
Northeast	36.28	97	19.4
Midwest	34.39	92	22.0
South	41.12	110	38.5
West	35.27	95	20.1

Note: For definitions of best and biggest customers, see introduction or glossary.
Source: Calculations by New Strategist based on the 1997 Consumer Expenditure Survey

Ice Cream and Related Products

Best customers:
- Married couples with children

Customer trends:
- The growing number of families with children will boost spending.

Families with children are the best customers of ice cream and related products. Some of this higher spending is due to the demands of children, but adults also love ice cream. Householders spanning the ages from 35 to 74 spend more than the average household on ice cream. Married couples with preschoolers spend 37 percent more than average, while couples with school-aged children spend 45 percent more and those with adult children at home spend 49 percent more.

The growing number of school-aged children should boost spending on ice cream. In addition, after years of trying to lower their fat intake, Americans are once again letting themselves indulge a bit. This change of heart should spur spending on ice cream.

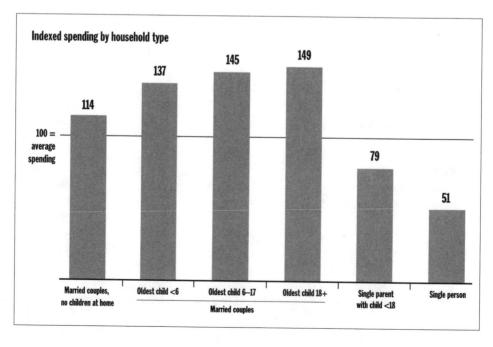

Indexed spending by household type

114	137	145	149	79	51

100 = average spending

Married couples, no children at home | Oldest child <6 | Oldest child 6–17 | Oldest child 18+ | Single parent with child <18 | Single person

Married couples

ICE CREAM AND RELATED PRODUCTS

Total household spending	$5,586,026,160
Average household spends	52.91

	average spending	best customers (index)	biggest customers (market share)
AGE OF HOUSEHOLDER			
Total households	**$52.91**	**100**	**100.0%**
Under age 25	24.45	46	3.3
Aged 25 to 34	44.52	84	15.9
Aged 35 to 44	63.18	119	27.8
Aged 45 to 54	60.40	114	20.9
Aged 55 to 64	60.52	114	13.3
Aged 65 to 74	57.32	108	12.4
Aged 75 or older	38.82	73	6.8
HOUSEHOLD INCOME			
Total households reporting income	**54.45**	**100**	**100.0**
Under $20,000	36.73	67	23.5
$20,000 to $29,999	48.51	89	13.0
$30,000 to $39,999	50.67	93	11.4
$40,000 to $49,999	56.39	104	9.7
$50,000 to $69,999	69.80	128	18.0
$70,000 or more	87.19	160	23.9
HOUSEHOLD TYPE			
Total households	**52.91**	**100**	**100.0**
Married couples	69.72	132	68.9
Married couples, no children	60.31	114	24.3
Married couples, with children	76.25	144	38.7
Oldest child under 6	72.59	137	7.1
Oldest child 6 to 17	76.54	145	21.0
Oldest child 18 or older	78.74	149	10.7
Single parent with child under 18	41.81	79	5.0
Single person	27.12	51	14.7
REGION			
Total households	**52.91**	**100**	**100.0**
Northeast	54.95	104	20.7
Midwest	48.88	92	22.1
South	49.36	93	32.5
West	61.05	115	24.5

Note: For definitions of best and biggest customers, see introduction or glossary.
Source: Calculations by New Strategist based on the 1997 Consumer Expenditure Survey

Jams, Preserves, and Other Sweets

Best customers:	• Married couples with children
Customer trends:	• Spending may increase slightly as the number of school-aged children rises.

Married couples with preschoolers spend 47 percent more than the average household on jams, preserves, and other sweets, while those with school-aged children spend 50 percent more. Peanut butter and jelly sandwiches are one reason why these households spend more. Married couples with adult children at home spend 33 percent more than average on this item. The higher spending of these households is due to their larger household size.

Spending may increase slightly as the number of school-aged children rises during the next few years.

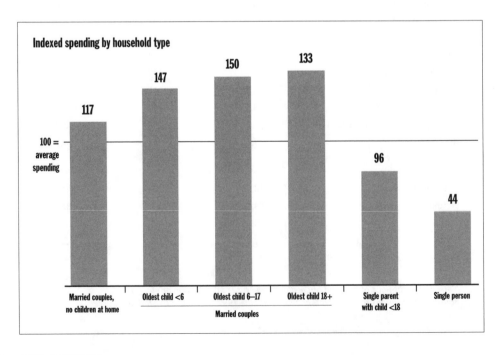

Indexed spending by household type

117	147	150	133	96	44

100 = average spending

Married couples, no children at home | Oldest child <6 | Oldest child 6–17 | Oldest child 18+ | Single parent with child <18 | Single person

Married couples

JAMS, PRESERVES, AND OTHER SWEETS

Total household spending	$2,389,184,880		
Average household spends	22.63		

	average spending	best customers (index)	biggest customers (market share)
AGE OF HOUSEHOLDER			
Total households	**$22.63**	**100**	**100.0%**
Under age 25	8.69	38	2.7
Aged 25 to 34	21.34	94	17.8
Aged 35 to 44	26.74	118	27.5
Aged 45 to 54	26.17	116	21.2
Aged 55 to 64	26.34	116	13.6
Aged 65 to 74	23.21	103	11.8
Aged 75 or older	14.61	65	6.0
HOUSEHOLD INCOME			
Total households reporting income	**23.32**	**100**	**100.0**
Under $20,000	16.29	70	24.3
$20,000 to $29,999	17.69	76	11.1
$30,000 to $39,999	27.77	119	14.6
$40,000 to $49,999	25.26	108	10.1
$50,000 to $69,999	29.08	125	17.5
$70,000 or more	34.03	146	21.8
HOUSEHOLD TYPE			
Total households	**22.63**	**100**	**100.0**
Married couples	30.23	134	69.9
Married couples, no children	26.59	117	25.1
Married couples, with children	32.74	145	38.9
Oldest child under 6	33.26	147	7.6
Oldest child 6 to 17	33.84	150	21.8
Oldest child 18 or older	30.10	133	9.6
Single parent with child under 18	21.68	96	6.0
Single person	9.99	44	12.7
REGION			
Total households	**22.63**	**100**	**100.0**
Northeast	21.92	97	19.3
Midwest	23.87	105	25.2
South	21.54	95	33.2
West	23.66	105	22.2

Note: For definitions of best and biggest customers, see introduction or glossary.
Source: Calculations by New Strategist based on the 1997 Consumer Expenditure Survey

Lunch Meats (Cold Cuts)

Best customers: • Married couples with school-aged or adult children

Customer trends: • If people buy lunch from restaurants and carry-outs more often, spending on lunch meats will decline.

Married couples with adult children at home spend 63 percent more than the average household on lunch meats. Behind this higher spending is their larger household size. Married couples with school-aged children spend 38 percent more than average on this item. Spending on lunch meats is above average for household-ers spanning the ages from 35 to 64.

Spending on lunch meats should remain stable unless a strong economy encourages more people to buy lunches from restaurants or carry-outs—in which case spending on lunch meats would decline.

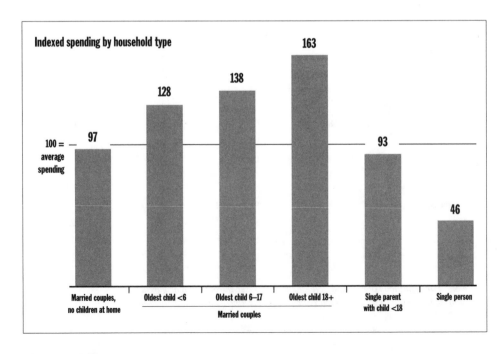

Indexed spending by household type

97	128	138	163	93	46
Married couples, no children at home	Oldest child <6	Oldest child 6–17	Oldest child 18+	Single parent with child <18	Single person

100 = average spending

Married couples

LUNCH MEATS (COLD CUTS)

Total household spending $6,920,506,800
Average household spends 65.55

	average spending	best customers (index)	biggest customers (market share)
AGE OF HOUSEHOLDER			
Total households	**$65.55**	**100**	**100.0%**
Under age 25	34.55	53	3.7
Aged 25 to 34	58.35	89	16.8
Aged 35 to 44	80.68	123	28.6
Aged 45 to 54	72.80	111	20.3
Aged 55 to 64	75.36	115	13.4
Aged 65 to 74	65.62	100	11.5
Aged 75 or older	42.31	65	6.0
HOUSEHOLD INCOME			
Total households reporting income	**67.48**	**100**	**100.0**
Under $20,000	49.12	73	25.4
$20,000 to $29,999	62.12	92	13.4
$30,000 to $39,999	67.14	99	12.2
$40,000 to $49,999	78.48	116	10.9
$50,000 to $69,999	81.58	121	17.0
$70,000 or more	93.18	138	20.6
HOUSEHOLD TYPE			
Total households	**65.55**	**100**	**100.0**
Married couples	82.37	126	65.7
Married couples, no children	63.68	97	20.7
Married couples, with children	93.11	142	38.2
Oldest child under 6	83.68	128	6.6
Oldest child 6 to 17	90.14	138	20.0
Oldest child 18 or older	106.94	163	11.7
Single parent with child under 18	60.74	93	5.8
Single person	30.29	46	13.3
REGION			
Total households	**65.55**	**100**	**100.0**
Northeast	74.40	114	22.7
Midwest	74.30	113	27.1
South	56.66	86	30.2
West	62.00	95	20.1

Note: For definitions of best and biggest customers, see introduction or glossary.
Source: Calculations by New Strategist based on the 1997 Consumer Expenditure Survey

Margarine

Best customers:
- Married couples with adult children
- Householders aged 55 to 64

Customer trends:
- Spending should increase as growing numbers of older householders try to lower their cholesterol.

Spending on margarine peaks among householders aged 55 to 64. These householders spend 27 percent more on margarine than the average household, substituting it for butter because of health concerns. Married couples with adult children at home are the best customers of margarine. Spending by these families is 58 percent higher than that of the average household.

Spending on margarine is likely to rise as the aging population becomes increasingly health conscious—particularly with new margarines entering the market which promise to lower cholesterol.

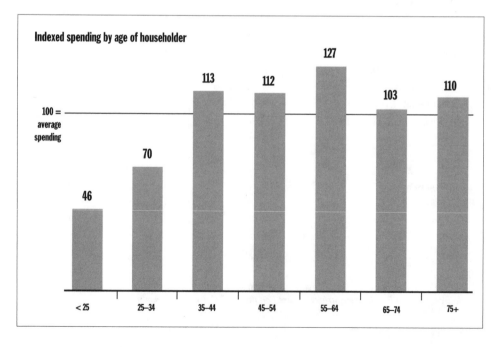

Indexed spending by age of householder

< 25	25–34	35–44	45–54	55–64	65–74	75+
46	70	113	112	127	103	110

100 = average spending

MARGARINE

Total household spending $1,239,462,240
Average household spends 11.74

	average spending	best customers (index)	biggest customers (market share)
AGE OF HOUSEHOLDER			
Total households	**$11.74**	**100**	**100.0%**
Under age 25	5.45	46	3.3
Aged 25 to 34	8.27	70	13.3
Aged 35 to 44	13.30	113	26.4
Aged 45 to 54	13.13	112	20.5
Aged 55 to 64	14.91	127	14.8
Aged 65 to 74	12.09	103	11.8
Aged 75 or older	12.91	110	10.2
HOUSEHOLD INCOME			
Total households reporting income	**12.25**	**100**	**100.0**
Under $20,000	10.68	87	30.4
$20,000 to $29,999	11.32	92	13.5
$30,000 to $39,999	12.98	106	13.0
$40,000 to $49,999	11.86	97	9.1
$50,000 to $69,999	11.74	96	13.5
$70,000 or more	16.54	135	20.2
HOUSEHOLD TYPE			
Total households	**11.74**	**100**	**100.0**
Married couples	14.84	126	66.1
Married couples, no children	13.99	119	25.4
Married couples, with children	14.65	125	33.5
Oldest child under 6	10.87	93	4.8
Oldest child 6 to 17	14.28	122	17.7
Oldest child 18 or older	18.57	158	11.4
Single parent with child under 18	11.22	96	6.0
Single person	5.44	46	13.3
REGION			
Total households	**11.74**	**100**	**100.0**
Northeast	11.08	94	18.9
Midwest	12.76	109	26.0
South	11.63	99	34.6
West	11.41	97	20.6

Note: For definitions of best and biggest customers, see introduction or glossary.
Source: Calculations by New Strategist based on the 1997 Consumer Expenditure Survey

Milk, Fresh

Best customers: • Married couples with children

Customer trends: • Spending is likely to decline as the population ages.

Not surprisingly, married couples with children are the best customers of milk. Those with school-aged children spend 55 percent more than the average household on this item, while those with adult children at home spend 49 percent more. Householders aged 35 to 44 spend 28 percent more than average on milk because most have children at home.

Spending on milk is likely to decline as the population ages and fewer households include children. The milk industry's efforts to promote its product to adults may limit the decline somewhat, but the campaigns are unlikely to reverse the trend.

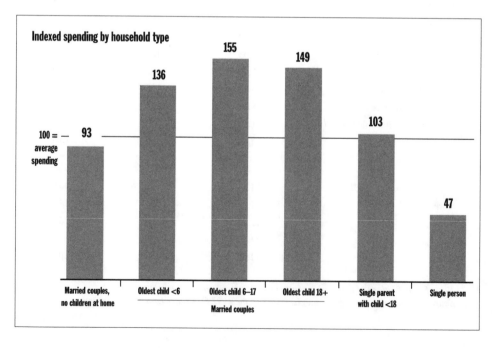

Indexed spending by household type

93	136	155	149	103	47

100 = average spending

Married couples, no children at home | Oldest child <6 | Oldest child 6–17 | Oldest child 18+ | Single parent with child <18 | Single person

Married couples

MILK, FRESH

Total household spending	$12,540,317,280
Average household spends	118.78

	average spending	best customers (index)	biggest customers (market share)
AGE OF HOUSEHOLDER			
Total households	**$118.78**	**100**	**100.0%**
Under age 25	73.01	61	4.4
Aged 25 to 34	115.76	97	18.4
Aged 35 to 44	152.57	128	29.9
Aged 45 to 54	126.85	107	19.6
Aged 55 to 64	112.93	95	11.1
Aged 65 to 74	110.23	93	10.6
Aged 75 or older	83.44	70	6.5
HOUSEHOLD INCOME			
Total households reporting income	**124.37**	**100**	**100.0**
Under $20,000	93.84	75	26.3
$20,000 to $29,999	122.71	99	14.4
$30,000 to $39,999	133.19	107	13.1
$40,000 to $49,999	141.68	114	10.7
$50,000 to $69,999	141.81	114	16.0
$70,000 or more	158.01	127	19.0
HOUSEHOLD TYPE			
Total households	**118.78**	**100**	**100.0**
Married couples	151.59	128	66.7
Married couples, no children	110.36	93	19.8
Married couples, with children	177.48	149	40.2
Oldest child under 6	161.36	136	7.0
Oldest child 6 to 17	184.55	155	22.6
Oldest child 18 or older	176.71	149	10.7
Single parent with child under 18	122.78	103	6.5
Single person	55.53	47	13.4
REGION			
Total households	**118.78**	**100**	**100.0**
Northeast	119.47	101	20.1
Midwest	119.28	100	24.0
South	112.20	94	33.0
West	128.02	108	22.9

Note: For definitions of best and biggest customers, see introduction or glossary.
Source: Calculations by New Strategist based on the 1997 Consumer Expenditure Survey

Nondairy Cream and Imitation Milk

Best customers:

- Married couples without children
- Married couples with adult children
- Householders aged 55 to 74

Customer trends:

- A spending decline is likely as younger generations, who drink much less coffee, replace older coffee drinkers.

Older householders are the best customers of nondairy creamers. Those aged 55 to 74 spend 20 to 29 percent more than the average household on this item. Married couples with adult children at home spend 44 percent more than average on nondairy cream and imitation milk. Couples without children at home, most of whom are older, spend 39 percent more than average.

Nondairy cream and imitation milk have never caught on with younger consumers. One reason for this disinterest is that younger generations aren't as fond of coffee, which is a primary use of nondairy cream. Spending on nondairy cream and imitation milk is likely to decline as younger generations replace older coffee drinkers.

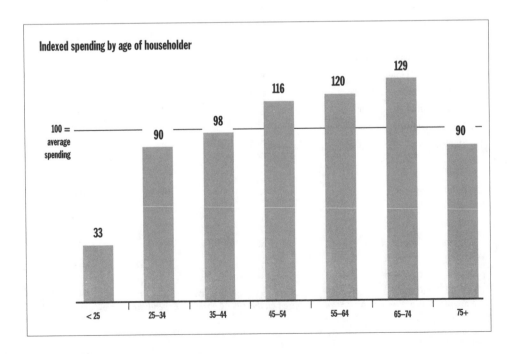

Indexed spending by age of householder

100 = average spending

| < 25 | 25–34 | 35–44 | 45–54 | 55–64 | 65–74 | 75+ |
| 33 | 90 | 98 | 116 | 120 | 129 | 90 |

NONDAIRY CREAM AND IMITATION MILK

Total household spending	$897,396,000		
Average household spends	8.50		

	average spending	best customers (index)	biggest customers (market share)
AGE OF HOUSEHOLDER			
Total households	**$8.50**	**100**	**100.0%**
Under age 25	2.78	33	2.3
Aged 25 to 34	7.63	90	16.9
Aged 35 to 44	8.35	98	22.9
Aged 45 to 54	9.83	116	21.2
Aged 55 to 64	10.20	120	14.0
Aged 65 to 74	10.97	129	14.8
Aged 75 or older	7.63	90	8.4
HOUSEHOLD INCOME			
Total households reporting income	**8.56**	**100**	**100.0**
Under $20,000	6.00	70	24.4
$20,000 to $29,999	8.62	101	14.7
$30,000 to $39,999	10.93	128	15.6
$40,000 to $49,999	9.45	110	10.3
$50,000 to $69,999	8.48	99	13.9
$70,000 or more	11.53	135	20.1
HOUSEHOLD TYPE			
Total households	**8.50**	**100**	**100.0**
Married couples	10.75	126	66.1
Married couples, no children	11.78	139	29.6
Married couples, with children	9.52	112	30.1
Oldest child under 6	6.91	81	4.2
Oldest child 6 to 17	9.24	109	15.8
Oldest child 18 or older	12.26	144	10.4
Single parent with child under 18	6.25	74	4.6
Single person	4.44	52	15.0
REGION			
Total households	**8.50**	**100**	**100.0**
Northeast	7.63	90	17.9
Midwest	8.31	98	23.4
South	7.88	93	32.3
West	10.47	123	26.2

Note: For definitions of best and biggest customers, see introduction or glossary.
Source: Calculations by New Strategist based on the 1997 Consumer Expenditure Survey

Nuts

Best customers:
- Householders aged 55 to 64
- Married couples without children
- Married couples with adult children

Customer trends:
- Spending is likely to rise as boomers age into the prime nut-consuming age groups.

Older householders spend the most on nuts. Householders aged 55 to 64 spend 37 percent more than the average householder on this item. Married couples without children at home, most of whom are older, spend 44 percent more than average. Those with adult children in the household spend 46 percent more than average.

While many people limit their consumption of nuts because of concerns about fat and calories, researchers are discovering that many nuts have health benefits. Consequently, as boomers age into the prime nut-consuming age groups, spending on nuts is likely to rise.

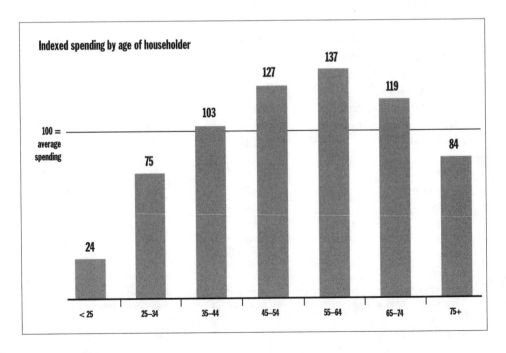

Indexed spending by age of householder

100 = average spending

< 25	25–34	35–44	45–54	55–64	65–74	75+
24	75	103	127	137	119	84

NUTS

Total household spending	$1,868,695,200
Average household spends	17.70

	average spending	best customers (index)	biggest customers (market share)
AGE OF HOUSEHOLDER			
Total households	**$17.70**	**100**	**100.0%**
Under age 25	4.26	24	1.7
Aged 25 to 34	13.24	75	14.1
Aged 35 to 44	18.30	103	24.1
Aged 45 to 54	22.40	127	23.2
Aged 55 to 64	24.23	137	16.0
Aged 65 to 74	21.06	119	13.6
Aged 75 or older	14.82	84	7.8
HOUSEHOLD INCOME			
Total households reporting income	**18.27**	**100**	**100.0**
Under $20,000	11.75	64	22.4
$20,000 to $29,999	14.30	78	11.4
$30,000 to $39,999	21.69	119	14.5
$40,000 to $49,999	22.84	125	11.7
$50,000 to $69,999	20.98	115	16.1
$70,000 or more	28.07	154	23.0
HOUSEHOLD TYPE			
Total households	**17.70**	**100**	**100.0**
Married couples	23.37	132	69.0
Married couples, no children	25.48	144	30.7
Married couples, with children	21.74	123	33.0
Oldest child under 6	18.49	104	5.4
Oldest child 6 to 17	21.07	119	17.3
Oldest child 18 or older	25.81	146	10.5
Single parent with child under 18	12.94	73	4.6
Single person	8.88	50	14.4
REGION			
Total households	**17.70**	**100**	**100.0**
Northeast	16.70	94	18.8
Midwest	18.88	107	25.5
South	14.70	83	29.0
West	22.08	125	26.5

Note: For definitions of best and biggest customers, see introduction or glossary.
Source: Calculations by New Strategist based on the 1997 Consumer Expenditure Survey

Olives, Pickles, and Relishes

Best customers: • Married couples with school-aged or older children

Customer trends: • Spending is likely to rise as food preferences become increasingly diverse.

Married couples with adult children at home spend 68 percent more than the average household on olives, pickles, and relishes. Those with school-aged children spend 40 percent more. Above-average household size is the reason for the higher spending of these households.

Spending in this category is likely to rise in the years ahead because of the nation's changing food preferences. As the country's racial and ethnic diversity increases, so does the variety of foods enjoyed by the population. Immigrants aren't the only ones driving this trend. Younger generations of native-born Americans have embraced novel foods from different cultures, and their wide-ranging tastes will boost spending on olives, pickles, and relishes.

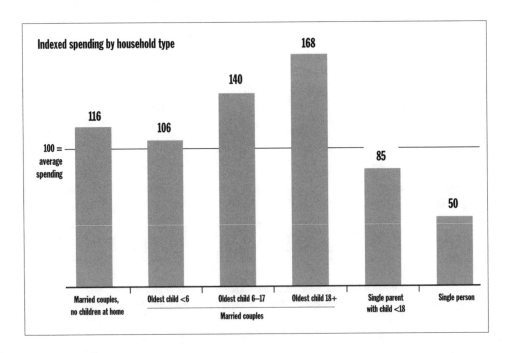

Indexed spending by household type

Married couples, no children at home	116
Married couples, Oldest child <6	106
Married couples, Oldest child 6–17	140
Married couples, Oldest child 18+	168
Single parent with child <18	85
Single person	50

100 = average spending

OLIVES, PICKLES, RELISHES

Total household spending	$1,112,771,040		
Average household spends	10.54		

	average spending	best customers (index)	biggest customers (market share)
AGE OF HOUSEHOLDER			
Total households	**$10.54**	**100**	**100.0%**
Under age 25	4.84	46	3.3
Aged 25 to 34	8.83	84	15.8
Aged 35 to 44	13.00	123	28.7
Aged 45 to 54	11.91	113	20.7
Aged 55 to 64	12.01	114	13.3
Aged 65 to 74	9.41	89	10.2
Aged 75 or older	9.53	90	8.4
HOUSEHOLD INCOME			
Total households reporting income	**11.26**	**100**	**100.0**
Under $20,000	7.81	69	24.2
$20,000 to $29,999	8.79	78	11.4
$30,000 to $39,999	10.38	92	11.3
$40,000 to $49,999	13.92	124	11.6
$50,000 to $69,999	13.28	118	16.6
$70,000 or more	18.25	162	24.2
HOUSEHOLD TYPE			
Total households	**10.54**	**100**	**100.0**
Married couples	13.89	132	68.9
Married couples, no children	12.24	116	24.8
Married couples, with children	14.78	140	37.7
Oldest child under 6	11.22	106	5.5
Oldest child 6 to 17	14.80	140	20.4
Oldest child 18 or older	17.72	168	12.1
Single parent with child under 18	8.98	85	5.3
Single person	5.22	50	14.2
REGION			
Total households	**10.54**	**100**	**100.0**
Northeast	8.84	84	16.8
Midwest	10.74	102	24.3
South	10.38	98	34.4
West	12.12	115	24.4

Note: For definitions of best and biggest customers, see introduction or glossary.
Source: Calculations by New Strategist based on the 1997 Consumer Expenditure Survey

Pasta, Cornmeal, and Other Cereal Products

Best customers: • Married couples with children

Customer trends: • Spending is likely to rise as an aging population shifts to a healthier diet.

Married couples with children are the best customers of pasta, cornmeal, and other cereal products. Not only do these households have more mouths to feed, but pasta is the favorite dish of many children. Couples with school-aged children spend 46 percent more than average on pasta, while those with adult children at home spend 44 percent more.

Spending on pasta is likely to rise, even as the children of the baby-boom generation leave home. Behind the increase will be the growing interest of aging boomers in healthy eating.

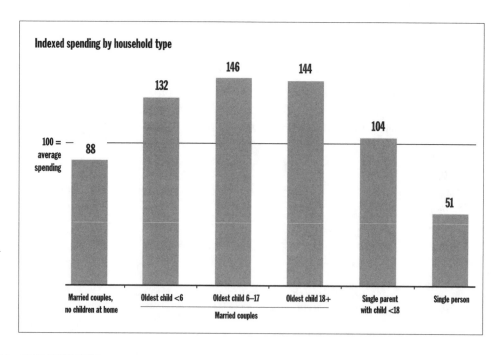

Indexed spending by household type

		146	144		
132					
100 = average spending	88			104	
					51
Married couples, no children at home	Oldest child <6	Oldest child 6–17	Oldest child 18+	Single parent with child <18	Single person
		Married couples			

PASTA, CORNMEAL, AND OTHER CEREAL PRODUCTS

Total household spending $2,959,295,280
Average household spends   28.03

	average spending	best customers (index)	biggest customers (market share)
AGE OF HOUSEHOLDER			
Total households	**$28.03**	**100**	**100.0%**
Under age 25	17.45	62	4.4
Aged 25 to 34	30.89	110	20.8
Aged 35 to 44	35.07	125	29.1
Aged 45 to 54	31.78	113	20.8
Aged 55 to 64	27.70	99	11.5
Aged 65 to 74	20.93	75	8.6
Aged 75 or older	15.93	57	5.3
HOUSEHOLD INCOME			
Total households reporting income	**29.13**	**100**	**100.0**
Under $20,000	21.58	74	25.8
$20,000 to $29,999	24.88	85	12.5
$30,000 to $39,999	31.18	107	13.1
$40,000 to $49,999	28.47	98	9.1
$50,000 to $69,999	35.92	123	17.3
$70,000 or more	42.22	145	21.7
HOUSEHOLD TYPE			
Total households	**28.03**	**100**	**100.0**
Married couples	34.31	122	64.0
Married couples, no children	24.65	88	18.8
Married couples, with children	39.96	143	38.3
Oldest child under 6	37.03	132	6.8
Oldest child 6 to 17	40.95	146	21.3
Oldest child 18 or older	40.44	144	10.4
Single parent with child under 18	29.17	104	6.5
Single person	14.20	51	14.6
REGION			
Total households	**28.03**	**100**	**100.0**
Northeast	33.17	118	23.6
Midwest	26.67	95	22.7
South	25.57	91	31.8
West	28.74	103	21.8

Note: For definitions of best and biggest customers, see introduction or glossary.
Source: Calculations by New Strategist based on the 1997 Consumer Expenditure Survey

Peanut Butter

Best customers: • Married couples with children

Customer trends: • Spending should increase along with the number of families with children, but concerns about peanut allergies may limit the rise.

Most kids love peanut butter, which is why married couples with children are the best customers of this item, accounting for 40 percent of the market. Married couples with preschoolers spend 41 percent more than the average household on peanut butter. Married couples with school-aged children spend 53 percent more, and those with adult children at home spend 51 percent more.

Spending on peanut butter should rise as the number of households with school-aged children increases. Concerns about peanut allergies may limit the spending increase, however, especially if a large number of schools banned the product.

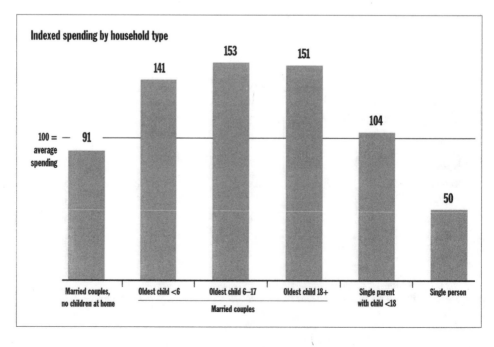

Indexed spending by household type

Married couples, no children at home	Oldest child <6	Oldest child 6–17	Oldest child 18+	Single parent with child <18	Single person
91	141	153	151	104	50

Married couples

100 = average spending

PEANUT BUTTER

Total household spending	$1,227,848,880
Average household spends	11.63

	average spending	best customers (index)	biggest customers (market share)
AGE OF HOUSEHOLDER			
Total households	**$11.63**	**100**	**100.0%**
Under age 25	6.67	57	4.1
Aged 25 to 34	11.82	102	19.2
Aged 35 to 44	13.89	119	27.8
Aged 45 to 54	12.34	106	19.4
Aged 55 to 64	12.18	105	12.2
Aged 65 to 74	10.44	90	10.3
Aged 75 or older	9.32	80	7.5
HOUSEHOLD INCOME			
Total households reporting income	**11.50**	**100**	**100.0**
Under $20,000	9.36	81	28.3
$20,000 to $29,999	9.24	80	11.7
$30,000 to $39,999	12.16	106	12.9
$40,000 to $49,999	11.39	99	9.3
$50,000 to $69,999	16.14	140	19.7
$70,000 or more	13.79	120	17.9
HOUSEHOLD TYPE			
Total households	**11.63**	**100**	**100.0**
Married couples	14.67	126	66.0
Married couples, no children	10.62	91	19.5
Married couples, with children	17.44	150	40.3
Oldest child under 6	16.39	141	7.2
Oldest child 6 to 17	17.82	153	22.3
Oldest child 18 or older	17.58	151	10.9
Single parent with child under 18	12.05	104	6.5
Single person	5.83	50	14.4
REGION			
Total households	**11.63**	**100**	**100.0**
Northeast	12.88	111	22.1
Midwest	11.25	97	23.1
South	11.91	102	35.7
West	10.48	90	19.1

Note: For definitions of best and biggest customers, see introduction or glossary.
Source: Calculations by New Strategist based on the 1997 Consumer Expenditure Survey

Pies, Tarts, and Turnovers

Best customers:	• Householders aged 45 to 64
	• Married couples with school-aged or older children
Customer trends:	• Spending is likely to rise as prepared desserts replace home cooking.

The best customers of pies, tarts, and turnovers are older householders as well as married couples with school-aged or older children. Householders aged 45 to 64 spend 25 to 29 percent more than average on this item. Couples with adult children at home spend 85 percent more than average, while those with school-aged children spend 43 percent more.

Spending on pies, tarts, and turnovers is likely to rise in the years ahead as busy two-earner couples buy more prepared desserts rather than bake from scratch.

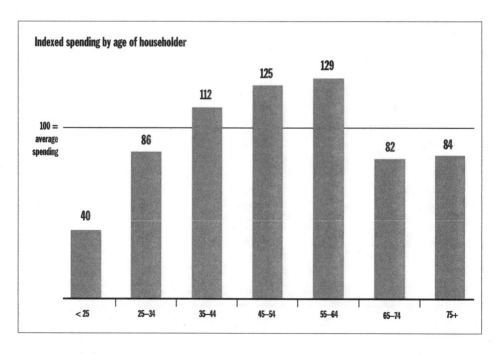

Indexed spending by age of householder

PIES, TARTS, AND TURNOVERS

Total household spending	$1,425,276,000		
Average household spends	13.50		

	average spending	best customers (index)	biggest customers (market share)
AGE OF HOUSEHOLDER			
Total households	**$13.50**	**100**	**100.0%**
Under age 25	5.34	40	2.8
Aged 25 to 34	11.60	86	16.2
Aged 35 to 44	15.17	112	26.1
Aged 45 to 54	16.84	125	22.9
Aged 55 to 64	17.46	129	15.1
Aged 65 to 74	11.10	82	9.4
Aged 75 or older	11.35	84	7.8
HOUSEHOLD INCOME			
Total households reporting income	**14.11**	**100**	**100.0**
Under $20,000	9.45	67	23.3
$20,000 to $29,999	10.21	72	10.6
$30,000 to $39,999	13.17	93	11.4
$40,000 to $49,999	17.70	125	11.7
$50,000 to $69,999	17.79	126	17.7
$70,000 or more	23.26	165	24.6
HOUSEHOLD TYPE			
Total households	**13.50**	**100**	**100.0**
Married couples	18.02	133	69.8
Married couples, no children	16.80	124	26.6
Married couples, with children	19.46	144	38.8
Oldest child under 6	13.10	97	5.0
Oldest child 6 to 17	19.33	143	20.8
Oldest child 18 or older	25.03	185	13.3
Single parent with child under 18	8.97	66	4.2
Single person	5.15	38	11.0
REGION			
Total households	**13.50**	**100**	**100.0**
Northeast	14.49	107	21.4
Midwest	12.97	96	23.0
South	12.52	93	32.4
West	14.72	109	23.2

Note: For definitions of best and biggest customers, see introduction or glossary.
Source: Calculations by New Strategist based on the 1997 Consumer Expenditure Survey

Pork Chops

Best customers:
- Householders aged 35 to 44
- Married couples with children
- Single parents
- Households in the South

Customer trends:
- Spending should remain stable as long as the number of families with children continues to grow.

Families with children are the best customers of pork chops. Married couples with children spend from 33 to 51 percent more than the average household on pork chops. Single-parent families spend 27 percent more than average on this item. Householders spanning the ages from 25 to 54 spend more than average on pork chops because they are likely to have children at home. Households in the South spend 15 percent more than average on pork chops.

Spending on pork chops is likely to remain stable because of the growing number of families with children. In the years ahead, however, average household spending on this item may decline because of the aging population's growing concern about healthy eating.

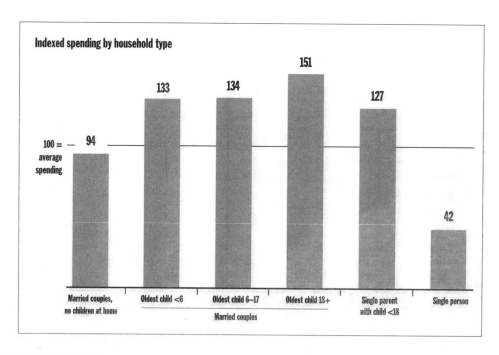

Indexed spending by household type

94	133	134	151	127	42

100 = average spending

Married couples, no children at home | Oldest child <6 | Oldest child 6–17 | Oldest child 18+ | Single parent with child <18 | Single person

Married couples

PORK CHOPS

Total household spending	$4,141,746,480		
Average household spends	39.23		

	average spending	best customers (index)	biggest customers (market share)
AGE OF HOUSEHOLDER			
Total households	**$39.23**	**100**	**100.0%**
Under age 25	20.10	51	3.6
Aged 25 to 34	43.82	112	21.1
Aged 35 to 44	48.05	122	28.5
Aged 45 to 54	45.91	117	21.4
Aged 55 to 64	38.33	98	11.4
Aged 65 to 74	30.62	78	9.0
Aged 75 or older	23.48	60	5.6
HOUSEHOLD INCOME			
Total households reporting income	**39.60**	**100**	**100.0**
Under $20,000	33.91	86	29.8
$20,000 to $29,999	39.35	99	14.5
$30,000 to $39,999	40.05	101	12.4
$40,000 to $49,999	33.32	84	7.9
$50,000 to $69,999	49.30	124	17.5
$70,000 or more	46.86	118	17.7
HOUSEHOLD TYPE			
Total households	**39.23**	**100**	**100.0**
Married couples	48.69	124	64.9
Married couples, no children	36.88	94	20.1
Married couples, with children	54.26	138	37.2
Oldest child under 6	52.07	133	6.8
Oldest child 6 to 17	52.63	134	19.5
Oldest child 18 or older	59.37	151	10.9
Single parent with child under 18	49.77	127	8.0
Single person	16.55	42	12.1
REGION			
Total households	**39.23**	**100**	**100.0**
Northeast	40.22	103	20.5
Midwest	34.28	87	20.9
South	45.11	115	40.1
West	34.43	88	18.6

Note: For definitions of best and biggest customers, see introduction or glossary.
Source: Calculations by New Strategist based on the 1997 Consumer Expenditure Survey

Pork, Except Bacon, Frankfurters, Ham, Pork Chops, and Sausage

Best customers:
- Householders aged 45 to 74
- Married couples with adult children

Customer trends:
- Spending is likely to decline as an aging population becomes increasingly concerned with healthy eating.

The pork industry has marketed its product as the alternative to red meat, and its efforts have paid off. Pork consumption has increased over the past few years. Nevertheless, the best customers of pork (excluding bacon, frankfurters, ham, pork chops, and sausage) are older Americans. Householders aged 45 to 74 spend 10 to 36 percent more than the average householder on this item. Married couples with adult children at home spend 41 percent more, in part because their households are larger.

Spending on pork (excluding bacon, frankfurters, ham, pork chops, and sausage) is likely to decline as boomers age into the prime pork-eating age groups. Not only are boomers less likely to cook meals at home, but they are more willing than today's older Americans to forego meat at the dinner table.

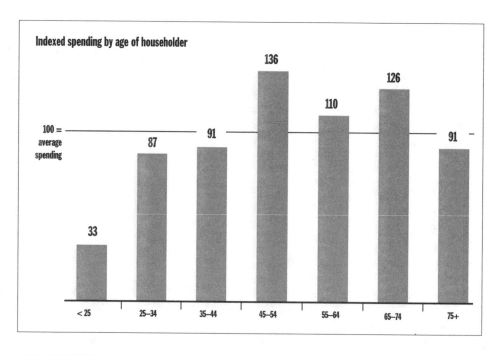

Indexed spending by age of householder

100 = average spending

< 25	25–34	35–44	45–54	55–64	65–74	75+
33	87	91	136	110	126	91

PORK, EXCEPT BACON, FRANKFURTERS, HAM, PORK CHOPS, AND SAUSAGE

Total household spending	$3,280,246,320
Average household spends	31.07

	average spending	best customers (index)	biggest customers (market share)
AGE OF HOUSEHOLDER			
Total households	**$31.07**	**100**	**100.0%**
Under age 25	10.22	33	2.3
Aged 25 to 34	27.03	87	16.4
Aged 35 to 44	28.38	91	21.2
Aged 45 to 54	42.13	136	24.8
Aged 55 to 64	34.10	110	12.8
Aged 65 to 74	39.13	126	14.4
Aged 75 or older	28.15	91	8.4
HOUSEHOLD INCOME			
Total households reporting income	**31.75**	**100**	**100.0**
Under $20,000	26.91	85	29.5
$20,000 to $29,999	32.52	102	15.0
$30,000 to $39,999	33.80	106	13.0
$40,000 to $49,999	35.68	112	10.5
$50,000 to $69,999	28.06	88	12.4
$70,000 or more	40.09	126	18.9
HOUSEHOLD TYPE			
Total households	**31.07**	**100**	**100.0**
Married couples	39.05	126	65.7
Married couples, no children	34.91	112	24.0
Married couples, with children	36.93	119	32.0
Oldest child under 6	31.13	100	5.2
Oldest child 6 to 17	35.99	116	16.9
Oldest child 18 or older	43.67	141	10.1
Single parent with child under 18	21.67	70	4.4
Single person	16.72	54	15.5
REGION			
Total households	**31.07**	**100**	**100.0**
Northeast	24.16	78	15.5
Midwest	34.06	110	26.2
South	31.59	102	35.5
West	33.30	107	22.8

Note: For definitions of best and biggest customers, see introduction or glossary.
Source: Calculations by New Strategist based on the 1997 Consumer Expenditure Survey

Potato Chips and Other Snacks

Best customers: • Married couples with school-aged or older children

Customer trends: • Spending is likely to increase as the affluence of the population grows and a greater variety of snacks tempts shoppers.

Married couples with school-aged children spend 82 percent more than the average household on potato chips and other snacks. Married couples with adult children at home spend 52 percent more than average on chips and snacks. Although children play a role in the higher spending of these households, household size is also a factor since Americans of all ages eat chips and other snack foods.

While it's hard to imagine people snacking more than they do now, the growing affluence of the population should boost spending on this item as Americans buy higher-priced snacks. In addition, the growing variety of snacks will tempt shoppers to buy more.

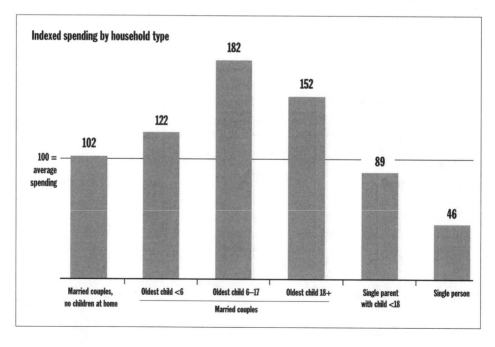

Indexed spending by household type

102	122	182	152	89	46
Married couples, no children at home	Oldest child <6	Oldest child 6–17	Oldest child 18+	Single parent with child <18	Single person

100 = average spending

Married couples

POTATO CHIPS AND OTHER SNACKS

Total household spending $7,055,644,080
Average household spends   66.83

	average spending	best customers (index)	biggest customers (market share)
AGE OF HOUSEHOLDER			
Total households	**$66.83**	**100**	**100.0%**
Under age 25	33.63	50	3.6
Aged 25 to 34	65.67	98	18.5
Aged 35 to 44	94.45	141	32.9
Aged 45 to 54	79.48	119	21.8
Aged 55 to 64	65.12	97	11.4
Aged 65 to 74	49.96	75	8.6
Aged 75 or older	28.03	42	3.9
HOUSEHOLD INCOME			
Total households reporting income	**70.36**	**100**	**100.0**
Under $20,000	40.42	57	20.0
$20,000 to $29,999	58.06	83	12.1
$30,000 to $39,999	72.21	103	12.5
$40,000 to $49,999	91.19	130	12.1
$50,000 to $69,999	93.26	133	18.6
$70,000 or more	112.16	159	23.8
HOUSEHOLD TYPE			
Total households	**66.83**	**100**	**100.0**
Married couples	90.00	135	70.4
Married couples, no children	67.99	102	21.7
Married couples, with children	107.78	161	43.4
Oldest child under 6	81.55	122	6.3
Oldest child 6 to 17	121.63	182	26.5
Oldest child 18 or older	101.83	152	11.0
Single parent with child under 18	59.47	89	5.6
Single person	30.87	46	13.3
REGION			
Total households	**66.83**	**100**	**100.0**
Northeast	55.31	83	16.5
Midwest	73.44	110	26.3
South	65.83	99	34.4
West	71.72	107	22.8

Note: For definitions of best and biggest customers, see introduction or glossary.
Source: Calculations by New Strategist based on the 1997 Consumer Expenditure Survey

Poultry

The best customers of poultry are the largest households. Married couples with children spend 21 to 61 percent more than the average household on this item. Single parents spend 18 percent more than average on poultry. Householders aged 35 to 54 spend 19 to 20 percent more than average on this item because most have children, which makes their households relatively large. Households in the Northeast spend 22 percent more than average on poultry.

Spending on this item is likely to rise as aging boomers, concerned with eating a healthy diet, substitute poultry for red meat at the dinner table.

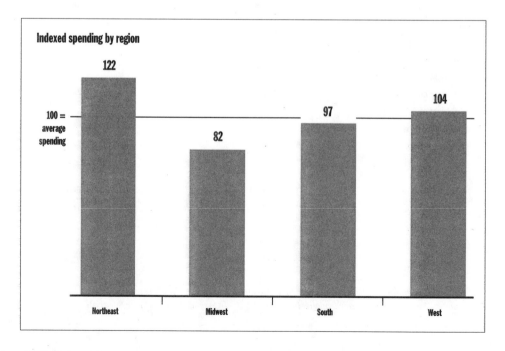

Indexed spending by region

100 = average spending

Northeast	Midwest	South	West
122	82	97	104

POULTRY

Total household spending	$15,309,575,760	
Average household spends	145.01	

	average spending	best customers (index)	biggest customers (market share)
AGE OF HOUSEHOLDER			
Total households	**$145.01**	**100**	**100.0%**
Under age 25	77.67	54	3.8
Aged 25 to 34	145.75	101	19.0
Aged 35 to 44	174.47	120	28.0
Aged 45 to 54	172.34	119	21.8
Aged 55 to 64	149.87	103	12.1
Aged 65 to 74	135.42	93	10.7
Aged 75 or older	81.01	56	5.2
HOUSEHOLD INCOME			
Total households reporting income	**145.61**	**100**	**100.0**
Under $20,000	111.70	77	26.7
$20,000 to $29,999	132.12	91	13.3
$30,000 to $39,999	146.91	101	12.3
$40,000 to $49,999	151.89	104	9.8
$50,000 to $69,999	168.79	116	16.3
$70,000 or more	206.52	142	21.2
HOUSEHOLD TYPE			
Total households	**145.01**	**100**	**100.0**
Married couples	181.95	125	65.6
Married couples, no children	140.16	97	20.6
Married couples, with children	208.09	144	38.6
Oldest child under 6	175.63	121	6.2
Oldest child 6 to 17	208.73	144	20.9
Oldest child 18 or older	233.90	161	11.6
Single parent with child under 18	170.88	118	7.4
Single person	61.31	42	12.1
REGION			
Total households	**145.01**	**100**	**100.0**
Northeast	176.72	122	24.3
Midwest	118.80	82	19.6
South	141.20	97	34.0
West	150.69	104	22.1

Note: For definitions of best and biggest customers, see introduction or glossary.
Source: Calculations by New Strategist based on the 1997 Consumer Expenditure Survey

Rice

Best customers:
- Householders aged 45 to 64
- Married couples with adult children
- Single parents
- Households in the Northeast and West

Customer trends:
- Spending will climb as the Hispanic and Asian populations grow.

The best customers of rice are married couples with adult children at home. They spend 95 percent more than the average household on this item. Single parents spend 76 percent more than average. Householders aged 45 to 64 spend 28 to 29 percent more than average. Households in the Northeast and in the West spend 24 to 39 percent more, in part because many Hispanic and Asian immigrants—for whom rice is a dietary staple—live in these regions.

Spending on rice will rise as the Hispanic and Asian populations grow and as boomers age into the prime rice-eating age groups.

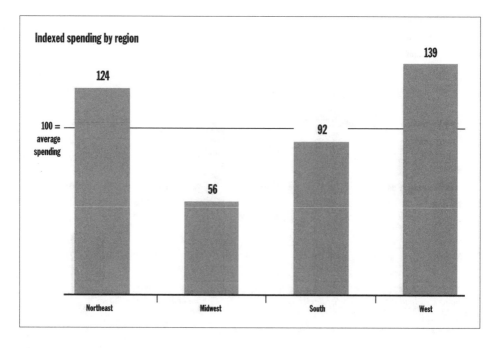

Indexed spending by region

100 = average spending

| Northeast | Midwest | South | West |
| 124 | 56 | 92 | 139 |

RICE

Total household spending	$1,939,431,120
Average household spends	18.37

	average spending	best customers (index)	biggest customers (market share)
AGE OF HOUSEHOLDER			
Total households	**$18.37**	**100**	**100.0%**
Under age 25	11.88	65	4.6
Aged 25 to 34	19.60	107	20.1
Aged 35 to 44	19.05	104	24.1
Aged 45 to 54	23.60	128	23.5
Aged 55 to 64	23.62	129	15.0
Aged 65 to 74	12.73	69	7.9
Aged 75 or older	9.66	53	4.9
HOUSEHOLD INCOME			
Total households reporting income	**18.21**	**100**	**100.0**
Under $20,000	15.68	86	30.0
$20,000 to $29,999	19.31	106	15.5
$30,000 to $39,999	21.25	117	14.3
$40,000 to $49,999	17.56	96	9.0
$50,000 to $69,999	18.47	101	14.2
$70,000 or more	20.30	111	16.7
HOUSEHOLD TYPE			
Total households	**18.37**	**100**	**100.0**
Married couples	21.86	119	62.2
Married couples, no children	16.76	91	19.5
Married couples, with children	24.21	132	35.4
Oldest child under 6	21.61	118	6.1
Oldest child 6 to 17	19.56	106	15.5
Oldest child 18 or older	35.75	195	14.0
Single parent with child under 18	32.38	176	11.1
Single person	6.53	36	10.2
REGION			
Total households	**18.37**	**100**	**100.0**
Northeast	22.76	124	24.7
Midwest	10.21	56	13.3
South	16.91	92	32.1
West	25.60	139	29.6

Note: For definitions of best and biggest customers, see introduction or glossary.
Source: Calculations by New Strategist based on the 1997 Consumer Expenditure Survey

Salad Dressings

Best customers:
- Householders aged 45 to 64
- Married couples with school-aged or older children

Customer trends:
- Spending should remain stable as boomers buy prepared salads and dressings from grocery stores.

The best customers of salad dressings are householders aged 45 to 64. They spend 25 to 30 percent more than the average household on this item. Married couples with school-aged children spend 51 percent more than average, while those with adult children at home spend 49 percent more. Couples with children spend more on salad dressing because their households are larger than average.

The rise of takeout food has limited spending on salad dressings. But as more grocery stores offer prepared salads as a takeout option, spending on salad dressing is likely to remain stable or even rise in the years ahead because aging boomers opt for more healthful eating.

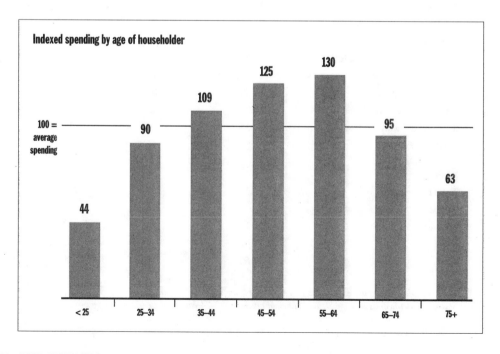

Indexed spending by age of householder

100 = average spending

< 25	25–34	35–44	45–54	55–64	65–74	75+
44	90	109	125	130	95	63

SALAD DRESSINGS

Total household spending	$2,605,615,680	
Average household spends	24.68	

	average spending	best customers (index)	biggest customers (market share)
AGE OF HOUSEHOLDER			
Total households	**$24.68**	**100**	**100.0%**
Under age 25	10.75	44	3.1
Aged 25 to 34	22.26	90	17.0
Aged 35 to 44	26.84	109	25.3
Aged 45 to 54	30.97	125	23.0
Aged 55 to 64	32.10	130	15.2
Aged 65 to 74	23.53	95	10.9
Aged 75 or older	15.55	63	5.9
HOUSEHOLD INCOME			
Total households reporting income	**26.02**	**100**	**100.0**
Under $20,000	17.44	67	23.3
$20,000 to $29,999	22.18	85	12.5
$30,000 to $39,999	30.44	117	14.3
$40,000 to $49,999	29.84	115	10.7
$50,000 to $69,999	34.09	131	18.4
$70,000 or more	35.11	135	20.2
HOUSEHOLD TYPE			
Total households	**24.68**	**100**	**100.0**
Married couples	32.14	130	68.1
Married couples, no children	27.84	113	24.1
Married couples, with children	34.50	140	37.6
Oldest child under 6	25.11	102	5.2
Oldest child 6 to 17	37.24	151	22.0
Oldest child 18 or older	36.83	149	10.7
Single parent with child under 18	20.38	83	5.2
Single person	11.05	45	12.9
REGION			
Total households	**24.68**	**100**	**100.0**
Northeast	25.22	102	20.4
Midwest	22.68	92	22.0
South	23.64	96	33.4
West	28.02	114	24.1

Note: For definitions of best and biggest customers, see introduction or glossary.
Source: Calculations by New Strategist based on the 1997 Consumer Expenditure Survey

Salads, Prepared

Best customers:
- Householders aged 45 to 54
- Married couples with adult children
- Married couples without children

Customer trends:
- Spending will rise as busy two-earner couples seek healthier takeout foods.

Prepared salads have become popular as busy two-earner couples try to reduce meal preparation time. Because prepared salads are relatively expensive, however, the best customers are those in their peak-earning years. Householders aged 45 to 54 spend 41 percent more than the average household on this item. Married couples with adult children at home spend 50 percent more than average, while those without children at home spend 35 percent more.

The health concerns of an aging population ensures greater spending on salads. Spending on prepared salads will rise accordingly as more grocery stores offer this option to their busy customers.

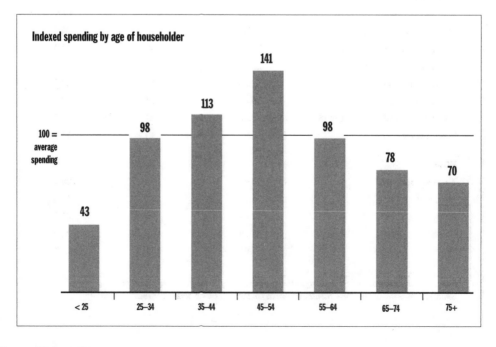

Indexed spending by age of householder

100 = average spending

< 25	25–34	35–44	45–54	55–64	65–74	75+
43	98	113	141	98	78	70

SALADS, PREPARED

Total household spending	$1,588,918,800		
Average household spends	15.05		

	average spending	best customers (index)	biggest customers (market share)
AGE OF HOUSEHOLDER			
Total households	**$15.05**	**100**	**100.0%**
Under age 25	6.50	43	3.1
Aged 25 to 34	14.79	98	18.5
Aged 35 to 44	16.97	113	26.2
Aged 45 to 54	21.22	141	25.8
Aged 55 to 64	14.81	98	11.5
Aged 65 to 74	11.73	78	8.9
Aged 75 or older	10.50	70	6.5
HOUSEHOLD INCOME			
Total households reporting income	**15.30**	**100**	**100.0**
Under $20,000	7.75	51	17.6
$20,000 to $29,999	12.56	82	12.0
$30,000 to $39,999	15.08	99	12.1
$40,000 to $49,999	16.00	105	9.8
$50,000 to $69,999	25.13	164	23.1
$70,000 or more	25.54	167	25.0
HOUSEHOLD TYPE			
Total households	**15.05**	**100**	**100.0**
Married couples	19.63	130	68.2
Married couples, no children	20.26	135	28.7
Married couples, with children	19.22	128	34.3
Oldest child under 6	16.39	109	5.6
Oldest child 6 to 17	18.70	124	18.1
Oldest child 18 or older	22.63	150	10.8
Single parent with child under 18	8.76	58	3.7
Single person	8.71	58	16.6
REGION			
Total households	**15.05**	**100**	**100.0**
Northeast	13.86	92	18.4
Midwest	17.39	116	27.6
South	14.43	96	33.4
West	14.57	97	20.6

Note: For definitions of best and biggest customers, see introduction or glossary.
Source: Calculations by New Strategist based on the 1997 Consumer Expenditure Survey

Salt, Spices, and Other Seasonings

Best customers:
- Householders aged 35 to 54
- Married couples with school-aged or older children
- Households in the West

Customer trends:
- Spending will rise as the Hispanic and Asian populations grow and as a greater variety of foods become staples of the American diet.

The best customers of salt, spices, and other seasonings are households in the West. They spend 28 percent more than average on this item, mainly because of the many Hispanic and Asian households in the West, whose diet is typically spicy. Householders aged 35 to 54 spend 20 to 23 percent more than average on salt, spices, and other seasonings. Married couples with school-aged or older children at home spend 34 to 44 percent more, in part because their households are larger.

Spending on spices will rise in the years ahead as the Hispanic and Asian populations grow, and as the foods enjoyed by immigrants become staples of the American diet.

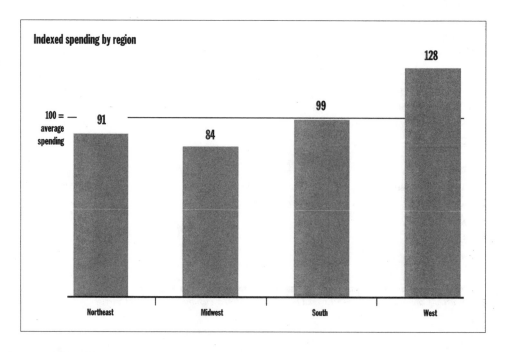

Indexed spending by region

100 = average spending

Northeast	Midwest	South	West
91	84	99	128

SALT, SPICES, AND OTHER SEASONINGS

Total household spending	$2,013,334,320
Average household spends	19.07

	average spending	best customers (index)	biggest customers (market share)
AGE OF HOUSEHOLDER			
Total households	**$19.07**	**100**	**100.0%**
Under age 25	9.82	51	3.7
Aged 25 to 34	17.29	91	17.1
Aged 35 to 44	22.92	120	28.0
Aged 45 to 54	23.40	123	22.5
Aged 55 to 64	20.77	109	12.7
Aged 65 to 74	16.96	89	10.2
Aged 75 or older	13.02	68	6.4
HOUSEHOLD INCOME			
Total households reporting income	**20.23**	**100**	**100.0**
Under $20,000	14.80	73	25.5
$20,000 to $29,999	18.47	91	13.3
$30,000 to $39,999	20.04	99	12.1
$40,000 to $49,999	23.38	116	10.8
$50,000 to $69,999	23.61	117	16.4
$70,000 or more	28.85	143	21.3
HOUSEHOLD TYPE			
Total households	**19.07**	**100**	**100.0**
Married couples	24.22	127	66.4
Married couples, no children	21.38	112	23.9
Married couples, with children	25.16	132	35.5
Oldest child under 6	21.24	111	5.7
Oldest child 6 to 17	25.64	134	19.6
Oldest child 18 or older	27.49	144	10.4
Single parent with child under 18	20.15	106	6.6
Single person	7.78	41	11.7
REGION			
Total households	**19.07**	**100**	**100.0**
Northeast	17.34	91	18.2
Midwest	15.96	84	20.0
South	18.88	99	34.5
West	24.36	128	27.1

Note: For definitions of best and biggest customers, see introduction or glossary.
Source: Calculations by New Strategist based on the 1997 Consumer Expenditure Survey

Sauces and Gravies

Best customers:
- Householders aged 35 to 54
- Married couples with children

Customer trends:
- Spending is likely to remain stable while the baby-boom generation is raising children.

The best customers of sauces and gravies, married couples with children, spend 51 percent more than average on this item. Behind this higher spending are the larger households of couples with kids, as well as children's taste for tomato sauce. Householders aged 35 to 54 spend 26 to 30 percent more than average on this item because they are likely to have children at home.

Spending on sauces and gravies will remain stable while the children of the baby-boom generation are at home. Spending by the average household may decline when boomers become empty-nesters.

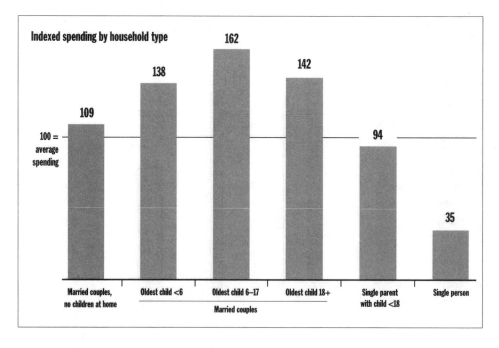

Indexed spending by household type

109	138	162	142	94	35

100 = average spending

Married couples, no children at home | Oldest child <6 | Oldest child 6–17 | Oldest child 18+ | Single parent with child <18 | Single person

Married couples

SAUCES AND GRAVIES

Total household spending $4,208,259,360
Average household spends   39.86

	average spending	best customers (index)	biggest customers (market share)
AGE OF HOUSEHOLDER			
Total households	**$39.86**	**100**	**100.0%**
Under age 25	22.69	57	4.0
Aged 25 to 34	42.79	107	20.3
Aged 35 to 44	50.09	126	29.2
Aged 45 to 54	51.69	130	23.8
Aged 55 to 64	38.66	97	11.3
Aged 65 to 74	27.46	69	7.9
Aged 75 or older	17.32	43	4.0
HOUSEHOLD INCOME			
Total households reporting income	**43.18**	**100**	**100.0**
Under $20,000	26.00	60	21.0
$20,000 to $29,999	38.83	90	13.1
$30,000 to $39,999	42.74	99	12.1
$40,000 to $49,999	53.57	124	11.6
$50,000 to $69,999	52.20	121	17.0
$70,000 or more	70.24	163	24.3
HOUSEHOLD TYPE			
Total households	**39.86**	**100**	**100.0**
Married couples	53.91	135	70.7
Married couples, no children	43.26	109	23.2
Married couples, with children	60.34	151	40.7
Oldest child under 6	54.87	138	7.1
Oldest child 6 to 17	64.51	162	23.5
Oldest child 18 or older	56.55	142	10.2
Single parent with child under 18	37.49	94	5.9
Single person	13.95	35	10.1
REGION			
Total households	**39.86**	**100**	**100.0**
Northeast	36.49	92	18.3
Midwest	38.94	98	23.3
South	38.73	97	33.9
West	45.75	115	24.4

Note: For definitions of best and biggest customers, see introduction or glossary.
Source: Calculations by New Strategist based on the 1997 Consumer Expenditure Survey

Sausage

Best customers:
- Householders aged 55 to 64
- Married couples with children

Customer trends:
- Spending will decline as the aging population becomes more concerned about healthy eating.

The best customers of sausage are married couples with children. These households spend 30 to 48 percent more than the average household on this item. Behind the higher spending is the larger size of those households. Householders aged 55 to 64 spend 39 percent more than the average household on sausage. Older householders, many of whom were raised on a meat-and-potatoes diet, often find it hard to give up foods they love despite the need to eat heathier.

Boomers are less likely than older Americans to follow a meat-and-potatoes diet. As the baby-boom generation enters the prime sausage-eating age groups, spending on sausage is likely to decline.

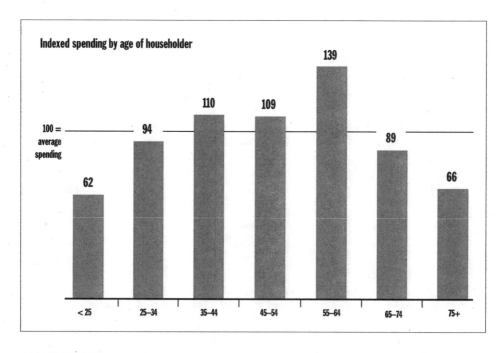

Indexed spending by age of householder

100 = average spending

| < 25 | 25–34 | 35–44 | 45–54 | 55–64 | 65–74 | 75+ |
| 62 | 94 | 110 | 109 | 139 | 89 | 66 |

SAUSAGE

Total household spending	$2,546,493,120
Average household spends	24.12

	average spending	best customers (index)	biggest customers (market share)
AGE OF HOUSEHOLDER			
Total households	**$24.12**	**100**	**100.0%**
Under age 25	14.90	62	4.4
Aged 25 to 34	22.79	94	17.8
Aged 35 to 44	26.42	110	25.5
Aged 45 to 54	26.27	109	20.0
Aged 55 to 64	33.52	139	16.2
Aged 65 to 74	21.36	89	10.2
Aged 75 or older	15.92	66	6.1
HOUSEHOLD INCOME			
Total households reporting income	**25.09**	**100**	**100.0**
Under $20,000	21.99	88	30.5
$20,000 to $29,999	27.19	108	15.8
$30,000 to $39,999	25.81	103	12.6
$40,000 to $49,999	26.82	107	10.0
$50,000 to $69,999	22.97	92	12.9
$70,000 or more	29.59	118	17.6
HOUSEHOLD TYPE			
Total households	**24.12**	**100**	**100.0**
Married couples	31.41	130	68.1
Married couples, no children	25.45	106	22.5
Married couples, with children	33.28	138	37.1
Oldest child under 6	35.34	147	7.5
Oldest child 6 to 17	31.26	130	18.9
Oldest child 18 or older	35.62	148	10.6
Single parent with child under 18	20.94	87	5.4
Single person	9.25	38	11.0
REGION			
Total households	**24.12**	**100**	**100.0**
Northeast	19.85	82	16.4
Midwest	26.55	110	26.3
South	26.41	109	38.2
West	21.75	90	19.2

Note: For definitions of best and biggest customers, see introduction or glossary.
Source: Calculations by New Strategist based on the 1997 Consumer Expenditure Survey

Soup, Canned and Packaged

Best customers:
- Married couples with children
- Households in the West

Customer trends:
- Spending is likely to decline as shoppers buy fresh soups prepared by groceries and delis.

Spending on soup does not vary much by demographic segment. Householders aged 35 to 44 spend 14 percent more than average on soup because they have children at home and their households are larger than average. For the same reason, married couples with children spend 33 percent more than average on canned and packaged soup. Householders in the West spend 14 percent more than average on this item.

Spending on canned and packaged soup is likely to decline as shoppers substitute fresh soups bought in delis and grocery stores for the canned and packaged variety.

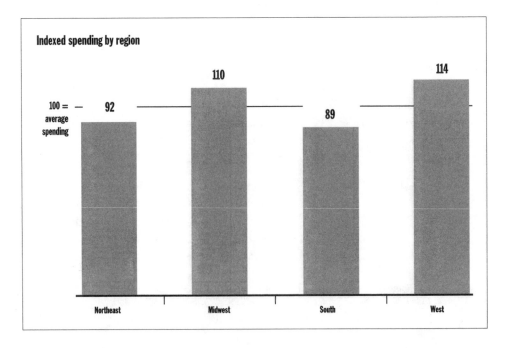

Indexed spending by region

100 = average spending

Northeast	Midwest	South	West
92	110	89	114

SOUP, CANNED AND PACKAGED

Total household spending	$3,470,283,120		
Average household spends	32.87		

	average spending	best customers (index)	biggest customers (market share)
AGE OF HOUSEHOLDER			
Total households	**$32.87**	**100**	**100.0%**
Under age 25	19.37	59	4.2
Aged 25 to 34	28.98	88	16.6
Aged 35 to 44	37.51	114	26.5
Aged 45 to 54	33.39	102	18.6
Aged 55 to 64	37.87	115	13.4
Aged 65 to 74	35.86	109	12.5
Aged 75 or older	29.56	90	8.4
HOUSEHOLD INCOME			
Total households reporting income	**33.24**	**100**	**100.0**
Under $20,000	24.87	75	26.1
$20,000 to $29,999	30.23	91	13.3
$30,000 to $39,999	32.54	98	12.0
$40,000 to $49,999	34.99	105	9.8
$50,000 to $69,999	45.09	136	19.0
$70,000 or more	43.42	131	19.5
HOUSEHOLD TYPE			
Total households	**32.87**	**100**	**100.0**
Married couples	41.10	125	65.4
Married couples, no children	35.86	109	23.3
Married couples, with children	43.71	133	35.7
Oldest child under 6	42.06	128	6.6
Oldest child 6 to 17	44.06	134	19.5
Oldest child 18 or older	44.39	135	9.7
Single parent with child under 18	27.28	83	5.2
Single person	19.10	58	16.7
REGION			
Total households	**32.87**	**100**	**100.0**
Northeast	30.25	92	18.4
Midwest	36.03	110	26.2
South	29.34	89	31.1
West	37.39	114	24.2

Note: For definitions of best and biggest customers, see introduction or glossary.
Source: Calculations by New Strategist based on the 1997 Consumer Expenditure Survey

Sugar

Married couples with school-aged children spend 40 percent more than the average household on sugar. Married couples with adult children at home spend 39 percent more than average. Behind this higher spending on sugar are the demands of children for cookies and other home-baked goods.

Baking cookies and other desserts at home has become less frequent thanks to the busy lives of today's parents and the growing availability of prepared desserts. Spending on sugar is unlikely to grow unless home baking makes a comeback.

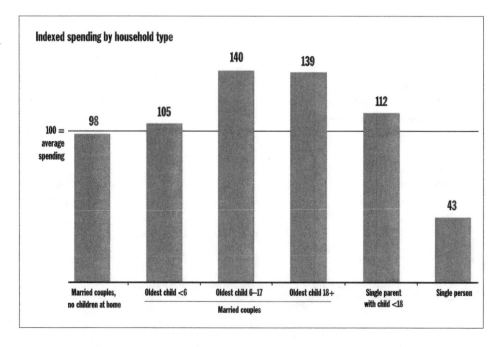

Indexed spending by household type

| | 98 | 105 | 140 | 139 | 112 | 43 |

100 = average spending

| Married couples, no children at home | Oldest child <6 | Oldest child 6–17 | Oldest child 18+ | Single parent with child <18 | Single person |

Married couples

SUGAR

Total household spending	$1,998,553,680		
Average household spends	18.93		

	average spending	best customers (index)	biggest customers (market share)
AGE OF HOUSEHOLDER			
Total households	**$18.93**	**100**	**100.0%**
Under age 25	11.96	63	4.5
Aged 25 to 34	19.00	100	18.9
Aged 35 to 44	20.54	109	25.2
Aged 45 to 54	21.03	111	20.4
Aged 55 to 64	20.07	106	12.4
Aged 65 to 74	19.48	103	11.8
Aged 75 or older	14.57	77	7.2
HOUSEHOLD INCOME			
Total households reporting income	**19.59**	**100**	**100.0**
Under $20,000	19.86	101	35.3
$20,000 to $29,999	20.51	105	15.3
$30,000 to $39,999	18.83	96	11.8
$40,000 to $49,999	17.72	90	8.5
$50,000 to $69,999	20.37	104	14.6
$70,000 or more	18.92	97	14.4
HOUSEHOLD TYPE			
Total households	**18.93**	**100**	**100.0**
Married couples	23.52	124	65.0
Married couples, no children	18.58	98	20.9
Married couples, with children	25.03	132	35.5
Oldest child under 6	19.82	105	5.4
Oldest child 6 to 17	26.58	140	20.4
Oldest child 18 or older	26.27	139	10.0
Single parent with child under 18	21.19	112	7.0
Single person	8.07	43	12.2
REGION			
Total households	**18.93**	**100**	**100.0**
Northeast	19.18	101	20.2
Midwest	17.00	90	21.5
South	22.16	117	40.8
West	15.70	83	17.6

Note: For definitions of best and biggest customers, see introduction or glossary.
Source: Calculations by New Strategist based on the 1997 Consumer Expenditure Survey

Sweet Rolls, Coffee Cakes, and Doughnuts

Best customers: • Married couples with school-aged or older children

Customer trends: • Spending is likely to remain stable as manufacturers tempt shoppers with a
                                     growing variety of products.

Married couples with adult children at home spend 58 percent more than the average household on sweet rolls, coffee cakes, and doughnuts. Spending by married couples with school-aged children is 34 percent greater than average. Behind the higher spending of these households is their larger size and the sweet tooth of children.

Although aging Americans will be trying to eat healthier in the years ahead, they will continue to indulge their sweet tooth—particularly as manufacturers tempt them with a growing variety of products. Consequently, spending on this item is likely to remain stable.

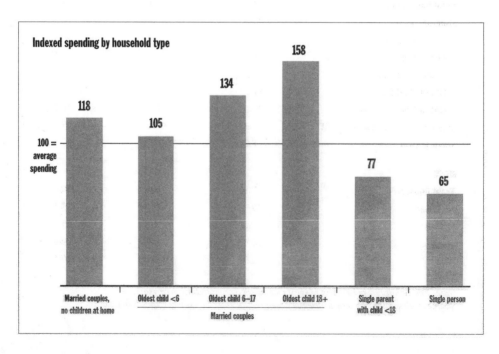

Indexed spending by household type

118	105	134	158	77	65
Married couples, no children at home	Oldest child <6	Oldest child 6–17	Oldest child 18+	Single parent with child <18	Single person

100 = average spending

Married couples

SWEET ROLLS, COFFEE CAKES, AND DOUGHNUTS

Total household spending	$2,441,972,880	
Average household spends	23.13	

	average spending	best customers (index)	biggest customers (market share)
AGE OF HOUSEHOLDER			
Total households	**$23.13**	**100**	**100.0%**
Under age 25	8.83	38	2.7
Aged 25 to 34	24.48	106	20.0
Aged 35 to 44	26.44	114	26.6
Aged 45 to 54	25.53	110	20.2
Aged 55 to 64	26.03	113	13.1
Aged 65 to 74	20.85	90	10.3
Aged 75 or older	18.81	81	7.6
HOUSEHOLD INCOME			
Total households reporting income	**23.58**	**100**	**100.0**
Under $20,000	15.26	65	22.5
$20,000 to $29,999	30.72	130	19.0
$30,000 to $39,999	25.10	106	13.0
$40,000 to $49,999	23.64	100	9.4
$50,000 to $69,999	25.50	108	15.2
$70,000 or more	31.63	134	20.1
HOUSEHOLD TYPE			
Total households	**23.13**	**100**	**100.0**
Married couples	29.59	128	66.9
Married couples, no children	27.19	118	25.1
Married couples, with children	31.00	134	36.0
Oldest child under 6	24.29	105	5.4
Oldest child 6 to 17	31.04	134	19.5
Oldest child 18 or older	36.55	158	11.4
Single parent with child under 18	17.87	77	4.8
Single person	15.11	65	18.8
REGION			
Total households	**23.13**	**100**	**100.0**
Northeast	26.12	113	22.6
Midwest	28.29	122	29.2
South	18.71	81	28.2
West	21.78	94	20.0

Note: For definitions of best and biggest customers, see introduction or glossary.
Source: Calculations by New Strategist based on the 1997 Consumer Expenditure Survey

Tea

Best customers:
- Householders aged 45 to 64
- Married couples with adult children
- Households in the Northeast

Customer trends:
- Spending may rise because of the growing popularity of herbal teas and flavored iced tea.

Older Americans are the best customers of tea. Householders aged 45 to 74 spend 18 to 38 percent more than average on tea. Married couples with adult children at home spend 77 percent more than the average household. Households in the Northeast spend 43 percent more than average on tea.

Herbal teas and flavored iced tea have given the tea market a boost. Spending on tea may rise if more young adults become regular tea drinkers.

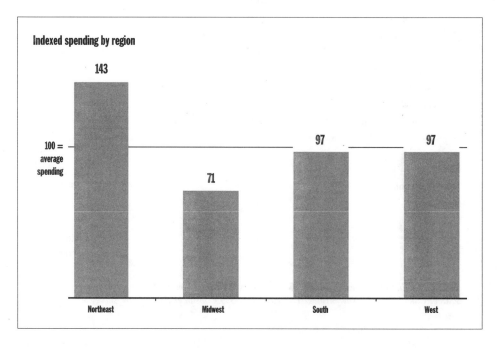

Indexed spending by region

Northeast 143
Midwest 71
South 97
West 97

100 = average spending

TEA

| | Total household spending | $1,558,301,760 |
| Average household spends | 14.76 |

	average spending	best customers (index)	biggest customers (market share)
AGE OF HOUSEHOLDER			
Total households	**$14.76**	**100**	**100.0%**
Under age 25	5.98	41	2.9
Aged 25 to 34	12.52	85	16.0
Aged 35 to 44	14.34	97	22.6
Aged 45 to 54	17.93	121	22.3
Aged 55 to 64	20.30	138	16.0
Aged 65 to 74	17.40	118	13.5
Aged 75 or older	11.11	75	7.0
HOUSEHOLD INCOME			
Total households reporting income	**15.22**	**100**	**100.0**
Under $20,000	10.59	70	24.2
$20,000 to $29,999	14.41	95	13.8
$30,000 to $39,999	19.19	126	15.4
$40,000 to $49,999	18.03	118	11.1
$50,000 to $69,999	18.32	120	16.9
$70,000 or more	17.99	118	17.7
HOUSEHOLD TYPE			
Total households	**14.76**	**100**	**100.0**
Married couples	18.52	125	65.6
Married couples, no children	16.79	114	24.3
Married couples, with children	18.58	126	33.8
Oldest child under 6	12.83	87	4.5
Oldest child 6 to 17	17.24	117	17.0
Oldest child 18 or older	26.07	177	12.7
Single parent with child under 18	12.61	85	5.4
Single person	8.91	60	17.3
REGION			
Total households	**14.76**	**100**	**100.0**
Northeast	21.13	143	28.6
Midwest	10.44	71	16.9
South	14.31	97	33.8
West	14.37	97	20.7

Note: For definitions of best and biggest customers, see introduction or glossary.
Source: Calculations by New Strategist based on the 1997 Consumer Expenditure Survey

Vegetable Juices

Best customers:
- Householders aged 55 to 64
- Married couples with children

Customer trends:
- Spending may rise as the population ages.

The best customers of vegetable juices are married couples with children. These households spend from 31 to 60 percent more than average on this item, in part because their households are larger. Householders aged 55 to 64 spend 20 percent more than average on this item.

Spending on vegetable juices is likely to rise in the years ahead as the population ages. As manufacturers produce a greater variety of vegetable juices to compete with the growing fruit juice market, more consumers will be tempted to buy.

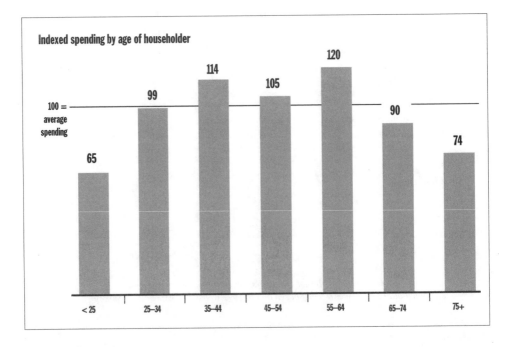

Indexed spending by age of householder

100 = average spending

< 25	25–34	35–44	45–54	55–64	65–74	75+
65	99	114	105	120	90	74

VEGETABLE JUICES

Total household spending	$791,820,000		
Average household spends	7.50		

	average spending	best customers (index)	biggest customers (market share)
AGE OF HOUSEHOLDER			
Total households	$7.50	100	100.0%
Under age 25	4.90	65	4.6
Aged 25 to 34	7.41	99	18.6
Aged 35 to 44	8.55	114	26.5
Aged 45 to 54	7.86	105	19.2
Aged 55 to 64	9.01	120	14.0
Aged 65 to 74	6.75	90	10.3
Aged 75 or older	5.55	74	6.9
HOUSEHOLD INCOME			
Total households reporting income	7.47	100	100.0
Under $20,000	6.35	85	29.6
$20,000 to $29,999	6.11	82	11.9
$30,000 to $39,999	6.82	91	11.2
$40,000 to $49,999	8.82	118	11.0
$50,000 to $69,999	7.22	97	13.6
$70,000 or more	10.96	147	21.9
HOUSEHOLD TYPE			
Total households	7.50	100	100.0
Married couples	9.38	125	65.4
Married couples, no children	7.71	103	21.9
Married couples, with children	10.54	141	37.8
Oldest child under 6	9.82	131	6.7
Oldest child 6 to 17	10.10	135	19.6
Oldest child 18 or older	12.00	160	11.5
Single parent with child under 18	7.71	103	6.5
Single person	3.39	45	13.0
REGION			
Total households	7.50	100	100.0
Northeast	7.82	104	20.8
Midwest	6.07	81	19.3
South	6.89	92	32.0
West	9.73	130	27.6

Note: For definitions of best and biggest customers, see introduction or glossary.
Source: Calculations by New Strategist based on the 1997 Consumer Expenditure Survey

Vegetables, Canned

Best customers:
- Married couples with school-aged or older children
- Householders aged 35 to 64
- Households in the South

Customer trends:
- Spending is likely to decline as the older buyers of canned vegetables are replaced by younger shoppers accustomed to the fresh variety.

The best customers of canned vegetables are older householders. Those aged 55 to 64 spend 21 percent more than the average household on this item. Married couples with school-aged children spend 46 percent more than average, while those with adult children at home spend 37 percent more—in part because these households are larger than average. Households in the South spend 17 percent more than the average household on canned vegetables.

Spending on canned vegetables will decline in the years ahead as the best customers age and are replaced by shoppers who prefer fresh vegetables.

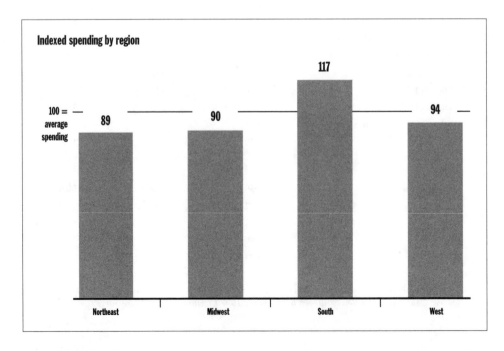

Indexed spending by region

100 = average spending

Northeast 89 | Midwest 90 | South 117 | West 94

VEGETABLES, CANNED

Total household spending	$3,784,899,600	
Average household spends	35.85	

	average spending	best customers ('index)	biggest customers (market share)
AGE OF HOUSEHOLDER			
Total households	**$35.85**	**100**	**100.0%**
Under age 25	17.18	48	3.4
Aged 25 to 34	34.48	96	18.1
Aged 35 to 44	40.29	112	26.1
Aged 45 to 54	41.08	115	21.0
Aged 55 to 64	43.22	121	14.1
Aged 65 to 74	34.46	96	11.0
Aged 75 or older	25.46	71	6.6
HOUSEHOLD INCOME			
Total households reporting income	**36.57**	**100**	**100.0**
Under $20,000	29.06	79	27.7
$20,000 to $29,999	37.99	104	15.2
$30,000 to $39,999	35.81	98	12.0
$40,000 to $49,999	41.56	114	10.6
$50,000 to $69,999	40.52	111	15.6
$70,000 or more	45.26	124	18.5
HOUSEHOLD TYPE			
Total households	**35.85**	**100**	**100.0**
Married couples	45.24	126	66.0
Married couples, no children	38.90	109	23.2
Married couples, with children	48.06	134	36.0
Oldest child under 6	36.52	102	5.2
Oldest child 6 to 17	52.24	146	21.2
Oldest child 18 or older	49.29	137	9.9
Single parent with child under 18	33.34	93	5.8
Single person	16.79	47	13.5
REGION			
Total households	**35.85**	**100**	**100.0**
Northeast	31.80	89	17.7
Midwest	32.39	90	21.6
South	41.89	117	40.8
West	33.74	94	20.0

Note: For definitions of best and biggest customers, see introduction or glossary.
Source: Calculations by New Strategist based on the 1997 Consumer Expenditure Survey

Vegetables, Fresh

The best customers of fresh vegetables are health-conscious older people. Householders aged 55 to 64 spend 30 percent more than the average household on fresh vegetables. Married couples with adult children at home spend 51 percent more than average on this item.

After their children have grown up and householders no longer have to please their kids' picky palates, the consumption of fresh vegetables increases. With health-conscious baby boomers nearing the empty-nest stage of life, spending on fresh vegetables is poised to rise.

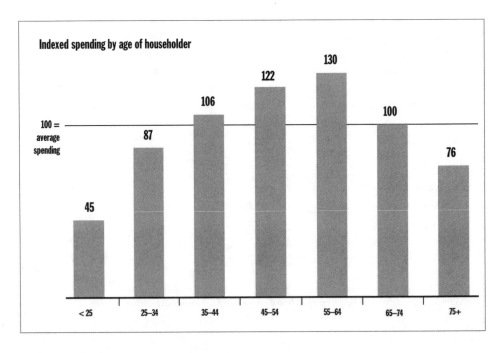

Indexed spending by age of householder

100 = average spending

< 25	25–34	35–44	45–54	55–64	65–74	75+
45	87	106	122	130	100	76

VEGETABLES, FRESH

Total household spending	$15,070,974,000
Average household spends	142.75

	average spending	best customers (index)	biggest customers (market share)
AGE OF HOUSEHOLDER			
Total households	**$142.75**	**100**	**100.0%**
Under age 25	64.41	45	3.2
Aged 25 to 34	124.32	87	16.4
Aged 35 to 44	151.18	106	24.6
Aged 45 to 54	173.82	122	22.3
Aged 55 to 64	185.04	130	15.1
Aged 65 to 74	143.46	100	11.5
Aged 75 or older	108.95	76	7.1
HOUSEHOLD INCOME			
Total households reporting income	**145.02**	**100**	**100.0**
Under $20,000	107.35	74	25.8
$20,000 to $29,999	139.46	96	14.0
$30,000 to $39,999	138.24	95	11.7
$40,000 to $49,999	134.88	93	8.7
$50,000 to $69,999	159.27	110	15.4
$70,000 or more	230.97	159	23.8
HOUSEHOLD TYPE			
Total households	**142.75**	**100**	**100.0**
Married couples	178.99	125	65.6
Married couples, no children	164.81	115	24.6
Married couples, with children	180.33	126	34.0
Oldest child under 6	162.21	114	5.8
Oldest child 6 to 17	170.29	119	17.4
Oldest child 18 or older	215.62	151	10.9
Single parent with child under 18	163.00	114	7.2
Single person	71.68	50	14.4
REGION			
Total households	**142.75**	**100**	**100.0**
Northeast	161.94	113	22.7
Midwest	121.72	85	20.4
South	125.27	88	30.6
West	175.86	123	26.2

Note: For definitions of best and biggest customers, see introduction or glossary.
Source: Calculations by New Strategist based on the 1997 Consumer Expenditure Survey

Vegetables, Frozen

Best customers:
- Married couples with children
- Householders aged 35 to 54

Customer trends:
- Spending is likely to remain stable because frozen vegetables are more convenient to prepare than fresh vegetables.

Married couples with children are the best customers of frozen vegetables, largely because they have more mouths to feed. Another factor driving the higher spending of families with children on frozen vegetables is their convenience. Couples with children spend 33 to 59 percent more than average on this item. Householders aged 35 to 54 spend 22 to 27 percent more than average on frozen vegetables because most have children at home, which boosts their household size.

Spending on frozen vegetables is likely to remain stable because of the convenience they offer busy householders.

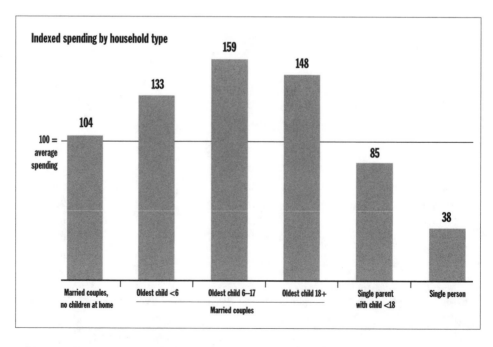

Indexed spending by household type

Married couples, no children at home	Oldest child <6	Oldest child 6–17	Oldest child 18+	Single parent with child <18	Single person
104	133	159	148	85	38

Married couples

100 = average spending

VEGETABLES, FROZEN

Total household spending	$2,805,154,320
Average household spends	26.57

	average spending	best customers (index)	biggest customers (market share)
AGE OF HOUSEHOLDER			
Total households	**$26.57**	**100**	**100.0%**
Under age 25	14.86	56	4.0
Aged 25 to 34	24.53	92	17.4
Aged 35 to 44	33.80	127	29.6
Aged 45 to 54	32.33	122	22.3
Aged 55 to 64	25.99	98	11.4
Aged 65 to 74	24.51	92	10.6
Aged 75 or older	14.98	56	5.2
HOUSEHOLD INCOME			
Total households reporting income	**27.14**	**100**	**100.0**
Under $20,000	17.41	64	22.3
$20,000 to $29,999	20.42	75	11.0
$30,000 to $39,999	29.24	108	13.2
$40,000 to $49,999	36.84	136	12.7
$50,000 to $69,999	29.98	110	15.5
$70,000 or more	44.52	164	24.5
HOUSEHOLD TYPE			
Total households	**26.57**	**100**	**100.0**
Married couples	35.26	133	69.4
Married couples, no children	27.69	104	22.2
Married couples, with children	39.92	150	40.4
Oldest child under 6	35.29	133	6.8
Oldest child 6 to 17	42.14	159	23.1
Oldest child 18 or older	39.30	148	10.6
Single parent with child under 18	22.51	85	5.3
Single person	10.22	38	11.1
REGION			
Total households	**26.57**	**100**	**100.0**
Northeast	30.44	115	22.9
Midwest	22.63	85	20.4
South	29.06	109	38.2
West	23.38	88	18.7

Note: For definitions of best and biggest customers, see introduction or glossary.
Source: Calculations by New Strategist based on the 1997 Consumer Expenditure Survey

Chapter 8.

Food Away From Home

Food Away From Home

The average American household spent $1,921.35 on food-away-from-home in 1997, amounting to 40 percent of the food budget. Some of this total is spent on board while at college, some is spent on catered affairs, and some is devoted to food purchased while on trips (shown separately in the Travel chapter). That leaves $1,477.51 spent by the average household on restaurant and carry-out food in their local area in 1997.

Spending on food away from home by the average household fell 13.1 percent between 1987 and 1997, after adjusting for inflation. This decline was far greater than the 2.9 percent drop in spending on food purchased at grocery stores, which is called food-at-home spending. Consequently, the food-away-from-home share of the food budget is shrinking. Behind this decline are the efforts made by the supermarket industry to woo customers, with many stores offering prepared meals and even sit-down dining areas.

Prepared meals have become a necessity to working parents. To regain lost ground, restaurants will have to offer convenience to busy families while also creating an appealing experience for those with the time to enjoy dining out.

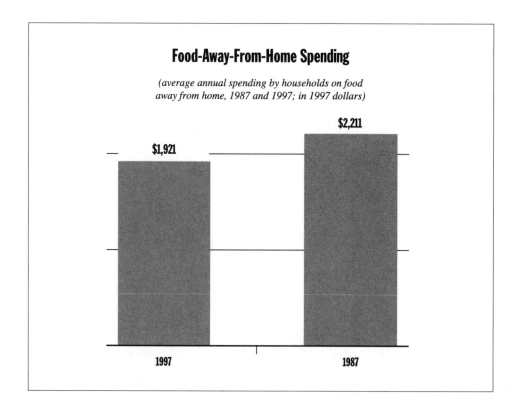

Food-Away-From-Home Spending

(average annual spending by households on food away from home, 1987 and 1997; in 1997 dollars)

$1,921 — 1997

$2,211 — 1987

Food-Away-From-Home Spending

(average annual spending of households on food away from home, and percent distribution of spending by type, 1997)

Total spending on food away from home	**$1,921.35**	**100.0%**
Total spending at restaurants, carry-outs	1,477.51	76.9
Dinner at restaurants, carry-outs	740.70	38.6
Lunch at restaurants, carry-outs	501.92	26.1
Snacks and nonalcoholic beverages purchased at restaurants, carry-outs	119.38	6.2
Breakfast and brunch at restaurants, carry-outs	115.51	6.0

Note: Numbers will not add to total because not all categories are shown, including board while at school, catered affairs, and food purchased on trips which is in the Travel chapter.

Breakfast and Brunch at Restaurants, Carry-Outs

Best customers:	• Householders aged 35 to 54
	• Married couples with school-aged or older children
	• Married couples without children
Customer trends:	• As more men and women go to work, buying a restaurant or carry-out breakfast will remain popular.

Working people, particularly those with children, are the best breakfast customers at restaurants and carry-outs. Married couples with children aged 18 or older at home spend 59 percent more than average on breakfast away from home. Couples with school-aged children spend 28 percent more, while those without children at home spend 15 percent more. Householders aged 35 to 54 spend more than average on this item because most are working parents.

The biggest threat to breakfast away from home is in the freezer case. But so far, microwavable breakfasts aren't as tasty and don't travel as well as restaurant food. As long as men and women have to rush off to work in the morning, breakfast away from home will continue to be popular.

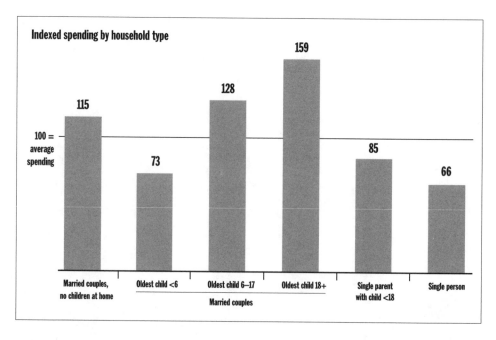

Indexed spending by household type

Married couples, no children at home	115
Oldest child <6	73
Oldest child 6–17	128
Oldest child 18+	159
Single parent with child <18	85
Single person	66

100 = average spending

Married couples

BREAKFAST AND BRUNCH AT RESTAURANTS, CARRY-OUTS

Total household spending $12,195,083,760
Average household spends   115.51

	average spending	best customers (index)	biggest customers (market share)
AGE OF HOUSEHOLDER			
Total households	**$115.51**	**100**	**100.0%**
Under age 25	62.84	54	3.9
Aged 25 to 34	110.84	96	18.1
Aged 35 to 44	142.17	123	28.6
Aged 45 to 54	132.53	115	21.0
Aged 55 to 64	114.47	99	11.6
Aged 65 to 74	123.81	107	12.3
Aged 75 or older	62.78	54	5.1
HOUSEHOLD INCOME			
Total households reporting income	**116.35**	**100**	**100.0**
Under $20,000	56.92	49	17.0
$20,000 to $29,999	105.62	91	13.3
$30,000 to $39,999	129.31	111	13.6
$40,000 to $49,999	162.27	139	13.0
$50,000 to $69,999	156.33	134	18.9
$70,000 or more	180.96	156	23.2
HOUSEHOLD TYPE			
Total households	**115.51**	**100**	**100.0**
Married couples	139.16	120	63.0
Married couples, no children	132.92	115	24.6
Married couples, with children	143.70	124	33.4
Oldest child under 6	84.39	73	3.8
Oldest child 6 to 17	148.15	128	18.7
Oldest child 18 or older	184.22	159	11.5
Single parent with child under 18	97.97	85	5.3
Single person	76.43	66	19.0
REGION			
Total households	**115.51**	**100**	**100.0**
Northeast	123.33	107	21.3
Midwest	124.70	108	25.8
South	96.82	84	29.2
West	127.94	111	23.5

Note: For definitions of best and biggest customers, see introduction or glossary.
Source: Calculations by New Strategist based on the 1997 Consumer Expenditure Survey

Dinner at Restaurants, Carry-Outs

Best customers:
- Householders aged 35 to 54
- Married couples with school-aged or older children

Customer trends:
- Little growth because of competition with supermarkets, more of which are offering prepared meals for busy families.

Working parents have been a boon to restaurants and carry-outs. After a long day at the office, going out to eat or picking up a carry-out dinner is a lot more appealing than cooking and washing dishes. Married couples with children aged 18 or older at home spend 45 percent more than the average household on dinner at restaurants and carry-outs. Those with school-aged children spend 23 percent more than average. Householders aged 35 to 54, most of whom are parents, spend 19 to 24 percent more than average.

Supermarkets are pulling ahead in the battle with restaurants over the consumer's food dollar. With a growing number of supermarkets offering convenient meals for busy families, spending on restaurant and carry-out dinners is not likely to grow much in the near future.

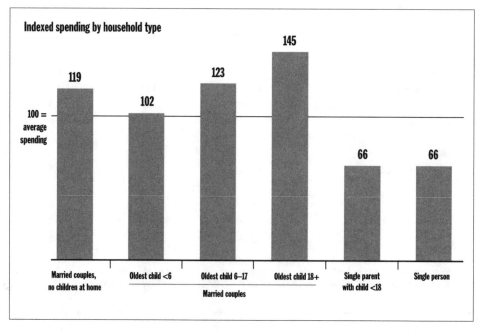

Indexed spending by household type

		Married couples			Single parent with child <18	Single person
Married couples, no children at home	Oldest child <6	Oldest child 6–17	Oldest child 18+			
119	102	123	145		66	66

100 = average spending

DINNER AT RESTAURANTS, CARRY-OUTS

Total household spending	$78,200,143,200
Average household spends	740.70

	average spending	best customers (index)	biggest customers (market share)
AGE OF HOUSEHOLDER			
Total households	**$740.70**	**100**	**100.0%**
Under age 25	481.54	65	4.6
Aged 25 to 34	731.20	99	18.6
Aged 35 to 44	881.45	119	27.7
Aged 45 to 54	918.48	124	22.7
Aged 55 to 64	779.05	105	12.3
Aged 65 to 74	645.38	87	10.0
Aged 75 or older	357.11	48	4.5
HOUSEHOLD INCOME			
Total households reporting income	**753.30**	**100**	**100.0**
Under $20,000	369.45	49	17.1
$20,000 to $29,999	541.94	72	10.5
$30,000 to $39,999	722.73	96	11.7
$40,000 to $49,999	870.85	116	10.8
$50,000 to $69,999	1,039.69	138	19.4
$70,000 or more	1,498.26	199	29.7
HOUSEHOLD TYPE			
Total households	**740.70**	**100**	**100.0**
Married couples	899.18	121	63.5
Married couples, no children	878.06	119	25.3
Married couples, with children	919.76	124	33.4
Oldest child under 6	752.06	102	5.2
Oldest child 6 to 17	911.63	123	17.9
Oldest child 18 or older	1,076.06	145	10.4
Single parent with child under 18	491.63	66	4.2
Single person	486.80	66	18.9
REGION			
Total households	**740.70**	**100**	**100.0**
Northeast	809.80	109	21.8
Midwest	776.12	105	25.0
South	648.49	88	30.5
West	785.05	106	22.5

Note: For definitions of best and biggest customers, see introduction or glossary.
Source: Calculations by New Strategist based on the 1997 Consumer Expenditure Survey

Lunch at Restaurants, Carry-Outs

Best customers:	• Householders aged 25 to 54
	• Married couples with school-aged or older children
Customer trends:	• If the economy remains strong, spending in this category is likely to increase.

Working people frequently buy lunch at restaurants or from carry-outs. This explains why householders aged 25 to 54—in their prime working years—spend more than average on this item. The best customers in the category are married couples with school-aged or older children at home. Most of these households have at least two earners, so they generally have more money than time. Married couples with adult children at home spend 52 percent more than average on lunch at restaurants and carry-outs. Those with school-aged children spend 46 percent more.

Bringing a bag lunch to work is a less expensive alternative to buying lunch from a restaurant or carry-out, but as long as the economy remains strong, spending on lunch from restaurants or carry-outs is likely to rise.

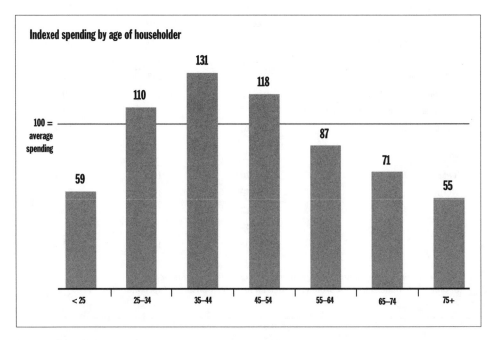

Indexed spending by age of householder

100 = average spending

< 25	25–34	35–44	45–54	55–64	65–74	75+
59	110	131	118	87	71	55

LUNCH AT RESTAURANTS, CARRY-OUTS

Total household spending $52,990,705,920
Average household spends   501.92

	average spending	best customers (index)	biggest customers (market share)
AGE OF HOUSEHOLDER			
Total households	**$501.92**	**100**	**100.0%**
Under age 25	298.02	59	4.2
Aged 25 to 34	553.50	110	20.8
Aged 35 to 44	658.91	131	30.5
Aged 45 to 54	593.04	118	21.6
Aged 55 to 64	434.30	87	10.1
Aged 65 to 74	354.99	71	8.1
Aged 75 or older	278.25	55	5.2
HOUSEHOLD INCOME			
Total households reporting income	**517.92**	**100**	**100.0**
Under $20,000	242.45	47	16.3
$20,000 to $29,999	434.38	84	12.3
$30,000 to $39,999	498.84	96	11.8
$40,000 to $49,999	599.68	116	10.8
$50,000 to $69,999	721.86	139	19.6
$70,000 or more	986.14	190	28.5
HOUSEHOLD TYPE			
Total households	**501.92**	**100**	**100.0**
Married couples	619.49	123	64.5
Married couples, no children	514.56	103	21.9
Married couples, with children	695.88	139	37.3
Oldest child under 6	530.37	106	5.4
Oldest child 6 to 17	730.72	146	21.2
Oldest child 18 or older	763.96	152	10.9
Single parent with child under 18	370.88	74	4.6
Single person	306.23	61	17.5
REGION			
Total households	**501.92**	**100**	**100.0**
Northeast	542.35	108	21.6
Midwest	488.65	97	23.3
South	499.01	99	34.7
West	484.08	96	20.5

Note: For definitions of best and biggest customers, see introduction or glossary.
Source: Calculations by New Strategist based on the 1997 Consumer Expenditure Survey

Snacks and Nonalcoholic Beverages at Restaurants, Carry-Outs

Best customers:
- Householders aged 25 to 54
- Married couples with children

Customer trends:
- The number of teens and young adults is growing, boosting sales of snacks and nonalcoholic beverages at restaurants and carry-outs.

Married couples with children are the best customers of snacks and nonalcoholic beverages at restaurants and carry-outs. Married couples with children of any age at home spend 48 percent more than the average household on snacks and beverages. Householders aged 25 to 54, most of whom have children, spend from 17 to 39 percent more than the average household on this item.

Teens are big eaters, spending not only family money but also their own funds on snacks and nonalcoholic beverages. As the number of teens and young adults rises, sales of snacks and beverages at restaurants and carry-outs should grow.

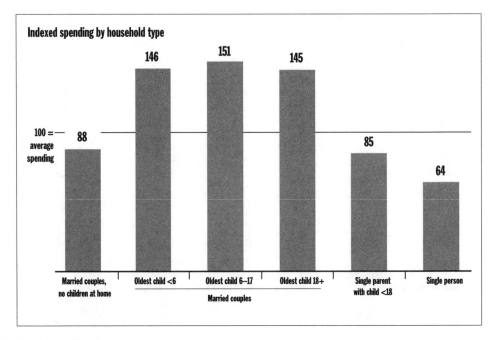

Indexed spending by household type

Married couples, no children at home	Oldest child <6	Oldest child 6–17	Oldest child 18+	Single parent with child <18	Single person
88	146	151	145	85	64

100 = average spending

Married couples

SNACKS AND NONALCOHOLIC BEVERAGES PURCHASED AT RESTAURANTS, CARRY-OUTS

Total household spending $12,603,662,880
Average household spends   119.38

	average spending	best customers (index)	biggest customers (market share)
AGE OF HOUSEHOLDER			
Total households	**$119.38**	**100**	**100.0%**
Under age 25	108.77	91	6.5
Aged 25 to 34	146.75	123	23.2
Aged 35 to 44	166.43	139	32.4
Aged 45 to 54	140.26	117	21.5
Aged 55 to 64	101.08	85	9.9
Aged 65 to 74	53.14	45	5.1
Aged 75 or older	22.85	19	1.8
HOUSEHOLD INCOME			
Total households reporting income	**128.93**	**100**	**100.0**
Under $20,000	66.53	52	18.0
$20,000 to $29,999	96.28	75	10.9
$30,000 to $39,999	133.69	104	12.7
$40,000 to $49,999	176.93	137	12.8
$50,000 to $69,999	163.68	127	17.8
$70,000 or more	231.59	180	26.9
HOUSEHOLD TYPE			
Total households	**119.38**	**100**	**100.0**
Married couples	147.11	123	64.4
Married couples, no children	104.86	88	18.7
Married couples, with children	177.27	148	39.9
Oldest child under 6	174.25	146	7.5
Oldest child 6 to 17	180.83	151	22.0
Oldest child 18 or older	172.64	145	10.4
Single parent with child under 18	102.03	85	5.4
Single person	76.23	64	18.3
REGION			
Total households	**119.38**	**100**	**100.0**
Northeast	130.85	110	21.9
Midwest	129.69	109	26.0
South	101.06	85	29.5
West	126.67	106	22.5

Note: For definitions of best and biggest customers, see introduction or glossary.
Source: Calculations by New Strategist based on the 1997 Consumer Expenditure Survey

Chapter 9.

Gifts

Gifts

Gift purchasing patterns are changing, with Americans increasingly likely to give gifts of experiences (such as travel packages, massages, and so on) rather than sweaters, ties, and blenders. Consequently, spending on traditional gifts, such as apparel, has declined over the past decade. Spending on gifts of clothing fell more than 20 percent between 1987 and 1997, after adjusting for inflation. Spending on gifts of household textiles (sheets, towels, etc.) plummeted 53 percent during those years.

The biggest spenders on many gifts are the most affluent householders, typically those aged 45 to 54. But the most traditional gift givers are older householders. They are the ones most likely to spend on gifts of apparel and household items. As the experiential baby-boom generation enters its fifties and sixties in the years ahead, it's likely that a growing share of gift spending will be devoted to experiences.

Readers should note that the gift spending shown here is limited to gifts given to people living in other households, not within the same household. Gift spending is also included in individual product and service categories.

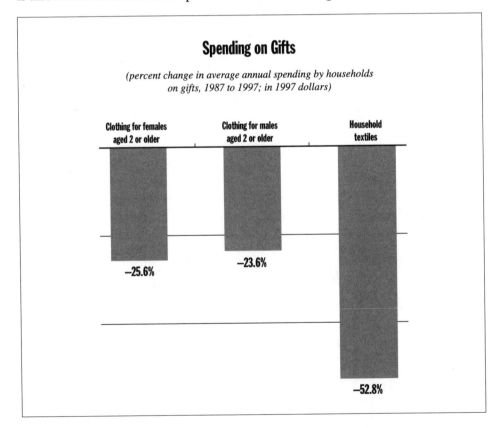

Spending on Gifts

(percent change in average annual spending by households on gifts, 1987 to 1997; in 1997 dollars)

Clothing for females aged 2 or older: −25.6%
Clothing for males aged 2 or older: −23.6%
Household textiles: −52.8%

Gift Spending

(average annual spending of households on gifts, and percent distribution of spending by type, 1997)

Total spending on gifts	**$1,059.44**	**100.0%**
Gifts of women's and girls' apparel	81.19	7.7
Gifts of men's and boys' apparel	61.29	5.8
Gifts of out-of-town trip expenses	46.85	4.4
Gifts of food	43.94	4.1
Gifts of jewelry	41.18	3.9
Gifts of toys, games, hobby supplies, and tricycles	40.95	3.9
Gifts of housekeeping supplies	36.73	3.5
Gifts of infants' apparel	32.52	3.1
Gifts of appliances and miscellaneous housewares	27.34	2.6
Gifts of stationery, stationery supplies, giftwrap	20.71	2.0
Gifts of plants and fresh flowers, indoor	16.63	1.6
Gifts of telephone service, excluding mobile phone service	16.34	1.5
Gifts of entertainment events, out-of-town trips	10.36	1.0
Gifts of household textiles	8.35	0.8
Gifts of airline fares	6.89	0.7
Gifts of infants' equipment and furniture	4.50	0.4

Note: Numbers will not add to total because not all categories are shown.

Gifts of Airline Fares

Best customers:
- Householders aged 45 to 54
- Married couples without children
- Households in the West

Customer trends:
- Increased spending is possible if the economy remains strong.

The middle-aged are the best customers of airline fares as gifts. Householders aged 45 to 54 spend 86 percent more than the average household on airline tickets purchased for others. Married couples without children at home spend 72 percent more than average on this item, many of them buying tickets for adult children traveling to and from college. Households in the West spend 85 percent more than the average household on gifts of airline fares.

Older boomers are in their peak earning years at a time when the economy is strong. This should boost spending on gifts of airline fares.

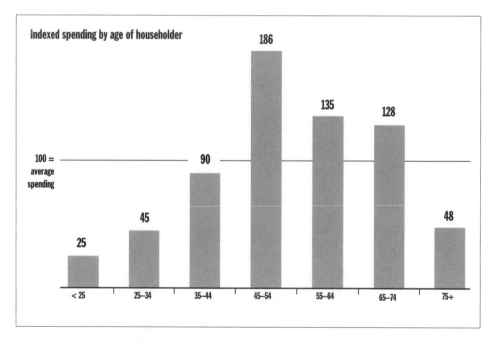

Indexed spending by age of householder

100 = average spending

| <25 | 25–34 | 35–44 | 45–54 | 55–64 | 65–74 | 75+ |
| 25 | 45 | 90 | 186 | 135 | 128 | 48 |

GIFTS OF AIRLINE FARES

Total household spending	$727,418,640		
Average household spends	6.89		

	average spending	best customers (index)	biggest customers (market share)
AGE OF HOUSEHOLDER			
Total households	**$6.89**	**100**	**100.0%**
Under age 25	1.74	25	1.8
Aged 25 to 34	3.07	45	8.4
Aged 35 to 44	6.20	90	20.9
Aged 45 to 54	12.83	186	34.1
Aged 55 to 64	9.27	135	15.7
Aged 65 to 74	8.81	128	14.7
Aged 75 or older	3.29	48	4.4
HOUSEHOLD INCOME			
Total households reporting income	**7.64**	**100**	**100.0**
Under $20,000	2.80	37	12.8
$20,000 to $29,999	5.59	73	10.7
$30,000 to $39,999	5.43	71	8.7
$40,000 to $49,999	7.58	99	9.3
$50,000 to $69,999	13.64	179	25.1
$70,000 or more	17.12	224	33.5
HOUSEHOLD TYPE			
Total households	**6.89**	**100**	**100.0**
Married couples	8.51	124	64.6
Married couples, no children	11.83	172	36.6
Married couples, with children	6.19	90	24.2
Oldest child under 6	4.13	60	3.1
Oldest child 6 to 17	8.15	118	17.2
Oldest child 18 or older	3.71	54	3.9
Single parent with child under 18	7.00	102	6.4
Single person	4.92	71	20.5
REGION			
Total households	**6.89**	**100**	**100.0**
Northeast	6.27	91	18.2
Midwest	6.92	100	24.0
South	3.67	53	18.6
West	12.74	185	39.3

Note: For definitions of best and biggest customers, see introduction or glossary.
Source: Calculations by New Strategist based on the 1997 Consumer Expenditure Survey

Gifts of Appliances and Miscellaneous Housewares

Best customers:
- Householders aged 45 to 64
- Married couples with adult children
- Married couples without children

Customer trends:
- Spending may rise as boomer parents buy appliances and housewares for grown children setting up their own households.

Householders aged 55 to 64 spend twice as much as the average household on gifts of appliances and miscellaneous housewares. Married couples without children at home and those with adult children at home spend 51 to 66 percent more than average on this item. Behind this spending are parents buying appliances and housewares for grown children who are setting up their own households.

As the children of boomers grow up and the young-adult population expands, spending on gifts of appliances and housewares is likely to rise.

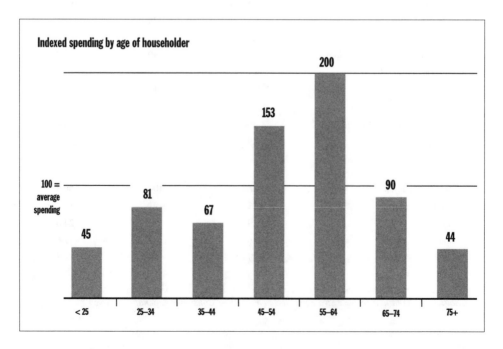

Indexed spending by age of householder

100 = average spending

| < 25 | 25–34 | 35–44 | 45–54 | 55–64 | 65–74 | 75+ |
| 45 | 81 | 67 | 153 | 200 | 90 | 44 |

GIFTS OF APPLIANCES AND MISCELLANEOUS HOUSEWARES

Total household spending	$2,886,447,840
Average household spends	27.34

	average spending	best customers (index)	biggest customers (market share)
AGE OF HOUSEHOLDER			
Total households	**$27.34**	**100**	**100.0%**
Under age 25	12.25	45	3.2
Aged 25 to 34	22.13	81	15.3
Aged 35 to 44	18.37	67	15.6
Aged 45 to 54	41.77	153	28.0
Aged 55 to 64	54.76	200	23.4
Aged 65 to 74	24.70	90	10.4
Aged 75 or older	12.08	44	4.1
HOUSEHOLD INCOME			
Total households reporting income	**30.20**	**100**	**100.0**
Under $20,000	15.29	51	17.6
$20,000 to $29,999	20.54	68	9.9
$30,000 to $39,999	27.06	90	11.0
$40,000 to $49,999	22.81	76	7.1
$50,000 to $69,999	39.95	132	18.6
$70,000 or more	71.56	237	35.4
HOUSEHOLD TYPE			
Total households	**27.34**	**100**	**100.0**
Married couples	34.47	126	65.9
Married couples, no children	41.25	151	32.2
Married couples, with children	29.17	107	28.7
Oldest child under 6	27.30	100	5.1
Oldest child 6 to 17	21.56	79	11.5
Oldest child 18 or older	45.31	166	11.9
Single parent with child under 18	10.83	40	2.5
Single person	23.40	86	24.6
REGION			
Total households	**27.34**	**100**	**100.0**
Northeast	30.55	112	22.3
Midwest	33.48	122	29.3
South	23.87	87	30.5
West	23.27	85	18.1

Note: For definitions of best and biggest customers, see introduction or glossary.
Source: Calculations by New Strategist based on the 1997 Consumer Expenditure Survey

Gifts of Entertainment Events, Out-of-Town Trips

Best customers:	• Householders aged 45 to 54
	• Households with incomes of $70,000 or more
	• Households in the West
Customer trends:	• Spending is likely to rise along with the number of affluent households.

When visiting friends and family out of town, many people show their gratitude by treating their hosts to entertainment events, such as movies or ball games. The affluent spend the most entertaining others while out of town. Households with incomes of $70,000 or more spend two and one-half times as much as the average household on this item. Householders aged 45 to 54 spend 81 percent more than average, while households in the West spend 44 percent more.

The number of affluent households should grow for another decade as boomers fill the peak-earning age groups. Consequently, spending on gifts of entertainment events while on out-of-town trips is likely to grow.

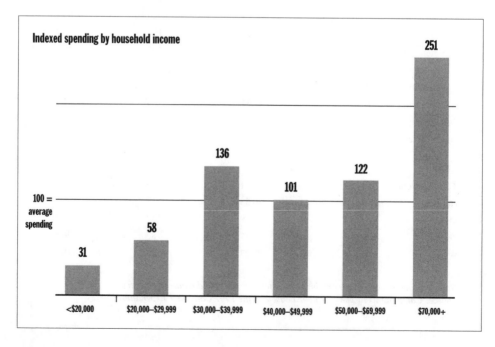

Indexed spending by household income

100 = average spending

<$20,000	$20,000–$29,999	$30,000–$39,999	$40,000–$49,999	$50,000–$69,999	$70,000+
31	58	136	101	122	251

GIFTS OF ENTERTAINMENT EVENTS, OUT-OF-TOWN TRIPS

Total household spending $1,093,767,360
Average household spends   10.36

	average spending	best customers (index)	biggest customers (market share)
AGE OF HOUSEHOLDER			
Total households	**$10.36**	**100**	**100.0%**
Under age 25	6.84	66	4.7
Aged 25 to 34	7.32	71	13.3
Aged 35 to 44	9.08	88	20.4
Aged 45 to 54	18.79	181	33.2
Aged 55 to 64	14.43	139	16.2
Aged 65 to 74	7.65	74	8.5
Aged 75 or older	4.04	39	3.6
HOUSEHOLD INCOME			
Total households reporting income	**11.41**	**100**	**100.0**
Under $20,000	3.59	31	11.0
$20,000 to $29,999	6.61	58	8.5
$30,000 to $39,999	15.49	136	16.6
$40,000 to $49,999	11.56	101	9.5
$50,000 to $69,999	13.88	122	17.1
$70,000 or more	28.60	251	37.5
HOUSEHOLD TYPE			
Total households	**10.36**	**100**	**100.0**
Married couples	12.57	121	63.4
Married couples, no children	13.67	132	28.2
Married couples, with children	12.53	121	32.5
Oldest child under 6	6.33	61	3.1
Oldest child 6 to 17	13.49	130	18.9
Oldest child 18 or older	15.04	145	10.4
Single parent with child under 18	2.07	20	1.3
Single person	9.55	92	26.5
REGION			
Total households	**10.36**	**100**	**100.0**
Northeast	11.85	114	22.8
Midwest	10.87	105	25.1
South	6.41	62	21.6
West	14.87	144	30.5

Note: For definitions of best and biggest customers, see introduction or glossary.
Source: Calculations by New Strategist based on the 1997 Consumer Expenditure Survey

Gifts of Food

Best customers:
- Householders aged 35 to 64
- Married couples without children

Customer trends:
- Little growth is likely as cooking-averse boomers become empty nesters.

Married couples without children at home spend 68 percent more than the average household on gifts of food. Giving a gift of food is a nurturing act. Many of these typically older couples are taking soups, casseroles, and desserts to grown children living elsewhere. This also explains why householders aged 35 to 64 spend at least 30 percent more than average on gifts of food. Many in the age group are parents of grown children.

As boomers become empty nesters, spending on gifts of food is likely to remain stable. Although boomers cook less than older generations, takeout and prepared food are likely to substitute for gifts of home-cooked meals.

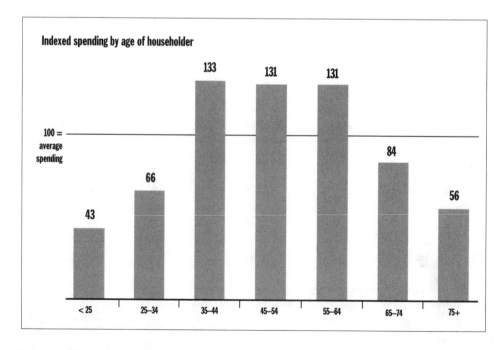

Indexed spending by age of householder

100 = average spending

< 25	25–34	35–44	45–54	55–64	65–74	75+
43	66	133	131	131	84	56

GIFTS OF FOOD

Total household spending	$4,639,009,440
Average household spends	43.94

	average spending	best customers (index)	biggest customers (market share)
AGE OF HOUSEHOLDER			
Total households	**$43.94**	**100**	**100.0%**
Under age 25	18.83	43	3.0
Aged 25 to 34	28.96	66	12.4
Aged 35 to 44	58.24	133	30.8
Aged 45 to 54	57.58	131	24.0
Aged 55 to 64	57.41	131	15.2
Aged 65 to 74	36.93	84	9.6
Aged 75 or older	24.62	56	5.2
HOUSEHOLD INCOME			
Total households reporting income	**43.17**	**100**	**100.0**
Under $20,000	17.46	40	14.1
$20,000 to $29,999	33.39	77	11.3
$30,000 to $39,999	34.19	79	9.7
$40,000 to $49,999	40.55	94	8.8
$50,000 to $69,999	79.19	183	25.7
$70,000 or more	86.38	200	29.9
HOUSEHOLD TYPE			
Total households	**43.94**	**100**	**100.0**
Married couples	56.97	130	67.8
Married couples, no children	73.87	168	35.9
Married couples, with children	46.86	107	28.7
Oldest child under 6	–	–	–
Oldest child 6 to 17	50.68	115	16.8
Oldest child 18 or older	42.24	96	6.9
Single parent with child under 18	14.67	33	2.1
Single person	30.26	69	19.8
REGION			
Total households	**43.94**	**100**	**100.0**
Northeast	43.06	98	19.6
Midwest	42.36	96	23.0
South	42.16	96	33.5
West	49.30	112	23.8

Note: (–) means sample is too small to make a reliable estimate. For definitions of best and biggest customers, see introduction or glossary.
Source: Calculations by New Strategist based on the 1997 Consumer Expenditure Survey

Gifts of Household Textiles

Best customers:
- Householders aged 55 to 64
- Married couples without children

Customer trends:
- Little change in spending until the children of boomers set up house and their parents buy them sheets and towels.

The best customers of household textile gifts are older householders and married couples without children at home, many of whom are older. Householders aged 55 to 64 spend 78 percent more than the average householder on gifts of household textiles. Married couples without children at home spend 65 percent more than average. For both groups, the primary recipients of these gifts are grown children setting up house.

Spending on gifts of household textiles is unlikely to change much in the near future. Within a decade, however, the large Millennial generation (the children of baby boomers) will reach the age of independence. As they do, spending on gifts of household textiles should increase substantially.

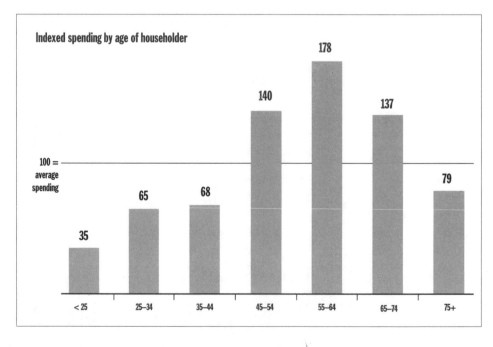

GIFTS OF HOUSEHOLD TEXTILES

Total household spending	$881,559,600		
Average household spends	8.35		

	average spending	best customers (index)	biggest customers (market share)
AGE OF HOUSEHOLDER			
Total households	**$8.35**	**100**	**100.0%**
Under age 25	2.92	35	2.5
Aged 25 to 34	5.40	65	12.2
Aged 35 to 44	5.66	68	15.8
Aged 45 to 54	11.71	140	25.7
Aged 55 to 64	14.86	178	20.8
Aged 65 to 74	11.46	137	15.7
Aged 75 or older	6.62	79	7.4
HOUSEHOLD INCOME			
Total households reporting income	**9.02**	**100**	**100.0**
Under $20,000	4.93	55	19.0
$20,000 to $29,999	6.40	71	10.4
$30,000 to $39,999	6.05	67	8.2
$40,000 to $49,999	10.03	111	10.4
$50,000 to $69,999	12.74	141	19.8
$70,000 or more	19.43	215	32.2
HOUSEHOLD TYPE			
Total households	**8.35**	**100**	**100.0**
Married couples	10.25	123	64.2
Married couples, no children	13.77	165	35.2
Married couples, with children	8.12	97	26.1
Oldest child under 6	3.92	47	2.4
Oldest child 6 to 17	7.63	91	13.3
Oldest child 18 or older	12.10	145	10.4
Single parent with child under 18	2.34	28	1.8
Single person	8.00	96	27.5
REGION			
Total households	**8.35**	**100**	**100.0**
Northeast	9.93	119	23.8
Midwest	8.50	102	24.3
South	6.74	81	28.2
West	9.36	112	23.8

Note: For definitions of best and biggest customers, see introduction or glossary.
Source: Calculations by New Strategist based on the 1997 Consumer Expenditure Survey

Gifts of Housekeeping Supplies

Best customers:
- Married couples without children
- Householders in the Midwest

Customer trends:
- Spending is not likely to change much in the near future.

Housekeeping supplies are frequently given as gifts, particularly between parents and grown children. The best customers of this item are married couples without children at home, spending 45 percent more than the average household. Many of these householders are older and they are giving housekeeping supplies to adult children living elsewhere. Householders in the Midwest spend 31 percent more than average on this item.

Spending on gifts of housekeeping supplies is likely to remain stable for the next few years. As the children of boomers grow up and leave home, spending may rise because boomer parents will be buying supplies for their children.

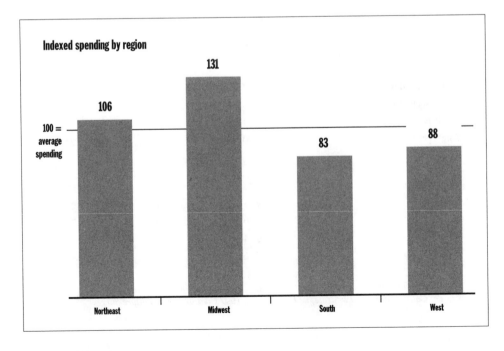

Indexed spending by region

100 = average spending

Northeast 106 Midwest 131 South 83 West 88

GIFTS OF HOUSEKEEPING SUPPLIES

Total household spending $3,877,806,480
Average household spends   36.73

	average spending	best customers (index)	biggest customers (market share)
AGE OF HOUSEHOLDER			
Total households	**$36.73**	**100**	**100.0%**
Under age 25	12.95	35	2.5
Aged 25 to 34	31.73	86	16.3
Aged 35 to 44	46.50	127	29.5
Aged 45 to 54	38.84	106	19.4
Aged 55 to 64	44.02	120	14.0
Aged 65 to 74	41.26	112	12.9
Aged 75 or older	23.90	65	6.1
HOUSEHOLD INCOME			
Total households reporting income	**39.84**	**100**	**100.0**
Under $20,000	21.58	54	18.9
$20,000 to $29,999	30.73	77	11.3
$30,000 to $39,999	38.54	97	11.8
$40,000 to $49,999	42.38	106	9.9
$50,000 to $69,999	45.95	115	16.2
$70,000 or more	82.63	207	31.0
HOUSEHOLD TYPE			
Total households	**36.73**	**100**	**100.0**
Married couples	46.00	125	65.5
Married couples, no children	53.36	145	31.0
Married couples, with children	43.51	118	31.8
Oldest child under 6	36.01	98	5.0
Oldest child 6 to 17	46.32	126	18.3
Oldest child 18 or older	44.14	120	8.6
Single parent with child under 18	20.94	57	3.6
Single person	28.98	79	22.7
REGION			
Total households	**36.73**	**100**	**100.0**
Northeast	38.80	106	21.1
Midwest	48.14	131	31.3
South	30.40	83	28.9
West	32.41	88	18.7

Note: For definitions of best and biggest customers, see introduction or glossary.
Source: Calculations by New Strategist based on the 1997 Consumer Expenditure Survey

Gifts of Infants' Apparel

Best customers:
- Householders aged 25 to 34
- Married couples with children under age 6

Customer trends:
- A spending decline is likely until the Millennial generation begins to have children.

Although grandparents often dote on grandchildren, they are not the best customers of infant apparel gifts. That distinction belongs to married couples with young children. Couples with children under age 6 spend nearly three times as much as the average household on gifts of infants' apparel as their friends become new parents. Householders aged 25 to 34, the age when most Americans have children, spend 35 percent more than average.

The number of young couples is down because the small Generation X is in its twenties. This will mean less spending on gifts of infants' apparel. When the Millennial generation (the children of baby boomers) begins to have children in about five years, spending on gifts of baby clothes will rise again.

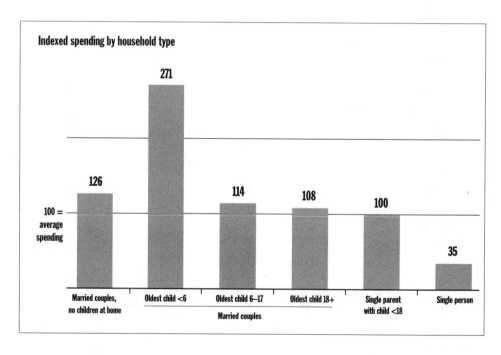

Indexed spending by household type

271	Oldest child <6
126	Married couples, no children at home
114	Oldest child 6–17
108	Oldest child 18+
100	Single parent with child <18
35	Single person

100 = average spending

Married couples

GIFTS OF INFANTS' APPAREL

Total household spending	$3,433,331,520	
Average household spends	32.52	

	average spending	best customers (index)	biggest customers (market share)
AGE OF HOUSEHOLDER			
Total households	**$32.52**	**100**	**100.0%**
Under age 25	21.89	67	4.8
Aged 25 to 34	44.06	135	25.6
Aged 35 to 44	33.27	102	23.8
Aged 45 to 54	38.58	119	21.7
Aged 55 to 64	32.24	99	11.6
Aged 65 to 74	23.24	71	8.2
Aged 75 or older	16.55	51	4.7
HOUSEHOLD INCOME			
Total households reporting income	**33.37**	**100**	**100.0**
Under $20,000	18.49	55	19.3
$20,000 to $29,999	27.17	81	11.9
$30,000 to $39,999	38.46	115	14.1
$40,000 to $49,999	39.89	120	11.2
$50,000 to $69,999	44.75	134	18.8
$70,000 or more	53.42	160	23.9
HOUSEHOLD TYPE			
Total households	**32.52**	**100**	**100.0**
Married couples	44.05	135	70.8
Married couples, no children	40.94	126	26.9
Married couples, with children	47.52	146	39.3
Oldest child under 6	88.16	271	13.9
Oldest child 6 to 17	36.93	114	16.5
Oldest child 18 or older	34.99	108	7.7
Single parent with child under 18	32.68	100	6.3
Single person	11.39	35	10.1
REGION			
Total households	**32.52**	**100**	**100.0**
Northeast	35.11	108	21.6
Midwest	27.20	84	20.0
South	29.72	91	31.9
West	40.44	124	26.4

Note: For definitions of best and biggest customers, see introduction or glossary.
Source: Calculations by New Strategist based on the 1997 Consumer Expenditure Survey

Gifts of Infants' Equipment and Furniture

Best customers:
- Householders aged 55 to 64
- Married couples without children
- Households with incomes of $70,000 or more

Customer trends:
- Spending should remain stable until boomers become grandparents.

The best customers of infants' equipment and furniture gifts are new grandparents. Householders aged 55 to 64, the age at which many people become grandparents for the first time, spend twice as much as the average household on gifts of infants' equipment and furniture. Married couples without children in the household, most of whom are older, spend twice the average on this item. Households with incomes of $70,000 or more spend three times as much as the average household, and account for half the market.

Although some boomers are already grandparents, most will have to wait a few more years for grandchildren. Spending on gifts of infants' equipment and furniture will be remain stable until then.

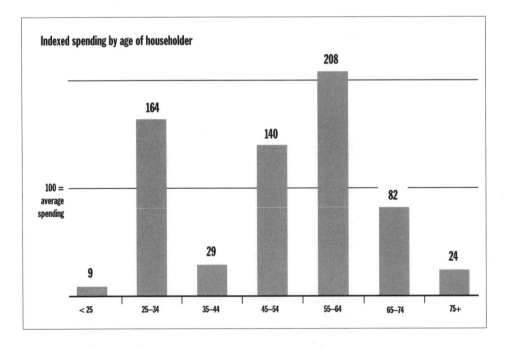

Indexed spending by age of householder

100 = average spending

| <25 | 25–34 | 35–44 | 45–54 | 55–64 | 65–74 | 75+ |
| 9 | 164 | 29 | 140 | 208 | 82 | 24 |

GIFTS OF INFANTS' EQUIPMENT AND FURNITURE

Total household spending	$475,092,000
Average household spends	4.50

	average spending	best customers (index)	biggest customers (market share)
AGE OF HOUSEHOLDER			
Total households	**$4.50**	**100**	**100.0%**
Under age 25	0.40	9	0.6
Aged 25 to 34	7.38	164	30.9
Aged 35 to 44	1.30	29	6.7
Aged 45 to 54	6.29	140	25.6
Aged 55 to 64	9.38	208	24.3
Aged 65 to 74	3.69	82	9.4
Aged 75 or older	1.10	24	2.3
HOUSEHOLD INCOME			
Total households reporting income	**5.05**	**100**	**100.0**
Under $20,000	1.83	36	12.6
$20,000 to $29,999	2.75	54	8.0
$30,000 to $39,999	1.42	28	3.4
$40,000 to $49,999	6.20	123	11.5
$50,000 to $69,999	4.79	95	13.3
$70,000 or more	16.74	331	49.6
HOUSEHOLD TYPE			
Total households	**4.50**	**100**	**100.0**
Married couples	5.75	128	66.8
Married couples, no children	9.59	213	45.5
Married couples, with children	3.41	76	20.4
Oldest child under 6	1.18	26	1.3
Oldest child 6 to 17	2.94	65	9.5
Oldest child 18 or older	6.05	134	9.7
Single parent with child under 18	5.56	124	7.8
Single person	3.44	76	22.0
REGION			
Total households	**4.50**	**100**	**100.0**
Northeast	3.33	74	14.8
Midwest	6.15	137	32.7
South	2.32	52	18.0
West	7.30	162	34.5

Note: For definitions of best and biggest customers, see introduction or glossary.
Source: Calculations by New Strategist based on the 1997 Consumer Expenditure Survey

Gifts of Jewelry

Best customers:
- Households with incomes of $50,000 or more
- Householders aged 45 to 54
- Married couples with adult children

Customer trends:
- Increased spending is likely as a growing number of affluent boomers enjoy their wealth.

The best customers of jewelry gifts are households with incomes of $50,000 or more, spending two to three times as much as the average household on this item. Households with incomes of $50,000 or more account for nearly three-quarters of all spending on gifts of jewelry. Householders aged 45 to 54, who are in their peak-earning years, spend more than twice as much as the average household on gifts of jewelry. Married couples with adult children at home spend nearly two and one-half times as much as the average on this item.

The number of affluent households is growing as boomers enter their peak-earning years. Spending on gifts of jewelry is likely to grow with the expanding ranks of affluent households.

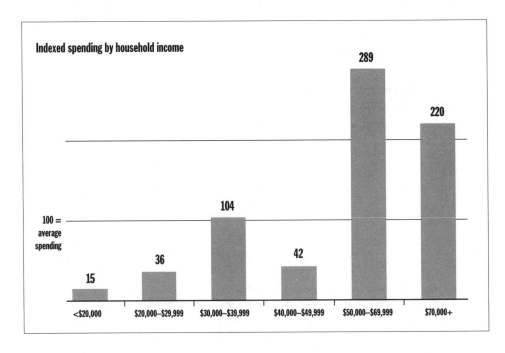

Indexed spending by household income

<$20,000	$20,000–$29,999	$30,000–$39,999	$40,000–$49,999	$50,000–$69,999	$70,000+
15	36	104	42	289	220

100 = average spending

GIFTS OF JEWELRY

Total household spending $4,347,619,680
Average household spends   41.18

	average spending	best customers (index)	biggest customers (market share)
AGE OF HOUSEHOLDER			
Total households	**$41.18**	**100**	**100.0%**
Under age 25	41.66	101	7.2
Aged 25 to 34	17.33	42	7.9
Aged 35 to 44	24.82	60	14.0
Aged 45 to 54	95.12	231	42.3
Aged 55 to 64	55.08	134	15.6
Aged 65 to 74	38.00	92	10.6
Aged 75 or older	9.40	23	2.1
HOUSEHOLD INCOME			
Total households reporting income	**43.57**	**100**	**100.0**
Under $20,000	6.39	15	5.1
$20,000 to $29,999	15.50	36	5.2
$30,000 to $39,999	45.39	104	12.7
$40,000 to $49,999	18.39	42	3.9
$50,000 to $69,999	126.08	289	40.6
$70,000 or more	95.98	220	32.9
HOUSEHOLD TYPE			
Total households	**41.18**	**100**	**100.0**
Married couples	57.87	141	73.5
Married couples, no children	44.49	108	23.1
Married couples, with children	73.08	177	47.7
Oldest child under 6	34.00	83	4.2
Oldest child 6 to 17	75.81	184	26.8
Oldest child 18 or older	100.20	243	17.5
Single parent with child under 18	12.91	31	2.0
Single person	16.61	40	11.6
REGION			
Total households	**41.18**	**100**	**100.0**
Northeast	43.29	105	21.0
Midwest	27.66	67	16.1
South	49.94	121	42.3
West	40.13	97	20.7

Note: For definitions of best and biggest customers, see introduction or glossary.
Source: Calculations by New Strategist based on the 1997 Consumer Expenditure Survey

Gifts of Men's and Boys' Apparel

Best customers:
- Householders aged 45 to 64
- Married couples without children

Customer trends:
- Spending on gifts of apparel is unlikely to grow because men and boys prefer to receive electronic gadgets and toys.

Householders aged 45 to 64 spend 42 to 55 percent more than the average household on gifts of men's and boys' apparel. Married couples without children in the household spend 46 percent more than average. Many of them are older couples buying gifts for grandsons and adult sons.

Boys do not particularly appreciate gifts of clothing, but prefer toys, video games, and other fun things. Men, too, prefer to receive electronic gadgets rather than sweaters or ties. Because of these preferences, spending on gifts of men's and boys' apparel is unlikely to grow.

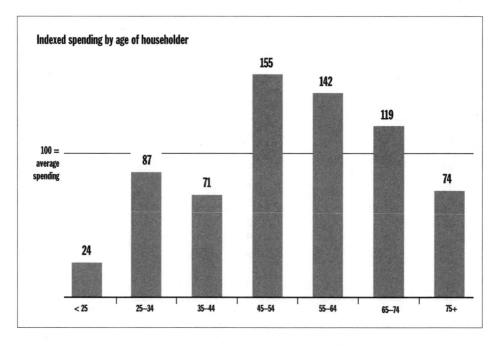

Indexed spending by age of householder

100 = average spending

< 25	25–34	35–44	45–54	55–64	65–74	75+
24	87	71	155	142	119	74

GIFTS OF MEN'S AND BOYS' APPAREL

Total household spending $6,470,753,040
Average household spends   61.29

	average spending	best customers (index)	biggest customers (market share)
AGE OF HOUSEHOLDER			
Total households	**$61.29**	**100**	**100.0%**
Under age 25	14.67	24	1.7
Aged 25 to 34	53.45	87	16.5
Aged 35 to 44	43.80	71	16.6
Aged 45 to 54	94.76	155	28.3
Aged 55 to 64	87.32	142	16.6
Aged 65 to 74	73.16	119	13.7
Aged 75 or older	45.61	74	6.9
HOUSEHOLD INCOME			
Total households reporting income	**60.59**	**100**	**100.0**
Under $20,000	30.53	50	17.5
$20,000 to $29,999	51.77	85	12.5
$30,000 to $39,999	58.45	96	11.8
$40,000 to $49,999	63.48	105	9.8
$50,000 to $69,999	60.71	100	14.1
$70,000 or more	135.02	223	33.3
HOUSEHOLD TYPE			
Total households	**61.29**	**100**	**100.0**
Married couples	77.89	127	66.5
Married couples, no children	89.58	146	31.2
Married couples, with children	67.99	111	29.8
Oldest child under 6	73.45	120	6.2
Oldest child 6 to 17	60.90	99	14.5
Oldest child 18 or older	77.36	126	9.1
Single parent with child under 18	34.18	56	3.5
Single person	38.62	63	18.1
REGION			
Total households	**61.29**	**100**	**100.0**
Northeast	62.31	102	20.3
Midwest	71.48	117	27.9
South	53.58	87	30.5
West	61.49	100	21.3

Note: For definitions of best and biggest customers, see introduction or glossary.
Source: Calculations by New Strategist based on the 1997 Consumer Expenditure Survey

Gifts of Out-of-Town Trip Expenses

Best customers:

- Householders aged 55 to 64
- Married couples without children

Customer trends:

- Spending is likely to rise as boomers become empty nesters and help their children pay for visits home.

Householders aged 55 to 64 spend nearly two and one-half times as much as the average household on gifts of out-of-town trip expenses. Married couples without children at home, many of whom are older, spend 66 percent more than average on this item. Many older householders are paying travel expenses for their grown children, encouraging them to visit. A few are even giving their children vacation packages as gifts.

Americans are increasingly giving gifts of experiences—such as travel—rather than sweaters, blenders, or other products. This trend is likely to intensify as affluent boomers become empty nesters.

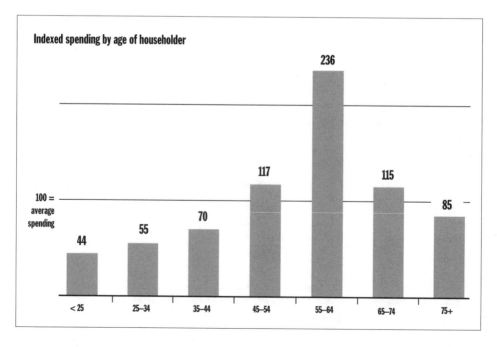

Indexed spending by age of householder

100 = average spending

| < 25 | 25–34 | 35–44 | 45–54 | 55–64 | 65–74 | 75+ |
| 44 | 55 | 70 | 117 | 236 | 115 | 85 |

GIFTS OF OUT-OF-TOWN TRIP EXPENSES

Total household spending $4,946,235,600
Average household spends   46.85

	average spending	best customers (index)	biggest customers (market share)
AGE OF HOUSEHOLDER			
Total households	**$46.85**	**100**	**100.0%**
Under age 25	20.57	44	3.1
Aged 25 to 34	25.96	55	10.5
Aged 35 to 44	32.74	70	16.3
Aged 45 to 54	54.98	117	21.5
Aged 55 to 64	110.67	236	27.6
Aged 65 to 74	53.78	115	13.2
Aged 75 or older	39.96	85	7.9
HOUSEHOLD INCOME			
Total households reporting income	**132.91**	**100**	**100.0**
Under $20,000	68.40	51	17.9
$20,000 to $29,999	104.24	78	11.5
$30,000 to $39,999	223.36	168	20.5
$40,000 to $49,999	98.61	74	6.9
$50,000 to $69,999	146.50	110	15.5
$70,000 or more	241.41	182	27.2
HOUSEHOLD TYPE			
Total households	**46.85**	**100**	**100.0**
Married couples	47.60	102	53.1
Married couples, no children	77.95	166	35.5
Married couples, with children	27.02	58	15.5
Oldest child under 6	14.56	31	1.6
Oldest child 6 to 17	26.47	56	8.2
Oldest child 18 or older	37.07	79	5.7
Single parent with child under 18	19.32	41	2.6
Single person	53.19	114	32.6
REGION			
Total households	**46.85**	**100**	**100.0**
Northeast	63.41	135	27.0
Midwest	50.06	107	25.5
South	27.91	60	20.8
West	58.77	125	26.6

Note: For definitions of best and biggest customers, see introduction or glossary.
Source: Calculations by New Strategist based on the 1997 Consumer Expenditure Survey

Gifts of Plants and Fresh Flowers, Indoor

Best customers:
- Households with incomes of $70,000 or more
- Householders aged 45 to 54
- Married couples without children

Customer trends:
- Spending should grow along with the number of affluent households.

Plants and fresh flowers make good gifts for all sorts of occasions, and they have the advantage of being easily obtained on a moment's notice. The best customers of gifts of plants and fresh flowers are the affluent. Households with incomes of $70,000 or more spend twice as much as the average household on this item. Householders aged 45 to 54 spend 55 percent more than the average householder on this item because many of them are in their peak-earning years. Married couples without children at home, many of whom are older, spend 46 percent more than average.

Plants and fresh flowers are perennial gifts. They are as suitable for near strangers as they are for intimate acquaintances. Spending on this item is likely to grow along with the ranks of affluent households.

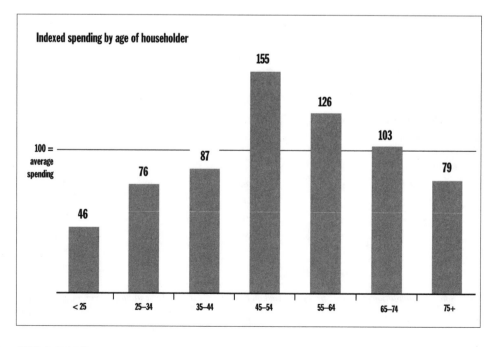

Indexed spending by age of householder

100 = average spending

| < 25 | 25–34 | 35–44 | 45–54 | 55–64 | 65–74 | 75+ |
| 46 | 76 | 87 | 155 | 126 | 103 | 79 |

GIFTS OF PLANTS AND FRESH FLOWERS, INDOOR

Total household spending $1,755,728,880
Average household spends   16.63

	average spending	best customers (index)	biggest customers (market share)
AGE OF HOUSEHOLDER			
Total households	**$16.63**	**100**	**100.0%**
Under age 25	7.61	46	3.3
Aged 25 to 34	12.61	76	14.3
Aged 35 to 44	14.40	87	20.1
Aged 45 to 54	25.75	155	28.4
Aged 55 to 64	21.03	126	14.8
Aged 65 to 74	17.08	103	11.8
Aged 75 or older	13.18	79	7.4
HOUSEHOLD INCOME			
Total households reporting income	**17.81**	**100**	**100.0**
Under $20,000	10.13	57	19.8
$20,000 to $29,999	13.81	78	11.3
$30,000 to $39,999	15.48	87	10.6
$40,000 to $49,999	17.97	101	9.4
$50,000 to $69,999	21.23	119	16.7
$70,000 or more	38.22	215	32.1
HOUSEHOLD TYPE			
Total households	**16.63**	**100**	**100.0**
Married couples	19.19	115	60.3
Married couples, no children	24.33	146	31.2
Married couples, with children	15.44	93	25.0
Oldest child under 6	11.61	70	3.6
Oldest child 6 to 17	14.55	87	12.7
Oldest child 18 or older	19.99	120	8.6
Single parent with child under 18	5.64	34	2.1
Single person	15.13	91	26.1
REGION			
Total households	**16.63**	**100**	**100.0**
Northeast	20.19	121	24.3
Midwest	16.11	97	23.1
South	14.62	88	30.7
West	17.15	103	21.9

Note: For definitions of best and biggest customers, see introduction or glossary.
Source: Calculations by New Strategist based on the 1997 Consumer Expenditure Survey

Gifts of Stationery, Stationery Supplies, Giftwrap

Best customers:
- **Married couples without children**
- **Households in the Midwest**

Customer trends:
- **A spending decline is likely as more people turn to e-mail for correspondence.**

Married couples without children at home spend 42 percent more than the average household on gifts of stationery, stationery supplies, and giftwrap. Undoubtedly, some are older couples giving writing supplies to grown children in the hope that they will write. Households in the Midwest spend 44 percent more than average on stationery, stationery supplies, and giftwrap.

Stationery and boxed sets of greeting cards were once common gift items. But e-mail is overtaking written correspondence, and even greeting cards are threatened by electronic versions. Spending on gifts of stationery, stationery supplies, and gift wrap is likely to decline as a result.

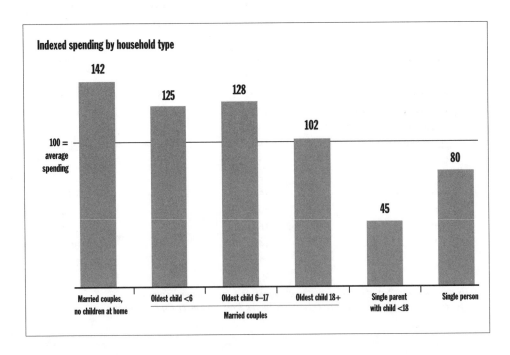

Indexed spending by household type

100 = average spending

Married couples, no children at home	Oldest child <6	Oldest child 6–17	Oldest child 18+	Single parent with child <18	Single person
142	125	128	102	45	80
		Married couples			

GIFTS OF STATIONERY, STATIONERY SUPPLIES, GIFTWRAP

Total household spending $2,186,478,960
Average household spends   20.71

	average spending	best customers (index)	biggest customers (market share)
AGE OF HOUSEHOLDER			
Total households	**$20.71**	**100**	**100.0%**
Under age 25	6.51	31	2.2
Aged 25 to 34	19.75	95	18.0
Aged 35 to 44	26.30	127	29.5
Aged 45 to 54	23.52	114	20.8
Aged 55 to 64	23.31	113	13.1
Aged 65 to 74	21.67	105	12.0
Aged 75 or older	11.07	53	5.0
HOUSEHOLD INCOME			
Total households reporting income	**23.05**	**100**	**100.0**
Under $20,000	11.91	52	18.0
$20,000 to $29,999	17.29	75	11.0
$30,000 to $39,999	23.18	101	12.3
$40,000 to $49,999	24.78	108	10.1
$50,000 to $69,999	24.18	105	14.7
$70,000 or more	50.72	220	32.9
HOUSEHOLD TYPE			
Total households	**20.71**	**100**	**100.0**
Married couples	26.09	126	65.9
Married couples, no children	29.50	142	30.4
Married couples, with children	24.96	121	32.4
Oldest child under 6	25.88	125	6.4
Oldest child 6 to 17	26.51	128	18.6
Oldest child 18 or older	21.07	102	7.3
Single parent with child under 18	9.30	45	2.8
Single person	16.58	80	23.0
REGION			
Total households	**20.71**	**100**	**100.0**
Northeast	21.10	102	20.4
Midwest	29.91	144	34.5
South	15.94	77	26.9
West	17.88	86	18.3

Note: For definitions of best and biggest customers, see introduction or glossary.
Source: Calculations by New Strategist based on the 1997 Consumer Expenditure Survey

Gifts of Telephone Service, Excluding Mobile Phone Service

Best customers:
- Householders under age 25
- Households with incomes under $20,000
- Single-person households

Customer trends:
- Because the number of low-income households is relatively stable, spending on this item is not likely to change much in the near future.

Telephone service is a truly utilitarian gift. Those most likely to pay someone else's telephone bill tend to be young, low-income householders helping out friends and relatives. Householders under age 25, a segment of the population that is disproportionately poor, spend three times as much as the average householder on gifts of telephone service. Households with incomes below $20,000 spend 73 percent more than average, and account for fully 60 percent of spending on this item. Single-person households spend 50 percent more than average.

Nationally, the share of households with low incomes is stable, suggesting that spending on this item is unlikely to change much in the near future.

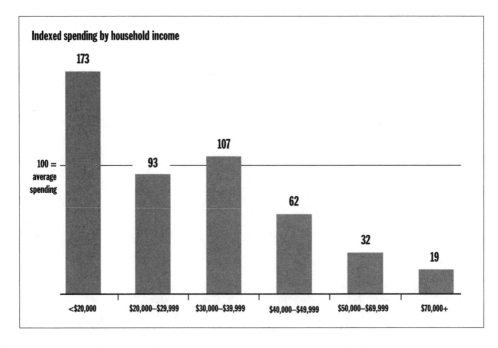

Indexed spending by household income

<$20,000	$20,000–$29,999	$30,000–$39,999	$40,000–$49,999	$50,000–$69,999	$70,000+
173	93	107	62	32	19

100 = average spending

GIFTS OF TELEPHONE SERVICE, EXCLUDING MOBILE PHONE SERVICE

Total household spending $1,725,111,840
Average household spends   16.34

	average spending	best customers (index)	biggest customers (market share)
AGE OF HOUSEHOLDER			
Total households	**$16.34**	**100**	**100.0%**
Under age 25	54.51	334	23.7
Aged 25 to 34	23.89	146	27.6
Aged 35 to 44	10.81	66	15.4
Aged 45 to 54	13.32	82	14.9
Aged 55 to 64	10.55	65	7.5
Aged 65 to 74	8.72	53	6.1
Aged 75 or older	8.27	51	4.7
HOUSEHOLD INCOME			
Total households reporting income	**16.09**	**100**	**100.0**
Under $20,000	27.81	173	60.2
$20,000 to $29,999	14.96	93	13.6
$30,000 to $39,999	17.24	107	13.1
$40,000 to $49,999	9.93	62	5.8
$50,000 to $69,999	5.18	32	4.5
$70,000 or more	3.07	19	2.9
HOUSEHOLD TYPE			
Total households	**16.34**	**100**	**100.0**
Married couples	10.89	67	34.8
Married couples, no children	8.57	52	11.2
Married couples, with children	11.48	70	18.9
Oldest child under 6	15.80	97	5.0
Oldest child 6 to 17	12.13	74	10.8
Oldest child 18 or older	7.09	43	3.1
Single parent with child under 18	18.22	112	7.0
Single person	24.45	150	43.0
REGION			
Total households	**16.34**	**100**	**100.0**
Northeast	20.54	126	25.1
Midwest	10.43	64	15.3
South	19.65	120	42.0
West	13.59	83	17.7

Note: For definitions of best and biggest customers, see introduction or glossary.
Source: Calculations by New Strategist based on the 1997 Consumer Expenditure Survey

Gifts of Toys, Games, Hobby Supplies, and Tricycles

Best customers:	• Householders aged 55 to 64
	• Married couples without children
	• Married couples with adult children
Customer trends:	• Spending should surge as baby boomers become grandparents.

The best customers of gifts of toys, games, hobby supplies, and tricycles are grandparents. Married couples with adult children at home spend twice as much as the average household on this item. Married couples without children at home spend 54 percent more than average, while householders aged 55 to 64 spend 58 percent more.

As the Millennial generation enters its twenties, their boomer parents are about to become grandparents. Spending on gifts of toys, games, hobby supplies, and tricycles will rise sharply as boomers enter this new lifestage.

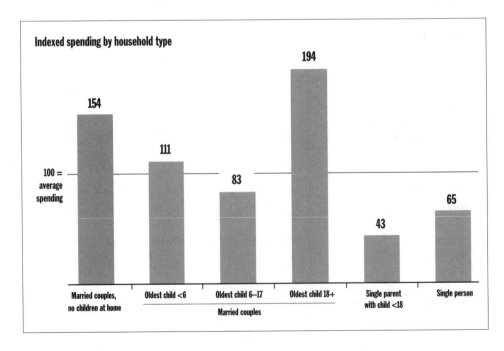

Indexed spending by household type

100 = average spending

Married couples, no children at home	Oldest child <6	Oldest child 6–17	Oldest child 18+	Single parent with child <18	Single person
154	111	83	194	43	65

Married couples

GIFTS OF TOYS, GAMES, HOBBY SUPPLIES, TRICYCLES

Total household spending $4,323,337,200
Average household spends   40.95

	average spending	best customers (index)	biggest customers (market share)
AGE OF HOUSEHOLDER			
Total households	**$40.95**	**100**	**100.0%**
Under age 25	9.64	24	1.7
Aged 25 to 34	48.15	118	22.2
Aged 35 to 44	35.38	86	20.1
Aged 45 to 54	44.22	108	19.8
Aged 55 to 64	64.86	158	18.5
Aged 65 to 74	39.68	97	11.1
Aged 75 or older	30.78	75	7.0
HOUSEHOLD INCOME			
Total households reporting income	**41.69**	**100**	**100.0**
Under $20,000	18.07	43	15.1
$20,000 to $29,999	31.95	77	11.2
$30,000 to $39,999	50.19	120	14.7
$40,000 to $49,999	39.03	94	8.8
$50,000 to $69,999	78.26	188	26.3
$70,000 or more	65.31	157	23.4
HOUSEHOLD TYPE			
Total households	**40.95**	**100**	**100.0**
Married couples	54.19	132	69.2
Married couples, no children	63.23	154	33.0
Married couples, with children	48.45	118	31.8
Oldest child under 6	45.62	111	5.7
Oldest child 6 to 17	34.14	83	12.1
Oldest child 18 or older	79.59	194	14.0
Single parent with child under 18	17.74	43	2.7
Single person	26.68	65	18.7
REGION			
Total households	**40.95**	**100**	**100.0**
Northeast	33.25	81	16.2
Midwest	51.34	125	30.0
South	38.85	95	33.1
West	39.99	98	20.7

Note: For definitions of best and biggest customers, see introduction or glossary.
Source: Calculations by New Strategist based on the 1997 Consumer Expenditure Survey

Gifts of Women's and Girls' Apparel

Best customers:
- Householders aged 45 to 54
- Married couples without children
- Married couples with adult children

Customer trends:
- Spending on gifts of apparel is likely to decline as experiential gifts become more popular.

Married couples without children at home spend 60 percent more than the average household on gifts of women's and girls' apparel. Many of these couples are older, and the recipients of these gifts are granddaughters and adult daughters living elsewhere. Married couples with adult children at home spend 38 percent more than average on this item. Householders aged 45 to 54 spend 35 percent more than average on gifts of women's and girls' apparel.

Gift giving has changed over the past few decades. Boomers and younger generations favor gifts of experiences—such as vacation packages or facials—over gifts of apparel or other products. While clothing will always remain on the gift list, spending on gifts of apparel is not likely to rise.

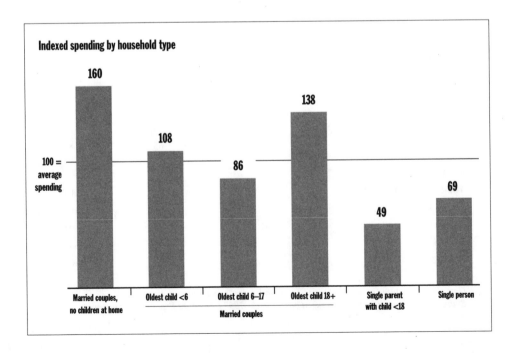

Indexed spending by household type

Married couples, no children at home	Oldest child <6	Oldest child 6–17	Oldest child 18+	Single parent with child <18	Single person
160	108	86	138	49	69

100 = average spending

Married couples

GIFTS OF WOMEN'S AND GIRLS' APPAREL

Total household spending $8,571,715,440
Average household spends   81.19

	average spending	best customers (index)	biggest customers (market share)
AGE OF HOUSEHOLDER			
Total households	**$81.19**	**100**	**100.0%**
Under age 25	50.92	63	4.5
Aged 25 to 34	56.69	70	13.2
Aged 35 to 44	82.98	102	23.8
Aged 45 to 54	109.95	135	24.8
Aged 55 to 64	100.80	124	14.5
Aged 65 to 74	99.18	122	14.0
Aged 75 or older	48.04	59	5.5
HOUSEHOLD INCOME			
Total households reporting income	**82.34**	**100**	**100.0**
Under $20,000	43.48	53	18.4
$20,000 to $29,999	63.90	78	11.3
$30,000 to $39,999	93.81	114	13.9
$40,000 to $49,999	83.48	101	9.5
$50,000 to $69,999	122.98	149	21.0
$70,000 or more	140.93	171	25.6
HOUSEHOLD TYPE			
Total households	**81.19**	**100**	**100.0**
Married couples	105.03	129	67.6
Married couples, no children	129.55	160	34.1
Married couples, with children	84.82	104	28.1
Oldest child under 6	88.01	108	5.6
Oldest child 6 to 17	69.69	86	12.5
Oldest child 18 or older	112.25	138	9.9
Single parent with child under 18	39.58	49	3.1
Single person	56.33	69	19.9
REGION			
Total households	**81.19**	**100**	**100.0**
Northeast	88.41	109	21.8
Midwest	90.56	112	26.7
South	72.57	89	31.2
West	77.98	96	20.4

Note: For definitions of best and biggest customers, see introduction or glossary.
Source: Calculations by New Strategist based on the 1997 Consumer Expenditure Survey

Chapter 10.

Health Care

Health Care

Health care costs have been rising relentlessly for years. In 1997, the $1,840.71 spent out-of-pocket by the average household on health care consumed a larger share of the household budget than did entertainment or clothes. Between 1987 and 1997, health care spending rose 15 percent, after adjusting for inflation. Households spent 59 percent more out-of-pocket on health insurance in 1997 than in 1987. Out-of-pocket expenses for drugs rose 12 percent, while medical supplies cost the average household 5 percent more. Medical services was the only category of health care spending for which the average household spent less in 1997 than in 1987—down 20 percent—as the growth of health maintenance organizations and managed care reduced these out-of-pocket costs.

The biggest out-of-pocket spenders on health care are Americans aged 65 or older, despite the fact that their health insurance is provided by the government. Medicare co-payments (not analyzed in this book) as well as commercial Medicare supplements purchased by many add up to a considerable out-of-pocket expense. In addition, older Americans spend much more than others on prescription drugs, which are not covered by Medicare. As the baby-boom generation ages into its sixties, beginning in less than a decade, out-of-pocket spending on health care will soar.

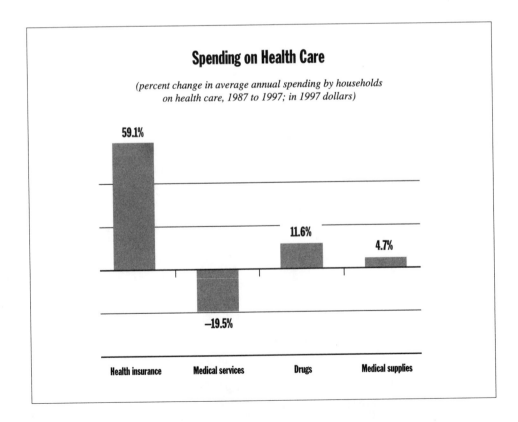

Spending on Health Care

(percent change in average annual spending by households on health care, 1987 to 1997; in 1997 dollars)

- Health insurance: 59.1%
- Medical services: −19.5%
- Drugs: 11.6%
- Medical supplies: 4.7%

Health Care Spending

(average annual spending of households on health care, and percent distribution of spending by type, 1997)

Total spending on health care	**$1,840.71**	**100.0%**
Health insurance, health maintenance organization	276.46	15.0
Drugs, prescription	216.58	11.8
Dental services	203.56	11.1
Health insurance, traditional fee for service	163.02	8.9
Health insurance, preferred provider plan	149.74	8.1
Physician services	133.59	7.3
Health insurance, commercial Medicare supplements	92.58	5.0
Drugs, nonprescription	75.43	4.1
Eyeglasses and contact lenses	59.73	3.2
Nonphysician health care professional services	37.03	2.0
Vitamins, nonprescription	28.43	1.5
Eye care services	27.14	1.5
Lab tests, X-rays	22.93	1.2
Hearing aids	11.42	0.6
Medical equipment	7.32	0.4

Note: Numbers will not add to total because not all categories are shown, including Medicare payments.

Dental Services

Best customers:
- Householders aged 45 to 74
- Married couples with school-aged or older children

Customer trends:
- Spending will rise as boomers reach the age at which people require more dental care.

Older people concerned about saving their teeth spend more than average on dental services. Householders aged 45 to 74 spend 20 to 38 percent more than the average household on this item. Married couples with children also spend more than the average household on dental services. Not only do they have more teeth to care for, but children often require expensive orthodontic treatments. Married couples with school-aged children spend 77 percent more than average on dental services, while those with adult children at home spend twice as much as the average household.

Spending on dental care will rise as growing numbers of older Americans try to save their teeth.

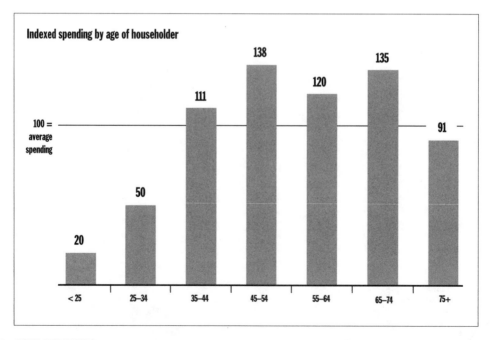

Indexed spending by age of householder

< 25	25–34	35–44	45–54	55–64	65–74	75+
20	50	111	138	120	135	91

100 = average spending

DENTAL SERVICES

Total household spending	$21,491,050,560
Average household spends	203.56

	average spending	best customers (index)	biggest customers (market share)
AGE OF HOUSEHOLDER			
Total households	**$203.56**	**100**	**100.0%**
Under age 25	39.96	20	1.4
Aged 25 to 34	102.73	50	9.5
Aged 35 to 44	225.91	111	25.8
Aged 45 to 54	280.79	138	25.3
Aged 55 to 64	244.82	120	14.0
Aged 65 to 74	274.25	135	15.5
Aged 75 or older	186.07	91	8.5
HOUSEHOLD INCOME			
Total households reporting income	**209.60**	**100**	**100.0**
Under $20,000	92.56	44	15.4
$20,000 to $29,999	154.00	73	10.7
$30,000 to $39,999	167.11	80	9.7
$40,000 to $49,999	255.45	122	11.4
$50,000 to $69,999	302.69	144	20.3
$70,000 or more	455.30	217	32.5
HOUSEHOLD TYPE			
Total households	**203.56**	**100**	**100.0**
Married couples	287.62	141	73.9
Married couples, no children	259.38	127	27.2
Married couples, with children	321.86	158	42.5
Oldest child under 6	114.22	56	2.9
Oldest child 6 to 17	361.20	177	25.8
Oldest child 18 or older	390.79	192	13.8
Single parent with child under 18	107.59	53	3.3
Single person	96.36	47	13.6
REGION			
Total households	**203.56**	**100**	**100.0**
Northeast	217.94	107	21.4
Midwest	187.73	92	22.0
South	181.34	89	31.1
West	244.31	120	25.5

Note: For definitions of best and biggest customers, see introduction or glossary.
Source: Calculations by New Strategist based on the 1997 Consumer Expenditure Survey

Drugs, Nonprescription

Best customers:
- Householders aged 55 or older
- Married couples without children

Customer trends:
- Spending will rise as the aging population seeks new remedies for what ails them.

Spending on nonprescription drugs rises with age. Householders aged 55 or older spend 28 to 44 percent more than the average householder on over-the-counter drugs. Married couples without children at home, who tend to be older, spend 36 percent more than average on this item.

Americans are always searching for magic bullets to help them fight acute and chronic illnesses. Spending in this market will rise substantially in the years ahead as an increasing variety of drugs become available in over-the-counter formulations and as the aging population seeks new remedies for its ailments.

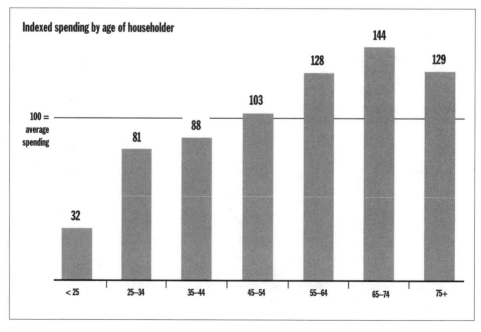

Indexed spending by age of householder

< 25	25–34	35–44	45–54	55–64	65–74	75+
32	81	88	103	128	144	129

100 = average spending

DRUGS, NONPRESCRIPTION

Total household spending $7,963,597,680
Average household spends   75.43

	average spending	best customers (index)	biggest customers (market share)
AGE OF HOUSEHOLDER			
Total households	**$75.43**	**100**	**100.0%**
Under age 25	24.17	32	2.3
Aged 25 to 34	61.37	81	15.3
Aged 35 to 44	66.55	88	20.5
Aged 45 to 54	77.32	103	18.8
Aged 55 to 64	96.36	128	14.9
Aged 65 to 74	108.32	144	16.5
Aged 75 or older	97.63	129	12.0
HOUSEHOLD INCOME			
Total households reporting income	**84.09**	**100**	**100.0**
Under $20,000	71.53	85	29.6
$20,000 to $29,999	84.07	100	14.6
$30,000 to $39,999	89.02	106	12.9
$40,000 to $49,999	81.17	97	9.0
$50,000 to $69,999	84.93	101	14.2
$70,000 or more	108.18	129	19.2
HOUSEHOLD TYPE			
Total households	**75.43**	**100**	**100.0**
Married couples	91.17	121	63.2
Married couples, no children	102.46	136	29.0
Married couples, with children	82.99	110	29.6
Oldest child under 6	65.12	86	4.4
Oldest child 6 to 17	89.74	119	17.3
Oldest child 18 or older	84.33	112	8.0
Single parent with child under 18	55.27	73	4.6
Single person	53.15	70	20.2
REGION			
Total households	**75.43**	**100**	**100.0**
Northeast	62.19	82	16.5
Midwest	75.93	101	24.1
South	75.27	100	34.8
West	87.25	116	24.6

Note: For definitions of best and biggest customers, see introduction or glossary.
Source: Calculations by New Strategist based on the 1997 Consumer Expenditure Survey

Drugs, Prescription

Best customers:	• **Householders aged 65 or older**
	• **Married couples without children**
	• **Households in the South**
Customer trends:	• **Spending will increase as aging boomers manage their chronic conditions.**

Aging brings on a variety of health problems, many of which require medication. Consequently, householders aged 65 or older are the best customers of prescription drugs, spending twice the average amount on this item. Married couples without children at home, who tend to be older, spend 84 percent more than average. Incomes are lower in the South, and poor health tends to accompany low incomes. This is one reason why Southerners spend 27 percent more than average on prescription drugs.

Pharmaceutical companies know the aging of the baby-boom generation brings unprecedented opportunities for them. As they develop new products that promise to alleviate various problems of aging, spending on drugs will increase.

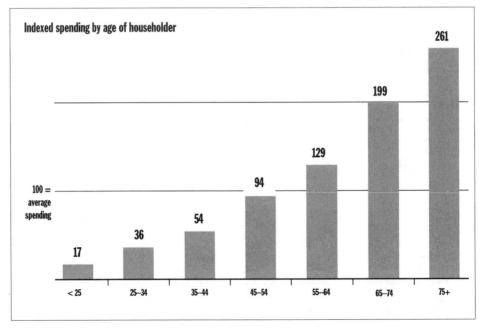

Indexed spending by age of householder

					199	261
				129		
100 = average spending			94			
		54				
	36					
17						
< 25	25–34	35–44	45–54	55–64	65–74	75+

DRUGS, PRESCRIPTION

Total household spending	$22,865,650,080
Average household spends	216.58

	average spending	best customers (index)	biggest customers (market share)
AGE OF HOUSEHOLDER			
Total households	**$216.58**	**100**	**100.0%**
Under age 25	36.85	17	1.2
Aged 25 to 34	78.16	36	6.8
Aged 35 to 44	117.65	54	12.6
Aged 45 to 54	203.01	94	17.2
Aged 55 to 64	280.20	129	15.1
Aged 65 to 74	430.80	199	22.8
Aged 75 or older	564.54	261	24.3
HOUSEHOLD INCOME			
Total households reporting income	**223.69**	**100**	**100.0**
Under $20,000	248.96	111	38.8
$20,000 to $29,999	269.35	120	17.6
$30,000 to $39,999	200.13	89	10.9
$40,000 to $49,999	190.98	85	8.0
$50,000 to $69,999	190.14	85	11.9
$70,000 or more	191.45	86	12.8
HOUSEHOLD TYPE			
Total households	**216.58**	**100**	**100.0**
Married couples	267.08	123	64.5
Married couples, no children	398.58	184	39.3
Married couples, with children	156.42	72	19.4
Oldest child under 6	103.13	48	2.4
Oldest child 6 to 17	122.09	56	8.2
Oldest child 18 or older	264.01	122	8.8
Single parent with child under 18	78.62	36	2.3
Single person	170.52	79	22.6
REGION			
Total households	**216.58**	**100**	**100.0**
Northeast	150.64	70	13.9
Midwest	246.81	114	27.2
South	274.37	127	44.2
West	149.65	69	14.7

Note: For definitions of best and biggest customers, see introduction or glossary.
Source: Calculations by New Strategist based on the 1997 Consumer Expenditure Survey

Eye Care Services

Best customers:
- Householders aged 55 or older
- Married couples with adult children
- Married couples without children

Customer trends:
- Spending will increase as older boomers seek high-tech solutions to vision problems.

Householders aged 55 or older spend 20 to 72 percent more than the average household on eye care services. At this age, many people find their eyesight changing—and not for the better. This prompts an increase in visits to eye care professionals. Married couples without children at home spend 45 percent more than average on this item, primarily because many are older. Married couples with adult children at home spend twice as much as the average household on eye care services.

Boomers and younger generations are likely to embrace high-tech—and more expensive—solutions to vision and eye problems, such as laser surgery to correct nearsightedness. This will boost spending on eye care services.

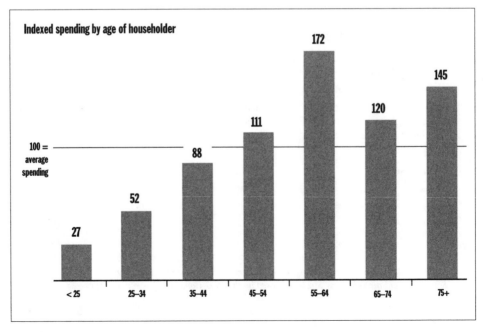

Indexed spending by age of householder

100 = average spending

< 25	25–34	35–44	45–54	55–64	65–74	75+
27	52	88	111	172	120	145

EYE CARE SERVICES

Total household spending	$2,865,332,640
Average household spends	27.14

	average spending	best customers (index)	biggest customers (market share)
AGE OF HOUSEHOLDER			
Total households	**$27.14**	**100**	**100.0%**
Under age 25	7.41	27	1.9
Aged 25 to 34	14.03	52	9.8
Aged 35 to 44	24.01	88	20.6
Aged 45 to 54	30.17	111	20.4
Aged 55 to 64	46.63	172	20.0
Aged 65 to 74	32.61	120	13.8
Aged 75 or older	39.42	145	13.5
HOUSEHOLD INCOME			
Total households reporting income	**27.68**	**100**	**100.0**
Under $20,000	19.68	71	24.8
$20,000 to $29,999	25.40	92	13.4
$30,000 to $39,999	22.71	82	10.0
$40,000 to $49,999	25.23	91	8.5
$50,000 to $69,999	28.59	103	14.5
$70,000 or more	53.30	193	28.8
HOUSEHOLD TYPE			
Total households	**27.14**	**100**	**100.0**
Married couples	36.94	136	71.2
Married couples, no children	39.26	145	30.9
Married couples, with children	37.19	137	36.8
Oldest child under 6	17.45	64	3.3
Oldest child 6 to 17	34.33	126	18.4
Oldest child 18 or older	57.09	210	15.1
Single parent with child under 18	20.11	74	4.7
Single person	16.49	61	17.5
REGION			
Total households	**27.14**	**100**	**100.0**
Northeast	26.08	96	19.2
Midwest	29.40	108	25.9
South	25.19	93	32.4
West	28.78	106	22.5

Note: For definitions of best and biggest customers, see introduction or glossary.
Source: Calculations by New Strategist based on the 1997 Consumer Expenditure Survey

Eyeglasses and Contact Lenses

Best customers:
- Householders aged 45 to 54
- Married couples with adult children

Customer trends:
- Boomers are reaching the age when eyesight deteriorates, which means more spending on eyeglasses and contact lenses.

After age 40, many people find their vision changing. Presbyopia, or farsightedness, is the bane of people in their late forties and early fifties, and their spending on eyeglasses and contact lenses reflects this fact. Householders aged 45 to 54 spend 52 percent more than the average householder on glasses and contact lenses. Married couples with adult children at home spend 86 percent more than average, in part because those households have more family members.

As people get older they find it harder to read the fine print. With the huge baby-boom generation now joining the bifocal crowd, spending on eyeglasses and contact lenses will rise substantially in the years ahead.

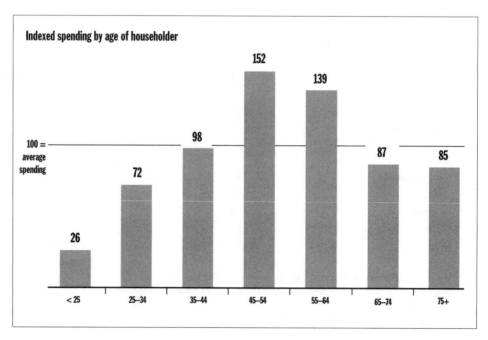

Indexed spending by age of householder

< 25	25–34	35–44	45–54	55–64	65–74	75+
26	72	98	152	139	87	85

100 = average spending

EYEGLASSES AND CONTACT LENSES

Total household spending $6,306,054,480
Average household spends   59.73

	average spending	best customers (index)	biggest customers (market share)
AGE OF HOUSEHOLDER			
Total households	**$59.73**	**100**	**100.0%**
Under age 25	15.80	26	1.9
Aged 25 to 34	42.79	72	13.5
Aged 35 to 44	58.33	98	22.7
Aged 45 to 54	90.51	152	27.8
Aged 55 to 64	82.91	139	16.2
Aged 65 to 74	52.08	87	10.0
Aged 75 or older	50.89	85	7.9
HOUSEHOLD INCOME			
Total households reporting income	**61.25**	**100**	**100.0**
Under $20,000	32.69	53	18.6
$20,000 to $29,999	47.69	78	11.4
$30,000 to $39,999	55.17	90	11.0
$40,000 to $49,999	64.73	106	9.9
$50,000 to $69,999	81.11	132	18.6
$70,000 or more	125.22	204	30.6
HOUSEHOLD TYPE			
Total households	**59.73**	**100**	**100.0**
Married couples	81.33	136	71.2
Married couples, no children	78.84	132	28.2
Married couples, with children	84.26	141	37.9
Oldest child under 6	48.43	81	4.2
Oldest child 6 to 17	83.59	140	20.4
Oldest child 18 or older	111.26	186	13.4
Single parent with child under 18	38.24	64	4.0
Single person	33.70	56	16.2
REGION			
Total households	**59.73**	**100**	**100.0**
Northeast	56.71	95	19.0
Midwest	67.20	113	26.9
South	58.43	98	34.1
West	56.30	94	20.0

Note: For definitions of best and biggest customers, see introduction or glossary.
Source: Calculations by New Strategist based on the 1997 Consumer Expenditure Survey

Health Insurance, Commercial Medicare Supplements

Best customers:
- Householders aged 65 or older
- Married couples without children

Customer trends:
- Spending will increase as health care costs rise and insurers pass more costs on to consumers.

The oldest Americans have higher medical expenses than any other segment of society. Householders aged 75 or older spend five times the average on out-of-pocket expenses for commercial Medicare supplement insurance. Those aged 65 to 74 spend three and one-half times as much as the average on this item. Married couples without children at home, many of whom are older, spend more than twice the average on these insurance policies.

Although Medicare provides substantial benefits to older Americans, the coverage excludes many products and services—which is why older Americans purchase commercial Medicare supplement policies. Out-of-pocket costs for commercial Medicare supplements will rise in the years ahead, along with health care costs in general.

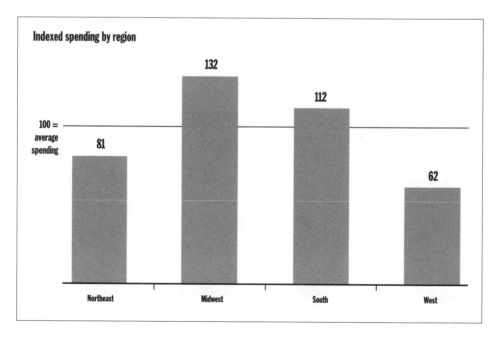

Indexed spending by region

Northeast	Midwest	South	West
81	132	112	62

100 = average spending

HEALTH INSURANCE, COMMERCIAL MEDICARE SUPPLEMENTS

Total household spending $9,774,226,080
Average household spends   92.58

	average spending	best customers (index)	biggest customers (market share)
AGE OF HOUSEHOLDER			
Total households	**$92.58**	**100**	**100.0%**
Under age 25	9.29	10	0.7
Aged 25 to 34	3.60	4	0.7
Aged 35 to 44	9.55	10	2.4
Aged 45 to 54	8.85	10	1.8
Aged 55 to 64	37.63	41	4.7
Aged 65 to 74	337.01	364	41.8
Aged 75 or older	476.53	515	47.9
HOUSEHOLD INCOME			
Total households reporting income	**100.04**	**100**	**100.0**
Under $20,000	145.85	146	50.8
$20,000 to $29,999	159.08	159	23.2
$30,000 to $39,999	64.23	64	7.9
$40,000 to $49,999	53.26	53	5.0
$50,000 to $69,999	54.35	54	7.6
$70,000 or more	37.10	37	5.5
HOUSEHOLD TYPE			
Total households	**92.58**	**100**	**100.0**
Married couples	103.88	112	58.7
Married couples, no children	215.20	232	49.6
Married couples, with children	18.60	20	5.4
Oldest child under 6	10.35	11	0.6
Oldest child 6 to 17	6.11	7	1.0
Oldest child 18 or older	49.80	54	3.9
Single parent with child under 18	3.25	4	0.2
Single person	102.00	110	31.7
REGION			
Total households	**92.58**	**100**	**100.0**
Northeast	74.80	81	16.1
Midwest	122.21	132	31.5
South	103.74	112	39.1
West	57.64	62	13.2

Note: For definitions of best and biggest customers, see introduction or glossary.
Source: Calculations by New Strategist based on the 1997 Consumer Expenditure Survey

Health Insurance, Health Maintenance Organization

Best customers:
- Married couples with children

Customer trends:
- Spending is likely to increase as more families opt for the most affordable health insurance.

Married couples with school-aged or older children spend 66 percent more than the average household on out-of-pocket costs for health insurance through health maintenance organizations (HMOs). Those with children under age 6 spend 50 percent more than average on this item. Families spend more because they have more people to cover, and HMOs are often more affordable than other types of coverage.

Although HMOs are not always people's first choice among health care plans, for many they are the most affordable choice. Consequently, spending on HMOs will continue to rise.

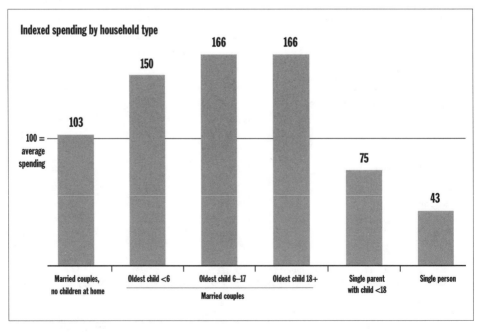

Indexed spending by household type

Married couples, no children at home	Oldest child <6	Oldest child 6–17	Oldest child 18+	Single parent with child <18	Single person
103	150	166	166	75	43

100 = average spending

Married couples

HEALTH INSURANCE, HEALTH MAINTENANCE ORGANIZATION

Total household spending $29,187,540,960
Average household spends   276.46

	average spending	best customers (index)	biggest customers (market share)
AGE OF HOUSEHOLDER			
Total households	**$276.46**	**100**	**100.0%**
Under age 25	109.90	40	2.8
Aged 25 to 34	287.97	104	19.7
Aged 35 to 44	366.72	133	30.9
Aged 45 to 54	358.57	130	23.8
Aged 55 to 64	325.74	118	13.7
Aged 65 to 74	153.31	55	6.4
Aged 75 or older	83.09	30	2.8
HOUSEHOLD INCOME			
Total households reporting income	**281.34**	**100**	**100.0**
Under $20,000	110.04	39	13.6
$20,000 to $29,999	251.38	89	13.1
$30,000 to $39,999	303.73	108	13.2
$40,000 to $49,999	410.42	146	13.6
$50,000 to $69,999	425.93	151	21.3
$70,000 or more	474.88	169	25.2
HOUSEHOLD TYPE			
Total households	**276.46**	**100**	**100.0**
Married couples	379.90	137	71.9
Married couples, no children	286.11	103	22.1
Married couples, with children	450.19	163	43.8
Oldest child under 6	413.37	150	7.7
Oldest child 6 to 17	458.61	166	24.1
Oldest child 18 or older	459.49	166	12.0
Single parent with child under 18	207.21	75	4.7
Single person	119.59	43	12.4
REGION			
Total households	**276.46**	**100**	**100.0**
Northeast	307.38	111	22.2
Midwest	250.30	91	21.6
South	263.62	95	33.3
West	297.93	108	22.9

Note: For definitions of best and biggest customers, see introduction or glossary.
Source: Calculations by New Strategist based on the 1997 Consumer Expenditure Survey

Health Insurance, Preferred Provider Plan

Best customers:
- Married couples with children under 18

Customer trends:
- Spending is likely to increase unless HMOs improve their services.

The best customers of preferred provider health insurance plans are families with children. With more household members to cover, out-of-pocket health insurance premiums and copayments add up. Married couples with children under age 6 spend 61 percent more than the average household on preferred provider health insurance plans. Married couples with school-aged children spend 56 percent more than average.

Preferred provider plans generally allow more choices among health care providers than health maintenance organizations (HMOs) do, but they are less expensive than traditional plans that allow complete freedom of choice. With many consumers increasingly dissatisfied with HMOs, preferred provider plans are likely to attract more customers, which would boost spending in this category.

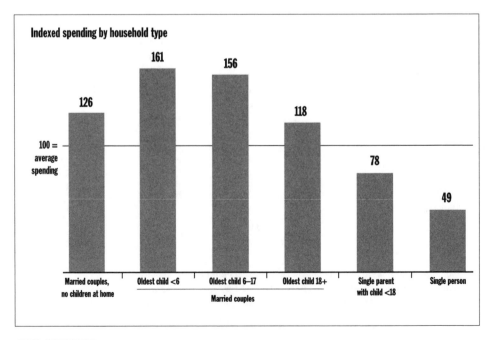

Indexed spending by household type

Married couples, no children at home	Oldest child <6	Oldest child 6–17	Oldest child 18+	Single parent with child <18	Single person
126	161	156	118	78	49

100 = average spending

Married couples

HEALTH INSURANCE, PREFERRED PROVIDER PLAN

Total household spending $15,808,950,240
Average household spends   149.74

	average spending	best customers (index)	biggest customers (market share)
AGE OF HOUSEHOLDER			
Total households	**$149.74**	**100**	**100.0%**
Under age 25	36.62	24	1.7
Aged 25 to 34	134.28	90	16.9
Aged 35 to 44	175.11	117	27.2
Aged 45 to 54	201.76	135	24.7
Aged 55 to 64	201.91	135	15.7
Aged 65 to 74	144.23	96	11.0
Aged 75 or older	42.96	29	2.7
HOUSEHOLD INCOME			
Total households reporting income	**155.09**	**100**	**100.0**
Under $20,000	43.50	28	9.8
$20,000 to $29,999	126.81	82	11.9
$30,000 to $39,999	127.49	82	10.1
$40,000 to $49,999	202.95	131	12.2
$50,000 to $69,999	336.05	217	30.4
$70,000 or more	265.36	171	25.6
HOUSEHOLD TYPE			
Total households	**149.74**	**100**	**100.0**
Married couples	208.73	139	72.9
Married couples, no children	189.18	126	27.0
Married couples, with children	219.83	147	39.5
Oldest child under 6	240.72	161	8.3
Oldest child 6 to 17	233.60	156	22.7
Oldest child 18 or older	177.02	118	8.5
Single parent with child under 18	116.19	78	4.9
Single person	74.02	49	14.2
REGION			
Total households	**149.74**	**100**	**100.0**
Northeast	103.60	69	13.8
Midwest	152.91	102	24.4
South	191.15	128	44.5
West	121.52	81	17.2

Note: For definitions of best and biggest customers, see introduction or glossary.
Source: Calculations by New Strategist based on the 1997 Consumer Expenditure Survey

Health Insurance, Traditional Fee for Service

Best customers:

- Householders aged 55 to 64
- Married couples without children
- Married couples with adult children

Customer trends:

- Spending will decline as people switch to more affordable types of insurance.

Out-of-pocket expenses for traditional fee-for-service health insurance plans are generally higher than those for preferred provider plans or health maintenance organizations. Consequently, older householders who do not need dependent coverage spend the most on this item. Householders aged 55 to 64 spend 51 percent more than average out-of-pocket expenses on traditional fee-for-service plans. Married couples without children at home spend 61 percent more than average, while married couples with adult children at home spend 63 percent more.

Traditional fee-for-service plans are no longer affordable for many Americans. As more people choose other types of plans, overall spending in this category is likely to decline. Those who remain covered by traditional plans will bear more of the costs, however, offsetting some of the decline.

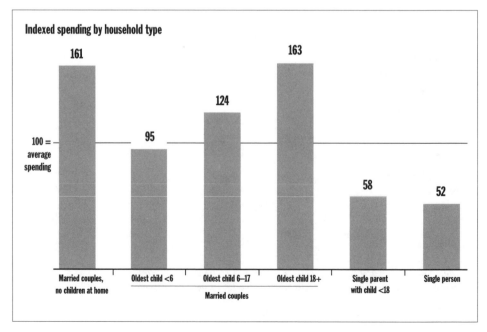

Indexed spending by household type

100 = average spending

| Married couples, no children at home | Oldest child <6 | Oldest child 6–17 | Oldest child 18+ | Single parent with child <18 | Single person |
| 161 | 95 | 124 | 163 | 58 | 52 |

Married couples

HEALTH INSURANCE, TRADITIONAL FEE FOR SERVICE

Total household spending $17,210,999,520
Average household spends   163.02

	average spending	best customers (index)	biggest customers (market share)
AGE OF HOUSEHOLDER			
Total households	**$163.02**	**100**	**100.0%**
Under age 25	29.66	18	1.3
Aged 25 to 34	118.89	73	13.8
Aged 35 to 44	141.36	87	20.2
Aged 45 to 54	204.24	125	23.0
Aged 55 to 64	245.92	151	17.6
Aged 65 to 74	211.88	130	14.9
Aged 75 or older	163.06	100	9.3
HOUSEHOLD INCOME			
Total households reporting income	**156.23**	**100**	**100.0**
Under $20,000	107.31	69	23.9
$20,000 to $29,999	126.22	81	11.8
$30,000 to $39,999	187.16	120	14.6
$40,000 to $49,999	183.54	117	11.0
$50,000 to $69,999	173.34	111	15.6
$70,000 or more	241.11	154	23.1
HOUSEHOLD TYPE			
Total households	**163.02**	**100**	**100.0**
Married couples	229.29	141	73.5
Married couples, no children	261.90	161	34.3
Married couples, with children	210.47	129	34.7
Oldest child under 6	155.12	95	4.9
Oldest child 6 to 17	202.90	124	18.1
Oldest child 18 or older	265.39	163	11.7
Single parent with child under 18	95.33	58	3.7
Single person	84.29	52	14.9
REGION			
Total households	**163.02**	**100**	**100.0**
Northeast	185.51	114	22.7
Midwest	175.40	108	25.7
South	160.52	98	34.4
West	132.01	81	17.2

Note: For definitions of best and biggest customers, see introduction or glossary.
Source: Calculations by New Strategist based on the 1997 Consumer Expenditure Survey

Hearing Aids

Best customers:
- Householders aged 55 or older
- Married couples without children

Customer trends:
- Spending will increase as boomers encounter hearing problems and technological advances boost hearing aid sales.

Hearing loss increases with age, which explains why householders aged 75 or older spend four times as much as the average householder on hearing aids. Those aged 55 to 64 spend two and one-half times as much as average. Married couples without children, most of whom are older, spend twice as much as average on hearing aids.

Spending on hearing aids will rise substantially as boomers age and technological advances make hearing aids not only more effective but also less noticeable.

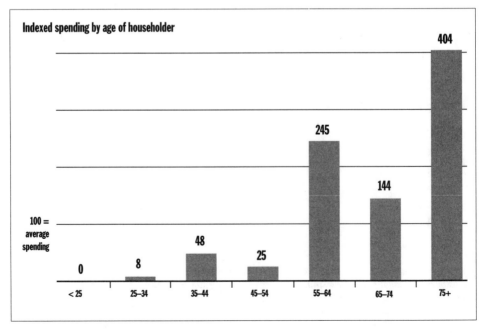

Indexed spending by age of householder

100 = average spending

| < 25 | 25–34 | 35–44 | 45–54 | 55–64 | 65–74 | 75+ |
| 0 | 8 | 48 | 25 | 245 | 144 | 404 |

HEARING AIDS

Total household spending $1,205,677,920
Average household spends   11.42

	average spending	best customers (index)	biggest customers (market share)
AGE OF HOUSEHOLDER			
Total households	**$11.42**	**100**	**100.0%**
Under age 25	0.02	0	0.0
Aged 25 to 34	0.93	8	1.5
Aged 35 to 44	5.44	48	11.1
Aged 45 to 54	2.90	25	4.7
Aged 55 to 64	28.02	245	28.6
Aged 65 to 74	16.41	144	16.5
Aged 75 or older	46.11	404	37.6
HOUSEHOLD INCOME			
Total households reporting income	**12.21**	**100**	**100.0**
Under $20,000	9.65	79	27.5
$20,000 to $29,999	23.44	192	28.0
$30,000 to $39,999	13.59	111	13.6
$40,000 to $49,999	23.15	190	17.7
$50,000 to $69,999	9.35	77	10.7
$70,000 or more	1.93	16	2.4
HOUSEHOLD TYPE			
Total households	**11.42**	**100**	**100.0**
Married couples	15.25	134	69.8
Married couples, no children	23.51	206	43.9
Married couples, with children	10.36	91	24.4
Oldest child under 6	13.70	120	6.2
Oldest child 6 to 17	4.41	39	5.6
Oldest child 18 or older	20.02	175	12.6
Single parent with child under 18	1.37	12	0.8
Single person	11.33	99	28.5
REGION			
Total households	**11.42**	**100**	**100.0**
Northeast	20.68	181	36.2
Midwest	11.73	103	24.5
South	5.76	50	17.6
West	11.64	102	21.7

Note: For definitions of best and biggest customers, see introduction or glossary.
Source: Calculations by New Strategist based on the 1997 Consumer Expenditure Survey

Lab Tests, X-Rays

Best customers:	• **Householders aged 55 to 64**
	• **Married couples with adult children**
Customer trends:	• **Spending will increase substantially as health-conscious adults opt for more medical tests to prevent and manage diseases.**

Householders in their fifties and sixties are of the age when health care professionals recommend regular diagnostic checkups, which often include lab tests and X-rays, to prevent health problems. Many health insurance plans do not cover preventive care, however, which is why householders are paying out-of-pocket for lab tests and X-rays. Householders aged 55 to 64 spend twice as much as the average householder on this item. Married couples with adult children at home, who tend to be older, also spend much more than average on lab tests and X-rays.

Americans know the value of prevention and early detection of diseases. Out-of-pocket spending on lab tests and X-rays is likely to increase as health-conscious boomers enter the 55-to-64 age group.

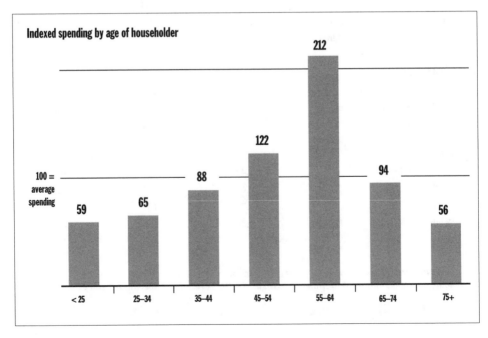

Indexed spending by age of householder

< 25	25–34	35–44	45–54	55–64	65–74	75+
59	65	88	122	212	94	56

100 = average spending

LAB TESTS, X-RAYS

Total household spending $2,420,857,680
Average household spends   22.93

	average spending	best customers (index)	biggest customers (market share)
AGE OF HOUSEHOLDER			
Total households	**$22.93**	**100**	**100.0%**
Under age 25	13.42	59	4.2
Aged 25 to 34	14.92	65	12.3
Aged 35 to 44	20.16	88	20.5
Aged 45 to 54	28.00	122	22.4
Aged 55 to 64	48.61	212	24.7
Aged 65 to 74	21.64	94	10.8
Aged 75 or older	12.80	56	5.2
HOUSEHOLD INCOME			
Total households reporting income	**24.56**	**100**	**100.0**
Under $20,000	16.28	66	23.1
$20,000 to $29,999	27.74	113	16.5
$30,000 to $39,999	15.81	64	7.9
$40,000 to $49,999	20.86	85	7.9
$50,000 to $69,999	33.09	135	18.9
$70,000 or more	42.17	172	25.7
HOUSEHOLD TYPE			
Total households	**22.93**	**100**	**100.0**
Married couples	30.35	132	69.2
Married couples, no children	33.36	145	31.0
Married couples, with children	27.88	122	32.7
Oldest child under 6	20.64	90	4.6
Oldest child 6 to 17	21.18	92	13.4
Oldest child 18 or older	46.61	203	14.6
Single parent with child under 18	17.34	76	4.7
Single person	13.54	59	17.0
REGION			
Total households	**22.93**	**100**	**100.0**
Northeast	16.97	74	14.8
Midwest	20.49	89	21.4
South	29.06	127	44.2
West	21.23	93	19.7

Note: For definitions of best and biggest customers, see introduction or glossary.
Source: Calculations by New Strategist based on the 1997 Consumer Expenditure Survey

Medical Equipment

Best customers:
- Householders aged 65 or older
- Married couples without children

Customer trends:
- Spending should be stable for now, but increases are likely when today's younger generations demand high-tech help for their health problems.

The oldest householders spend the most on medical equipment, such as walkers, wheelchairs, blood pressure monitors, and so on. Householders aged 65 or older spend more than two and one-half times as much as the average householder on medical equipment. Married couples without children at home, most of whom are older, spend twice the average on this item.

Because the small Depression-era generation is now entering the oldest age groups, spending on medical equipment should remain stable for the next few years. But as boomers age, spending in this category is likely to surge. Comfortable with technology, boomers will become eager customers of high-tech medical equipment.

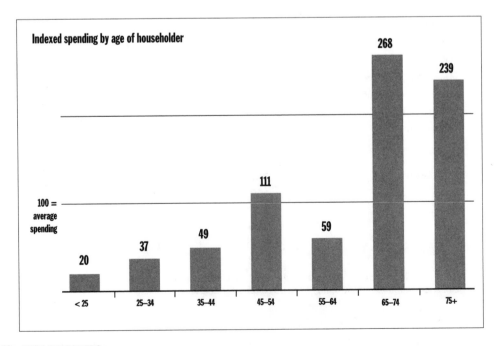

Indexed spending by age of householder

100 = average spending

< 25	25–34	35–44	45–54	55–64	65–74	75+
20	37	49	111	59	268	239

MEDICAL EQUIPMENT

Total household spending	$772,816,320
Average household spends	7.32

	average spending	best customers (index)	biggest customers (market share)
AGE OF HOUSEHOLDER			
Total households	**$7.32**	**100**	**100.0%**
Under age 25	1.48	20	1.4
Aged 25 to 34	2.74	37	7.1
Aged 35 to 44	3.61	49	11.5
Aged 45 to 54	8.13	111	20.3
Aged 55 to 64	4.30	59	6.9
Aged 65 to 74	19.62	268	30.7
Aged 75 or older	17.47	239	22.2
HOUSEHOLD INCOME			
Total households reporting income	**7.90**	**100**	**100.0**
Under $20,000	9.84	125	43.4
$20,000 to $29,999	12.91	163	23.9
$30,000 to $39,999	5.49	69	8.5
$40,000 to $49,999	6.74	85	8.0
$50,000 to $69,999	2.16	27	3.8
$70,000 or more	6.61	84	12.5
HOUSEHOLD TYPE			
Total households	**7.32**	**100**	**100.0**
Married couples	8.87	121	63.4
Married couples, no children	14.83	203	43.2
Married couples, with children	4.52	62	16.6
Oldest child under 6	7.28	99	5.1
Oldest child 6 to 17	2.75	38	5.5
Oldest child 18 or older	6.09	83	6.0
Single parent with child under 18	9.86	135	8.5
Single person	4.90	67	19.2
REGION			
Total households	**7.32**	**100**	**100.0**
Northeast	11.97	164	32.7
Midwest	6.92	95	22.6
South	5.22	71	24.9
West	6.90	94	20.0

Note: For definitions of best and biggest customers, see introduction or glossary.
Source: Calculations by New Strategist based on the 1997 Consumer Expenditure Survey

Nonphysician Health Care Professional Services

Best customers:	• Householders aged 35 to 64
	• Married couples with adult children
	• Households in the West
Customer trends:	• Spending is likely to increase as more people seek alternative medical care.

Householders aged 35 to 64 and married couples with adult children at home spend about one-third more than the average householder on health care services provided by professionals other than physicians. Households in the West spend 41 percent more than average on nonphysician professional services.

Alternative health care has become popular over the past few decades, with millions of Americans seeking the medical advice of nonphysicians such as chiropractors, acupuncturists, and nurse practitioners. This trend shows no sign of reversing. Spending on nonphysician health care services will rise substantially in the years ahead as aging boomers seek remedies for their health problems.

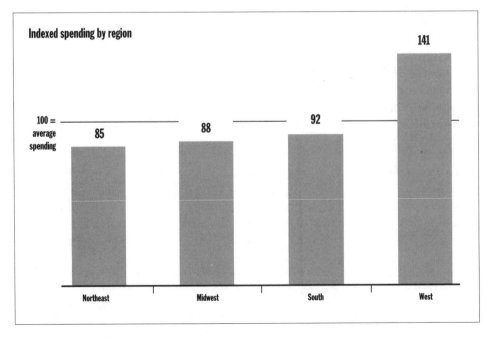

Indexed spending by region

100 = average spending

Northeast	Midwest	South	West
85	88	92	141

NONPHYSICIAN HEALTH CARE PROFESSIONAL SERVICES

Total household spending $3,909,479,280
Average household spends   37.03

	average spending	best customers (index)	biggest customers (market share)
AGE OF HOUSEHOLDER			
Total households	**$37.03**	**100**	**100.0%**
Under age 25	8.54	23	1.6
Aged 25 to 34	25.72	69	13.1
Aged 35 to 44	50.13	135	31.5
Aged 45 to 54	48.84	132	24.2
Aged 55 to 64	48.83	132	15.4
Aged 65 to 74	24.37	66	7.5
Aged 75 or older	26.51	72	6.7
HOUSEHOLD INCOME			
Total households reporting income	**40.94**	**100**	**100.0**
Under $20,000	24.69	60	21.0
$20,000 to $29,999	38.71	95	13.8
$30,000 to $39,999	40.97	100	12.2
$40,000 to $49,999	51.07	125	11.7
$50,000 to $69,999	48.62	119	16.7
$70,000 or more	67.42	165	24.6
HOUSEHOLD TYPE			
Total households	**37.03**	**100**	**100.0**
Married couples	43.93	119	62.0
Married couples, no children	45.24	122	26.1
Married couples, with children	45.45	123	33.0
Oldest child under 6	47.82	129	6.6
Oldest child 6 to 17	42.31	114	16.6
Oldest child 18 or older	50.09	135	9.7
Single parent with child under 18	25.03	68	4.2
Single person	33.93	92	26.3
REGION			
Total households	**37.03**	**100**	**100.0**
Northeast	31.51	85	17.0
Midwest	32.66	88	21.1
South	34.02	92	32.1
West	52.08	141	29.9

Note: For definitions of best and biggest customers, see introduction or glossary.
Source: Calculations by New Strategist based on the 1997 Consumer Expenditure Survey

Physician Services

Best customers:
- Married couples with children under age 6
- Married couples with adult children

Customer trends:
- As health care costs go up and insurance coverage declines, spending in this category will increase.

The best customers of physician services are parents of young children. Married couples with preschoolers spend 63 percent more out-of-pocket on this item than the average household. Spending by families with preschoolers is higher because young children visit doctors so frequently. Married couples with adult children at home spend 46 percent more than the average household on this item.

Out-of-pocket spending on physician services is likely to rise because health care costs are going up and insurance plans are passing on more of those costs to consumers.

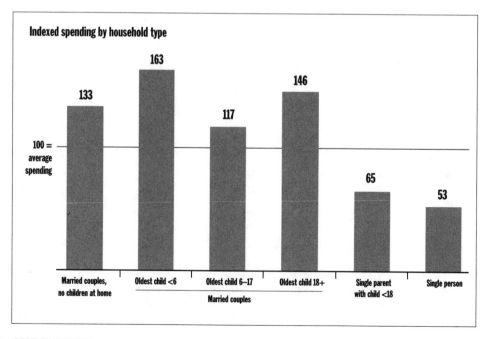

Indexed spending by household type

133	163	117	146	65	53

100 = average spending

Married couples, no children at home | Oldest child <6 | Oldest child 6–17 | Oldest child 18+ | Single parent with child <18 | Single person

Married couples

PHYSICIAN SERVICES

Total household spending	$14,103,897,840	
Average household spends	133.59	

	average spending	best customers (index)	biggest customers (market share)
AGE OF HOUSEHOLDER			
Total households	**$133.59**	**100**	**100.0%**
Under age 25	31.71	24	1.7
Aged 25 to 34	122.94	92	17.4
Aged 35 to 44	150.05	112	26.1
Aged 45 to 54	160.27	120	22.0
Aged 55 to 64	168.03	126	14.7
Aged 65 to 74	134.74	101	11.6
Aged 75 or older	94.67	71	6.6
HOUSEHOLD INCOME			
Total households reporting income	**137.85**	**100**	**100.0**
Under $20,000	80.90	59	20.4
$20,000 to $29,999	123.70	90	13.1
$30,000 to $39,999	147.79	107	13.1
$40,000 to $49,999	169.66	123	11.5
$50,000 to $69,999	180.43	131	18.4
$70,000 or more	216.35	157	23.5
HOUSEHOLD TYPE			
Total households	**133.59**	**100**	**100.0**
Married couples	179.04	134	70.1
Married couples, no children	177.04	133	28.3
Married couples, with children	178.16	133	35.9
Oldest child under 6	217.67	163	8.4
Oldest child 6 to 17	155.65	117	17.0
Oldest child 18 or older	195.44	146	10.5
Single parent with child under 18	87.28	65	4.1
Single person	70.21	53	15.1
REGION			
Total households	**133.59**	**100**	**100.0**
Northeast	102.99	77	15.4
Midwest	135.38	101	24.2
South	141.13	106	36.9
West	147.96	111	23.5

Note: For definitions of best and biggest customers, see introduction or glossary.
Source: Calculations by New Strategist based on the 1997 Consumer Expenditure Survey

Vitamins, Nonprescription

Best customers:
- Householders aged 65 to 74
- Married couples without children
- Single parents

Customer trends:
- Spending on vitamins will increase substantially as boomers age.

As people age, they become more health conscious. Consequently, older people are the best customers of nonprescription vitamins. Householders aged 65 to 74 spend nearly twice as much as the average householder on vitamins. Married couples without children at home, most of whom are older, spend 61 percent more. Single parents spend 65 percent more than average.

Evidence that vitamins are beneficial continues to mount. Spending on this item is likely to rise substantially as boomers age and seek to prevent ailments through better nutrition.

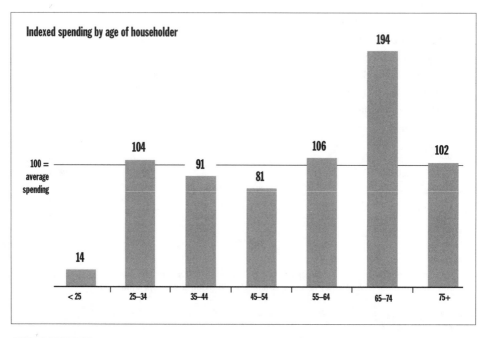

Indexed spending by age of householder

100 = average spending

< 25	25–34	35–44	45–54	55–64	65–74	75+
14	104	91	81	106	194	102

VITAMINS, NONPRESCRIPTION

Total household spending $3,001,525,680
Average household spends   28.43

	average spending	best customers (index)	biggest customers (market share)
AGE OF HOUSEHOLDER			
Total households	**$28.43**	**100**	**100.0%**
Under age 25	4.04	14	1.0
Aged 25 to 34	29.65	104	19.7
Aged 35 to 44	25.88	91	21.2
Aged 45 to 54	22.90	81	14.8
Aged 55 to 64	30.15	106	12.4
Aged 65 to 74	55.07	194	22.2
Aged 75 or older	29.09	102	9.5
HOUSEHOLD INCOME			
Total households reporting income	**33.82**	**100**	**100.0**
Under $20,000	10.65	31	11.0
$20,000 to $29,999	46.31	137	20.0
$30,000 to $39,999	57.19	169	20.7
$40,000 to $49,999	49.70	147	13.7
$50,000 to $69,999	33.89	100	14.1
$70,000 or more	42.11	125	18.6
HOUSEHOLD TYPE			
Total households	**28.43**	**100**	**100.0**
Married couples	35.45	125	65.2
Married couples, no children	45.67	161	34.3
Married couples, with children	22.96	81	21.7
Oldest child under 6	23.17	81	4.2
Oldest child 6 to 17	25.61	90	13.1
Oldest child 18 or older	17.47	61	4.4
Single parent with child under 18	46.92	165	10.4
Single person	16.70	59	16.9
REGION			
Total households	**28.43**	**100**	**100.0**
Northeast	27.58	97	19.4
Midwest	34.55	122	29.0
South	17.19	60	21.1
West	40.33	142	30.1

Note: For definitions of best and biggest customers, see introduction or glossary.
Source: Calculations by New Strategist based on the 1997 Consumer Expenditure Survey

Chapter 11.

Household Furnishings and Equipment

Household Furnishings and Equipment

The average American household spent $1,512.44 feathering its nest in 1997. These expenses include everything from computers to indoor plants and fresh flowers, mattresses, microwave ovens, telephone answering machines, and vacuum cleaners. Between 1987 and 1997, households boosted their spending on furnishings and equipment by 4 percent, after adjusting for inflation. Many items within this category experienced steep spending declines, however. The average household spent 39 percent less on household textiles (sheets, towels, etc.) in 1997 than in 1987, 20 percent less on floor coverings, and 25 percent less on major appliances. In contrast, the average household spent 14 percent more on small appliances and 47 percent more on miscellaneous household equipment—a category that includes computer hardware and software for nonbusiness use (shown separately in the Computer chapter), office furniture and business equipment for home use, as well as telephones, clocks, lamps, lawn and garden equipment, and other items.

During the past decade, the pattern of spending on household furnishings and equipment has shifted. As computers and home offices have become more popular, Americans are devoting more dollars to those items and less to the basics such as furniture, linens, and other traditional household products. Spending may revert back to the basics once computer spending slows, especially as baby boomers become empty nesters and redecorate their homes to accomodate their new, child free lifestyle.

Household Furnishings and Equipment Spending

(average annual spending of households on household furnishings and equipment, and percent distribution of spending by type, 1997)

Total spending on household furnishings and equipment	**$1,512.44**	**100.0%**
Decorative items for the home	134.12	8.9
Telephones and accessories	96.54	6.4
Sofas	93.81	6.2
Bedroom furniture, except mattresses and springs	63.99	4.2
Refrigerators and freezers	57.60	3.8
Plants and fresh flowers, indoor	52.33	3.5
Kitchen and dining room furniture	48.69	3.2

Living room chairs	$ 47.42	3.1%
Mattresses and springs	46.56	3.1
Wall units, cabinets, miscellaneous furniture	42.81	2.8
Lawn and garden equipment	39.37	2.6
Rugs, nonpermanent	38.93	2.6
Carpeting, wall-to-wall	38.82	2.6
Kitchenware and cookware, nonelectric	38.53	2.5
Bedroom linens	34.28	2.3
Washing machines	23.02	1.5
Cooking stoves, ovens	22.06	1.5
Living room tables	20.60	1.4
Infants' furniture and equipment	16.92	1.1
Curtains and draperies	16.73	1.1
Kitchen appliances, small electric	16.67	1.1
Power tools	16.31	1.1
Clothes dryers	16.22	1.1
Floor cleaning equipment, electric	15.68	1.0
Outdoor furniture	13.61	0.9
Business equipment and office furniture for home use	12.94	0.9
Lamps and lighting fixtures	12.53	0.8
Dishwashers	12.47	0.8
Bathroom linens	11.13	0.7
Dinnerware	10.61	0.7
Microwave ovens	9.59	0.6
Closet and storage items	8.94	0.6
Glassware	8.25	0.5
Air conditioners, window units	4.93	0.3
Flatware	4.68	0.3
Sewing machines	3.55	0.2
Furniture rental	3.41	0.2
Telephone answering devices	3.31	0.2
Kitchen and dining room linens	2.40	0.2
Slipcovers and decorative pillows	2.10	0.1
Calculators	1.92	0.1
Smoke alarms	1.05	0.1

Note: Numbers will not add to total because not all categories are shown, including computers and computer hardware for nonbusiness use, and computer software for nonbusiness use which are in the Computer chapter.

Air Conditioners, Window Units

Best customers:	• Householders aged 55 to 64
	• Married couples with adult children
	• Households in the Northeast
Customer trends:	• Growing market as boomers become empty nesters, able to spend on themselves again.

Married couples with adult children at home are the best customers of window unit air conditioners. These households spend 84 percent more than average on window units. Householders aged 55 to 64 (many of whom have adult children at home) spend 68 percent more than average on this item. Households in the Northeast, where summers are relatively short but sometimes quite hot, spend 58 percent more than average on window air conditioners.

As their children grow up and boomers can spend on themselves again, spending on window air conditioners should rise.

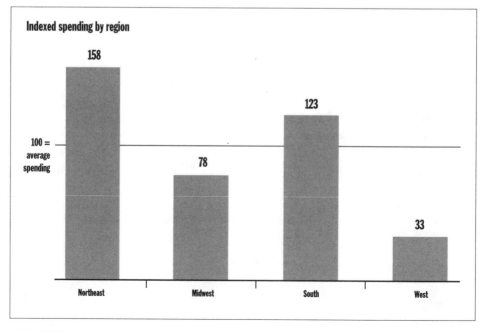

Indexed spending by region

Northeast: 158
Midwest: 78
South: 123
West: 33

100 = average spending

AIR CONDITIONERS, WINDOW UNITS

Total household spending $520,489,680
Average household spends   4.93

	average spending	best customers (index)	biggest customers (market share)
AGE OF HOUSEHOLDER			
Total households	**$4.93**	**100**	**100.0%**
Under age 25	1.85	38	2.7
Aged 25 to 34	4.39	89	16.8
Aged 35 to 44	7.19	146	33.9
Aged 45 to 54	4.46	90	16.6
Aged 55 to 64	8.26	168	19.5
Aged 65 to 74	2.27	46	5.3
Aged 75 or older	2.81	57	5.3
HOUSEHOLD INCOME			
Total households reporting income	**5.82**	**100**	**100.0**
Under $20,000	4.09	70	24.5
$20,000 to $29,999	6.38	110	16.0
$30,000 to $39,999	7.15	123	15.0
$40,000 to $49,999	4.58	79	7.4
$50,000 to $69,999	6.48	111	15.6
$70,000 or more	8.40	144	21.6
HOUSEHOLD TYPE			
Total households	**4.93**	**100**	**100.0**
Married couples	5.69	115	60.4
Married couples, no children	4.55	92	19.7
Married couples, with children	6.29	128	34.3
Oldest child under 6	3.40	69	3.5
Oldest child 6 to 17	5.95	121	17.6
Oldest child 18 or older	9.07	184	13.2
Single parent with child under 18	2.60	53	3.3
Single person	2.60	53	15.2
REGION			
Total households	**4.93**	**100**	**100.0**
Northeast	7.79	158	31.6
Midwest	3.83	78	18.6
South	6.06	123	42.9
West	1.64	33	7.1

Note: For definitions of best and biggest customers, see introduction or glossary.
Source: Calculations by New Strategist based on the 1997 Consumer Expenditure Survey

Bathroom Linens

Best customers:
- Householders aged 45 to 54
- Married couples with adult children

Customer trends:
- The growing number of householders in their peak-earning years could spur spending on bathroom linens.

The bathroom is no longer merely a functional room. With amenities such as whirlpool baths, it is becoming a quiet haven for relaxation. Those who can afford to do so are adding bathrooms or redecorating existing ones, often purchasing new bathroom linens. Those who can most afford to spend on bathrooms are middle-aged couples in their peak-earning years. This explains why married couples with adult children at home spend 58 percent more than average on this item, and why householders aged 45 to 54 spend 27 percent more than average. Both are likely to be in their peak-earning years.

With the large baby-boom generation expanding the ranks of the nation's affluent households, spending on bathroom linens may rise.

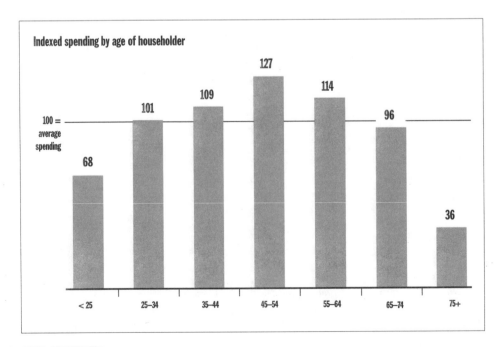

Indexed spending by age of householder

68	101	109	127	114	96	36
< 25	25–34	35–44	45–54	55–64	65–74	75+

100 = average spending

BATHROOM LINENS

Total household spending	$1,175,060,880	
Average household spends	11.13	

	average spending	best customers (index)	biggest customers (market share)
AGE OF HOUSEHOLDER			
Total households	**$11.13**	**100**	**100.0%**
Under age 25	7.60	68	4.9
Aged 25 to 34	11.23	101	19.0
Aged 35 to 44	12.10	109	25.3
Aged 45 to 54	14.11	127	23.2
Aged 55 to 64	12.65	114	13.3
Aged 65 to 74	10.71	96	11.0
Aged 75 or older	3.96	36	3.3
HOUSEHOLD INCOME			
Total households reporting income	**12.07**	**100**	**100.0**
Under $20,000	6.04	50	17.4
$20,000 to $29,999	11.73	97	14.2
$30,000 to $39,999	10.76	89	10.9
$40,000 to $49,999	10.78	89	8.4
$50,000 to $69,999	16.46	136	19.1
$70,000 or more	24.22	201	30.0
HOUSEHOLD TYPE			
Total households	**11.13**	**100**	**100.0**
Married couples	13.57	122	63.8
Married couples, no children	13.16	118	25.2
Married couples, with children	14.05	126	33.9
Oldest child under 6	11.40	102	5.3
Oldest child 6 to 17	13.25	119	17.3
Oldest child 18 or older	17.56	158	11.3
Single parent with child under 18	10.48	94	5.9
Single person	8.01	72	20.7
REGION			
Total households	**11.13**	**100**	**100.0**
Northeast	13.04	117	23.4
Midwest	10.74	96	23.1
South	9.89	89	31.0
West	11.83	106	22.6

Note: For definitions of best and biggest customers, see introduction or glossary.
Source: Calculations by New Strategist based on the 1997 Consumer Expenditure Survey

Bedroom Furniture, Except Mattresses and Springs

Best customers:	• **Married couples with children under 18**
	• **Householders aged 35 to 54**
Customer trends:	• **Little if any growth because most boomers have outfitted their children's bedrooms by now. Teen demand for redecorating could boost spending somewhat, however.**

Married couples with preschoolers spend 41 percent more than average on bedroom furniture not including mattresses and box springs. Those with school-aged children spend 45 percent more. This is no surprise since children's bedrooms need furnishings. Householders aged 35 to 54 spend 31 to 61 percent more than average on bedroom furniture because most have children.

Spending on bedroom furniture is not likely to grow much because most baby boomers have already outfitted their children's bedrooms. If teenagers demand their rooms be redecorated, however, spending could increase somewhat.

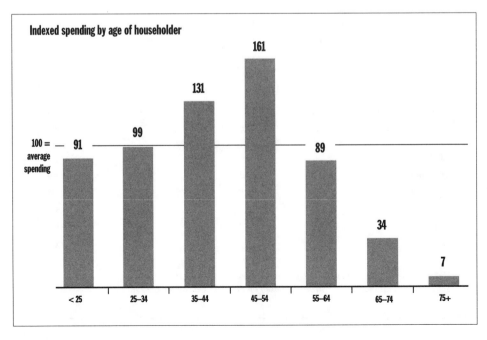

Indexed spending by age of householder

100 = average spending

< 25	25–34	35–44	45–54	55–64	65–74	75+
91	99	131	161	89	34	7

BEDROOM FURNITURE, EXCEPT MATTRESSES AND SPRINGS

Total household spending	$6,755,808,240
Average household spends	63.99

	average spending	best customers (index)	biggest customers (market share)
AGE OF HOUSEHOLDER			
Total households	**$63.99**	**100**	**100.0%**
Under age 25	57.96	91	6.4
Aged 25 to 34	63.06	99	18.6
Aged 35 to 44	84.12	131	30.6
Aged 45 to 54	102.91	161	29.5
Aged 55 to 64	57.14	89	10.4
Aged 65 to 74	21.79	34	3.9
Aged 75 or older	4.18	7	0.6
HOUSEHOLD INCOME			
Total households reporting income	**60.38**	**100**	**100.0**
Under $20,000	16.46	27	9.5
$20,000 to $29,999	24.45	40	5.9
$30,000 to $39,999	38.92	64	7.9
$40,000 to $49,999	55.20	91	8.6
$50,000 to $69,999	120.02	199	27.9
$70,000 or more	162.64	269	40.3
HOUSEHOLD TYPE			
Total households	**63.99**	**100**	**100.0**
Married couples	83.67	131	68.4
Married couples, no children	82.01	128	27.4
Married couples, with children	84.66	132	35.6
Oldest child under 6	89.92	141	7.2
Oldest child 6 to 17	92.58	145	21.0
Oldest child 18 or older	64.86	101	7.3
Single parent with child under 18	57.89	90	5.7
Single person	30.86	48	13.9
REGION			
Total households	**63.99**	**100**	**100.0**
Northeast	70.05	109	21.9
Midwest	50.23	78	18.8
South	72.86	114	39.7
West	59.22	93	19.7

Note: For definitions of best and biggest customers, see introduction or glossary.
Source: Calculations by New Strategist based on the 1997 Consumer Expenditure Survey

Bedroom Linens

Best customers:
- Householders aged 45 to 54
- Households with incomes of $70,000 or more
- Married couples with adult children

Customer trends:
- Strong growth in the future as older boomers experiment with new looks for their bedroom.

Householders aged 45 to 54 spend 43 percent more than the average household on bedroom linens. Married couples with adult children at home (many of whom are in the 45-to-54 age group) spend 40 percent more than average on this item. The most affluent households—those with incomes of $70,000 or more—spend twice as much as the average household on bedroom linens.

Many middle-aged householders whose children are grown spend more money on themselves, making them the best customers of new bedroom linens. The market for bedroom linens is likely to grow as children leave home and boomers change the look of their bedrooms.

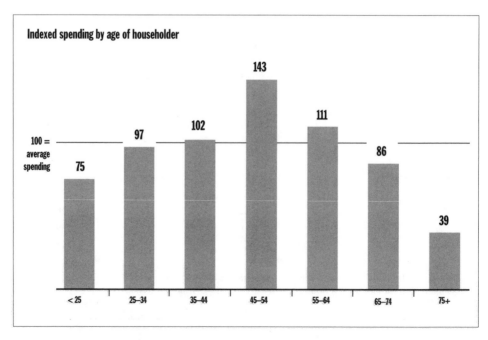

Indexed spending by age of householder

<25	25–34	35–44	45–54	55–64	65–74	75+
75	97	102	143	111	86	39

100 = average spending

BEDROOM LINENS

Total household spending	$3,619,145,280		
Average household spends	34.28		

	average spending	best customers (index)	biggest customers (market share)
AGE OF HOUSEHOLDER			
Total households	**$34.28**	**100**	**100.0%**
Under age 25	25.63	75	5.3
Aged 25 to 34	33.12	97	18.2
Aged 35 to 44	35.09	102	23.8
Aged 45 to 54	48.97	143	26.2
Aged 55 to 64	37.95	111	12.9
Aged 65 to 74	29.61	86	9.9
Aged 75 or older	13.40	39	3.6
HOUSEHOLD INCOME			
Total households reporting income	**35.52**	**100**	**100.0**
Under $20,000	16.45	46	16.1
$20,000 to $29,999	22.53	63	9.3
$30,000 to $39,999	29.67	84	10.2
$40,000 to $49,999	41.09	116	10.8
$50,000 to $69,999	53.43	150	21.1
$70,000 or more	77.13	217	32.5
HOUSEHOLD TYPE			
Total households	**34.28**	**100**	**100.0**
Married couples	44.08	129	67.2
Married couples, no children	43.66	127	27.2
Married couples, with children	41.51	121	32.6
Oldest child under 6	39.17	114	5.9
Oldest child 6 to 17	39.10	114	16.6
Oldest child 18 or older	48.08	140	10.1
Single parent with child under 18	28.05	82	5.1
Single person	21.23	62	17.8
REGION			
Total households	**34.28**	**100**	**100.0**
Northeast	37.71	110	22.0
Midwest	31.76	93	22.1
South	28.53	83	29.0
West	43.30	126	26.8

Note: For definitions of best and biggest customers, see introduction or glossary.
Source: Calculations by New Strategist based on the 1997 Consumer Expenditure Survey

Business Equipment and Office Furniture for Home Use

Best customers:
- Householders aged 45 to 64
- Households with incomes of $70,000 or more
- Married couples with school-aged children
- Households in the West

Customer trends:
- Spending on business equipment and office furniture for the home will increase sharply as home computers become universal.

Whether they telecommute or just need a place to park the home computer, an increasing number of Americans are setting up home offices. Households with incomes of $70,000 or more spend more than three times the average amount on business equipment and office furniture. Married couples with school-aged children also spend three times the average on this item as they buy computer desks for their children's use. Householders aged 45 to 54 spend more than twice the average on this item, while households in the West spend almost three times the average.

Home offices are becoming a standard fixture in American houses. Spending on business furniture for home use will grow rapidly as computers become universal and more people work at home.

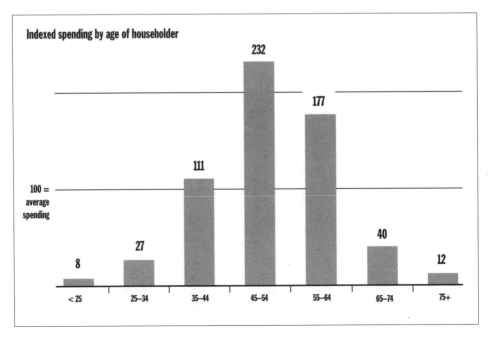

Indexed spending by age of householder

100 = average spending

< 25	25–34	35–44	45–54	55–64	65–74	75+
8	27	111	232	177	40	12

BUSINESS EQUIPMENT AND OFFICE FURNITURE FOR HOME USE

Total household spending $1,366,153,440
Average household spends   12.94

	average spending	best customers (index)	biggest customers (market share)
AGE OF HOUSEHOLDER			
Total households	$12.94	100	100.0%
Under age 25	1.07	8	0.6
Aged 25 to 34	3.55	27	5.2
Aged 35 to 44	14.39	111	25.9
Aged 45 to 54	29.96	232	42.4
Aged 55 to 64	22.90	177	20.6
Aged 65 to 74	5.19	40	4.6
Aged 75 or older	1.52	12	1.1
HOUSEHOLD INCOME			
Total households reporting income	15.33	100	100.0
Under $20,000	2.51	16	5.7
$20,000 to $29,999	3.76	25	3.6
$30,000 to $39,999	4.88	32	3.9
$40,000 to $49,999	2.46	16	1.5
$50,000 to $69,999	34.64	226	31.7
$70,000 or more	54.95	358	53.6
HOUSEHOLD TYPE			
Total households	12.94	100	100.0
Married couples	18.31	141	74.0
Married couples, no children	9.94	77	16.4
Married couples, with children	26.14	202	54.3
Oldest child under 6	2.43	19	1.0
Oldest child 6 to 17	40.51	313	45.5
Oldest child 18 or older	16.70	129	9.3
Single parent with child under 18	1.27	10	0.6
Single person	5.68	44	12.6
REGION			
Total households	12.94	100	100.0
Northeast	6.02	47	9.3
Midwest	6.27	48	11.6
South	7.50	58	20.2
West	35.15	272	57.7

Note: For definitions of best and biggest customers, see introduction or glossary.
Source: Calculations by New Strategist based on the 1997 Consumer Expenditure Survey

Calculators

Best customers:	• Householders aged 35 to 45
	• Married couples with school-aged or older children
	• Households in the West
Customer trends:	• Stable for now, but the calculator market will shrink as multifunction, hand-held devices proliferate.

Despite the proliferation of high-powered computers, there is still a place for calculators. The main users of calculators are school children learning higher mathematics, such as algebra and calculus. Consequently, the best customers of calculators are married couples with school-aged or older children. These households spend more than twice as much as the average household on calculators. Householders aged 35 to 44 spend 72 percent more than average, and those aged 45 to 54 spend 35 percent more, because most of them are parents. Households in the West spend 40 percent more than average on calculators.

Computers have not replaced calculators, but new technologies threaten the market. When personal digital assistants or similar hand-held devices with multiple capabilities become more affordable, they will replace calculators on the desks of school children.

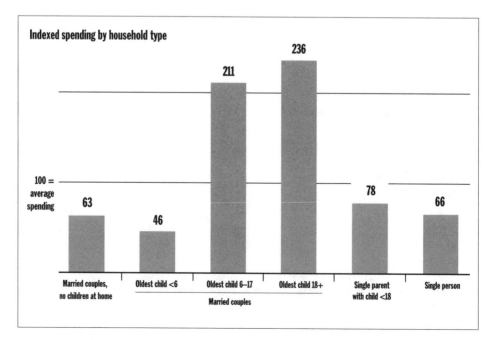

Indexed spending by household type

100 = average spending

- Married couples, no children at home: 63
- Married couples, Oldest child <6: 46
- Married couples, Oldest child 6–17: 211
- Married couples, Oldest child 18+: 236
- Single parent with child <18: 78
- Single person: 66

CALCULATORS

Total household spending	$202,705,920	
Average household spends	1.92	

	average spending	best customers (index)	biggest customers (market share)
AGE OF HOUSEHOLDER			
Total households	**$1.92**	**100**	**100.0%**
Under age 25	2.89	151	10.7
Aged 25 to 34	1.56	81	15.3
Aged 35 to 44	3.30	172	40.0
Aged 45 to 54	2.60	135	24.8
Aged 55 to 64	1.14	59	6.9
Aged 65 to 74	0.25	13	1.5
Aged 75 or older	0.16	8	0.8
HOUSEHOLD INCOME			
Total households reporting income	**2.10**	**100**	**100.0**
Under $20,000	0.97	46	16.1
$20,000 to $29,999	0.87	41	6.1
$30,000 to $39,999	2.44	116	14.2
$40,000 to $49,999	2.23	106	9.9
$50,000 to $69,999	3.46	165	23.1
$70,000 or more	4.27	203	30.4
HOUSEHOLD TYPE			
Total households	**1.92**	**100**	**100.0**
Married couples	2.52	131	68.6
Married couples, no children	1.21	63	13.4
Married couples, with children	3.57	186	50.0
Oldest child under 6	0.89	46	2.4
Oldest child 6 to 17	4.05	211	30.7
Oldest child 18 or older	4.53	236	17.0
Single parent with child under 18	1.50	78	4.9
Single person	1.26	66	18.9
REGION			
Total households	**1.92**	**100**	**100.0**
Northeast	1.74	91	18.1
Midwest	2.10	109	26.1
South	1.42	74	25.8
West	2.69	140	29.8

Note: For definitions of best and biggest customers, see introduction or glossary.
Source: Calculations by New Strategist based on the 1997 Consumer Expenditure Survey

Carpeting, Wall-to-Wall

Best customers:
- Householders aged 55 to 64
- Married couples with preschoolers
- Married couples without children

Customer trends:
- The growing number of older householders will boost spending on wall-to-wall carpeting.

Wall-to-wall carpeting is not a purchase people make often. The best customers are empty nesters and couples with preschoolers. Not surprisingly, households with incomes of $70,000 or more also spend well above average on wall-to-wall carpeting. Married couples with children under age 6 spend more than twice as much as the average household on wall-to-wall carpeting as they "kid-proof" their house. Empty nesters spend 73 percent more than average on this item as they replace worn carpets after their children leave home. People aged 55 to 64, many of whom are empty nesters, spend 87 percent more than average on carpeting.

With the empty-nest population poised to expand as the children of boomers grow up, spending on wall-to-wall carpeting should rise.

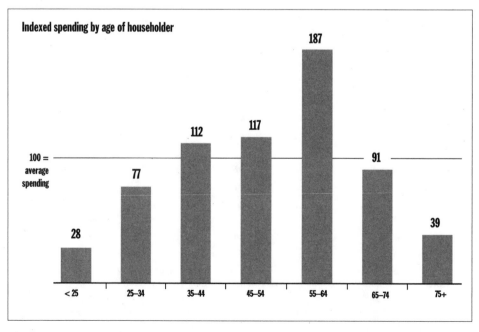

Indexed spending by age of householder

100 = average spending

< 25	25–34	35–44	45–54	55–64	65–74	75+
28	77	112	117	187	91	39

CARPETING, WALL-TO-WALL

Total household spending	$4,098,460,320	
Average household spends	38.82	

	average spending	best customers (index)	biggest customers (market share)
AGE OF HOUSEHOLDER			
Total households	**$38.82**	**100**	**100.0%**
Under age 25	10.93	28	2.0
Aged 25 to 34	30.01	77	14.6
Aged 35 to 44	43.57	112	26.1
Aged 45 to 54	45.34	117	21.4
Aged 55 to 64	72.71	187	21.8
Aged 65 to 74	35.38	91	10.5
Aged 75 or older	14.95	39	3.6
HOUSEHOLD INCOME			
Total households reporting income	**37.36**	**100**	**100.0**
Under $20,000	12.79	34	11.9
$20,000 to $29,999	15.02	40	5.9
$30,000 to $39,999	30.36	81	9.9
$40,000 to $49,999	32.71	88	8.2
$50,000 to $69,999	60.49	162	22.7
$70,000 or more	103.34	277	41.3
HOUSEHOLD TYPE			
Total households	**38.82**	**100**	**100.0**
Married couples	58.52	151	78.8
Married couples, no children	67.10	173	36.9
Married couples, with children	51.14	132	35.4
Oldest child under 6	87.39	225	11.6
Oldest child 6 to 17	41.38	107	15.5
Oldest child 18 or older	44.97	116	8.3
Single parent with child under 18	41.62	107	6.7
Single person	14.46	37	10.7
REGION			
Total households	**38.82**	**100**	**100.0**
Northeast	47.73	123	24.6
Midwest	38.24	99	23.5
South	28.93	75	26.0
West	47.29	122	25.9

Note: For definitions of best and biggest customers, see introduction or glossary.
Source: Calculations by New Strategist based on the 1997 Consumer Expenditure Survey

Closet and Storage Items

Best customers:
- Householders aged 65 to 74
- Householders aged 45 to 54

Customer trends:
- Spending on closet and storage items will rise as people look for ways to organize all their belongings.

The American home is becoming increasingly crowded as gadgets proliferate and our growing affluence leads to the accumulation of more and more stuff. All this stuff needs to be put somewhere, spurring spending on closet and storage items. Spending on these items peaks during times of transitions—when children leave home or after retirement, for example. This explains why some of the best customers of closet and storage items are householders aged 65 to 74 (spending 66 percent more than average) and householders aged 45 to 54 (spending 45 percent more).

Manufacturers of closet and storage items will be the beneficiaries of America's rising affluence as people look for ways to store their growing number of possessions.

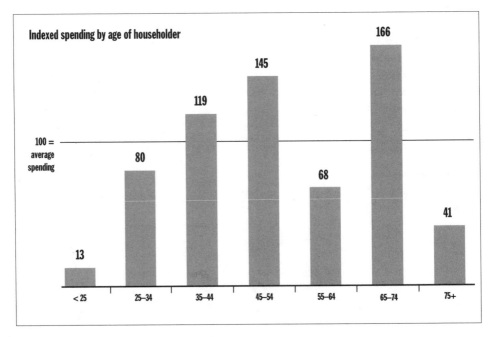

Indexed spending by age of householder

100 = average spending

< 25	25–34	35–44	45–54	55–64	65–74	75+
13	80	119	145	68	166	41

CLOSET AND STORAGE ITEMS

Total household spending $943,849,440
Average household spends   8.94

	average spending	best customers (index)	biggest customers (market share)
AGE OF HOUSEHOLDER			
Total households	**$8.94**	**100**	**100.0%**
Under age 25	1.15	13	0.9
Aged 25 to 34	7.16	80	15.1
Aged 35 to 44	10.62	119	27.6
Aged 45 to 54	12.98	145	26.6
Aged 55 to 64	6.08	68	7.9
Aged 65 to 74	14.88	166	19.1
Aged 75 or older	3.70	41	3.9
HOUSEHOLD INCOME			
Total households reporting income	**9.57**	**100**	**100.0**
Under $20,000	7.68	80	28.0
$20,000 to $29,999	6.89	72	10.5
$30,000 to $39,999	7.63	80	9.7
$40,000 to $49,999	8.07	84	7.9
$50,000 to $69,999	6.85	72	10.0
$70,000 or more	21.22	222	33.1
HOUSEHOLD TYPE			
Total households	**8.94**	**100**	**100.0**
Married couples	10.59	118	61.9
Married couples, no children	9.20	103	22.0
Married couples, with children	10.85	121	32.6
Oldest child under 6	11.27	126	6.5
Oldest child 6 to 17	9.74	109	15.9
Oldest child 18 or older	12.72	142	10.2
Single parent with child under 18	3.57	40	2.5
Single person	9.12	102	29.3
REGION			
Total households	**8.94**	**100**	**100.0**
Northeast	9.93	111	22.2
Midwest	7.04	79	18.8
South	6.24	70	24.4
West	14.38	161	34.2

Note: For definitions of best and biggest customers, see introduction or glossary.
Source: Calculations by New Strategist based on the 1997 Consumer Expenditure Survey

Clothes Dryers

Best customers:

- Married couples with preschoolers

Customer trends:

- Unchanging market because of stability in the number of couples with preschoolers.

While many young adults don't mind heading to a laundromat, couples with young children much prefer doing laundry at home. Consequently, married couples with preschoolers are the best customers of clothes dryers, spending 81 percent more than the average household on this item. Couples without children at home (many of whom are older) spend 24 percent more than average on clothes dryers because many are replacing machines purchased when they were young.

The number of couples with preschoolers is stable right now as the small Generation X moves through its twenties. Spending on clothes dryers should begin to rise once the larger Millennial generation has children—still a few years away.

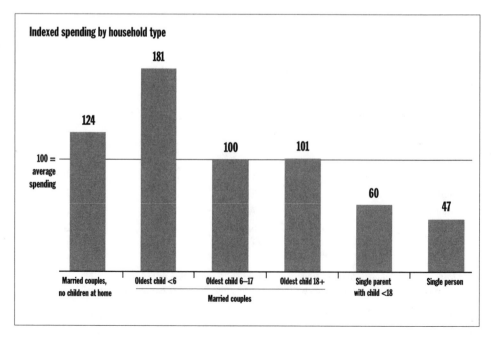

Indexed spending by household type

| 124 | 181 | 100 | 101 | 60 | 47 |

100 = average spending

- Married couples, no children at home
- Oldest child <6
- Oldest child 6–17
- Oldest child 18+

Married couples

- Single parent with child <18
- Single person

CLOTHES DRYERS

Total household spending	$1,712,442,720
Average household spends	16.22

	average spending	best customers (index)	biggest customers (market share)
AGE OF HOUSEHOLDER			
Total households	**$16.22**	**100**	**100.0%**
Under age 25	11.28	70	4.9
Aged 25 to 34	17.81	110	20.7
Aged 35 to 44	20.59	127	29.5
Aged 45 to 54	17.31	107	19.6
Aged 55 to 64	16.12	99	11.6
Aged 65 to 74	12.83	79	9.1
Aged 75 or older	8.02	49	4.6
HOUSEHOLD INCOME			
Total households reporting income	**16.71**	**100**	**100.0**
Under $20,000	8.36	50	17.4
$20,000 to $29,999	14.20	85	12.4
$30,000 to $39,999	24.20	145	17.7
$40,000 to $49,999	13.82	83	7.7
$50,000 to $69,999	28.05	168	23.6
$70,000 or more	23.69	142	21.2
HOUSEHOLD TYPE			
Total households	**16.22**	**100**	**100.0**
Married couples	20.68	127	66.7
Married couples, no children	20.17	124	26.5
Married couples, with children	18.78	116	31.1
Oldest child under 6	29.36	181	9.3
Oldest child 6 to 17	16.24	100	14.6
Oldest child 18 or older	16.34	101	7.2
Single parent with child under 18	9.72	60	3.8
Single person	7.65	47	13.5
REGION			
Total households	**16.22**	**100**	**100.0**
Northeast	15.80	97	19.5
Midwest	14.48	89	21.3
South	17.88	110	38.5
West	15.86	98	20.8

Note: For definitions of best and biggest customers, see introduction or glossary.
Source: Calculations by New Strategist based on the 1997 Consumer Expenditure Survey

Cooking Stoves, Ovens

Best customers:
- Householders aged 55 to 64
- Married couples without children at home

Customer trends:
- The growing number of middle-aged householders may mean more spending in this category.

Householders aged 55 to 64 spend 78 percent more than the average household on cooking stoves and ovens. At this age, many people are renovating their homes, particularly kitchens and bathrooms. Others are simply replacing old appliances. Married couples without children at home, most of whom are older householders, spend 61 percent more than average on stoves and ovens.

As the large baby-boom generation is reaching its empty-nest years, when many people remodel their homes, sales of stoves and ovens may increase.

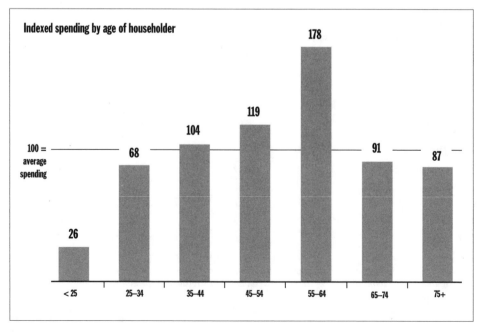

Indexed spending by age of householder

100 = average spending

< 25	25–34	35–44	45–54	55–64	65–74	75+
26	68	104	119	178	91	87

COOKING STOVES, OVENS

Total household spending	$2,329,006,560
Average household spends	22.06

	average spending	best customers (index)	biggest customers (market share)
AGE OF HOUSEHOLDER			
Total households	**$22.06**	**100**	**100.0%**
Under age 25	5.72	26	1.8
Aged 25 to 34	15.03	68	12.9
Aged 35 to 44	22.99	104	24.2
Aged 45 to 54	26.22	119	21.8
Aged 55 to 64	39.32	178	20.8
Aged 65 to 74	20.05	91	10.4
Aged 75 or older	19.17	87	8.1
HOUSEHOLD INCOME			
Total households reporting income	**21.86**	**100**	**100.0**
Under $20,000	11.05	51	17.6
$20,000 to $29,999	20.92	96	14.0
$30,000 to $39,999	27.57	126	15.4
$40,000 to $49,999	17.84	82	7.6
$50,000 to $69,999	25.58	117	16.4
$70,000 or more	42.35	194	29.0
HOUSEHOLD TYPE			
Total households	**22.06**	**100**	**100.0**
Married couples	28.63	130	67.9
Married couples, no children	35.60	161	34.4
Married couples, with children	24.01	109	29.3
Oldest child under 6	26.09	118	6.1
Oldest child 6 to 17	24.84	113	16.4
Oldest child 18 or older	20.83	94	6.8
Single parent with child under 18	5.27	24	1.5
Single person	12.35	56	16.1
REGION			
Total households	**22.06**	**100**	**100.0**
Northeast	21.12	96	19.1
Midwest	22.12	100	24.0
South	26.95	122	42.6
West	14.86	67	14.3

Note: For definitions of best and biggest customers, see introduction or glossary.
Source: Calculations by New Strategist based on the 1997 Consumer Expenditure Survey

Curtains and Draperies

Best customers:
- Married couples without children
- Householders aged 45 to 64
- Households with incomes of $70,000 or more

Customer trends:
- Older householders who want a new look for their home should boost spending in this category.

The best customers of curtains and draperies are householders aged 45 to 64, spending from 45 to 54 percent more than the average household on this item. Many are empty nesters in their peak-earning years. With their children grown, they want a new look for their home. Households with incomes of $70,000 or more spend three times the average on curtains and drapes. Married couples without children at home, many of whom are older, spend 89 percent more than average on this item.

Older householders often redecorate after their children have moved out of the house. Spending in this category should get a boost as the number of older householders expands.

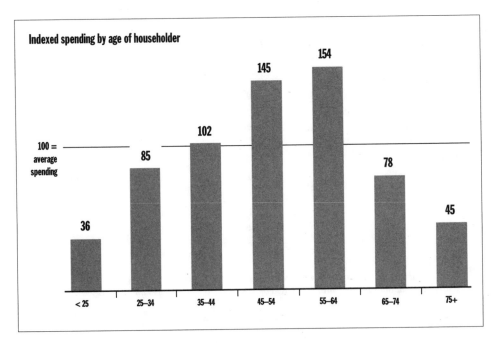

Indexed spending by age of householder

< 25	25–34	35–44	45–54	55–64	65–74	75+
36	85	102	145	154	78	45

100 = average spending

CURTAINS AND DRAPERIES

Total household spending	$1,766,286,480
Average household spends	16.73

	average spending	best customers (index)	biggest customers (market share)
AGE OF HOUSEHOLDER			
Total households	**$16.73**	**100**	**100.0%**
Under age 25	6.05	36	2.6
Aged 25 to 34	14.24	85	16.1
Aged 35 to 44	17.01	102	23.7
Aged 45 to 54	24.34	145	26.7
Aged 55 to 64	25.72	154	17.9
Aged 65 to 74	13.02	78	8.9
Aged 75 or older	7.58	45	4.2
HOUSEHOLD INCOME			
Total households reporting income	**16.52**	**100**	**100.0**
Under $20,000	7.64	46	16.1
$20,000 to $29,999	7.73	47	6.8
$30,000 to $39,999	8.95	54	6.6
$40,000 to $49,999	13.28	80	7.5
$50,000 to $69,999	17.85	108	15.2
$70,000 or more	52.78	319	47.8
HOUSEHOLD TYPE			
Total households	**16.73**	**100**	**100.0**
Married couples	23.92	143	74.8
Married couples, no children	31.66	189	40.4
Married couples, with children	18.96	113	30.5
Oldest child under 6	25.80	154	7.9
Oldest child 6 to 17	18.35	110	16.0
Oldest child 18 or older	15.31	92	6.6
Single parent with child under 18	9.92	59	3.7
Single person	6.24	37	10.7
REGION			
Total households	**16.73**	**100**	**100.0**
Northeast	17.25	103	20.6
Midwest	16.02	96	22.9
South	13.10	78	27.3
West	23.01	138	29.2

Note: For definitions of best and biggest customers, see introduction or glossary.
Source: Calculations by New Strategist based on the 1997 Consumer Expenditure Survey

Decorative Items for the Home

Best customers:
- Married couples without children
- Married couples with adult children

Customer trends:
- More middle-aged empty nesters spell growth for this market.

Older couples without young children at home are the best customers of decorative items. Married couples without children, most of whom are older people, spend 62 percent more than average on decorative items for the home. Those with adult children at home spend 61 percent more. Householders aged 45 to 54 and householders aged 65 to 74 also spend well above average on this item.

When children are grown, many people seize the opportunity to redecorate their homes. Finally, they can buy the breakable items they've always wanted. As the number of middle-aged empty nesters grows in the next few years, spending on decorative items for the home should increase.

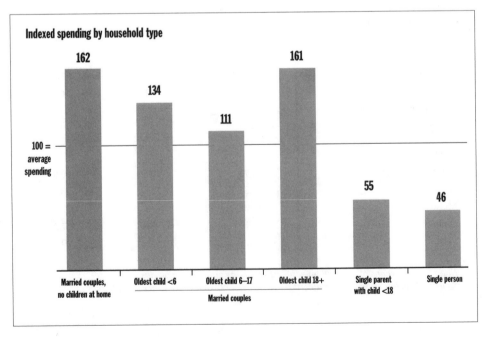

Indexed spending by household type

162	134	111	161	55	46
Married couples, no children at home	Oldest child <6	Oldest child 6–17	Oldest child 18+	Single parent with child <18	Single person

Married couples

100 = average spending

DECORATIVE ITEMS FOR THE HOME

Total household spending		$14,159,853,120	
Average household spends		134.12	

	average spending	best customers (index)	biggest customers (market share)
AGE OF HOUSEHOLDER			
Total households	**$134.12**	**100**	**100.0%**
Under age 25	31.52	24	1.7
Aged 25 to 34	130.54	97	18.4
Aged 35 to 44	127.85	95	22.2
Aged 45 to 54	193.95	145	26.5
Aged 55 to 64	137.95	103	12.0
Aged 65 to 74	182.61	136	15.6
Aged 75 or older	63.89	48	4.4
HOUSEHOLD INCOME			
Total households reporting income	**134.65**	**100**	**100.0**
Under $20,000	56.08	42	14.5
$20,000 to $29,999	98.59	73	10.7
$30,000 to $39,999	79.23	59	7.2
$40,000 to $49,999	196.14	146	13.6
$50,000 to $69,999	209.47	156	21.8
$70,000 or more	283.45	211	31.5
HOUSEHOLD TYPE			
Total households	**134.12**	**100**	**100.0**
Married couples	189.13	141	73.7
Married couples, no children	217.37	162	34.6
Married couples, with children	173.11	129	34.7
Oldest child under 6	179.27	134	6.9
Oldest child 6 to 17	149.35	111	16.2
Oldest child 18 or older	215.74	161	11.6
Single parent with child under 18	73.40	55	3.4
Single person	61.26	46	13.1
REGION			
Total households	**134.12**	**100**	**100.0**
Northeast	136.71	102	20.4
Midwest	162.25	121	28.9
South	97.88	73	25.5
West	158.47	118	25.1

Note: For definitions of best and biggest customers, see introduction or glossary.
Source: Calculations by New Strategist based on the 1997 Consumer Expenditure Survey

Dinnerware

The best customers of dinnerware are families with school-aged and older children. They spend twice as much as the average household on this item. Householders aged 45 to 54—a group likely to have school-aged children—spend 85 percent more than average on dinnerware. One factor behind this high level of spending is the need to replace dinnerware broken by children.

Spending on dinnerware is not likely to change much, unless the strong economy encourages people to spend their discretionary dollars on this item.

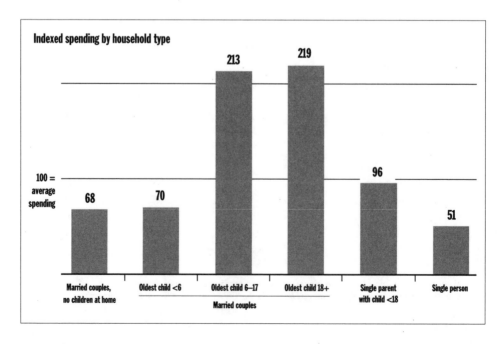

Indexed spending by household type

Married couples, no children at home	Oldest child <6	Oldest child 6–17	Oldest child 18+	Single parent with child <18	Single person
68	70	213	219	96	51

Married couples

100 = average spending

DINNERWARE

Total household spending	$1,120,161,360		
Average household spends	10.61		

	average spending	best customers (index)	biggest customers (market share)
AGE OF HOUSEHOLDER			
Total households	**$10.61**	**100**	**100.0%**
Under age 25	2.30	22	1.5
Aged 25 to 34	7.88	74	14.0
Aged 35 to 44	15.90	150	34.9
Aged 45 to 54	19.62	185	33.9
Aged 55 to 64	8.16	77	9.0
Aged 65 to 74	3.30	31	3.6
Aged 75 or older	4.71	44	4.1
HOUSEHOLD INCOME			
Total households reporting income	**11.54**	**100**	**100.0**
Under $20,000	3.50	30	10.6
$20,000 to $29,999	5.19	45	6.6
$30,000 to $39,999	16.09	139	17.0
$40,000 to $49,999	8.85	77	7.2
$50,000 to $69,999	16.89	146	20.5
$70,000 or more	28.76	249	37.3
HOUSEHOLD TYPE			
Total households	**10.61**	**100**	**100.0**
Married couples	14.28	135	70.4
Married couples, no children	7.18	68	14.4
Married couples, with children	19.51	184	49.4
Oldest child under 6	7.40	70	3.6
Oldest child 6 to 17	22.59	213	31.0
Oldest child 18 or older	23.21	219	15.7
Single parent with child under 18	10.15	96	6.0
Single person	5.42	51	14.7
REGION			
Total households	**10.61**	**100**	**100.0**
Northeast	7.72	73	14.5
Midwest	13.27	125	29.9
South	7.51	71	24.7
West	15.28	144	30.6

Note: For definitions of best and biggest customers, see introduction or glossary.
Source: Calculations by New Strategist based on the 1997 Consumer Expenditure Survey

Dishwashers

Best customers:
- Householders aged 55 to 64
- Married couples without children

Customer trends:
- Spending on dishwashers will rise in the coming years as the number of older householders increases.

A dishwasher is one of the conveniences few households want to do without. After thousands of cycles, however, dishwashers eventually wear out. This is why older householders are the best customers of dishwashers. Householders aged 55 to 64 spend 82 percent more than the average household on this item. Married couples without children at home, most of whom are older, spend nearly twice the average.

The number of older households with aging appliances is poised to rise in the near future. In addition, the strong economy is encouraging many householders to renovate their homes. These factors point to more spending on dishwashers in the years ahead.

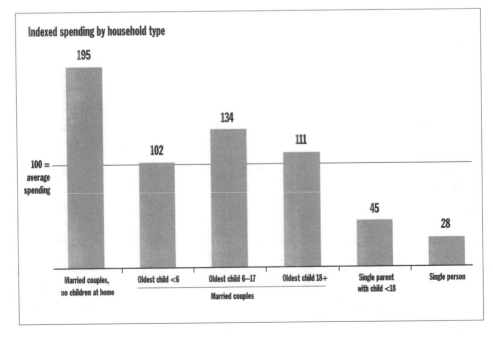

Indexed spending by household type

Married couples, no children at home	Oldest child <6	Oldest child 6–17	Oldest child 18+	Single parent with child <18	Single person
195	102	134	111	45	28

100 = average spending

Married couples

DISHWASHERS

Total household spending	$1,316,532,720
Average household spends	12.47

	average spending	best customers (index)	biggest customers (market share)
AGE OF HOUSEHOLDER			
Total households	**$12.47**	**100**	**100.0%**
Under age 25	1.57	13	0.9
Aged 25 to 34	8.66	69	13.1
Aged 35 to 44	10.69	86	19.9
Aged 45 to 54	13.29	107	19.5
Aged 55 to 64	22.75	182	21.3
Aged 65 to 74	15.31	123	14.1
Aged 75 or older	14.96	120	11.2
HOUSEHOLD INCOME			
Total households reporting income	**12.07**	**100**	**100.0**
Under $20,000	3.84	32	11.1
$20,000 to $29,999	12.98	108	15.7
$30,000 to $39,999	18.04	149	18.3
$40,000 to $49,999	6.36	53	4.9
$50,000 to $69,999	20.73	172	24.1
$70,000 or more	20.92	173	25.9
HOUSEHOLD TYPE			
Total households	**12.47**	**100**	**100.0**
Married couples	18.09	145	75.9
Married couples, no children	24.35	195	41.7
Married couples, with children	15.14	121	32.6
Oldest child under 6	12.75	102	5.3
Oldest child 6 to 17	16.65	134	19.4
Oldest child 18 or older	13.79	111	8.0
Single parent with child under 18	5.55	45	2.8
Single person	3.46	28	8.0
REGION			
Total households	**12.47**	**100**	**100.0**
Northeast	14.04	113	22.5
Midwest	14.79	119	28.3
South	11.08	89	31.0
West	10.66	85	18.2

Note: For definitions of best and biggest customers, see introduction or glossary.
Source: Calculations by New Strategist based on the 1997 Consumer Expenditure Survey

Flatware

Best customers:
- Householders aged 55 to 64
- Married couples without children
- Married couples with adult children

Customer trends:
- Rising number of older Americans could boost this market—if boomers can be convinced to buy.

The first set of flatware people acquire is usually a hand-me-down from their parents or an inexpensive set from a discount store. Eventually, however, the desire for better flatware takes hold. Older householders (aged 55 to 64) spend 90 percent more than average on flatware. Married couples without children at home (most of whom are older) spend 50 percent more than average, while those with adult children at home spend 46 percent more.

Spending on flatware could get a boost from the coming expansion of the 55-to-64 age group. But boomers have been slow to buy a variety of housewares—including furniture, linen, and china—preferring to spend on computers and other electronic gadgets. If they can be convinced to buy, the market should grow.

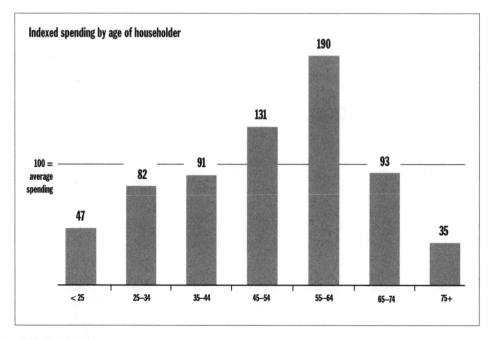

Indexed spending by age of householder

< 25	25–34	35–44	45–54	55–64	65–74	75+
47	82	91	131	190	93	35

100 = average spending

FLATWARE

Total household spending	$494,095,680		
Average household spends	4.68		

	average spending	best customers (index)	biggest customers (market share)
AGE OF HOUSEHOLDER			
Total households	**$4.68**	**100**	**100.0%**
Under age 25	2.19	47	3.3
Aged 25 to 34	3.84	82	15.5
Aged 35 to 44	4.24	91	21.1
Aged 45 to 54	6.15	131	24.1
Aged 55 to 64	8.90	190	22.2
Aged 65 to 74	4.35	93	10.7
Aged 75 or older	1.62	35	3.2
HOUSEHOLD INCOME			
Total households reporting income	**4.42**	**100**	**100.0**
Under $20,000	1.58	36	12.5
$20,000 to $29,999	2.91	66	9.6
$30,000 to $39,999	2.80	63	7.7
$40,000 to $49,999	3.99	90	8.4
$50,000 to $69,999	7.66	173	24.3
$70,000 or more	11.03	250	37.3
HOUSEHOLD TYPE			
Total households	**4.68**	**100**	**100.0**
Married couples	5.96	127	66.6
Married couples, no children	7.03	150	32.1
Married couples, with children	5.47	117	31.4
Oldest child under 6	5.49	117	6.0
Oldest child 6 to 17	4.78	102	14.9
Oldest child 18 or older	6.85	146	10.5
Single parent with child under 18	1.58	34	2.1
Single person	3.64	78	22.3
REGION			
Total households	**4.68**	**100**	**100.0**
Northeast	5.30	113	22.6
Midwest	4.20	90	21.4
South	4.28	91	31.9
West	5.29	113	24.0

Note: For definitions of best and biggest customers, see introduction or glossary.
Source: Calculations by New Strategist based on the 1997 Consumer Expenditure Survey

Floor Cleaning Equipment, Electric

Best customers:	• Married couples without children
	• Married couples with adult children
	• Households in the West
Customer trends:	• Declining housekeeping standards may hurt this market.

Older married couples spend the most on electrical floor cleaning equipment (i.e., vacuum cleaners) because they are the ones most concerned with having a clean home. Married couples with adult children at home spend 38 percent more than average on this item, while those without children at home (most of whom are older) spend 34 percent more. Households in the West spend 44 percent more than average on electric floor cleaning equipment.

Boomers and younger adults have lower housekeeping standards than older Americans because they are too busy to worry much about cleaning. This could dampen spending on electric floor cleaning equipment in the years ahead.

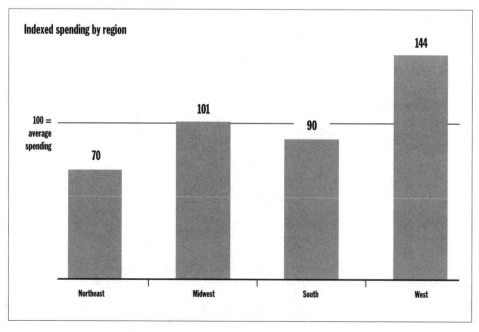

Indexed spending by region

100 = average spending

Northeast	Midwest	South	West
70	101	90	144

FLOOR CLEANING EQUIPMENT, ELECTRIC

Total household spending $1,655,431,680
Average household spends   15.68

	average spending	best customers (index)	biggest customers (market share)
AGE OF HOUSEHOLDER			
Total households	**$15.68**	**100**	**100.0%**
Under age 25	11.94	76	5.4
Aged 25 to 34	15.90	101	19.1
Aged 35 to 44	13.31	85	19.7
Aged 45 to 54	19.31	123	22.6
Aged 55 to 64	17.75	113	13.2
Aged 65 to 74	18.09	115	13.2
Aged 75 or older	11.26	72	6.7
HOUSEHOLD INCOME			
Total households reporting income	**16.13**	**100**	**100.0**
Under $20,000	7.17	44	15.5
$20,000 to $29,999	14.08	87	12.8
$30,000 to $39,999	25.63	159	19.4
$40,000 to $49,999	18.11	112	10.5
$50,000 to $69,999	18.82	117	16.4
$70,000 or more	27.51	171	25.5
HOUSEHOLD TYPE			
Total households	**15.68**	**100**	**100.0**
Married couples	19.75	126	65.9
Married couples, no children	21.03	134	28.6
Married couples, with children	17.45	111	29.9
Oldest child under 6	16.51	105	5.4
Oldest child 6 to 17	15.68	100	14.5
Oldest child 18 or older	21.70	138	10.0
Single parent with child under 18	13.11	84	5.2
Single person	9.22	59	16.9
REGION			
Total households	**15.68**	**100**	**100.0**
Northeast	10.99	70	14.0
Midwest	15.85	101	24.2
South	14.05	90	31.3
West	22.55	144	30.5

Note: For definitions of best and biggest customers, see introduction or glossary.
Source: Calculations by New Strategist based on the 1997 Consumer Expenditure Survey

Furniture Rental

Best Customers:	• Householders aged 25 to 34
	• Households with incomes below $20,000
	• Single parents
	• Households in the South
Customer Trends:	• Little or no increase since more young adults are living with their parents rather than setting up their own households

Young, low-income households are the best customers of furniture rental. Single parents, in particular, need furniture for themselves and their children. These households spend four times the average on furniture rental. Householders aged 25 to 34 spend twice as much as the average household on this item. Households with incomes below $20,000 spend 56 percent more than average. Southerners spend 28 percent more than average because of the high proportion of low-income households in the region.

The number of young adults is rising as the children of boomers grow up. But the proportion of young adults who live with their parents rather than set up their own household is also increasing. The market for furniture rental is not likely to grow much, if at all.

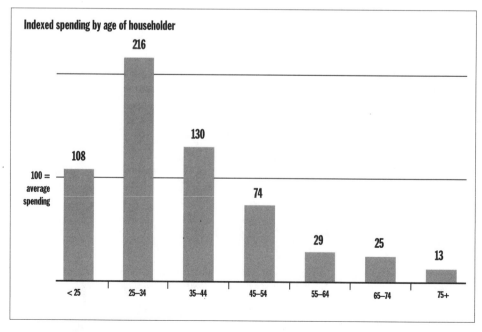

Indexed spending by age of householder

100 = average spending

| < 25 | 25–34 | 35–44 | 45–54 | 55–64 | 65–74 | 75+ |
| 108 | 216 | 130 | 74 | 29 | 25 | 13 |

FURNITURE RENTAL

Total household spending	$360,014,160
Average household spends	3.41

	average spending	best customers (index)	biggest customers (market share)
AGE OF HOUSEHOLDER			
Total households	**$3.41**	**100**	**100.0%**
Under age 25	3.68	108	7.7
Aged 25 to 34	7.38	216	40.8
Aged 35 to 44	4.44	130	30.3
Aged 45 to 54	2.54	74	13.6
Aged 55 to 64	0.98	29	3.4
Aged 65 to 74	0.85	25	2.9
Aged 75 or older	0.44	13	1.2
HOUSEHOLD INCOME			
Total households reporting income	**3.50**	**100**	**100.0**
Under $20,000	5.46	156	54.3
$20,000 to $29,999	1.65	47	6.9
$30,000 to $39,999	2.94	84	10.3
$40,000 to $49,999	4.09	117	10.9
$50,000 to $69,999	2.34	67	9.4
$70,000 or more	1.96	56	8.4
HOUSEHOLD TYPE			
Total households	**3.41**	**100**	**100.0**
Married couples	2.14	63	32.8
Married couples, no children	1.04	30	6.5
Married couples, with children	2.67	78	21.0
Oldest child under 6	3.18	93	4.8
Oldest child 6 to 17	3.42	100	14.6
Oldest child 18 or older	0.80	23	1.7
Single parent with child under 18	13.47	395	24.8
Single person	1.95	57	16.4
REGION			
Total households	**3.41**	**100**	**100.0**
Northeast	3.26	96	19.1
Midwest	2.62	77	18.4
South	4.38	128	44.8
West	2.82	83	17.6

Note: For definitions of best and biggest customers, see introduction or glossary.
Source: Calculations by New Strategist based on the 1997 Consumer Expenditure Survey

Glassware

Best customers:	• Householders aged 45 to 74
	• Married couples without children
	• Households in the Northeast
Customer trends:	• Stable spending with little chance of growth.

In this era of casual entertaining, few people worry about serving drinks to their guests in the proper type of glass. Families with children often use plastic or paper cups instead. Consequently, the best customers of glassware are older householders. Those aged 45 to 74 spend from 43 to 66 percent more than the average householder on this item. Married couples without children at home (most of whom are older) spend 73 percent more than average on glassware.

Boomers and younger generations have been slow to buy many of the housewares that older generations once invested in, such as china, linens, flatware, and glassware. Consequently, the market for glassware is likely to remain stable or even decline as boomers age.

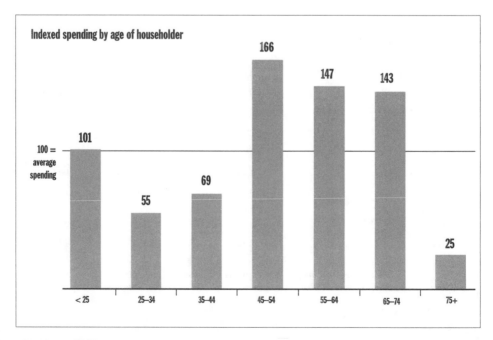

Indexed spending by age of householder

Age	Index
< 25	101
25–34	55
35–44	69
45–54	166
55–64	147
65–74	143
75+	25

100 = average spending

GLASSWARE

Total household spending	$871,002,000
Average household spends	8.25

	average spending	best customers (index)	biggest customers (market share)
AGE OF HOUSEHOLDER			
Total households	**$8.25**	**100**	**100.0%**
Under age 25	8.31	101	7.2
Aged 25 to 34	4.53	55	10.4
Aged 35 to 44	5.66	69	16.0
Aged 45 to 54	13.70	166	30.4
Aged 55 to 64	12.14	147	17.2
Aged 65 to 74	11.78	143	16.4
Aged 75 or older	2.07	25	2.3
HOUSEHOLD INCOME			
Total households reporting income	**8.60**	**100**	**100.0**
Under $20,000	5.21	61	21.1
$20,000 to $29,999	5.18	60	8.8
$30,000 to $39,999	7.90	92	11.2
$40,000 to $49,999	7.25	84	7.9
$50,000 to $69,999	9.14	106	14.9
$70,000 or more	20.56	239	35.7
HOUSEHOLD TYPE			
Total households	**8.25**	**100**	**100.0**
Married couples	10.66	129	67.6
Married couples, no children	14.28	173	36.9
Married couples, with children	8.51	103	27.7
Oldest child under 6	5.89	71	3.7
Oldest child 6 to 17	8.65	105	15.3
Oldest child 18 or older	10.44	127	9.1
Single parent with child under 18	2.59	31	2.0
Single person	6.11	74	21.3
REGION			
Total households	**8.25**	**100**	**100.0**
Northeast	11.21	136	27.1
Midwest	8.02	97	23.2
South	8.80	107	37.2
West	4.93	60	12.7

Note: For definitions of best and biggest customers, see introduction or glossary.
Source: Calculations by New Strategist based on the 1997 Consumer Expenditure Survey

Infants' Furniture and Equipment

Best customers:
- Householders aged 25 to 34
- Married couples with preschoolers

Customer trends:
- A stable market until the large Millennial generation (the children of boomers) begins to have children and spending rises.

The best customers of infants' furniture and equipment are, naturally, households with infants. Married couples with preschoolers spend four times the average amount on infants' furniture and equipment. Householders aged 25 to 34 spend nearly three times the average on this item because many people in the age group have infants.

The number of newborns has declined slightly in the past few years because small Generation X is occupying most of the twentysomething age group. But the larger Millennial generation is now entering its twenties and will begin making grandparents out of baby boomers. This should boost spending on infants' furniture and equipment.

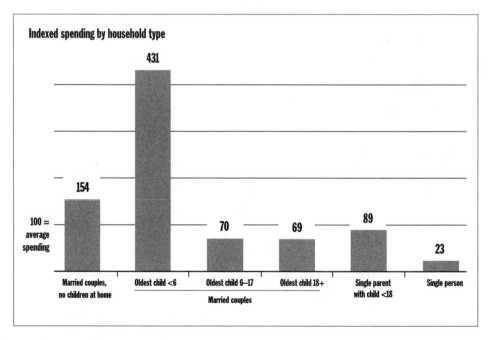

Indexed spending by household type

154	431	70	69	89	23
Married couples, no children at home	Oldest child <6	Oldest child 6–17	Oldest child 18+	Single parent with child <18	Single person
		Married couples			

100 = average spending

INFANTS' FURNITURE AND EQUIPMENT

Total household spending $1,786,345,920
Average household spends   16.92

	average spending	best customers (index)	biggest customers (market share)
AGE OF HOUSEHOLDER			
Total households	**$16.92**	**100**	**100.0%**
Under age 25	6.64	39	2.8
Aged 25 to 34	48.24	285	53.8
Aged 35 to 44	13.20	78	18.1
Aged 45 to 54	10.52	62	11.4
Aged 55 to 64	15.63	92	10.8
Aged 65 to 74	4.34	26	2.9
Aged 75 or older	1.10	7	0.6
HOUSEHOLD INCOME			
Total households reporting income	**19.44**	**100**	**100.0**
Under $20,000	6.35	33	11.4
$20,000 to $29,999	18.63	96	14.0
$30,000 to $39,999	12.07	62	7.6
$40,000 to $49,999	17.13	88	8.2
$50,000 to $69,999	18.94	97	13.7
$70,000 or more	57.50	296	44.2
HOUSEHOLD TYPE			
Total households	**16.92**	**100**	**100.0**
Married couples	26.38	156	81.5
Married couples, no children	26.09	154	32.9
Married couples, with children	24.30	144	38.6
Oldest child under 6	72.86	431	22.2
Oldest child 6 to 17	11.77	70	10.1
Oldest child 18 or older	11.64	69	4.9
Single parent with child under 18	15.01	89	5.6
Single person	3.94	23	6.7
REGION			
Total households	**16.92**	**100**	**100.0**
Northeast	17.46	103	20.6
Midwest	15.95	94	22.5
South	13.89	82	28.6
West	22.29	132	28.0

Note: For definitions of best and biggest customers, see introduction or glossary.
Source: Calculations by New Strategist based on the 1997 Consumer Expenditure Survey

Kitchen and Dining Room Furniture

Best customers:
- Married couples without children
- Married couples with preschoolers

Customer trends:
- More spending is likely as Millennials fill the twentysomething age group and boomers become empty nesters.

Two demographic segments comprise the market for kitchen and dining room furniture: young couples furnishing their first home and older couples redecorating after their children have left home. Married couples with preschoolers spend 55 percent more than average on kitchen and dining room furniture, while those without children at home spend 69 percent more. Householders aged 25 to 34 spend 45 percent more than average on this item because many are establishing their first home. Those aged 45 to 64 spend more because many are redecorating.

Spending on kitchen and dining room furniture is likely to rise as the Millennial generation sets up house and boomers become empty nesters.

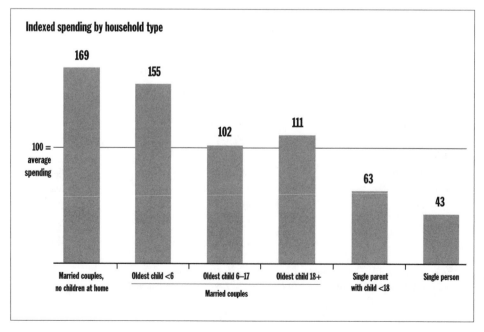

KITCHEN AND DINING ROOM FURNITURE

Total household spending	$5,140,495,440
Average household spends	48.69

	average spending	best customers (index)	biggest customers (market share)
AGE OF HOUSEHOLDER			
Total households	**$48.69**	**100**	**100.0%**
Under age 25	23.53	48	3.4
Aged 25 to 34	70.66	145	27.4
Aged 35 to 44	43.19	89	20.6
Aged 45 to 54	64.61	133	24.3
Aged 55 to 64	60.36	124	14.5
Aged 65 to 74	37.34	77	8.8
Aged 75 or older	5.11	10	1.0
HOUSEHOLD INCOME			
Total households reporting income	**46.41**	**100**	**100.0**
Under $20,000	19.11	41	14.3
$20,000 to $29,999	34.96	75	11.0
$30,000 to $39,999	46.38	100	12.2
$40,000 to $49,999	36.75	79	7.4
$50,000 to $69,999	59.18	128	17.9
$70,000 or more	115.26	248	37.1
HOUSEHOLD TYPE			
Total households	**48.69**	**100**	**100.0**
Married couples	70.16	144	75.3
Married couples, no children	82.10	169	36.0
Married couples, with children	55.72	114	30.8
Oldest child under 6	75.47	155	8.0
Oldest child 6 to 17	49.64	102	14.8
Oldest child 18 or older	53.88	111	8.0
Single parent with child under 18	30.81	63	4.0
Single person	21.18	43	12.5
REGION			
Total households	**48.69**	**100**	**100.0**
Northeast	77.39	159	31.8
Midwest	39.99	82	19.6
South	39.30	81	28.2
West	46.89	96	20.5

Note: For definitions of best and biggest customers, see introduction or glossary.
Source: Calculations by New Strategist based on the 1997 Consumer Expenditure Survey

Kitchen and Dining Room Linens

Best customers:	• **Householders aged 45 to 64**
	• **Married couples with school-aged children**
	• **Households in the Midwest**
Customer trends:	• **Possible rise in spending as aging boomers redecorate.**

Householders aged 45 to 64 spend 35 to 68 percent more than the average householder on kitchen and dining room linens. Parents of school-aged children spend 72 percent more as they replace linens made threadbare by children. Households in the Midwest spend 30 percent more than average on this item. Households with incomes of $70,000 or more spend over twice the average on kitchen and dining room linens.

Moving to a new home or renovating an old one triggers spending on kitchen and dining room linens. With older boomers in their peak-earning years and many buying larger homes, spending on kitchen and dining room linens may get a boost.

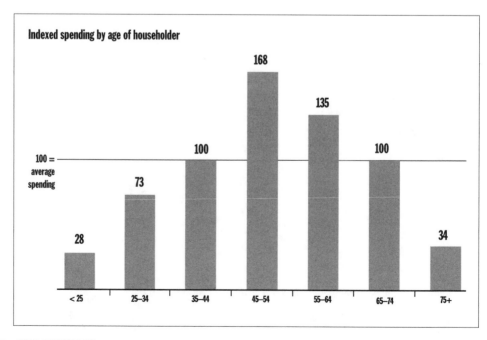

Indexed spending by age of householder

<25	25–34	35–44	45–54	55–64	65–74	75+
28	73	100	168	135	100	34

100 = average spending

KITCHEN AND DINING ROOM LINENS

Total household spending	$253,382,400	
Average household spends	2.40	

	average spending	best customers (index)	biggest customers (market share)
AGE OF HOUSEHOLDER			
Total households	**$2.40**	**100**	**100.0%**
Under age 25	0.67	28	2.0
Aged 25 to 34	1.75	73	13.8
Aged 35 to 44	2.39	100	23.2
Aged 45 to 54	4.04	168	30.8
Aged 55 to 64	3.24	135	15.7
Aged 65 to 74	2.40	100	11.5
Aged 75 or older	0.81	34	3.1
HOUSEHOLD INCOME			
Total households reporting income	**2.39**	**100**	**100.0**
Under $20,000	0.95	40	13.8
$20,000 to $29,999	1.16	49	7.1
$30,000 to $39,999	2.96	124	15.1
$40,000 to $49,999	1.77	74	6.9
$50,000 to $69,999	2.91	122	17.1
$70,000 or more	6.37	267	39.8
HOUSEHOLD TYPE			
Total households	**2.40**	**100**	**100.0**
Married couples	3.35	140	73.0
Married couples, no children	3.53	147	31.4
Married couples, with children	3.55	148	39.8
Oldest child under 6	2.17	90	4.7
Oldest child 6 to 17	4.13	172	25.0
Oldest child 18 or older	3.36	140	10.1
Single parent with child under 18	1.98	83	5.2
Single person	1.33	55	15.9
REGION			
Total households	**2.40**	**100**	**100.0**
Northeast	2.46	103	20.5
Midwest	3.11	130	31.0
South	1.71	71	24.9
West	2.69	112	23.8

Note: For definitions of best and biggest customers, see introduction or glossary.
Source: Calculations by New Strategist based on the 1997 Consumer Expenditure Survey

Kitchen Appliances, Small Electric

Best customers:	• Householders aged 55 to 64 • Married couples without children • Married couples with adult children
Customer trends:	• Stable market because of Americans' desire for well-equipped kitchens.

Older householders are the best customers of small electric kitchen appliances, such as espresso machines, bread makers, food processors, and can openers. In part, this is because older people are more likely to actually use their kitchen for cooking rather than simply as a place to gather while eating takeout food. Householders aged 55 to 64 spend 34 percent more than the average household on small electric kitchen appliances. Married couples with adult children at home spend 42 percent more than average. Those without children at home, most of whom are older couples, spend 33 percent more.

The market for small, electric kitchen appliances should remain healthy despite the rise of takeout because Americans want their kitchens to be well-equipped, whether they use the equipment or not.

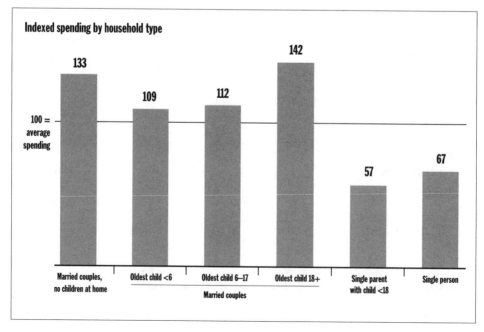

Indexed spending by household type

Married couples, no children at home	Oldest child <6	Oldest child 6–17	Oldest child 18+	Single parent with child <18	Single person
133	109	112	142	57	67

100 = average spending

Married couples

KITCHEN APPLIANCES, SMALL ELECTRIC

Total household spending	$1,759,951,920
Average household spends	16.67

	average spending	best customers (index)	biggest customers (market share)
AGE OF HOUSEHOLDER			
Total households	**$16.67**	**100**	**100.0%**
Under age 25	11.70	70	5.0
Aged 25 to 34	15.36	92	17.4
Aged 35 to 44	15.57	93	21.7
Aged 45 to 54	20.74	124	22.8
Aged 55 to 64	22.34	134	15.6
Aged 65 to 74	18.04	108	12.4
Aged 75 or older	9.04	54	5.0
HOUSEHOLD INCOME			
Total households reporting income	**17.50**	**100**	**100.0**
Under $20,000	10.81	62	21.5
$20,000 to $29,999	12.30	70	10.3
$30,000 to $39,999	19.11	109	13.4
$40,000 to $49,999	18.94	108	10.1
$50,000 to $69,999	23.83	136	19.1
$70,000 or more	29.98	171	25.6
HOUSEHOLD TYPE			
Total households	**16.67**	**100**	**100.0**
Married couples	20.81	125	65.3
Married couples, no children	22.24	133	28.5
Married couples, with children	19.94	120	32.2
Oldest child under 6	18.25	109	5.6
Oldest child 6 to 17	18.67	112	16.3
Oldest child 18 or older	23.71	142	10.2
Single parent with child under 18	9.43	57	3.6
Single person	11.20	67	19.3
REGION			
Total households	**16.67**	**100**	**100.0**
Northeast	16.21	97	19.4
Midwest	18.87	113	27.0
South	13.50	81	28.3
West	19.83	119	25.3

Note: For definitions of best and biggest customers, see introduction or glossary.
Source: Calculations by New Strategist based on the 1997 Consumer Expenditure Survey

Kitchenware and Cookware, Nonelectric

Best customers:	• Householders aged 45 to 54
	• Married couples with school-aged children
	• Households in the West
Customer trends:	• Stable market, even though less cooking is taking place in American homes. Future upswing possible as Millennial generation sets up house.

Married couples with school-aged children spend 74 percent more than average on nonelectric kitchenware and cookware. Householders aged 45 to 54 spend 50 percent more. Many people in this age group have school-aged children. Spending by households in the West is 55 percent higher than average, in part because the region is home to many recent movers, and cookware items are often purchased after a move.

Although home-cooked meals are less common than ever in American homes, cookware is as popular as ever. Demand may rise as the large Millennial generation begins to establish its own households in a few years.

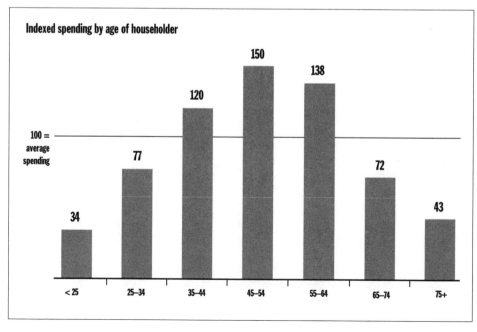

Indexed spending by age of householder

100 = average spending

< 25	25–34	35–44	45–54	55–64	65–74	75+
34	77	120	150	138	72	43

KITCHENWARE AND COOKWARE, NONELECTRIC

Total household spending	$4,067,843,280
Average household spends	38.53

	average spending	best customers (index)	biggest customers (market share)
AGE OF HOUSEHOLDER			
Total households	**$38.53**	**100**	**100.0%**
Under age 25	13.17	34	2.4
Aged 25 to 34	29.58	77	14.5
Aged 35 to 44	46.05	120	27.8
Aged 45 to 54	57.65	150	27.4
Aged 55 to 64	53.11	138	16.1
Aged 65 to 74	27.67	72	8.2
Aged 75 or older	16.51	43	4.0
HOUSEHOLD INCOME			
Total households reporting income	**43.20**	**100**	**100.0**
Under $20,000	35.03	81	28.2
$20,000 to $29,999	31.30	72	10.6
$30,000 to $39,999	34.96	81	9.9
$40,000 to $49,999	26.59	62	5.8
$50,000 to $69,999	65.20	151	21.2
$70,000 or more	74.32	172	25.7
HOUSEHOLD TYPE			
Total households	**38.53**	**100**	**100.0**
Married couples	49.24	128	66.8
Married couples, no children	42.73	111	23.7
Married couples, with children	56.14	146	39.2
Oldest child under 6	44.72	116	6.0
Oldest child 6 to 17	66.90	174	25.3
Oldest child 18 or older	44.01	114	8.2
Single parent with child under 18	35.39	92	5.8
Single person	21.78	57	16.2
REGION			
Total households	**38.53**	**100**	**100.0**
Northeast	36.45	95	18.9
Midwest	38.11	99	23.6
South	26.68	69	24.2
West	59.65	155	32.9

Note: For definitions of best and biggest customers, see introduction or glossary.
Source: Calculations by New Strategist based on the 1997 Consumer Expenditure Survey

Lamps and Lighting Fixtures

Best customers:
- Married couples with school-aged children
- Households with incomes of $70,000 or more

Customer trends:
- Stable as long as the economy remains strong.

Households with incomes of $70,000 or more spend nearly three times the average on lamps and lighting fixtures, accounting for 44 percent of the market. Married couples with school-aged children spend 52 percent more than average on this item as parents buy lamps for children's desks and bedside tables. Households in the West spend 52 percent more than average on lamps.

Because the number of families with school-aged children is at a peak, spending on lamps and lighting fixtures should remain stable if the economy continues to be strong.

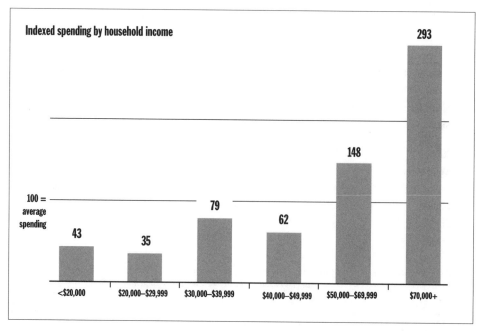

Indexed spending by household income

43	35	79	62	148	293
<$20,000	$20,000–$29,999	$30,000–$39,999	$40,000–$49,999	$50,000–$69,999	$70,000+

100 = average spending

LAMPS AND LIGHTING FIXTURES

Total household spending $1,322,867,280
Average household spends   12.53

	average spending	best customers (index)	biggest customers (market share)
AGE OF HOUSEHOLDER			
Total households	**$12.53**	**100**	**100.0%**
Under age 25	7.40	59	4.2
Aged 25 to 34	10.27	82	15.5
Aged 35 to 44	15.43	123	28.6
Aged 45 to 54	16.24	130	23.7
Aged 55 to 64	11.33	90	10.5
Aged 65 to 74	16.74	134	15.3
Aged 75 or older	2.76	22	2.1
HOUSEHOLD INCOME			
Total households reporting income	**13.73**	**100**	**100.0**
Under $20,000	5.86	43	14.9
$20,000 to $29,999	4.82	35	5.1
$30,000 to $39,999	10.88	79	9.7
$40,000 to $49,999	8.50	62	5.8
$50,000 to $69,999	20.32	148	20.8
$70,000 or more	40.18	293	43.7
HOUSEHOLD TYPE			
Total households	**12.53**	**100**	**100.0**
Married couples	16.28	130	67.9
Married couples, no children	15.57	124	26.5
Married couples, with children	17.15	137	36.8
Oldest child under 6	14.46	115	5.9
Oldest child 6 to 17	19.02	152	22.1
Oldest child 18 or older	15.31	122	8.8
Single parent with child under 18	7.48	60	3.7
Single person	8.10	65	18.6
REGION			
Total households	**12.53**	**100**	**100.0**
Northeast	10.99	88	17.5
Midwest	14.23	114	27.1
South	8.25	66	23.0
West	19.10	152	32.4

Note: For definitions of best and biggest customers, see introduction or glossary.
Source: Calculations by New Strategist based on the 1997 Consumer Expenditure Survey

Lawn and Garden Equipment

Best customers:
- Married couples without children
- Householders aged 45 to 64

Customer trends:
- A growing market as boomers gain more free time to indulge in hobbies such as gardening.

Middle-aged people with children and jobs don't have much time to garden or work in the yard. Households without children, however, have the luxury of keeping the grass trimmed and flower beds watered. Married couples without children at home spend 78 percent more than the average household on lawn and garden equipment. Householders aged 45 to 64, many of whom are empty nesters and early retirees, spend 38 to 57 percent more than average on this item.

Now at the peak of their careers, boomers have little time for hobbies. But the time squeeze will ease within the next ten years for the oldest boomers, boosting sales of lawn and garden equipment.

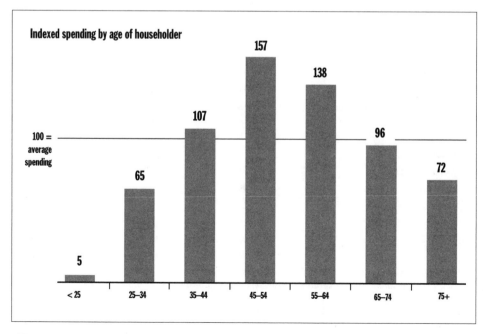

Indexed spending by age of householder

100 = average spending

< 25	25–34	35–44	45–54	55–64	65–74	75+
5	65	107	157	138	96	72

LAWN AND GARDEN EQUIPMENT

Total household spending	$4,156,527,120
Average household spends	39.37

	average spending	best customers (index)	biggest customers (market share)
AGE OF HOUSEHOLDER			
Total households	**$39.37**	**100**	**100.0%**
Under age 25	1.94	5	0.4
Aged 25 to 34	25.68	65	12.3
Aged 35 to 44	42.12	107	24.9
Aged 45 to 54	61.66	157	28.7
Aged 55 to 64	54.16	138	16.0
Aged 65 to 74	37.64	96	11.0
Aged 75 or older	28.50	72	6.7
HOUSEHOLD INCOME			
Total households reporting income	**40.53**	**100**	**100.0**
Under $20,000	18.85	47	16.2
$20,000 to $29,999	20.92	52	7.5
$30,000 to $39,999	33.83	83	10.2
$40,000 to $49,999	54.82	135	12.7
$50,000 to $69,999	76.69	189	26.6
$70,000 or more	72.82	180	26.9
HOUSEHOLD TYPE			
Total households	**39.37**	**100**	**100.0**
Married couples	60.42	153	80.2
Married couples, no children	70.25	178	38.1
Married couples, with children	49.77	126	34.0
Oldest child under 6	37.19	94	4.9
Oldest child 6 to 17	53.20	135	19.7
Oldest child 18 or older	51.81	132	9.5
Single parent with child under 18	11.59	29	1.8
Single person	14.21	36	10.4
REGION			
Total households	**39.37**	**100**	**100.0**
Northeast	51.15	130	26.0
Midwest	44.58	113	27.1
South	39.10	99	34.6
West	22.86	58	12.3

Note: For definitions of best and biggest customers, see introduction or glossary.
Source: Calculations by New Strategist based on the 1997 Consumer Expenditure Survey

Living Room Chairs

Best customers: • Married couples without children

Customer trends: • A bright future as the nest empties and boomers replace their worn-out furniture.

Married couples without children at home spend 51 percent more than average on living room chairs. Most are older couples whose grown children live elsewhere. After their children have left home, many older couples spend on themselves, indulging in redecorating their homes and buying new furniture. Spending on living room chairs is above average for householders in the age groups from 45 to 74.

The number of empty nesters is poised to expand in the years ahead as the children of boomers grow up. This will boost spending on living room chairs as older householders replace worn items.

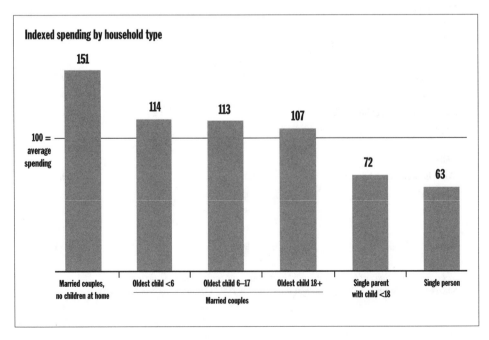

Indexed spending by household type

Married couples, no children at home	Oldest child <6	Oldest child 6–17	Oldest child 18+	Single parent with child <18	Single person
151	114	113	107	72	63

100 = average spending

Married couples

LIVING ROOM CHAIRS

Total household spending $5,006,413,920
Average household spends   47.42

	average spending	best customers (index)	biggest customers (market share)
AGE OF HOUSEHOLDER			
Total households	**$47.42**	**100**	**100.0%**
Under age 25	19.55	41	2.9
Aged 25 to 34	49.81	105	19.8
Aged 35 to 44	42.02	89	20.6
Aged 45 to 54	62.43	132	24.1
Aged 55 to 64	52.12	110	12.8
Aged 65 to 74	54.74	115	13.2
Aged 75 or older	32.89	69	6.5
HOUSEHOLD INCOME			
Total households reporting income	**51.17**	**100**	**100.0**
Under $20,000	28.42	56	19.3
$20,000 to $29,999	29.65	58	8.5
$30,000 to $39,999	51.44	101	12.3
$40,000 to $49,999	55.27	108	10.1
$50,000 to $69,999	64.39	126	17.7
$70,000 or more	110.03	215	32.1
HOUSEHOLD TYPE			
Total households	**47.42**	**100**	**100.0**
Married couples	61.45	130	67.8
Married couples, no children	71.44	151	32.2
Married couples, with children	52.75	111	29.9
Oldest child under 6	53.97	114	5.9
Oldest child 6 to 17	53.41	113	16.4
Oldest child 18 or older	50.54	107	7.7
Single parent with child under 18	34.28	72	4.5
Single person	29.79	63	18.0
REGION			
Total households	**47.42**	**100**	**100.0**
Northeast	54.24	114	22.8
Midwest	46.07	97	23.2
South	46.97	99	34.6
West	43.27	91	19.4

Note: For definitions of best and biggest customers, see introduction or glossary.
Source: Calculations by New Strategist based on the 1997 Consumer Expenditure Survey

Living Room Tables

The best customers of living room tables are younger home buyers furnishing their first home or empty nesters redecorating after their children have left home. Couples with preschoolers spend 56 percent more than average on living room tables, while couples without children at home (most of them older) spend 41 percent more.

The number of people of prime home-buying age is declining as the small Generation X moves into the age group. This contraction could dampen spending on living room tables.

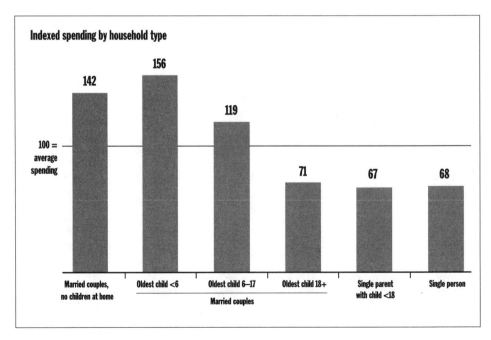

Indexed spending by household type

Married couples, no children at home	Oldest child <6	Oldest child 6–17	Oldest child 18+	Single parent with child <18	Single person
142	156	119	71	67	68

100 = average spending

Married couples

LIVING ROOM TABLES

Total household spending	$2,174,865,600		
Average household spends	20.60		

	average spending	best customers (index)	biggest customers (market share)
AGE OF HOUSEHOLDER			
Total households	**$20.60**	**100**	**100.0%**
Under age 25	13.43	65	4.6
Aged 25 to 34	25.00	121	22.9
Aged 35 to 44	29.02	141	32.8
Aged 45 to 54	21.79	106	19.4
Aged 55 to 64	16.96	82	9.6
Aged 65 to 74	16.78	81	9.3
Aged 75 or older	3.00	15	1.4
HOUSEHOLD INCOME			
Total households reporting income	**21.35**	**100**	**100.0**
Under $20,000	8.14	38	13.3
$20,000 to $29,999	8.66	41	5.9
$30,000 to $39,999	16.12	76	9.2
$40,000 to $49,999	23.09	108	10.1
$50,000 to $69,999	28.34	133	18.6
$70,000 or more	61.16	286	42.8
HOUSEHOLD TYPE			
Total households	**20.60**	**100**	**100.0**
Married couples	27.33	133	69.4
Married couples, no children	29.18	142	30.2
Married couples, with children	23.32	113	30.4
Oldest child under 6	32.14	156	8.0
Oldest child 6 to 17	24.47	119	17.3
Oldest child 18 or older	14.70	71	5.1
Single parent with child under 18	13.74	67	4.2
Single person	13.93	68	19.4
REGION			
Total households	**20.60**	**100**	**100.0**
Northeast	21.25	103	20.6
Midwest	19.06	93	22.1
South	19.01	92	32.2
West	24.31	118	25.1

Note: For definitions of best and biggest customers, see introduction or glossary.
Source: Calculations by New Strategist based on the 1997 Consumer Expenditure Survey

Mattresses and Springs

Best customers:
- Householders aged 25 to 34
- Householders aged 45 to 54
- Married couples without children
- Married couples with school-aged children

Customer trends:
- Spending should rise as growing numbers of empty nesters trade in worn-out mattresses for more expensive ones to relieve their aches and pains.

Two demographic segments comprise the best customers of mattresses—parents of school-aged children who need more mattresses for their growing families, and empty nesters who are replacing worn out mattresses with new models. Married couples with school-aged children spend 25 percent more than average on mattresses, while those without children at home spend 29 percent more. Householders aged 25 to 34 (many of whom are parents of school-aged children) spend 29 percent more than average on this item, while those aged 45 to 54 (many of whom are empty nesters) spend 31 percent more.

As the number of empty nesters expands, spending on mattresses—especially higher-quality products that promise relief from aches and pains—should rise.

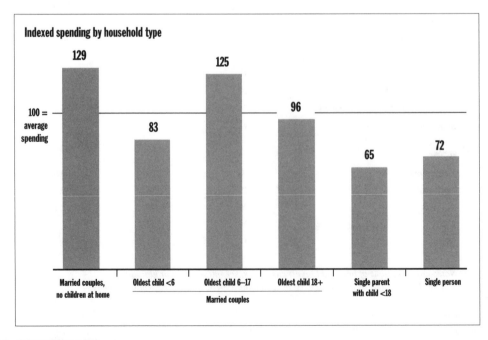

Indexed spending by household type

129	83	125	96	65	72

100 = average spending

Married couples, no children at home | Oldest child <6 | Oldest child 6–17 | Oldest child 18+ | Single parent with child <18 | Single person

Married couples

MATTRESSES AND SPRINGS

Total household spending	$4,915,618,560		
Average household spends	46.56		

	average spending	best customers (index)	biggest customers (market share)
AGE OF HOUSEHOLDER			
Total households	**$46.56**	**100**	**100.0%**
Under age 25	31.16	67	4.8
Aged 25 to 34	59.85	129	24.3
Aged 35 to 44	48.26	104	24.1
Aged 45 to 54	61.05	131	24.0
Aged 55 to 64	51.38	110	12.9
Aged 65 to 74	30.47	65	7.5
Aged 75 or older	12.36	27	2.5
HOUSEHOLD INCOME			
Total households reporting income	**45.54**	**100**	**100.0**
Under $20,000	24.62	54	18.8
$20,000 to $29,999	29.74	65	9.5
$30,000 to $39,999	28.07	62	7.5
$40,000 to $49,999	50.69	111	10.4
$50,000 to $69,999	85.11	187	26.2
$70,000 or more	83.60	184	27.4
HOUSEHOLD TYPE			
Total households	**46.56**	**100**	**100.0**
Married couples	55.11	118	61.9
Married couples, no children	59.95	129	27.5
Married couples, with children	50.78	109	29.3
Oldest child under 6	38.77	83	4.3
Oldest child 6 to 17	58.06	125	18.1
Oldest child 18 or older	44.64	96	6.9
Single parent with child under 18	30.15	65	4.1
Single person	33.44	72	20.6
REGION			
Total households	**46.56**	**100**	**100.0**
Northeast	45.40	98	19.5
Midwest	44.70	96	22.9
South	52.18	112	39.1
West	40.51	87	18.5

Note: For definitions of best and biggest customers, see introduction or glossary.
Source: Calculations by New Strategist based on the 1997 Consumer Expenditure Survey

Microwave Ovens

Best customers:

- Married couples with adult children

Customer trends:

- Little growth, since most households already own a microwave oven and will spend on a new one only when it needs to be replaced.

The microwave oven didn't take long to catch on. As the lives of Americans got busier, the demand for convenience rose, and there are few things more convenient than a microwave oven. The best customers of microwave ovens are married couples with adult children at home. These households spend 70 percent more than the average household on this item. Some are replacing aging microwave ovens, while others are buying them for college-bound children.

Microwave ovens have become a standard fixture in most American homes. Spending on this item is likely to remain stable as households replace older machines.

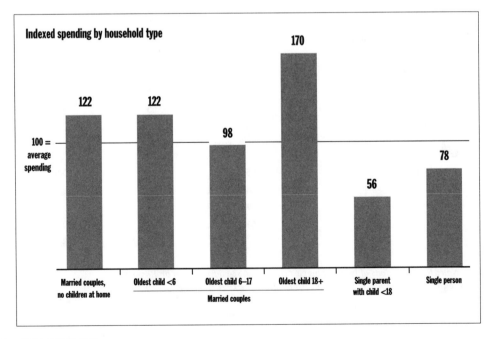

Indexed spending by household type

122	122	98	170	56	78
Married couples, no children at home	Oldest child <6	Oldest child 6–17	Oldest child 18+	Single parent with child <18	Single person

100 = average spending

Married couples

MICROWAVE OVENS

Total household spending	$1,012,473,840		
Average household spends	9.59		

	average spending	best customers (index)	biggest customers (market share)
AGE OF HOUSEHOLDER			
Total households	**$9.59**	**100**	**100.0%**
Under age 25	7.55	79	5.6
Aged 25 to 34	10.51	110	20.7
Aged 35 to 44	9.63	100	23.4
Aged 45 to 54	10.47	109	20.0
Aged 55 to 64	11.09	116	13.5
Aged 65 to 74	8.55	89	10.2
Aged 75 or older	6.80	71	6.6
HOUSEHOLD INCOME			
Total households reporting income	**10.12**	**100**	**100.0**
Under $20,000	6.49	64	22.3
$20,000 to $29,999	7.42	73	10.7
$30,000 to $39,999	14.68	145	17.7
$40,000 to $49,999	12.12	120	11.2
$50,000 to $69,999	10.96	108	15.2
$70,000 or more	15.48	153	22.9
HOUSEHOLD TYPE			
Total households	**9.59**	**100**	**100.0**
Married couples	11.55	120	63.0
Married couples, no children	11.67	122	26.0
Married couples, with children	11.70	122	32.8
Oldest child under 6	11.73	122	6.3
Oldest child 6 to 17	9.43	98	14.3
Oldest child 18 or older	16.29	170	12.2
Single parent with child under 18	5.38	56	3.5
Single person	7.48	78	22.4
REGION			
Total households	**9.59**	**100**	**100.0**
Northeast	7.04	73	14.7
Midwest	9.36	98	23.3
South	10.14	106	36.9
West	11.31	118	25.1

Note: For definitions of best and biggest customers, see introduction or glossary.
Source: Calculations by New Strategist based on the 1997 Consumer Expenditure Survey

Outdoor Furniture

Best customers:
- Householders aged 45 to 54
- Households with incomes of $70,000 or more
- Married couples without children
- Households in the West

Customer trends:
- Increased spending is likely as affluent boomers enjoy the good life.

Outdoor furniture is a discretionary expense. Consequently, households with incomes of $70,000 or more spend three times the average amount on outdoor furniture, accounting for 48 percent of the market. Married couples without children at home spend more than twice the average on this item. Householders aged 45 to 54, who are in their peak-earning years, spend 79 percent more than average on outdoor furniture. Households in the West spend 74 percent more than average.

Heightened interest in gardening is one factor that will contribute to increased sales of outdoor furniture. In addition, rising affluence among older boomers will allow them to spend more on these items as they enjoy the good life in their own backyards.

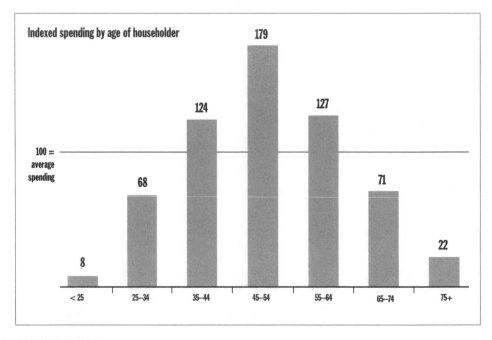

Indexed spending by age of householder

< 25	8
25–34	68
35–44	124
45–54	179
55–64	127
65–74	71
75+	22

100 = average spending

OUTDOOR FURNITURE

Total household spending	$1,436,889,360
Average household spends	13.61

	average spending	best customers (index)	biggest customers (market share)
AGE OF HOUSEHOLDER			
Total households	**$13.61**	**100**	**100.0%**
Under age 25	1.13	8	0.6
Aged 25 to 34	9.19	68	12.7
Aged 35 to 44	16.82	124	28.7
Aged 45 to 54	24.41	179	32.9
Aged 55 to 64	17.33	127	14.9
Aged 65 to 74	9.71	71	8.2
Aged 75 or older	2.95	22	2.0
HOUSEHOLD INCOME			
Total households reporting income	**12.33**	**100**	**100.0**
Under $20,000	2.74	22	7.7
$20,000 to $29,999	4.26	35	5.0
$30,000 to $39,999	11.16	91	11.1
$40,000 to $49,999	10.68	87	8.1
$50,000 to $69,999	17.71	144	20.2
$70,000 or more	39.48	320	47.9
HOUSEHOLD TYPE			
Total households	**13.61**	**100**	**100.0**
Married couples	21.72	160	83.4
Married couples, no children	29.33	216	46.0
Married couples, with children	17.75	130	35.1
Oldest child under 6	14.56	107	5.5
Oldest child 6 to 17	20.67	152	22.1
Oldest child 18 or older	14.14	104	7.5
Single parent with child under 18	7.69	57	3.5
Single person	3.61	27	7.6
REGION			
Total households	**13.61**	**100**	**100.0**
Northeast	11.15	82	16.4
Midwest	10.42	77	18.3
South	11.09	81	28.4
West	23.63	174	36.9

Note: For definitions of best and biggest customers, see introduction or glossary.
Source: Calculations by New Strategist based on the 1997 Consumer Expenditure Survey

Plants and Fresh Flowers, Indoor

Best customers:
- Householders aged 45 to 54
- Households with incomes of $70,000 or more
- Married couples without children

Customer trends:
- Older boomers with disposable income should keep the market healthy.

Spending on fresh flowers and indoor plants by households with incomes of $70,000 or more is twice the average. These households have the money to spend on this entirely discretionary purchase. Married couples without children at home, who have time to tend indoor plants, spend 62 percent more than average on this item. Householders aged 45 to 54, who are in their peak earning years, also enjoy adding greenery and flowers to their homes, spending 45 percent more than average.

Most grocery stores now include a florist shop, making it easy to pick up a fresh bouquet, and flowers and plants remain popular gifts. If the economy remains strong, the growing number of householders in their peak-earning years should keep this market growing.

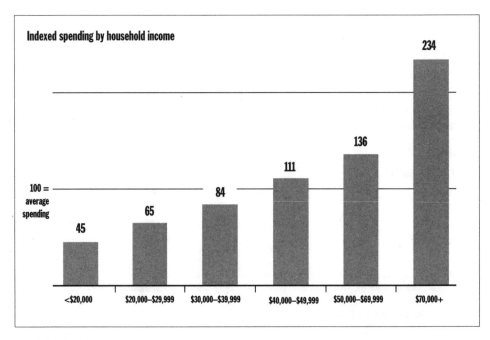

Indexed spending by household income

100 = average spending

<$20,000	$20,000–$29,999	$30,000–$39,999	$40,000–$49,999	$50,000–$69,999	$70,000+
45	65	84	111	136	234

PLANTS AND FRESH FLOWERS, INDOOR

Total household spending	$5,524,792,080
Average household spends	52.33

	average spending	best customers (index)	biggest customers (market share)
AGE OF HOUSEHOLDER			
Total households	**$52.33**	**100**	**100.0%**
Under age 25	18.46	35	2.5
Aged 25 to 34	43.49	83	15.7
Aged 35 to 44	52.73	101	23.4
Aged 45 to 54	76.05	145	26.6
Aged 55 to 64	65.14	124	14.5
Aged 65 to 74	54.11	103	11.9
Aged 75 or older	30.14	58	5.4
HOUSEHOLD INCOME			
Total households reporting income	**53.57**	**100**	**100.0**
Under $20,000	24.32	45	15.8
$20,000 to $29,999	34.71	65	9.5
$30,000 to $39,999	45.11	84	10.3
$40,000 to $49,999	59.30	111	10.4
$50,000 to $69,999	72.86	136	19.1
$70,000 or more	125.36	234	35.0
HOUSEHOLD TYPE			
Total households	**52.33**	**100**	**100.0**
Married couples	69.43	133	69.4
Married couples, no children	84.69	162	34.5
Married couples, with children	60.72	116	31.2
Oldest child under 6	49.95	95	4.9
Oldest child 6 to 17	60.85	116	16.9
Oldest child 18 or older	68.18	130	9.4
Single parent with child under 18	25.82	49	3.1
Single person	32.79	63	18.0
REGION			
Total households	**52.33**	**100**	**100.0**
Northeast	66.81	128	25.5
Midwest	54.40	104	24.8
South	39.26	75	26.2
West	57.84	111	23.5

Note: For definitions of best and biggest customers, see introduction or glossary.
Source: Calculations by New Strategist based on the 1997 Consumer Expenditure Survey

Power Tools

Best customers:
- Householders aged 35 to 54
- Married couples without children
- Married couples with school-aged children
- Households in the Midwest

Customer trends:
- Potential gains as the growing number of empty nesters take up woodworking as a hobby.

Home repair projects require power tools. Those most likely to tackle home repairs and remodeling are householders aged 35 to 54. The fact that many people in the age group have school-aged children accounts for the 60 percent above-average spending on power tools by married couples with school-aged children. Married couples without children at home spend 75 percent more than average on this item as empty nesters find time to enjoy woodworking as a hobby. Households in the Midwest spend 34 percent more than average on this item.

With the number of empty nesters poised to rise, more men and women may take up woodworking as a hobby. This trend should increase spending on power tools.

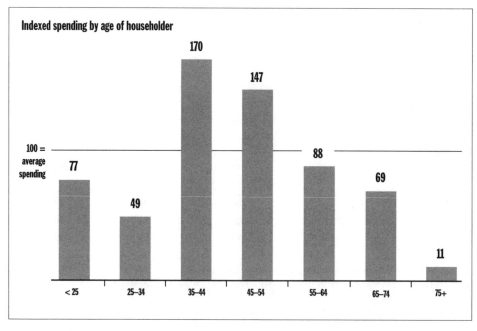

Indexed spending by age of householder

100 = average spending

| < 25 | 25–34 | 35–44 | 45–54 | 55–64 | 65–74 | 75+ |
| 77 | 49 | 170 | 147 | 88 | 69 | 11 |

POWER TOOLS

Total household spending	$1,721,944,560	
Average household spends	16.31	

	average spending	best customers (index)	biggest customers (market share)
AGE OF HOUSEHOLDER			
Total households	**$16.31**	**100**	**100.0%**
Under age 25	12.50	77	5.4
Aged 25 to 34	8.03	49	9.3
Aged 35 to 44	27.76	170	39.6
Aged 45 to 54	23.96	147	26.9
Aged 55 to 64	14.42	88	10.3
Aged 65 to 74	11.28	69	7.9
Aged 75 or older	1.83	11	1.0
HOUSEHOLD INCOME			
Total households reporting income	**17.48**	**100**	**100.0**
Under $20,000	6.49	37	12.9
$20,000 to $29,999	25.84	148	21.6
$30,000 to $39,999	12.77	73	8.9
$40,000 to $49,999	28.67	164	15.3
$50,000 to $69,999	10.95	63	8.8
$70,000 or more	35.48	203	30.3
HOUSEHOLD TYPE			
Total households	**16.31**	**100**	**100.0**
Married couples	24.66	151	79.1
Married couples, no children	28.48	175	37.3
Married couples, with children	20.89	128	34.4
Oldest child under 6	12.23	75	3.9
Oldest child 6 to 17	26.17	160	23.3
Oldest child 18 or older	17.51	107	7.7
Single parent with child under 18	1.95	12	0.8
Single person	4.61	28	8.1
REGION			
Total households	**16.31**	**100**	**100.0**
Northeast	8.99	55	11.0
Midwest	21.78	134	31.9
South	15.06	92	32.2
West	19.02	117	24.8

Note: For definitions of best and biggest customers, see introduction or glossary.
Source: Calculations by New Strategist based on the 1997 Consumer Expenditure Survey

Refrigerators and Freezers

Best customers:
- Householders aged 55 to 64
- Married couples with school-aged children

Customer trends:
- Possible growth as the number of older Americans expands—if manufacturers can convince them to replace their worn-out appliances.

The best customers of refrigerators are older people replacing worn-out appliances. Householders aged 55 to 64 spend 71 percent more than the average householder on refrigerators and freezers. Another best-customer segment is married couples with young children—some of them are furnishing their first home, while others are buying bigger refrigerators for their expanding families. Married couples with children under age 6 spend 48 percent more than average on this item.

Spending on refrigerators may get a boost as the 55-to-64 age group expands—if manufacturers can convince people to replace their old machines. Greater energy efficiency and add-ons such as ice makers and indoor water dispensers may spur replacement sales.

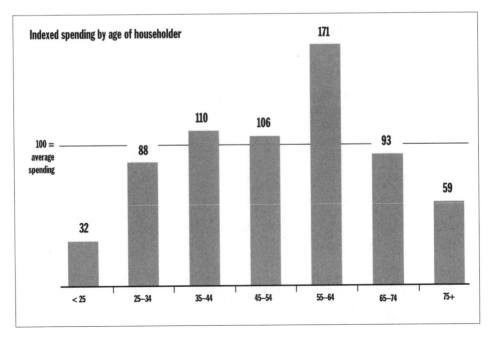

Indexed spending by age of householder

< 25	25–34	35–44	45–54	55–64	65–74	75+
32	88	110	106	171	93	59

100 = average spending

REFRIGERATORS AND FREEZERS

Total household spending $6,081,177,600
Average household spends   57.60

	average spending	best customers (index)	biggest customers (market share)
AGE OF HOUSEHOLDER			
Total households	**$57.60**	**100**	**100.0%**
Under age 25	18.71	32	2.3
Aged 25 to 34	50.47	88	16.5
Aged 35 to 44	63.47	110	25.6
Aged 45 to 54	61.06	106	19.4
Aged 55 to 64	98.67	171	20.0
Aged 65 to 74	53.48	93	10.6
Aged 75 or older	33.88	59	5.5
HOUSEHOLD INCOME			
Total households reporting income	**59.67**	**100**	**100.0**
Under $20,000	42.51	71	24.8
$20,000 to $29,999	36.19	61	8.9
$30,000 to $39,999	58.64	98	12.0
$40,000 to $49,999	55.49	93	8.7
$50,000 to $69,999	73.06	122	17.2
$70,000 or more	113.43	190	28.4
HOUSEHOLD TYPE			
Total households	**57.60**	**100**	**100.0**
Married couples	73.78	128	67.0
Married couples, no children	74.13	129	27.5
Married couples, with children	75.28	131	35.1
Oldest child under 6	85.24	148	7.6
Oldest child 6 to 17	71.61	124	18.1
Oldest child 18 or older	75.59	131	9.4
Single parent with child under 18	38.90	68	4.2
Single person	28.56	50	14.2
REGION			
Total households	**57.60**	**100**	**100.0**
Northeast	47.74	83	16.6
Midwest	50.19	87	20.8
South	63.21	110	38.3
West	66.01	115	24.3

Note: For definitions of best and biggest customers, see introduction or glossary.
Source: Calculations by New Strategist based on the 1997 Consumer Expenditure Survey

Rugs, Nonpermanent

Best customers:
- Householders aged 65 or older
- Married couples without children

Customer trends:
- Little growth or possible decline in spending during the next few years because of stability in the number of Americans aged 65 or older.

Older Americans are the best customers of rugs. Householders aged 65 or older spend more than twice the average on them because many elderly people live in older homes, which usually lack wall-to-wall carpeting. Married couples without children at home, most of whom are older, spend three times the average on this item.

Spending on rugs is likely to remain stable or even decline somewhat as the small Depression-era cohort fills the older age groups.

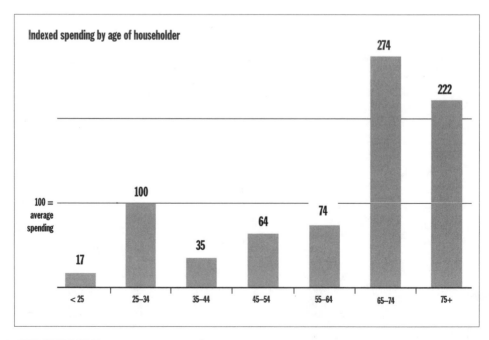

Indexed spending by age of householder

< 25	25–34	35–44	45–54	55–64	65–74	75+
17	100	35	64	74	274	222

100 = average spending

RUGS, NONPERMANENT

Total household spending	$4,110,073,680
Average household spends	38.93

	average spending	best customers (index)	biggest customers (market share)
AGE OF HOUSEHOLDER			
Total households	**$38.93**	**100**	**100.0%**
Under age 25	6.75	17	1.2
Aged 25 to 34	38.77	100	18.8
Aged 35 to 44	13.69	35	8.2
Aged 45 to 54	24.86	64	11.7
Aged 55 to 64	28.75	74	8.6
Aged 65 to 74	106.62	274	31.4
Aged 75 or older	86.56	222	20.7
HOUSEHOLD INCOME			
Total households reporting income	**45.41**	**100**	**100.0**
Under $20,000	7.53	17	5.8
$20,000 to $29,999	10.58	23	3.4
$30,000 to $39,999	99.06	218	26.7
$40,000 to $49,999	104.70	231	21.6
$50,000 to $69,999	35.85	79	11.1
$70,000 or more	86.17	190	28.4
HOUSEHOLD TYPE			
Total households	**38.93**	**100**	**100.0**
Married couples	60.81	156	81.7
Married couples, no children	124.29	319	68.1
Married couples, with children	15.55	40	10.7
Oldest child under 6	13.69	35	1.8
Oldest child 6 to 17	13.62	35	5.1
Oldest child 18 or older	20.99	54	3.9
Single parent with child under 18	6.33	16	1.0
Single person	14.38	37	10.6
REGION			
Total households	**38.93**	**100**	**100.0**
Northeast	53.83	138	27.6
Midwest	47.11	121	28.9
South	33.75	87	30.2
West	24.58	63	13.4

Note: For definitions of best and biggest customers, see introduction or glossary.
Source: Calculations by New Strategist based on the 1997 Consumer Expenditure Survey

Sewing Machines

Best customers:	• **Householders aged 55 to 74**
	• **Married couples without children**
	• **Married couples with children under age 6**
	• **Households in the Midwest**
Customer trends:	• **Declining sales because fewer people have the time or skill to sew.**

The sewing room is giving way to the home office in American households, but older people still buy sewing machines. Married couples without children at home, most of whom are older, spend more than twice the average on sewing machines. Householders aged 55 to 64 spend 59 percent more, while those aged 65 to 74 spend 53 percent more on sewing machines. The only exception to this pattern is the above-average spending by married couples with preschoolers, who spend 68 percent more than average on this item.

Sewing is nearly a lost art in America. As ready-made clothing and household items such as curtains and pillows became increasingly affordable over the past few decades, fewer people learned to sew. Sales of sewing machines are likely to decline since young adults have neither the time nor the skills to use them.

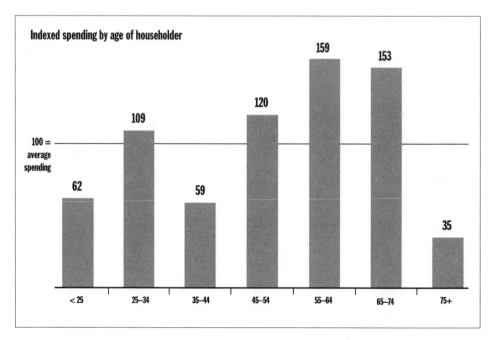

Indexed spending by age of householder

100 = average spending

< 25	25–34	35–44	45–54	55–64	65–74	75+
62	109	59	120	159	153	35

SEWING MACHINES

Total household spending	$374,794,800		
Average household spends	3.55		

	average spending	best customers (index)	biggest customers (market share)
AGE OF HOUSEHOLDER			
Total households	**$3.55**	**100**	**100.0%**
Under age 25	2.20	62	4.4
Aged 25 to 34	3.87	109	20.6
Aged 35 to 44	2.11	59	13.8
Aged 45 to 54	4.27	120	22.0
Aged 55 to 64	5.64	159	18.5
Aged 65 to 74	5.42	153	17.5
Aged 75 or older	1.23	35	3.2
HOUSEHOLD INCOME			
Total households reporting income	**3.49**	**100**	**100.0**
Under $20,000	0.70	20	7.0
$20,000 to $29,999	6.81	195	28.5
$30,000 to $39,999	2.59	74	9.1
$40,000 to $49,999	2.99	86	8.0
$50,000 to $69,999	3.82	109	15.4
$70,000 or more	7.47	214	32.0
HOUSEHOLD TYPE			
Total households	**3.55**	**100**	**100.0**
Married couples	5.05	142	74.4
Married couples, no children	7.87	222	47.3
Married couples, with children	3.32	94	25.1
Oldest child under 6	5.96	168	8.6
Oldest child 6 to 17	3.48	98	14.3
Oldest child 18 or older	1.12	32	2.3
Single parent with child under 18	5.16	145	9.1
Single person	1.36	38	11.0
REGION			
Total households	**3.55**	**100**	**100.0**
Northeast	2.26	64	12.7
Midwest	4.65	131	31.3
South	3.41	96	33.5
West	3.77	106	22.6

Note: For definitions of best and biggest customers, see introduction or glossary.
Source: Calculations by New Strategist based on the 1997 Consumer Expenditure Survey

Slipcovers and Decorative Pillows

Best customers:	• **Married couples without children**
Customer trends:	• **The rising number of affluent empty nesters means more spending on the home, which will include spending on slipcovers and decorative pillows.**

Married couples without children at home spend 72 percent more than average on slipcovers and decorative pillows. Most have grown children who have moved out of the home, spurring these householders to redecorate with new pillows and slipcovers. Spending on this item is also above average among householders aged 25 to 34, many of whom are buying them as they establish their first household.

The number of empty nesters will increase in the coming years as boomers enter the lifestage. This should boost spending on pillows and slipcovers.

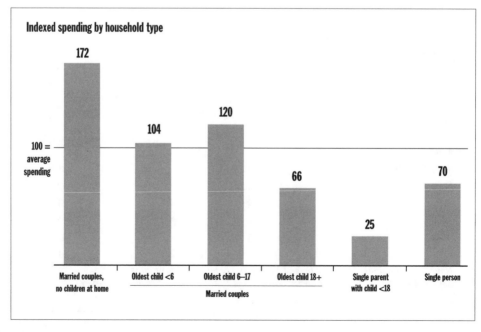

Indexed spending by household type

Household type	Index
Married couples, no children at home	172
Oldest child <6	104
Oldest child 6–17	120
Oldest child 18+	66
Single parent with child <18	25
Single person	70

100 = average spending

Married couples (Oldest child <6, Oldest child 6–17, Oldest child 18+)

SLIPCOVERS AND DECORATIVE PILLOWS

Total household spending	$221,709,600	
Average household spends	2.10	

	average spending	best customers (index)	biggest customers (market share)
AGE OF HOUSEHOLDER			
Total households	**$2.10**	**100**	**100.0%**
Under age 25	0.86	41	2.9
Aged 25 to 34	2.72	130	24.4
Aged 35 to 44	2.05	98	22.7
Aged 45 to 54	2.51	120	21.9
Aged 55 to 64	2.60	124	14.4
Aged 65 to 74	1.89	90	10.3
Aged 75 or older	0.73	35	3.2
HOUSEHOLD INCOME			
Total households reporting income	**2.40**	**100**	**100.0**
Under $20,000	1.11	46	16.0
$20,000 to $29,999	1.15	48	7.0
$30,000 to $39,999	1.84	77	9.4
$40,000 to $49,999	2.10	88	8.2
$50,000 to $69,999	5.05	210	29.5
$70,000 or more	4.78	199	29.8
HOUSEHOLD TYPE			
Total households	**2.10**	**100**	**100.0**
Married couples	2.72	130	67.7
Married couples, no children	3.62	172	36.8
Married couples, with children	2.15	102	27.5
Oldest child under 6	2.19	104	5.4
Oldest child 6 to 17	2.52	120	17.5
Oldest child 18 or older	1.39	66	4.8
Single parent with child under 18	0.52	25	1.6
Single person	1.48	70	20.2
REGION			
Total households	**2.10**	**100**	**100.0**
Northeast	2.26	108	21.5
Midwest	1.81	86	20.6
South	1.85	88	30.7
West	2.69	128	27.2

Note: For definitions of best and biggest customers, see introduction or glossary.
Source: Calculations by New Strategist based on the 1997 Consumer Expenditure Survey

Smoke Alarms

Best customers:

- Householders aged 65 to 74
- Married couples with school-aged children

Customer trends:

- The public's growing safety consciousness should boost spending on smoke alarms.

The best customers of smoke alarms are older householders and parents of school-aged children. Householders aged 65 to 74 spend twice the average on smoke alarms. Married couples with school-aged children spend 83 percent more than average. Nearly all public schools teach children about fire safety, including the importance of smoke alarms. In many families, school children are encouraging their parents to buy smoke alarms.

Public campaigns to promote fire safety have been effective in convincing Americans of their need for smoke alarms. The market for alarms is likely to grow because Americans are increasingly safety conscious.

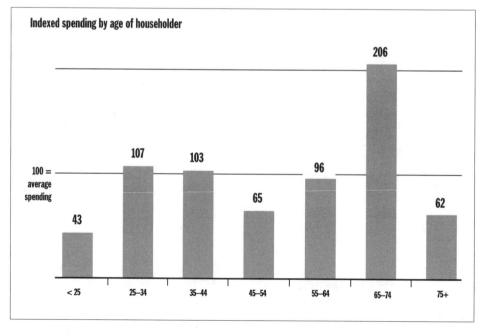

Indexed spending by age of householder

100 = average spending

< 25	25–34	35–44	45–54	55–64	65–74	75+
43	107	103	65	96	206	62

SMOKE ALARMS

Total household spending	$110,854,800		
Average household spends	1.05		

	average spending	best customers (index)	biggest customers (market share)
AGE OF HOUSEHOLDER			
Total households	**$1.05**	**100**	**100.0%**
Under age 25	0.45	43	3.0
Aged 25 to 34	1.12	107	20.1
Aged 35 to 44	1.08	103	23.9
Aged 45 to 54	0.68	65	11.9
Aged 55 to 64	1.01	96	11.2
Aged 65 to 74	2.16	206	23.6
Aged 75 or older	0.65	62	5.8
HOUSEHOLD INCOME			
Total households reporting income	**1.12**	**100**	**100.0**
Under $20,000	0.43	38	13.3
$20,000 to $29,999	1.80	161	23.5
$30,000 to $39,999	1.48	132	16.2
$40,000 to $49,999	1.20	107	10.0
$50,000 to $69,999	1.60	143	20.1
$70,000 or more	1.28	114	17.1
HOUSEHOLD TYPE			
Total households	**1.05**	**100**	**100.0**
Married couples	1.22	116	60.8
Married couples, no children	0.97	92	19.7
Married couples, with children	1.53	146	39.2
Oldest child under 6	1.28	122	6.3
Oldest child 6 to 17	1.92	183	26.6
Oldest child 18 or older	0.92	88	6.3
Single parent with child under 18	0.34	32	2.0
Single person	1.01	96	27.6
REGION			
Total households	**1.05**	**100**	**100.0**
Northeast	0.98	93	18.6
Midwest	1.41	134	32.1
South	0.85	81	28.2
West	1.03	98	20.8

Note: For definitions of best and biggest customers, see introduction or glossary.
Source: Calculations by New Strategist based on the 1997 Consumer Expenditure Survey

Sofas

Best customers: • Householders aged 25 to 34
                     • Married couples with school-aged children

Customer trends: • Spending could rise if boomers decided to replace worn sofas when their
                       children leave home.

Most people purchase a sofa when they establish their first household, and that accounts for the 30 percent-above-average spending on sofas by householders aged 25 to 34. Married couples with children under age 18 also spend more than average on sofas because many are purchasing their first home, an activity that often triggers furniture buying.

Sofa buying is below average in the older age groups. This pattern may change, however, because many boomers have never replaced their starter sofas. Spending by boomers on replacement sofas could boost the market.

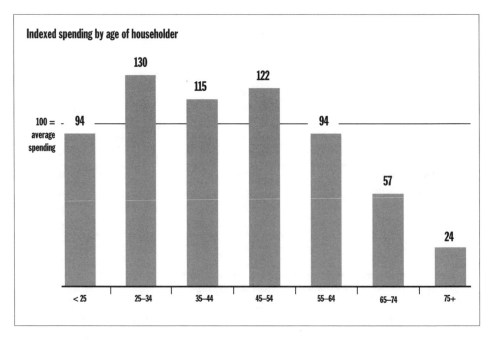

Indexed spending by age of householder

< 25	25–34	35–44	45–54	55–64	65–74	75+
94	130	115	122	94	57	24

100 = average spending

SOFAS

Total household spending	$9,904,084,560		
Average household spends	93.81		

	average spending	best customers (index)	biggest customers (market share)
AGE OF HOUSEHOLDER			
Total households	**$93.81**	**100**	**100.0%**
Under age 25	87.86	94	6.7
Aged 25 to 34	122.10	130	24.6
Aged 35 to 44	108.04	115	26.8
Aged 45 to 54	114.42	122	22.3
Aged 55 to 64	87.80	94	10.9
Aged 65 to 74	53.10	57	6.5
Aged 75 or older	22.50	24	2.2
HOUSEHOLD INCOME			
Total households reporting income	**89.42**	**100**	**100.0**
Under $20,000	36.71	41	14.3
$20,000 to $29,999	48.60	54	7.9
$30,000 to $39,999	71.91	80	9.8
$40,000 to $49,999	97.02	108	10.1
$50,000 to $69,999	130.57	146	20.5
$70,000 or more	223.02	249	37.3
HOUSEHOLD TYPE			
Total households	**93.81**	**100**	**100.0**
Married couples	122.36	130	68.2
Married couples, no children	118.22	126	26.9
Married couples, with children	121.35	129	34.8
Oldest child under 6	112.16	120	6.2
Oldest child 6 to 17	132.15	141	20.5
Oldest child 18 or older	106.08	113	8.1
Single parent with child under 18	80.98	86	5.4
Single person	56.19	60	17.2
REGION			
Total households	**93.81**	**100**	**100.0**
Northeast	89.91	96	19.1
Midwest	99.13	106	25.3
South	87.21	93	32.4
West	102.31	109	23.2

Note: For definitions of best and biggest customers, see introduction or glossary.
Source: Calculations by New Strategist based on the 1997 Consumer Expenditure Survey

Telephone Answering Devices

Best customers:	• Married couples with school-aged children
	• Households in the Northeast
Customer trends:	• Telecommunications is evolving, and the future of today's telephone answering devices is, at best, uncertain.

Telephone answering machines are now almost as common as tables and chairs in American homes. Most purchasing is for replacement, as people upgrade to take advantage of new features or replace broken machines. Households with school-aged children spend 34 percent more than average on answering machines, in part because their teenagers are demanding the ability to stay in touch with friends. Households in the Northeast spend 58 percent more than average on this item.

Telephone answering machines are now common in American homes, but will they be common in ten years? As telecommunications evolves, it's likely that other devices, such as home computers or personal digital assistants, will absorb the functions of today's answering machines.

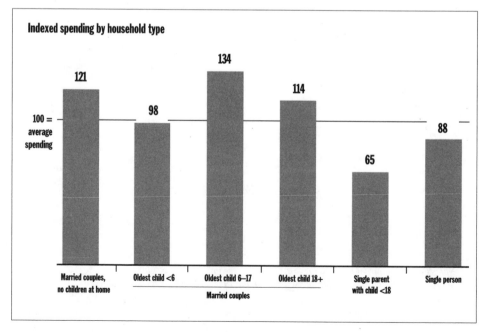

Indexed spending by household type

100 = average spending

Married couples, no children at home	Oldest child <6	Oldest child 6–17	Oldest child 18+	Single parent with child <18	Single person
121	98	134	114	65	88

Married couples

TELEPHONE ANSWERING DEVICES

Total household spending	$349,456,560
Average household spends	3.31

	average spending	best customers (index)	biggest customers (market share)
AGE OF HOUSEHOLDER			
Total households	**$3.31**	**100**	**100.0%**
Under age 25	3.93	119	8.4
Aged 25 to 34	3.44	104	19.6
Aged 35 to 44	3.88	117	27.3
Aged 45 to 54	4.01	121	22.2
Aged 55 to 64	3.95	119	13.9
Aged 65 to 74	1.50	45	5.2
Aged 75 or older	1.19	36	3.3
HOUSEHOLD INCOME			
Total households reporting income	**3.52**	**100**	**100.0**
Under $20,000	1.55	44	15.4
$20,000 to $29,999	2.49	71	10.3
$30,000 to $39,999	3.59	102	12.5
$40,000 to $49,999	5.90	168	15.7
$50,000 to $69,999	4.36	124	17.4
$70,000 or more	6.78	193	28.8
HOUSEHOLD TYPE			
Total households	**3.31**	**100**	**100.0**
Married couples	3.81	115	60.2
Married couples, no children	3.99	121	25.7
Married couples, with children	4.02	121	32.6
Oldest child under 6	3.23	98	5.0
Oldest child 6 to 17	4.42	134	19.4
Oldest child 18 or older	3.77	114	8.2
Single parent with child under 18	2.14	65	4.1
Single person	2.92	88	25.3
REGION			
Total households	**3.31**	**100**	**100.0**
Northeast	5.22	158	31.5
Midwest	2.84	86	20.5
South	2.37	72	25.0
West	3.59	108	23.0

Note: For definitions of best and biggest customers, see introduction or glossary.
Source: Calculations by New Strategist based on the 1997 Consumer Expenditure Survey

Telephones and Accessories

Best customers:
- Householders aged 45 to 64
- Single parents

Customer trends:
- Telephones loaded with features are replacing older models, boosting sales in what would otherwise be a saturated market.

It's hard to imagine that households could accommodate any more phones. Yet Americans can't seem to get enough of them. The biggest spenders on telephones and accessories are householders aged 45 to 54, who spend 39 percent more than average. Those aged 55 to 64 spend 26 percent more. Single parents spend 29 percent more than the average household on this item.

Many households are replacing older, simple phones with portables, speaker phones, caller-ID boxes, and other high-tech telecommunications devices. This trend will continue, boosting sales of telephones and accessories for years to come.

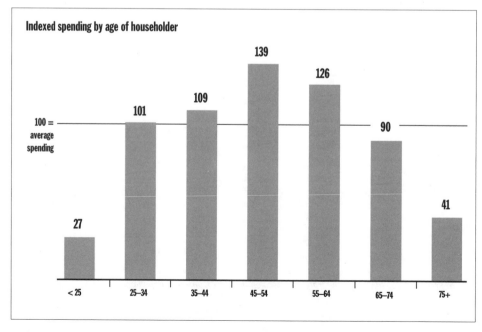

Indexed spending by age of householder

100 = average spending

< 25	25–34	35–44	45–54	55–64	65–74	75+
27	101	109	139	126	90	41

TELEPHONES AND ACCESSORIES

Total household spending $10,192,307,040
Average household spends   96.54

	average spending	best customers (index)	biggest customers (market share)
AGE OF HOUSEHOLDER			
Total households	**$96.54**	**100**	**100.0%**
Under age 25	26.05	27	1.9
Aged 25 to 34	97.32	101	19.0
Aged 35 to 44	105.33	109	25.4
Aged 45 to 54	133.82	139	25.4
Aged 55 to 64	122.09	126	14.8
Aged 65 to 74	86.81	90	10.3
Aged 75 or older	39.45	41	3.8
HOUSEHOLD INCOME			
Total households reporting income	**103.30**	**100**	**100.0**
Under $20,000	76.96	75	25.9
$20,000 to $29,999	74.60	72	10.5
$30,000 to $39,999	112.06	108	13.3
$40,000 to $49,999	61.17	59	5.5
$50,000 to $69,999	140.51	136	19.1
$70,000 or more	173.21	168	25.1
HOUSEHOLD TYPE			
Total households	**96.54**	**100**	**100.0**
Married couples	120.38	125	65.2
Married couples, no children	100.82	104	22.3
Married couples, with children	108.06	112	30.1
Oldest child under 6	93.14	96	5.0
Oldest child 6 to 17	111.49	115	16.8
Oldest child 18 or older	113.59	118	8.5
Single parent with child under 18	124.40	129	8.1
Single person	55.06	57	16.4
REGION			
Total households	**96.54**	**100**	**100.0**
Northeast	76.69	79	15.9
Midwest	87.77	91	21.7
South	109.89	114	39.7
West	103.06	107	22.7

Note: For definitions of best and biggest customers, see introduction or glossary.
Source: Calculations by New Strategist based on the 1997 Consumer Expenditure Survey

Wall Units, Cabinets, Miscellaneous Furniture

Best customers:
- Married couples with children under age 18

Customer trends:
- Spending on wall units and cabinets is likely to grow as boomers try to organize their homes.

For most parents, it's a struggle to figure out what to do with all those toys. The solution for many is to buy wall units and cabinets in which to store them. That's one reason why married couples with preschoolers spend 62 percent more than the average household on wall units and cabinets, while those with school-age children spend 51 percent more. The growing importance of the entertainment center is another reason for spending on this item. Wall units housing TVs, VCRs, and stereos are becoming common in American homes.

With homes becoming ever more crowded with toys, TVs, and other electronics, spending on wall units and cabinets will rise. Also driving this growth will be family heirlooms that require display space, which boomers are likely to inherit during the next decade.

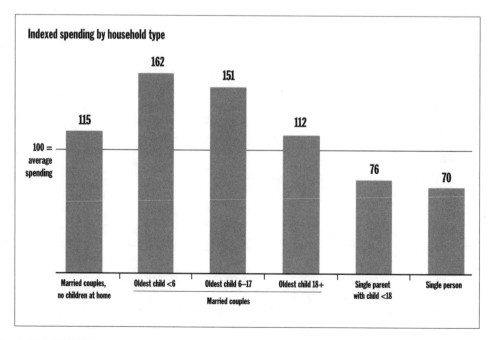

Indexed spending by household type

Married couples, no children at home	Oldest child <6	Oldest child 6–17	Oldest child 18+	Single parent with child <18	Single person
115	162	151	112	76	70

100 = average spending

Married couples

WALL UNITS, CABINETS, MISCELLANEOUS FURNITURE

Total household spending $4,519,708,560
Average household spends   42.81

	average spending	best customers (index)	biggest customers (market share)
AGE OF HOUSEHOLDER			
Total households	**$42.81**	**100**	**100.0%**
Under age 25	17.08	40	2.8
Aged 25 to 34	48.34	113	21.3
Aged 35 to 44	52.23	122	28.4
Aged 45 to 54	55.67	130	23.8
Aged 55 to 64	38.11	89	10.4
Aged 65 to 74	40.75	95	10.9
Aged 75 or older	10.82	25	2.4
HOUSEHOLD INCOME			
Total households reporting income	**42.67**	**100**	**100.0**
Under $20,000	22.49	53	18.4
$20,000 to $29,999	15.53	36	5.3
$30,000 to $39,999	38.26	90	11.0
$40,000 to $49,999	37.90	89	8.3
$50,000 to $69,999	58.64	137	19.3
$70,000 or more	107.84	253	37.8
HOUSEHOLD TYPE			
Total households	**42.81**	**100**	**100.0**
Married couples	56.32	132	68.8
Married couples, no children	49.38	115	24.6
Married couples, with children	61.05	143	38.3
Oldest child under 6	69.27	162	8.3
Oldest child 6 to 17	64.71	151	22.0
Oldest child 18 or older	47.76	112	8.0
Single parent with child under 18	32.68	76	4.8
Single person	29.93	70	20.1
REGION			
Total households	**42.81**	**100**	**100.0**
Northeast	43.61	102	20.3
Midwest	36.93	86	20.6
South	47.07	110	38.4
West	41.67	97	20.7

Note: For definitions of best and biggest customers, see introduction or glossary.
Source: Calculations by New Strategist based on the 1997 Consumer Expenditure Survey

Washing Machines

Best customers: • Married couples with children under age 6

Customer trends: • Little change for now, but spending could increase as the children of boomers start families.

Laundromats are not convenient for parents with young children. Consequently, the best customers of washing machines are married couples with children under age 6. These households spend 55 percent more than average on this item. Householders aged 35 to 44 spend 23 percent more than average on washing machines because many have preschoolers. Householders aged 65 to 74 spend 26 percent more than average on washing machines as they replace worn-out appliances.

Generation X now occupies the age group of family formation. In several years, however, the larger Millennial generation will begin to have children and sales of washing machines should rise accordingly.

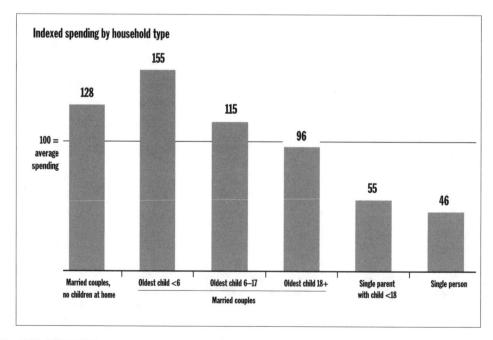

Indexed spending by household type

Married couples, no children at home	Oldest child <6	Oldest child 6–17	Oldest child 18+	Single parent with child <18	Single person
128	155	115	96	55	46

100 = average spending

Married couples

WASHING MACHINES

Total household spending	$2,430,359,520
Average household spends	23.02

	average spending	best customers (index)	biggest customers (market share)
AGE OF HOUSEHOLDER			
Total households	**$23.02**	**100**	**100.0%**
Under age 25	11.37	49	3.5
Aged 25 to 34	21.65	94	17.7
Aged 35 to 44	28.27	123	28.6
Aged 45 to 54	24.52	107	19.5
Aged 55 to 64	25.63	111	13.0
Aged 65 to 74	28.98	126	14.4
Aged 75 or older	8.00	35	3.2
HOUSEHOLD INCOME			
Total households reporting income	**23.03**	**100**	**100.0**
Under $20,000	19.43	84	29.4
$20,000 to $29,999	16.33	71	10.4
$30,000 to $39,999	19.49	85	10.3
$40,000 to $49,999	24.59	107	10.0
$50,000 to $69,999	34.10	148	20.8
$70,000 or more	29.42	128	19.1
HOUSEHOLD TYPE			
Total households	**23.02**	**100**	**100.0**
Married couples	28.70	125	65.2
Married couples, no children	29.51	128	27.4
Married couples, with children	27.00	117	31.5
Oldest child under 6	35.60	155	8.0
Oldest child 6 to 17	26.39	115	16.7
Oldest child 18 or older	22.08	96	6.9
Single parent with child under 18	12.61	55	3.4
Single person	10.67	46	13.3
REGION			
Total households	**23.02**	**100**	**100.0**
Northeast	17.48	76	15.2
Midwest	21.80	95	22.6
South	26.92	117	40.8
West	23.21	101	21.4

Note: For definitions of best and biggest customers, see introduction or glossary.
Source: Calculations by New Strategist based on the 1997 Consumer Expenditure Survey

Chapter 12.

Household Services

Household Services

Spending on household services is dominated by day care needs. Spending on day care centers and babysitters accounts for 42 percent of the $548.50 devoted to this category. While the $160 spent by the average household on day care centers in 1997 seems low, the 6 percent of households who actually purchased this item paid an average of $693 per quarter (see Appendix B), for an estimated annual cost of $2,772—a much more realistic figure.

Spending by the average household on household services increased 4.5 percent between 1987 and 1997, after adjusting for inflation. Spending on personal care services—most of it day care—rose 9.5 percent, while spending on other types of household services barely changed.

Those who spend the most in this category are households with young children. Apart from day care and babysitting, however, the best customers of household services are older Americans—particularly for housekeeping and lawn and garden services. Spending in this category is likely to stablize along with the number of families with young children. But spending on adult day care, house-keeping services, and lawn and garden services should expand with the aging of the population.

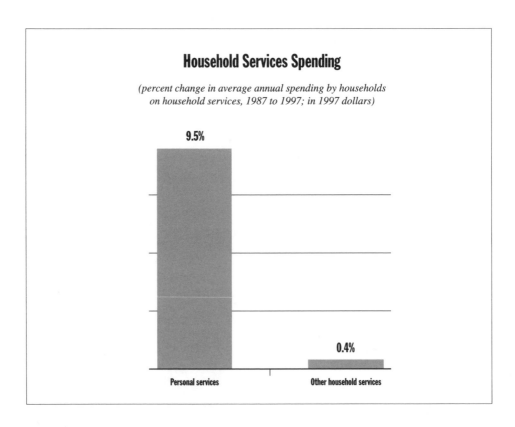

Household Services Spending

(percent change in average annual spending by households on household services, 1987 to 1997; in 1997 dollars)

9.5%

0.4%

Personal services   Other household services

Household Services Spending

(average annual spending of households on household services, and percent distribution of spending by type, 1997)

Total spending on household services	**$548.50**	**100.0%**
Day care centers, nursery schools, preschools	160.60	29.3
Housekeeping services	75.34	13.7
Gardening and lawn care service	72.44	13.2
Babysitting and childcare, other home	37.37	6.8
Babysitting and childcare, own home	34.39	6.3
Day care, adult	30.74	5.6
Laundry and dry cleaning, nonapparel	15.11	2.8
Appliance repair, including service center	13.50	2.5
Reupholstering and furniture repair	10.87	2.0
Water softening service	4.51	0.8

Note: Numbers will not add to total because not all categories are shown, including repair of computer systems for nonbusiness use, and computer information services which are in the Computer chapter.

Appliance Repair, including Service Center

Best customers:
- Householders aged 55 to 64
- Married couples without children
- Married couples with adult children

Customer trends:
- Little change during the next few years as some boomers replace their appliances while others opt for repair.

Because older householders have older appliances, they are the best customers of appliance repair. Householders aged 55 to 64 spend 64 percent more than the average household on appliance repair. Married couples with adult children at home spend 66 percent more than average, while those without children at home spend 63 percent more. Many of them are older householders.

The market for appliance repair is likely to remain stable. While some boomers will replace older appliances, especially as they become empty nesters, others will opt for repair unless convinced of the benefits of replacement—such as greater energy efficiency, more convenience, or new features.

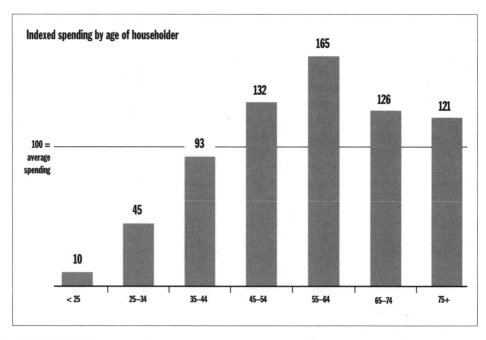

Indexed spending by age of householder

< 25	25–34	35–44	45–54	55–64	65–74	75+
10	45	93	132	165	126	121

100 = average spending

APPLIANCE REPAIR, INCLUDING SERVICE CENTER

Total household spending $1,425,276,000
Average household spends   13.50

	average spending	best customers (index)	biggest customers (market share)
AGE OF HOUSEHOLDER			
Total households	**$13.50**	**100**	**100.0%**
Under age 25	1.40	10	0.7
Aged 25 to 34	6.03	45	8.4
Aged 35 to 44	12.51	93	21.6
Aged 45 to 54	17.87	132	24.3
Aged 55 to 64	22.32	165	19.3
Aged 65 to 74	16.97	126	14.4
Aged 75 or older	16.40	121	11.3
HOUSEHOLD INCOME			
Total households reporting income	**13.77**	**100**	**100.0**
Under $20,000	7.54	55	19.1
$20,000 to $29,999	10.93	79	11.6
$30,000 to $39,999	13.28	96	11.8
$40,000 to $49,999	14.03	102	9.5
$50,000 to $69,999	18.20	132	18.6
$70,000 or more	27.17	197	29.5
HOUSEHOLD TYPE			
Total households	**13.50**	**100**	**100.0**
Married couples	19.06	141	73.8
Married couples, no children	21.95	163	34.7
Married couples, with children	16.47	122	32.8
Oldest child under 6	13.71	102	5.2
Oldest child 6 to 17	14.52	108	15.6
Oldest child 18 or older	22.39	166	11.9
Single parent with child under 18	9.30	69	4.3
Single person	5.99	44	12.7
REGION			
Total households	**13.50**	**100**	**100.0**
Northeast	10.50	78	15.5
Midwest	12.90	96	22.8
South	14.04	104	36.3
West	16.10	119	25.3

Note: For definitions of best and biggest customers, see introduction or glossary.
Source: Calculations by New Strategist based on the 1997 Consumer Expenditure Survey

Babysitting and Childcare, Other Home

Best customers:	• **Married couples with preschoolers**
	• **Single parents**
	• **Householders aged 25 to 34**
Customer trends:	• **Working parents who cannot afford or do not like center-based care will keep spending strong in this category.**

Childcare is one of the largest expenses parents face. The best customers of babysitting and childcare in someone else's home are married couples with preschoolers and single parents. Couples with children under age 6 spend nearly seven times as much as the average household on babysitting and childcare in someone else's home. Single parents spend three times the average on this item. Householders aged 25 to 34 spend more than twice the average on babysitting and childcare in someone else's home because many in the age group have preschoolers.

Finding affordable, high-quality day care is difficult for many parents. Day care centers are relatively expensive, and many parents prefer a home setting. With so many parents in the workforce, the market for babysitting and childcare in someone else's home will continue to be strong.

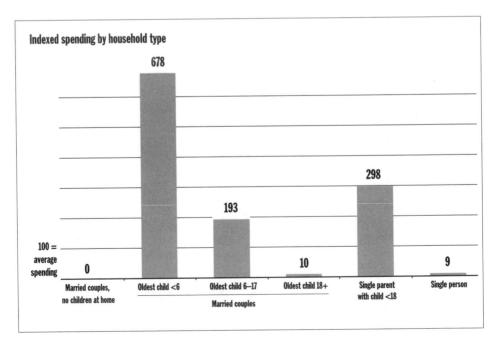

Indexed spending by household type

678 — Oldest child <6 (Married couples)
193 — Oldest child 6–17 (Married couples)
10 — Oldest child 18+ (Married couples)
298 — Single parent with child <18
9 — Single person
0 — Married couples, no children at home

100 = average spending

BABYSITTING AND CHILDCARE, OTHER HOME

Total household spending	$3,945,375,120	
Average household spends	37.37	

	average spending	best customers (index)	biggest customers (market share)
AGE OF HOUSEHOLDER			
Total households	**$37.37**	**100**	**100.0%**
Under age 25	43.32	116	8.2
Aged 25 to 34	95.53	256	48.2
Aged 35 to 44	55.40	148	34.5
Aged 45 to 54	17.45	47	8.6
Aged 55 to 64	0.52	1	0.2
Aged 65 to 74	0.16	0	0.0
Aged 75 or older	1.12	3	0.3
HOUSEHOLD INCOME			
Total households reporting income	**41.43**	**100**	**100.0**
Under $20,000	21.25	51	17.9
$20,000 to $29,999	28.64	69	10.1
$30,000 to $39,999	38.66	93	11.4
$40,000 to $49,999	57.52	139	13.0
$50,000 to $69,999	76.90	186	26.1
$70,000 or more	59.87	145	21.6
HOUSEHOLD TYPE			
Total households	**37.37**	**100**	**100.0**
Married couples	49.28	132	69.0
Married couples, no children	0.13	0	0.1
Married couples, with children	88.60	237	63.7
Oldest child under 6	253.51	678	34.9
Oldest child 6 to 17	72.18	193	28.1
Oldest child 18 or older	3.85	10	0.7
Single parent with child under 18	111.45	298	18.7
Single person	3.55	9	2.7
REGION			
Total households	**37.37**	**100**	**100.0**
Northeast	28.34	76	15.1
Midwest	49.03	131	31.4
South	35.07	94	32.7
West	36.52	98	20.8

Note: For definitions of best and biggest customers, see introduction or glossary.
Source: Calculations by New Strategist based on the 1997 Consumer Expenditure Survey

Babysitting and Childcare, Own Home

Best customers:
- Married couples with preschoolers
- Households with incomes of $70,000 or more
- Households in the West

Customer trends:
- A shrinking market as the number of older, affluent parents declines with the aging of the baby-boom generation.

The best customers of babysitting and childcare services in their own home are affluent married couples aged 35 to 44. Households with incomes of $70,000 or more spend nearly four times as much as the average household on babysitting and childcare in their home. Married couples with preschoolers spend more than eight times the average amount on this item, while householders aged 35 to 44 spend more than twice the average. Households in the West spend twice as much as average on in-home childcare because of the availability of the many Hispanic immigrants in the region, who make up a large share of in-home childcare workers.

The market for in-home child care is likely to shrink as boomers age out of their childbearing years and are replaced by the less numerous Generation X.

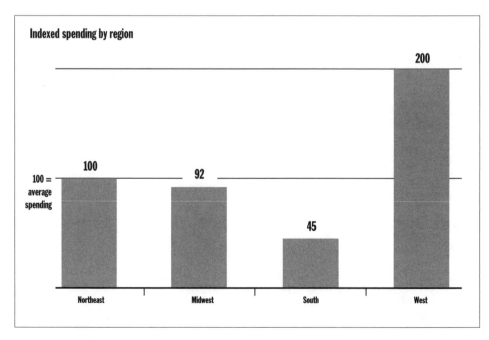

Indexed spending by region

100 = average spending

Northeast	Midwest	South	West
100	92	45	200

BABYSITTING AND CHILDCARE, OWN HOME

Total household spending $3,630,758,640
Average household spends   34.39

	average spending	best customers (index)	biggest customers (market share)
AGE OF HOUSEHOLDER			
Total households	**$34.39**	**100**	**100.0%**
Under age 25	18.31	53	3.8
Aged 25 to 34	60.49	176	33.2
Aged 35 to 44	79.36	231	53.7
Aged 45 to 54	15.01	44	8.0
Aged 55 to 64	2.83	8	1.0
Aged 65 to 74	1.21	4	0.4
Aged 75 or older	0.02	0	0.0
HOUSEHOLD INCOME			
Total households reporting income	**35.51**	**100**	**100.0**
Under $20,000	7.60	21	7.5
$20,000 to $29,999	20.51	58	8.4
$30,000 to $39,999	15.82	45	5.4
$40,000 to $49,999	24.80	70	6.5
$50,000 to $69,999	46.45	131	18.4
$70,000 or more	127.72	360	53.8
HOUSEHOLD TYPE			
Total households	**34.39**	**100**	**100.0**
Married couples	54.01	157	82.1
Married couples, no children	0.02	0	0.0
Married couples, with children	94.97	276	74.2
Oldest child under 6	294.58	857	44.1
Oldest child 6 to 17	70.93	206	30.0
Oldest child 18 or older	0.80	2	0.2
Single parent with child under 18	63.66	185	11.6
Single person	0.21	1	0.2
REGION			
Total households	**34.39**	**100**	**100.0**
Northeast	34.27	100	19.9
Midwest	31.71	92	22.0
South	15.33	45	15.6
West	68.84	200	42.5

Note: For definitions of best and biggest customers, see introduction or glossary.
Source: Calculations by New Strategist based on the 1997 Consumer Expenditure Survey

Day Care Centers, Nursery Schools, Preschools

Best customers:
- Householders aged 25 to 44
- Households with incomes of $70,000 or more
- Married couples with children under age 18
- Single parents

Customer trends:
- Continued growth is likely as more parents of young children enter the workforce.

With most parents now in the workforce, day care centers, nursery schools, and preschools are big business. The best customers of these centers, married couples with preschoolers, spend nearly eight times as much as the average household. Married couples with school-aged children and single parents spend twice as much as average. Spending by householders aged 25 to 44 is well above average because most have preschoolers at home. Households with incomes of $70,000 or more spend nearly three times as much as the average household on this item.

The number of preschoolers is projected to decline slightly in the near future. But the proportion of parents who work continues to rise, offsetting the decline in the number of young children.

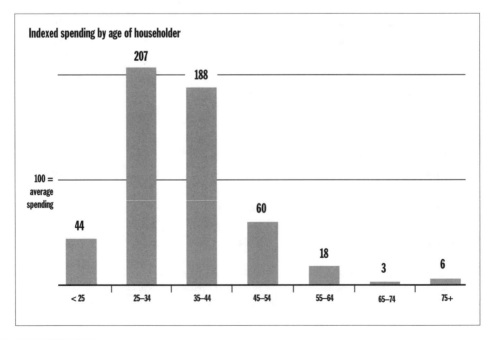

Indexed spending by age of householder

100 = average spending

< 25	25–34	35–44	45–54	55–64	65–74	75+
44	207	188	60	18	3	6

DAY CARE CENTERS, NURSERY SCHOOLS, PRESCHOOLS

Total household spending $16,955,505,600
Average household spends   160.60

	average spending	best customers (index)	biggest customers (market share)
AGE OF HOUSEHOLDER			
Total households	**$160.60**	**100**	**100.0%**
Under age 25	69.98	44	3.1
Aged 25 to 34	332.23	207	39.0
Aged 35 to 44	302.58	188	43.8
Aged 45 to 54	96.36	60	11.0
Aged 55 to 64	29.26	18	2.1
Aged 65 to 74	5.08	3	0.4
Aged 75 or older	9.69	6	0.6
HOUSEHOLD INCOME			
Total households reporting income	**169.14**	**100**	**100.0**
Under $20,000	43.23	26	8.9
$20,000 to $29,999	90.20	53	7.8
$30,000 to $39,999	100.42	59	7.3
$40,000 to $49,999	177.46	105	9.8
$50,000 to $69,999	300.14	177	24.9
$70,000 or more	467.64	276	41.3
HOUSEHOLD TYPE			
Total households	**160.60**	**100**	**100.0**
Married couples	239.64	149	78.0
Married couples, no children	5.38	3	0.7
Married couples, with children	430.39	268	72.0
Oldest child under 6	1,255.56	782	40.2
Oldest child 6 to 17	341.36	213	30.9
Oldest child 18 or older	20.20	13	0.9
Single parent with child under 18	317.79	198	12.4
Single person	9.34	6	1.7
REGION			
Total households	**160.60**	**100**	**100.0**
Northeast	133.93	83	16.7
Midwest	151.35	94	22.5
South	164.30	102	35.7
West	189.98	118	25.1

Note: For definitions of best and biggest customers, see introduction or glossary.
Source: Calculations by New Strategist based on the 1997 Consumer Expenditure Survey

Day Care, Adult

Best customers:
- Householders aged 65 or older
- Households with incomes under $20,000

Customer trends:
- Rapid growth as the nation ages and middle-aged working women seek relief from caretaking tasks.

Older Americans want to maintain their independence as long as possible. But for many, a time comes when they need some assistance, and their caretakers (usually adult daughters) need relief. Adult day care provides help at a much lower cost than a nursing home or retirement community. Householders aged 75 or older spend four and one-half times as much as the average household on adult day care. Those aged 65 to 74 spend more than twice the average on this item. Households with incomes below $20,000 spend 45 percent more than average on adult day care because older people are overrepresented in this segment.

The elderly population is growing rapidly. At the same time, more middle-aged women—who traditionally care for older family members—are in the labor force. Spending on adult day care is likely to grow rapidly for years to come.

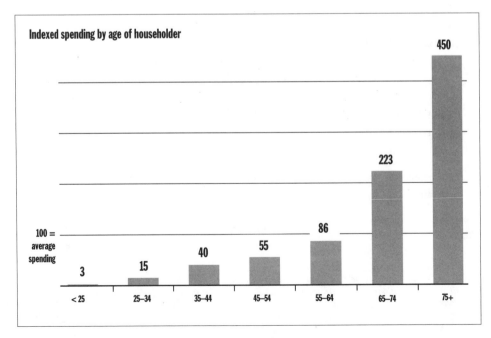

Indexed spending by age of householder

| <25 | 25–34 | 35–44 | 45–54 | 55–64 | 65–74 | 75+ |
| 3 | 15 | 40 | 55 | 86 | 223 | 450 |

100 = average spending

DAY CARE, ADULT

Total household spending	$3,245,406,240		
Average household spends	30.74		

	average spending	best customers (index)	biggest customers (market share)
AGE OF HOUSEHOLDER			
Total households	**$30.74**	**100**	**100.0%**
Under age 25	0.85	3	0.2
Aged 25 to 34	4.57	15	2.8
Aged 35 to 44	12.44	40	9.4
Aged 45 to 54	17.00	55	10.1
Aged 55 to 64	26.32	86	10.0
Aged 65 to 74	68.52	223	25.6
Aged 75 or older	138.35	450	41.9
HOUSEHOLD INCOME			
Total households reporting income	**26.84**	**100**	**100.0**
Under $20,000	39.01	145	50.6
$20,000 to $29,999	34.29	128	18.7
$30,000 to $39,999	24.60	92	11.2
$40,000 to $49,999	11.43	43	4.0
$50,000 to $69,999	9.96	37	5.2
$70,000 or more	18.57	69	10.3
HOUSEHOLD TYPE			
Total households	**30.74**	**100**	**100.0**
Married couples	25.20	82	42.9
Married couples, no children	33.75	110	23.4
Married couples, with children	5.74	19	5.0
Oldest child under 6	10.99	36	1.8
Oldest child 6 to 17	5.45	18	2.6
Oldest child 18 or older	2.55	8	0.6
Single parent with child under 18	0.61	2	0.1
Single person	43.84	143	41.0
REGION			
Total households	**30.74**	**100**	**100.0**
Northeast	22.13	72	14.4
Midwest	15.65	51	12.2
South	33.81	110	38.4
West	50.76	165	35.1

Note: For definitions of best and biggest customers, see introduction or glossary.
Source: Calculations by New Strategist based on the 1997 Consumer Expenditure Survey

Gardening and Lawn Care Service

Best customers:
- Householders aged 45 or older
- Households with incomes of $70,000 or more
- Households in the West

Customer trends:
- Affluent boomers and an aging population mean growing demand for gardening and lawn care services.

Households pay for gardening and lawn care service either because they need to or because they can afford to. Households with incomes of $70,000 or more spend three times as much as the average household on these services. Many older householders can no longer care for their yards, which explains why they spend much more than average on lawn and garden services. Households in the West spend 46 percent more than average because recent immigrants in the region provide a large pool of inexpensive labor.

Demographic trends point to growing demand for gardening and lawn care services. Not only is the population aging, but many boomers in their peak-earning years will be willing to trade a portion of their paychecks for more free time.

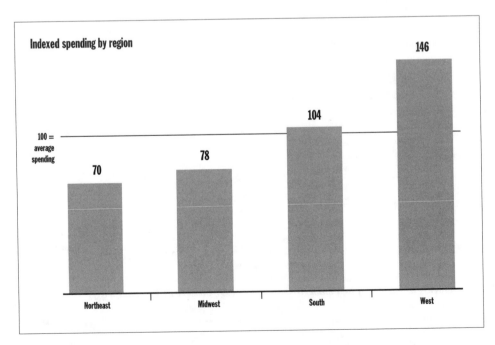

Indexed spending by region

100 = average spending

Northeast	Midwest	South	West
70	78	104	146

GARDENING AND LAWN CARE SERVICE

Total household spending	$7,647,925,440	
Average household spends	72.44	

	average spending	best customers (index)	biggest customers (market share)
AGE OF HOUSEHOLDER			
Total households	**$72.44**	**100**	**100.0%**
Under age 25	3.35	5	0.3
Aged 25 to 34	20.97	29	5.5
Aged 35 to 44	50.56	70	16.2
Aged 45 to 54	111.63	154	28.2
Aged 55 to 64	90.44	125	14.6
Aged 65 to 74	99.57	137	15.8
Aged 75 or older	151.07	209	19.4
HOUSEHOLD INCOME			
Total households reporting income	**73.37**	**100**	**100.0**
Under $20,000	42.78	58	20.3
$20,000 to $29,999	48.90	67	9.7
$30,000 to $39,999	36.27	49	6.0
$40,000 to $49,999	64.18	87	8.2
$50,000 to $69,999	68.15	93	13.0
$70,000 or more	209.56	286	42.7
HOUSEHOLD TYPE			
Total households	**72.44**	**100**	**100.0**
Married couples	86.13	119	62.2
Married couples, no children	112.49	155	33.1
Married couples, with children	67.79	94	25.2
Oldest child under 6	47.10	65	3.3
Oldest child 6 to 17	69.56	96	14.0
Oldest child 18 or older	79.00	109	7.8
Single parent with child under 18	36.61	51	3.2
Single person	62.31	86	24.7
REGION			
Total households	**72.44**	**100**	**100.0**
Northeast	50.73	70	14.0
Midwest	56.67	78	18.7
South	75.38	104	36.3
West	105.79	146	31.0

Note: For definitions of best and biggest customers, see introduction or glossary.
Source: Calculations by New Strategist based on the 1997 Consumer Expenditure Survey

Housekeeping Services

Best customers:
- Householders aged 45 to 54
- Householders aged 75 or older
- Households with incomes of $70,000 or more

Customer trends:
- Stable market despite growing affluence because of higher comfort levels with messy homes.

Households with incomes of $70,000 or more spend four times as much as the average household on housekeeping services. Many of them are dual-income couples who have neither the time nor the inclination to clean house after a long day at the office. Householders aged 45 to 54, most of whom are married couples in their peak-earning years, spend 64 percent more than average on housekeeping services. Householders aged 75 or older spend 71 percent more than average on this item as they try to maintain their independence.

The busy American lifestyle has benefited the housekeeping service market, but not as much as one might imagine. Working families have learned to live with a little dirt and mess. While the affluent will continue to buy housekeeping services, the market isn't likely to grow much unless housekeeping standards rise.

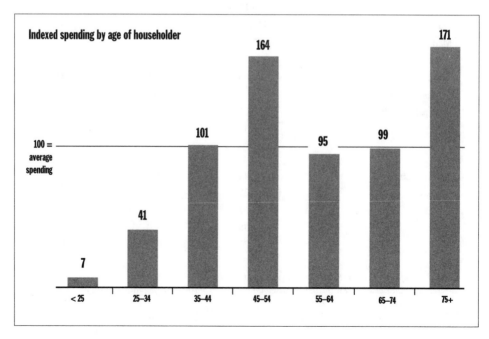

Indexed spending by age of householder

<25	25–34	35–44	45–54	55–64	65–74	75+
7	41	101	164	95	99	171

100 = average spending

HOUSEKEEPING SERVICES

Total household spending	$7,954,095,840		
Average household spends	75.34		

	average spending	best customers (index)	biggest customers (market share)
AGE OF HOUSEHOLDER			
Total households	**$75.34**	**100**	**100.0%**
Under age 25	5.31	7	0.5
Aged 25 to 34	30.70	41	7.7
Aged 35 to 44	76.38	101	23.6
Aged 45 to 54	123.30	164	30.0
Aged 55 to 64	71.29	95	11.0
Aged 65 to 74	74.29	99	11.3
Aged 75 or older	128.59	171	15.9
HOUSEHOLD INCOME			
Total households reporting income	**76.51**	**100**	**100.0**
Under $20,000	31.53	41	14.4
$20,000 to $29,999	33.84	44	6.5
$30,000 to $39,999	30.09	39	4.8
$40,000 to $49,999	37.47	49	4.6
$50,000 to $69,999	58.94	77	10.8
$70,000 or more	301.90	395	59.0
HOUSEHOLD TYPE			
Total households	**75.34**	**100**	**100.0**
Married couples	99.57	132	69.1
Married couples, no children	105.42	140	29.9
Married couples, with children	102.70	136	36.6
Oldest child under 6	110.56	147	7.5
Oldest child 6 to 17	113.87	151	22.0
Oldest child 18 or older	74.47	99	7.1
Single parent with child under 18	44.24	59	3.7
Single person	50.44	67	19.2
REGION			
Total households	**75.34**	**100**	**100.0**
Northeast	72.92	97	19.3
Midwest	45.33	60	14.4
South	72.89	97	33.8
West	115.40	153	32.5

Note: For definitions of best and biggest customers, see introduction or glossary.
Source: Calculations by New Strategist based on the 1997 Consumer Expenditure Survey

Laundry and Dry Cleaning, Nonapparel

Best customers:
- Householders aged 25 to 54
- Married couples with children under age 18
- Single parents

Customer trends:
- Spending is likely to rise as the number of households with teenagers grows.

Households with children are the best customers of nonapparel laundry and dry cleaning. Both married couples and single parents with children under age 18 at home spend much more than average on this item. Behind their higher spending is the mess their children make. Householders aged 45 to 54 also spend more than average on nonapparel laundry and dry cleaning. Now that their children are growing up, these householders are cleaning up after them.

The number of households with teenagers will peak in a few years, boosting spending on nonapparel laundry and dry cleaning.

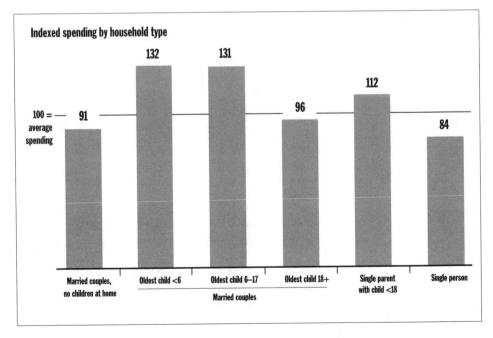

Indexed spending by household type

Married couples, no children at home	91	
Oldest child <6	132	
Oldest child 6–17	131	
Oldest child 18+	96	
Single parent with child <18	112	
Single person	84	

100 = average spending

LAUNDRY AND DRY CLEANING, NONAPPAREL

Total household spending	$1,595,253,360
Average household spends	15.11

	average spending	best customers (index)	biggest customers (market share)
AGE OF HOUSEHOLDER			
Total households	**$15.11**	**100**	**100.0%**
Under age 25	11.79	78	5.5
Aged 25 to 34	18.49	122	23.1
Aged 35 to 44	16.63	110	25.6
Aged 45 to 54	20.96	139	25.4
Aged 55 to 64	13.48	89	10.4
Aged 65 to 74	8.31	55	6.3
Aged 75 or older	6.66	44	4.1
HOUSEHOLD INCOME			
Total households reporting income	**15.08**	**100**	**100.0**
Under $20,000	8.43	56	19.5
$20,000 to $29,999	12.40	82	12.0
$30,000 to $39,999	15.33	102	12.4
$40,000 to $49,999	6.91	46	4.3
$50,000 to $69,999	21.84	145	20.3
$70,000 or more	31.53	209	31.3
HOUSEHOLD TYPE			
Total households	**15.11**	**100**	**100.0**
Married couples	16.45	109	56.9
Married couples, no children	13.70	91	19.3
Married couples, with children	18.43	122	32.8
Oldest child under 6	19.96	132	6.8
Oldest child 6 to 17	19.78	131	19.0
Oldest child 18 or older	14.51	96	6.9
Single parent with child under 18	16.99	112	7.1
Single person	12.67	84	24.1
REGION			
Total households	**15.11**	**100**	**100.0**
Northeast	22.04	146	29.1
Midwest	13.13	87	20.8
South	12.18	81	28.1
West	15.62	103	22.0

Note: For definitions of best and biggest customers, see introduction or glossary.
Source: Calculations by New Strategist based on the 1997 Consumer Expenditure Survey

Reupholstering and Furniture Repair

Best customers:	• Householders aged 55 to 74
	• Households with incomes of $70,000 or more
	• Married couples without children
Customer trends:	• Declining market as boomers and younger generations replace rather than repair.

Older Americans are more likely to repair appliances and furniture than younger generations are. This is why householders aged 65 to 74 spend 90 percent more than the average household on reupholstering and furniture repair. Those aged 55 to 64 spend 67 percent more. Households with incomes of $70,000 or more spend nearly three times as much as the average household on furniture repair and reupholstery. Married couples without children at home, most of whom are older couples, spend 74 percent more than average on this item.

Younger generations are more inclined than their elders to replace rather than repair furniture. This suggests less spending on this category in the future.

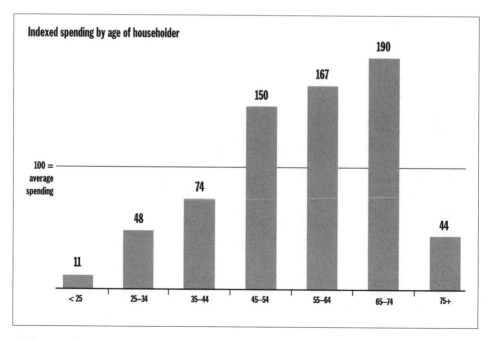

Indexed spending by age of householder

100 = average spending

< 25	25–34	35–44	45–54	55–64	65–74	75+
11	48	74	150	167	190	44

REUPHOLSTERING AND FURNITURE REPAIR

Total household spending	$1,147,611,120
Average household spends	10.87

	average spending	best customers (index)	biggest customers (market share)
AGE OF HOUSEHOLDER			
Total households	**$10.87**	**100**	**100.0%**
Under age 25	1.19	11	0.8
Aged 25 to 34	5.27	48	9.1
Aged 35 to 44	8.03	74	17.2
Aged 45 to 54	16.31	150	27.5
Aged 55 to 64	18.14	167	19.5
Aged 65 to 74	20.69	190	21.8
Aged 75 or older	4.75	44	4.1
HOUSEHOLD INCOME			
Total households reporting income	**11.78**	**100**	**100.0**
Under $20,000	7.02	60	20.8
$20,000 to $29,999	3.62	31	4.5
$30,000 to $39,999	8.35	71	8.7
$40,000 to $49,999	11.10	94	8.8
$50,000 to $69,999	13.46	114	16.0
$70,000 or more	32.48	276	41.2
HOUSEHOLD TYPE			
Total households	**10.87**	**100**	**100.0**
Married couples	14.42	133	69.4
Married couples, no children	18.87	174	37.0
Married couples, with children	12.50	115	30.9
Oldest child under 6	8.91	82	4.2
Oldest child 6 to 17	12.55	115	16.8
Oldest child 18 or older	14.95	138	9.9
Single parent with child under 18	6.99	64	4.0
Single person	5.72	53	15.1
REGION			
Total households	**10.87**	**100**	**100.0**
Northeast	10.86	100	20.0
Midwest	9.42	87	20.7
South	10.42	96	33.4
West	13.24	122	25.9

Note: For definitions of best and biggest customers, see introduction or glossary.
Source: Calculations by New Strategist based on the 1997 Consumer Expenditure Survey

Water Softening Service

Best customers:
- Married couples
- Households in the Midwest

Customer trends:
- Businesses offering water softening service could boost spending by addressing water purity concerns.

The need for water softening services is highly dependent on geography. Households in the Midwest spend 63 percent more than average on this item because water in the region is more likely to be hard. Households in the West also spend more than average on water softening services. Married couples spend more than single parents or single persons on this item because they can better afford it, as can households with incomes of $70,000 or more.

Demand for water softening services will remain stable in areas with hard water, which can cause plumbing problems. Businesses offering these services could boost spending by addressing Americans' growing concern with water purity.

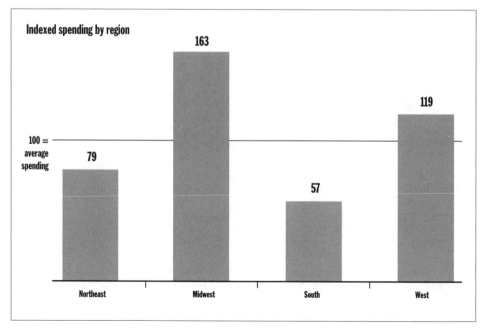

Indexed spending by region

100 = average spending

Northeast	Midwest	South	West
79	163	57	119

WATER SOFTENING SERVICE

Total household spending	$476,147,760
Average household spends	4.51

	average spending	best customers (index)	biggest customers (market share)
AGE OF HOUSEHOLDER			
Total households	**$4.51**	**100**	**100.0%**
Under age 25	0.98	22	1.5
Aged 25 to 34	4.30	95	18.0
Aged 35 to 44	4.67	104	24.1
Aged 45 to 54	4.85	108	19.7
Aged 55 to 64	4.42	98	11.4
Aged 65 to 74	6.29	139	16.0
Aged 75 or older	4.53	100	9.3
HOUSEHOLD INCOME			
Total households reporting income	**5.11**	**100**	**100.0**
Under $20,000	3.06	60	20.9
$20,000 to $29,999	4.25	83	12.1
$30,000 to $39,999	2.80	55	6.7
$40,000 to $49,999	4.62	90	8.5
$50,000 to $69,999	5.45	107	15.0
$70,000 or more	12.59	246	36.8
HOUSEHOLD TYPE			
Total households	**4.51**	**100**	**100.0**
Married couples	7.03	156	81.5
Married couples, no children	7.52	167	35.6
Married couples, with children	6.42	142	38.3
Oldest child under 6	7.20	160	8.2
Oldest child 6 to 17	5.08	113	16.4
Oldest child 18 or older	8.57	190	13.7
Single parent with child under 18	1.43	32	2.0
Single person	1.38	31	8.8
REGION			
Total households	**4.51**	**100**	**100.0**
Northeast	3.56	79	15.8
Midwest	7.37	163	39.0
South	2.57	57	19.9
West	5.38	119	25.3

Note: For definitions of best and biggest customers, see introduction or glossary.
Source: Calculations by New Strategist based on the 1997 Consumer Expenditure Survey

Chapter 13.

Housekeeping Supplies

Housekeeping Supplies

The average household spent $454.93 on housekeeping supplies in 1997, a category that includes disposable household products such as laundry and cleaning supplies, toilet tissue, paper towels, garden seeds, lawn fertilizer, postage, and stationery. Spending in this category fell 6 percent between 1987 and 1997, after adjusting for inflation. The biggest decline was for laundry and cleaning supplies, down 15 percent. Postage and stationery spending fell 13 percent as younger householders shifted away from letter writing towards e-mail.

With two-earner couples now the norm, Americans have less time to attend to housekeeping chores such as cleaning. Consequently, they are spending less on these products. As younger generations age, spending on many of these products will continue to decline.

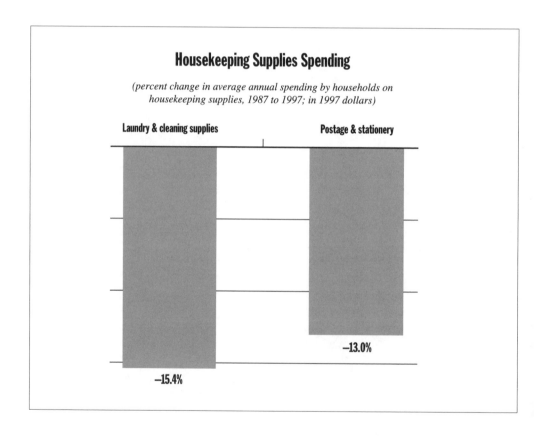

Housekeeping Supplies Spending

(percent change in average annual spending by households on housekeeping supplies, 1987 to 1997; in 1997 dollars)

Laundry & cleaning supplies — −15.4%

Postage & stationery — −13.0%

Housekeeping Supplies Spending

(average annual spending of households on housekeeping supplies, and percent distribution of spending by type, 1997)

Total spending on housekeeping supplies	**$454.93**	**100.0%**
Laundry and cleaning supplies	115.85	25.5
Cleansing and toilet tissues, paper towels, and napkins	64.42	14.2
Stationery, stationery supplies, giftwrap	62.61	13.8
Postage	62.53	13.7
Lawn and garden supplies	55.74	12.3

Note: Numbers will not add to total because not all categories are shown.

Cleansing and Toilet Tissues, Paper Towels, and Napkins

Best customers: • Married couples with school-aged or older children

Customer trends: • Average household spending on these items is unlikely to grow.

Every household needs paper products, but those with children use more than average. Married couples with school-aged children spend 43 percent more than the average household on cleansing and toilet tissues, paper towels, and napkins. Those with children aged 18 or older at home spend 45 percent more on these items.

Americans like the convenience of disposable paper towels and napkins, and every household needs toilet tissue. Spending on these products will rise as the number of households increases. The average household, however, is not likely to spend more on these items.

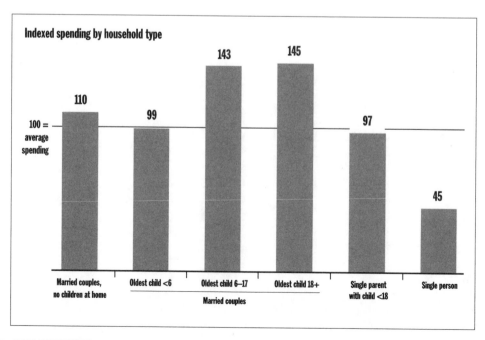

Indexed spending by household type

110	99	143	145	97	45

100 = average spending

| Married couples, no children at home | Oldest child <6 | Oldest child 6–17 | Oldest child 18+ | Single parent with child <18 | Single person |

Married couples

CLEANSING AND TOILET TISSUES, PAPER TOWELS, AND NAPKINS

Total household spending $6,801,205,920
Average household spends   64.42

	average spending	best customers (index)	biggest customers (market share)
AGE OF HOUSEHOLDER			
Total households	**$64.42**	**100**	**100.0%**
Under age 25	22.71	35	2.5
Aged 25 to 34	55.86	87	16.4
Aged 35 to 44	76.90	119	27.8
Aged 45 to 54	74.20	115	21.1
Aged 55 to 64	75.06	117	13.6
Aged 65 to 74	67.92	105	12.1
Aged 75 or older	49.29	77	7.1
HOUSEHOLD INCOME			
Total households reporting income	**69.32**	**100**	**100.0**
Under $20,000	51.73	75	26.0
$20,000 to $29,999	65.52	95	13.8
$30,000 to $39,999	67.42	97	11.9
$40,000 to $49,999	62.14	90	8.4
$50,000 to $69,999	78.99	114	16.0
$70,000 or more	108.73	157	23.4
HOUSEHOLD TYPE			
Total households	**64.42**	**100**	**100.0**
Married couples	82.22	128	66.7
Married couples, no children	70.96	110	23.5
Married couples, with children	86.33	134	36.0
Oldest child under 6	63.91	99	5.1
Oldest child 6 to 17	92.13	143	20.8
Oldest child 18 or older	93.36	145	10.4
Single parent with child under 18	62.39	97	6.1
Single person	29.29	45	13.1
REGION			
Total households	**64.42**	**100**	**100.0**
Northeast	66.65	103	20.7
Midwest	61.40	95	22.8
South	60.86	94	33.0
West	71.34	111	23.5

Note: For definitions of best and biggest customers, see introduction or glossary.
Source: Calculations by New Strategist based on the 1997 Consumer Expenditure Survey

Laundry and Cleaning Supplies

Best customers:
- Householders aged 35 to 54
- Married couples with school-aged or older children

Customer trends:
- As boomers enter the empty-nest years, spending in this category could decline. New products that clean better or more conveniently could boost sales, however.

The American household is getting dirtier. Younger families, in particular, have less time to clean because both husband and wife are in the labor force. But that doesn't mean they don't buy laundry and cleaning supplies. Married couples with school-aged children spend 54 percent more than the average household on this item, and those with adult children at home spend 43 percent more. Householders aged 35 to 54, most of whom have children, spend 18 to 20 percent more than average.

As baby boomers become empty nesters and no longer have to clean up after children, spending in this category is likely to decline. Manufacturers could boost spending, however, by offering solutions to the housecleaning problems of dual-income couples.

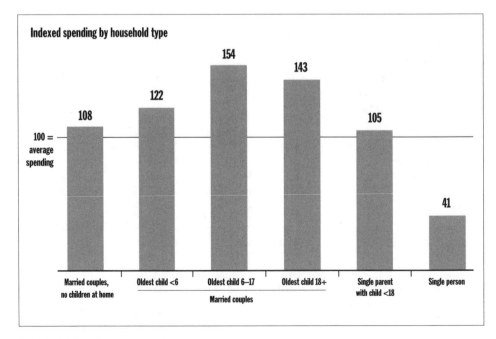

Indexed spending by household type

Married couples, no children at home	Oldest child <6	Oldest child 6–17	Oldest child 18+	Single parent with child <18	Single person
108	122	154	143	105	41

100 = average spending

Married couples

LAUNDRY AND CLEANING SUPPLIES

Total household spending $12,230,979,600
Average household spends   115.85

	average spending	best customers (index)	biggest customers (market share)
AGE OF HOUSEHOLDER			
Total households	**$115.85**	**100**	**100.0%**
Under age 25	55.58	48	3.4
Aged 25 to 34	112.35	97	18.3
Aged 35 to 44	138.58	120	27.8
Aged 45 to 54	136.88	118	21.6
Aged 55 to 64	129.90	112	13.1
Aged 65 to 74	104.57	90	10.4
Aged 75 or older	72.98	63	5.9
HOUSEHOLD INCOME			
Total households reporting income	**124.91**	**100**	**100.0**
Under $20,000	84.80	68	23.6
$20,000 to $29,999	109.05	87	12.8
$30,000 to $39,999	128.07	103	12.5
$40,000 to $49,999	145.20	116	10.9
$50,000 to $69,999	161.71	129	18.2
$70,000 or more	179.07	143	21.4
HOUSEHOLD TYPE			
Total households	**115.85**	**100**	**100.0**
Married couples	151.45	131	68.4
Married couples, no children	125.21	108	23.1
Married couples, with children	167.22	144	38.8
Oldest child under 6	141.88	122	6.3
Oldest child 6 to 17	178.31	154	22.4
Oldest child 18 or older	166.06	143	10.3
Single parent with child under 18	121.33	105	6.6
Single person	47.91	41	11.9
REGION			
Total households	**115.85**	**100**	**100.0**
Northeast	111.49	96	19.2
Midwest	112.11	97	23.1
South	116.89	101	35.2
West	122.26	106	22.4

Note: For definitions of best and biggest customers, see introduction or glossary.
Source: Calculations by New Strategist based on the 1997 Consumer Expenditure Survey

Lawn and Garden Supplies

Best customers:
- Householders aged 45 to 74
- Married couples without children
- Married couples with adult children

Customer trends:
- Expanding market thanks to the rising number of older adults.

Empty nesters and the recently retired have time to putter around in the garden. Consequently, people aged 45 to 74 spend more than the average household on lawn and garden supplies—up to 49 percent more. Married couples without children at home spend 84 percent more than average on this item, while those with adult children at home spend 62 percent more. Both types of households are likely to be headed by older people.

Baby boomers have already shown a strong interest in gardening. As their children grow up and they gain more free time, spending on lawn and garden supplies will rise.

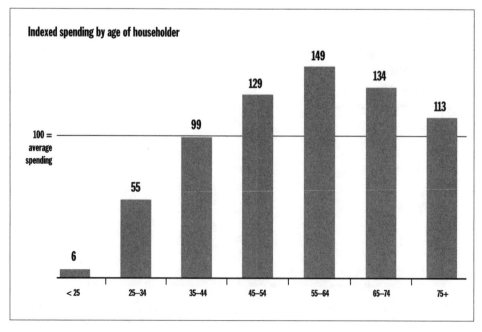

Indexed spending by age of householder

100 = average spending

| < 25 | 25–34 | 35–44 | 45–54 | 55–64 | 65–74 | 75+ |
| 6 | 55 | 99 | 129 | 149 | 134 | 113 |

LAWN AND GARDEN SUPPLIES

Total household spending	$5,884,806,240
Average household spends	55.74

	average spending	best customers (index)	biggest customers (market share)
AGE OF HOUSEHOLDER			
Total households	**$55.74**	**100**	**100.0%**
Under age 25	3.23	6	0.4
Aged 25 to 34	30.51	55	10.3
Aged 35 to 44	54.98	99	22.9
Aged 45 to 54	71.77	129	23.6
Aged 55 to 64	82.83	149	17.3
Aged 65 to 74	74.68	134	15.4
Aged 75 or older	62.91	113	10.5
HOUSEHOLD INCOME			
Total households reporting income	**59.02**	**100**	**100.0**
Under $20,000	31.60	54	18.6
$20,000 to $29,999	28.87	49	7.1
$30,000 to $39,999	51.26	87	10.6
$40,000 to $49,999	61.44	104	9.7
$50,000 to $69,999	115.02	195	27.4
$70,000 or more	105.07	178	26.6
HOUSEHOLD TYPE			
Total households	**55.74**	**100**	**100.0**
Married couples	79.38	142	74.5
Married couples, no children	102.54	184	39.3
Married couples, with children	68.04	122	32.8
Oldest child under 6	63.31	114	5.8
Oldest child 6 to 17	59.04	106	15.4
Oldest child 18 or older	90.07	162	11.6
Single parent with child under 18	23.30	42	2.6
Single person	29.15	52	15.0
REGION			
Total households	**55.74**	**100**	**100.0**
Northeast	47.50	85	17.0
Midwest	69.11	124	29.6
South	49.38	89	30.9
West	58.76	105	22.4

Note: For definitions of best and biggest customers, see introduction or glossary.
Source: Calculations by New Strategist based on the 1997 Consumer Expenditure Survey

Postage

Best customers:
- Householders aged 45 to 74
- Married couples without children
- Married couples with adult children

Customer trends:
- Continuing decline as more households use e-mail.

Older Americans still send cards and letters to friends and family via the postal service, but younger people prefer to zap e-mails and electronic greeting cards through the Internet. Householders aged 65 to 74 spend 36 percent more than average on postage. Those aged 45 to 64 spend nearly 30 percent more than average. Married couples without children at home spend 38 percent more than the average household on postage, while those with adult children at home spend 36 percent more. Behind their higher spending is the fact that many are older householders.

Spending on postage will continue to decline as more households get e-mail accounts. Technology allowing people to send photographs electronically also will reduce postage spending.

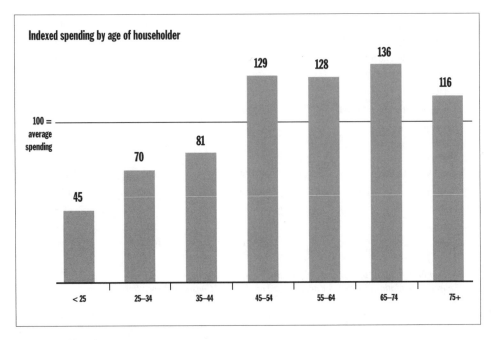

Indexed spending by age of householder

100 = average spending

< 25	25–34	35–44	45–54	55–64	65–74	75+
45	70	81	129	128	136	116

POSTAGE

Total household spending $6,601,667,280
Average household spends   62.53

	average spending	best customers (index)	biggest customers (market share)
AGE OF HOUSEHOLDER			
Total households	**$62.53**	**100**	**100.0%**
Under age 25	27.97	45	3.2
Aged 25 to 34	43.91	70	13.2
Aged 35 to 44	50.79	81	18.9
Aged 45 to 54	80.45	129	23.6
Aged 55 to 64	79.94	128	14.9
Aged 65 to 74	85.01	136	15.6
Aged 75 or older	72.73	116	10.8
HOUSEHOLD INCOME			
Total households reporting income	**66.50**	**100**	**100.0**
Under $20,000	39.28	59	20.6
$20,000 to $29,999	76.13	114	16.7
$30,000 to $39,999	65.89	99	12.1
$40,000 to $49,999	67.12	101	9.4
$50,000 to $69,999	80.40	121	17.0
$70,000 or more	104.39	157	23.5
HOUSEHOLD TYPE			
Total households	**62.53**	**100**	**100.0**
Married couples	75.91	121	63.5
Married couples, no children	86.40	138	29.5
Married couples, with children	66.90	107	28.8
Oldest child under 6	71.96	115	5.9
Oldest child 6 to 17	55.84	89	13.0
Oldest child 18 or older	84.92	136	9.8
Single parent with child under 18	32.03	51	3.2
Single person	39.72	64	18.2
REGION			
Total households	**62.53**	**100**	**100.0**
Northeast	62.72	100	20.0
Midwest	63.25	101	24.2
South	53.63	86	29.9
West	75.65	121	25.7

Note: For definitions of best and biggest customers, see introduction or glossary.
Source: Calculations by New Strategist based on the 1997 Consumer Expenditure Survey

Stationery, Stationery Supplies, Giftwrap

Best customers:
- Married couples with children
- Householders aged 35 to 44
- Households with incomes of $70,000 or more
- Households in the Midwest

Customer trends:
- Stable for now, but electronic communications will reduce spending in the future.

Married couples with preschoolers spend 69 percent more than the average household on stationery, stationery supplies, and giftwrap. Those with school-aged children spend 27 percent more, while those with adult children at home spend 55 percent more than average. As children's birthday parties have become more elaborate (and more expensive), so have the invitations, gift bags, wrapping paper, and related supplies. Householders aged 35 to 44 spend 32 percent more than average on this item because most are parents.

With letter writing becoming less common, spending on traditional stationery has declined. But spending on greeting cards and invitations has expanded and takes up some of the slack. Eventually, however, electronic greeting cards will cut into the market, and spending will decline.

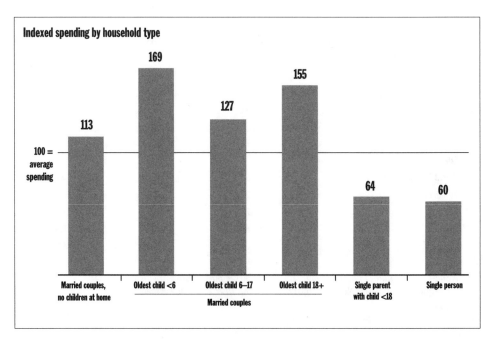

Indexed spending by household type

Married couples, no children at home	Oldest child <6	Oldest child 6–17	Oldest child 18+	Single parent with child <18	Single person
113	169	127	155	64	60

100 = average spending

Married couples

STATIONERY, STATIONERY SUPPLIES, GIFTWRAP

Total household spending $6,610,113,360
Average household spends   62.61

	average spending	best customers (index)	biggest customers (market share)
AGE OF HOUSEHOLDER			
Total households	**$62.61**	**100**	**100.0%**
Under age 25	18.71	30	2.1
Aged 25 to 34	63.92	102	19.3
Aged 35 to 44	82.64	132	30.7
Aged 45 to 54	72.13	115	21.1
Aged 55 to 64	59.18	95	11.0
Aged 65 to 74	50.66	81	9.3
Aged 75 or older	48.67	78	7.2
HOUSEHOLD INCOME			
Total households reporting income	**67.06**	**100**	**100.0**
Under $20,000	33.97	51	17.6
$20,000 to $29,999	49.29	74	10.7
$30,000 to $39,999	79.15	118	14.4
$40,000 to $49,999	66.78	100	9.3
$50,000 to $69,999	70.33	105	14.7
$70,000 or more	143.42	214	32.0
HOUSEHOLD TYPE			
Total households	**62.61**	**100**	**100.0**
Married couples	79.94	128	66.8
Married couples, no children	70.77	113	24.1
Married couples, with children	89.77	143	38.5
Oldest child under 6	105.63	169	8.7
Oldest child 6 to 17	79.71	127	18.5
Oldest child 18 or older	96.78	155	11.1
Single parent with child under 18	40.04	64	4.0
Single person	37.29	60	17.1
REGION			
Total households	**62.61**	**100**	**100.0**
Northeast	53.92	86	17.2
Midwest	79.36	127	30.3
South	50.86	81	28.3
West	70.86	113	24.0

Note: For definitions of best and biggest customers, see introduction or glossary.
Source: Calculations by New Strategist based on the 1997 Consumer Expenditure Survey

Chapter 14.

Personal Care

Personal Care

The average household spent $527.62 in 1997 on personal care products and services. This category includes everything from hair cuts, facials, and manicures to cosmetics, shampoo, toothpaste, electric shavers, and hair dryers. Spending on personal care products and services rose 13 percent between 1987 and 1997, after adjusting for inflation.

Behind the spending growth in this category is the expanding number of products and services with which Americans can pamper themselves. Personal care services for women command the largest share of this catgory, accounting for more than one-third of personal care spending. The best customers of personal care services for females are older women. This fact guarantees continued spending growth in the category as aging baby-boom women gain the free time to indulge themselves.

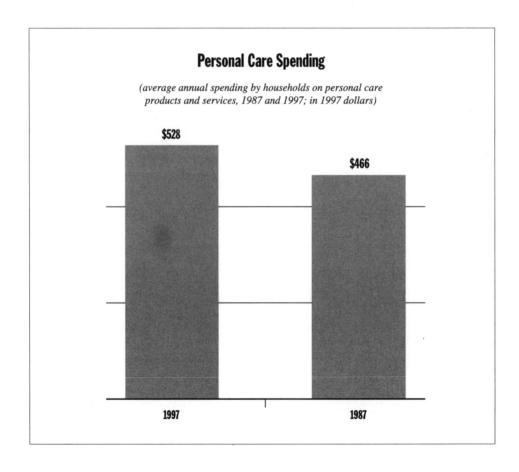

Personal Care Spending

(average annual spending by households on personal care products and services, 1987 and 1997; in 1997 dollars)

$528 — 1997

$466 — 1987

Personal Care Products and Services Spending

(average annual spending of households on personal care products and services, and percent distribution of spending by type, 1997)

Total spending on personal care products and services	**$527.62**	**100.0%**
Personal care services, female	188.30	35.7
Cosmetics, perfume, and bath products	109.99	20.8
Personal care services, male	97.25	18.4
Hair care products	51.00	9.7
Deodorants, feminine hygiene, miscellaneous products	29.80	5.6
Oral hygiene products	26.96	5.1
Shaving products	11.45	2.2
Personal care appliances, electric	4.56	0.9

Note: Numbers will not add to total because not all categories are shown.

Cosmetics, Perfume, and Bath Products

Best customers: • Householders aged 45 to 54
                   • Married couples with school-aged or older children

Customer trends: • A spending decline is likely as consumers become increasingly savvy shoppers.

Married couples with adult children at home spend 43 percent more than the average household on cosmetics, perfume, and bath products, mostly because there are more people in those households. Householders aged 45 to 54 spend 26 percent more than average on this item, as do married couples with school-aged children.

Spending on cosmetics, perfume, and bath products is likely to decline because increasingly savvy consumers will be shopping around for the best prices. To compete effectively, manufacturers will have to add value to their products.

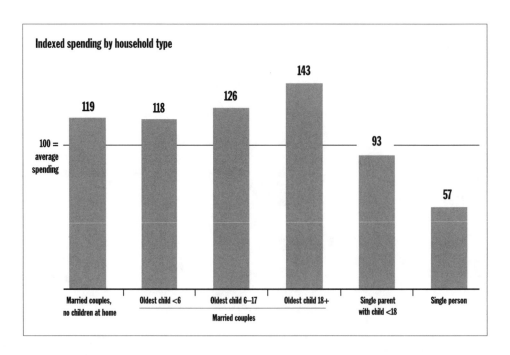

Indexed spending by household type

Married couples, no children at home	Oldest child <6	Oldest child 6–17	Oldest child 18+	Single parent with child <18	Single person
119	118	126	143	93	57

Married couples

100 = average spending

COSMETICS, PERFUME, AND BATH PRODUCTS

Total household spending $11,612,304,240
Average household spends   109.99

	average spending	best customers (index)	biggest customers (market share)
AGE OF HOUSEHOLDER			
Total households	**$109.99**	**100**	**100.0%**
Under age 25	58.23	53	3.8
Aged 25 to 34	109.33	99	18.8
Aged 35 to 44	123.63	112	26.1
Aged 45 to 54	138.76	126	23.1
Aged 55 to 64	113.08	103	12.0
Aged 65 to 74	108.90	99	11.4
Aged 75 or older	63.38	58	5.4
HOUSEHOLD INCOME			
Total households reporting income	**120.23**	**100**	**100.0**
Under $20,000	59.20	49	17.2
$20,000 to $29,999	119.81	100	14.6
$30,000 to $39,999	153.02	127	15.6
$40,000 to $49,999	103.48	86	8.0
$50,000 to $69,999	148.48	123	17.3
$70,000 or more	211.31	176	26.3
HOUSEHOLD TYPE			
Total households	**109.99**	**100**	**100.0**
Married couples	137.17	125	65.2
Married couples, no children	131.25	119	25.5
Married couples, with children	141.91	129	34.7
Oldest child under 6	129.98	118	6.1
Oldest child 6 to 17	139.10	126	18.4
Oldest child 18 or older	157.54	143	10.3
Single parent with child under 18	102.80	93	5.9
Single person	63.20	57	16.5
REGION			
Total households	**109.99**	**100**	**100.0**
Northeast	87.97	80	16.0
Midwest	113.47	103	24.7
South	117.84	107	37.4
West	113.84	104	22.0

Note: For definitions of best and biggest customers, see introduction or glossary.
Source: Calculations by New Strategist based on the 1997 Consumer Expenditure Survey

Deodorants, Feminine Hygiene, Miscellaneous Products

Best customers:	• **Married couples with school-aged or older children**
Customer trends:	• **Stable spending because of the growing teen population.**

Married couples with school-aged children spend 41 percent more than the average household on deodorants, feminine hygiene products, and other personal care items. Married couples with adult children at home spend 39 percent more than average on this item, mostly because there are more people in those households.

As boomer women approach menopause, the feminine hygiene market is being transformed. But household spending in this category should remain stable because of the growing teen population.

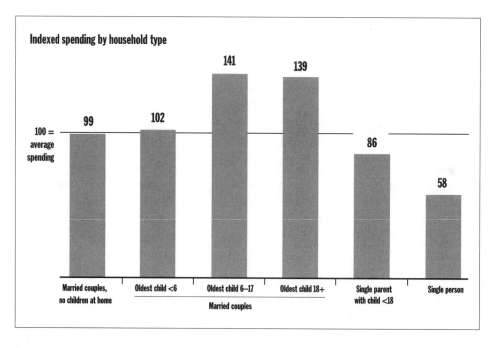

Indexed spending by household type

Married couples, no children at home	Oldest child <6	Oldest child 6–17	Oldest child 18+	Single parent with child <18	Single person
99	102	141	139	86	58

100 = average spending

Married couples

DEODORANTS, FEMININE HYGIENE, MISCELLANEOUS PRODUCTS

Total household spending $3,146,164,800
Average household spends   29.80

	average spending	best customers (index)	biggest customers (market share)
AGE OF HOUSEHOLDER			
Total households	**$29.80**	**100**	**100.0%**
Under age 25	16.67	56	4.0
Aged 25 to 34	31.80	107	20.1
Aged 35 to 44	37.87	127	29.6
Aged 45 to 54	37.32	125	22.9
Aged 55 to 64	26.93	90	10.5
Aged 65 to 74	19.22	64	7.4
Aged 75 or older	19.16	64	6.0
HOUSEHOLD INCOME			
Total households reporting income	**32.35**	**100**	**100.0**
Under $20,000	21.18	65	22.8
$20,000 to $29,999	28.66	89	12.9
$30,000 to $39,999	43.19	134	16.3
$40,000 to $49,999	34.99	108	10.1
$50,000 to $69,999	38.26	118	16.6
$70,000 or more	43.92	136	20.3
HOUSEHOLD TYPE			
Total households	**29.80**	**100**	**100.0**
Married couples	35.77	120	62.8
Married couples, no children	29.61	99	21.2
Married couples, with children	39.36	132	35.5
Oldest child under 6	30.49	102	5.3
Oldest child 6 to 17	41.95	141	20.5
Oldest child 18 or older	41.57	139	10.0
Single parent with child under 18	25.52	86	5.4
Single person	17.18	58	16.6
REGION			
Total households	**29.80**	**100**	**100.0**
Northeast	27.42	92	18.4
Midwest	26.51	89	21.3
South	35.30	118	41.3
West	26.83	90	19.1

Note: For definitions of best and biggest customers, see introduction or glossary.
Source: Calculations by New Strategist based on the 1997 Consumer Expenditure Survey

Hair Care Products

Best customers: • Married couples with children under 18

Customer trends: • The graying of the baby boom is likely to boost spending on hair care products.

Although some families share one bottle of shampoo, others have shower stalls crowded with hair care products. The latter is particularly true for families with children, which explains why married couples with preschoolers spend 67 percent more than the average household on hair care products. Those with school-aged children spend 40 percent more than average.

The most promising development for manufacturers of hair care products is the aging of the baby-boom generation. While some boomers will age quietly, others will search the hair care aisle to find remedies for their graying and thinning manes, boosting spending on hair care products.

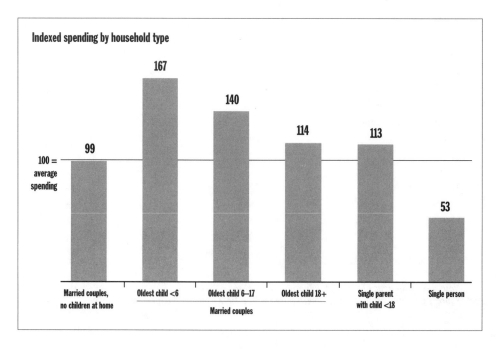

Indexed spending by household type

Married couples, no children at home	99
Oldest child <6 (Married couples)	167
Oldest child 6–17 (Married couples)	140
Oldest child 18+ (Married couples)	114
Single parent with child <18	113
Single person	53

100 = average spending

HAIR CARE PRODUCTS

Total household spending	$5,384,376,000		
Average household spends	51.00		

	average spending	best customers (index)	biggest customers (market share)
AGE OF HOUSEHOLDER			
Total households	**$51.00**	**100**	**100.0%**
Under age 25	36.47	72	5.1
Aged 25 to 34	62.55	123	23.1
Aged 35 to 44	65.04	128	29.7
Aged 45 to 54	54.57	107	19.6
Aged 55 to 64	45.52	89	10.4
Aged 65 to 74	34.56	68	7.8
Aged 75 or older	26.17	51	4.8
HOUSEHOLD INCOME			
Total households reporting income	**55.39**	**100**	**100.0**
Under $20,000	33.57	61	21.1
$20,000 to $29,999	58.40	105	15.4
$30,000 to $39,999	59.18	107	13.1
$40,000 to $49,999	68.05	123	11.5
$50,000 to $69,999	68.49	124	17.4
$70,000 or more	76.81	139	20.7
HOUSEHOLD TYPE			
Total households	**51.00**	**100**	**100.0**
Married couples	62.21	122	63.8
Married couples, no children	50.54	99	21.1
Married couples, with children	71.01	139	37.4
Oldest child under 6	85.17	167	8.6
Oldest child 6 to 17	71.64	140	20.4
Oldest child 18 or older	57.92	114	8.2
Single parent with child under 18	57.81	113	7.1
Single person	27.07	53	15.2
REGION			
Total households	**51.00**	**100**	**100.0**
Northeast	49.27	97	19.3
Midwest	46.44	91	21.8
South	51.80	102	35.4
West	56.28	110	23.4

Note: For definitions of best and biggest customers, see introduction or glossary.
Source: Calculations by New Strategist based on the 1997 Consumer Expenditure Survey

Oral Hygiene Products

Best customers: • Married couples with school-aged or older children

Customer trends: • Spending will increase as Americans seek healthier—and better looking—teeth.

Oral hygiene products are found in every household. The primary determinant of spending on this item is household size—the larger the household the greater the spending. Married couples with adult children at home spend 30 percent more than the average household on oral hygiene products. Those with school-aged children spend 29 percent more than average.

Consumers are better educated about dental health than ever before, and this means more spending on oral hygiene products. In the years ahead, growing numbers of householders will pay more for products that promise not only healthier teeth and gums but also whiter and brighter smiles.

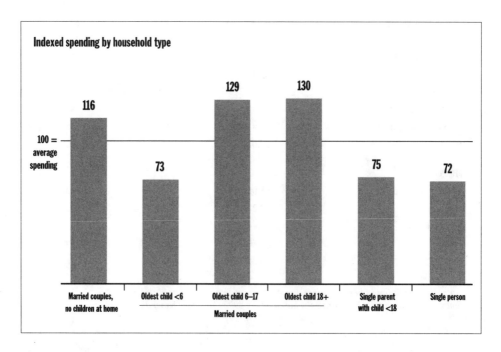

Indexed spending by household type

116	73	129	130	75	72
Married couples, no children at home	Oldest child <6	Oldest child 6–17	Oldest child 18+	Single parent with child <18	Single person

100 = average spending

Married couples

ORAL HYGIENE PRODUCTS

Total household spending $2,846,328,960
Average household spends 26.96

	average spending	best customers (index)	biggest customers (market share)
AGE OF HOUSEHOLDER			
Total households	**$26.96**	**100**	**100.0%**
Under age 25	14.67	54	3.9
Aged 25 to 34	25.21	94	17.6
Aged 35 to 44	33.38	124	28.8
Aged 45 to 54	29.82	111	20.3
Aged 55 to 64	29.71	110	12.9
Aged 65 to 74	23.62	88	10.0
Aged 75 or older	20.08	74	6.9
HOUSEHOLD INCOME			
Total households reporting income	**29.26**	**100**	**100.0**
Under $20,000	17.19	59	20.5
$20,000 to $29,999	29.96	102	15.0
$30,000 to $39,999	42.74	146	17.9
$40,000 to $49,999	28.36	97	9.1
$50,000 to $69,999	32.43	111	15.6
$70,000 or more	41.18	141	21.0
HOUSEHOLD TYPE			
Total households	**26.96**	**100**	**100.0**
Married couples	31.89	118	61.9
Married couples, no children	31.26	116	24.7
Married couples, with children	31.59	117	31.5
Oldest child under 6	19.77	73	3.8
Oldest child 6 to 17	34.75	129	18.8
Oldest child 18 or older	35.07	130	9.4
Single parent with child under 18	20.27	75	4.7
Single person	19.44	72	20.7
REGION			
Total households	**26.96**	**100**	**100.0**
Northeast	25.20	93	18.7
Midwest	23.38	87	20.7
South	30.49	113	39.5
West	26.88	100	21.2

Note: For definitions of best and biggest customers, see introduction or glossary.
Source: Calculations by New Strategist based on the 1997 Consumer Expenditure Survey

Personal Care Appliances, Electric

Best customers: • Married couples with school-aged or older children.

Customer trends: • Spending could increase if marketers target the expanding teen population.

Households with children are the best customers of electric personal care appliances, such as hair dryers. Larger households are understandably bigger spenders, but the presence of teenagers in a household also spurs spending on this item. Married couples with school-aged children spend 47 percent more than the average household on electric personal care appliances. Those with adult children at home spend 41 percent more than average.

Spending on electric personal care appliances may rise as the teen population expands, particularly if manufacturers design and market products specifically for teens.

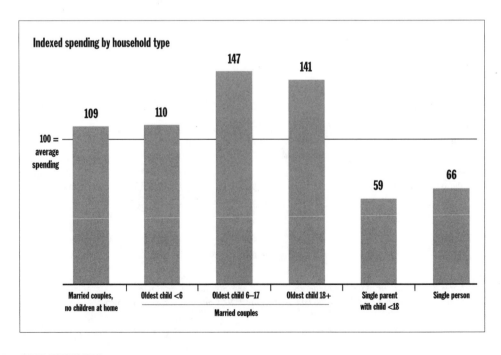

Indexed spending by household type

109	110	147	141	59	66

100 = average spending

Married couples, no children at home | Oldest child <6 | Oldest child 6–17 | Oldest child 18+ | Single parent with child <18 | Single person

Married couples

PERSONAL CARE APPLIANCES, ELECTRIC

Total household spending $481,426,560
Average household spends   4.56

	average spending	best customers (index)	biggest customers (market share)
AGE OF HOUSEHOLDER			
Total households	**$4.56**	**100**	**100.0%**
Under age 25	3.91	86	6.1
Aged 25 to 34	5.43	119	22.5
Aged 35 to 44	5.26	115	26.8
Aged 45 to 54	5.18	114	20.8
Aged 55 to 64	4.08	89	10.4
Aged 65 to 74	3.53	77	8.9
Aged 75 or older	2.22	49	4.5
HOUSEHOLD INCOME			
Total households reporting income	**4.80**	**100**	**100.0**
Under $20,000	2.89	60	21.0
$20,000 to $29,999	3.05	64	9.3
$30,000 to $39,999	6.38	133	16.3
$40,000 to $49,999	4.78	100	9.3
$50,000 to $69,999	6.56	137	19.2
$70,000 or more	8.04	168	25.0
HOUSEHOLD TYPE			
Total households	**4.56**	**100**	**100.0**
Married couples	5.87	129	67.3
Married couples, no children	4.95	109	23.2
Married couples, with children	6.31	138	37.2
Oldest child under 6	5.01	110	5.7
Oldest child 6 to 17	6.71	147	21.4
Oldest child 18 or older	6.41	141	10.1
Single parent with child under 18	2.69	59	3.7
Single person	2.99	66	18.8
REGION			
Total households	**4.56**	**100**	**100.0**
Northeast	3.56	78	15.6
Midwest	5.36	118	28.1
South	3.45	76	26.4
West	6.44	141	30.0

Note: For definitions of best and biggest customers, see introduction or glossary.
Source: Calculations by New Strategist based on the 1997 Consumer Expenditure Survey

Personal Care Services, Female

Best customers:
- Householders aged 45 to 74
- Married couples with adult children

Customer trends:
- Spending should rise sharply as baby-boom women get older and have more time to pamper themselves.

Older women are the best customers of personal care service providers, such as hairdressers and manicurists. Householders aged 45 to 74 spend 15 to 18 percent more than the average householder on this item. Married couples with adult children at home spend 37 percent more than average not only because their households are larger, but also because these householders are older.

As the women of the baby-boom generation age and have more time to pamper themselves, spending on personal care services for females should rise sharply.

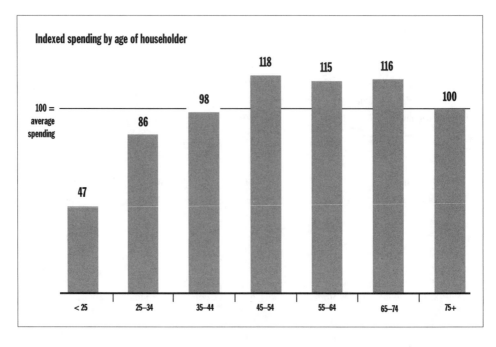

Indexed spending by age of householder

100 = average spending

< 25	25–34	35–44	45–54	55–64	65–74	75+
47	86	98	118	115	116	100

PERSONAL CARE SERVICES, FEMALE

Total household spending $19,879,960,800
Average household spends   188.30

	average spending	best customers (index)	biggest customers (market share)
AGE OF HOUSEHOLDER			
Total households	**$188.30**	**100**	**100.0%**
Under age 25	88.97	47	3.4
Aged 25 to 34	162.67	86	16.3
Aged 35 to 44	184.46	98	22.8
Aged 45 to 54	221.30	118	21.5
Aged 55 to 64	215.67	115	13.4
Aged 65 to 74	218.87	116	13.3
Aged 75 or older	188.78	100	9.3
HOUSEHOLD INCOME			
Total households reporting income	**190.41**	**100**	**100.0**
Under $20,000	113.74	60	20.8
$20,000 to $29,999	155.29	82	11.9
$30,000 to $39,999	165.95	87	10.7
$40,000 to $49,999	198.98	105	9.8
$50,000 to $69,999	248.48	130	18.3
$70,000 or more	363.48	191	28.5
HOUSEHOLD TYPE			
Total households	**188.30**	**100**	**100.0**
Married couples	231.14	123	64.2
Married couples, no children	238.68	127	27.1
Married couples, with children	221.75	118	31.7
Oldest child under 6	189.49	101	5.2
Oldest child 6 to 17	214.85	114	16.6
Oldest child 18 or older	258.79	137	9.9
Single parent with child under 18	160.33	85	5.3
Single person	117.02	62	17.9
REGION			
Total households	**188.30**	**100**	**100.0**
Northeast	207.67	110	22.0
Midwest	179.59	95	22.8
South	185.91	99	34.4
West	183.83	98	20.7

Note: For definitions of best and biggest customers, see introduction or glossary.
Source: Calculations by New Strategist based on the 1997 Consumer Expenditure Survey

Personal Care Services, Male

Best customers:
- Householders aged 25 to 54
- Married couples with children

Customer trends:
- Because younger men are concerned about their looks, spending on personal care services for males will increase.

Householders aged 25 to 54 spend 14 to 26 percent more than average on personal care services for males. Married couples with adult children at home spend 56 percent more than the average household on this item. Those with school-aged children spend 49 percent more than average, while couples with preschoolers spend 34 percent more. Behind the higher spending on this item by households with children is their larger size.

Not long ago, few men would have admitted to worrying about their looks. Beginning with boomer men, however, catering to male vanity has become big business. Spending on personal care services for males is likely to rise as boomers and younger men strive to look their best.

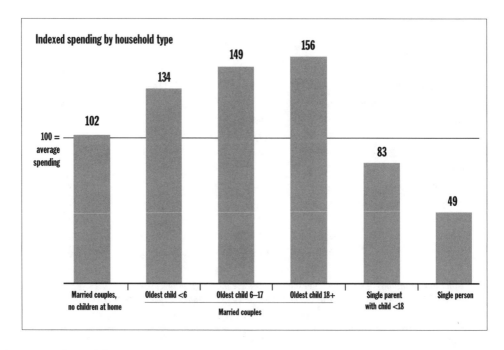

Indexed spending by household type

Married couples, no children at home	Oldest child <6	Oldest child 6–17	Oldest child 18+	Single parent with child <18	Single person
102	134	149	156	83	49

Married couples

100 = average spending

PERSONAL CARE SERVICES, MALE

Total household spending $10,267,266,000
Average household spends   97.25

	average spending	best customers (index)	biggest customers (market share)
AGE OF HOUSEHOLDER			
Total households	**$97.25**	**100**	**100.0%**
Under age 25	61.13	63	4.5
Aged 25 to 34	111.06	114	21.5
Aged 35 to 44	113.67	117	27.2
Aged 45 to 54	122.49	126	23.1
Aged 55 to 64	88.03	91	10.6
Aged 65 to 74	72.32	74	8.5
Aged 75 or older	48.41	50	4.6
HOUSEHOLD INCOME			
Total households reporting income	**97.86**	**100**	**100.0**
Under $20,000	49.18	50	17.5
$20,000 to $29,999	82.92	85	12.4
$30,000 to $39,999	97.40	100	12.2
$40,000 to $49,999	113.02	115	10.8
$50,000 to $69,999	137.27	140	19.7
$70,000 or more	179.79	184	27.5
HOUSEHOLD TYPE			
Total households	**97.25**	**100**	**100.0**
Married couples	125.38	129	67.4
Married couples, no children	99.62	102	21.9
Married couples, with children	143.64	148	39.7
Oldest child under 6	129.88	134	6.9
Oldest child 6 to 17	144.47	149	21.6
Oldest child 18 or older	151.81	156	11.2
Single parent with child under 18	80.57	83	5.2
Single person	48.05	49	14.2
REGION			
Total households	**97.25**	**100**	**100.0**
Northeast	104.19	107	21.4
Midwest	92.64	95	22.8
South	98.25	101	35.2
West	94.28	97	20.6

Note: For definitions of best and biggest customers, see introduction or glossary.
Source: Calculations by New Strategist based on the 1997 Consumer Expenditure Survey

Shaving Products

The more people live in a household, the more it spends on shaving products. Married couples with adult children at home spend 71 percent more than the average household on shaving products, while householders aged 45 to 54 spend 44 percent more. Both household segments are likely to include children old enough to use shaving products.

As the young-adult population grows, spending on shaving products is likely to rise.

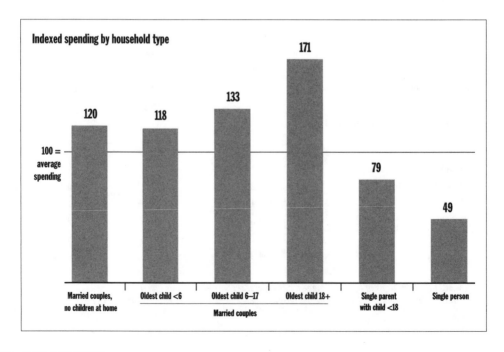

Indexed spending by household type

100 = average spending

| Married couples, no children at home | Oldest child <6 | Oldest child 6–17 | Oldest child 18+ | Single parent with child <18 | Single person |
| 120 | 118 | 133 | 171 | 79 | 49 |

Married couples

SHAVING PRODUCTS

Total household spending	$1,208,845,200
Average household spends	11.45

	average spending	best customers (index)	biggest customers (market share)
AGE OF HOUSEHOLDER			
Total households	**$11.45**	**100**	**100.0%**
Under age 25	5.92	52	3.7
Aged 25 to 34	11.40	100	18.8
Aged 35 to 44	12.94	113	26.3
Aged 45 to 54	16.47	144	26.4
Aged 55 to 64	11.26	98	11.5
Aged 65 to 74	10.16	89	10.2
Aged 75 or older	4.67	41	3.8
HOUSEHOLD INCOME			
Total households reporting income	**11.85**	**100**	**100.0**
Under $20,000	6.62	56	19.5
$20,000 to $29,999	9.56	81	11.8
$30,000 to $39,999	14.92	126	15.4
$40,000 to $49,999	10.46	88	8.3
$50,000 to $69,999	15.54	131	18.4
$70,000 or more	20.47	173	25.8
HOUSEHOLD TYPE			
Total households	**11.45**	**100**	**100.0**
Married couples	14.91	130	68.1
Married couples, no children	13.78	120	25.7
Married couples, with children	16.01	140	37.6
Oldest child under 6	13.55	118	6.1
Oldest child 6 to 17	15.25	133	19.4
Oldest child 18 or older	19.59	171	12.3
Single parent with child under 18	9.00	79	4.9
Single person	5.57	49	14.0
REGION			
Total households	**11.45**	**100**	**100.0**
Northeast	9.38	82	16.4
Midwest	10.10	88	21.1
South	13.35	117	40.7
West	11.79	103	21.9

Note: For definitions of best and biggest customers, see introduction or glossary.
Source: Calculations by New Strategist based on the 1997 Consumer Expenditure Survey

Chapter 15.

Reading Material

Reading Material

Americans spent $163.58 on newspapers, magazines, and books in 1997. Spending on reading material fell a steep 18 percent between 1987 and 1997, after adjusting for inflation. Behind this decline is the rise of electronic media (television and the Internet), which has reduced reading among younger generations.

The best customers of reading material are older Americans. Americans aged 55 or older are the biggest spenders on newspapers and magazine subscriptions. Middle-aged and younger adults spend the most on books and newsstand magazines. The market for books has a healthy future because electronic media provide no adequate substitute, but newspapers and magazines face uncertainty as computer-savvy younger generations replace older customers. Spending on reading material is likely to decline.

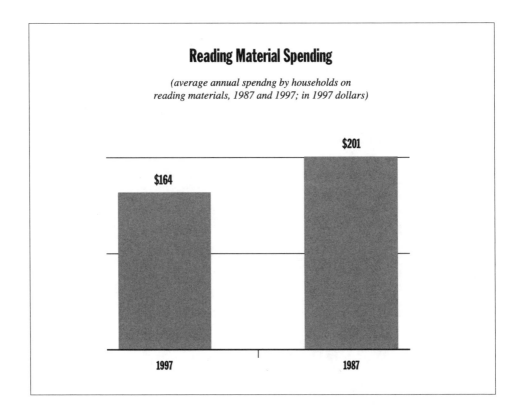

Reading Material Spending

*(average annual spendng by households on
reading materials, 1987 and 1997; in 1997 dollars)*

$201

$164

1997   1987

Reading Material Spending

(average annual spending of households on reading material, and percent distribution of spending by type, 1997)

Total spending on reading material	**$163.58**	**100.0%**
Newspaper subscriptions	51.70	31.6
Books, except book clubs	49.50	30.3
Magazine subscriptions	22.62	13.8
Newspapers, nonsubscription	17.18	10.5
Magazines, nonsubscription	11.55	7.1
Books purchased through book clubs	10.18	6.2

Note: Numbers will not add to total because not all categories are shown.

Books Purchased through Book Clubs

Best customers:	• Householders aged 65 to 74
	• Married couples with children under age 6
	• Married couples with adult children
Customer trends:	• Spending is likely to decline because busy younger generations will not subscribe to book clubs as readily as today's older Americans.

Book clubs have the advantage of being able to target the interests of specific consumer segments. Clubs targeting parents of young children, for example, have enjoyed a ready market, and married couples with children under age 6 spend 38 percent more than the average household on books purchased through book clubs. Older Americans are even better customers, however. Householders aged 65 to 74 spend 32 percent more than average on book clubs. Married couples with adult children at home spend 52 percent more.

Book clubs offer convenience by bringing bookstores into the home, but they are also inconvenient because their mailings require a response. It is unlikely that busy younger generations will subscribe to book clubs as readily as the current generation of older Americans, suggesting a spending decline in the years ahead.

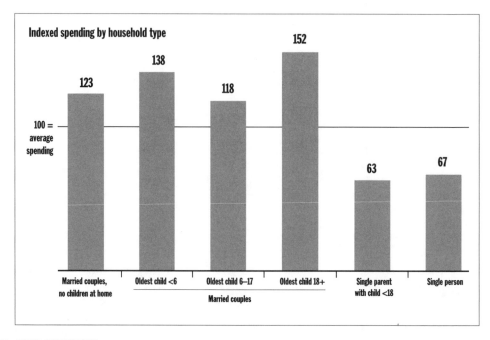

Indexed spending by household type

Married couples, no children at home	Oldest child <6	Oldest child 6–17	Oldest child 18+	Single parent with child <18	Single person
123	138	118	152	63	67

Married couples

100 = average spending

BOOKS PURCHASED THROUGH BOOK CLUBS

Total household spending $1,074,763,680
Average household spends   10.18

	average spending	best customers (index)	biggest customers (market share)
AGE OF HOUSEHOLDER			
Total households	**$10.18**	**100**	**100.0%**
Under age 25	2.89	28	2.0
Aged 25 to 34	10.07	99	18.7
Aged 35 to 44	8.67	85	19.8
Aged 45 to 54	12.62	124	22.7
Aged 55 to 64	11.73	115	13.4
Aged 65 to 74	13.39	132	15.1
Aged 75 or older	9.07	89	8.3
HOUSEHOLD INCOME			
Total households reporting income	**11.18**	**100**	**100.0**
Under $20,000	4.51	40	14.1
$20,000 to $29,999	9.92	89	13.0
$30,000 to $39,999	12.41	111	13.6
$40,000 to $49,999	10.41	93	8.7
$50,000 to $69,999	19.72	176	24.8
$70,000 or more	19.39	173	25.9
HOUSEHOLD TYPE			
Total households	**10.18**	**100**	**100.0**
Married couples	12.47	122	64.1
Married couples, no children	12.54	123	26.3
Married couples, with children	13.34	131	35.2
Oldest child under 6	14.06	138	7.1
Oldest child 6 to 17	12.04	118	17.2
Oldest child 18 or older	15.46	152	10.9
Single parent with child under 18	6.42	63	4.0
Single person	6.82	67	19.2
REGION			
Total households	**10.18**	**100**	**100.0**
Northeast	10.11	99	19.8
Midwest	11.79	116	27.7
South	8.41	83	28.8
West	11.37	112	23.7

Note: For definitions of best and biggest customers, see introduction or glossary.
Source: Calculations by New Strategist based on the 1997 Consumer Expenditure Survey

Books, except Book Clubs

Best customers:
- Householders aged 45 to 54
- Households in the West
- Households with incomes of $70,000 or more

Customer trends:
- Stable for now, but other forms of entertainment and reference pose a threat.

Householders aged 45 to 54 are the best customers of books. Not only are they in their peak-earning years, but they are also highly educated—and the greater the education, the more people spend on books. Householders aged 45 to 54 spend 41 percent more than average on books. Those with household incomes of $70,000 or more spend twice the average amount on books. Households in the West, where the population is relatively well-educated, spend 37 percent more than average on books.

The aging of the well-educated baby-boom generation is a positive trend for the book industry. Spending on books is likely to rise in the older age groups as they fill with boomers. But competition from other forms of leisure entertainment and the availability of alternative reference materials could threaten the book market.

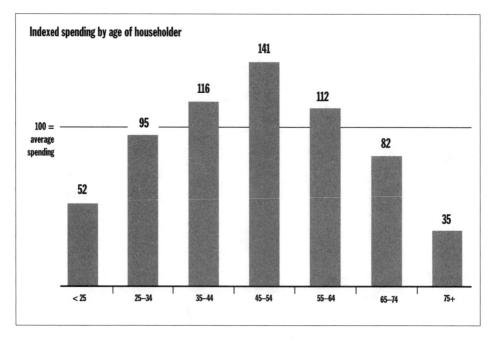

Indexed spending by age of householder

< 25	25–34	35–44	45–54	55–64	65–74	75+
52	95	116	141	112	82	35

100 = average spending

BOOKS, EXCEPT BOOK CLUBS

Total household spending $5,226,012,000
Average household spends   49.50

	average spending	best customers (index)	biggest customers (market share)
AGE OF HOUSEHOLDER			
Total households	**$49.50**	**100**	**100.0%**
Under age 25	25.89	52	3.7
Aged 25 to 34	47.02	95	17.9
Aged 35 to 44	57.22	116	26.9
Aged 45 to 54	69.60	141	25.8
Aged 55 to 64	55.41	112	13.1
Aged 65 to 74	40.58	82	9.4
Aged 75 or older	17.26	35	3.2
HOUSEHOLD INCOME			
Total households reporting income	**52.79**	**100**	**100.0**
Under $20,000	19.41	37	12.8
$20,000 to $29,999	36.15	68	10.0
$30,000 to $39,999	43.56	83	10.1
$40,000 to $49,999	51.87	98	9.2
$50,000 to $69,999	74.90	142	19.9
$70,000 or more	134.15	254	38.0
HOUSEHOLD TYPE			
Total households	**49.50**	**100**	**100.0**
Married couples	60.93	123	64.4
Married couples, no children	63.29	128	27.3
Married couples, with children	62.19	126	33.8
Oldest child under 6	53.93	109	5.6
Oldest child 6 to 17	64.74	131	19.0
Oldest child 18 or older	62.92	127	9.1
Single parent with child under 18	25.79	52	3.3
Single person	40.74	82	23.6
REGION			
Total households	**49.50**	**100**	**100.0**
Northeast	54.71	111	22.1
Midwest	45.95	93	22.2
South	37.74	76	26.6
West	67.90	137	29.1

Note: For definitions of best and biggest customers, see introduction or glossary.
Source: Calculations by New Strategist based on the 1997 Consumer Expenditure Survey

Magazine Subscriptions

Best customers:
- Married couples without children
- Householders aged 55 to 74

Customer trends:
- Spending may decline because of competition with other forms of leisure entertainment.

The best customers of magazine subscriptions are older Americans. Householders aged 55 to 74 spend 27 to 33 percent more than the average householder on this item. Married couples without children at home, most of whom are older, spend 63 percent more than average on magazine subscriptions. Magazine subscriptions are more popular among older Americans because they are the ones who have the time to read magazines.

Americans are suffering from information overload. Magazines now compete not only with other magazines, but with television and the Internet for people's limited reading time. Younger generations, in particular, have little interest in subscribing to magazines, suggesting a spending decline in the years ahead.

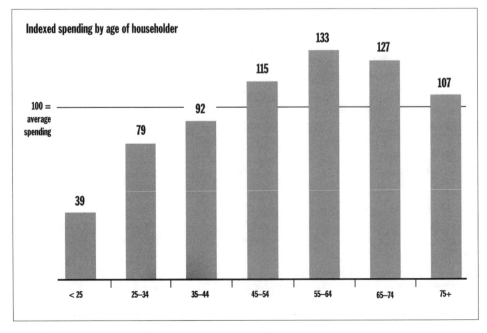

Indexed spending by age of householder

< 25	25–34	35–44	45–54	55–64	65–74	75+
39	79	92	115	133	127	107

100 = average spending

MAGAZINE SUBSCRIPTIONS

Total household spending	$2,388,129,120		
Average household spends	22.62		

	average spending	best customers (index)	biggest customers (market share)
AGE OF HOUSEHOLDER			
Total households	**$22.62**	**100**	**100.0%**
Under age 25	8.74	39	2.7
Aged 25 to 34	17.84	79	14.9
Aged 35 to 44	20.76	92	21.4
Aged 45 to 54	25.95	115	21.0
Aged 55 to 64	30.00	133	15.5
Aged 65 to 74	28.77	127	14.6
Aged 75 or older	24.13	107	9.9
HOUSEHOLD INCOME			
Total households reporting income	**24.01**	**100**	**100.0**
Under $20,000	11.60	48	16.8
$20,000 to $29,999	21.49	90	13.1
$30,000 to $39,999	25.03	104	12.7
$40,000 to $49,999	24.38	102	9.5
$50,000 to $69,999	32.93	137	19.3
$70,000 or more	45.93	191	28.6
HOUSEHOLD TYPE			
Total households	**22.62**	**100**	**100.0**
Married couples	29.47	130	68.1
Married couples, no children	36.82	163	34.7
Married couples, with children	25.56	113	30.4
Oldest child under 6	19.26	85	4.4
Oldest child 6 to 17	27.89	123	17.9
Oldest child 18 or older	25.35	112	8.1
Single parent with child under 18	11.17	49	3.1
Single person	15.71	69	20.0
REGION			
Total households	**22.62**	**100**	**100.0**
Northeast	21.86	97	19.3
Midwest	25.90	115	27.4
South	18.69	83	28.8
West	26.08	115	24.5

Note: For definitions of best and biggest customers, see introduction or glossary.
Source: Calculations by New Strategist based on the 1997 Consumer Expenditure Survey

Magazines, Nonsubscription

Best customers:
- Householders aged 35 to 54
- Married couples with school-aged children

Customer trends:
- Nonsubscription spending on magazines will erode subscription spending as younger householders age.

The best customers of magazines purchased at newsstands and other outlets are busy middle-aged householders who buy on impulse as they rush from one activity to another. Householders aged 35 to 54 spend 16 to 32 percent more than average on nonsubscription magazines. Households with school-aged children spend 33 percent more, partly because of the magazine purchases of teenagers. The affluent are most likely to succumb to impulse buying, which accounts for the above-average spending of householders with incomes of $70,000 or more on this item.

The best customers of magazines purchased at newsstands and other outlets are younger than the best customers of magazines purchased by subscription. This suggests that impulse purchasing may erode subscription spending as younger generations age.

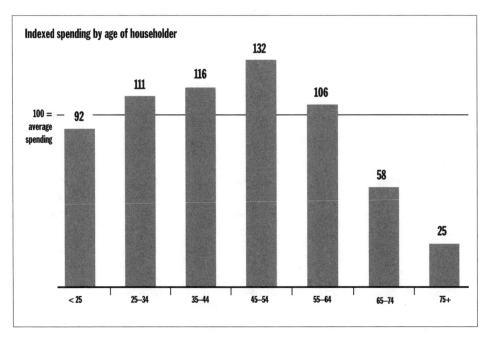

Indexed spending by age of householder

100 = average spending

Age	Index
< 25	92
25–34	111
35–44	116
45–54	132
55–64	106
65–74	58
75+	25

MAGAZINES, NONSUBSCRIPTION

Total household spending	$1,219,402,800	
Average household spends	11.55	

	average spending	best customers (index)	biggest customers (market share)
AGE OF HOUSEHOLDER			
Total households	**$11.55**	**100**	**100.0%**
Under age 25	10.59	92	6.5
Aged 25 to 34	12.80	111	20.9
Aged 35 to 44	13.41	116	27.0
Aged 45 to 54	15.30	132	24.3
Aged 55 to 64	12.21	106	12.3
Aged 65 to 74	6.73	58	6.7
Aged 75 or older	2.87	25	2.3
HOUSEHOLD INCOME			
Total households reporting income	**12.35**	**100**	**100.0**
Under $20,000	6.22	50	17.5
$20,000 to $29,999	9.64	78	11.4
$30,000 to $39,999	13.15	106	13.0
$40,000 to $49,999	12.01	97	9.1
$50,000 to $69,999	16.82	136	19.1
$70,000 or more	24.65	200	29.8
HOUSEHOLD TYPE			
Total households	**11.55**	**100**	**100.0**
Married couples	13.43	116	60.8
Married couples, no children	12.14	105	22.4
Married couples, with children	14.42	125	33.6
Oldest child under 6	12.73	110	5.7
Oldest child 6 to 17	15.39	133	19.4
Oldest child 18 or older	13.67	118	8.5
Single parent with child under 18	7.98	69	4.3
Single person	9.44	82	23.5
REGION			
Total households	**11.55**	**100**	**100.0**
Northeast	10.62	92	18.4
Midwest	10.87	94	22.5
South	10.19	88	30.8
West	15.44	134	28.4

Note: For definitions of best and biggest customers, see introduction or glossary.
Source: Calculations by New Strategist based on the 1997 Consumer Expenditure Survey

Newspaper Subscriptions

Best customers: • Householders aged 65 or older
• Married couples without children

Customer trends: • Continued spending decline because of competition from other information sources.

Older householders are by far the best customers of newspaper subscriptions. Householders aged 65 to 74 spend 62 percent more than the average household on newspaper subscriptions. Those aged 75 or older spend 68 percent more than average. Married couples without children, who are disproportionately older, spend 58 percent more than average.

Younger generations are much more likely than their elders to get their news from media other than newspapers, especially television. Internet news is also competing with printed papers. Spending on newspaper subscriptions is likely to decline as younger, computer-savvy generations enter the older age groups.

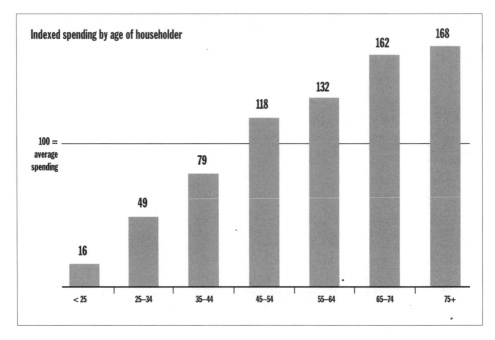

Indexed spending by age of householder

100 = average spending

| < 25 | 25–34 | 35–44 | 45–54 | 55–64 | 65–74 | 75+ |
| 16 | 49 | 79 | 118 | 132 | 162 | 168 |

NEWSPAPER SUBSCRIPTIONS

Total household spending	$5,458,279,200	
Average household spends	51.70	

	average spending	best customers (index)	biggest customers (market share)
AGE OF HOUSEHOLDER			
Total households	**$51.70**	**100**	**100.0%**
Under age 25	8.03	16	1.1
Aged 25 to 34	25.17	49	9.2
Aged 35 to 44	41.03	79	18.5
Aged 45 to 54	61.18	118	21.7
Aged 55 to 64	68.18	132	15.4
Aged 65 to 74	83.73	162	18.6
Aged 75 or older	86.75	168	15.6
HOUSEHOLD INCOME			
Total households reporting income	**52.31**	**100**	**100.0**
Under $20,000	34.91	67	23.2
$20,000 to $29,999	45.04	86	12.6
$30,000 to $39,999	44.65	85	10.4
$40,000 to $49,999	48.45	93	8.7
$50,000 to $69,999	65.80	126	17.7
$70,000 or more	95.96	183	27.4
HOUSEHOLD TYPE			
Total households	**51.70**	**100**	**100.0**
Married couples	66.95	129	67.7
Married couples, no children	81.66	158	33.7
Married couples, with children	57.31	111	29.8
Oldest child under 6	45.22	87	4.5
Oldest child 6 to 17	54.88	106	15.4
Oldest child 18 or older	70.89	137	9.9
Single parent with child under 18	19.32	37	2.3
Single person	37.79	73	21.0
REGION			
Total households	**51.70**	**100**	**100.0**
Northeast	60.51	117	23.4
Midwest	58.93	114	27.2
South	41.29	80	27.9
West	52.40	101	21.5

Note: For definitions of best and biggest customers, see introduction or glossary.
Source: Calculations by New Strategist based on the 1997 Consumer Expenditure Survey

Newspapers, Nonsubscription

Best customers:	• **Households in the Northeast**
	• **Married couples without children**
	• **Married couples with adult children**
	• **Householders aged 45 to 74**
Customer trends:	• **Spending may decline as news sources with greater immediacy threaten impulse buying.**

The best customers of nonsubscription newspapers are residents of the Northeast's commuter-friendly cities. Households in the Northeast spend 93 percent more than average on this item, many buying from newsstands or vending machines. Householders aged 45 to 74 spend 16 to 19 percent more than the average household on nonsubscription newspapers. Older married couples are also more likely than average to buy newspapers. Couples without children at home, most of whom are older, spend 23 percent more than average on this item, while those with adult children at home spend 22 percent more.

Spending on nonsubscription newspapers may decline as other news sources with greater immediacy—the Internet in particular—threaten impulse purchases.

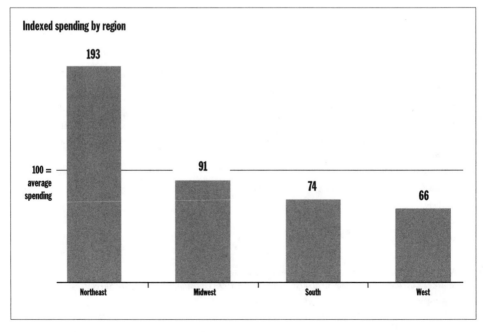

Indexed spending by region

Northeast 193
Midwest 91
South 74
West 66

100 = average spending

NEWSPAPERS, NONSUBSCRIPTION

Total household spending $1,813,795,680
Average household spends   17.18

	average spending	best customers (index)	biggest customers (market share)
AGE OF HOUSEHOLDER			
Total households	**$17.18**	**100**	**100.0%**
Under age 25	7.77	45	3.2
Aged 25 to 34	17.60	102	19.3
Aged 35 to 44	18.20	106	24.6
Aged 45 to 54	20.08	117	21.4
Aged 55 to 64	19.99	116	13.6
Aged 65 to 74	20.53	119	13.7
Aged 75 or older	7.63	44	4.1
HOUSEHOLD INCOME			
Total households reporting income	**17.67**	**100**	**100.0**
Under $20,000	10.89	62	21.5
$20,000 to $29,999	17.88	101	14.8
$30,000 to $39,999	19.79	112	13.7
$40,000 to $49,999	22.29	126	11.8
$50,000 to $69,999	22.89	130	18.2
$70,000 or more	23.72	134	20.1
HOUSEHOLD TYPE			
Total households	**17.18**	**100**	**100.0**
Married couples	19.93	116	60.7
Married couples, no children	21.20	123	26.3
Married couples, with children	19.18	112	30.0
Oldest child under 6	19.08	111	5.7
Oldest child 6 to 17	18.38	107	15.6
Oldest child 18 or older	20.88	122	8.7
Single parent with child under 18	11.89	69	4.3
Single person	13.69	80	22.9
REGION			
Total households	**17.18**	**100**	**100.0**
Northeast	33.14	193	38.5
Midwest	15.64	91	21.8
South	12.66	74	25.7
West	11.33	66	14.0

Note: For definitions of best and biggest customers, see introduction or glossary.
Source: Calculations by New Strategist based on the 1997 Consumer Expenditure Survey

Chapter 16.

Shelter and Utilities

Shelter and Utilities

Americans spend more on shelter and utilities than they do on any other major category, a total of $8,756.10 in 1997. One-fourth of this total is spent on mortgage interest, while 11 percent is devoted to property taxes. The average household spent 8 percent more on shelter in 1997 than in 1987, after adjusting for inflation. Spending on utilities, fuels, and public services rose 2 percent. Property taxes increased the most, up 48 percent during those years. Spending on fuel oil and other fuels fell 19 percent as oil prices declined. Spending on telephone service rose 15 percent, while spending on water and other public services was up 32 percent.

The biggest spenders on shelter and utilities are the most affluent household-ers who tend to buy the most expensive homes. But the biggest spenders on many items, such as homeowner's insurance and property taxes, are older householders because they have the highest homeownership rate. Older homeowners are also the biggest spenders on maintentance and repair services since they are more likely than younger homeowners to hire others to do the work rather than do it themselves. Spending on shelter will continue to rise along with the homeowership rate.

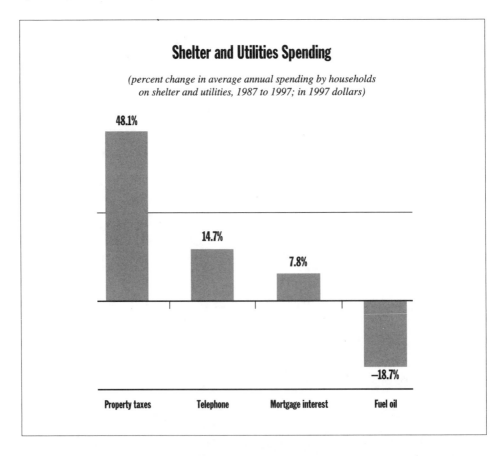

Shelter and Utilities Spending

(percent change in average annual spending by households on shelter and utilities, 1987 to 1997; in 1997 dollars)

48.1%

14.7%

7.8%

−18.7%

Property taxes   Telephone   Mortgage interest   Fuel oil

Shelter and Utilities Spending

(average annual spending of households on shelter and utilities, and percent distribution of spending by type, 1997)

Total spending on shelter and utilities	**$8,756.10**	**100.0%**
Mortgage interest	2,109.06	24.1
Rent	1,876.81	21.4
Property taxes	971.15	11.1
Electricity	908.67	10.4
Telephone service in home city, excluding mobile phone	756.44	8.6
Maintenance and repair services, owned homes	365.61	4.2
Natural gas	300.96	3.4
Insurance, homeowners	230.91	2.6
Water and sewerage maintenance	207.28	2.4
Vacation homes, owned	133.69	1.5
Home equity loan/line of credit interest	116.05	1.3
Fuel oil and other fuels	107.72	1.2
Maintenance and repair materials, owned homes	83.91	1.0
Trash collection	76.00	0.9
Telephone service for mobile phone	52.61	0.6
Property management, owned homes	16.49	0.2
Insurance, tenants	9.76	0.1
Property security, owned homes	3.09	0.0

Note: Numbers will not add to total because not all categories are shown, including lodging on out-of-town trips which is in the Travel chapter.

Electricity

Best customers:
- Households in the South
- Married couples with adult children

Customer trends:
- A spending decline is likely as the push for deregulation of the electric industry picks up steam.

Spending on electricity doesn't differ much from household to household, but there are a few exceptions. Households in the South spend 20 percent more than the average household on electricity. Climate is the reason. During the South's long, hot summer, electric meters whirl as air conditioners hum. Married couples with adult children at home spend 42 percent more than average on electricity, primarily because they have larger than average homes.

Electric utility deregulation is already a reality in some areas and is gaining support in others. Utility companies are likely to respond by holding rates stable or cutting them, bringing average spending on electricity down.

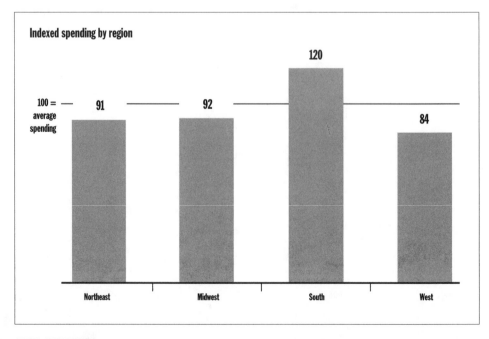

Indexed spending by region

Northeast	Midwest	South	West
91	92	120	84

100 = average spending

ELECTRICITY

Total household spending	$95,933,743,920		
Average household spends	908.67		

	average spending	best customers (index)	biggest customers (market share)
AGE OF HOUSEHOLDER			
Total households	**$908.67**	**100**	**100.0%**
Under age 25	389.61	43	3.0
Aged 25 to 34	785.27	86	16.3
Aged 35 to 44	1,014.56	112	26.0
Aged 45 to 54	1,114.46	123	22.5
Aged 55 to 64	1,013.36	112	13.0
Aged 65 to 74	910.88	100	11.5
Aged 75 or older	751.39	83	7.7
HOUSEHOLD INCOME			
Total households reporting income	**899.68**	**100**	**100.0**
Under $20,000	690.62	77	26.7
$20,000 to $29,999	841.52	94	13.7
$30,000 to $39,999	890.92	99	12.1
$40,000 to $49,999	972.64	108	10.1
$50,000 to $69,999	1,080.33	120	16.9
$70,000 or more	1,235.50	137	20.5
HOUSEHOLD TYPE			
Total households	**908.67**	**100**	**100.0**
Married couples	1,105.49	122	63.6
Married couples, no children	1,000.56	110	23.5
Married couples, with children	1,159.22	128	34.3
Oldest child under 6	912.61	100	5.2
Oldest child 6 to 17	1,183.80	130	19.0
Oldest child 18 or older	1,285.90	142	10.2
Single parent with child under 18	888.50	98	6.1
Single person	554.76	61	17.5
REGION			
Total households	**908.67**	**100**	**100.0**
Northeast	829.60	91	18.2
Midwest	834.46	92	21.9
South	1,093.85	120	42.0
West	762.38	84	17.8

Note: For definitions of best and biggest customers, see introduction or glossary.
Source: Calculations by New Strategist based on the 1997 Consumer Expenditure Survey

Fuel Oil and Other Fuels

Best customers:
- Households in the Northeast
- Married couples with adult children

Customer trends:
- Spending may decline slightly because the population of the Northeast is growing more slowly than that of other regions.

Households in the Northeast spend almost two and one-half times as much as the average household on fuel oil and other fuels. Houses in the Northeast, many of which are older, are more likely than those in other regions to use fuel oil for heat. Married couples with adult children at home spend 69 percent more than average on this item, primarily because their homes are larger.

Because the population of the Northeast is growing more slowly than those of other regions, spending on this item by the average household may decline slightly—unless oil prices rise.

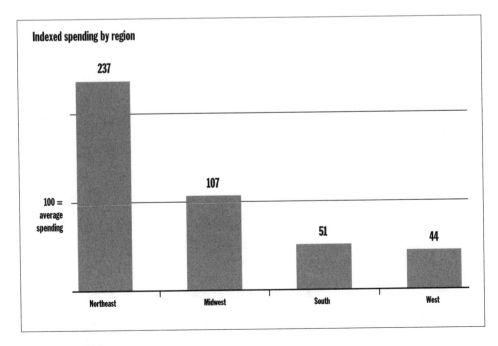

Indexed spending by region

Northeast	237
Midwest	107
South	51
West	44

100 = average spending

FUEL OIL AND OTHER FUELS

Total household spending	$11,372,646,720		
Average household spends	107.72		

	average spending	best customers (index)	biggest customers (market share)
AGE OF HOUSEHOLDER			
Total households	**$107.72**	**100**	**100.0%**
Under age 25	10.68	10	0.7
Aged 25 to 34	69.01	64	12.1
Aged 35 to 44	108.35	101	23.4
Aged 45 to 54	146.87	136	25.0
Aged 55 to 64	126.00	117	13.6
Aged 65 to 74	133.88	124	14.3
Aged 75 or older	126.52	117	10.9
HOUSEHOLD INCOME			
Total households reporting income	**109.11**	**100**	**100.0**
Under $20,000	84.16	77	26.9
$20,000 to $29,999	97.63	89	13.1
$30,000 to $39,999	107.20	98	12.0
$40,000 to $49,999	111.22	102	9.5
$50,000 to $69,999	126.16	116	16.2
$70,000 or more	162.66	149	22.3
HOUSEHOLD TYPE			
Total households	**107.72**	**100**	**100.0**
Married couples	139.33	129	67.6
Married couples, no children	133.98	124	26.5
Married couples, with children	145.71	135	36.4
Oldest child under 6	101.52	94	4.8
Oldest child 6 to 17	143.38	133	19.4
Oldest child 18 or older	182.04	169	12.2
Single parent with child under 18	59.23	55	3.5
Single person	66.49	62	17.7
REGION			
Total households	**107.72**	**100**	**100.0**
Northeast	254.76	237	47.2
Midwest	115.06	107	25.5
South	54.98	51	17.8
West	47.82	44	9.4

Note: For definitions of best and biggest customers, see introduction or glossary.
Source: Calculations by New Strategist based on the 1997 Consumer Expenditure Survey

Home Equity Loan/Line of Credit Interest

Best customers:
- Householders aged 45 to 54
- Households with incomes of $70,000 or more
- Married couples with school-aged or older children

Customer trends:
- Spending will increase as boomers borrow to pay their children's college costs.

Affluent households spend the most on interest for a home equity loan or line of credit. Households with incomes of $70,000 or more spend more than two and one-half times as much as the average household on this item. Householders aged 45 to 54 spend more than twice the average. Married couples with school-aged or older children spend about 120 percent more than average.

Boomers are trying to save for retirement and for their children's college tuition at the same time. Because many will come up short when the bills are due, home equity loans will become an increasingly popular way to pay for college. Consequently, spending on home equity interest will rise.

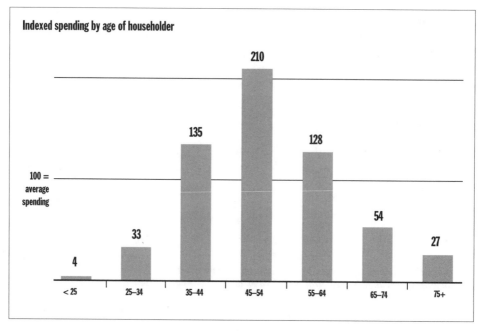

Indexed spending by age of householder

Age	Index
< 25	4
25–34	33
35–44	135
45–54	210
55–64	128
65–74	54
75+	27

100 = average spending

HOME EQUITY LOAN/LINE OF CREDIT INTEREST

Total household spending	$12,252,094,800
Average household spends	116.05

	average spending	best customers (index)	biggest customers (market share)
AGE OF HOUSEHOLDER			
Total households	$116.05	100	100.0%
Under age 25	4.11	4	0.3
Aged 25 to 34	38.63	33	6.3
Aged 35 to 44	156.22	135	31.3
Aged 45 to 54	243.89	210	38.5
Aged 55 to 64	148.78	128	15.0
Aged 65 to 74	62.62	54	6.2
Aged 75 or older	31.20	27	2.5
HOUSEHOLD INCOME			
Total households reporting income	119.90	100	100.0
Under $20,000	31.62	26	9.2
$20,000 to $29,999	60.19	50	7.3
$30,000 to $39,999	87.60	73	8.9
$40,000 to $49,999	149.54	125	11.7
$50,000 to $69,999	199.30	166	23.3
$70,000 or more	317.27	265	39.6
HOUSEHOLD TYPE			
Total households	116.05	100	100.0
Married couples	175.74	151	79.2
Married couples, no children	128.82	111	23.7
Married couples, with children	223.73	193	51.8
Oldest child under 6	88.67	76	3.9
Oldest child 6 to 17	255.04	220	32.0
Oldest child 18 or older	257.01	221	15.9
Single parent with child under 18	24.63	21	1.3
Single person	42.55	37	10.5
REGION			
Total households	116.05	100	100.0
Northeast	153.46	132	26.4
Midwest	120.63	104	24.8
South	70.09	60	21.1
West	151.22	130	27.7

Note: For definitions of best and biggest customers, see introduction or glossary.
Source: Calculations by New Strategist based on the 1997 Consumer Expenditure Survey

Insurance, Homeowners

Best customers:
- Householders aged 65 to 74
- Married couples with adult children

Customer trends:
- Spending will grow as the homeownership rate rises, homes grow in size, and disaster-related insurance claims increase.

Homeownership peaks among 65-to-74-year-olds, which explains why they are among the best customers of homeowner's insurance. Householders aged 65 to 74 spend 43 percent more than the average household on this item. Married couples with adult children at home spend 58 percent more than average because of their older age and higher-than-average homeownership rates.

Several factors point to increased spending on homeowner's insurance. The proportion of Americans who own homes is at an all-time high and rising. Homes are getting larger and more expensive, which boosts insurance rates. And the insurance industry paid out record amounts during the past few years due to weather-related disasters, including hurricanes and tornadoes.

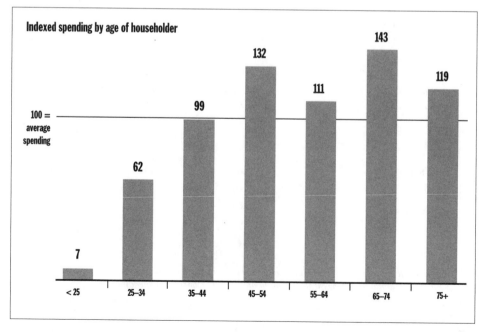

Indexed spending by age of householder

100 = average spending

< 25	25–34	35–44	45–54	55–64	65–74	75+
7	62	99	132	111	143	119

INSURANCE, HOMEOWNERS

Total household spending	$24,378,554,160
Average household spends	230.91

	average spending	best customers (index)	biggest customers (market share)
AGE OF HOUSEHOLDER			
Total households	**$230.91**	**100**	**100.0%**
Under age 25	16.48	7	0.5
Aged 25 to 34	144.24	62	11.8
Aged 35 to 44	229.49	99	23.1
Aged 45 to 54	305.76	132	24.3
Aged 55 to 64	255.53	111	12.9
Aged 65 to 74	329.10	143	16.3
Aged 75 or older	274.59	119	11.1
HOUSEHOLD INCOME			
Total households reporting income	**233.28**	**100**	**100.0**
Under $20,000	137.82	59	20.6
$20,000 to $29,999	167.96	72	10.5
$30,000 to $39,999	224.05	96	11.7
$40,000 to $49,999	246.10	105	9.9
$50,000 to $69,999	319.75	137	19.2
$70,000 or more	437.86	188	28.1
HOUSEHOLD TYPE			
Total households	**230.91**	**100**	**100.0**
Married couples	306.22	133	69.3
Married couples, no children	310.89	135	28.7
Married couples, with children	305.16	132	35.5
Oldest child under 6	243.18	105	5.4
Oldest child 6 to 17	297.19	129	18.7
Oldest child 18 or older	365.60	158	11.4
Single parent with child under 18	104.15	45	2.8
Single person	137.66	60	17.1
REGION			
Total households	**230.91**	**100**	**100.0**
Northeast	232.51	101	20.1
Midwest	213.94	93	22.1
South	245.43	106	37.1
West	224.64	97	20.7

Note: For definitions of best and biggest customers, see introduction or glossary.
Source: Calculations by New Strategist based on the 1997 Consumer Expenditure Survey

Insurance, Tenant's

Best customers:
- Householders aged 25 to 34
- Married couples with children under age 6
- People living alone

Customer trends:
- Spending on tenant's insurance might increase if insurers put more effort into educating renters about its benefits.

Householders aged 25 to 34 spend 41 percent more than the average household on tenant's insurance. Married couples with preschoolers spend 40 percent more. Single-person households spend 31 percent more than average on this item. All of these demographic segments have one thing in common: they are more likely than average to be renters.

Many renters do not buy insurance, however. Some can't afford it, but others don't realize they need it. Spending on tenant's insurance probably would increase if the insurance industry marketed these products more heavily.

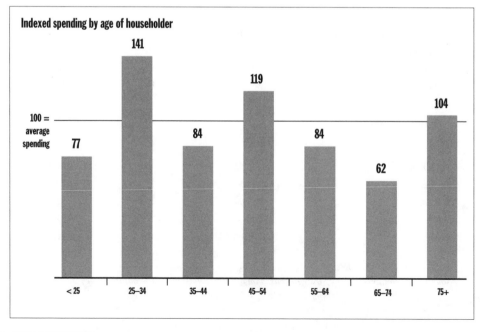

Indexed spending by age of householder

Age	< 25	25–34	35–44	45–54	55–64	65–74	75+
Index	77	141	84	119	84	62	104

100 = average spending

INSURANCE, TENANT'S

Total household spending $1,030,421,760
Average household spends 9.76

	average spending	best customers (index)	biggest customers (market share)
AGE OF HOUSEHOLDER			
Total households	**$9.76**	**100**	**100.0%**
Under age 25	7.47	77	5.4
Aged 25 to 34	13.78	141	26.6
Aged 35 to 44	8.17	84	19.5
Aged 45 to 54	11.66	119	21.9
Aged 55 to 64	8.16	84	9.8
Aged 65 to 74	6.09	62	7.2
Aged 75 or older	10.13	104	9.7
HOUSEHOLD INCOME			
Total households reporting income	**10.07**	**100**	**100.0**
Under $20,000	6.83	68	23.6
$20,000 to $29,999	7.94	79	11.5
$30,000 to $39,999	13.96	139	17.0
$40,000 to $49,999	12.26	122	11.4
$50,000 to $69,999	11.73	116	16.4
$70,000 or more	13.62	135	20.2
HOUSEHOLD TYPE			
Total households	**9.76**	**100**	**100.0**
Married couples	8.55	88	45.8
Married couples, no children	8.81	90	19.3
Married couples, with children	8.71	89	24.0
Oldest child under 6	13.65	140	7.2
Oldest child 6 to 17	7.85	80	11.7
Oldest child 18 or older	6.93	71	5.1
Single parent with child under 18	6.76	69	4.3
Single person	12.75	131	37.5
REGION			
Total households	**9.76**	**100**	**100.0**
Northeast	10.19	104	20.9
Midwest	10.05	103	24.6
South	10.60	109	37.9
West	7.66	78	16.7

Note: For definitions of best and biggest customers, see introduction or glossary.
Source: Calculations by New Strategist based on the 1997 Consumer Expenditure Survey

Maintenance and Repair Materials, Owned Homes

Best customers:
- Married couples with children
- Householders aged 35 to 44

Customer trends:
- Spending is likely to rise as more people become homeowners.

Married couples with children are the best customers of maintenance and repair materials for owned homes. Behind this higher spending is the need for housing additions and remodeling as families expand. Married couples with adult children at home spend 74 percent more than the average household on this item. Couples with children under age 6 spend 58 percent more than average, while those with school-aged children spend 50 percent more. Householders aged 35 to 44—most of them married, with children—are more likely than older householders to tackle repair and remodeling projects themselves rather than hire someone else to do the work.

Spending on maintenance and repair materials for owned homes is likely to rise along with the homeownership rate.

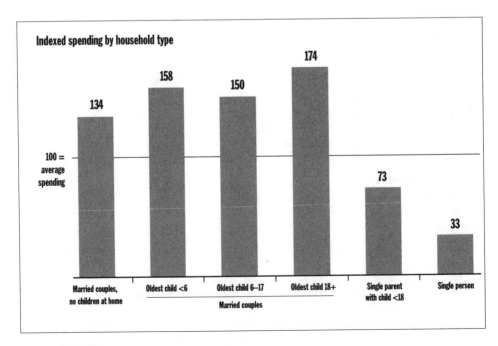

Indexed spending by household type

134	158	150	174	73	33

100 = average spending

Married couples, no children at home | Oldest child <6 | Oldest child 6–17 | Oldest child 18+ | Single parent with child <18 | Single person

Married couples

MAINTENANCE AND REPAIR MATERIALS, OWNED HOMES

Total household spending	$8,858,882,160
Average household spends	83.91

	average spending	best customers (index)	biggest customers (market share)
AGE OF HOUSEHOLDER			
Total households	**$83.91**	**100**	**100.0%**
Under age 25	9.52	11	0.8
Aged 25 to 34	65.26	78	14.7
Aged 35 to 44	114.86	137	31.8
Aged 45 to 54	104.74	125	22.9
Aged 55 to 64	105.57	126	14.7
Aged 65 to 74	79.79	95	10.9
Aged 75 or older	38.07	45	4.2
HOUSEHOLD INCOME			
Total households reporting income	**88.29**	**100**	**100.0**
Under $20,000	48.49	55	19.1
$20,000 to $29,999	74.92	85	12.4
$30,000 to $39,999	90.01	102	12.5
$40,000 to $49,999	101.86	115	10.8
$50,000 to $69,999	149.10	169	23.7
$70,000 or more	127.07	144	21.5
HOUSEHOLD TYPE			
Total households	**83.91**	**100**	**100.0**
Married couples	122.18	146	76.1
Married couples, no children	112.13	134	28.5
Married couples, with children	132.47	158	42.4
Oldest child under 6	132.84	158	8.1
Oldest child 6 to 17	125.60	150	21.8
Oldest child 18 or older	146.11	174	12.5
Single parent with child under 18	61.34	73	4.6
Single person	28.10	33	9.6
REGION			
Total households	**83.91**	**100**	**100.0**
Northeast	90.05	107	21.4
Midwest	108.66	129	30.9
South	63.46	76	26.4
West	83.88	100	21.2

Note: For definitions of best and biggest customers, see introduction or glossary.
Source: Calculations by New Strategist based on the 1997 Consumer Expenditure Survey

Maintenance and Repair Services, Owned Homes

Best customers:	• Householders aged 55 or older
	• Married couples without children
Customer trends:	• Spending should surge as affluent boomers hire help to maintain and repair their homes.

The best customers of maintenance and repair services for owned homes are householders aged 55 or older. Older householders whose children are grown can better afford to hire contractors to do repairs. Some are physically unable to maintain a home themselves. Householders aged 55 or older spend 36 to 49 percent more than the average household on maintenance and repair services for owned homes. Married couples without children at home, most of whom are older, spend 54 percent more than average.

With the baby-boom generation in its peak-earning years and about to enter the 55-and-older age group, spending on maintenance and repair services for owned homes should surge.

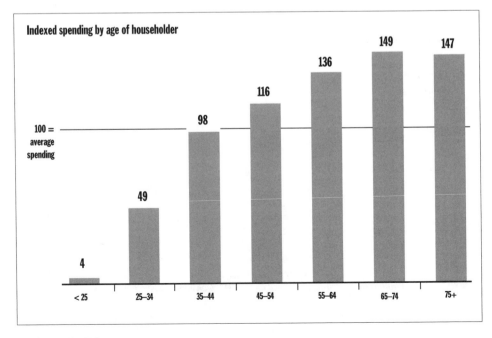

Indexed spending by age of householder

100 = average spending

| < 25 | 25–34 | 35–44 | 45–54 | 55–64 | 65–74 | 75+ |
| 4 | 49 | 98 | 116 | 136 | 149 | 147 |

MAINTENANCE AND REPAIR SERVICES, OWNED HOMES

Total household spending $38,599,641,360
Average household spends   365.61

	average spending	best customers (index)	biggest customers (market share)
AGE OF HOUSEHOLDER			
Total households	**$365.61**	**100**	**100.0%**
Under age 25	13.02	4	0.3
Aged 25 to 34	179.79	49	9.3
Aged 35 to 44	357.04	98	22.7
Aged 45 to 54	423.07	116	21.2
Aged 55 to 64	496.81	136	15.9
Aged 65 to 74	543.75	149	17.1
Aged 75 or older	535.78	147	13.6
HOUSEHOLD INCOME			
Total households reporting income	**369.97**	**100**	**100.0**
Under $20,000	194.15	52	18.3
$20,000 to $29,999	266.08	72	10.5
$30,000 to $39,999	370.76	100	12.3
$40,000 to $49,999	389.99	105	9.9
$50,000 to $69,999	375.30	101	14.2
$70,000 or more	862.99	233	34.9
HOUSEHOLD TYPE			
Total households	**365.61**	**100**	**100.0**
Married couples	466.13	127	66.7
Married couples, no children	562.34	154	32.8
Married couples, with children	421.91	115	31.0
Oldest child under 6	261.31	71	3.7
Oldest child 6 to 17	482.06	132	19.2
Oldest child 18 or older	415.11	114	8.2
Single parent with child under 18	122.62	34	2.1
Single person	277.66	76	21.8
REGION			
Total households	**365.61**	**100**	**100.0**
Northeast	416.40	114	22.8
Midwest	385.33	105	25.2
South	298.32	82	28.5
West	406.19	111	23.6

Note: For definitions of best and biggest customers, see introduction or glossary.
Source: Calculations by New Strategist based on the 1997 Consumer Expenditure Survey

Mortgage Interest

Best customers:
- Married couples with children under age 6
- Married couples with school-aged children
- Households with incomes of $70,000 or more

Customer trends:
- Spending is likely to increase because the homeownership rate is rising.

The longer people have owned their home, the less mortgage interest they pay. Married couples with children under age 18 pay more than average in mortgage interest because they are relatively young and haven't owned their home for long. Affluent households spend more than average because they tend to have larger mortgages. Households with incomes of $70,000 or more spend nearly three times as much as the average household on mortgage interest.

With homeownership at an all-time high and continuing to increase, spending by the average household on mortgage interest will rise.

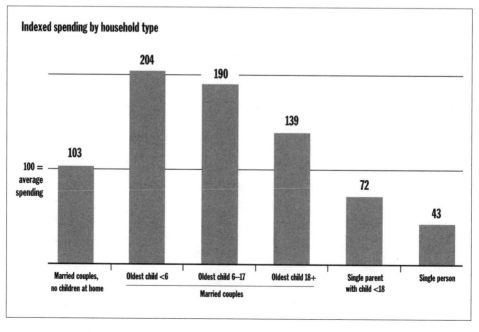

Indexed spending by household type

Married couples, no children at home	Oldest child <6	Oldest child 6–17	Oldest child 18+	Single parent with child <18	Single person
103	204	190	139	72	43

100 = average spending

Married couples

MORTGAGE INTEREST

Total household spending	$222,666,118,560
Average household spends	2,109.06

	average spending	best customers (index)	biggest customers (market share)
AGE OF HOUSEHOLDER			
Total households	**$2,109.06**	**100**	**100.0%**
Under age 25	219.56	10	0.7
Aged 25 to 34	2,328.75	110	20.8
Aged 35 to 44	3,291.39	156	36.3
Aged 45 to 54	3,152.04	149	27.4
Aged 55 to 64	1,778.23	84	9.8
Aged 65 to 74	716.27	34	3.9
Aged 75 or older	229.03	11	1.0
HOUSEHOLD INCOME			
Total households reporting income	**2,114.98**	**100**	**100.0**
Under $20,000	480.65	23	7.9
$20,000 to $29,999	999.28	47	6.9
$30,000 to $39,999	1,682.00	80	9.7
$40,000 to $49,999	2,506.43	119	11.1
$50,000 to $69,999	3,443.01	163	22.9
$70,000 or more	5,875.34	278	41.5
HOUSEHOLD TYPE			
Total households	**2,109.06**	**100**	**100.0**
Married couples	3,044.52	144	75.5
Married couples, no children	2,181.87	103	22.1
Married couples, with children	3,771.43	179	48.1
Oldest child under 6	4,298.65	204	10.5
Oldest child 6 to 17	3,997.87	190	27.6
Oldest child 18 or older	2,936.05	139	10.0
Single parent with child under 18	1,508.06	72	4.5
Single person	898.53	43	12.2
REGION			
Total households	**2,109.06**	**100**	**100.0**
Northeast	2,197.49	104	20.8
Midwest	1,834.37	87	20.8
South	1,709.06	81	28.3
West	2,991.84	142	30.1

Note: For definitions of best and biggest customers, see introduction or glossary.
Source: Calculations by New Strategist based on the 1997 Consumer Expenditure Survey

Natural Gas

Households in the Northeast and the Midwest are the best customers of natural gas. Those in the Northeast spend 32 percent more than the average household on natural gas, those in the Midwest, 48 percent. Married couples with adult children at home spend 36 percent more than average on natural gas, primarily because their houses tend to be larger.

Barring a hike in natural gas prices, spending on natural gas by the average household is not likely to rise much because of slow population growth in the regions where natural gas is most popular.

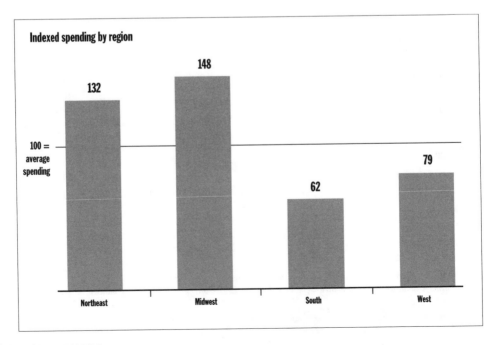

Indexed spending by region

Northeast	Midwest	South	West
132	148	62	79

100 = average spending

NATURAL GAS

Total household spending	$31,774,152,960
Average household spends	300.96

	average spending	best customers (index)	biggest customers (market share)
AGE OF HOUSEHOLDER			
Total households	**$300.96**	**100**	**100.0%**
Under age 25	87.79	29	2.1
Aged 25 to 34	263.63	88	16.5
Aged 35 to 44	326.66	109	25.2
Aged 45 to 54	320.97	107	19.5
Aged 55 to 64	342.15	114	13.3
Aged 65 to 74	341.20	113	13.0
Aged 75 or older	334.48	111	10.3
HOUSEHOLD INCOME			
Total households reporting income	**298.08**	**100**	**100.0**
Under $20,000	215.40	72	25.2
$20,000 to $29,999	279.14	94	13.7
$30,000 to $39,999	299.50	100	12.3
$40,000 to $49,999	337.35	113	10.6
$50,000 to $69,999	347.89	117	16.4
$70,000 or more	436.75	147	21.9
HOUSEHOLD TYPE			
Total households	**300.96**	**100**	**100.0**
Married couples	355.32	118	61.7
Married couples, no children	331.74	110	23.5
Married couples, with children	374.66	124	33.5
Oldest child under 6	316.30	105	5.4
Oldest child 6 to 17	378.64	126	18.3
Oldest child 18 or older	408.35	136	9.8
Single parent with child under 18	278.48	93	5.8
Single person	196.88	65	18.8
REGION			
Total households	**300.96**	**100**	**100.0**
Northeast	396.41	132	26.3
Midwest	445.77	148	35.4
South	185.32	62	21.5
West	238.21	79	16.8

Note: For definitions of best and biggest customers, see introduction or glossary.
Source: Calculations by New Strategist based on the 1997 Consumer Expenditure Survey

Property Management, Owned Homes

Best customers:
- Householders aged 65 or older
- Households in the West

Customer trends:
- Spending is likely to rise as boomers buy second homes.

The oldest householders are the best customers of property management for owned homes. Householders aged 75 or older spend twice as much as the average householder on property management. Those aged 65 to 74 spend 52 percent more than average. Many are snowbirds with winter and summer homes. Others own rental property and hire property managers to tend their buildings. Households in the West spend 49 percent more than average on this item.

As boomers enter their peak-earning years, the second-home market is likely to surge. This should boost spending on property management services.

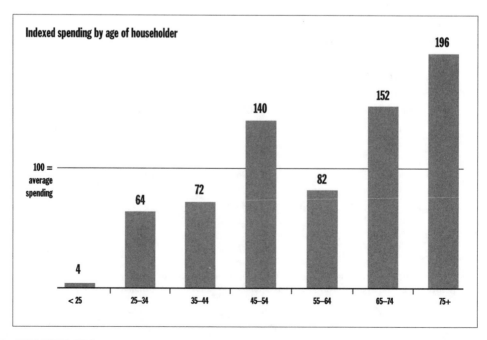

Indexed spending by age of householder

Age	Index
< 25	4
25–34	64
35–44	72
45–54	140
55–64	82
65–74	152
75+	196

100 = average spending

PROPERTY MANAGEMENT, OWNED HOMES

Total household spending $1,740,948,240
Average household spends   16.49

	average spending	best customers (index)	biggest customers (market share)
AGE OF HOUSEHOLDER			
Total households	**$16.49**	**100**	**100.0%**
Under age 25	0.72	4	0.3
Aged 25 to 34	10.59	64	12.1
Aged 35 to 44	11.80	72	16.6
Aged 45 to 54	23.14	140	25.7
Aged 55 to 64	13.56	82	9.6
Aged 65 to 74	24.99	152	17.4
Aged 75 or older	32.28	196	18.2
HOUSEHOLD INCOME			
Total households reporting income	**17.75**	**100**	**100.0**
Under $20,000	9.97	56	19.6
$20,000 to $29,999	11.44	64	9.4
$30,000 to $39,999	18.42	104	12.7
$40,000 to $49,999	16.02	90	8.4
$50,000 to $69,999	21.06	119	16.7
$70,000 or more	39.47	222	33.2
HOUSEHOLD TYPE			
Total households	**16.49**	**100**	**100.0**
Married couples	16.57	100	52.5
Married couples, no children	23.54	143	30.5
Married couples, with children	13.18	80	21.5
Oldest child under 6	22.05	134	6.9
Oldest child 6 to 17	11.59	70	10.2
Oldest child 18 or older	10.06	61	4.4
Single parent with child under 18	6.22	38	2.4
Single person	18.21	110	31.7
REGION			
Total households	**16.49**	**100**	**100.0**
Northeast	22.94	139	27.8
Midwest	11.15	68	16.2
South	11.51	70	24.4
West	24.58	149	31.7

Note: For definitions of best and biggest customers, see introduction or glossary.
Source: Calculations by New Strategist based on the 1997 Consumer Expenditure Survey

Property Security, Owned Homes

Best customers:	• Householders aged 65 or older
	• Married couples without children
	• Households in the Northeast
Customer trends:	• Spending will increase as the population ages.

Householders aged 65 or older are the best customers of property security for owned homes. Those aged 75 or older spend twice as much as the average household on property security, while householders aged 65 to 74 spend 83 percent more than average. Married couples without children at home, most of them older, spend 76 percent more than average on this item, while households in the Northeast spend 58 percent more.

As people age, they become more concerned with security. The expanding ranks of older Americans point to increased spending on property security.

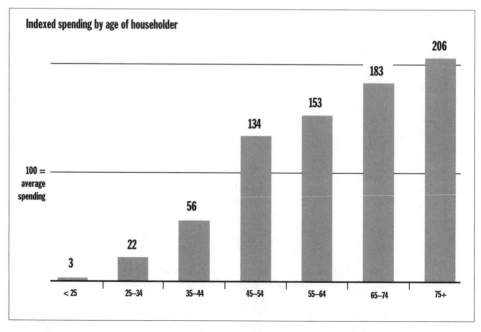

Indexed spending by age of householder

100 = average spending

< 25	25–34	35–44	45–54	55–64	65–74	75+
3	22	56	134	153	183	206

PROPERTY SECURITY, OWNED HOMES

Total household spending	$326,229,840
Average household spends	3.09

	average spending	best customers (index)	biggest customers (market share)
AGE OF HOUSEHOLDER			
Total households	**$3.09**	**100**	**100.0%**
Under age 25	0.09	3	0.2
Aged 25 to 34	0.69	22	4.2
Aged 35 to 44	1.74	56	13.1
Aged 45 to 54	4.15	134	24.6
Aged 55 to 64	4.73	153	17.9
Aged 65 to 74	5.65	183	21.0
Aged 75 or older	6.35	206	19.1
HOUSEHOLD INCOME			
Total households reporting income	**3.12**	**100**	**100.0**
Under $20,000	1.98	63	22.1
$20,000 to $29,999	2.01	64	9.4
$30,000 to $39,999	1.56	50	6.1
$40,000 to $49,999	3.89	125	11.7
$50,000 to $69,999	3.71	119	16.7
$70,000 or more	7.09	227	34.0
HOUSEHOLD TYPE			
Total households	**3.09**	**100**	**100.0**
Married couples	3.29	106	55.7
Married couples, no children	5.43	176	37.5
Married couples, with children	2.08	67	18.1
Oldest child under 6	2.47	80	4.1
Oldest child 6 to 17	2.16	70	10.2
Oldest child 18 or older	1.65	53	3.8
Single parent with child under 18	0.88	28	1.8
Single person	2.78	90	25.8
REGION			
Total households	**3.09**	**100**	**100.0**
Northeast	4.88	158	31.5
Midwest	1.29	42	10.0
South	2.80	91	31.6
West	3.90	126	26.8

Note: For definitions of best and biggest customers, see introduction or glossary.
Source: Calculations by New Strategist based on the 1997 Consumer Expenditure Survey

Property Taxes

Best customers:
- Married couples with school-aged or older children
- Households in the Northeast

Customer trends:
- Spending is not likely to rise much in the next few years because homeowners are resisting property tax hikes.

Households in the Northeast spend 62 percent more than the average household on property taxes. Higher home values in the region are one reason for this, as are higher tax rates. Married couples with adult children at home spend 53 percent more than average on property taxes, while those with school-aged children spend 43 percent more. Families with children tend to own larger and more expensive homes, which increases their property taxes.

Property taxes have risen sharply during the past few years, and homeowners are beginning to resist further hikes. Because of this resistance, spending on property taxes is unlikely to rise much in the next few years.

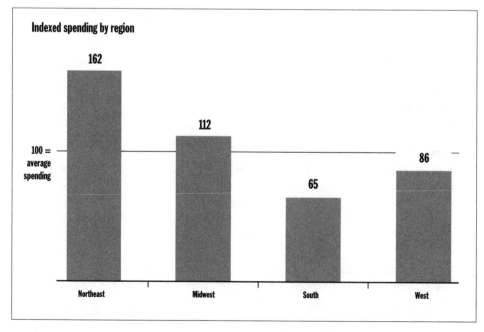

Indexed spending by region

- Northeast: 162
- Midwest: 112
- South: 65
- West: 86

100 = average spending

PROPERTY TAXES

Total household spending	$102,530,132,400
Average household spends	971.15

	average spending	best customers (index)	biggest customers (market share)
AGE OF HOUSEHOLDER			
Total households	**$971.15**	**100**	**100.0%**
Under age 25	100.95	10	0.7
Aged 25 to 34	638.84	66	12.4
Aged 35 to 44	1,053.52	108	25.2
Aged 45 to 54	1,302.73	134	24.6
Aged 55 to 64	1,195.34	123	14.4
Aged 65 to 74	1,197.12	123	14.1
Aged 75 or older	890.99	92	8.5
HOUSEHOLD INCOME			
Total households reporting income	**946.59**	**100**	**100.0**
Under $20,000	477.84	50	17.6
$20,000 to $29,999	639.70	68	9.9
$30,000 to $39,999	734.44	78	9.5
$40,000 to $49,999	989.89	105	9.8
$50,000 to $69,999	1,251.10	132	18.6
$70,000 or more	2,199.11	232	34.7
HOUSEHOLD TYPE			
Total households	**971.15**	**100**	**100.0**
Married couples	1,333.24	137	71.8
Married couples, no children	1,325.05	136	29.1
Married couples, with children	1,382.80	142	38.3
Oldest child under 6	1,225.16	126	6.5
Oldest child 6 to 17	1,389.11	143	20.8
Oldest child 18 or older	1,482.81	153	11.0
Single parent with child under 18	507.14	52	3.3
Single person	550.00	57	16.3
REGION			
Total households	**971.15**	**100**	**100.0**
Northeast	1,568.97	162	32.3
Midwest	1,087.81	112	26.8
South	629.73	65	22.6
West	838.44	86	18.3

Note: For definitions of best and biggest customers, see introduction or glossary.
Source: Calculations by New Strategist based on the 1997 Consumer Expenditure Survey

Rent

Best customers:
- Householders under age 35
- Single parents
- Households in the West

Customer trends:
- Spending is likely to rise as the young-adult population expands.

Young adults are the best customers of rental housing. Householders under age 25 spend 54 percent more than average on rent, while those aged 35 to 44 spend 67 percent more. Single parents spend 50 percent more than average on rent. Households in the West spend 39 percent more than average on this item. Expensive housing in the region not only drives up rental prices, it creates a larger proportion of renters.

Spending on rent by the average household is likely to rise as the young-adult population expands with the Millennial generation.

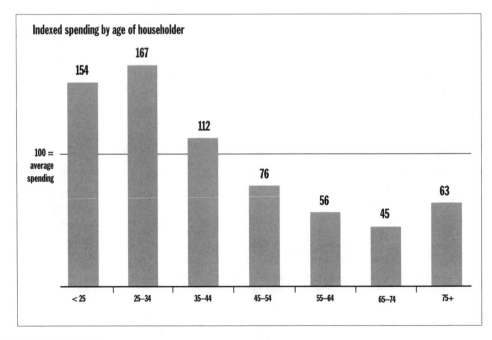

Indexed spending by age of householder

| < 25 | 25–34 | 35–44 | 45–54 | 55–64 | 65–74 | 75+ |
| 154 | 167 | 112 | 76 | 56 | 45 | 63 |

100 = average spending

RENT

Total household spending	$198,146,092,560		
Average household spends	1,876.81		

	average spending	best customers (index)	biggest customers (market share)
AGE OF HOUSEHOLDER			
Total households	**$1,876.81**	**100**	**100.0%**
Under age 25	2,882.42	154	10.9
Aged 25 to 34	3,143.34	167	31.6
Aged 35 to 44	2,103.55	112	26.1
Aged 45 to 54	1,422.79	76	13.9
Aged 55 to 64	1,042.51	56	6.5
Aged 65 to 74	846.89	45	5.2
Aged 75 or older	1,183.83	63	5.9
HOUSEHOLD INCOME			
Total households reporting income	**1,867.90**	**100**	**100.0**
Under $20,000	1,905.64	102	35.5
$20,000 to $29,999	2,278.20	122	17.8
$30,000 to $39,999	2,390.71	128	15.6
$40,000 to $49,999	2,039.40	109	10.2
$50,000 to $69,999	1,477.96	79	11.1
$70,000 or more	1,210.28	65	9.7
HOUSEHOLD TYPE			
Total households	**1,876.81**	**100**	**100.0**
Married couples	1,279.05	68	35.6
Married couples, no children	1,065.90	57	12.1
Married couples, with children	1,374.03	73	19.7
Oldest child under 6	2,110.92	112	5.8
Oldest child 6 to 17	1,401.78	75	10.9
Oldest child 18 or older	790.71	42	3.0
Single parent with child under 18	2,815.56	150	9.4
Single person	2,382.48	127	36.5
REGION			
Total households	**1,876.81**	**100**	**100.0**
Northeast	2,199.76	117	23.4
Midwest	1,393.21	74	17.7
South	1,572.11	84	29.2
West	2,617.53	139	29.6

Note: For definitions of best and biggest customers, see introduction or glossary.
Source: Calculations by New Strategist based on the 1997 Consumer Expenditure Survey

Telephone Service for Mobile Phone

Best customers:
- Householders aged 45 to 54
- Married couples with children
- Households in the South

Customer trends:
- Spending will surge as mobile phones become universally owned.

The best customers of mobile phones are families with children. Many families have more than one mobile phone so that children and parents can stay in touch. Married couples with children spend 53 percent more than the average household on mobile phones. Mobile phones have caught on big in the South. Households in the region spend 38 percent more than average on mobile phones.

Spending on mobile phone service will increase substantially as these items become universally owned.

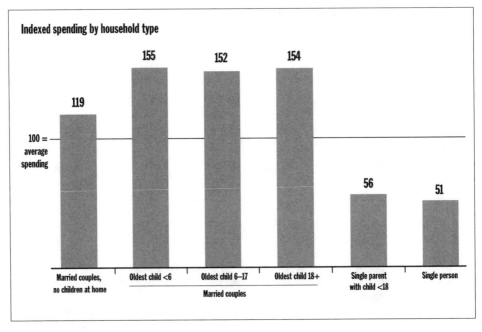

Indexed spending by household type

119	155	152	154	56	51
Married couples, no children at home	Oldest child <6	Oldest child 6–17	Oldest child 18+	Single parent with child <18	Single person
		Married couples			

100 = average spending

TELEPHONE SERVICE FOR MOBILE PHONE

Total household spending	$5,554,353,360
Average household spends	52.61

	average spending	best customers (index)	biggest customers (market share)
AGE OF HOUSEHOLDER			
Total households	**$52.61**	**100**	**100.0%**
Under age 25	20.65	39	2.8
Aged 25 to 34	63.80	121	22.9
Aged 35 to 44	64.98	124	28.7
Aged 45 to 54	73.93	141	25.7
Aged 55 to 64	59.83	114	13.3
Aged 65 to 74	25.39	48	5.5
Aged 75 or older	5.89	11	1.0
HOUSEHOLD INCOME			
Total households reporting income	**54.00**	**100**	**100.0**
Under $20,000	14.52	27	9.4
$20,000 to $29,999	34.10	63	9.2
$30,000 to $39,999	46.76	87	10.6
$40,000 to $49,999	57.82	107	10.0
$50,000 to $69,999	99.44	184	25.8
$70,000 or more	126.30	234	35.0
HOUSEHOLD TYPE			
Total households	**52.61**	**100**	**100.0**
Married couples	72.23	137	71.8
Married couples, no children	62.78	119	25.5
Married couples, with children	80.66	153	41.2
Oldest child under 6	81.39	155	8.0
Oldest child 6 to 17	80.19	152	22.2
Oldest child 18 or older	81.11	154	11.1
Single parent with child under 18	29.58	56	3.5
Single person	26.59	51	14.5
REGION			
Total households	**52.61**	**100**	**100.0**
Northeast	41.37	79	15.7
Midwest	44.61	85	20.3
South	72.42	138	48.0
West	39.62	75	16.0

Note: For definitions of best and biggest customers, see introduction or glossary.
Source: Calculations by New Strategist based on the 1997 Consumer Expenditure Survey

Telephone Service in Home City, excluding Mobile Phone

Best customers: • Married couples with adult children

Customer trends: • Spending is likely to rise as more households install additional phone lines for online use.

Spending on phone service does not vary much among demographic segments with one exception: household type. Married couples with adult children at home spend 32 percent more than the average household on telephone service. Behind this higher spending is that more adults use the telephone and, in some households, the need for an additional phone line.

With most households now owning a computer, a second phone line is becoming a necessity for those who spend a lot of time online. Rapidly rising Internet usage should boost spending on telephone service.

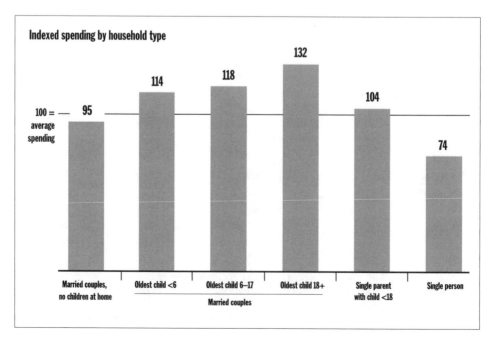

Indexed spending by household type

95	114	118	132	104	74

100 = average spending

Married couples, no children at home | Oldest child <6 | Oldest child 6–17 | Oldest child 18+ | Single parent with child <18 | Single person

Married couples

TELEPHONE SERVICE IN HOME CITY, EXCLUDING MOBILE PHONE

Total household spending $79,861,909,440
Average household spends 756.44

	average spending	best customers (index)	biggest customers (market share)
AGE OF HOUSEHOLDER			
Total households	**$756.44**	**100**	**100.0%**
Under age 25	528.99	70	5.0
Aged 25 to 34	829.57	110	20.7
Aged 35 to 44	856.35	113	26.3
Aged 45 to 54	877.67	116	21.3
Aged 55 to 64	782.37	103	12.1
Aged 65 to 74	601.41	80	9.1
Aged 75 or older	452.06	60	5.6
HOUSEHOLD INCOME			
Total households reporting income	**755.32**	**100**	**100.0**
Under $20,000	569.68	75	26.3
$20,000 to $29,999	708.03	94	13.7
$30,000 to $39,999	787.17	104	12.7
$40,000 to $49,999	801.39	106	9.9
$50,000 to $69,999	901.52	119	16.8
$70,000 or more	1,041.90	138	20.6
HOUSEHOLD TYPE			
Total households	**756.44**	**100**	**100.0**
Married couples	846.86	112	58.5
Married couples, no children	718.68	95	20.3
Married couples, with children	916.06	121	32.6
Oldest child under 6	858.59	114	5.8
Oldest child 6 to 17	896.34	118	17.2
Oldest child 18 or older	997.10	132	9.5
Single parent with child under 18	787.99	104	6.5
Single person	556.46	74	21.1
REGION			
Total households	**756.44**	**100**	**100.0**
Northeast	743.38	98	19.6
Midwest	733.54	97	23.2
South	766.56	101	35.4
West	777.87	103	21.8

Note: For definitions of best and biggest customers, see introduction or glossary.
Source: Calculations by New Strategist based on the 1997 Consumer Expenditure Survey

Trash Collection

Best customers:
- Married couples with school-aged or older children
- Households in the West

Customer trends:
- Spending will increase as it becomes more expensive to dispose of garbage.

The larger the household, the more trash it generates. Married couples with school-aged children spend 31 percent more than the average household on trash collection, while couples with adult children at home spend 33 percent more. Households in the West spend 38 percent more than average on this item.

The cost of garbage disposal is rising as the nation's landfills fill up and environmental regulations tighten. Consequently, spending on trash collection is likely to rise.

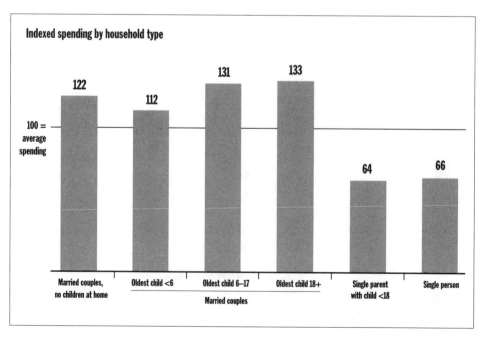

Indexed spending by household type

Married couples, no children at home	Oldest child <6	Oldest child 6–17	Oldest child 18+	Single parent with child <18	Single person
122	112	131	133	64	66

100 = average spending

Married couples

TRASH COLLECTION

Total household spending	$8,023,776,000	
Average household spends	76.00	

	average spending	best customers (index)	biggest customers (market share)
AGE OF HOUSEHOLDER			
Total households	**$76.00**	**100**	**100.0%**
Under age 25	14.39	19	1.3
Aged 25 to 34	58.54	77	14.5
Aged 35 to 44	81.47	107	24.9
Aged 45 to 54	93.56	123	22.6
Aged 55 to 64	88.39	116	13.6
Aged 65 to 74	83.53	110	12.6
Aged 75 or older	85.33	112	10.5
HOUSEHOLD INCOME			
Total households reporting income	**78.22**	**100**	**100.0**
Under $20,000	53.83	69	24.0
$20,000 to $29,999	70.48	90	13.2
$30,000 to $39,999	70.96	91	11.1
$40,000 to $49,999	82.68	106	9.9
$50,000 to $69,999	98.39	126	17.7
$70,000 or more	126.83	162	24.2
HOUSEHOLD TYPE			
Total households	**76.00**	**100**	**100.0**
Married couples	95.35	125	65.6
Married couples, no children	92.54	122	26.0
Married couples, with children	97.27	128	34.4
Oldest child under 6	84.97	112	5.8
Oldest child 6 to 17	99.78	131	19.1
Oldest child 18 or older	100.98	133	9.6
Single parent with child under 18	48.34	64	4.0
Single person	50.24	66	19.0
REGION			
Total households	**76.00**	**100**	**100.0**
Northeast	45.80	60	12.0
Midwest	74.46	98	23.4
South	76.72	101	35.2
West	104.93	138	29.3

Note: For definitions of best and biggest customers, see introduction or glossary.
Source: Calculations by New Strategist based on the 1997 Consumer Expenditure Survey

Vacation Homes, Owned

Best customers:	• **Householders aged 45 to 64**
	• **Households with incomes of $70,000 or more**
	• **Married couples without children**
	• **Married couples with adult children**
Customer trends:	• **Spending should surge as affluent boomers buy second homes.**

Not surprisingly, the affluent are the best customers of vacation homes. Households with incomes of $70,000 or more spend four times as much as the average household on owned vacation homes. Householders aged 45 to 54, who are in their peak earning years, spend 74 percent more than average, while those aged 55 to 64 spend 87 percent more. Married couples without children at home and those with adult children in the household spend nearly twice as much as average. Most of these households are headed by older people.

Spending on this item is likely to surge as affluent boomers invest in second homes for fun and profit.

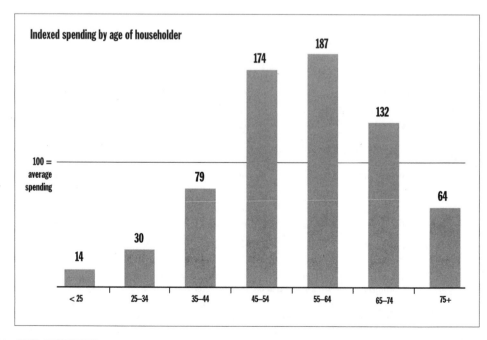

Indexed spending by age of householder

<25	25–34	35–44	45–54	55–64	65–74	75+
14	30	79	174	187	132	64

100 = average spending

VACATION HOMES, OWNED

Total household spending $14,114,455,440
Average household spends   133.69

	average spending	best customers (index)	biggest customers (market share)
AGE OF HOUSEHOLDER			
Total households	$133.69	100	100.0%
Under age 25	18.16	14	1.0
Aged 25 to 34	40.20	30	5.7
Aged 35 to 44	105.91	79	18.4
Aged 45 to 54	232.71	174	31.9
Aged 55 to 64	250.32	187	21.8
Aged 65 to 74	177.11	132	15.2
Aged 75 or older	86.23	64	6.0
HOUSEHOLD INCOME			
Total households reporting income	135.60	100	100.0
Under $20,000	33.21	24	8.5
$20,000 to $29,999	67.98	50	7.3
$30,000 to $39,999	56.14	41	5.1
$40,000 to $49,999	118.39	87	8.2
$50,000 to $69,999	116.71	86	12.1
$70,000 or more	533.74	394	58.8
HOUSEHOLD TYPE			
Total households	133.69	100	100.0
Married couples	207.77	155	81.3
Married couples, no children	261.26	195	41.7
Married couples, with children	173.52	130	34.9
Oldest child under 6	35.61	27	1.4
Oldest child 6 to 17	181.44	136	19.7
Oldest child 18 or older	256.14	192	13.8
Single parent with child under 18	74.93	56	3.5
Single person	50.17	38	10.8
REGION			
Total households	133.69	100	100.0
Northeast	178.01	133	26.6
Midwest	101.18	76	18.1
South	94.86	71	24.8
West	192.36	144	30.6

Note: For definitions of best and biggest customers, see introduction or glossary.
Source: Calculations by New Strategist based on the 1997 Consumer Expenditure Survey

Water and Sewerage Maintenance

Best customers:	• Married couples with school-aged or older children
Customer trends:	• Increases are likely as clean water becomes more expensive and aging water and sewer systems must be replaced.

The more people live in a household, the more water the household uses. This is especially true if some of those people are teenagers or young adults. Married couples with school-aged children spend 41 percent more than the average household on water and sewerage maintenance. Married couples with adult children at home spend 58 percent more.

Spending on water and sewerage maintenance is likely to rise as clean water becomes more expensive and aging sewerage systems must be replaced.

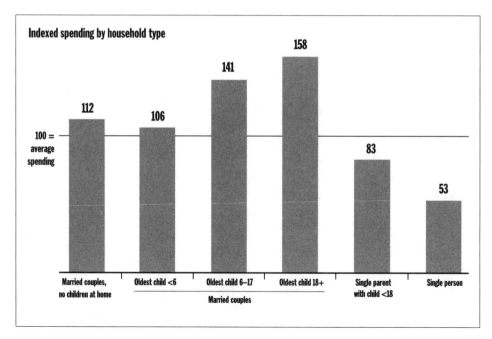

Indexed spending by household type

- Married couples, no children at home: 112
- Oldest child <6: 106
- Oldest child 6–17: 141
- Oldest child 18+: 158
- Single parent with child <18: 83
- Single person: 53

100 = average spending

Married couples

WATER AND SEWERAGE MAINTENANCE

Total household spending | $21,883,793,280
Average household spends | 207.28

	average spending	best customers (index)	biggest customers (market share)
AGE OF HOUSEHOLDER			
Total households	$207.28	100	100.0%
Under age 25	40.11	19	1.4
Aged 25 to 34	158.88	77	14.5
Aged 35 to 44	237.82	115	26.7
Aged 45 to 54	260.01	125	23.0
Aged 55 to 64	237.58	115	13.4
Aged 65 to 74	222.19	107	12.3
Aged 75 or older	196.56	95	8.8
HOUSEHOLD INCOME			
Total households reporting income	210.76	100	100.0
Under $20,000	136.74	65	22.6
$20,000 to $29,999	184.46	88	12.8
$30,000 to $39,999	198.65	94	11.5
$40,000 to $49,999	230.77	109	10.2
$50,000 to $69,999	276.88	131	18.4
$70,000 or more	344.20	163	24.4
HOUSEHOLD TYPE			
Total households	207.28	100	100.0
Married couples	267.66	129	67.5
Married couples, no children	231.37	112	23.8
Married couples, with children	288.20	139	37.4
Oldest child under 6	219.23	106	5.4
Oldest child 6 to 17	292.95	141	20.6
Oldest child 18 or older	327.93	158	11.4
Single parent with child under 18	171.75	83	5.2
Single person	110.74	53	15.3
REGION			
Total households	207.28	100	100.0
Northeast	165.75	80	16.0
Midwest	200.40	97	23.1
South	211.67	102	35.6
West	246.88	119	25.3

Note: For definitions of best and biggest customers, see introduction or glossary.
Source: Calculations by New Strategist based on the 1997 Consumer Expenditure Survey

Chapter 17.

Tobacco Products

Tobacco Products

The average household spent $263.69 on tobacco products in 1997, more than it spent on reading material, computers, or alcoholic beverages. Between 1987 and 1997, spending on tobacco products fell 19.5 percent, after adjusting for inflation as cigarette prices rose and many people gave up smoking altogether.

Spending on tobacco products will continue to decline as public smoking becomes increasingly restricted, tobacco becomes more expensive, and more smokers give up the habit.

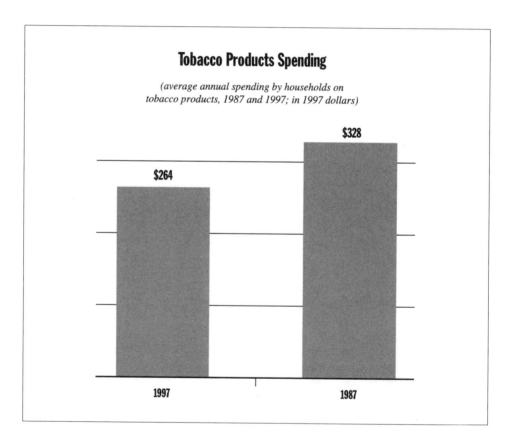

Tobacco Products Spending

(average annual spending by households on tobacco products, 1987 and 1997; in 1997 dollars)

$264 — 1997

$328 — 1987

Tobacco Products Spending

(average annual spending of households on tobacco products, and percent distribution of spending by type, 1997)

Total spending on tobacco products	**$263.69**	**100.0%**
Cigarettes	232.31	88.1
Tobacco products, except cigarettes	28.78	10.9
Smoking accessories	2.60	1.0

Cigarettes

Best customers:
- Householders aged 35 to 44
- Married couples with adult children

Customer trends:
- Increased cigarette prices are likely to prompt some people to kick the habit, resulting in a decline in spending.

People aged 35 to 44 are most likely to smoke, which is why they spend more on cigarettes. Householders in this age group spend 29 percent more than the average household on cigarettes, and account for 30 percent of the market. Married couples with adult children at home spend 39 percent more than average on cigarettes, largely because there are more adults in these households.

The proportion of people who smoke had been falling for decades, but has now leveled off. Recent increases in cigarette prices are likely to prompt some people to kick the habit, however, resulting in less spending.

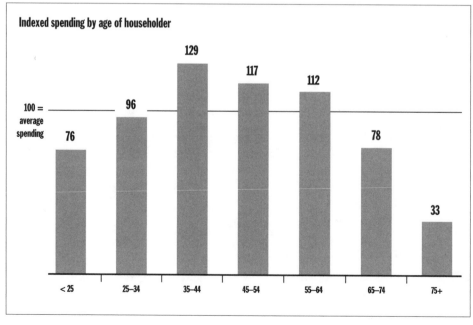

Indexed spending by age of householder

< 25	25–34	35–44	45–54	55–64	65–74	75+
76	96	129	117	112	78	33

100 = average spending

CIGARETTES

Total household spending	$24,526,360,560
Average household spends	232.31

	average spending	best customers (index)	biggest customers (market share)
AGE OF HOUSEHOLDER			
Total households	**$232.31**	**100**	**100.0%**
Under age 25	177.48	76	5.4
Aged 25 to 34	223.58	96	18.2
Aged 35 to 44	298.85	129	29.9
Aged 45 to 54	270.93	117	21.4
Aged 55 to 64	260.95	112	13.1
Aged 65 to 74	181.97	78	9.0
Aged 75 or older	75.73	33	3.0
HOUSEHOLD INCOME			
Total households reporting income	**237.35**	**100**	**100.0**
Under $20,000	214.94	91	31.5
$20,000 to $29,999	240.98	102	14.8
$30,000 to $39,999	284.83	120	14.7
$40,000 to $49,999	253.61	107	10.0
$50,000 to $69,999	264.35	111	15.6
$70,000 or more	211.65	89	13.3
HOUSEHOLD TYPE			
Total households	**232.31**	**100**	**100.0**
Married couples	251.23	108	56.5
Married couples, no children	209.24	90	19.2
Married couples, with children	266.15	115	30.8
Oldest child under 6	195.85	84	4.3
Oldest child 6 to 17	262.84	113	16.5
Oldest child 18 or older	323.16	139	10.0
Single parent with child under 18	179.67	77	4.9
Single person	150.58	65	18.6
REGION			
Total households	**232.31**	**100**	**100.0**
Northeast	236.07	102	20.3
Midwest	273.24	118	28.1
South	230.20	99	34.6
West	186.21	80	17.0

Note: For definitions of best and biggest customers, see introduction or glossary.
Source: Calculations by New Strategist based on the 1997 Consumer Expenditure Survey

Smoking Accessories

Best customers:
- Householders aged 45 to 54
- Householders aged 25 to 34
- Households with incomes of $30,000 to $39,999

Customer trends:
- Some increase is possible if more people roll their own in response to rising cigarette prices.

This category includes cigarette papers and pipes. The best customers of these products are households with incomes of $30,000 to $39,999, which spend twice the average amount on smoking accessories. Householders aged 45 to 54 spend 80 percent more than average, while those aged 25 to 34 spend 52 percent more.

Cigarette prices have taken a huge jump recently. This has prompted some smokers to try rolling their own. In response to rising prices, however, it's likely that more people will give up cigarettes entirely rather than resort to making their own. Consequently, there will be little change in spending on this category.

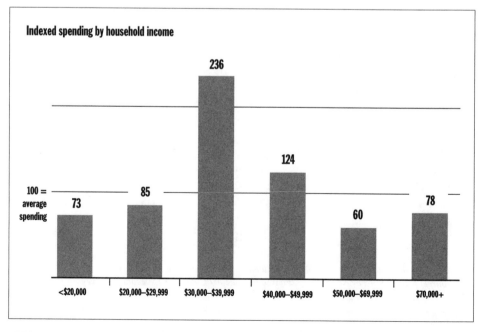

Indexed spending by household income

73	85	236	124	60	78
<$20,000	$20,000–$29,999	$30,000–$39,999	$40,000–$49,999	$50,000–$69,999	$70,000+

100 = average spending

SMOKING ACCESSORIES

Total household spending	$274,497,600		
Average household spends	2.60		

	average spending	best customers (index)	biggest customers (market share)
AGE OF HOUSEHOLDER			
Total households	**$2.60**	**100**	**100.0%**
Under age 25	3.96	152	10.8
Aged 25 to 34	1.72	66	12.5
Aged 35 to 44	2.15	83	19.2
Aged 45 to 54	4.68	180	33.0
Aged 55 to 64	1.49	57	6.7
Aged 65 to 74	3.26	125	14.4
Aged 75 or older	0.91	35	3.3
HOUSEHOLD INCOME			
Total households reporting income	**2.35**	**100**	**100.0**
Under $20,000	1.72	73	25.5
$20,000 to $29,999	2.00	85	12.4
$30,000 to $39,999	5.54	236	28.8
$40,000 to $49,999	2.92	124	11.6
$50,000 to $69,999	1.42	60	8.5
$70,000 or more	1.83	78	11.6
HOUSEHOLD TYPE			
Total households	**2.60**	**100**	**100.0**
Married couples	2.20	85	44.2
Married couples, no children	2.99	115	24.5
Married couples, with children	1.65	63	17.1
Oldest child under 6	1.09	42	2.2
Oldest child 6 to 17	1.43	55	8.0
Oldest child 18 or older	2.53	97	7.0
Single parent with child under 18	1.23	47	3.0
Single person	1.94	75	21.4
REGION			
Total households	**2.60**	**100**	**100.0**
Northeast	1.96	75	15.1
Midwest	2.75	106	25.3
South	2.57	99	34.5
West	3.06	118	25.0

Note: For definitions of best and biggest customers, see introduction or glossary.
Source: Calculations by New Strategist based on the 1997 Consumer Expenditure Survey

Tobacco Products, except Cigarettes

Best customers:
- Married couples with preschoolers
- Married couples with adult children
- Households in the South

Customer trends:
- Flat or declining spending as cigars lose some of their cachet due to health concerns.

This category includes cigars, chewing tobacco, and pipe tobacco. The best customers of these products are householders aged 25 to 34 and householders aged 45 to 54, spending one-quarter more than average. Married couples with preschoolers spend 63 percent more than average on tobacco products, while those with adult children at home spend 38 percent more. Spending by households in the South is 23 percent higher than average. Southerners have long been more likely than people living in other regions to indulge in snuff and chewing tobacco.

During the past few years, cigars have enjoyed a surprising popularity among young to middle-aged men, but this is unlikely to last. The cigar craze will lose steam as health concerns reassert themselves. Spending on tobacco products other than cigarettes is likely to be flat or decline in the coming years.

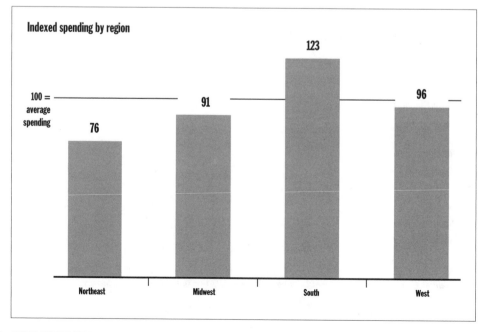

Indexed spending by region

Northeast	Midwest	South	West
76	91	123	96

100 = average spending

TOBACCO PRODUCTS, EXCEPT CIGARETTES

Total household spending $3,038,477,280
Average household spends   28.78

	average spending	best customers (index)	biggest customers (market share)
AGE OF HOUSEHOLDER			
Total households	**$28.78**	**100**	**100.0%**
Under age 25	18.43	64	4.5
Aged 25 to 34	35.77	124	23.4
Aged 35 to 44	28.06	97	22.7
Aged 45 to 54	36.40	126	23.2
Aged 55 to 64	29.30	102	11.9
Aged 65 to 74	27.29	95	10.9
Aged 75 or older	10.49	36	3.4
HOUSEHOLD INCOME			
Total households reporting income	**31.47**	**100**	**100.0**
Under $20,000	22.10	70	24.5
$20,000 to $29,999	20.46	65	9.5
$30,000 to $39,999	30.51	97	11.9
$40,000 to $49,999	29.89	95	8.9
$50,000 to $69,999	50.26	160	22.4
$70,000 or more	48.20	153	22.9
HOUSEHOLD TYPE			
Total households	**28.78**	**100**	**100.0**
Married couples	39.91	139	72.5
Married couples, no children	36.35	126	27.0
Married couples, with children	36.53	127	34.1
Oldest child under 6	46.85	163	8.4
Oldest child 6 to 17	31.37	109	15.9
Oldest child 18 or older	39.61	138	9.9
Single parent with child under 18	6.68	23	1.5
Single person	16.95	59	16.9
REGION			
Total households	**28.78**	**100**	**100.0**
Northeast	21.79	76	15.1
Midwest	26.10	91	21.7
South	35.30	123	42.8
West	27.65	96	20.4

Note: For definitions of best and biggest customers, see introduction or glossary.
Source: Calculations by New Strategist based on the 1997 Consumer Expenditure Survey

Chapter 18.

Transportation

Transportation

The average household spent $6,456.86 on transportation in 1997, making it one of the biggest expenses. Spending on transportation fell 0.6 percent between 1987 and 1997, despite rising prices for new vehicles and automotive insurance.

Transportation spending remained fairly stable between 1987 and 1997 because the price of gasoline (which accounts for the largest share of transportation spending) fell during the decade. Spending on gasoline and motor oil was 12.5 percent lower in 1997 than in 1987, after adjusting for inflation. Spending on vehicle finance charges also fell, down 26 percent as interest rates declined. And Americans increasingly purchased used cars and trucks, which also limited growth in transportation spending.

The best customers of most transportation categories are the largest households because they have the greatest number of vehicles. In the years ahead, transportation spending will rise as the children of baby boomers reach driving age. It's likely that many boomer households will buy cars for their kids, spending more on vehicles, insurance, and gasoline.

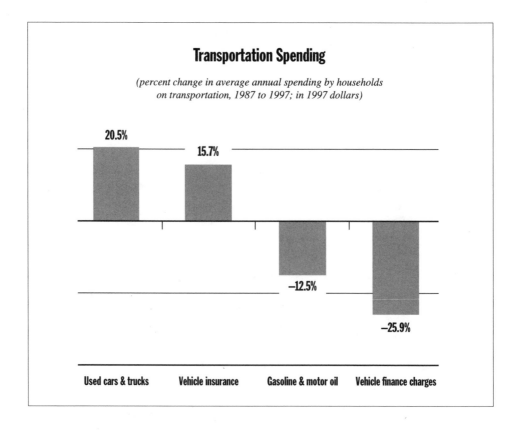

Transportation Spending

(percent change in average annual spending by households on transportation, 1987 to 1997; in 1997 dollars)

Used cars & trucks	Vehicle insurance	Gasoline & motor oil	Vehicle finance charges
20.5%	15.7%	−12.5%	−25.9%

Transportation Spending

(average annual spending of households on transportation, and percent distribution of spending by type, 1997)

Total spending on transportation	**$6,456.86**	**100.0%**
Gasoline and motor oil	1,087.42	16.8
Cars, used	895.31	13.9
Insurance, vehicle	754.99	11.7
Cars, new	700.22	10.8
Vehicle maintenance and repairs	681.62	10.6
Trucks, used	568.22	8.8
Trucks, new	528.67	8.2
Finance charges, vehicle	292.81	4.5
Car lease payments	180.25	2.8
Truck lease payments	109.97	1.7
Mass transit, intracity fares	55.77	0.9
Car rental	34.51	0.5
Parking fees in home city	24.37	0.4
Taxi fares and limousine service	9.51	0.1
Automobile service clubs	8.19	0.1
Towing charges	5.04	0.1

Note: Numbers will not add to total because not all categories are shown, including airline fares; bus fares, intercity; train fares, intercity; ship fares; and out-of-town transportation costs which are in the Travel chapter.

Automobile Service Clubs

Best customers:
- Householders aged 45 to 74
- Married couples without children
- Married couples with adult children
- Households in the West

Customer trends:
- Spending is likely to decline because automotive manufacturers and credit card companies are offering automotive services, luring away customers.

Older householders are the best customers of automobile service clubs, especially those with adult children at home. Householders aged 45 to 74 spend 31 to 47 percent more than the average household on automobile service clubs. Married couples with adult children at home spend 52 percent more than average on this item, while those without children, most of whom are older, spend 44 percent more. Households in the West, where the car culture is more prevalent, spend 39 percent more than average.

Auto manufacturers and credit card companies are offering many of the same services as automobile service clubs, luring younger generations away from this product. Because of growing competition, spending on automobile service clubs is likely to decline.

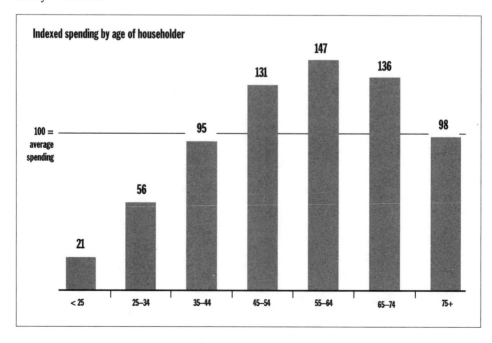

Indexed spending by age of householder

100 = average spending

< 25	25–34	35–44	45–54	55–64	65–74	75+
21	56	95	131	147	136	98

AUTOMOBILE SERVICE CLUBS

Total household spending	$864,667,440		
Average household spends	8.19		

	average spending	best customers (index)	biggest customers (market share)
AGE OF HOUSEHOLDER			
Total households	**$8.19**	**100**	**100.0%**
Under age 25	1.72	21	1.5
Aged 25 to 34	4.62	56	10.6
Aged 35 to 44	7.75	95	22.0
Aged 45 to 54	10.72	131	24.0
Aged 55 to 64	12.07	147	17.2
Aged 65 to 74	11.12	136	15.6
Aged 75 or older	8.05	98	9.1
HOUSEHOLD INCOME			
Total households reporting income	**8.68**	**100**	**100.0**
Under $20,000	4.61	53	18.5
$20,000 to $29,999	6.75	78	11.4
$30,000 to $39,999	7.54	87	10.6
$40,000 to $49,999	11.02	127	11.9
$50,000 to $69,999	10.08	116	16.3
$70,000 or more	18.22	210	31.4
HOUSEHOLD TYPE			
Total households	**8.19**	**100**	**100.0**
Married couples	10.25	125	65.4
Married couples, no children	11.79	144	30.7
Married couples, with children	9.28	113	30.5
Oldest child under 6	6.81	83	4.3
Oldest child 6 to 17	8.59	105	15.3
Oldest child 18 or older	12.44	152	10.9
Single parent with child under 18	3.28	40	2.5
Single person	6.19	76	21.7
REGION			
Total households	**8.19**	**100**	**100.0**
Northeast	8.84	108	21.6
Midwest	8.57	105	25.0
South	5.63	69	24.0
West	11.38	139	29.5

Note: For definitions of best and biggest customers, see introduction or glossary.
Source: Calculations by New Strategist based on the 1997 Consumer Expenditure Survey

Car Lease Payments

Best customers:
- Households with incomes of $70,000 or more
- Householders aged 45 to 54
- Married couples with adult children

Customer trends:
- Spending is likely to rise as more people opt for this payment method and as the children of boomers grow up and acquire their first cars.

The affluent are most likely to lease automobiles. Households with incomes of $70,000 or more spend three times as much as the average household on car lease payments, and account for 46 percent of the market. Householders aged 45 to 54 spend 66 percent more than average because they are in their peak-earning years. Married couples with adult children at home, who tend to have more cars than the average household, spend more than twice the average on this item.

Spending on car leases is likely to rise as more people opt for this payment method and as the children of boomers grow up and acquire their first cars.

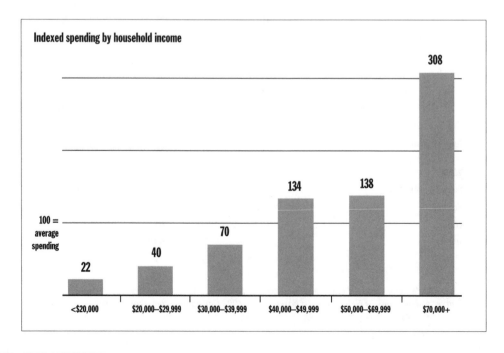

Indexed spending by household income

22	40	70	134	138	308
<$20,000	$20,000–$29,999	$30,000–$39,999	$40,000–$49,999	$50,000–$69,999	$70,000+

100 = average spending

CAR LEASE PAYMENTS

Total household spending $19,030,074,000
Average household spends   180.25

	average spending	best customers (index)	biggest customers (market share)
AGE OF HOUSEHOLDER			
Total households	**$180.25**	**100**	**100.0%**
Under age 25	66.78	37	2.6
Aged 25 to 34	196.43	109	20.6
Aged 35 to 44	179.81	100	23.2
Aged 45 to 54	298.93	166	30.4
Aged 55 to 64	189.55	105	12.3
Aged 65 to 74	93.68	52	6.0
Aged 75 or older	96.62	54	5.0
HOUSEHOLD INCOME			
Total households reporting income	**171.51**	**100**	**100.0**
Under $20,000	38.30	22	7.8
$20,000 to $29,999	68.32	40	5.8
$30,000 to $39,999	119.59	70	8.5
$40,000 to $49,999	229.78	134	12.5
$50,000 to $69,999	236.62	138	19.4
$70,000 or more	527.55	308	46.0
HOUSEHOLD TYPE			
Total households	**180.25**	**100**	**100.0**
Married couples	248.98	138	72.2
Married couples, no children	214.08	119	25.3
Married couples, with children	279.98	155	41.8
Oldest child under 6	301.29	167	8.6
Oldest child 6 to 17	207.32	115	16.7
Oldest child 18 or older	411.71	228	16.4
Single parent with child under 18	92.81	51	3.2
Single person	87.02	48	13.9
REGION			
Total households	**180.25**	**100**	**100.0**
Northeast	281.87	156	31.2
Midwest	168.85	94	22.4
South	121.47	67	23.5
West	194.07	108	22.9

Note: For definitions of best and biggest customers, see introduction or glossary.
Source: Calculations by New Strategist based on the 1997 Consumer Expenditure Survey

Car Rental

(includes spending on car rentals while on out-of-town trips, also shown separately in the Travel chapter)

Best customers: • Households with incomes of $70,000 or more
• Householders aged 45 to 64
• Married couples with adult children

Customer trends: • Spending will rise as boomers enter the peak-traveling age groups.

The affluent spend more on rental cars than anyone else. Households with incomes of $70,000 or more spend three times as much as the average household on rental cars, accounting for 48 percent of the market. Householders aged 45 to 64 spend 41 to 56 percent more on this item because they are in their peak-earning and -traveling years. Married couples with adult children at home spend 54 percent more than average on this item.

Most people rent cars while on out-of-town trips. As boomers enter the ages at which people travel the most, spending on car rentals should rise.

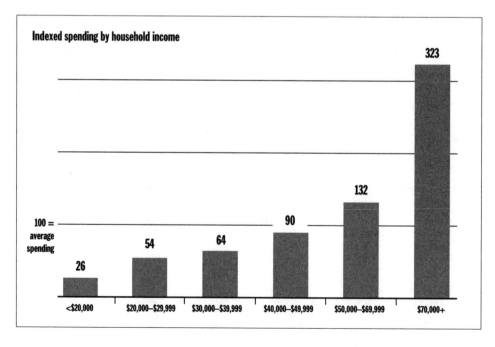

Indexed spending by household income

26	54	64	90	132	323
<$20,000	$20,000–$29,999	$30,000–$39,999	$40,000–$49,999	$50,000–$69,999	$70,000+

100 = average spending

CAR RENTAL

Total household spending	$3,643,427,760
Average household spends	34.51

	average spending	best customers (index)	biggest customers (market share)
AGE OF HOUSEHOLDER			
Total households	**$34.51**	**100**	**100.0%**
Under age 25	6.62	19	1.4
Aged 25 to 34	34.47	100	18.8
Aged 35 to 44	36.22	105	24.4
Aged 45 to 54	53.87	156	28.6
Aged 55 to 64	48.68	141	16.5
Aged 65 to 74	17.77	51	5.9
Aged 75 or older	16.39	47	4.4
HOUSEHOLD INCOME			
Total households reporting income	**34.32**	**100**	**100.0**
Under $20,000	8.91	26	9.0
$20,000 to $29,999	18.54	54	7.9
$30,000 to $39,999	22.11	64	7.9
$40,000 to $49,999	30.90	90	8.4
$50,000 to $69,999	45.29	132	18.5
$70,000 or more	110.74	323	48.2
HOUSEHOLD TYPE			
Total households	**34.51**	**100**	**100.0**
Married couples	44.64	129	67.6
Married couples, no children	47.48	138	29.4
Married couples, with children	42.68	124	33.2
Oldest child under 6	34.92	101	5.2
Oldest child 6 to 17	40.23	117	17.0
Oldest child 18 or older	53.22	154	11.1
Single parent with child under 18	14.11	41	2.6
Single person	23.54	68	19.6
REGION			
Total households	**34.51**	**100**	**100.0**
Northeast	41.66	121	24.1
Midwest	26.67	77	18.5
South	23.82	69	24.1
West	44.18	128	27.2

Note: For definitions of best and biggest customers, see introduction or glossary.
Source: Calculations by New Strategist based on the 1997 Consumer Expenditure Survey

Cars, New

Best customers:	• Householders aged 45 to 54
	• Married couples without children
	• Married couples with children under age 6
Customer trends:	• Spending on new cars will decline as trucks capture more of the young-adult market, leasing grows in popularity, and car buyers opt for used cars.

The new car market faces stiff competition from the growing popularity of trucks—especially among younger adults. In addition, the rise of leasing has flooded the market with high-quality used cars, siphoning off customers. Consequently, the buyers of new cars are getting older. Among age groups, householders aged 45 to 64 are the only ones who spend more than average on new cars. Couples without children at home, most of whom are older, spend 51 percent more than average on new cars. Married couples with preschoolers spend 72 percent more than average on this item.

Spending on new cars is likely to decline as leasing becomes more popular, as trucks capture more buyers, and as the pool of high-quality used cars grows.

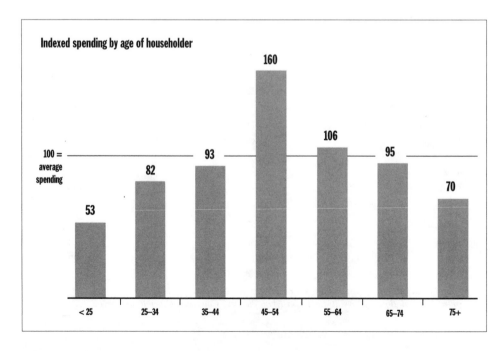

Indexed spending by age of householder

100 = average spending

< 25	25–34	35–44	45–54	55–64	65–74	75+
53	82	93	160	106	95	70

CARS, NEW

Total household spending	$73,926,426,720
Average household spends	700.22

	average spending	best customers (index)	biggest customers (market share)
AGE OF HOUSEHOLDER			
Total households	**$700.22**	**100**	**100.0%**
Under age 25	368.01	53	3.7
Aged 25 to 34	572.99	82	15.4
Aged 35 to 44	653.04	93	21.7
Aged 45 to 54	1,118.89	160	29.3
Aged 55 to 64	744.40	106	12.4
Aged 65 to 74	668.54	95	11.0
Aged 75 or older	489.12	70	6.5
HOUSEHOLD INCOME			
Total households reporting income	**748.92**	**100**	**100.0**
Under $20,000	219.44	29	10.2
$20,000 to $29,999	717.48	96	14.0
$30,000 to $39,999	797.95	107	13.0
$40,000 to $49,999	893.55	119	11.2
$50,000 to $69,999	803.95	107	15.1
$70,000 or more	1,831.06	244	36.5
HOUSEHOLD TYPE			
Total households	**700.22**	**100**	**100.0**
Married couples	906.73	129	67.7
Married couples, no children	1,054.06	151	32.1
Married couples, with children	862.05	123	33.1
Oldest child under 6	1,206.01	172	8.9
Oldest child 6 to 17	820.30	117	17.0
Oldest child 18 or older	700.46	100	7.2
Single parent with child under 18	530.64	76	4.8
Single person	488.50	70	20.0
REGION			
Total households	**700.22**	**100**	**100.0**
Northeast	574.00	82	16.4
Midwest	687.86	98	23.5
South	809.05	116	40.3
West	654.08	93	19.8

Note: For definitions of best and biggest customers, see introduction or glossary.
Source: Calculations by New Strategist based on the 1997 Consumer Expenditure Survey

Cars, Used

Best customers:
- Householders aged 25 to 34
- Married couples with adult children

Customer trends:
- Spending is likely to rise as the children of boomers grow up and acquire their first cars.

The best customers of used cars are parents buying vehicles for their teenaged or young-adult children. Married couples with adult children at home spend twice as much as the average household on used cars. Householders aged 25 to 34 spend 36 percent more than average on this item.

The quality of used cars has improved as leasing has become more popular. Spending on used cars is likely to increase—especially as the children of boomers get their driver's license and acquire a car of their own.

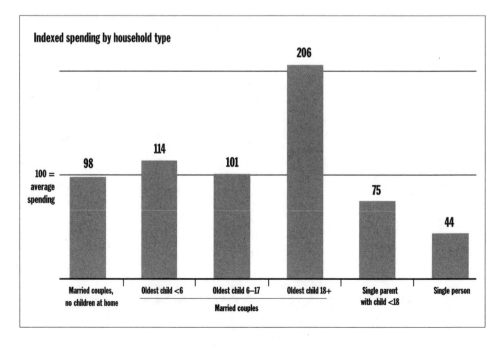

Indexed spending by household type

			206		
98	114	101		75	44
Married couples, no children at home	Oldest child <6	Oldest child 6–17	Oldest child 18+	Single parent with child <18	Single person
		Married couples			

100 = average spending

CARS, USED

Total household spending $94,523,248,560
Average household spends   895.31

	average spending	best customers (index)	biggest customers (market share)
AGE OF HOUSEHOLDER			
Total households	**$895.31**	**100**	**100.0%**
Under age 25	826.28	92	6.6
Aged 25 to 34	1,213.91	136	25.6
Aged 35 to 44	881.13	98	22.9
Aged 45 to 54	1,123.41	125	23.0
Aged 55 to 64	807.91	90	10.5
Aged 65 to 74	579.11	65	7.4
Aged 75 or older	387.84	43	4.0
HOUSEHOLD INCOME			
Total households reporting income	**935.75**	**100**	**100.0**
Under $20,000	596.68	64	22.2
$20,000 to $29,999	879.67	94	13.7
$30,000 to $39,999	1,014.05	108	13.3
$40,000 to $49,999	1,264.49	135	12.6
$50,000 to $69,999	1,326.37	142	19.9
$70,000 or more	1,144.04	122	18.3
HOUSEHOLD TYPE			
Total households	**895.31**	**100**	**100.0**
Married couples	1,067.50	119	62.3
Married couples, no children	877.59	98	20.9
Married couples, with children	1,178.01	132	35.4
Oldest child under 6	1,019.30	114	5.9
Oldest child 6 to 17	902.73	101	14.7
Oldest child 18 or older	1,848.55	206	14.8
Single parent with child under 18	673.62	75	4.7
Single person	393.90	44	12.6
REGION			
Total households	**895.31**	**100**	**100.0**
Northeast	692.09	77	15.4
Midwest	979.72	109	26.1
South	914.24	102	35.6
West	960.36	107	22.8

Note: For definitions of best and biggest customers, see introduction or glossary.
Source: Calculations by New Strategist based on the 1997 Consumer Expenditure Survey

Finance Charges, Vehicle

Best customers:	• Householders aged 25 to 34
	• Married couples with children under age 6
	• Married couples with adult children
Customer trends:	• Spending increases are likely as the children of boomers buy cars and as vehicle prices continue to rise.

The best customers of vehicle finance charges are those who have little savings, those who buy the most expensive vehicles, and those who need the most vehicles. Householders aged 25 to 34, who have little savings, spend 43 percent more than the average householder on vehicle finance charges. Householders aged 45 to 54, who are in their peak-earnings years and typically buy the most expensive vehicles, spend 33 percent more than average on this item. Married couples with children spend 61 percent more than average on finance charges because they have the largest number of vehicles.

The price of vehicles keeps rising, boosting spending on finance charges. In addition, spending will increase because boomers will be buying cars for their children.

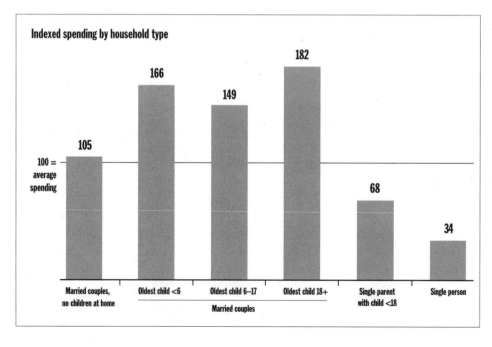

Indexed spending by household type

FINANCE CHARGES, VEHICLE

Total household spending	$30,913,708,560	
Average household spends	292.81	

	average spending	best customers (index)	biggest customers (market share)
AGE OF HOUSEHOLDER			
Total households	**$292.81**	**100**	**100.0%**
Under age 25	162.04	55	3.9
Aged 25 to 34	418.50	143	27.0
Aged 35 to 44	349.36	119	27.8
Aged 45 to 54	387.98	133	24.3
Aged 55 to 64	259.54	89	10.3
Aged 65 to 74	136.66	47	5.4
Aged 75 or older	43.33	15	1.4
HOUSEHOLD INCOME			
Total households reporting income	**304.80**	**100**	**100.0**
Under $20,000	98.04	32	11.2
$20,000 to $29,999	233.51	77	11.2
$30,000 to $39,999	359.70	118	14.4
$40,000 to $49,999	446.92	147	13.7
$50,000 to $69,999	509.91	167	23.5
$70,000 or more	529.81	174	26.0
HOUSEHOLD TYPE			
Total households	**292.81**	**100**	**100.0**
Married couples	401.65	137	71.7
Married couples, no children	306.47	105	22.3
Married couples, with children	471.43	161	43.3
Oldest child under 6	486.48	166	8.5
Oldest child 6 to 17	435.83	149	21.7
Oldest child 18 or older	532.68	182	13.1
Single parent with child under 18	200.34	68	4.3
Single person	100.42	34	9.9
REGION			
Total households	**292.81**	**100**	**100.0**
Northeast	213.63	73	14.6
Midwest	307.42	105	25.1
South	335.09	114	39.9
West	281.40	96	20.4

Note: For definitions of best and biggest customers, see introduction or glossary.
Source: Calculations by New Strategist based on the 1997 Consumer Expenditure Survey

Gasoline and Motor Oil

(includes spending on gasoline and motor oil on out-of-town trips, also shown separately in the Travel chapter)

Best customers:
- Married couples with children
- Householders aged 45 to 54

Customer trends:
- Spending is likely to increase because Americans are driving more than ever and gas prices are going up.

The more vehicles a household owns, the more it spends on gasoline and motor oil. Married couples with children, who tend to have more cars than the average household, spend the most on gasoline and motor oil—77 percent more than the average household. Most of these households have at least two cars and many have three or more. Married couples with school-aged children spend 38 percent more than average on gasoline and motor oil. Householders aged 45 to 54, who tend to own more cars than other age groups, spend 30 percent more than average on gasoline and motor oil.

In recent years, motorists have enjoyed record-low gasoline prices, but prices are now going up, boosting spending on gasoline. Spending will also increase because Americans are driving more than ever, a trend that shows no sign of reversing.

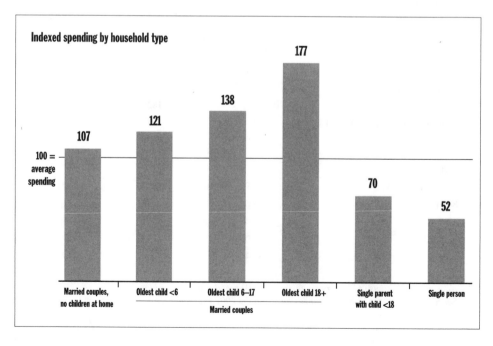

Indexed spending by household type

Married couples, no children at home	Oldest child <6	Oldest child 6–17	Oldest child 18+	Single parent with child <18	Single person
107	121	138	177	70	52

100 = average spending

Married couples

GASOLINE AND MOTOR OIL

Total household spending $114,805,453,920
Average household spends   1,087.42

	average spending	best customers (index)	biggest customers (market share)
AGE OF HOUSEHOLDER			
Total households	**$1,087.42**	**100**	**100.0%**
Under age 25	690.48	63	4.5
Aged 25 to 34	1,115.12	103	19.3
Aged 35 to 44	1,285.85	118	27.5
Aged 45 to 54	1,412.79	130	23.8
Aged 55 to 64	1,170.68	108	12.6
Aged 65 to 74	793.82	73	8.4
Aged 75 or older	455.36	42	3.9
HOUSEHOLD INCOME			
Total households reporting income	**1,099.26**	**100**	**100.0**
Under $20,000	628.59	57	19.9
$20,000 to $29,999	951.93	87	12.6
$30,000 to $39,999	1,170.65	106	13.0
$40,000 to $49,999	1,319.65	120	11.2
$50,000 to $69,999	1,534.79	140	19.6
$70,000 or more	1,734.61	158	23.6
HOUSEHOLD TYPE			
Total households	**1,087.42**	**100**	**100.0**
Married couples	1,415.51	130	68.1
Married couples, no children	1,167.74	107	22.9
Married couples, with children	1,580.87	145	39.1
Oldest child under 6	1,313.65	121	6.2
Oldest child 6 to 17	1,504.99	138	20.1
Oldest child 18 or older	1,925.56	177	12.7
Single parent with child under 18	757.54	70	4.4
Single person	564.66	52	14.9
REGION			
Total households	**1,087.42**	**100**	**100.0**
Northeast	974.78	90	17.9
Midwest	1,100.96	101	24.2
South	1,097.64	101	35.2
West	1,161.34	107	22.7

Note: For definitions of best and biggest customers, see introduction or glossary.
Source: Calculations by New Strategist based on the 1997 Consumer Expenditure Survey

Insurance, Vehicle

Best customers:	• **Householders aged 45 to 54**
	• **Married couples with children**
Customer trends:	• **Spending is likely to rise because more households will include teen drivers, but competition in the insurance industry will limit the increase.**

The best customers of vehicle insurance are families with children. Married couples with children at home spend 41 percent more than the average household on vehicle insurance because rates are higher for additional drivers—especially teens and young adults. Householders aged 45 to 54, many of whom have teenagers in the household, spend 32 percent more than average on this item.

Spending on vehicle insurance by the average household is likely to rise as boomer children start to drive. One factor that may keep spending down, however, is greater competition, especially as Internet sales of insurance become more common.

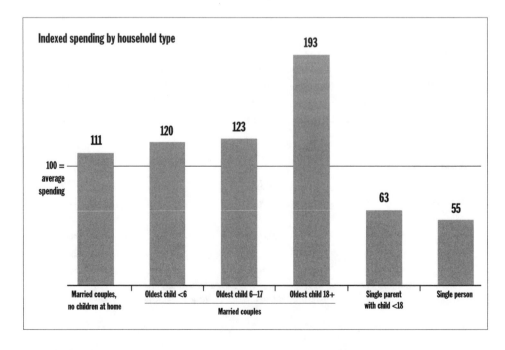

Indexed spending by household type

Married couples, no children at home	Oldest child <6	Oldest child 6–17	Oldest child 18+	Single parent with child <18	Single person
111	120	123	193	63	55

Married couples

100 = average spending

INSURANCE, VEHICLE

Total household spending	$79,708,824,240
Average household spends	754.99

	average spending	best customers (index)	biggest customers (market share)
AGE OF HOUSEHOLDER			
Total households	**$754.99**	**100**	**100.0%**
Under age 25	340.80	45	3.2
Aged 25 to 34	745.60	99	18.6
Aged 35 to 44	836.91	111	25.8
Aged 45 to 54	993.69	132	24.1
Aged 55 to 64	851.14	113	13.2
Aged 65 to 74	661.03	88	10.0
Aged 75 or older	410.90	54	5.1
HOUSEHOLD INCOME			
Total households reporting income	**779.47**	**100**	**100.0**
Under $20,000	375.93	48	16.8
$20,000 to $29,999	666.50	86	12.5
$30,000 to $39,999	848.89	109	13.3
$40,000 to $49,999	915.02	117	11.0
$50,000 to $69,999	1,113.92	143	20.1
$70,000 or more	1,374.46	176	26.4
HOUSEHOLD TYPE			
Total households	**754.99**	**100**	**100.0**
Married couples	973.76	129	67.4
Married couples, no children	836.68	111	23.7
Married couples, with children	1,065.94	141	38.0
Oldest child under 6	902.34	120	6.1
Oldest child 6 to 17	929.82	123	17.9
Oldest child 18 or older	1,458.42	193	13.9
Single parent with child under 18	477.79	63	4.0
Single person	417.08	55	15.9
REGION			
Total households	**754.99**	**100**	**100.0**
Northeast	808.43	107	21.4
Midwest	683.89	91	21.6
South	727.00	96	33.6
West	830.71	110	23.4

Note: For definitions of best and biggest customers, see introduction or glossary.
Source: Calculations by New Strategist based on the 1997 Consumer Expenditure Survey

Mass Transit, Intracity Fares

Best customers:	• Householders aged 25 to 34
	• Single parents
	• Households in the Northeast
Customer trends:	• Spending will increase as fares rise to pay for needed maintenance and improvements.

Households in the Northeast are the best customers of intracity mass-transit fares. Northeasterners spend three times as much as the average household on public transportation. Single parents spend 51 percent more than average. Householders aged 25 to 34 spend 35 percent more than average on this item. Because of their low incomes, many single parents and young householders do not own a vehicle. In addition, they are overrepresented in urban settings, where mass transit is more common.

Mass transit fares are likely to rise because of the cost of much-needed maintenance and repairs as well as improvements to the systems. Consequently, spending on mass transit is likely to rise.

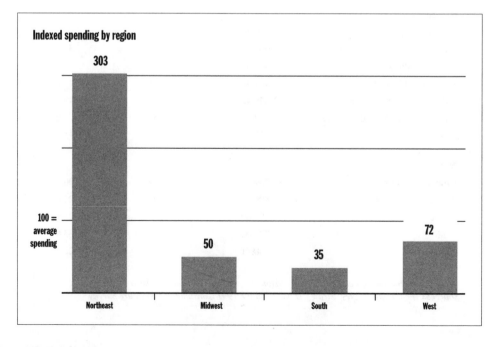

Indexed spending by region

Northeast	Midwest	South	West
303	50	35	72

100 = average spending

MASS TRANSIT, INTRACITY FARES

Total household spending	$5,887,973,520		
Average household spends	55.77		

	average spending	best customers (index)	biggest customers (market share)
AGE OF HOUSEHOLDER			
Total households	**$55.77**	**100**	**100.0%**
Under age 25	45.49	82	5.8
Aged 25 to 34	75.44	135	25.5
Aged 35 to 44	56.95	102	23.8
Aged 45 to 54	70.11	126	23.0
Aged 55 to 64	58.89	106	12.3
Aged 65 to 74	34.54	62	7.1
Aged 75 or older	14.84	27	2.5
HOUSEHOLD INCOME			
Total households reporting income	**54.55**	**100**	**100.0**
Under $20,000	39.13	72	25.0
$20,000 to $29,999	53.28	98	14.3
$30,000 to $39,999	52.42	96	11.7
$40,000 to $49,999	53.49	98	9.2
$50,000 to $69,999	48.22	88	12.4
$70,000 or more	100.05	183	27.4
HOUSEHOLD TYPE			
Total households	**55.77**	**100**	**100.0**
Married couples	51.60	93	48.4
Married couples, no children	35.04	63	13.4
Married couples, with children	59.15	106	28.5
Oldest child under 6	62.49	112	5.8
Oldest child 6 to 17	49.23	88	12.8
Oldest child 18 or older	76.83	138	9.9
Single parent with child under 18	84.41	151	9.5
Single person	42.86	77	22.1
REGION			
Total households	**55.77**	**100**	**100.0**
Northeast	168.99	303	60.5
Midwest	27.66	50	11.9
South	19.62	35	12.3
West	40.30	72	15.3

Note: For definitions of best and biggest customers, see introduction or glossary.
Source: Calculations by New Strategist based on the 1997 Consumer Expenditure Survey

Parking Fees in Home City

Best customers:
- Households with incomes of $70,000 or more
- Married couples with children under age 6
- Householders aged 25 to 34

Customer trends:
- Little change in spending as suburbs compete with cities for shoppers.

While everyone else is circling the block looking for a parking space, the affluent cruise into their reserved spots in lots and garages. Households with incomes of $70,000 or more spend more than two and one-half times as much as the average household on parking fees in their home city. Married couples with preschoolers spend 85 percent more than average on parking fees, while householders aged 25 to 34 spend 45 percent more. Young adults, and young families, are more likely than other demographic segments to live in urban areas, where they must pay to park.

One amenity that makes suburban living and shopping more attractive is free parking. Spending on parking fees is not likely to change much in the years ahead as suburbs compete with cities for shoppers.

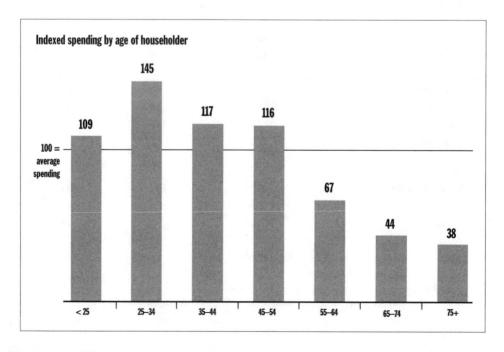

Indexed spending by age of householder

< 25	25–34	35–44	45–54	55–64	65–74	75+
109	145	117	116	67	44	38

100 = average spending

PARKING FEES IN HOME CITY

Total household spending	$2,572,887,120
Average household spends	24.37

	average spending	best customers (index)	biggest customers (market share)
AGE OF HOUSEHOLDER			
Total households	**$24.37**	**100**	**100.0%**
Under age 25	26.57	109	7.7
Aged 25 to 34	35.38	145	27.4
Aged 35 to 44	28.61	117	27.3
Aged 45 to 54	28.26	116	21.2
Aged 55 to 64	16.29	67	7.8
Aged 65 to 74	10.61	44	5.0
Aged 75 or older	9.22	38	3.5
HOUSEHOLD INCOME			
Total households reporting income	**26.27**	**100**	**100.0**
Under $20,000	10.76	41	14.3
$20,000 to $29,999	11.98	46	6.7
$30,000 to $39,999	23.95	91	11.1
$40,000 to $49,999	31.83	121	11.3
$50,000 to $69,999	31.99	122	17.1
$70,000 or more	69.46	264	39.5
HOUSEHOLD TYPE			
Total households	**24.37**	**100**	**100.0**
Married couples	27.00	111	57.9
Married couples, no children	24.23	99	21.2
Married couples, with children	30.89	127	34.1
Oldest child under 6	45.09	185	9.5
Oldest child 6 to 17	28.64	118	17.1
Oldest child 18 or older	25.28	104	7.5
Single parent with child under 18	9.63	40	2.5
Single person	24.03	99	28.3
REGION			
Total households	**24.37**	**100**	**100.0**
Northeast	32.60	134	26.7
Midwest	21.99	90	21.6
South	17.12	70	24.5
West	31.21	128	27.2

Note: For definitions of best and biggest customers, see introduction or glossary.
Source: Calculations by New Strategist based on the 1997 Consumer Expenditure Survey

Taxi Fares and Limousine Service

Best customers:
- Householders aged 25 to 34
- People living alone
- Households in the Northeast

Customer trends:
- Improved mass transit systems and lower crime may reduce spending.

Households in the highly urbanized Northeast are the best customers of taxi fares and limousine service, spending twice as much as the average household on this item. Householders aged 25 to 34 spend 45 percent more than average, while people who live alone spend 38 percent more. Households in the Northeast, young adults, and people who live alone are less likely to own a vehicle than other householders, making them dependent on taxi service.

Spending on taxi and limousine service may fall in the years ahead as improved mass transit systems and reduced crime convince more urban residents to ride the bus or subway.

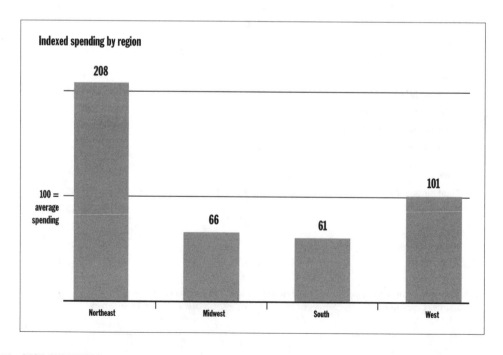

Indexed spending by region

100 = average spending

Northeast	Midwest	South	West
208	66	61	101

TAXI FARES AND LIMOUSINE SERVICE

Total household spending $1,004,027,760
Average household spends   9.51

	average spending	best customers (index)	biggest customers (market share)
AGE OF HOUSEHOLDER			
Total households	**$9.51**	**100**	**100.0%**
Under age 25	6.55	69	4.9
Aged 25 to 34	13.79	145	27.4
Aged 35 to 44	10.21	107	25.0
Aged 45 to 54	10.58	111	20.4
Aged 55 to 64	6.80	72	8.3
Aged 65 to 74	6.06	64	7.3
Aged 75 or older	6.85	72	6.7
HOUSEHOLD INCOME			
Total households reporting income	**9.81**	**100**	**100.0**
Under $20,000	9.07	92	32.2
$20,000 to $29,999	10.24	104	15.2
$30,000 to $39,999	6.08	62	7.6
$40,000 to $49,999	9.76	99	9.3
$50,000 to $69,999	6.24	64	8.9
$70,000 or more	17.54	179	26.7
HOUSEHOLD TYPE			
Total households	**9.51**	**100**	**100.0**
Married couples	5.96	63	32.8
Married couples, no children	6.22	65	14.0
Married couples, with children	5.96	63	16.8
Oldest child under 6	4.21	44	2.3
Oldest child 6 to 17	6.92	73	10.6
Oldest child 18 or older	5.29	56	4.0
Single parent with child under 18	9.50	100	6.3
Single person	13.11	138	39.6
REGION			
Total households	**9.51**	**100**	**100.0**
Northeast	19.77	208	41.5
Midwest	6.29	66	15.8
South	5.80	61	21.3
West	9.57	101	21.4

Note: For definitions of best and biggest customers, see introduction or glossary.
Source: Calculations by New Strategist based on the 1997 Consumer Expenditure Survey

Towing Charges

Best customers: • Married couples with adult children

Customer trends: • A decline in spending is possible as vehicles become more reliable and a greater variety of organizations provide roadside assistance.

The more cars a household owns, the more it spends on towing charges. This is especially true for households with older vehicles. Married couples with adult children at home spend 63 percent more than the average household on towing charges. Not only do these households have more cars than average, they tend to have older cars belonging to teenaged or young-adult drivers.

Spending on towing charges is likely to decline because vehicle reliability is increasing. In addition, fewer of those who require a tow truck will pay out-of-pocket for the service since a growing variety of organizations are offering free towing for their members.

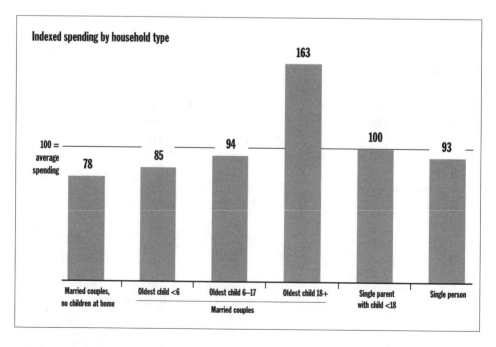

Indexed spending by household type

Married couples, no children at home	78
Oldest child <6	85
Oldest child 6–17	94
Oldest child 18+	163
Single parent with child <18	100
Single person	93

100 = average spending

Married couples

TOWING CHARGES

Total household spending	$532,103,040
Average household spends	5.04

	average spending	best customers (index)	biggest customers (market share)
AGE OF HOUSEHOLDER			
Total households	**$5.04**	**100**	**100.0%**
Under age 25	7.44	148	10.5
Aged 25 to 34	4.58	91	17.1
Aged 35 to 44	6.29	125	29.0
Aged 45 to 54	6.48	129	23.6
Aged 55 to 64	3.74	74	8.7
Aged 65 to 74	3.58	71	8.1
Aged 75 or older	1.60	32	3.0
HOUSEHOLD INCOME			
Total households reporting income	**5.24**	**100**	**100.0**
Under $20,000	4.95	95	32.9
$20,000 to $29,999	2.86	55	8.0
$30,000 to $39,999	5.45	104	12.7
$40,000 to $49,999	4.96	95	8.9
$50,000 to $69,999	6.72	128	18.0
$70,000 or more	6.84	131	19.5
HOUSEHOLD TYPE			
Total households	**5.04**	**100**	**100.0**
Married couples	5.14	102	53.3
Married couples, no children	3.94	78	16.7
Married couples, with children	5.57	111	29.7
Oldest child under 6	4.30	85	4.4
Oldest child 6 to 17	4.73	94	13.7
Oldest child 18 or older	8.19	163	11.7
Single parent with child under 18	5.05	100	6.3
Single person	4.68	93	26.7
REGION			
Total households	**5.04**	**100**	**100.0**
Northeast	4.64	92	18.4
Midwest	5.00	99	23.7
South	5.13	102	35.5
West	5.32	106	22.4

Note: For definitions of best and biggest customers, see introduction or glossary.
Source: Calculations by New Strategist based on the 1997 Consumer Expenditure Survey

Truck Lease Payments

Best customers:
- Households with incomes of $70,000 or more
- Married couples with children

Customer trends:
- As leasing grows in popularity, spending on truck leases will rise.

Households with incomes of $70,000 or more spend more than three times as much as the average household on truck lease payments, and account for 48 percent of the market. Married couples with children spend twice as much as average on this item. For many, leasing makes it possible to afford bigger and better trucks, since monthly lease payments are lower than purchase installments.

The growing popularity of trucks and of leasing guarantees increased spending on this item.

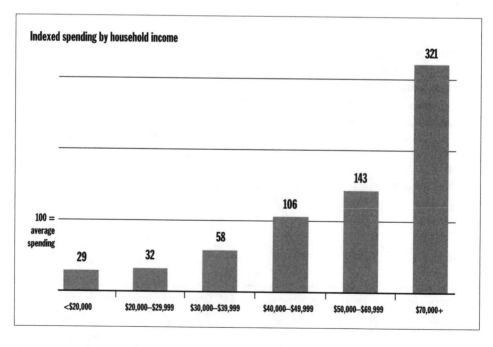

Indexed spending by household income

<$20,000	29
$20,000–$29,999	32
$30,000–$39,999	58
$40,000–$49,999	106
$50,000–$69,999	143
$70,000+	321

100 = average spending

TRUCK LEASE PAYMENTS

Total household spending $11,610,192,720
Average household spends   109.97

	average spending	best customers (index)	biggest customers (market share)
AGE OF HOUSEHOLDER			
Total households	**$109.97**	**100**	**100.0%**
Under age 25	79.52	72	5.1
Aged 25 to 34	120.54	110	20.7
Aged 35 to 44	163.30	148	34.5
Aged 45 to 54	184.74	168	30.8
Aged 55 to 64	63.12	57	6.7
Aged 65 to 74	18.35	17	1.9
Aged 75 or older	3.00	3	0.3
HOUSEHOLD INCOME			
Total households reporting income	**112.72**	**100**	**100.0**
Under $20,000	33.24	29	10.3
$20,000 to $29,999	35.70	32	4.6
$30,000 to $39,999	65.71	58	7.1
$40,000 to $49,999	119.53	106	9.9
$50,000 to $69,999	161.05	143	20.1
$70,000 or more	361.94	321	48.0
HOUSEHOLD TYPE			
Total households	**109.97**	**100**	**100.0**
Married couples	163.03	148	77.5
Married couples, no children	100.52	91	19.5
Married couples, with children	221.51	201	54.1
Oldest child under 6	247.26	225	11.6
Oldest child 6 to 17	219.75	200	29.1
Oldest child 18 or older	206.65	188	13.5
Single parent with child under 18	78.56	71	4.5
Single person	19.60	18	5.1
REGION			
Total households	**109.97**	**100**	**100.0**
Northeast	118.76	108	21.6
Midwest	123.85	113	26.9
South	69.27	63	22.0
West	152.95	139	29.5

Note: For definitions of best and biggest customers, see introduction or glossary.
Source: Calculations by New Strategist based on the 1997 Consumer Expenditure Survey

Trucks, New

Best customers:
- Married couples with children
- Householders aged 35 to 54

Customer trends:
- Spending will continue to rise, especially with the growing popularity smaller sport utility vehicles.

Americans have fallen in love with trucks, which range in style from family-friendly minivans to hip sport utilities and macho pickups. Boomers are especially partial to trucks, and householders aged 35 to 54 spend 30 to 37 percent more than average on new trucks. Married couples with children are the best customers of new trucks, however. Those with adult children at home spend 87 percent more than the average household on this item, while those with preschoolers spend 86 percent more than average.

Spending on new trucks will continue to rise because the truck market is adapting more readily to the preferences of younger generations than the car market. Although boomers could regain an interest in cars once their children are grown, smaller sport utility vehicles are likely to retain these customers.

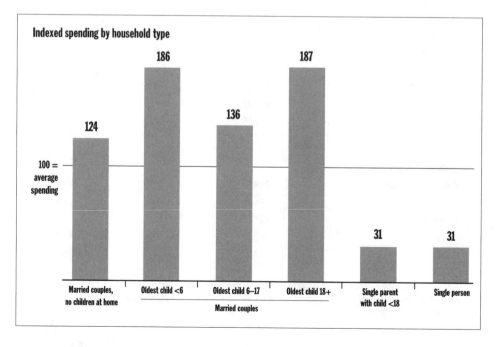

Indexed spending by household type

Married couples, no children at home	Oldest child <6	Oldest child 6–17	Oldest child 18+	Single parent with child <18	Single person
124	186	136	187	31	31

100 = average spending

Married couples

TRUCKS, NEW

Total household spending	$55,814,863,920		
Average household spends	528.67		

	average spending	best customers (index)	biggest customers (market share)
AGE OF HOUSEHOLDER			
Total households	**$528.67**	100	100.0%
Under age 25	145.46	28	2.0
Aged 25 to 34	586.35	111	20.9
Aged 35 to 44	724.82	137	31.9
Aged 45 to 54	689.35	130	23.9
Aged 55 to 64	630.06	119	13.9
Aged 65 to 74	273.62	52	5.9
Aged 75 or older	84.98	16	1.5
HOUSEHOLD INCOME			
Total households reporting income	**561.19**	100	100.0
Under $20,000	125.85	22	7.8
$20,000 to $29,999	258.25	46	6.7
$30,000 to $39,999	780.58	139	17.0
$40,000 to $49,999	788.19	140	13.1
$50,000 to $69,999	1,110.63	198	27.8
$70,000 or more	1,034.14	184	27.5
HOUSEHOLD TYPE			
Total households	**528.67**	100	100.0
Married couples	755.07	143	74.7
Married couples, no children	655.32	124	26.5
Married couples, with children	841.38	159	42.8
Oldest child under 6	984.68	186	9.6
Oldest child 6 to 17	718.13	136	19.8
Oldest child 18 or older	988.26	187	13.4
Single parent with child under 18	166.36	31	2.0
Single person	161.35	31	8.8
REGION			
Total households	**528.67**	100	100.0
Northeast	399.06	75	15.1
Midwest	527.80	100	23.9
South	676.73	128	44.7
West	408.36	77	16.4

Note: For definitions of best and biggest customers, see introduction or glossary.
Source: Calculations by New Strategist based on the 1997 Consumer Expenditure Survey

Trucks, Used

The best customers of used trucks are families with young children. Married couples with children under age 6 spend two and one-half times as much as the average household on used minivans, sport utility vehicles, and pickups. Typically, these are young householders who cannot afford or do not want to invest in a new vehicle. Married couples with adult children at home spend 69 percent more than average on this item, while those with school-aged children spend 66 percent more.

Trucks, especially sport utility vehicles, are becoming more expensive as manufacturers add more amenities. At the same time, the quality of used trucks is increasing thanks to the popularity of leasing. Consequently, spending on used trucks is likely to increase.

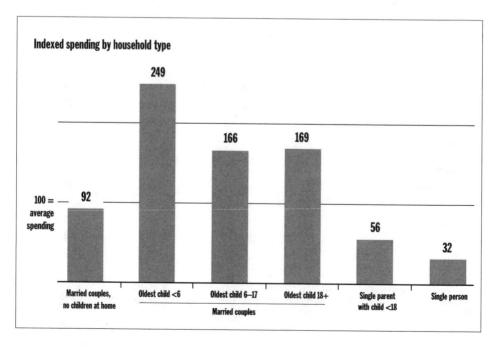

Indexed spending by household type

92	249	166	169	56	32

100 = average spending

Married couples, no children at home | Oldest child <6 | Oldest child 6–17 | Oldest child 18+ | Single parent with child <18 | Single person

Married couples

TRUCKS, USED

Total household spending	$59,990,394,720
Average household spends	568.22

	average spending	best customers (index)	biggest customers (market share)
AGE OF HOUSEHOLDER			
Total households	**$568.22**	**100**	**100.0%**
Under age 25	369.47	65	4.6
Aged 25 to 34	793.31	140	26.3
Aged 35 to 44	712.88	125	29.2
Aged 45 to 54	725.13	128	23.4
Aged 55 to 64	459.06	81	9.4
Aged 65 to 74	270.44	48	5.5
Aged 75 or older	97.04	17	1.6
HOUSEHOLD INCOME			
Total households reporting income	**563.97**	**100**	**100.0**
Under $20,000	264.81	47	16.4
$20,000 to $29,999	376.34	67	9.7
$30,000 to $39,999	764.68	136	16.6
$40,000 to $49,999	1,063.68	189	17.6
$50,000 to $69,999	788.33	140	19.6
$70,000 or more	756.85	134	20.1
HOUSEHOLD TYPE			
Total households	**568.22**	**100**	**100.0**
Married couples	819.40	144	75.4
Married couples, no children	525.08	92	19.7
Married couples, with children	1,037.17	183	49.1
Oldest child under 6	1,415.83	249	12.8
Oldest child 6 to 17	940.49	166	24.1
Oldest child 18 or older	961.90	169	12.2
Single parent with child under 18	320.57	56	3.5
Single person	184.01	32	9.3
REGION			
Total households	**568.22**	**100**	**100.0**
Northeast	359.81	63	12.6
Midwest	564.24	99	23.7
South	626.63	110	38.5
West	672.76	118	25.1

Note: For definitions of best and biggest customers, see introduction or glossary.
Source: Calculations by New Strategist based on the 1997 Consumer Expenditure Survey

Vehicle Maintenance and Repairs

Best customers: • Married couples with school-aged or older children

Customer trends: • Spending is unlikely to change since today's cars are more reliable than ever.

The households with the most vehicles spend the most on maintenance and repairs. Married couples with adult children at home spend 57 percent more than the average household on the maintenance and repairs of their cars and trucks. Married couples with school-aged children spend 46 percent more than average.

Today's vehicles are better than those of the past. Behind the improvements are more informed consumers, giving a competitive edge to automotive manufacturers that build the most reliable machines. Because of improving quality, spending on vehicle maintenance and repairs is unlikely to change.

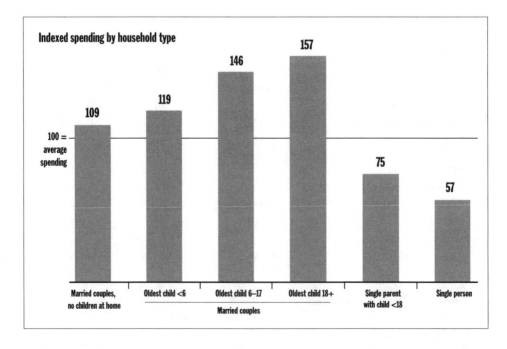

Indexed spending by household type

109	119	146	157	75	57

100 = average spending

Married couples, no children at home | Oldest child <6 | Oldest child 6–17 | Oldest child 18+ | Single parent with child <18 | Single person

Married couples

VEHICLE MAINTENANCE AND REPAIRS

Total household spending	$71,962,713,120
Average household spends	681.62

	average spending	best customers (index)	biggest customers (market share)
AGE OF HOUSEHOLDER			
Total households	**$681.62**	**100**	**100.0%**
Under age 25	324.12	48	3.4
Aged 25 to 34	597.92	88	16.5
Aged 35 to 44	788.13	116	26.9
Aged 45 to 54	941.73	138	25.3
Aged 55 to 64	759.53	111	13.0
Aged 65 to 74	570.64	84	9.6
Aged 75 or older	393.31	58	5.4
HOUSEHOLD INCOME			
Total households reporting income	**719.82**	**100**	**100.0**
Under $20,000	388.80	54	18.8
$20,000 to $29,999	599.73	83	12.2
$30,000 to $39,999	698.77	97	11.9
$40,000 to $49,999	738.93	103	9.6
$50,000 to $69,999	981.03	136	19.1
$70,000 or more	1,368.84	190	28.4
HOUSEHOLD TYPE			
Total households	**681.62**	**100**	**100.0**
Married couples	880.30	129	67.5
Married couples, no children	742.85	109	23.3
Married couples, with children	980.11	144	38.7
Oldest child under 6	811.29	119	6.1
Oldest child 6 to 17	994.98	146	21.2
Oldest child 18 or older	1,072.66	157	11.3
Single parent with child under 18	509.90	75	4.7
Single person	391.40	57	16.5
REGION			
Total households	**681.62**	**100**	**100.0**
Northeast	584.15	86	17.1
Midwest	659.18	97	23.1
South	656.96	96	33.6
West	838.20	123	26.1

Note: For definitions of best and biggest customers, see introduction or glossary.
Source: Calculations by New Strategist based on the 1997 Consumer Expenditure Survey

Chapter 19.

Travel

Travel

Travel is one of the most popular leisure-time activities of Americans. In 1997, the average household spent $1,130.10 on travel, including airline fares, lodging, luggage, food, and recreation expenses while on trips. Food purchased on trips, airline fares, and lodging account for two-thirds of all travel spending. Another 12 percent is devoted to recreational expenses such as greens fees and theme park admissions.

The best customers of travel are older Americans, particularly householders aged 45 to 64. They are the biggest spenders on food, airline fares, train fares, rental cars, lodging, luggage, and recreation expenses on trips. As the large, baby-boom generation fills the 45-to-64 age group, spending on travel will rise substantially.

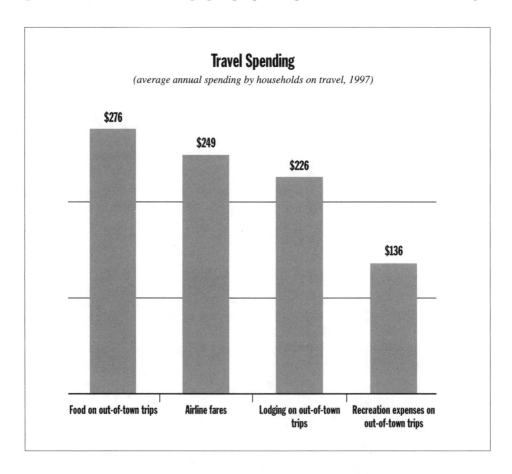

Travel Spending
(average annual spending by households on travel, 1997)

$276 — Food on out-of-town trips
$249 — Airline fares
$226 — Lodging on out-of-town trips
$136 — Recreation expenses on out-of-town trips

Travel Spending

(average annual spending of households on travel, and percent distribution of spending by type, 1997)

Total spending on travel	**$1,130.10**	**100.0%**
Food on out-of-town trips	275.55	24.4
Airline fares	248.82	22.0
Lodging on out-of-town trips	225.77	20.0
Recreation expenses, out-of-town trips	135.61	12.0
Gasoline on out-of-town trips	89.11	7.9
Alcohol purchased on trips	32.48	2.9
Auto rental on out-of-town trips	26.78	2.4
Ship fares	26.40	2.3
Train fares, intercity	21.19	1.9
Transportation, local, on out-of-town trips	20.01	1.8
Bus fares, intercity	10.51	0.9
Luggage	9.72	0.9
Parking fees and tolls on out-of-town trips	8.15	0.7

Airline Fares

Best customers: • Householders aged 45 to 64
                   • Married couples without children
                   • Married couples with adult children
                   • Households in the West

Customer trends: • As boomers enter the peak-travel years, spending on airline fares will rise.

As Americans have become more affluent, airline travel has surged. The biggest spenders on airline travel are those who travel the most—older Americans. Householders aged 45 to 64 spend 32 to 36 percent more on airline fares than the average householder. Married couples with adult children at home spend 71 percent more than average on this item, while those without children—many of whom are older—spend 36 percent more. Households in the West spend 46 percent more than average on airline fares.

As boomers enter their fifties and sixties, the peak years of travel, spending on airline fares will rise.

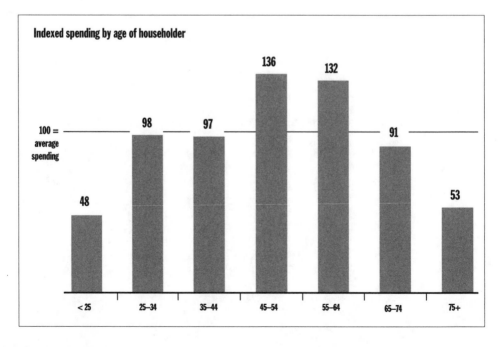

Indexed spending by age of householder

100 = average spending

< 25	25–34	35–44	45–54	55–64	65–74	75+
48	98	97	136	132	91	53

AIRLINE FARES

Total household spending $26,269,420,320
Average household spends 248.82

	average spending	best customers (index)	biggest customers (market share)
AGE OF HOUSEHOLDER			
Total households	**$248.82**	**100**	**100.0%**
Under age 25	119.92	48	3.4
Aged 25 to 34	243.68	98	18.5
Aged 35 to 44	240.65	97	22.5
Aged 45 to 54	337.67	136	24.9
Aged 55 to 64	327.78	132	15.4
Aged 65 to 74	226.35	91	10.4
Aged 75 or older	131.85	53	4.9
HOUSEHOLD INCOME			
Total households reporting income	**253.59**	**100**	**100.0**
Under $20,000	93.07	37	12.8
$20,000 to $29,999	152.29	60	8.8
$30,000 to $39,999	187.86	74	9.1
$40,000 to $49,999	225.19	89	8.3
$50,000 to $69,999	325.94	129	18.0
$70,000 or more	730.21	288	43.0
HOUSEHOLD TYPE			
Total households	**248.82**	**100**	**100.0**
Married couples	329.35	132	69.2
Married couples, no children	338.77	136	29.1
Married couples, with children	336.27	135	36.3
Oldest child under 6	303.08	122	6.3
Oldest child 6 to 17	303.52	122	17.7
Oldest child 18 or older	426.29	171	12.3
Single parent with child under 18	111.29	45	2.8
Single person	170.98	69	19.7
REGION			
Total households	**248.82**	**100**	**100.0**
Northeast	294.77	118	23.7
Midwest	229.41	92	22.0
South	166.85	67	23.4
West	362.06	146	30.9

Note: For definitions of best and biggest customers, see introduction or glossary.
Source: Calculations by New Strategist based on the 1997 Consumer Expenditure Survey

Alcohol Purchased on Trips

Best customers:
- Householders aged 25 to 34
- Householders aged 45 to 54
- Married couples without children
- Households in the Northeast and West

Customer trends:
- Spending may rise along with the number of empty-nest boomers on the road.

Two age groups spend the most on alcohol while on trips—young adults and travelers in their peak-earning years. Householders aged 25 to 34 spend 20 percent more than average on this item, while those aged 45 to 54 spend 28 percent more. Married couples without children at home spend 46 percent more than average on alcohol while on trips. No longer responsible for children, empty nesters can relax with a drink more easily than those caring for kids. Households in the West and Northeast, where incomes tend to be higher, spend 31 to 39 percent more than average on alcohol while traveling.

Spending on alcoholic beverages while on trips may rise as the children of boomers grow up and empty nesters have more opportunities to indulge.

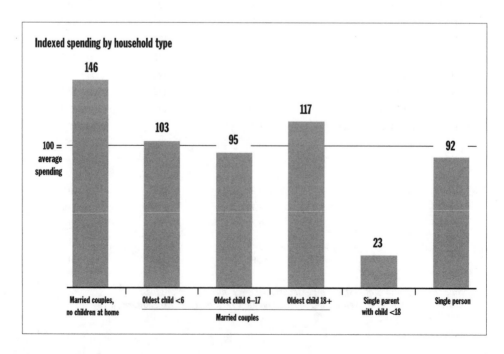

Indexed spending by household type

100 = average spending

Married couples, no children at home	Oldest child <6	Oldest child 6–17	Oldest child 18+	Single parent with child <18	Single person
146	103	95	117	23	92

Married couples

ALCOHOL PURCHASED ON TRIPS

Total household spending $3,429,108,480
Average household spends   32.48

	average spending	best customers (index)	biggest customers (market share)
AGE OF HOUSEHOLDER			
Total households	**$32.48**	**100**	**100.0%**
Under age 25	35.52	109	7.8
Aged 25 to 34	39.09	120	22.7
Aged 35 to 44	30.39	94	21.8
Aged 45 to 54	41.70	128	23.5
Aged 55 to 64	34.61	107	12.4
Aged 65 to 74	24.30	75	8.6
Aged 75 or older	11.29	35	3.2
HOUSEHOLD INCOME			
Total households reporting income	**34.93**	**100**	**100.0**
Under $20,000	13.29	38	13.3
$20,000 to $29,999	22.51	64	9.4
$30,000 to $39,999	24.58	70	8.6
$40,000 to $49,999	34.96	100	9.4
$50,000 to $69,999	43.81	125	17.6
$70,000 or more	97.61	279	41.8
HOUSEHOLD TYPE			
Total households	**32.48**	**100**	**100.0**
Married couples	38.46	118	61.9
Married couples, no children	47.38	146	31.1
Married couples, with children	33.22	102	27.5
Oldest child under 6	33.57	103	5.3
Oldest child 6 to 17	30.70	95	13.8
Oldest child 18 or older	38.07	117	8.4
Single parent with child under 18	7.38	23	1.4
Single person	30.03	92	26.6
REGION			
Total households	**32.48**	**100**	**100.0**
Northeast	42.69	131	26.3
Midwest	30.08	93	22.1
South	20.58	63	22.1
West	45.13	139	29.5

Note: For definitions of best and biggest customers, see introduction or glossary.
Source: Calculations by New Strategist based on the 1997 Consumer Expenditure Survey

Auto Rental on Out-of-Town Trips

Best customers:	• Householders aged 45 to 64
	• Married couples without children
	• Married couples with adult children
	• Households with incomes of $70,000 or more
	• Households in the West
Customer trends:	• Spending should increase substantially as the peak-travel age groups fill with boomers.

Many travelers rent a car once they reach their destination. Those who spend the most on this item are households with incomes of $70,000 or more, accounting for 50 percent of the market. Householders aged 45 to 64, the ages of peak travel, spend 29 to 51 percent more than average on this item. Married couples without children at home, many of them older, spend 43 percent more than average, while those with adult children at home spend 55 percent more. Households in the West, where incomes tend to be higher, spend 61 percent more.

As the large baby-boom generation enters its fifties and sixties—the peak-travel age groups—spending on rental cars while traveling should rise.

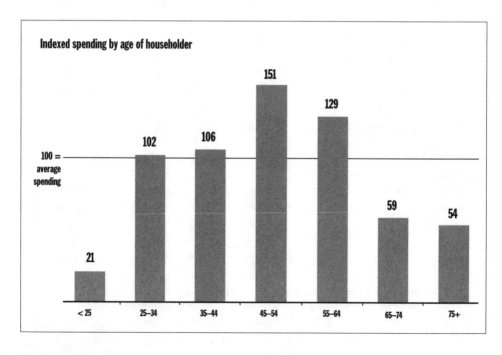

Indexed spending by age of householder

AUTO RENTAL ON OUT-OF-TOWN TRIPS

Total household spending $2,827,325,280
Average household spends   26.78

	average spending	best customers (index)	biggest customers (market share)
AGE OF HOUSEHOLDER			
Total households	**$26.78**	**100**	**100.0%**
Under age 25	5.53	21	1.5
Aged 25 to 34	27.31	102	19.2
Aged 35 to 44	28.46	106	24.7
Aged 45 to 54	40.57	151	27.8
Aged 55 to 64	34.62	129	15.1
Aged 65 to 74	15.71	59	6.7
Aged 75 or older	14.40	54	5.0
HOUSEHOLD INCOME			
Total households reporting income	**27.04**	**100**	**100.0**
Under $20,000	6.32	23	8.1
$20,000 to $29,999	12.24	45	6.6
$30,000 to $39,999	18.16	67	8.2
$40,000 to $49,999	23.66	88	8.2
$50,000 to $69,999	35.94	133	18.7
$70,000 or more	90.80	336	50.2
HOUSEHOLD TYPE			
Total households	**26.78**	**100**	**100.0**
Married couples	35.12	131	68.6
Married couples, no children	38.17	143	30.4
Married couples, with children	33.53	125	33.7
Oldest child under 6	28.58	107	5.5
Oldest child 6 to 17	31.33	117	17.0
Oldest child 18 or older	41.53	155	11.2
Single parent with child under 18	11.50	43	2.7
Single person	16.92	63	18.2
REGION			
Total households	**26.78**	**100**	**100.0**
Northeast	30.99	116	23.1
Midwest	21.37	80	19.1
South	18.16	68	23.7
West	43.07	161	34.2

Note: For definitions of best and biggest customers, see introduction or glossary.
Source: Calculations by New Strategist based on the 1997 Consumer Expenditure Survey

Bus Fares, Intercity

Best customers:
- Householders aged 55 to 74
- Married couples with adult children
- Households in the Northeast

Customer trends:
- A spending decline is likely because younger generations prefer to travel by air or car.

Older householders are the biggest spenders on intercity bus fares. Those aged 55 to 74 spend 32 to 36 percent more than average on this item. Married couples with adult children at home, many of whom are older, spend 36 percent more than average on intercity bus fares. Some are buying bus fares for children going to and from college. Households in the Northeast spend 59 percent more than average on intercity bus fares. The close proximity of large Northeastern cities makes bus service more convenient than other modes of transportation for travelers in the region.

Unless bus companies can boost their business by offering innovative services, spending on bus fares is likely to decline. Today's older bus riders will soon be replaced by younger people who prefer traveling by air or car.

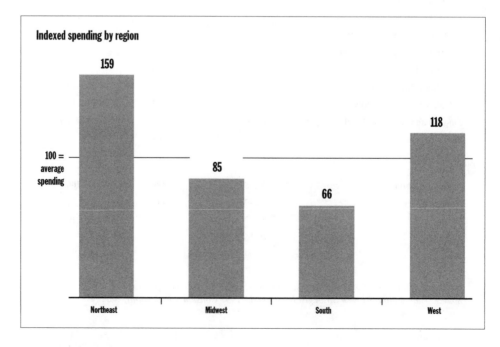

Indexed spending by region

100 = average spending

Northeast 159
Midwest 85
South 66
West 118

BUS FARES, INTERCITY

Total household spending $1,109,603,760
Average household spends 10.51

	average spending	best customers (index)	biggest customers (market share)
AGE OF HOUSEHOLDER			
Total households	**$10.51**	**100**	**100.0%**
Under age 25	9.53	91	6.4
Aged 25 to 34	7.12	68	12.8
Aged 35 to 44	9.16	87	20.3
Aged 45 to 54	13.34	127	23.3
Aged 55 to 64	14.25	136	15.8
Aged 65 to 74	13.89	132	15.2
Aged 75 or older	7.13	68	6.3
HOUSEHOLD INCOME			
Total households reporting income	**11.46**	**100**	**100.0**
Under $20,000	10.75	94	32.7
$20,000 to $29,999	10.01	87	12.8
$30,000 to $39,999	6.20	54	6.6
$40,000 to $49,999	5.96	52	4.9
$50,000 to $69,999	13.32	116	16.3
$70,000 or more	20.53	179	26.8
HOUSEHOLD TYPE			
Total households	**10.51**	**100**	**100.0**
Married couples	12.68	121	63.1
Married couples, no children	12.04	115	24.4
Married couples, with children	12.39	118	31.7
Oldest child under 6	8.61	82	4.2
Oldest child 6 to 17	12.77	122	17.7
Oldest child 18 or older	14.31	136	9.8
Single parent with child under 18	5.69	54	3.4
Single person	9.23	88	25.2
REGION			
Total households	**10.51**	**100**	**100.0**
Northeast	16.67	159	31.7
Midwest	8.92	85	20.3
South	6.92	66	23.0
West	12.42	118	25.1

Note: For definitions of best and biggest customers, see introduction or glossary.
Source: Calculations by New Strategist based on the 1997 Consumer Expenditure Survey

Food on Out-of-Town Trips

Best customers:

- Householders aged 45 to 64
- Married couples with adult children
- Married couples without children

Customer trends:

- Spending will rise substantially as boomers enter the peak ages of travel.

Spending on food accounts for a large share of the travel budget, ranking third after only airline fares and lodging expenses. The best customers of food purchased on trips are the biggest travelers. Householders aged 45 to 64 spend 33 to 41 percent more than the average householder on food while on trips. Married couples with adult children at home spend 53 percent more, while those without children, many of whom are older, spend 49 percent more.

Spending on food while on trips will rise substantially as the large baby-boom generation enters its fifties and sixties—the peak years of travel.

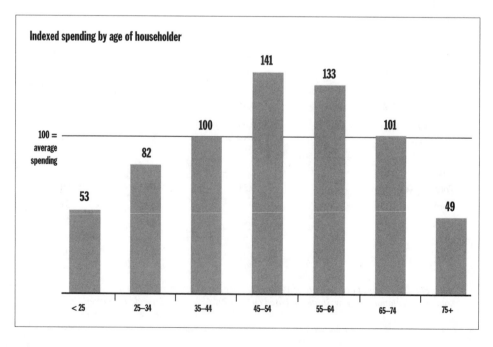

Indexed spending by age of householder

100 = average spending

| < 25 | 25–34 | 35–44 | 45–54 | 55–64 | 65–74 | 75+ |
| 53 | 82 | 100 | 141 | 133 | 101 | 49 |

FOOD ON OUT-OF-TOWN TRIPS

Total household spending $29,091,466,800
Average household spends   275.55

	average spending	best customers (index)	biggest customers (market share)
AGE OF HOUSEHOLDER			
Total households	**$275.55**	**100**	**100.0%**
Under age 25	147.38	53	3.8
Aged 25 to 34	227.05	82	15.5
Aged 35 to 44	274.99	100	23.2
Aged 45 to 54	387.59	141	25.8
Aged 55 to 64	366.00	133	15.5
Aged 65 to 74	279.57	101	11.6
Aged 75 or older	134.22	49	4.5
HOUSEHOLD INCOME			
Total households reporting income	**290.51**	**100**	**100.0**
Under $20,000	114.24	39	13.7
$20,000 to $29,999	168.71	58	8.5
$30,000 to $39,999	219.10	75	9.2
$40,000 to $49,999	302.07	104	9.7
$50,000 to $69,999	391.95	135	18.9
$70,000 or more	776.11	267	39.9
HOUSEHOLD TYPE			
Total households	**275.55**	**100**	**100.0**
Married couples	379.45	138	72.0
Married couples, no children	410.90	149	31.8
Married couples, with children	372.38	135	36.3
Oldest child under 6	285.20	104	5.3
Oldest child 6 to 17	378.29	137	20.0
Oldest child 18 or older	422.79	153	11.0
Single parent with child under 18	115.24	42	2.6
Single person	157.46	57	16.4
REGION			
Total households	**275.55**	**100**	**100.0**
Northeast	316.33	115	22.9
Midwest	272.77	99	23.7
South	221.48	80	28.0
West	329.14	119	25.4

Note: For definitions of best and biggest customers, see introduction or glossary.
Source: Calculations by New Strategist based on the 1997 Consumer Expenditure Survey

Gasoline on Out-of-Town Trips

Best customers:
- Householders aged 45 to 64
- Married couples with adult children
- Married couples without children
- Households in the West

Customer trends:
- Spending will increase as the ranks of travelers expand with the aging of the baby-boom generation.

Most people travel by car, and cars require gasoline. The best customers of gasoline on out-of-town trips are the biggest travelers. Householders aged 45 to 64 spend 25 to 32 percent more than the average householder on gasoline while traveling. Married couples with adult children and those without children at home—many of them in the 45-to-64 age group—spend 43 to 56 percent more than average on this item. Households in the wide open West spend 23 percent more than average on gasoline while on trips.

Spending on gasoline on out-of-town trips will rise along with the ranks of travelers as boomers enter the peak traveling age groups.

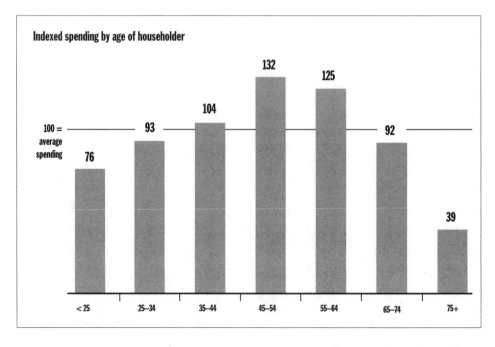

Indexed spending by age of householder

< 25	25–34	35–44	45–54	55–64	65–74	75+
76	93	104	132	125	92	39

100 = average spending

GASOLINE ON OUT-OF-TOWN TRIPS

Total household spending	$9,407,877,360
Average household spends	89.11

	average spending	best customers (index)	biggest customers (market share)
AGE OF HOUSEHOLDER			
Total households	**$89.11**	**100**	**100.0%**
Under age 25	67.54	76	5.4
Aged 25 to 34	82.66	93	17.5
Aged 35 to 44	92.56	104	24.2
Aged 45 to 54	117.67	132	24.2
Aged 55 to 64	111.36	125	14.6
Aged 65 to 74	82.04	92	10.6
Aged 75 or older	34.63	39	3.6
HOUSEHOLD INCOME			
Total households reporting income	**94.78**	**100**	**100.0**
Under $20,000	47.70	50	17.5
$20,000 to $29,999	76.58	81	11.8
$30,000 to $39,999	85.51	90	11.0
$40,000 to $49,999	110.50	117	10.9
$50,000 to $69,999	133.27	141	19.7
$70,000 or more	183.88	194	29.0
HOUSEHOLD TYPE			
Total households	**89.11**	**100**	**100.0**
Married couples	118.66	133	69.6
Married couples, no children	127.48	143	30.5
Married couples, with children	115.67	130	34.9
Oldest child under 6	85.21	96	4.9
Oldest child 6 to 17	115.07	129	18.8
Oldest child 18 or older	138.68	156	11.2
Single parent with child under 18	49.30	55	3.5
Single person	55.08	62	17.8
REGION			
Total households	**89.11**	**100**	**100.0**
Northeast	68.23	77	15.3
Midwest	95.29	107	25.6
South	84.24	95	33.0
West	109.79	123	26.2

Note: For definitions of best and biggest customers, see introduction or glossary.
Source: Calculations by New Strategist based on the 1997 Consumer Expenditure Survey

Lodging on Out-of-Town Trips

Best customers:	• Householders aged 45 to 64
	• Households with incomes of $70,000 or more
	• Married couples with school-aged or older children
	• Married couples without children
Customer trends:	• Spending will soar as affluent boomers enter the peak years of travel.

While traveling, many people stay with relatives. But if they can afford to do so, travelers stay in hotels and motels. The biggest spenders on lodging on out-of-town trips are the affluent in the peak-traveling age groups. Households with incomes of $70,000 or more account for 46 percent of the lodging market. Householders aged 45 to 64 spend 25 to 46 percent more than average on this item. Married couples without children, many of whom are older, as well as couples with school-aged or older children spend at least 50 percent more than the average household on lodging while on trips.

Spending on lodging should soar as the affluence of Americans grows and boomers enter the peak-traveling age groups.

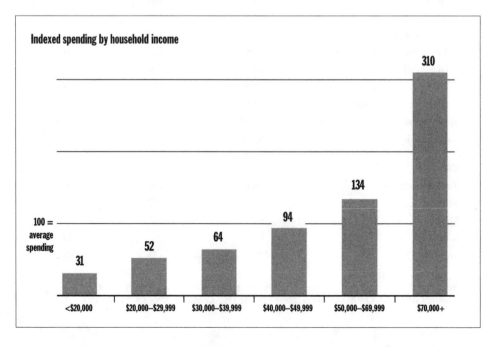

Indexed spending by household income

100 = average spending

<$20,000	$20,000–$29,999	$30,000–$39,999	$40,000–$49,999	$50,000–$69,999	$70,000+
31	52	64	94	134	310

LODGING ON OUT-OF-TOWN TRIPS

Total household spending $23,835,893,520
Average household spends   225.77

	average spending	best customers (index)	biggest customers (market share)
AGE OF HOUSEHOLDER			
Total households	**$225.77**	**100**	**100.0%**
Under age 25	74.28	33	2.3
Aged 25 to 34	163.33	72	13.6
Aged 35 to 44	237.89	105	24.5
Aged 45 to 54	330.57	146	26.8
Aged 55 to 64	283.15	125	14.6
Aged 65 to 74	241.73	107	12.3
Aged 75 or older	139.84	62	5.8
HOUSEHOLD INCOME			
Total households reporting income	**233.48**	**100**	**100.0**
Under $20,000	71.24	31	10.6
$20,000 to $29,999	120.94	52	7.6
$30,000 to $39,999	149.22	64	7.8
$40,000 to $49,999	218.71	94	8.8
$50,000 to $69,999	313.38	134	18.8
$70,000 or more	724.62	310	46.4
HOUSEHOLD TYPE			
Total households	**225.77**	**100**	**100.0**
Married couples	319.60	142	74.0
Married couples, no children	346.20	153	32.7
Married couples, with children	316.81	140	37.7
Oldest child under 6	196.33	87	4.5
Oldest child 6 to 17	340.22	151	21.9
Oldest child 18 or older	355.64	158	11.3
Single parent with child under 18	102.60	45	2.9
Single person	113.00	50	14.4
REGION			
Total households	**225.77**	**100**	**100.0**
Northeast	259.30	115	22.9
Midwest	220.84	98	23.4
South	178.57	79	27.6
West	277.32	123	26.1

Note: For definitions of best and biggest customers, see introduction or glossary.
Source: Calculations by New Strategist based on the 1997 Consumer Expenditure Survey

Luggage

Best customers:
- Householders aged 45 to 54
- Married couples with adult children
- Households in the West
- Households with incomes of $70,000 or more

Customer trends:
- Spending should rise as boomers buy luggage for children leaving home, and as improvements in luggage spur replacement sales.

Luggage is a lot lighter and easier to tote today than it was a few years ago. Luggage manufacturers have improved their products just in time to capture a growing tide of travelers as boomers enter the peak years of travel. Spending on luggage is greatest among the most affluent householders—those aged 45 to 54 spend 48 percent more on luggage than the average householder. Married couples with adult children at home spend 70 percent more than average on this item as they buy luggage for children going away to college. Households in the West, where incomes tend to be higher, spend 67 percent more than average on luggage.

Spending on luggage should rise as boomers buy for their own travels as well as for their college-bound children. Replacement sales will also spur spending as households upgrade their bags.

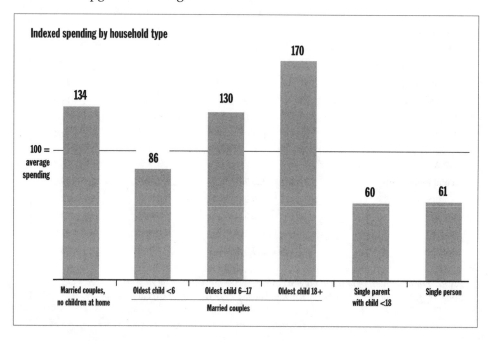

Indexed spending by household type

LUGGAGE

Total household spending	$1,026,198,720
Average household spends	9.72

	average spending	best customers (index)	biggest customers (market share)
AGE OF HOUSEHOLDER			
Total households	**$9.72**	**100**	**100.0%**
Under age 25	4.07	42	3.0
Aged 25 to 34	7.34	76	14.2
Aged 35 to 44	10.12	104	24.2
Aged 45 to 54	14.38	148	27.1
Aged 55 to 64	11.41	117	13.7
Aged 65 to 74	11.06	114	13.1
Aged 75 or older	4.92	51	4.7
HOUSEHOLD INCOME			
Total households reporting income	**10.01**	**100**	**100.0**
Under $20,000	2.95	29	10.3
$20,000 to $29,999	5.29	53	7.7
$30,000 to $39,999	7.98	80	9.7
$40,000 to $49,999	9.73	97	9.1
$50,000 to $69,999	12.66	126	17.8
$70,000 or more	30.38	303	45.4
HOUSEHOLD TYPE			
Total households	**9.72**	**100**	**100.0**
Married couples	12.59	130	67.7
Married couples, no children	13.06	134	28.7
Married couples, with children	12.86	132	35.6
Oldest child under 6	8.40	86	4.4
Oldest child 6 to 17	12.65	130	18.9
Oldest child 18 or older	16.49	170	12.2
Single parent with child under 18	5.83	60	3.8
Single person	5.91	61	17.5
REGION			
Total households	**9.72**	**100**	**100.0**
Northeast	10.39	107	21.4
Midwest	7.23	74	17.8
South	7.09	73	25.4
West	16.21	167	35.4

Note: For definitions of best and biggest customers, see introduction or glossary.
Source: Calculations by New Strategist based on the 1997 Consumer Expenditure Survey

Parking Fees and Tolls on Out-of-Town Trips

Best customers:
- Householders aged 45 to 64
- Married couples with adult children
- Households in the Northeast

Customer trends:
- Spending is likely to rise as travel increases.

The best customers of parking fees and tolls on trips are the biggest travelers. Householders aged 45 to 64 spend 30 to 38 percent more than average on this item. Married couples with adult children at home spend 67 percent more than average on parking fees and tolls on trips, primarily because there are more travelers in these households. Residents of the Northeast spend 71 percent more than average on this item because toll roads are much more common in the Northeast than in other regions.

Spending on parking fees and tolls while traveling will rise along with the number of travelers as boomers enter their fifties and sixties—the peak-travel years.

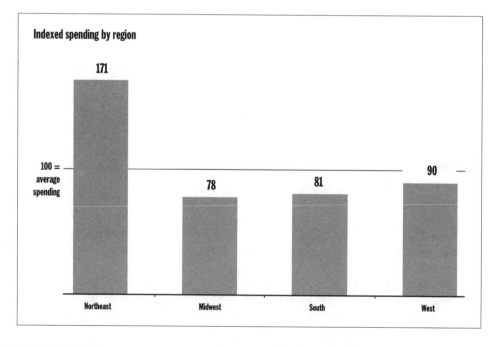

Indexed spending by region

Northeast	Midwest	South	West
171	78	81	90

100 = average spending

PARKING FEES AND TOLLS ON OUT-OF-TOWN TRIPS

Total household spending $860,444,400
Average household spends   8.15

	average spending	best customers (index)	biggest customers (market share)
AGE OF HOUSEHOLDER			
Total households	**$8.15**	**100**	**100.0%**
Under age 25	4.15	51	3.6
Aged 25 to 34	8.62	106	20.0
Aged 35 to 44	8.07	99	23.0
Aged 45 to 54	11.25	138	25.3
Aged 55 to 64	10.57	130	15.1
Aged 65 to 74	7.48	92	10.5
Aged 75 or older	2.17	27	2.5
HOUSEHOLD INCOME			
Total households reporting income	**8.48**	**100**	**100.0**
Under $20,000	3.59	42	14.7
$20,000 to $29,999	4.75	56	8.2
$30,000 to $39,999	7.64	90	11.0
$40,000 to $49,999	9.82	116	10.8
$50,000 to $69,999	10.05	119	16.6
$70,000 or more	21.94	259	38.7
HOUSEHOLD TYPE			
Total households	**8.15**	**100**	**100.0**
Married couples	10.91	134	70.0
Married couples, no children	11.43	140	29.9
Married couples, with children	11.39	140	37.6
Oldest child under 6	10.02	123	6.3
Oldest child 6 to 17	10.76	132	19.2
Oldest child 18 or older	13.62	167	12.0
Single parent with child under 18	3.17	39	2.4
Single person	5.55	68	19.6
REGION			
Total households	**8.15**	**100**	**100.0**
Northeast	13.93	171	34.1
Midwest	6.34	78	18.6
South	6.60	81	28.3
West	7.31	90	19.1

Note: For definitions of best and biggest customers, see introduction or glossary.
Source: Calculations by New Strategist based on the 1997 Consumer Expenditure Survey

Recreation Expenses, Out-of-Town Trips

Best customers:	• **Householders aged 45 to 54**
	• **Married couples with school-aged or older children**
Customer trends:	• **Spending should rise along with the number of householders traveling with teens and young adults.**

When they travel, Americans spend a lot of money having fun. Recreational costs, in fact, are the fourth largest expense of travel, following airline fares, lodging, and food. Recreational expenses while traveling include everything from a movie admission to a Disney World pass, greens fees, and baseball tickets. Householders aged 45 to 54, the most affluent, spend 42 percent more than average on recreational expenses while traveling. Those aged 55 to 64 spend 20 percent more. Married couples with school-aged or older children spend at least 50 percent more than average on this item as families look for ways to have fun.

Spending on recreational expenses while traveling will increase in the years ahead as affluent boomers travel with their families and as travel destinations invent more ways for people to spend their money.

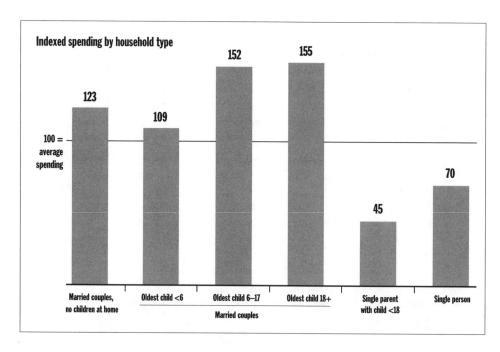

Indexed spending by household type

- Married couples, no children at home: 123
- Oldest child <6: 109
- Oldest child 6–17: 152
- Oldest child 18+: 155
- Single parent with child <18: 45
- Single person: 70

100 = average spending

Married couples

RECREATION EXPENSES, OUT-OF-TOWN TRIPS

Total household spending $14,317,161,360
Average household spends   135.61

	average spending	best customers (index)	biggest customers (market share)
AGE OF HOUSEHOLDER			
Total households	**$135.61**	**100**	**100.0%**
Under age 25	69.73	51	3.7
Aged 25 to 34	125.40	92	17.4
Aged 35 to 44	151.06	111	25.9
Aged 45 to 54	192.44	142	26.0
Aged 55 to 64	162.36	120	14.0
Aged 65 to 74	115.70	85	9.8
Aged 75 or older	47.09	35	3.2
HOUSEHOLD INCOME			
Total households reporting income	**141.98**	**100**	**100.0**
Under $20,000	48.93	34	12.0
$20,000 to $29,999	84.35	59	8.7
$30,000 to $39,999	122.68	86	10.6
$40,000 to $49,999	153.91	108	10.1
$50,000 to $69,999	185.32	131	18.3
$70,000 or more	382.71	270	40.3
HOUSEHOLD TYPE			
Total households	**135.61**	**100**	**100.0**
Married couples	179.33	132	69.1
Married couples, no children	167.21	123	26.3
Married couples, with children	196.17	145	38.9
Oldest child under 6	148.16	109	5.6
Oldest child 6 to 17	206.38	152	22.1
Oldest child 18 or older	209.86	155	11.1
Single parent with child under 18	60.90	45	2.8
Single person	94.99	70	20.1
REGION			
Total households	**135.61**	**100**	**100.0**
Northeast	156.43	115	23.0
Midwest	139.98	103	24.7
South	99.51	73	25.6
West	170.38	126	26.7

Note: For definitions of best and biggest customers, see introduction or glossary.
Source: Calculations by New Strategist based on the 1997 Consumer Expenditure Survey

Ship Fares

Best customers:
- Married couples without children
- Householders aged 65 to 74
- Households with incomes of $70,000 or more

Customer trends:
- Spending will increase as boomers enter the prime cruising age groups and as the cruise industry targets younger adults.

Empty nesters are the biggest spenders on ship fares. Married couples without children at home, most of whom are older, spend nearly three times as much as the average household on cruises. This household type accounts for 61.5 percent of all household spending on ship fares. The affluent can best afford to take a cruise, which explains why households with incomes of $70,000 or more spend more than three times as much as the average household on this item. Householders aged 65 to 74 spend 80 percent more than the average household on ship fares, while those aged 55 to 64 spend 53 percent more.

Spending on ship fares will increase rapidly in the years ahead because the baby-boom generation is about to enter the empty-nest life stage. In addition, the cruise industry is targeting younger adults as it builds more ships.

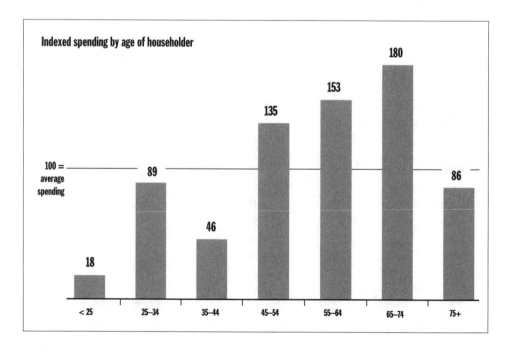

Indexed spending by age of householder

< 25	25–34	35–44	45–54	55–64	65–74	75+
18	89	46	135	153	180	86

100 = average spending

SHIP FARES

Total household spending	$2,787,206,400
Average household spends	26.40

	average spending	best customers (index)	biggest customers (market share)
AGE OF HOUSEHOLDER			
Total households	**$26.40**	**100**	**100.0%**
Under age 25	4.72	18	1.3
Aged 25 to 34	23.42	89	16.7
Aged 35 to 44	12.12	46	10.7
Aged 45 to 54	35.63	135	24.7
Aged 55 to 64	40.51	153	17.9
Aged 65 to 74	47.49	180	20.6
Aged 75 or older	22.81	86	8.0
HOUSEHOLD INCOME			
Total households reporting income	**18.98**	**100**	**100.0**
Under $20,000	1.34	7	2.5
$20,000 to $29,999	1.11	6	0.9
$30,000 to $39,999	9.53	50	6.1
$40,000 to $49,999	23.12	122	11.4
$50,000 to $69,999	37.93	200	28.1
$70,000 or more	64.88	342	51.1
HOUSEHOLD TYPE			
Total households	**26.40**	**100**	**100.0**
Married couples	39.91	151	79.0
Married couples, no children	76.11	288	61.5
Married couples, with children	15.10	57	15.4
Oldest child under 6	6.45	24	1.3
Oldest child 6 to 17	16.77	64	9.2
Oldest child 18 or older	17.89	68	4.9
Single parent with child under 18	4.90	19	1.2
Single person	12.66	48	13.8
REGION			
Total households	**26.40**	**100**	**100.0**
Northeast	33.48	127	25.3
Midwest	33.74	128	30.5
South	12.36	47	16.3
West	34.53	131	27.8

Note: For definitions of best and biggest customers, see introduction or glossary.
Source: Calculations by New Strategist based on the 1997 Consumer Expenditure Survey

Train Fares, Intercity

Best customers:
- Householders aged 45 to 64
- Married couples without children
- Married couples with adult children

Customer trends:
- Spending on train fares will rise if train service improves. Without improvements, spending will decline despite growing numbers of travelers.

Although many Americans would like to travel by rail, few do so because of the inconvenience. Older Americans spend the most on intercity train fares. Householders aged 45 to 64, the biggest travelers, spend 49 to 51 percent more than the average householder on this item. Married couples without children, most of whom are older, and those with adult children at home, spend 58 to 65 percent more than the average household on train fares.

Spending on train fares is likely to decline unless service improves and train travel becomes more convenient. As is true with bus passengers, the customers of train travel are aging because younger generations prefer to travel to their destinations by air or car.

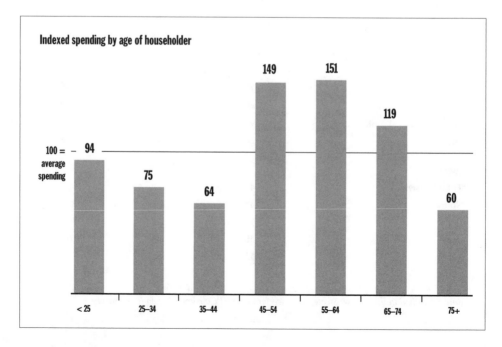

Indexed spending by age of householder

Age	Index
< 25	94
25–34	75
35–44	64
45–54	149
55–64	151
65–74	119
75+	60

100 = average spending

TRAIN FARES, INTERCITY

Total household spending	$2,237,155,440
Average household spends	21.19

	average spending	best customers (index)	biggest customers (market share)
AGE OF HOUSEHOLDER			
Total households	**$21.19**	**100**	**100.0%**
Under age 25	19.83	94	6.6
Aged 25 to 34	15.95	75	14.2
Aged 35 to 44	13.64	64	15.0
Aged 45 to 54	31.59	149	27.3
Aged 55 to 64	32.09	151	17.7
Aged 65 to 74	25.12	119	13.6
Aged 75 or older	12.75	60	5.6
HOUSEHOLD INCOME			
Total households reporting income	**21.26**	**100**	**100.0**
Under $20,000	9.09	43	14.9
$20,000 to $29,999	14.41	68	9.9
$30,000 to $39,999	12.98	61	7.5
$40,000 to $49,999	18.73	88	8.2
$50,000 to $69,999	28.68	135	18.9
$70,000 or more	57.69	271	40.6
HOUSEHOLD TYPE			
Total households	**21.19**	**100**	**100.0**
Married couples	28.05	132	69.2
Married couples, no children	35.01	165	35.3
Married couples, with children	22.53	106	28.6
Oldest child under 6	16.50	78	4.0
Oldest child 6 to 17	19.23	91	13.2
Oldest child 18 or older	33.53	158	11.4
Single parent with child under 18	5.69	27	1.7
Single person	14.69	69	19.9
REGION			
Total households	**21.19**	**100**	**100.0**
Northeast	27.71	131	26.1
Midwest	21.28	100	24.0
South	14.62	69	24.1
West	25.75	122	25.8

Note: For definitions of best and biggest customers, see introduction or glossary.
Source: Calculations by New Strategist based on the 1997 Consumer Expenditure Survey

Transportation, Local, on Out-of-Town Trips

Best customers:
- Householders aged 55 to 74
- Married couples with adult children
- Married couples without children

Customer trends:
- Spending will increase as a growing number of aging travelers avoid driving their cars in unfamiliar places.

The best customers of local transportation while on trips are older travelers. Householders aged 55 to 74 spend 21 to 41 percent more than the average householder on local transportation while on trips. Many are avoiding the stress of driving their own cars in unfamiliar places. Married couples without children, most of whom are older, and those with adult children at home spend 40 to 51 percent more than the average household on this item.

Spending on local transportation while traveling is likely to increase as a growing number of older travelers leave their car in the hotel parking garage and take a taxi. Falling crime rates will also encourage more spending on public transportation while on trips.

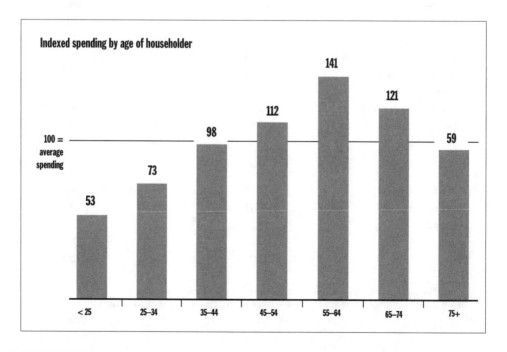

Indexed spending by age of householder

100 = average spending

<25	25–34	35–44	45–54	55–64	65–74	75+
53	73	98	112	141	121	59

TRANSPORTATION, LOCAL, ON OUT-OF-TOWN TRIPS

Total household spending $2,112,575,760
Average household spends   20.01

	average spending	best customers (index)	biggest customers (market share)
AGE OF HOUSEHOLDER			
Total households	**$20.01**	**100**	**100.0%**
Under age 25	10.60	53	3.8
Aged 25 to 34	14.57	73	13.7
Aged 35 to 44	19.64	98	22.8
Aged 45 to 54	22.32	112	20.4
Aged 55 to 64	28.28	141	16.5
Aged 65 to 74	24.30	121	13.9
Aged 75 or older	18.95	95	8.8
HOUSEHOLD INCOME			
Total households reporting income	**19.41**	**100**	**100.0**
Under $20,000	8.00	41	14.4
$20,000 to $29,999	14.33	74	10.8
$30,000 to $39,999	12.22	63	7.7
$40,000 to $49,999	19.95	103	9.6
$50,000 to $69,999	23.14	119	16.7
$70,000 or more	52.99	273	40.8
HOUSEHOLD TYPE			
Total households	**20.01**	**100**	**100.0**
Married couples	25.78	129	67.4
Married couples, no children	27.95	140	29.8
Married couples, with children	22.33	112	30.0
Oldest child under 6	20.83	104	5.4
Oldest child 6 to 17	18.97	95	13.8
Oldest child 18 or older	30.19	151	10.8
Single parent with child under 18	6.43	32	2.0
Single person	16.10	80	23.1
REGION			
Total households	**20.01**	**100**	**100.0**
Northeast	23.87	119	23.8
Midwest	16.70	83	19.9
South	16.62	83	29.0
West	25.68	128	27.3

Note: For definitions of best and biggest customers, see introduction or glossary.
Source: Calculations by New Strategist based on the 1997 Consumer Expenditure Survey

Appendix A

About the Consumer Expenditure Survey

History

The Consumer Expenditure Survey (CEX) is an ongoing study of the day-to-day spending of American households. In taking the survey, government interviewers collect spending data on products and services as well as the amount and sources of household income, changes in saving and debt, and demographic and economic characteristics of household members. Data collection for the CEX is done by the Bureau of the Census, under contract with the Bureau of Labor Statistics (BLS). The BLS is responsible for analysis and release of the survey data.

Since the late 19th century, the federal government has conducted expenditure surveys about every ten years. Although the results have been used for a variety of purposes, their primary application is to track consumer prices. Beginning in 1980, the CEX became a continuous survey with annual release of data (with a lag time of about two years between data collection and release). The survey is used to update prices for the market basket of products and services used in calculating the Consumer Price Index.

Description of the Consumer Expenditure Survey

The CEX is two surveys: an interview survey and a diary survey. In the interview portion of the survey, respondents are asked each quarter for five consecutive quarters to report their expenditures for the previous three months. The purchase of big-ticket items such as houses, cars, and major appliances, or recurring expenses such as insurance premiums, utility payments, and rent are recorded by the interview survey. About 95 percent of all expenditures are covered by the interview component.

Expenditures on small, frequently purchased items are recorded during a two-week period by the diary survey. These detailed records include expenses for food and beverages purchased in grocery stores and at restaurants, as well as other items such as tobacco, housekeeping supplies, nonprescription drugs, and personal care products and services. The diary survey is intended to capture expenditures that respondents are likely to forget or recall incorrectly over longer periods of time.

The average spending figures shown in this book are the integrated data from both the diary and interview components of the survey. Integrated data provide a more complete accounting of consumer expenditures than either component of the survey is designed to do alone.

Data Collection and Processing

Two separate, nationally representative samples are used for the interview and diary surveys. For the interview survey, about 5,000 consumer units are interviewed on a rotating panel basis each quarter for five consecutive quarters. Another 5,000 consumer units keep weekly diaries of spending for two consecutive weeks. The 10,000 diaries accumulated during a survey year are the basis for the diary survey. Data collection is carried out in 101 areas of the country.

The data are reviewed, audited, and cleaned by the BLS, and then weighted to reflect the number and characteristics of all U.S. consumer units. As with any sample survey, the CEX is subject to two major types of error. Nonsampling error occurs when respondents misinterpret questions or interviewers are inconsistent in the way they ask questions or record answers. Respondents may forget items, recall expenses incorrectly, or deliberately give wrong answers. A respondent may remember how much he or she spent at the grocery store but forget the items picked up at a local convenience store. Most surveys of alcohol consumption or spending on alcohol suffer from this type of underreporting, for example. Nonsampling error can also be caused by mistakes during the various stages of data processing and refinement.

Sampling error occurs when a sample does not accurately represent the population it is supposed to represent. This kind of error is present in every sample-based survey and is minimized by using a proper sampling procedure. As previously mentioned, standard error tables that document the extent of sampling error in the CEX are available from the BLS.

Although the CEX is the best source of information about the spending behavior of American households, it should be treated with caution because of the above problems. Comparisons with consumption data from other sources show that CEX data tend to underestimate expenditures except for rent, fuel, telephone service, furniture, transportation, and personal care services. Despite these problems, the data reveal important spending patterns by demographic segment that businesses can use to better market their products and services.

The Definition of Consumer Units

The CEX uses consumer units as its sampling unit instead of households, which are the sampling units used by the Census Bureau. The term "household" is used interchangeably with the term "consumer unit" in this book for convenience, although they are not exactly the same. Some households contain more than one consumer unit.

Consumer units are defined by the BLS as either: 1) members of a household who are related by blood, marriage, adoption, or other legal arrangements; 2) a person living alone or sharing a household with others or living as a roomer in a private home or lodging house or in permanent living quarters in a hotel or motel, but who is financially independent; or 3) two persons or more living together who pool their income to make joint expenditure decisions. The BLS defines financial independence in terms of "the three major expenses categories: housing, food, and other living expenses. To be considered financially independent, at least two of the three major expense categories have to be provided by the respondent."

The Census Bureau uses households as its sampling unit in the decennial census and in the monthly Current Population Survey. The Census Bureau's household "consists of all persons who occupy a housing unit. A house, an apartment or other groups of rooms, or a single room is regarded as a housing unit when it is occupied or intended for occupancy as separate living quarters; that is, when the occupants do not live and eat with any other persons in the structure and there is direct access from the outside or through a common hall."

The definition goes on to specify that "a household includes the related family members and all the unrelated persons, if any, such as lodgers, foster children, wards, or employees who share the housing unit. A person living alone in a housing unit or a group of unrelated persons sharing a housing unit as partners is also counted as a household. The count of households excludes group quarters."

Because there can be more than one consumer unit in a household, consumer units outnumber households by several million. Most of the excess consumer units are headed by young adults, under age 25.

For More Information

If you want to know more about the Consumer Expenditure Survey, contact the CEX specialists at the Bureau of Labor Statistics at (202) 606-6900, or visit the Consumer Expenditure Survey home page at <www.bls.gov/csxhome.htm>. The CEX web site includes news releases, technical documentation, and current and historical CEX data. The average spending figures for the 300 individual products and services analyzed in Best Customers are available only in printed reports from the BLS by special request.

Appendix B

Percent Reporting Expenditure and Average Amount Spent by Purchasers

(percent of households reporting expenditure and amount spent by purchasers during an average quarter, 1997)

	percent of households reporting expenditure during quarter	average amount spent per quarter
ALCOHOLIC BEVERAGES	**45.31%**	**$152.66**
At home	**35.09**	**103.18**
Beer and wine	33.64	87.57
Other alcoholic beverages	9.44	71.48
Away from home	**31.48**	**104.71**
Alcoholic beverages at restaurants, taverns	24.33	102.10
APPAREL	**84.79**	**405.76**
Men's apparel	**37.94**	**184.07**
Suits	2.46	357.52
Sportcoats and tailored jackets	2.25	168.78
Coats and jackets	5.61	122.46
Underwear	9.83	25.15
Hosiery	10.20	16.64
Nightwear	1.59	37.74
Accessories	7.29	37.96
Sweaters and vests	4.62	85.71
Active sportswear	4.98	56.78
Shirts	19.31	75.09
Pants	19.51	86.42
Shorts and shorts sets	6.01	47.38
Uniforms	1.19	96.43
Costumes	0.70	99.64
Boys' (aged 2 to 15) apparel	**14.90**	**134.16**
Coats and jackets	3.09	67.39
Sweaters	1.34	52.43
Shirts	7.61	56.73
Underwear	4.53	23.18
Nightwear	1.21	30.99

	percent of households reporting expenditure during quarter	average amount spent per quarter
Hosiery	4.43%	$13.77
Accessories	1.99	20.35
Suits, sportcoats, and vests	0.92	78.53
Pants	7.78	70.21
Shorts and shorts sets	4.20	51.55
Uniforms	2.75	40.09
Active sportswear	0.85	77.94
Costumes	1.10	30.23
Women's apparel	**51.98**	**206.52**
Coats and jackets	7.44	117.81
Dresses	15.47	119.49
Sportcoats and tailored jackets	2.73	95.05
Sweaters and vests	10.11	76.43
Shirts, blouses, and tops	23.33	61.46
Skirts	6.93	54.26
Pants	19.52	69.43
Shorts and shorts sets	8.60	48.72
Active sportswear	6.80	56.54
Nightwear	7.80	40.74
Undergarments	16.35	36.48
Hosiery	21.69	22.54
Suits	5.08	188.48
Accessories	9.89	40.52
Uniforms	1.92	81.77
Costumes	0.88	103.41
Girls' (aged 2 to 15) apparel	**15.70**	**146.02**
Coats and jackets	2.60	62.50
Dresses and suits	5.20	59.38
Shirts, blouses, and sweaters	8.18	65.16
Skirts and pants	7.32	66.56
Shorts and shorts sets	4.30	56.22
Active sportswear	2.82	38.48
Underwear and nightwear	5.88	28.70
Hosiery	4.88	14.34
Accessories	2.23	20.52
Uniforms	0.88	90.06
Costumes	1.49	58.39
Children under age 2	**17.23**	**102.70**
Coats, jackets, and snowsuits	2.31	35.50
Outerwear including dresses	10.34	59.33
Underwear	9.52	83.88

	percent of households reporting expenditure during quarter	average amount spent per quarter
Nightwear and loungewear	4.25%	$25.76
Accessories	5.55	29.86
Footwear	**38.52**	**97.71**
Men's	15.07	87.16
Boys'	7.39	61.47
Women's	22.59	71.57
Girls'	7.75	48.97
Other apparel products and services	**54.90**	**124.97**
Material for making clothes	2.74	52.10
Sewing patterns and notions	3.32	15.66
Watches	6.12	90.69
Jewelry	10.39	280.44
Shoe repair and other shoe services	2.42	24.59
Laundry and dry cleaning, coin-operated	18.52	47.98
Apparel alteration, repair, and tailoring services	4.20	36.31
Clothing rental	1.01	95.30
Watch and jewelry repair	4.25	29.88
Laundry and dry cleaning, professional	29.35	63.57
Clothing storage	0.12	62.50
COMPUTERS		
Computer information services	8.53	60.52
Computer software and accessories for nonbusiness use	4.19	147.49
Computer systems for nonbusiness use, repair	0.50	123.50
Computers and computer hardware for nonbusiness use	3.59	1,132.73
EDUCATION	**17.21**	**764.31**
College tuition	5.54	1,471.53
Elementary/high school tuition	2.40	938.96
Other schools tuition	1.11	433.78
Other school expenses including rentals	4.78	143.51
Books, supplies for college	5.31	225.38
Books, supplies for elementary, high school	4.22	72.39
Books, supplies for day care, nursery school	0.77	101.62
ENTERTAINMENT	**89.38**	**476.85**
Fees and admissions	**55.65**	**211.47**
Social, recreation, civic club membership	12.30	152.68
Fees for participant sports	14.71	123.42
Movie, theater, opera, ballet tickets	36.50	59.39

	percent of households reporting expenditure during quarter	average amount spent per quarter
Admission to sports events	8.98%	$93.29
Fees for recreational lessons	8.17	205.54
Television	**69.32**	**145.52**
Cable TV or community antenna	62.30	105.27
Black and white TV	0.11	152.27
Color TV, console	0.73	861.99
Color TV, portable, table model	2.77	360.65
VCRs and video disc players	2.28	291.45
Video cassettes, tapes, and discs	15.49	35.75
Video game hardware and software	4.13	119.49
Repair of TV, radio, and sound equipment	1.58	105.22
Rental of televisions	0.06	100.00
Radios and sound equipment	**47.49**	**86.50**
Radios	1.80	98.06
Tape recorders and players	0.45	107.22
Sound components and component systems	2.39	312.34
Compact disc, tape, record, video mail order clubs	5.17	51.21
Records, CDs, audio tapes, needles	20.42	48.25
Rental of VCR, radio, sound equipment	0.12	93.75
Musical instruments and accessories	2.07	289.37
Rental and repair of musical instruments	0.56	73.21
Rental of video cassettes, tapes, discs, films	35.49	28.39
Sound equipment accessories	0.91	153.30
Satellite dishes	0.23	370.65
Pets	**27.19**	**131.68**
Pet purchase, supplies, and medicines	20.88	86.88
Pet services	5.06	84.83
Veterinary services	9.78	136.73
Toys, games, hobbies, and tricycles	**21.14**	**158.61**
Playground equipment	**0.45**	**152.22**
OTHER ENTERTAINMENT SUPPLIES, EQUIPMENT, SERVICES	**40.04**	**241.13**
Unmotored recreational vehicles	**0.27**	**3,515.74**
Boat without motor and boat trailers	0.16	1,325.00
Trailer and other attachable campers	0.11	6,702.27
Motorized recreational vehicles	**0.31**	**11,770.97**
Motorized camper	0.04	16,356.25
Other vehicle	0.09	2,950.00
Motor boats	0.18	15,162.50

	percent of households reporting expenditure during quarter	average amount spent per quarter
Rental of recreational vehicles	**0.28%**	**$299.11**
Rental of noncamper trailer	0.02	37.50
Rental of boat	0.02	25.00
Rental of other RVs	0.01	300.00
Outboard motors	**0.06**	**1,362.50**
Docking and landing fees	**0.76**	**313.16**
Sports, recreation, exercise equipment	**14.46**	**208.71**
Athletic gear, game tables, exercise equipment	8.22	174.76
Bicycles	2.01	189.93
Camping equipment	0.97	91.49
Hunting and fishing equipment	2.75	147.45
Winter sports equipment	0.53	259.43
Water sports equipment	0.71	159.15
Other sports equipment	1.86	218.95
Rental and repair of miscellaneous sports equipment	0.52	91.83
Photographic equipment and supplies	**33.16**	**49.31**
Film	26.45	20.19
Film processing	24.86	29.53
Repair and rental of photographic equipment	0.12	102.08
Photographic equipment	2.06	172.21
FINANCIAL PRODUCTS & SERVICES		
Miscellaneous financial products and services	**46.24**	**408.10**
Legal fees	3.53	961.69
Funeral expenses	2.22	710.02
Safe deposit box rental	5.37	31.15
Checking accounts, other bank service charges	22.70	26.99
Cemetery lots, vaults, and maintenance fees	1.24	396.17
Accounting fees	6.01	203.79
Finance charges, except mortgage and vehicles	10.35	602.42
Occupational expenses	5.49	467.44
Expenses for other properties	6.93	359.34
Interest paid, home equity line of credit (other property)	0.02	612.50
Credit card memberships	2.07	48.07
Cash contributions	**12.76**	**1,961.01**
Cash contributions to non-household members, including students, alimony, child support	1.65	3,848.18
Gifts of cash, stocks, bonds to non-household members	3.54	1,589.19
Contributions to charities	6.44	395.77
Contributions to religious organizations	8.26	1,181.14
Contributions to educational organizations	1.43	295.10

	percent of households reporting expenditure during quarter	average amount spent per quarter
Contributions to political organizations	0.87%	$178.16
Other contributions	0.79	209.18
Personal insurance and pensions	**75.60**	**1,065.83**
Life and other personal insurance	38.81	243.90
Life, endowment, annuity, other personal insurance	37.99	243.14
Other nonhealth insurance	1.98	115.53
Pensions and Social Security	64.99	1,094.18
Deductions for government retirement	3.45	587.10
Deductions for railroad retirement	0.13	434.62
Deductions for private pensions	10.27	825.75
Non-payroll deposit to retirement plans	10.10	932.30
Deductions for Social Security	64.43	793.60
Personal taxes	**66.68**	**1,215.32**
Federal income taxes	62.25	991.12
State and local income taxes	45.56	353.82
Other taxes	14.09	228.50
FOOD	**99.94**	**1,216.88**
Food at home	**99.37**	**890.76**
Grocery stores	98.90	866.33
Convenience stores	30.03	201.22
Food away from home	**84.84**	**390.15**
Meals at restaurants, carryouts, and other	80.90	282.10
Board (including at school)	1.91	679.06
Catered affairs	1.48	858.11
School lunches	11.14	121.25
Meals as pay	2.44	312.60
GIFTS	**43.06**	**439.49**
Food	**1.46**	**582.88**
Housing	**21.08**	**240.93**
Household textiles	3.50	59.64
Appliances and miscellaneous housewares	4.15	116.20
Major appliances	0.54	292.59
Small appliances and miscellaneous housewares	3.80	85.39
Miscellaneous household equipment	11.05	95.32
Other housing	7.48	445.79
Apparel and services	**23.98**	**172.68**
Males 2 and older	7.46	141.22
Females 2 and older	9.35	141.28

	percent of households reporting expenditure during quarter	average amount spent per quarter
Children under 2	11.94%	$73.81
Other apparel products and services	6.46	137.00
Jewelry and watches	3.80	174.14
All other apparel products and services	3.16	70.57
Transportation	**6.47**	**205.80**
Health care	**1.80**	**368.06**
Entertainment	**13.98**	**143.87**
Toys, games, hobbies, and tricycles	7.36	112.67
Other entertainment	8.06	146.65
Education	**2.63**	**1,398.19**
All other gifts	**6.66**	**175.86**
HEALTH CARE	**80.47**	**530.25**
Health insurance	**62.95**	**349.99**
Commercial health insurance	15.50	328.02
Traditional fee for service health plan (not BCBS)	8.18	305.90
Preferred provider health plan (not BCBS)	7.75	333.19
Blue Cross, Blue Shield	14.46	332.83
Traditional fee for service health plan	4.30	365.87
Preferred provider health plan	3.66	317.28
Health maintenance organization	4.27	277.46
Commercial Medicare supplement	2.20	362.73
Other BCBS health insurance	0.67	142.54
Health maintenance plans (HMOs)	19.92	287.49
Medicare payments	23.46	171.48
Commercial Medicare supplements/other health insurance	10.77	221.45
Commercial Medicare supplement (not BCBS)	4.54	334.03
Other health insurance (not BCBS)	6.61	131.39
Medical services	**46.92**	**282.62**
Physician's services	29.99	111.36
Dental services	18.92	268.97
Eye care services	7.86	86.32
Service by professionals other than physician	4.77	194.08
Lab tests, X-rays	5.03	113.97
Hospital room	2.16	405.90
Hospital services other than room	4.04	324.07
Care in convalescent or nursing home	0.23	1,422.83
Other medical services	1.13	124.78
Prescription drugs	44.80	120.86

	percent of households reporting expenditure during quarter	average amount spent per quarter
Medical supplies	10.87%	$180.50
Eyeglasses and contact lenses	8.92	167.40
Hearing aids	0.81	352.47
Medical equipment for general use	0.80	75.94
Supportive/convalescent medical equipment	0.76	86.18
Rental of medical equipment	0.31	48.39
Rental of supportive, convalescent medical equipment	0.41	101.83
HOUSEHOLD FURNISHINGS & EQUIPMENT	**59.05**	**519.94**
Household textiles	**20.89**	**94.69**
Bathroom linens	7.23	38.49
Bedroom linens	10.14	84.52
Kitchen and dining room linens	2.47	24.29
Curtains and draperies	2.85	146.75
Slipcovers and decorative pillows	0.99	53.03
Sewing materials for household items	5.33	52.53
Other linens	0.73	43.84
Furniture	**13.00**	**744.88**
Mattresses and springs	2.43	479.01
Other bedroom furniture	2.70	592.50
Sofas	2.74	855.93
Living room chairs	2.46	481.91
Living room tables	1.77	290.96
Kitchen and dining room furniture	2.03	599.63
Infants' furniture	1.19	207.35
Outdoor furniture	1.87	181.95
Wall units, cabinets, and other furniture	2.96	361.57
Floor coverings	**3.68**	**372.89**
Wall-to-wall carpeting (renter)	0.18	269.44
Wall-to-wall carpeting, installed	0.05	685.00
Wall-to-wall carpeting, not installed carpet squares	0.14	100.00
Wall-to-wall carpeting, replacement (owner)	0.94	980.85
Wall-to-wall carpeting, not installed carpet squares	0.33	203.03
Wall-to-wall carpeting, installed	0.63	1,357.14
Room-size rugs and other floor covering, nonpermanent	2.63	152.76
Major appliances	**8.51**	**487.07**
Dishwashers (built-in), garbage disposals, range hoods (renter)	0.08	256.25
Dishwashers (built-in), garbage disposals, range hoods (owner)	0.76	383.22
Refrigerators and freezers (renter)	0.48	495.83
Refrigerators and freezers (owner)	1.60	751.25

	percent of households reporting expenditure during quarter	average amount spent per quarter
Washing machines (renter)	0.45%	$303.33
Washing machines (owner)	1.00	439.00
Clothes dryers (renter)	0.37	297.30
Clothes dryers (owner)	0.78	378.85
Cooking stoves, ovens (renter)	0.24	294.79
Cooking stoves, ovens (owner)	0.84	572.32
Microwave ovens (renter)	0.58	127.59
Microwave ovens (owner)	0.85	195.00
Portable dishwasher (renter)	0.03	341.67
Portable dishwasher (owner)	0.03	216.67
Window air conditioners (renter)	0.13	325.00
Window air conditioners (owner)	0.29	279.31
Electric floor cleaning equipment	1.90	206.32
Sewing machines	0.36	246.53
Small appliances and miscellaneous housewares	**18.44**	**83.62**
Housewares	11.41	78.66
Plastic dinnerware	1.45	30.17
China and other dinnerware	3.71	82.08
Flatware	1.98	59.09
Glassware	3.13	38.90
Silver serving pieces	0.08	40.63
Other serving pieces	1.05	41.43
Nonelectric cookware	4.06	64.90
Small appliances	9.44	68.30
Small electric kitchen appliances	7.83	53.22
Portable heating and cooling equipment	1.96	116.33
Miscellaneous household equipment	**43.22**	**277.23**
Window coverings	1.88	182.31
Infants' equipment	1.09	78.90
Outdoor equipment	0.76	136.51
Clocks	1.70	61.32
Lamps and lighting fixtures	3.36	93.23
Decorative items for the home	11.20	161.54
Telephones and accessories	5.38	75.19
Lawn and garden equipment	2.88	341.75
Power tools	2.35	165.53
Small miscellaneous furnishings	1.22	257.79
Hand tools	3.76	61.77
Plants and fresh flowers, indoor	21.48	60.91
Closet and storage items	1.68	63.24
Rental of furniture	0.36	236.81

	percent of households reporting expenditure during quarter	average amount spent per quarter
Telephone answering devices	1.32%	$62.69
Calculators	1.40	34.29
Business equipment for home use	0.34	171.32
Smoke alarms (owner)	0.50	43.00
Smoke alarms (renter)	0.10	47.50
Other household appliances (owner)	1.25	175.60
Other household appliances (renter)	0.53	69.34
HOUSEHOLD SERVICES	**41.63**	**323.17**
Personal services	**9.29**	**708.02**
Babysitting and child care in your own home	2.51	342.53
Babysitting and child care in someone else's home	1.94	481.57
Care for elderly, invalids, handicapped, etc.	0.44	1,531.25
Adult day care centers	0.07	1,353.57
Day care centers, nursery and preschools	5.79	693.44
Other household services	**36.61**	**187.82**
Housekeeping services	6.22	302.81
Gardening, lawn care service	12.67	142.94
Water softening service	1.39	81.12
Nonapparel laundry and dry cleaning, sent out	1.24	28.02
Nonapparel laundry and dry cleaning, coin-operated	6.91	17.76
Termite/pest control services	2.45	117.86
Other home services	2.76	144.38
Termite/pest control products	0.11	27.27
Moving, storage, and freight express	3.07	282.98
Appliance repair, including service center	3.37	100.15
Reupholstering and furniture repair	1.02	266.42
Repairs/rentals of lawn/garden equipment, hand/power tools, etc.	1.46	87.84
Appliance rental	0.25	105.00
Rental of office equipment for nonbusiness use	0.13	82.69
PERSONAL CARE PRODUCTS AND SERVICES	**74.82**	**97.41**
Wigs and hairpieces	0.59	51.69
Electric personal care appliances	3.32	34.34
Personal care services/female	54.14	86.95
Personal care services/male	54.86	44.32
Repair of personal care appliances	0.17	29.41
SHELTER	**98.18**	**1,615.37**
Owned dwellings	**64.05**	**1,535.86**
Mortgage interest and charges	38.61	1,440.86

	percent of households reporting expenditure during quarter	average amount spent per quarter
Mortgage interest	36.76%	$1,434.34
Interest paid, home equity loan	3.41	419.43
Interest paid, home equity line of credit	2.52	583.73
Prepayment penalty charge	0.05	80.00
Property taxes	63.44	382.70
Maintenance, repairs, insurance, other expenses	36.44	506.63
Homeowners and related insurance	24.71	233.62
Fire and extended coverage	1.16	172.84
Homeowners insurance	24.15	230.72
Ground rent	1.36	683.09
Maintenance and repair services	12.97	704.72
Painting and papering	1.53	740.36
Plumbing and water heating	3.87	236.50
Heat, air conditioning, electrical work	4.02	393.53
Roofing and gutters	1.06	1,721.46
Other repair and maintenance services	4.88	637.65
Repair/replacement of hard surface flooring	0.51	1,037.75
Repair of built-in appliances	0.47	95.21
Maintenance and repair materials	7.97	263.21
Paints, wallpaper and supplies	3.55	129.08
Tools/equipment for painting, wallpapering	3.55	13.87
Plumbing supplies and equipment	1.26	136.31
Electrical supplies, heating/cooling equipment	0.41	277.44
Hard surface flooring, repair and replacement	0.50	356.50
Roofing and gutters	0.44	441.48
Plaster, paneling, siding, windows, doors, screens, awnings	1.25	299.40
Patio, walk, fence, driveway, masonry, brick, and stucco work	0.42	54.76
Landscape maintenance	0.60	216.25
Miscellaneous supplies and equipment	1.85	219.05
Insulation, other maintenance/repair	1.58	145.89
Finish basement, remodel rooms, build patios, walks, etc.	0.31	563.71
Property management and security	3.17	154.42
Property management	2.98	138.34
Management and upkeep services for security	0.80	96.56
Parking	0.35	92.86
Rented dwellings	**34.72**	**1,427.98**
Rent	34.40	1,363.96
Rent as pay	1.51	1,198.01
Maintenance, insurance, and other expenses	4.04	210.52
Tenant's insurance	2.52	96.83

	percent of households reporting expenditure during quarter	average amount spent per quarter
Maintenance and repair services	0.63%	$659.52
Repair or maintenance services	0.58	664.66
Repair and replacement of hard surface flooring	0.05	585.00
Repair of built-in appliances	0.02	37.50
Maintenance and repair materials	1.23	155.08
Paint, wallpaper, and supplies	0.48	81.77
Painting and wallpapering	0.48	8.85
Plastering, paneling, roofing, gutters, etc.	0.17	179.41
Patio, walk, fence, driveway, masonry, brick, stucco work	0.02	25.00
Plumbing supplies and equipment	0.14	64.29
Electrical supplies, heating and cooling equipment	0.05	40.00
Miscellaneous supplies and equipment	0.41	179.27
Insulation, other maintenance and repair	0.30	86.67
Materials for additions, finishing basements, remodeling rooms	0.10	412.50
Construction materials for jobs not started	0.02	312.50
Hard surface flooring	0.06	308.33
Landscape maintenance	0.11	120.45
Other lodging	**21.83**	**487.65**
Owned vacation homes	4.29	779.08
Mortgage interest and charges	1.18	1,229.24
Mortgage interest	1.14	1,238.16
Interest paid, home equity loan	0.05	330.00
Interest paid, home equity line of credit	0.04	556.25
Property taxes	4.27	321.02
Maintenance, insurance and other expenses	1.26	413.49
Homeowners and related insurance	0.47	267.55
Homeowners insurance	0.43	271.51
Fire and extended coverage	0.05	180.00
Ground rent	0.07	582.14
Maintenance and repair services	0.66	365.91
Maintenance and repair materials	0.07	289.29
Property management and security	0.57	149.56
Property management	0.55	134.55
Management and upkeep services for security	0.20	56.25
Parking	0.08	90.63
Housing while attending school	1.42	1,168.13
UTILITIES	**98.10**	**614.76**
Natural gas	49.16	153.05
Electricity	90.87	249.99
Fuel oil and other fuels	11.31	238.11

	percent of households reporting expenditure during quarter	average amount spent per quarter
Telephone services	95.80%	$211.13
Telephone services in home city, excl. mobile phones	95.71	197.59
Telephone services for mobile phones	10.42	126.22
Water and other public services	58.76	121.64
Water and sewerage maintenance	52.78	98.18
Trash and garbage collection	36.74	51.71
Septic tank cleaning	0.36	181.94
READING MATERIAL	**65.33**	**62.60**
Newspaper subscriptions	30.89	41.84
Newspaper, nonsubscription	24.66	17.42
Magazine subscriptions	13.80	40.98
Magazines, nonsubscription	17.44	16.56
Books purchased through book clubs	4.91	51.83
Books not purchased through book clubs	24.33	50.86
Encyclopedia and other reference book sets	0.21	101.19
TOBACCO PRODUCTS	**29.70**	**219.77**
Cigarettes	26.87	216.14
Other tobacco products	4.76	145.90
TRANSPORTATION	**94.57**	**1,691.66**
Cars and trucks, new	**1.54**	**19,949.51**
New cars	0.91	19,236.81
New trucks	0.63	20,978.97
Cars and trucks, used	**4.87**	**7,512.94**
Used cars	3.36	6,661.53
Used trucks	1.65	8,609.39
Other vehicles	**0.17**	**6,404.41**
New motorcycles	0.06	10,995.83
Used motorcycles	0.10	3,830.00
Used aircraft	0.01	4,075.00
Gasoline and motor oil	**89.34**	**307.12**
Gasoline	88.24	279.16
Diesel fuel	1.25	202.00
Motor oil	17.91	16.89
Vehicle finance charges	**30.95**	**236.52**
Automobile finance charges	20.75	194.82
Truck finance charges	12.46	232.95
Motorcycle and plane finance charges	0.38	100.00
Other vehicle finance charges	1.43	235.84

	percent of households reporting expenditure during quarter	average amount spent per quarter
Maintenance and repairs	**58.61%**	**$271.78**
Coolant, additives, brake, transmission fluids	11.68	12.20
Tires	9.95	220.95
Parts, equipment, and accessories	14.37	89.27
Vehicle audio equipment	0.26	214.42
Body work and painting	1.81	445.99
Clutch, transmission repair	2.43	493.00
Drive shaft and rear-end repair	0.53	270.28
Brake work	6.96	200.50
Repair to steering or front-end	1.92	226.69
Repair to engine cooling system	2.89	172.84
Motor tune-up	6.96	161.82
Lube, oil change, and oil filters	33.45	40.58
Front-end alignment, wheel balance, rotation	3.10	97.82
Shock absorber replacement	0.71	175.35
Repair tires and other repair work	8.17	90.67
Exhaust system repair	2.79	165.95
Electrical system repair	4.20	174.64
Motor repair, replacement	3.82	493.78
Auto repair service policy	0.59	303.39
Vehicle accessories, including labor	1.08	214.58
Vehicle audio equipment, including labor	0.69	215.22
Vehicle air conditioning repair	1.93	247.02
Vehicle insurance	**48.80**	**386.78**
Vehicle rental, leases, licenses, other charges	**46.20**	**263.96**
Leased and rented vehicles	9.24	896.24
Rented vehicles	4.10	250.18
Auto rental	0.85	227.35
Truck rental	0.18	256.94
Truck rental, out-of-town trips	0.34	315.44
Leased vehicles	5.58	1,300.27
Car lease payments	3.70	1,096.49
Cash downpayment (car lease)	0.21	1,923.81
Termination fee (car lease)	0.04	1,131.25
Truck lease payments	2.18	1,128.10
Cash downpayment (truck lease)	0.16	1,660.94
Termination fee (truck lease)	0.03	808.33
State and local registration	19.84	119.23
Driver's license	7.67	24.19
Vehicle inspection	8.65	25.26
Parking fees in home city, excluding residence	12.04	50.60

	percent of households reporting expenditure during quarter	average amount spent per quarter
Towing charges	1.79%	$70.39
Automobile service clubs	3.72	55.04
Public transportation	**21.97**	**447.38**
Intracity mass transit fares	9.32	149.60
Taxi fares and limousine service	3.51	67.74
School bus	0.19	125.00
TRAVEL		
Admission to sports events, out-of-town trips	13.53	25.83
Airline fares	11.63	534.87
Alcohol purchased on trips	15.14	53.63
Auto rental on out-of-town trips	2.87	233.28
Bus fares, intercity	5.56	47.26
Food on out-of-town trips	33.20	168.60
Food prepared by household on out-of-town trips	18.24	70.79
Gasoline on out-of-town trips	29.19	76.32
Local transportation on out-of-town trips	6.30	50.04
Lodging on out-of-town trips	18.00	313.57
Luggage	2.40	101.25
Motor oil on out-of-town trips	29.19	0.77
Movie, other admissions, out-of-town trips	13.53	77.48
Other entertainment services, out-of-town trips	12.12	50.95
Parking fees, out-of-town trips	4.00	23.94
Participant sports, out-of-town trips	6.86	110.42
Recreation expenses, out of town trips	12.12	50.95
Ship fares	2.72	242.65
Taxi fares and limousine service on trips	6.30	29.37
Tolls on out-of-town trips	9.07	11.91
Train fares, intercity	5.04	105.11

Note: The categories listed here do not necessarily match the categories in this book.
Source: Bureau of Labor Statistics, unpublished data from the 1997 Consumer Expenditure Survey; calculations by New Strategist

Appendix C

Spending by Product and Service, 1997

(average annual spending of households on products and services, ranked by amount spent, 1997)

Federal income tax*	$2,467.90
Mortgage interest	2,109.06
Social Security*	2,045.27
Rent	1,876.81
Gasoline and motor oil	1,087.42
Property taxes	971.15
Electricity	908.67
Cars, used	895.31
Telephone service in home city, excluding mobile phone	756.44
Insurance, vehicle	754.99
Dinner at restaurants, carry-outs	740.70
Cars, new	700.22
Vehicle maintenance and repairs	681.62
State and local income tax*	644.81
Apparel, women's	574.26
Trucks, used	568.22
Trucks, new	528.67
Lunch at restaurants, carry-outs	501.92
Contributions to religious organizations	390.25
Insurance, life and other personal except health	378.63
Retirement accounts, nonpayroll deposits	376.65
Maintenance and repair services, owned homes	365.61
Pensions, deductions for private	339.22
Tuition, college	326.09
Apparel, men's	322.98
Natural gas	300.96
Finance charges, vehicle	292.81
Health insurance, health maintenance organization	276.46
Food on out-of-town trips	275.55
Cable TV or community antenna	262.34
Contributions of cash to nonhousehold members including students, alimony, child support	253.98
Finance charges, except mortgage and vehicle	249.40
Airline fares	248.82
Cigarettes	232.31

Insurance, homeowners	$230.91
Lodging on out-of-town trips	225.77
Gifts of cash, stocks, bonds to nonhousehold members	225.03
Beef	223.55
Drugs, prescription	216.58
Water and sewerage maintenance	207.28
Dental services	203.56
Apparel, children's	189.89
Personal care services, female	188.30
Car lease payments	180.25
Health insurance, traditional fee for service	163.02
Computers and computer hardware for nonbusiness use	162.66
Medicare*	160.92
Day care centers, nursery schools, preschools	160.60
Shoes, women's	157.11
Fruit, fresh	150.47
Health insurance, preferred provider plan	149.74
Poultry	145.01
Vegetables, fresh	142.75
Jewelry	142.02
Legal fees	135.79
Recreation expenses, out-of-town trips	135.61
Decorative items for the home	134.12
Vacation homes, owned	133.69
Physician services	133.59
Carbonated drinks	133.45
Beer and ale	130.42
Movie, theater, opera, ballet tickets	128.64
Toys, games, hobbies, and tricycles	127.68
Snacks and nonalcoholic beverages purchased at restaurants, carry-outs	119.38
Milk, fresh	118.78
Home equity loan/line of credit interest	116.05
Laundry and cleaning supplies	115.85
Breakfast and brunch at restaurants, carry-outs	115.51
Cosmetics, perfume, and bath products	109.99
Truck lease payments	109.97
Motor boats	109.17
Fuel oil and other fuels	107.72
Fees for participant sports	102.92
Occupational expenses, union and professional dues	102.65
Contributions to charities	101.95
Shoes, men	100.43
Personal care services, male	97.25
Telephones and accessories	96.54

Cheese	$94.33
Sofas	93.81
Health insurance, commercial Medicare supplements	92.58
Cereal, ready-to-eat and cooked	91.15
Tuition, elementary and high school	90.14
Fish and seafood	88.54
Pet food	87.23
Maintenance and repair materials, owned homes	83.91
Bread	83.43
Wine	79.62
Apparel, infants'	77.05
Trash collection	76.00
Drugs, nonprescription	75.43
Housekeeping services	75.34
Social, recreation, and civic club memberships	75.12
Gardening and lawn care service	72.44
Candy and chewing gum	69.26
Fees for recreational lessons	67.17
Potato chips and other snacks	66.83
Television sets	65.80
Lunch meats (cold cuts)	65.55
Cleansing and toilet tissues, paper towels, and napkins	64.42
Bedroom furniture, except mattresses and springs	63.99
Funeral expenses	63.05
Stationery, stationery supplies, giftwrap	62.61
Postage	62.53
Athletic gear, game tables, exercise equipment	60.02
Eyeglasses and contact lenses	59.73
Refrigerators and freezers	57.60
Pet purchase, supplies, medicine, services	57.32
Shoes, children	56.98
Mass transit, intracity fares	55.77
Lawn and garden supplies	55.74
Veterinary services	53.49
Ice cream and related products	52.91
Telephone service for mobile phone	52.61
Plants and fresh flowers, indoor	52.33
Newspaper subscriptions	51.70
Hair care products	51.00
Books, except book clubs	49.50
Accounting fees	48.99
Coffee	48.80
Kitchen and dining room furniture	48.69
Admission to sporting events	47.49

Books and supplies, college	$47.48
Fruit juice, canned and bottled	47.43
Living room chairs	47.42
Mattresses and springs	46.56
Cookies	45.01
Wall units, cabinets, miscellaneous furniture	42.81
Sound equipment and accessories	42.29
Biscuits and rolls	40.96
Videotape, disc, film rental	40.30
Sauces and gravies	39.86
CDs, audio tapes, records	39.41
Lawn and garden equipment	39.37
Pork chops	39.23
Rugs, nonpermanent	38.93
Carpeting, wall-to-wall	38.82
Kitchenware and cookware, nonelectric	38.53
Babysitting and childcare, other home	37.37
Ham	37.28
Nonphysician health care professional services	37.03
Vegetables, canned	35.85
Cakes and cupcakes	34.51
Car rental	34.51
Babysitting and childcare, own home	34.39
Bedroom linens	34.28
Soup, canned and packaged	32.87
Eggs	32.59
Alcohol purchased on trips	32.48
Laundry and dry cleaning of apparel, professional	31.24
Pork, except bacon, frankfurters, ham, pork chops, and sausage	31.07
Day care, adult	30.74
Deodorants, feminine hygiene, miscellaneous products	29.80
Watches	29.70
Film processing	29.36
Tobacco products, except cigarettes	28.78
Vitamins, nonprescription	28.43
Pasta, cornmeal, and other cereal products	28.03
Baby food	27.86
Eye care services	27.14
Oral hygiene products	26.96
VCRs and video disc players	26.58
Vegetables, frozen	26.57
Ship fares	26.40
Motorized campers	26.17
Bacon	25.42

Computer software and accessories for nonbusiness use	$24.72
Salad dressings	24.68
Bank service charges	24.51
Fats and oils	24.50
Parking fees in home city	24.37
Sausage	24.12
Musical instruments and accessories	23.96
Photographer's fees	23.45
Bakery products, frozen and refrigerated	23.35
Crackers	23.26
Sweetrolls, coffee cakes, and doughnuts	23.13
Washing machines	23.02
Lab tests, X-rays	22.93
Frankfurters	22.83
Jams, preserves, and other sweets	22.63
Magazine subscriptions	22.62
Video cassettes, tapes, and discs	22.15
Cooking stoves, ovens	22.06
Film	21.36
Train fares, intercity	21.19
Laundry and dry cleaning of apparel, coin-operated	20.79
Frozen meals	20.73
Computer information services	20.65
Living room tables	20.60
Transportation, local, on out-of-town trips	20.01
Fruit juice, fresh	19.82
Video game hardware and software	19.74
Cemetery lots, vaults, and maintenance fees	19.65
Fruit flavored drinks, noncarbonated	19.22
Salt, spices, and other seasonings	19.07
Sugar	18.93
Rice	18.37
Nuts	17.70
Newspaper, nonsubscription	17.18
Infants' furniture and equipment	16.92
Contributions to educational organizations	16.88
Curtains and draperies	16.73
Kitchen appliances, small electric	16.67
Baking needs and miscellaneous products	16.65
Property management, owned homes	16.49
Power tools	16.31
Clothes dryers	16.22
Hunting and fishing equipment	16.11
Floor cleaning equipment, electric	15.68

Bicycles	$15.27
Laundry and dry cleaning, nonapparel	15.11
Salads, prepared	15.05
Flour, prepared mixes	15.04
Tea	14.76
Butter	14.63
Photographic equipment	14.19
Fruit, canned	13.97
Outdoor furniture	13.61
Pies, tarts, and turnovers	13.50
Appliance repair, including service center	13.50
Whiskey	13.40
Fruit juice, frozen	13.01
Business equipment and office furniture for home use	12.94
Lamps and lighting fixtures	12.53
Dishwashers	12.47
Books and supplies, elementary and high school	12.22
Radios	11.76
Margarine	11.74
Peanut butter	11.63
Magazines, nonsubscription	11.55
Shaving products	11.45
Hearing aids	11.42
Bathroom linens	11.13
Reupholstering and furniture repair	10.87
Dinnerware	10.61
CD, tape, record, video, mail order clubs	10.59
Olives, pickles, and relishes	10.54
Bus fares, intercity	10.51
Books purchased through book clubs	10.18
Desserts, prepared	9.95
Insurance, tenants	9.76
Luggage	9.72
Microwave ovens	9.59
Docking and landing fees	9.52
Taxi fares and limousine service	9.51
Camping equipment	9.34
Closet and storage items	8.94
Sewing material, patterns, and notions for clothing	8.89
Flour	8.79
Nondairy cream and imitation milk	8.50
Glassware	8.25
Automobile service clubs	8.19
Parking fees and tolls on out-of-town trips	8.15

Vegetable juices	$7.50
Medical equipment	7.32
Safe deposit box rental	6.69
TV, radio, sound equipment repair	6.65
Contributions to political organizations	6.20
Apparel repair and tailoring	6.10
Winter sports equipment	5.50
Watch and jewelry repair	5.08
Towing charges	5.04
Air conditioners, window units	4.93
Flatware	4.68
Personal care appliances, electric	4.56
Water sports equipment	4.52
Water softening service	4.51
Credit card memberships	3.98
Clothing rental	3.85
Sewing machines	3.55
Artificial sweeteners	3.48
Satellite dishes	3.41
Furniture rental	3.41
Recreational vehicle rental	3.35
Telephone answering devices	3.31
Books and supplies, day care and nursery school	3.13
Property security, owned homes	3.09
Smoking accessories	2.60
Computer systems for nonbusiness use, repair	2.47
Kitchen and dining room linens	2.40
Shoe repair	2.38
Slipcovers and decorative pillows	2.10
Calculators	1.92
Musical instruments, rental and repair	1.64
Smoke alarms	1.05

* Not shown in book.
Note: Ranking does not show gift spending, which is included in each product and service category. Also not shown are gasoline on out-of-town trips and auto rental on out-of-town trips, which are included in the gasoline and auto rental categories.
Source: Calculations by New Strategist based on the 1997 Consumer Expenditure Survey

Appendix D

Spending Trends, 1987 to 1997

(average annual spending of households by product and service category, 1987 and 1997; percent change, 1987–97; in 1997 dollars)

	1997	1987	percent change 1987–97
Number of consumer units			
(in thousands, add 000)	**105,576**	**94,150**	**12.1%**
Average income before taxes	**$39,926**	**$38,608**	**3.4**
Average annual spending	**38,060**	**37,962**	**0.3**
ALCOHOLIC BEVERAGES	**$309**	**$408**	**−24.3%**
APPAREL	**1,729**	**2,043**	**−15.4**
Men and boys	**407**	**510**	**−20.2**
Men, 16 or older	323	417	−22.5
Boys, aged 2 to 15	84	93	−9.9
Women and girls	**680**	**835**	**−18.6**
Women, 16 or older	574	721	−20.3
Girls, aged 2 to 15	106	114	−7.4
Children under age 2	**77**	**82**	**−6.0**
Footwear	**315**	**260**	**21.2**
Other apparel products and services	**250**	**355**	**−29.5**
EDUCATION	**571**	**476**	**19.9**
ENTERTAINMENT	**1,813**	**1,686**	**7.6**
Fees and admissions	471	456	3.2
Television, radios, sound equipment	577	535	7.8
Pets, toys, and playground equipment	327	308	6.2
Other entertainment equip. and services	439	386	13.8
FINANCIAL PRODUCTS & SERVICES	**8,312**	**8,382**	**−0.8**
Miscellaneous financial	**847**	**794**	**6.7**
Cash contributions	**1,001**	**1,047**	**−4.4**
Personal insurance and pensions	**3,223**	**3,073**	**4.9**
Life and other personal insurance	379	415	−8.8
Pensions and Social Security	2,844	2,658	7.0
Personal taxes	**3,241**	**3,469**	**−6.6**
Federal income taxes	2,468	2,756	−10.5
State and local income taxes	645	641	0.6
Other taxes	129	71	82.6

	1997	1987	percent change 1987–97
FOOD AT HOME	**$2,880**	**$2,966**	**−2.9%**
Cereals and bakery products	**453**	**422**	**7.2**
Cereals and cereal products	161	147	9.6
Bakery products	292	274	6.5
Meats, poultry, fish, and eggs	**743**	**808**	**−8.1**
Beef	224	270	−17.0
Pork	157	164	−4.2
Other meats	96	117	−18.1
Poultry	145	123	18.0
Fish and seafood	89	93	−4.6
Eggs	33	40	−16.6
Dairy products	**314**	**387**	**−18.9**
Fresh milk and cream	128	186	−31.4
Other dairy products	186	201	−7.3
Fruits and vegetables	**476**	**503**	**−5.4**
Fresh fruits	150	160	−6.0
Fresh vegetables	143	155	−8.0
Processed fruits	102	110	−7.4
Processed vegetables	80	78	3.0
Other food at home	**895**	**801**	**11.7**
Sugar and other sweets	114	105	9.0
Fats and oils	81	72	12.4
Miscellaneous foods	403	350	15.0
Nonalcoholic beverages	245	274	−10.6
Food prepared by cu on out of town trips	52	44	18.7
FOOD AWAY FROM HOME	**1,921**	**2,211**	**−13.1**
GIFTS			
Clothing, males 2 or older	61	82	−25.6
Clothing, females 2 or older	81	106	−23.6
Clothing, infants under age 2	33	35	−6.6
Jewelry and watches	49	32	50.8
Small appliances & misc. housewares	21	23	−7.1
Household textiles	8	17	−52.8
HEALTH CARE	**1,841**	**1,604**	**14.8**
Health insurance	881	554	59.1
Medical services	531	660	−19.5
Drugs	320	287	11.6
Medical supplies	108	103	4.7

	1997	1987	percent change 1987–97
HOUSEHOLD FURNISHINGS AND EQUIPMENT	**$1,512**	**$1,458**	**3.7%**
Household textiles	79	129	−38.6
Furniture	387	445	−13.0
Floor coverings	78	97	−20.0
Major appliances	169	226	−25.2
Small appliances & misc. housewares	92	81	14.2
Miscellaneous household equipment	707	480	47.2
HOUSEHOLD SERVICES	**548**	**524**	**4.5**
Personal services	263	240	9.5
Other household services	285	284	0.4
HOUSEKEEPING SUPPLIES	**455**	**482**	**−5.6**
Laundry and cleaning supplies	116	137	−15.4
Other household products	210	196	6.9
Postage and stationery	129	148	−13.0
PERSONAL CARE	**528**	**466**	**13.2**
READING MATERIAL	**164**	**201**	**−18.3**
SHELTER AND UTILITIES	**8,756**	**8,230**	**6.4**
Shelter	**6,344**	**5,869**	**8.1**
Owned dwellings	3,935	3,356	17.3
Mortgage interest	2,225	2,064	7.8
Property taxes	971	656	48.1
Maintenance, repairs, insurance, other expenses	738	634	16.3
Rented dwellings	**1,983**	**1,900**	**4.4**
Other lodging	**426**	**613**	**−30.5**
Utilities	**2,412**	**2,361**	**2.2**
Natural gas	301	328	−8.2
Electricity	909	978	−7.0
Fuel oil and other fuels	108	133	−18.7
Telephone	809	705	14.7
Water and other public services	286	216	32.3
TOBACCO PRODUCTS	**264**	**328**	**−19.5**
TRANSPORTATION	**6,457**	**6,499**	**−0.6**
Vehicle purchases	**2,736**	**2,857**	**−4.2**
Cars and trucks, new	1,229	1,615	−23.9
Cars and trucks, used	1,464	1,215	20.5
Other vehicles	43	25	69.1
Gasoline and motor oil	**1,098**	**1,255**	**−12.5**

	1997	1987	percent change 1987–97
Vehicle finance charges	$293	$396	–25.9%
Maintenance and repairs	682	726	–6.1
Vehicle insurance	755	653	15.7
Vehicle rent, licenses, other charges	501	226	121.6
Public transportation	393	386	1.9

Note: The categories listed here do not necessarily match the categories in the book.
Source: Bureau of Labor Statistics, 1997 and 1987 Consumer Expenditure Surveys; calculations by New Strategist

Glossary

age The age of the reference person, also called the householder or head of household.

alcoholic beverages Includes beer and ale, wine, whiskey, gin, vodka, rum, and other alcoholic beverages.

apparel, accessories, and related services Includes the following:

• *men's and boys' apparel* Includes coats, jackets, sweaters, vests, sport coats, tailored jackets, slacks, shorts and short sets, sportswear, shirts, underwear, nightwear, hosiery, uniforms, and other accessories.

• *women's and girls' apparel* Includes coats, jackets, furs, sport coats, tailored jackets, sweaters, vests, blouses, shirts, dresses, dungarees, culottes, slacks, shorts, sportswear, underwear, nightwear, uniforms, hosiery, and other accessories.

• *infants' apparel* Includes coats, jackets, snowsuits, underwear, diapers, dresses, crawlers, sleeping garments, hosiery, footwear, and other accessories for children.

• *footwear* Includes articles such as shoes, slippers, boots, and other similar items. It excludes footwear for babies and footwear used for sports such as bowling or golf shoes.

• *other accessories, apparel products, and services* Includes material for making clothes, shoe repair, alterations and sewing patterns and notions, clothing rental, clothing storage, dry cleaning, sent-out laundry, watches, jewelry, and repairs to watches and jewelry.

average spending Average spending is the average amount spent per household. The Bureau of Labor Statistics calculates the average for all households in a segment, not just for those who purchased an item. For frequently purchased items—such as bread—the average spending figures give a fairly accurate account of the actual spending of purchasers. But for products and services purchased infrequently, the average amount is much less than what purchasers spend for an item. See Appendix B for percent reporting expenditure and average amount spent by purchasers.

baby boom People born from 1946 through 1964, aged 33 to 51 in 1997.

baby bust People born from 1965 through 1976, aged 21 to 32 in 1997. Also known as Generation X.

best customers Households that spend the most (highest index) on a product or service. See also indexed spending.

biggest customers Households that control the largest share of spending on a product or service. See also market share.

cash transfers and contributions Includes cash contributed to persons or organizations outside the consumer unit including alimony and child support payments, care of students away from home, and contributions to religious, educational, charitable, or political organizations.

complete income reporters Respondents who provided values for major sources of income, such as wages and salaries, self-employment income, and Social Security income. Even complete income reporters may not have given a full accounting of all income from all sources.

consumer unit Defined as follows:
• All members of a household who are related by blood, marriage, adoption, or other legal arrangements.

• A person living alone or sharing a household with others or living as a roomer in a private home or lodging house or in permanent living quarters in a hotel or motel, but who is financially independent.

• Two persons or more living together who pool their income to make joint expenditure decisions. Financial independence is determined by the three major expense categories: housing, food, and other living expenses. To be considered financially independent, at least two of the three major expense categories have to be provided by the respondent. For convenience, called households in the text of this book.

education Includes tuition, fees, books, supplies, and equipment for public and private nursery schools, elementary and high schools, colleges and universities, and other schools.

entertainment Includes the following:
• *fees and admissions* Includes fees for participant sports; admissions to sporting events, movies, concerts, plays; health, swimming, tennis, and country club memberships, and other social recreational and fraternal organizations; recreational lessons or instructions; rental of movies, and recreational expenses on trips.

• *television, radio, and sound equipment* Includes television sets, video recorders, video cassettes, tapes, discs, disc players, video game hardware, video game cartridges, cable TV, radios, phonographs, tape recorders and players, sound components, records and tapes, and records and tapes through record clubs, musical instruments, and rental and repair of TV and sound equipment.

• *pets, toys, hobbies, and playground equipment* Includes pet food, pet services, veterinary expenses, toys, games, hobbies, and playground equipment.

• *other entertainment equipment and services* Includes indoor exercise equipment, athletic shoes, bicycles, trailers, campers, camping equipment, rental of cameras and trailers, hunting and fishing equipment, sports equipment, winter sports equipment, water sports equipment, boats, boat motors and boat trailers, rental of boat, landing and docking fees, rental and repair of sports equipment, photographic equipment, film and film processing, photographer fees, repair and rental of photo equipment, fireworks, pinball and electronic video games.

expenditure The transaction cost including excise and sales taxes of goods and services acquired during the survey period. The full cost of each purchase is recorded even though full payment may not have been made at the date of purchase. Expenditure estimates include gifts. Excluded from expenditures are purchases or portions of purchases directly assignable to business purposes and periodic credit or installment payments on goods and services already acquired.

financial products and services Includes the following:
• *life and other personal insurance* Includes premiums from whole life and term insurance; endowments; income and other life insurance; mortgage guarantee insurance; mortgage life insurance; premiums for personal life liability, accident and disability;

and other nonhealth insurance other than homes and vehicles.

• *retirement, pensions, and Social Security* Includes all Social Security contributions paid by employees; employees' contributions to railroad retirement, government retirement and private pensions programs; retirement programs for self-employed.

financial, miscellaneous Includes union dues, professional dues and fees, other occupational expenses, funerals, cemetery lots, and unclassified fees and personal services.

food Includes the following:

• *food at home* Refers to the total expenditures for food at grocery stores or other food stores during the interview period. It is calculated by multiplying the number of visits to a grocery or other food store by the average amount spent per visit. It excludes the purchase of nonfood items.

• *food away from home* Includes all meals (breakfast, lunch, brunch, and dinner) at restaurants, carryouts, and vending machines, including tips, plus meals as pay, special catered affairs such as weddings, bar mitzvahs, and confirmations, and meals away from home on trips.

Generation X People born from 1965 through 1976, aged 21 to 32 in 1997. Also known as the baby bust.

gifts Products and services purchased as gifts for people living in other households. Gift spending is also included in each product and service category.

health care Includes the following:

• *health insurance* Includes health maintenance plans (HMOs), Blue Cross/Blue Shield, commercial health insurance, Medi-

care, Medicare supplemental insurance, and other health insurance.

• *medical services* Includes hospital room and services, physicians' services, services of a practitioner other than a physician, eye and dental care, lab tests, X-rays, nursing, therapy services, care in convalescent or nursing home, and other medical care.

• *drugs* Includes prescription and non-prescription drugs, internal and respiratory over-the-counter drugs.

• *medical supplies* Includes eyeglasses and contact lenses, topicals and dressings, antiseptics, bandages, cotton, first aid kits, contraceptives; medical equipment for general use such as syringes, ice bags, thermometers, vaporizers, heating pads; supportive or convalescent medical equipment such as hearing aids, braces, canes, crutches, and walkers.

household According to the Census Bureau, all the persons who occupy a household. A group of unrelated people who share a housing unit as roommates or unmarried partners is also counted as a household. Households do not include group quarters such as college dormitories, prisons, or nursing homes. A household may contain more than one consumer unit. The terms "household" and "consumer unit" are used interchangeably in this book.

household furnishings and equipment Includes the following:

• *household textiles* Includes bathroom, kitchen, dining room, and other linens, curtains and drapes, slipcovers and decorative pillows, and sewing materials.

• *furniture* Includes living room, dining room, kitchen, bedroom, nursery, porch, lawn, and other outdoor furniture.

• *carpet, rugs, and other floor coverings* Includes installation and replacement of wall-to-wall carpets, room-size rugs, and other soft floor coverings.

• *major appliances* Includes refrigerators, freezers, dishwashers, stoves, ovens, garbage disposals, vacuum cleaners, microwaves, air-conditioners, sewing machines, washing machines and dryers, and floor cleaning equipment.

• *small appliances and miscellaneous housewares* Includes small electrical kitchen appliances, portable heating and cooling equipment, china and other dinnerware, flatware, glassware, silver and other serving pieces, nonelectric cookware, and plastic dinnerware. Excludes personal care appliances.

• *miscellaneous household equipment* Includes typewriters, luggage, lamps and other light fixtures, window coverings, clocks, lawn mowers and gardening equipment, other hand and power tools, telephone answering devices, telephone accessories, computers and computer hardware for home use, calculators, office equipment for home use, floral arrangements and house plants, rental of furniture, closet and storage items, household decorative items, infants' equipment, outdoor equipment, smoke alarms, other household appliances and small miscellaneous furnishing.

household services Includes the following:

• *personal services* Includes baby sitting, day care, and care of elderly and handicapped persons.

• *other household services* Includes housekeeping services, gardening and lawn care services, coin-operated laundry and dry-cleaning of household textiles, termite and pest control products, moving, storage, and freight expenses, repair of household appliances and other household equipment, reupholstering and furniture repair, rental and repair of lawn and gardening tools, and rental of other household equipment.

housekeeping supplies Includes soaps, detergents, other laundry cleaning products, cleansing and toilet tissue, paper towels, napkins, and miscellaneous household products; lawn and garden supplies, postage, stationery, stationery supplies, and gift wrap.

indexed spending The indexed spending figures compare the spending of each demographic segment with that of the average household. To compute the indexes, the amount spent by each demographic segment on an item is divided by the amount spent on the item by the average household. An index of 100 is the average for all households. An index of 132 means average spending by households in a segment is 32 percent above average (100 plus 32). An index of 75 means average spending by households in a segment is 25 percent below average (100 minus 25). Indexed spending figures identify the best customers of a product or service.

market share The market share is the percentage of aggregate household spending on an item that is accounted for by a demographic segment. Market shares are calculated by dividing a demographic segment's total spending on an item by aggregate household spending on the item. Aggregate spending is calculated by mulitplying average spending on an item by the total number of households (105,576,000). Total spending for each demographic segment is calculated by mulitplying the segment's average spending on an item by the number of households in the segment. Market shares reveal the biggest customers—the demographic segments that account for the largest share of spending on a product or service.

Millennials People born from 1977 though 1994, and aged 3 through 20 in 1997.

personal care Includes products for the hair, oral hygiene products, shaving needs, cosmetics and bath products, suntan lotions and hand creams, electric personal care appliances, incontinence products, other personal care products, personal care services for males and females such as hair care services (haircuts, bleaching, tinting, coloring, conditioning treatments, permanents, press, and curls), styling and other services for wigs and hairpieces, body massages or slenderizing treatments, facials, manicures, pedicures, shaves, electrolysis.

reading material Includes subscriptions for newspapers, magazines, and books through book clubs; purchase of single-copy newspapers and magazines, books, and encyclopedias and other reference books.

reference person The first member mentioned by the respondent when asked to "Start with the name of the person or one of the persons who owns or rents the home." It is with respect to this person that the relationship of other consumer unit members is determined. Also called the householder or head of household.

region Consumer units are classified according to their address at the time of their participation in the survey. The four major census regions of the United States are the following state groupings:

• *Northeast* Connecticut, Maine, Massachusetts, New Hampshire, New Jersey, New York, Pennsylvania, Rhode Island, and Vermont.

• *Midwest* Illinois, Indiana, Iowa, Kansas, Michigan, Minnesota, Missouri, Nebraska, North Dakota, Ohio, South Dakota, and Wisconsin.

• *South* Alabama, Arkansas, Delaware, District of Columbia, Florida, Georgia, Kentucky, Louisiana, Maryland, Mississippi, North Carolina, Oklahoma, South Carolina, Tennessee, Texas, Virginia, and West Virginia.

• *West* Alaska, Arizona, California, Colorado, Hawaii, Idaho, Montana, Nevada, New Mexico, Oregon, Utah, Washington, and Wyoming.

shelter Includes the following:
• *owned dwellings* Includes interest on mortgages, property taxes and insurance, refinancing and prepayment charges, ground rent, expenses for property management/security, homeowners' insurance, fire insurance and extended coverage, landscaping expenses for repairs and maintenance contracted out (including periodic maintenance and service contracts), and expenses of materials for owner-performed repairs and maintenance for dwellings used or maintained by the consumer unit, but not dwellings maintained for business or rent.

• *rented dwellings* Includes rent paid for dwellings, rent received as pay, parking fees, maintenance, and other expenses.

• *other lodging* Includes all expenses for vacation homes, school, college, hotels, motels, cottages, trailer camps, and other lodging while out of town.

• *utilities, fuels, and public services* Includes natural gas, electricity, fuel oil, coal, bottled gas, wood, and other fuels; telephone charges; water, garbage and trash collection, sewerage maintenance, septic tank cleaning, and other public services.

tobacco and smoking supplies Includes cigarettes, cigars, snuff, loose smoking tobacco, chewing tobacco, and smoking accessories such as cigarette or cigar holders, pipes, flints, lighters, pipe cleaners, and other smoking products and accessories.

total income The before-tax combined income of all consumer unit members aged 14 or older during the 12 months preceding the interview. Sources of income may include wages and salaries; self-employment income; Social Security, private, and government retirement benefits; interest, dividends, rental and other property income; unemployment, workers' compensation, and veterans' benefits; public assistance, supplemental security income, and food stamps; alimony, child support, and other regular contributions for support; and other income such as scholarships or payment for support of foster children.

transportation Includes the following:
• *vehicle purchases (net outlay)* Includes the net outlay (purchase price minus trade-in value) on new and used domestic and imported cars and trucks and other vehicles, including motorcycles and private planes.

• *gasoline and motor oil* Includes gasoline, diesel fuel, and motor oil.

• *other vehicle expenses* Includes vehicle finance charges, maintenance and repairs, vehicle insurance, and vehicle rental licenses and other charges.

• *vehicle finance charges* Includes the dollar amount of interest paid for a loan con-

tracted for the purchase of vehicles described above.

• *maintenance and repairs* Includes tires, batteries, tubes, lubrication, filters, coolant, additives, brake and transmission fluids, oil change, brake adjustment and repair, front-end alignment, wheel balancing, steering repair, shock absorber replacement, clutch and transmission repair, electrical system repair, repair to cooling system, drive train repair, drive shaft and rear-end repair, tire repair, other maintenance and services, and auto repair policies.

• *vehicle insurance* Includes the premium paid for insuring cars, trucks, and other vehicles.

• *vehicle rental, licenses, and other charges* Includes leased and rented cars, trucks, motorcycles, and aircraft, inspection fees, state and local registration, drivers' license fees, parking fees, towing charges, and tolls on trips.

• *public transportation* Includes fares for mass transit, buses, trains, airlines, taxis, private school buses, and fares paid on train, boat, taxi, and bus trips.

Index